WINSTON S. CHURCHILL

Frontiers and Wars

HIS FOUR EARLY BOOKS

COVERING HIS LIFE AS SOLDIER AND

WAR CORRESPONDENT

EDITED INTO ONE VOLUME

KONECKY&KONECKY

Konecky & Konecky
156 Fifth Avenue
New York, N.Y. 10010

ISBN: 1-56852-057-3

Printed in the United States of A merica

CONTENTS

Publisher's Note   *page* 13

THE MALAKAND FIELD FORCE

	Introduction	17
I	The Malakand Camps	19
II	The Outbreak	28
III	The Attack on the Malakand	32
IV	The Relief of Chakdara	42
V	The Defence of Chakdara	49
VI	The Gate of Swat	57
VII	The Advance Against the Mohmands	65
VIII	Reconnaissance	73
IX	The March to Nawagai	79
X	The Action of the Mamund Valley, 16th September	83
XI	At Inayat Kila	94
XII	Nawagai	103
XIII	Back to the Mamund Valley	107
XIV	The Work of the Cavalry	117
XV	Submission	123

THE RIVER WAR

	Introduction	131
I	The Rebellion of the Mahdi	135
II	The Fate of the Envoy	154

CONTENTS

III   The Dervish Empire   *page* 175

IV   The Years of Preparation   187

V   The Beginning of the War   198

VI   Firket, 7th June 1896   209

VII   The Recovery of the Dongola Province   216

VIII   The Desert Railway   231

IX   Abu Hamed   246

X   Berber   258

XI   Reconnaissance   267

XII   The Grand Advance   279

XIII   The Operations of the First of September   287

XIV   The Battle of Omdurman, 2nd September 1898   295

XV   The Fall of the City   320

XVI   'The Fashoda Incident'   327

XVII   On the Blue Nile   338

XVIII   The End of the Khalifa   349

LONDON TO LADYSMITH   359

IAN HAMILTON'S MARCH   475

MAPS AND PLANS

THE MALAKAND FIELD FORCE

The Theatre of the Operations of the Malakand Field
   Force   *page* 16
The Malakand Position   33
Cavalry Fight at Malakand   46
The Operations in Bajaur   74–5
The Mamund Valley   89
The Attack upon Agrah   112

THE RIVER WAR

The Soudan and the Dervish Empire   181
Rail and River   234
The Nile from Atbara to Khartoum   265
The Battle of Atbara   275
The Battle of Omdurman – the First Attack   292
The Battle of Omdurman – the Khalifa's Attack   304
The Battle of Omdurman – Final Stage   322
The Campaign on the Blue Nile   344
The Action near Rosaires   346
The Shirkela Reconnaissance   351

LONDON TO LADYSMITH

Mr Churchill's Escape Route from Pretoria   360
Plan of States Model Schools   402
The Theatre of Operations in Natal   412
Potgieter's Ferry   421
Operations of the Natal Field Army, 11th January
   to 9th February   424–5

MAPS AND PLANS

Boer Position at Monte Cristo, 17th February   *page* 450

Operations of the Natal Field Army, 14th to 28th
    February   455

IAN HAMILTON'S MARCH

Ian Hamilton's Route from Bloemfontein to
    Pretoria   476

The Action at Israel's Poorte, 25th April   498

French's Operations round Thabanchu, 26th and 27th
    April   502

The Action of Houtnek   505

The Passage of the Sand River   514

Ian Hamilton's Action at the Sand River   517

The Action of Johannesburg   540

Operations at Diamond Hill – 1   560

Operations at Diamond Hill – 2   563

Eleven of the maps in this volume are reproduced
from the contemporary editions, and the remaining
twenty-one have been specially drawn for the present
edition by W. H. Bromage.

PUBLISHER'S NOTE

This volume contains the first four books written by Sir Winston Churchill. They have been, necessarily, abridged to get them into one manageable volume, but they retain, it is hoped, the splendid march of the narratives and the vigour of the author's style. The books appear in the order in which they were published; all of them were written while Sir Winston was a serving soldier and they are largely eye-witness accounts of actions in which he took part.

The first book, *The Story of the Malakand Field Force*, was written in 1897 and published in 1898. It has been out of print since 1911 and has, apparently, all but disappeared. It is exactly described by its sub-title: 'An episode of frontier war'. Frontier wars were endemic in India during the latter part of the nineteenth century. Their object, as described by the Government of India in a letter to the Secretary of State (No. 49, 1879) was 'to prevent at any cost the establishment within this out-lying country of the political preponderance of any other power'. The powers feared were Russia and Afghanistan. The effect of these wars was to advance the frontiers of British India up to the borders of Afghanistan, as is shown in the map on page 16. The 'Forward Policy', as it was called, had opponents among the Gladstonian liberals and the fluctuation of British policy according to the government in power sometimes had unfortunate results for military expeditions alternately sanctioned and withdrawn. Sir Bindon Blood's expedition against the tribes in the Swat Valley, which Sir Winston vigorously describes, was one of those carried through to a successful conclusion.

The River War was first published in two volumes in 1899. It is described as 'An account of the re-conquest of the Soudan' but it is much more than that. It is the author's first major historical work; it covers the history of the Soudan and its peoples; its decay under an ineffectively maintained Egyptian suzerainty; the rise of the famous

Mahdi, who was, as Sir Winston saw in 1899, the father of Arab nationalism; the murder of General Gordon and the extraordinary régime of fanaticism, plunder and slave raiding known as the Dervish Empire. The culmination of this luridly dramatic story is the account of the re-conquest and pacification by a mixed Anglo-Egyptian force under the Sirdar, General Sir Herbert, afterwards Lord Kitchener. The book has proved continuously popular and has been many times reprinted. For the last edition, revised in 1933 and still available, Sir Winston wrote a special introduction which is so characteristic that it has been retained in the present volume. It shows, more vividly than any comment, the change in the world political scene even since 1933.

London to Ladysmith and *Ian Hamilton's March* had their origins in the letters which Sir Winston sent to the *Morning Post* for which he was acting war correspondent in the South African War. Both were published in 1900 and have been out of print for nearly sixty years. *London to Ladysmith* contains the original account of his capture by the Boers and his escape; *Ian Hamilton's March* follows the fortunes of that General's army after the relief of Ladysmith. Both books reflect the intense patriotic sentiment engendered by the South African War, a sentiment exacerbated by unexpected military defeats, the hostility of most of Europe and America and the existence of a strong pro-Boer element among radicals at home. The conversation between the author and his Boer guard, reprinted on pages 392-5, vividly expresses the viewpoints of Briton and Boer. To re-read them, in circumstances which neither combatant dreamt of, is illuminating. Nor could anyone have foretold, in 1900, the astonishing future which awaited the ex-lieutenant of cavalry, just about to go into Parliament. Yet nothing he has since written is more characteristic of him than these early, half-forgotten books.

THE STORY OF

THE MALAKAND FIELD FORCE

An episode of frontier war

'They (Frontier Wars) are but the surf which
marks the edge and the advance of the wave of
civilisation.' *Lord Salisbury, in a speech at the
Guildhall,* 1892

Miles
0 10 20 30 40

THE THEATRE OF THE OPERATIONS OF THE MALAKAND FIELD FORCE

CHAPTER I

THE MALAKAND CAMPS

The town and cantonment of Nowshera was the base from which all the operations of the Malakand Field Force were conducted. It is situated on the India side of the Cabul River, and is six hours by rail from Rawal Pindi. In times of peace its garrison consists of one native cavalry regiment, one British, and one native infantry battalion. The road from Nowshera to the Malakand Pass and camps is forty-seven miles long, and divided into four stages. Usually there is an excellent *tonga* service, and the distance is covered in about six hours; but while the Field Force was mobilised so much traffic passed up and down the line, that the tonga ponies were soon reduced to a terrible condition of sores and emaciation, and could hardly drag the journey out in nine, ten, or even twelve hours. After leaving Nowshera, and crossing the Cabul River, a stage of fifteen miles brings the traveller to Mardan. This place – pronounced *Merdâne* – is the permanent station of the Corps of Guides. It is shady and agreeable, though terribly hot in the summer months.

After Mardan the mountains are approached, and as the tonga advances their shapes and colours are more distinctly seen. A few knolls and ridges rising from the level plain, mark the outposts of that great array of hills. Crossing a shallow stream – a tributary of the Cabul River, Jelala – the second stage is reached. In peace time a small mud fort is the only indication, but this is expanded by the proximity of war, to a considerable camp, with an entrenchment around it. Stopping only to change ponies the journey is resumed. The avenue of trees on either side has ceased. The road is traversed in a sweltering heat and choking dust. All around the country is red, sterile and burnt up. In front the great wall of hills rises up dark and ominous; at length Dargai at the foot of the pass is reached. It is another mud fort, swelled during the operations into an entrenched camp, and surrounded by a network of barbed wire entanglement. The Malakand Pass can now be seen – a great cleft in the line of mountains – and far up the gorge, the outline of the fort that guards it, is distinguishable.

The graded road winds up, and with many a turn, the long ascent from Dargai to the top of the pass. The driver flogs the wretched sore-backed ponies tirelessly. At length the summit is neared. The view is one worth stopping to look at. Behind and below, under the haze of the heat, is the wide expanse of open country – smooth, level, stretching away to the dim horizon. The tonga turns the corner, and enters a new world. A cooler breeze is blowing. On all sides the landscape is wild and rugged. As far as the eye can reach in every direction are jagged peaks and spurs.

The Malakand is like a great cup, of which the rim is broken into numerous clefts, and jagged points. At the bottom of this cup, is the crater camp. The deepest cleft is the Malakand Pass. The highest of the jagged points is Guides Hill, on a spur of which the fort stands. It needs no technical knowledge to see, that to defend such a place, the rim of the cup must be held. But in the Malakand, the bottom of the cup is too small to contain the necessary garrison. The whole position is therefore, from the military point of view, bad and indefensible. At the time this story opens the Malakand South Camp was an impossible place to put troops in. It was easy of access, it was cramped, and commanded by neighbouring heights.

The small area of the camp on the Kotal necessitated the formation of a second encampment in the plain of Khar. This was about two miles from the pass, and though it was close to Khar village, was called for political reasons North Malakand. The position of this camp was probably much stronger than that on the Kotal. Though situated in broken ground, and among rocks and nullahs, it was neither confined nor commanded. There was no danger of troops being shut up in it, and unable to deploy for action, as in the camp on the pass. It was, of course, of no strategic value, and was merely used as a habitation for the troops intended to hold Malakand, for whom there was no room in the crater and fort.

At first it was thought that the retention of the brigade in this advanced post, was only a matter of a few weeks. But as the months passed by the camp began to assume an appearance of permanency. The officers built themselves huts and mess rooms. Many officers brought their wives and families and the whole place was rapidly becoming a regular cantonment. No cases of Ghazi outrage broke the tranquillity. The revolvers, which all persons leaving camp were by regulations obliged to take, were either unloaded or carried by a native groom.

After crossing the Malakand Pass the first turning to the right leads to the Swat Valley. The traveller is now within the mountains. In every direction the view is restricted or terminated by walls of rock. The valley itself is broad, level and fertile. The river flows swiftly through the middle. On either side of it, is a broad strip of rice fields. Other crops occupy the drier ground. Numerous villages, some of which contain large populations, are scattered about.

In ancient times this region was the seat of a Buddhistic kingdom, and was known as Woo-Chang or 'Udyana', which means 'the Park', and proclaims the appreciation, which its former possessors had of their pleasant valley. 'The Park', which includes all the country on both banks of the Swat River, was famous for its forests, flowers and fruit. But though the valley retains much of its beauty, its forests have been destroyed by the improvidence, and its flowers and fruit have declined through the ignorance, of the fierce conquerors into whose hands it fell.

The reputation which its present inhabitants enjoy is evil. Among Pathans it is a common saying: 'Swat is heaven, but the Swatis are hell-fiends'. For many years they had lain under the stigma of cowardice, and were despised as well as distrusted by the tribes of the border; but their conduct in the recent fighting has cleared them at least from this imputation.

Several minor chieftains now divide authority in the Swat Valley, but till 1870 it was governed by a single ruler. The Ahkund of Swat was by origin a cowherd: an office considered most honourable in India. From such employment the future Ahkund received his inspiration. He sat for many years by the banks of the Indus, and meditated. Thus he became a saint. The fame of his holiness spread throughout all the region. The Swatis besought him to come and live in their valley. After dignified and diplomatic reluctance, he consented to exchange the banks of the Indus, for those of the Swat. For some years, he lived in the green valley, and enjoyed the reverence of its people. At the time of the great mutiny, Said Akbar, the King of Swat, died, and the saint succeeded to the temporal as well as the spiritual authority. In 1863 he preached the *Jehad* against the British, and headed the Swatis and Bunerwals in the Ambeyla campaign. The power which the Sirkar so extravagantly displayed to bring the war to an end, evidently impressed the old man, for at its close he made friends with the Government and received from them many tokens of respect.

Before he died in 1870, he summoned his people around him and declared to them that one day their valley would be the scene of a struggle between the Russians and the British. When that came he charged them to fight on our side.

His two sons are dead, but his two grandsons, both quite young, live on in the valley, and are the owners of the Ahkund's freeholds, which are in every section of the Swat country. They have very little political influence; but their persons and property are respected by the people and by the British for the sake of their grandfather, who sleeps in an odour of sanctity at Saidu, near Mingaora.

From the Malakand the signal tower of Chakdara can be seen eight miles away to the eastward. Thither the broad graded road runs like a ribbon across the plain. Seven miles from the Kotal Camp, it crosses the Amandara Pass, a gap in a considerable underfeature, which juts from the southern mountains. After this it turns more to the north and leads to the fortified bridge across the river. I invite the reader to remark this road, for it is historic. It is not only the route by which the Malakand Field Force was able to advance, but it is the very reason of their existence. Without this road there would have been no Malakand Camps, no fighting, no Malakand Field Force, no story. It is the road to Chitral.

Here then, at once, the whole vast question of frontier policy is raised. We hold the Malakand Pass to keep the Chitral road open. We keep the Chitral road open because we have retained Chitral. We retain Chitral in accordance with the 'forward policy'. I am thus confronted at the very outset of this book, which was intended to be devoted chiefly to the narration of military events, with that wide political question, on which the most valuable expert evidence is divided. But while the consideration of the advisability of the retention of Chitral may be deferred, a description of the means is necessary. Nowshera is the railway base of the road. Thence we have followed it to Mardan and across the frontier.

Here the new and disputed portion begins. Passing at first through the Lower Ranizai country, it climbs the Malakand Pass, descends into the valley beyond and runs thence through Upper Ranizai territory and Lower Swat to Chakdara. Here it crosses the Swat River by the fine suspension bridge which the fort guards. The three spans of this bridge are together nearly 1,500 feet long. It was constructed in 1895, during the operations, in about six weeks, and is a very remarkable piece of military engineering. Beyond the Swat the road runs, through the territories of the Khan of Dir, north and east to Sadu, an obscure village thirty-five miles from Malakand. This marks the end of the first section, and further than this, wheeled traffic cannot go. The road, now become a camel track, winds along the left bank of the Panjkora River to within five miles of Dir, where it crosses to the right bank by another suspension bridge. Thence it continues to the junction of the Dir stream, along which it finds its way to Dir itself, some fifty miles from Sadu. Beyond Dir camels cannot go; and here begins the third section – a path practicable only for mules, and about sixty miles long. From Dir the road is a triumph of engineering. In many places it is carried on wooden galleries perched on the faces of steep and tremendous cliffs, and at others it works round spurs by astounding zig-zags, or is scarped from the mountain side. At the end of the road is Fort Chitral with a garrison of two battalions, one company of sappers, and two mountain guns.

The road is maintained and protected by the tribes through whose territories it passes; but the two principal points where it might be closed are held by imperial garrisons. The Malakand Fort guards the passage of the mountains. Chakdara holds the bridge across the river. The rest is left to the tribal levies. The Ranizai tribe receive an annual subsidy from the Indian Government of 30,000 rupees, out of which they maintain 200 irregulars. These drive away marauders and discourage outrage and murder. The Khan of Dir, through whose territory it runs for seventy-three miles, also receives a subsidy from Government of 60,000 rupees, in consideration of which he provides 400 irregulars for the service of the road.

Until the great rising these arrangements worked admirably. The tribesmen interested in the maintenance of the route, were most reluctant to engage in hostilities against the Government. The elders of the Lower Ranizais, south of Malakand, collected all the arms of their

hot-headed youths, and forbade them to attack the troops. The Upper
Ranizais were induced by superstition and fear to join the Mullah; but
very half-heartedly. The Swatis were carried away by fanaticism. The
Khan of Dir throughout behaved loyally, as he is entirely dependent on
British support. The uncertainty and insecurity of their power, has
always led petty chiefs to seek the support of some powerful suzerain.
In 1876 the Mehtar of Chitral, Amman-al-Mulk, was encouraged to
seek the protection, and become the vassal of our vassal, the Maharaja
of Cashmere. In accordance with the general scheme of advance, a
British agency was at once established at Gilgit on the Chitral-Cashmere
frontier. Amman-al-Mulk was presented with a certain supply of arms
and ammunition, and an annual subsidy of 6,000 rupees, afterwards
raised to 12,000 rupees. The British thus obtained an interest in Chitral,
and a point of observation on its borders. In 1881 the agency was withdrawn, but the influence remained, and in 1889 it was re-established
with a much larger garrison. Meanwhile Amman-al-Mulk ruled in
Chitral, in the enjoyment of his subsidy and comparative peace. But
in 1892 he died, leaving many sons, all equally ferocious, ambitious and
unscrupulous. One of these, Afzal by name, seized the reins of power,
and having murdered as many of his brothers as he could catch, proclaimed himself Mehtar, and invited the recognition of the Indian
Government. He was acknowledged chief, as he seemed to be 'a man
of courage and determination', and his rule afforded a prospect of
settled government. His surviving brothers fled to neighbouring states.

Nizam, the eldest, came to Gilgit and appealed to the British. He got
no help. The blessing had already been bestowed. But in November
1892, Shere Afzul, a brother of the late Amman, returned by stealth to
Chitral, and killed the new Mehtar and another brother. The 'wicked
uncle', then ascended the throne, or its equivalent. He was, however,
opposed. The Indian Government refused to recognise him. Nizam, at
Gilgit, urged his claims. Finally, Nizam was allowed to go and try to
regain his inheritance. The moral support of 250 Cashmere rifles
brought him many adherents. Twelve hundred men sent by Shere
Afzul to oppose him, deserted to his side. The avuncular usurper fled
to Afghanistan, was received by the ruler with hospitality, and carefully
preserved as an element of future disorder.

Nizam now became Mehtar according to his desire. From the first he was poor and unpopular. With the support of the Government of India, however, he managed to maintain a weak, squalid rule for a space. To give him countenance, Captain Younghusband was sent to the country with a hundred bayonets. The Gilgit garrison was increased by a battalion, and several posts were established between that place and Mastuj.

Thus the imperial forces had entered Chitral. Their position was soon to become one of danger. They were separated from Gilgit by many miles of bad road, and warlike tribesmen. To move troops from Gilgit, would always be slow and difficult. Another route was however possible – a route northwards from Peshawar through Dir – shorter and easier, starting from British territory and the railway. Towards this line of communication the Indian Government now looked. If British troops or agents were to be retained in Chitral, if in other words their recognised policy was to be continued, this route must be opened up. They sounded the Home Government which declined to support such a scheme. At the same time it sanctioned the temporary retention of the troops, and the agent, in the hopes of strengthening Nizam.[1]

At this point Umra Khan must enter the story. The Gilgit agency report, dated 28th April 1890, speaks of this chief, who was the Khan of Jandol, as 'the most important man between Chitral and Peshawar'. To this powerful ruler, another of the sons of Amman, named Amir, had fled from the family massacre, which followed his father's death. Umra Khan protected him and determined to turn him to his own advantage. In May 1894, this youth – he was about twenty years of age – returned to Chitral, professing to have escaped from the hands of Umra Khan and was kindly received by Nizam, who seems to have been much hampered throughout his career by his virtue. On 1st January 1895, Amir availed himself of his welcome, to murder his brother, and the principal members of the Chitral Cabinet. He proclaimed himself Mehtar and asked for recognition. The imperial officers, though used to frontier politics, refused to commit themselves to any arrangement with such a villain, until the matter had been considered in India.

Umra Khan now advanced with a large force to the head of the Chitral Valley, nominally to assist his dear friend and ally, Amir, to

[1] Despatch from Secretary of State, No. 34, 1st September 1893.

consolidate his rule, really in the hopes of extending his own territories. But Amir, knowing Umra well, and having got his kingdom, did not desire to share it. Fighting ensued. The Chitralis were beaten. As he could not make any use of Amir, Umra Khan invited the wicked uncle to return. Shere Afzul accepted. A bargain was struck. Shere Afzul claimed to be made Mehtar. Umra supported his claims. Both threatened force in the event of opposition.

But the Imperial Government refused to have anything to do with the new claimant, and warned Umra Khan to leave Chitral territory forthwith or take the consequences. The answer was war. The scanty garrisons, and scattered parties of British troops were attacked. A company of the 14th Sikhs was cut to pieces. Fort Chitral, into which the rest of the Chitral mission and their escort had thrown themselves, was closely and fiercely besieged. To rescue them was imperative. A force of nearly 16,000 men crossed the frontier on the 1st of April, from Mardan, to advance to the relief by the shortest route – the route through Swat and Dir – the line of the present Chitral wall. The command of the expedition was confided to Sir Robert Low. Sir Bindon Blood was Chief of the Staff.

Now suddenly the Government of India with open eyes placed an obstacle in the path, which they had so long pursued, and to follow which they had made so many efforts and demanded so many sacrifices from their subjects. Probably to soothe the Liberal Government, by appearing to localise the disturbances, and disclaiming any further acquisition of territory, they issued a proclamation to 'all the people of Swat and the people of Bajans who do not side with Umra Khan', in which they declared that they had 'no intention of permanently occupying any territory through which Umra Khan's misconduct' might 'force them to pass, or of interfering with the independence of the tribes'.[1]

This proclamation had, however, no effect upon the tribesmen, who were infuriated by the sight of the troops and paid no attention to the protestations of the Government. They gathered accordingly, to oppose the advance of the troops. To the number of 12,000 they occupied the Malakand Pass – a tremendous position. From this they were driven with great slaughter on the 3rd of April, by the two lead-

[1] Proclamation, 14th March 1895.

ing brigades of Sir Robert Low's force. The road to Chitral was open. But the fort had already been relieved from Gilgit. Umra Khan fled to Afghanistan, and the question of future policy came before the Government of India.

Two alternatives presented themselves: either they must 'abandon the attempt to "keep up any effective control" ' over Chitral, or they must put a sufficient garrison there. In pursuance of their recognised policy, the Council decided unanimously that to maintain British influence in Chitral was 'a matter of first importance'. In a despatch[1] to the Home Government they set forth all their reasons, and at the same time declared that it was impossible to garrison Chitral without keeping up the road from Peshawar, by which the relief force had advanced.

On the 13th of June Lord Rosebery's Cabinet replied decisively, with courage if not with wisdom, that 'no military force or European agent should be kept at Chitral, that Chitral should not be fortified, and that no road should be made between Peshawar and Chitral'. By this they definitely and finally repudiated the policy, which had been consistently followed since 1876. They left Chitral to stew in its own juice. The Indian Government replied: 'We deeply regret but loyally accept decision', and began to gather up the severed strings of their policy and weave another web.

But in the nick of time the Liberal Government fell, and Lord Salisbury's Cabinet reversed their decision. 'It seemed' to the new ministry 'that the policy . . . continuously pursued by successive Governments ought not to be lightly abandoned unless its maintenance had become clearly impossible'.[2] Thus the retention of Chitral was sanctioned, and the road which that retention necessitated was made.

[1] Despatch of Government of India, No. 240, 8th May 1895.
[2] Despatch, Secretary of State, No. 30, 16th August 1895.

CHAPTER II

THE OUTBREAK

The historian of great events is always oppressed by the difficulty of tracing the silent, subtle influences, which in all communities precede and prepare the way for violent outbursts and uprisings. In an attempt to state the causes of the great tribal upheaval of 1897, these difficulties are increased by the fact that no European can gauge the motives or assume the points of view of Asiatics. It is, however, impossible to pass the question by, and ignoring the detail, I shall endeavour to indicate some at least of the most important and apparent forces.

During the two years that the British flag had floated over Chakdara and the Malakand the trade of the Swat Valley had nearly doubled. Most of the native population were content to bask in the genial warmth and enjoy the new-found riches and comforts. For two years reliefs had gone to and from Chitral without a shot being fired, not a post-bag had been stolen, not a messenger murdered. The political officers riding about freely among the fierce hill men were invited to settle many disputes, which would formerly have been left to armed force.

But a single class had viewed with quick intelligence and intense hostility the approach of the British power. The priesthood of the Afghan border instantly recognised the full meaning of the Chitral road. The cause of their antagonism is not hard to discern. Contact with civilisation assails the superstition, and credulity, on which the wealth and influence of the Mullah depend. A vast, but silent agitation was begun. Messengers passed to and fro among the tribes. Whispers of war, a holy war, were breathed to a race intensely passionate and fanatical. Vast and mysterious agencies, the force of which are incomprehensible to rational minds, were employed. The tribes were taught to expect prodigious events. A great day for their race and faith was at hand. Presently the moment would arrive. They must watch and be ready. The mountains became as full of explosives as a magazine.

A strange combination of circumstances operated to improve the opportunity. The victory of the Turks over the Greeks; the publication of the Amir's book on *Jehad*; his assumption of the position of a Caliph of Islam, and much indiscreet writing in the Anglo-Indian press, united to produce a 'boom' in Mohammedanism.

The moment was propitious; nor was the man wanting. What Peter the Hermit was to the regular bishops and cardinals of the Church, the Mad Mullah was to the ordinary priesthood of the Afghan border. A wild enthusiast, convinced alike of his Divine mission and miraculous powers, he preached a crusade, or *Jehad*, against the infidel. The mine was fired. The flame ran along the ground. The explosions burst forth in all directions.

Great and widespread as the preparations were, they were not visible to the watchful diplomatic agents who maintained the relation of the Government with the tribesmen. Among those able men who diligently collected information and observed the state of feeling, there were none who realised the latent forces that were being accumulated on all sides. It was not until the early days of July that it was noticed that there was a fanatical movement in Upper Swat. Even then its significance was disregarded and its importance underrated. That a Mad Fakir had arrived was known. His power was still a secret. It did not long remain so.

The rumours and reports which reached the Malakand of the agitation in Upper Swat and among the surrounding tribes were fully appreciated by the Pathan Sepoys of the garrison. As July advanced, several commanding officers were warned by their men that great events were impending. Major Deane, the political agent, watched with great anxiety, the daily progress of the fanatical movement. No one desires to be thought an alarmist, least of all on the frontier where there is always danger. At length, however, he felt compelled to officially report the disquieting signs. By the 23rd of July all the officers in charge of the various posts had been ordered to observe every precaution. But to the last everybody doubted that there would be a rising, nor did anyone imagine that even should one occur, it would lead to more than a skirmish. The natives were friendly and respectful. The valley smiled in fertile prosperity. Never was transformation scene more complete.

The bazaars of India are always full of marvellous tales. A single unimportant fact is exaggerated, and distorted. till it becomes unrecognisable. From it, a thousand wild, illogical, and fantastic conclusions, are drawn. These again are circulated as facts. So the game goes on. But amid all this falsehood, and idle report, there often lies important information. As July advanced, the bazaar at Malakand became full of tales of the Mad Fakir. A great day for Islam was at hand. A mighty man had arisen to lead them. The English would be swept away. By the time of the new moon, not one would remain.

On the afternoon of the 26th of July, the subalterns and younger officers of the Malakand garrison proceeded to Khar to play polo. Thither also came Lieutenant Rattray, riding over from Chakdara fort. The game was a good one, and the tribesmen of the neighbouring village watched it as usual in little groups, with a keen interest. Nothing in their demeanour betrayed their thoughts or intentions. The game ended, and the officers cantered back to their posts.

It was then that a strange incident occurred. As the *syces* were putting the rugs and clothing on the polo ponies, and loitering about the ground after the game, the watching natives drew near, and advised them to be off home at once, for there was going to be a fight. They knew, these Pathans, what was coming. The wave of fanaticism was sweeping down the valley. It would carry them away. Like one who feels a fit coming on, they waited. Nor did they care very much when the Mad Fakir arrived. They would fight and kill the infidels. In the meantime there was no necessity to deprive them of their ponies. And so with motives, partly callous, partly sportsmanlike, they warned the native grooms, and these taking the hint reached the camp in safety.

Late on this same afternoon Major Deane reported to Brigadier-General Meiklejohn, who commanded the Malakand garrison, that a great armed gathering had collected around the Mad Mullah's standard, and that an attack was probable. He advised that the Guides should be called up to reinforce the brigade. A telegram was immediately despatched to Mardan ordering them to march without delay. At 8.30 Lieutenant P. Eliott-Lockhart, who was the senior officer then with the regiment, received the order. At 1.30 a.m. they began their march.

After sending for the Guides, the brigadier, at about seven o'clock, interviewed his different commanding officers, and instructed them to be prepared to turn out at any moment. Major Deane now reported that the Mad Mullah and his gathering were advancing down the valley, and recommended that the Amandara Pass, four miles away, should be held. General Meiklejohn accordingly issued orders for a movable column, under command of Lieutenant-Colonel McRae, 45th Sikhs, which was to start at midnight and would be supported by the rest of the troops under command of the brigadier at 3 a.m.

All preparations were swiftly made. At 9.45, a telegram from Chakdara – which got through just before the wire was cut – reported that large forces of Pathans were rapidly moving towards the camps. A quarter of an hour later a jemadar of the Levies galloped in with the news that, to quote the official despatch: 'The Fakir had passed Khar and was advancing on Malakand, and that neither Levies nor people would act against him, and that the hills to the east of the camp were covered with Pathans'.

As soon as the officers had returned from polo, they found plenty of work waiting for them. Indents had to be made out for transport, rations and ammunition. At length the troops were in readiness for their early morning start. At 9.30 the officers sat down to dinner, still in their polo kit, which there had been no time to change. At ten o'clock they were discussing the prospects of the approaching march, and eagerly weighing the chances of a skirmish.

Suddenly in the stillness of the night a bugle-call sounded on the parade ground of the crater camp. Everyone sprang up. It was the 'Assembly'. For a moment there was silence while the officers seized their swords and belts and hurriedly fastened them on. Several, thinking that it was merely the warning for the movable column to fall in, waited to light their cigarettes. Then from many quarters the loud explosion of musketry burst forth, a sound which for six days and nights was to know no intermission.

The attack on the Malakand and the great frontier war had begun.

The noise of firing echoed among the hills. One valley caught the waves of sound and passed them to the next, till the whole wide mountain region rocked with the confusion of the tumult. Cables carried them to the far-off countries of the West. Distant populations on the Continent of Europe thought that in them they detected the dull, discordant tones of decline and fall. Diplomatists looked wise, economists anxious, stupid people mysterious and knowledgeable.

CHAPTER III

THE ATTACK ON THE MALAKAND

It has long been recognised by soldiers of every nation that, to resist a vigorous onslaught by night, is almost the hardest task that troops can be called upon to perform. Panics against which few brave men are proof, arise in a moment from such situations. Regiments that have marched unflinchingly to almost certain death on the battlefield, become in an instant terrified and useless.

In the attack on the Malakand camp, all the elements of danger and disorder were displayed. But there were men who were equal to the occasion. As soon as the alarm sounded Lieutenant-Colonel McRae of the 45th Sikhs, ran to the Quarter Guard, and collecting seven or eight men, sent them under command of Major Taylor, of the same regiment, down the Buddhist road to try and check the enemy's advance. Hurriedly assembling another dozen men, and leaving the Adjutant, Lieutenant Barff, with directions to bring on more, he ran with his little party after Taylor in the direction of the entrance gorge of the Kotal camp. Two roads give access to the Malakand camp, from the plain of Khar. At one point the Buddhist road, the higher of the two, passes through a narrow defile and turns a sharp corner. Here, if anywhere, the enemy might be held or at least delayed until the troops got under arms. Overtaking Major Taylor, Colonel McRae led the party, which then amounted to perhaps twenty men, swiftly down the road. It was a race on which the lives of hundreds depended. If the enemy could turn the corner, nothing could check their rush, and the few men who tried to oppose them would be cut to pieces. The Sikhs arrived first, but by a very little. As they turned the corner they met the mass of the enemy – nearly a thousand strong, armed chiefly with swords and knives, creeping silently and stealthily up the gorge, in the hope and assurance, of rushing the camp and massacring every soul in it. The whole road was crowded with the wild figures. McRae opened fire at once. Volley after volley was poured into the dense mass, at

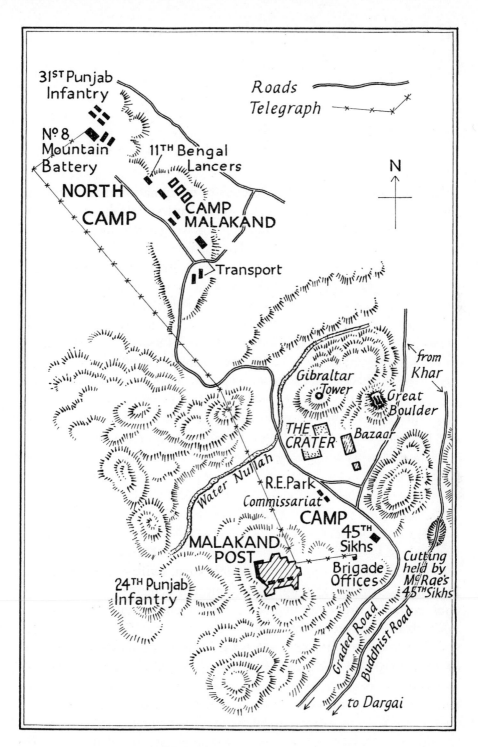

THE MALAKAND POSITION

deadly range. Then the Sikhs fired independently. This checked the enemy, who shouted and yelled in fury at being thus stopped. The small party of soldiers then fell back, pace by pace, firing incessantly, and took up a position in a cutting about fifty yards behind the corner. Their flanks were protected on the left by high rocks, and on the right by boulders and rough ground, over which in the darkness it was impossible to move. The road was about five yards wide. As fast as the tribesmen turned the corner they were shot down. It was a strong position.

Being thus effectively checked in their direct advance, the tribesmen began climbing up the hill to the left and throwing down rocks and stones on those who barred their path. They also fired their rifles round the corner, but as they were unable to see the soldiers without exposing themselves, most of their bullets went to the right.

The band of Sikhs were closely packed in the cutting, the front rank kneeling to fire. Nearly all were struck by stones and rocks. Major Taylor, displaying great gallantry, was mortally wounded. Several of the Sepoys were killed. Colonel McRae himself was accidentally stabbed in the neck by a bayonet and became covered with blood. But he called upon the men to maintain the good name of 'Rattray's Sikhs', and to hold their position till death or the regiment came up. And the soldiers replied by loudly shouting the Sikh war-cry, and defying the enemy to come on.

After twenty minutes of desperate fighting, Lieutenant Barff arrived with thirty more men. He was only just in time. The enemy had already worked round Colonel McRae's right, and the destruction of the few soldiers left alive could not long have been delayed. The reinforcement, climbing up the hillside, drove the enemy back and protected the flank. But the remainder of the regiment was now at hand. About 2 a.m., the tribesmen finding they could make no progress drew off, leaving many dead.

While these things were passing on the right, the glow of the star shells showed that the north camp was also engaged. The enemy had been checked on the Buddhist road, but another great mass of men forced their way along the Graded road in the centre of the position. On the first sound of firing the inlying picquet of the 24th Punjab Infantry doubled out, to reinforce the picquets on the road, and in the water-gorge. They only arrived in time to find these being driven in by overpowering numbers of the enemy. Hundreds of fierce swordsmen, swarmed into the bazaar, and into the *serai*, a small enclosure which adjoined. Sharpshooters scrambled up the surrounding hills, and kept up a tremendous fire. The defence of the left and centre of the camp was confided to the 24th Punjab Infantry.

One company of this regiment under Lieutenant Climo, charging across the football ground, cleared the bazaar at the point of the bayonet. The bazaar was crowded with tribesmen. The soldiers rushing forward amid loud cheers, plunged their bayonets into their furious adversaries. The sound of the hacking of swords, the screams of the unfortunate shopkeepers, the yells of the Ghazis were plainly heard above the ceaseless roll of musketry. The enemy now tried to force their way back into the bazaar, but the entrance was held against all assaults till about 10.45. The left flank of the company was now turned, and the pressure became so severe that they were withdrawn to a more interior line of defence. Another company held the approaches from the north camp. The remainder of the regiment and No. 5 company sappers and miners, were kept in readiness to reinforce any part of the line.

The enemy had attacked in tremendous strength along the two roads that gave access on the eastern side to the great cup of the Malakand. On the right road, they were checked by the brilliant movement of Colonel McRae and the courage of his regiment. Pouring in overwhelming force along the left road, they had burst into the camp itself, bearing down all opposition. The defenders, unable to hold the extended line of the rim, had been driven to take up a central position in the bottom of the cup. This central position comprised the sappers' and miners' enclosure, the commissariat lines and the Field Engineer Park. It was commanded on every side by the fire from the rim.

As the night wore on, the attack of the enemy became so vigorous, that the brigadier decided to call for a reinforcement of a hundred men, from the garrison of the fort. This work stood high on a hill, and was impregnable to an enemy unprovided with field guns. Lieutenant Rawlins volunteered to try and reach it with the order. Accompanied by three orderlies, he started. He had to make his way through much broken ground infested by the enemy. One man sprang at him and struck him on the wrist with a sword, but the subaltern, firing his revolver, shot him dead, reached the fort in safety, and brought back the sorely-needed reinforcement.

It was thought the enemy would make a final effort to capture the enclosure before dawn, that being the hour which Afghan tribesmen usually select. But they had lost heavily, and at about 3.30 a.m. began to carry away their dead and wounded. The firing did not, however, lessen until 4.15 a.m., when the sharpshooters withdrew to the heights, and the fusillade dwindled to 'sniping' at long range.

As soon as the first light of morning began to grow in the valley, two companies of the 24th advanced and cleared the bazaar of such of the enemy as had remained behind to plunder. The whole place had been thoroughly ransacked, and everything of value destroyed or carried off. The native manager had had a strange experience, and one which few men would envy. He had remained hidden in the back of a tent during the whole night in equal danger and terror of the bullets of the soldiers and swords of the enemy. Hearing the friendly voices he emerged uninjured from his retreat.

The evacuation of the north camp which had not been seriously involved in the fighting proceeded very slowly. The troops packed up their kits with great deliberation, and applications were made for transport. None was, however, available. All the camels were at Dargai, on the India side of the mountains. Repeated orders to hurry were sent from the Kotal. All hated leaving their belongings behind, having no confidence in the liberality of a paternal Government. As the afternoon passed the aspect of the enemy became very threatening and formidable. Great numbers drew near to the camp, and the guns were compelled to fire a good many rounds. At length, at four o'clock, imperative orders were sent that the north camp was to be at once abandoned, that the force there was to march to the Kotal, and that all baggage and stores not yet removed were to be left where they were.

It cannot be doubted that the concentration of the troops was a wise and judicious step. The garrison of the Kotal and south camp was insufficient, and whatever happened it was better for the troops to stand or fall together. The situation was also aggravated by the appearance of large numbers of tribesmen from the Utman Khel country, who crowded the hills to the west of the camp, and thus compelled the defenders to hold a greatly extended line. The abandonment of the north camp was carried out none too soon, for the enemy pressed the withdrawal of the troops, and they reached the south camp under cover of the fire of the 24th Punjab Infantry, and the Guides Cavalry. These had arrived in camp at 8.30 that morning after marching all night.

The telegraph had carried the news of the events of the night to all parts of the world. At Simla, the Government of India awoke to find themselves confronted with another heavy task. Messages recalled all officers to their regiments, and summoned reinforcements to the scene by road and rail. The 11th Bengal Lancers, the 38th Dogras and the 35th Sikhs started at dawn. No. 1 and No. 7 British Mountain Batteries were also ordered up. The Guides Cavalry had already arrived. Their infantry under Lieutenant Lockhart reached the Kotal at 7.30 p.m. on the 27th, having in spite of the intense heat and choking dust covered thirty-two miles in seventeen and a half hours. This wonderful feat was accomplished without impairing the efficiency of the soldiers. An officer who commanded the Dargai post told me that as they passed the guard there they shouldered arms with parade precision, to show that twenty-six miles under the hottest sun in the world, would not take the polish off the Corps of Guides.

Help in plenty was thus approaching as fast as eager men could march, but meanwhile the garrison had to face the danger as best they could alone. As the evening drew on the enemy were observed assembling in ever-increasing numbers. Great crowds of them could be seen streaming along the Chakdara road, and thickly dotting the hills with spots of white. They all wore white as yet. The sombre-clad warriors of Ambeyla were still absent. The glare of the flames from the north camp was soon to summon them to the attack of their ancient enemies. The spectacle as night fell, was strange, ominous, but not unpicturesque. Gay banners of every colour, shape and device, waved from the surrounding hills. The sunset caught the flashing of sword-blades behind the spurs and ridges. The numerous figures of the enemy moved busily about preparing for the attack. A dropping fire from the sharpshooters added an appropriate accompaniment. In the middle, at the bottom of the cup, was the crater camp, and the main enclosure with the smoke of the evening meal rising in the air. The troops moved to their stations, and as the shadows grew the firing swelled into a loud, incessant roar.

The disposition of the troops on the night of the 27th was as follows:

1. On the right Colonel McRae, with the 45th Sikhs and two guns supported by 100 men of the Guides Infantry, held almost the same position astride the Buddhist road as before.

2. In the centre the enclosure and Graded road were defended by
        31st Punjab Infantry.
        No. 5 Company Q.O. Sappers and Miners.
        The Guides.
        Two Guns.

3. On the left the 24th Punjab Infantry, with the two remaining guns under Lieutenant Climo, held the approaches from the abandoned north camp and the fort.

Most of this extended line, which occupied a great part of the rim, was formed by a chain of picquets, detached from one another and fortified by stone breastworks, with supports in rear. But in the centre the old line of the sappers' and miners' enclosure was adhered to. The bazaar was left to the enemy, but the *serai*, about a hundred yards in front of the main entrenchment, was held by a picquet of twenty-four men of the 31st Punjab Infantry under Subadar Syed Ahmed Shah. Here it was that the tragedy of the night occurred.

At eight o'clock the tribesmen attacked in tremendous force all along the line. The firing at once became intense and continuous. On the right Colonel McRae and his Sikhs were repeatedly charged by the swordsmen, many of whom succeeded in forcing their way into the picquets and perished by the bayonet.

All assaults were however beaten off. The tribesmen suffered terrible losses. The casualties among the Sikhs were also severe. In the morning Colonel McRae advanced from his defences, and covered by the fire of his two guns cleared the ground in his front of the enemy.

The centre was again the scene of severe fighting. The tribesmen poured into the bazaar and attacked the *serai* on all sides. This post was a mud-walled enclosure about fifty yards square. It was loopholed for musketry, but had no flank defences. The enemy made determined efforts to capture the place for several hours. Meanwhile so tremendous was the fire of the troops in the main enclosure that the attack upon the *serai* was hardly noticed. For six hours the picquet there held out against all assaults, but the absence of flank defences enabled the enemy to come close up to the walls. They then began to make holes through them, and to burrow underneath. The little garrison rushed from place to place repelling these attacks. But it was like caulking a sieve. At length the tribesmen burst in from several quarters, and the sheds inside caught fire. When all the defenders except four were killed or wounded, the subadar, himself struck by a bullet, ordered the place to be evacuated, and the survivors escaped by a ladder over the back wall, carrying their wounded with them. The bodies of the killed were found next morning extraordinarily mutilated.

The defence of this post to the bitter end must be regarded as a fine feat of arms. Subadar Syed Ahmed Shah was originally promoted to a commission for an act of conspicuous bravery, and his gallant conduct on this occasion is the subject of a special paragraph in despatches.

On the left, the 24th Punjab Infantry were also hotly engaged, and Lieutenant Costello received his first severe wound from a bullet, which passed through his back and arm. Towards morning the enemy began to press severely. Whereupon Lieutenant Climo, always inclined to bold and vigorous action, advanced from the breastworks to meet them with two companies. The tribesmen held their ground and maintained a continual fire from Martini-Henry rifles. They also rolled down great stones upon the companies. The 24th continued to advance, and drove the enemy from point to point, and position to position, pursuing them for a distance of two miles. 'Gallows Tree' hill, against which the first charge of the counter-attack was delivered, was held by nearly 1,000 tribesmen. On such crowded masses, the fire of the troops was deadly. The enemy left forty dead on the field of Lieutenant Climo's counter-attack, and were observed carrying off many wounded.

Thus the onslaught of the tribesmen had again been successfully repelled by the Malakand garrison. Many had been killed and wounded, but all the tribes for 100 miles around were hurrying to the attack, and their numbers momentarily increased. Great numbers of Bunerwals now joined the gathering. The garrison were able to distinguish these new-comers from the Swatis, Utman Khels, Mamunds, Salarzais and others, by the black or dark-blue clothes they wore. The troops were employed in strengthening the defences, and improving the shelters. The tribesmen kept up a harassing, and annoying long-range fire; towards evening they advanced to renew the attack, carrying hundreds of standards.

As darkness fell, heavy firing recommenced along the whole front. The enemy had apparently plenty of ammunition, and replied with effect, to the heavy fire of the troops. On the right Colonel McRae once more held his own against all attacks. In the centre the enemy charged again and again up to the breastwork of the enclosure. They did not succeed in penetrating. Three officers and several men were however wounded by the fire.

Lieutenant Ford was dangerously wounded in the shoulder. The bullet cut the artery, and he was bleeding to death when Surgeon-Lieutenant V. Hugo came to his aid. The fire was too hot to allow of lights being used. There was no cover of any sort. It was at the bottom of the cup. Nevertheless the surgeon struck a match at the peril of his life and examined the wound. The match went out amid a splutter of bullets, which kicked up the dust all around, but by its uncertain light he saw the nature of the injury. The officer had already fainted from the loss of blood. The doctor seized the artery, and, as no other ligature was forthcoming, he remained under fire for three hours holding a man's life, between his finger and thumb.

On the morning of the 29th signalling communication with Chakdara was for a few moments re-established. The garrison of the post announced their safety, and that all attacks had been repulsed with heavy loss, but they reported that ammunition and food were both running short. During the day the enemy again retired to the plain to rest, and prepare for the great attack which they intended making that night. The hour would be propitious. It was Jumarat, on which day the prophet watches with especial care over the interests of those who die for the faith. Besides, the moon was full, and had not the great Fakir declared that this should be the moment of victory? The Mullah declared that he would himself lead the assault. Tonight the infidels would be utterly destroyed.

Meanwhile the troops were busily employed in spite of their terrible fatigues in strengthening the defences. The bazaar and the *serai* were levelled. Trees were blown up and a clear field of fire was obtained in front of the central enclosure. Great bonfires were also prepared in front of the defences, to enable the soldiers to take good aim at their assailants while they were silhouetted against the light. In such occupations the day passed.

At four o'clock in the afternoon Major Stuart Beatson, commanding the 11th Bengal Lancers, arrived with his leading squadron. He brought a small supply of ammunition, which the garrison was in sore need of, the expenditure each night being tremendous. The 35th Sikhs and 38th Dogras under Colonel Reid arrived at Dargai, at the foot of the pass, in the evening. They had marched all day in the most intense heat. How terrible that march must have been, may be judged from the fact that in the 35th Sikhs twenty-one men actually died on the road of heat apoplexy. Brigadier-General Meiklejohn, feeling confidence in his ability to hold his own with the troops, had ordered them to remain halted at Dargai, and rest the next day.

The attack came with the night, but the defences in the centre had been much improved, and the tribesmen were utterly unable to cross the cleared glacis, which now stretched in front of the enclosure. They, however, assailed both flanks with determination, and the firing everywhere became heavy. At 2 a.m. the great attack was delivered. Along the whole front and from every side enormous numbers swarmed to the assault. On the right and left, hand-to-hand fighting took place. Colonel McRae again held his position, but many of the tribesmen died under the very muzzles of the rifles. The 24th Punjab Infantry on the left were the most severely engaged. The enemy succeeded in breaking into the breastworks, and close fighting ensued, but the fire of the troops was too hot for anything to live in their front. At 2.30 the Mad Mullah being wounded, another Mullah killed and several hundreds of tribesmen slain, the whole attack collapsed. The enemy recognised that their chance of taking the Malakand had passed.

In the morning the 38th Dogras, and 35th Sikhs, marched into the camp. The enemy continued firing into the entrenchments at long range, but without effect. They had evidently realised that the Malakand was too strong to be taken. The troops had a quiet night, and the weary, worn-out men got a little, needed sleep. Thus the long and persistent attack on the British frontier station of Malakand, languished and ceased. The tribesmen, sick of the slaughter at this point, concentrated their energies on Chakdara, which they believed must fall into their hands. To relieve this hard-pressed post now became the duty of the garrison of Malakand.

CHAPTER IV

THE RELIEF OF CHAKDARA

While the events described in the last chapter had been watched with interest and attention in all parts of the world, they were the subject of anxious consultation in the Council of the Governor-General. The Viceroy[1] belonged to that party in the State which has clung passionately, vainly, and often unwisely, to a policy of peace and retrenchment. He was supported in his reluctance to embark on warlike enterprises, by the whole force of the economic situation. No moment could have been less fitting: no man more disinclined.

On the 30th of July the following order was officially published: 'The Governor-General in Council sanctions the despatch of a force to be styled the Malakand Field Force, for the purpose of holding the Malakand, and the adjacent posts, and operating against the neighbouring tribes as may be required'.

The force was composed as follows:

1st Brigade
Commanding: COLONEL W. H. MEIKLEJOHN, C.B., C.M.G.,
with the local rank of Brigadier-General.
1st Border Royal West Kent Regiment
24th Punjab Infantry
31st Punjab Infantry
45th (Rattray's) Sikhs
Sections A and B of No. 1 British Field Hospital
No. 38 Native Field Hospital
Sections A and B of No. 50 Native Field Hospital

2nd Brigade
Commanding: BRIGADIER-GENERAL P. D. JEFFREYS, C.B.
1st Border East Kent Regiment (the Buffs)
35th Sikhs

[1] Lord Elgin.

38th Dogras
Guides Infantry
Sections C and D of No. 1 British Field Hospital
No. 37 Native Field Hospital
Sections C and D of No. 50 Native Field Hospital

Divisional Troops
4 Squadrons 11th Bengal Lancers
1   ,,   10th   ,,   ,,
2   ,,   Guides Cavalry
22nd Punjab Infantry
2 Companies 21st Punjab Infantry
10th Field Battery
6 Guns No. 1 British Mountain Battery
6 ,, No. 7   ,,   ,,   ,,
6 ,, No. 8 Bengal   ,,   ,,
No. 5 Company Madras Sappers and Miners
No. 3   ,,   Bombay   ,,   ,,   ,,
Section B of No. 13 British Field Hospital
Sections A and B of No. 35 Native Field Hospital

Line of Communications
No. 34 Native Field Hospital
Section B of No. 1 Native Field Hospital

This complete division amounted to a total available field strength of 6,800 bayonets, 700 lances or sabres, with 24 guns.

The command of this force was entrusted to Brigadier-General Sir Bindon Blood, K.C.B., who was granted the local rank of Major-General.

It would not be fitting for me, a subaltern of horse, to offer any criticism though eulogistic of the commander under whom I have had the honour to serve in the field. I shall content myself with saying that the general is one of that type of soldiers, and administrators, which the responsibilities and dangers of an empire produce.

Sir Bindon Blood was at Agra when on the evening of the 28th of July he received the telegram from the Adjutant-General in India, appointing him to the command of the Malakand Field Force, and instructing him to proceed at once to assume it. He started immediately, and on the 31st formally took command of the force at Nowshera. At

Mardan he halted to make arrangements for the onward march of the troops. Here at 3 a.m. on the 1st of August, he received a telegram from Army Headquarters informing him that Chakdara Fort was hard pressed, and directing him to hurry on to the Malakand, and attempt its relief at all costs. Sir Bindon Blood hurried on at once, and in spite of the disturbed state of the country reached the Malakand about noon on the 1st of August.

Sir Bindon Blood found General Meiklejohn busily engaged in organising a force of all arms which was to move to the relief of Chakdara on the following day. As it was dangerous to denude the Malakand position of troops, this force could not exceed 1,000 rifles, the available cavalry and four guns. Sir Bindon Blood relieved Brigadier-General Meiklejohn of the charge of the Malakand position, and gave him the command of the relieving column. Colonel Reid was then placed in command of Malakand, and instructed to strengthen the picquets at Castle Rock, as far as possible, and to be ready with a force taken from them, to clear the high ground on the right of the Graded road.

Sir Bindon Blood ordered General Meiklejohn to assemble his force before dark near the centre of the camp at a grove of trees called 'Gretna Green', to bivouac there for the night, and to be ready to start with the first light of morning. During the afternoon the enemy, encouraged by their success with the cavalry in the morning, advanced boldly to the picquets, and the firing was continuous. So heavy did the firing become between eleven and twelve o'clock at night, that the force at 'Gretna Green' got under arms. But towards morning the tribesmen retired. The reader may perhaps have in his own mind the description of the Malakand as a great cup with jagged clefts in the rim. Much of the rim was still held by the enemy. It was necessary for any force trying to get out of the cup, to fight their way along the narrow roads through the clefts, which were commanded by the heights on either side. For a considerable distance it was impossible to deploy. Therein lay the difficulty of the operation, which the General had now to perform. The relieving column was exposed to the danger of being stopped just as Colonel McRae had stopped the first attack of the tribesmen, along the Buddhist road.

Looking at the tangled, rugged nature of the country, it seems extraordinary to any untrained eye, that among so many peaks and points, one should be of more importance than another. Yet it is so. On the high ground, in front of the position that Colonel McRae and the 45th Sikhs had held so well, was a prominent spur. This was the key which would unlock the gate, and set free the troops who were cramped up within. Everyone realised afterwards how obvious this was, and wondered they had not thought of it before. Sir Bindon Blood selected the point as the object of his first attack, and it was against this that he directed Colonel Goldney with a force of about 300 men to move, as soon as he should give the signal to advance.

At half-past four in the morning of the 2nd of August, he proceeded to 'Gretna Green' and found the relieving column fallen in, and ready to march at daybreak. All expected a severe action. Oppressed with fatigue and sleeplessness, there were many who doubted that it would be successful. But though tired, they were determined, and braced themselves for a desperate struggle. The General-in-Chief was confident and serene. He summoned the different commanding officers, explained his plans, and shook hands all round. Slowly the first faint light of dawn grew in the eastern sky. Then the word was given to advance. Immediately the relieving column set off, fours deep, down the Graded road. Colonel Goldney simultaneously advanced to the attack of the spur, which will ever afterwards bear his name, with 250 men of the 35th Sikhs, and 50 of the 38th Dogras. He moved silently towards the stone shelters that the tribesmen had erected on the crest. He got to within 100 yards unperceived. The enemy, surprised, opened an irregular and ineffective fire. The Sikhs shouted, and dashed forward. The enemy fled in disorder, leaving seven dead and one prisoner on the ground.

The point now gained commanded the whole of the Graded road, right down to its junction with the road to the north camp. The relieving column moving down the road were enabled to deploy without loss or delay. The door was open. The enemy, utterly surprised and dumbfounded by this manœuvre, were seen running to and fro in the greatest confusion: in the graphic words of Sir Bindon Blood's despatch, 'Like ants in a disturbed ant-hill'. At length they seemed to realise the situation, and, descending from the high ground, took up a position near Bedford Hill in General Meiklejohn's front, and opened a heavy fire at close range; but the troops were now deployed, and able to

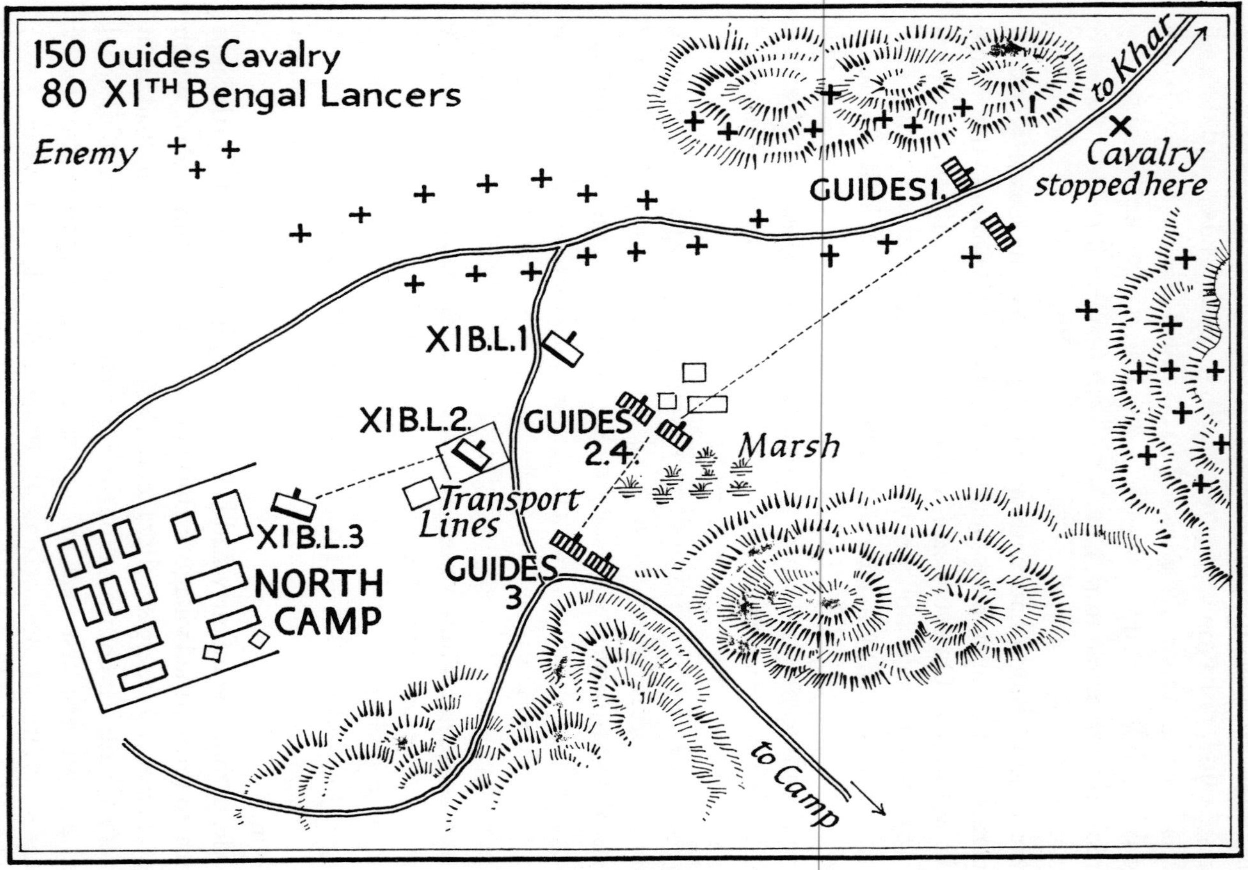

150 Guides Cavalry
80 XIᵀᴴ Bengal Lancers

to Khar

Cavalry stopped here

GUIDES 1.

Enemy

GUIDES 2.4.

Marsh

XIB.L.1

XIB.L.2

Transport Lines

GUIDES 3

XIB.L.3

NORTH CAMP

to Camp

CAVALRY FIGHT AT MALAKAND

bring their numbers to bear. Without wasting time in firing, they advanced with the bayonet. The leading company of the Guides stormed the hill in their front, with a loss of two killed and six wounded. The rest of the troops charged with even less loss. The enemy, thoroughly panic-stricken, began to fly, literally by thousands, along the heights to the right.

Sir Bindon Blood had with his staff ascended the Castle Rock, to superintend the operations generally. From this position the whole field was visible. On every side, and from every rock, the white figures of the enemy could be seen in full flight. The way was open. The passage was forced. Chakdara was saved. A great and brilliant success had been obtained. A thrill of exultation convulsed everyone. In that moment the general, who watched the triumphant issue of his plans, must have experienced as fine an emotion as is given to man on earth.

The victory had been gained, it remained to profit by it. The enemy would be compelled to retire across the plain. There at last was the chance of the cavalry. The four squadrons were hurried to the scene. The 11th Bengal Lancers, forming line across the plain, began a merciless pursuit up the valley. The Guides pushed on to seize the Amandara Pass, and relieve Chakdara. All along the rice fields and the rocks, the strong horsemen hunted the flying enemy. No quarter was asked or given, and every tribesman caught was speared or cut down at once. Their bodies lay thickly strewed about the fields, spotting with black and white patches, the bright green of the rice crop. It was a terrible lesson and one which the inhabitants of Swat and Bajaur will never forget.

Meanwhile the infantry had been advancing swiftly. The 45th Sikhs stormed the fortified village of Butkhela near the Amandara Pass, which the enemy held desperately. Lieut.-Colonel McRae, who had been relieved from the command of the regiment by the arrival of Colonel Sawyer, was the first man to enter the village. Eighty of the enemy were bayoneted in Butkhela alone. It was a terrible reckoning.

I am anxious to finish with this scene of carnage. The spectator who may gaze unmoved on the bloodshed of the battle, must avert his eyes from the horrors of the pursuit, unless, indeed, joining in it himself, he flings all scruples to the winds, and indulges to the full those deep-seated instincts of savagery, over which civilisation has but cast a veil of doubtful thickness.

The news of the relief of Chakdara was received with feelings of profound thankfulness throughout India. And in England, in the House of Commons, when the Secretary of State read out the telegram, there were few among the members who did not join in the cheers.

CHAPTER V

THE DEFENCE OF CHAKDARA

Chakdara holds the passage of the Swat River – a rapid, broad, and at most seasons of the year an unfordable torrent. It is built on a rocky knoll that rises abruptly from the plain about a hundred yards from the mountains. Sketches and photographs usually show only the knoll, and buildings, on it; and anyone looking at them will be struck by the picturesque, and impregnable aspect, of the little fort, without observing that its proportions are dwarfed, and its defences commanded, by the frowning cliffs, under which it stands. In its construction the principles of *Defilade* have been completely ignored. Standing on the mountain ridge occupied by the signal tower, it is possible to look or fire right into the fort. Every open space is commanded. Every parapet is exposed. Against an enemy unprovided with artillery, however, it could be held indefinitely; but the fact that all interior communications are open to fire, makes its defence painful to the garrison, and might by gradually weakening their numbers lead to its capture.

The narrow, swinging wire bridge across the Swat is nearly 500 yards long. At the southern end, it is closed by a massive iron door, loopholed for musketry, and flanked by two stone towers, in one of which a Maxim gun is mounted. On the further side is the fort itself, which consists of the fortified knoll, a strong stone-horn work, an enclosure for horses, protected by a loopholed wall and much tangled barbed wire, and the signal tower, a detached post 200 yards up the cliff.

The garrison of this place consisted at the time of the outbreak of twenty Sowars, of the 11th Bengal Lancers, and two strong companies of the 45th Sikhs, in all about 200 men, under the command of Lieutenant H. B. Rattray. As the rumours of an impending rising grew stronger and stronger, and the end of July approached, this officer made such preparations as he thought necessary for eventualities. On the 23rd he received an official warning from the D.A.A.G., Major Herbert (that a tribal rising was 'possible but not probable'). Every precaution was henceforth taken in the fort. On the 26th, a Sepoy who was out sketching hurried in with the news that a large body of tribesmen were advancing down the valley, and that he himself had been robbed of his compass, his field-glasses and some money.

The British officers of the Malakand garrison, though they took all military precautions for the defence of their posts, did not abandon their practice of riding freely about the valley armed only with revolvers; nor did they cease from their amusements. On the evening of the 26th, Lieutenant Rattray went over to Khar as usual to play polo. Just as the game was ended he received a letter brought in haste by two Sowars from Lieutenant Wheatley, the other subaltern at Chakdara, warning him that a great number of Pathans with flags were advancing on the fort. He at once galloped back at full speed, passing close to one large gathering of tribesmen, who for some reason of their own took no notice of him, and so reached the fort in safety, and just in time. Formidable masses of men were then closing in on it. He telegraphed to the D.A.A.G. at the Malakand reporting the impending attack. Immediately afterwards the wire was cut by the enemy and the little garrison got under arms.

A havildar of the Khan of Dir's Levies, had promised the political agent to give warning of any actual assault, by lighting a fire on the opposite hills. At 10.15 a solitary flame shot up. It was the signal. The alarm was sounded. The garrison went to their posts. For a space there was silence; and then out of the darkness began a fusillade, which did not stop until the 2nd of August. Immediately the figures of the tribesmen, as they advanced to the attack on the western face of the fort, became visible. The defenders opened fire with effect. The enemy pressed on vigorously. Their losses were severe. At length they retreated repulsed.

A second attack was immediately delivered against the north-east corner, and again beaten off by the garrison. At 4 a.m. a third assault was made upon the cavalry enclosure. The tribesmen, carrying scaling ladders, advanced with great determination. They were received with a deadly fire. They then drew off, and the first night of the siege was terminated by desultory firing.

Meanwhile, in spite of the vigorous attack that was being made on the Malakand, it was decided to send some assistance to the little band at Chakdara. Captain Wright and forty Sowars of the 11th Bengal Lancers with Captain Baker of the 2nd Bombay Grenadiers and transport officer at the Malakand, started at dawn on the 27th, by the road from the north camp. Before they had gone very far they came under the fire of the enemy on the hills. These did not dare to venture into the plain, but availed themselves of the broken nature of the country. As the squadron reached the road leading to the polo ground, Captain Wright received information that the enemy were collected on the plain, and immediately the pace was quickened in the hopes of a charge being possible. But the tribesmen ran to the hills at the sight of the Lancers, and maintained a constant, though luckily, an ill-aimed fire. At length the Amandara Pass came in sight. This is a gap in a long spur which runs from the southern side of the valley to the rapid river in the middle. As the river was then in full flood and unfordable, the only road to Chakdara lay over or through the spur. But the pass was held by the enemy.

Captain Wright had by this time realised what probably no one at the Malakand then knew, that the enemy's numbers were enormous. The whole way from Malakand to Amandara – every ridge and hill was crowned with their banners; wherever the ground protected them from the horsemen they gathered thickly. Cemeteries, nullahs and villages swarmed with men. Their figures could be seen in all directions. Far beyond the Amandara Pass bands of tribesmen, of varying strengths, could be seen hurrying, with their standards, to the attack.

Under a dropping fire from the cemetery on the right of the road, a brief consultation was held. The Amandara defile was occupied on both sides by the enemy. With the loss of perhaps a dozen men the squadron might gallop through. But this meant leaving all who fell, to perish miserably, by torture and mutilation. To attempt to pick up the wounded, would lead to the annihilation of the squadron. Any alternative was preferable, though if there were no other way, the dash would have to be made, and the wounded left. A Sowar now said there was a path round the rock by the bank of the river. Captain Wright determined to take it.

The path was bad. After about half the spur had been passed, it ended abruptly in a steep white rock. It was, in fact, a path leading to a point where the natives were in the habit of floating across the river upon *mussacks* (inflated skins). To go back now was to fail. Without hesitation the horsemen turned to the right up the hill and among the rocks, trusting to get through somehow. After passing over ground which would be difficult to move across on foot, they saw a gorge to their left which appeared as if it would lead to the open plain, on the other side of the ridge. Down this gorge forty horses huddled together, with no room to pick their way, were scrambling and jumping from rock to rock, apparently as conscious as their riders, that their lives depended on their cleverness – when, suddenly, the enemy appeared.

As soon as the tribesmen, who were holding the pass, saw the squadron trot off to their right towards the river, they realised that they intended to make a desperate effort to get through to Chakdara. They knew what the ground was like, and confident they would kill them all, if they could get there in time, ran swiftly along the spur. It was a race. The leading tribesmen arrived in time to fire on the cavalry while they were in the gorge. So close were they that the officers used their revolvers. But the Pathans were out of breath and shot badly. Several horses were hit, including Captain Wright's, but though the large thigh bone was shattered, the gallant beast held on, and carried his rider to Chakdara safely.

By the extraordinary activity of the horses the rocks were cleared before the enemy could collect in any strength. But to the dismay of all, the gorge was found to lead, not to the plain, but to a branch of the river. A broad, swift channel of water of unknown depth confronted the cavalry. To go back was now, however, out of the question. They plunged in. The 11th Bengal Lancers are perhaps better mounted than any native cavalry regiment in India. Their strong horses just held their own against the current. Several were nearly swept away. Captain Wright was the last to cross. All this time the enemy were firing and approaching. At length the passage was made, and the squadron collected on an island of flooded rice fields, in which the horses sank up to their hocks. Beyond this ran another arm of the river about fifty yards wide, and apparently almost as deep as the first. After passing this second torrent the squadron found themselves again in swampy ground on the same bank of the river as the enemy. Captain Wright dismounted his men and returned the fire. Then he turned back himself, and riding into the stream again, rescued the hospital assistant, whose pony, smaller than the other horses, was being carried off its legs by the force of the water. After this the march was resumed. The squadron kept in the heavy ground struggling along painfully. The enemy running along the edge of the rice fields, maintained a continual fire, kneeling down to take good aim. By slow degrees Chakdara was approached, and then the Bridgehead Maxim compelled the tribesmen to draw off.

Thus the garrison of the fort received a needed reinforcement. I have given a somewhat long description of this gallant ride, because it shows that there are few obstacles that can stop brave men and good horses. Captain Wright now assumed command of Chakdara, but the direction of the defence he still confided to Lieutenant Rattray.

At 11.30, in the heat of the day, the tribesmen attacked again. They surrounded the north and east sides of the fort, and made strenuous efforts to get in. They suffered heavy losses, from the musketry of the defence, and their dead lay scattered thickly on the approaches. Many Ghazis, mad with fanaticism, pressed on carrying standards until they fell riddled with bullets under the very walls.

To communicate with the Malakand was now almost impossible. To heliograph, it was necessary that the operator should be exposed to a terrible fire. In the evening the signal tower was surrounded by men in stone *sungars*, who kept up an incessant fusillade, and made all exposure, even for an instant, perilous.

At midday, after the repulse of the main attack, the guard of the signal tower was reinforced by six men, and food and water were also sent up. The difficult operation was protected by the fire of both the Maxims, and of all the garrison who could be spared from other points. Until the 1st of August water was sent up daily to the signal tower in this way. Looking at the ground it seems wonderful that supplies could have been got through at all.

Meanwhile every spare moment was devoted to improving the cover for the garrison. Captain Baker applied himself to this task, and used every expedient. Logs, sand bags, stones, boxes filled with earth were piled upon the walls. It is due to these precautions that the loss of life was no larger.

Continuous firing occupied the 28th, and at 5.30 p.m. the enemy again assaulted. As in previous attacks they at first advanced by twos and threes, making little dashes over the open ground, for bits of natural cover, and for the stone *sungars* they had built all round the fort under cover of darkness. Some of these were within 200 yards of the wall. In a great semi-circle round the face of the fort held by the cavalry, and displaying nearly 200 standards, whose gay colours were representative of every tribe on the border, they charged right up to the walls. Some of them actually got across the tangled barbed wire and were destroyed in the enclosure. But all efforts were defeated by the garrison, and towards morning the attack melted away.

Thursday morning dawned on similar scenes. At 3 p.m. the enemy came out of Chakdara village, and, carrying ladders to scale the walls, and bundles of grass to throw on the barbed wire, made a formidable effort. They directed the attack, mainly against the signal station. This building is a strong, square, stone tower. Its entrance is above six feet from the ground. All around the top runs a *machicoalis* gallery, a kind of narrow balcony, with holes in the floor to fire through. It is well provided with loopholes. At four o'clock it was closely assailed. The garrison of the fort aided the tower guard by their fire. So bold were the enemy in their efforts, that they rushed in under the fire of the defence, and lighted a great heap of grass about three yards from the doorway. The flames sprang up. A howl of ferocious delight arose. But the tribesmen relapsed into silence when they saw no real harm was done. At sunset the fore sight of the fort Maxim was shot away, and the defenders were temporarily deprived of the service of that powerful weapon. They soon managed, however, to rig up a makeshift which answered all practical purposes. At 8 p.m. the enemy wearied of the struggle, and the firing died away to desultory skirmishing.

The morning of the 30th brought no cessation of the fighting, but the enemy, disheartened by their losses of the previous night, did not attack until 7 p.m. At that hour they advanced and made a fresh effort. They were again repulsed. Perhaps the reader is tired of the long recital of the monotonous succession of assaults, and repulses. What must the garrison have been by the reality? Until this day – when they snatched a few hours' sleep – they had been continually fighting and watching for ninety-six hours.

During the whole time of the siege the difficulty of maintaining the signalling communication with the Malakand was extreme. But for the heroism of the signallers, it would have been insuperable. One man in particular, Sepoy Prem Singh, used every day at the risk of his life to come out through a porthole of the tower, establish his heliograph, and under a terrible fire from short range, flash urgent messages to the main force. The extreme danger, the delicacy of the operation of obtaining connection with a helio, the time consumed, the composure required, these things combined to make the action as brave as any which my pages record.[1] Early on Saturday morning a supply of water was sent to the guard of the signal tower. It was the last they got until 4.30 on Monday afternoon.

When the attack on the fort began the enemy numbered perhaps 1,500 men. Since then they had been increasing every day, until on the 1st and 2nd, they are estimated to have been between 12,000 and 14,000 strong. Matters now began to assume a still graver aspect. At five o'clock on the evening of the 31st a renewed attack was made in tremendous force on the east side of the fort. But it was beaten back with great loss by the Maxims, and the field gun. All night long the firing continued, and Sunday morning displayed the enemy in far larger numbers than hitherto. They now captured the Civil Hospital, a detached building, the walls of which they loopholed, and from which they maintained a galling fire. They also occupied the ridge, leading to the signal tower, thus cutting off all communication with its guard. No water reached those unfortunate men that day. The weather was intensely hot. The fire from the ridge made all interior communication difficult and dangerous. The enemy appeared, armed to a great extent with Martini-Henry rifles, and Sniders, and their musketry was most galling. The party in the tower kept sending by signal, pressing requests for water, which could not be supplied. The situation became critical.

At length the last day of the struggle came. At daybreak the enemy in tremendous numbers came on to the assault, as if resolute to take the

---

[1] A proposal has recently been made to give the Victoria Cross to native soldiers who shall deserve it. It would seem that the value of such a decoration must be enhanced by making it open to all British subjects. The keener the competition, the greater the honour of success. In sport, in courage, and in the sight of heaven, all men meet on equal terms.

place at any cost. They carried scaling ladders and bundles of grass. The firing became intense. In spite of the cover of the garrison several men were killed and wounded by the hail of bullets which was directed against the fort, and which splashed and scarred the walls in every direction.

Then suddenly as matters were approaching a crisis the cavalry of the relieving column appeared over the Amandara ridge. The strong horsemen mercilessly pursued and cut down all who opposed them. When they reached the Bridgehead, on the side of the river remote from the fort, the enemy began to turn and run. The garrison had held out stubbornly and desperately throughout the siege. Now that relief was at hand Lieutenant Rattray flung open the gate, and followed by half a dozen men charged the Civil Hospital. Captain Baker and Lieutenant Wheatley followed with a few more. The hospital was recaptured. The enemy occupying it, some thirty in number, were bayoneted. It was a finish in style.

CHAPTER VI

THE GATE OF SWAT

The Malakand Pass gives access to the valley of the Swat, a long and wide trough, running east and west, among the mountains. Six miles further to the east at Chakdara, the valley bifurcates. One branch runs northward, towards Uch, and turning again to the west ultimately leads to the Panjkora River, and beyond to the great valley of Nawagai. For some distance along this branch, lies the road to Chitral, and along it the Malakand Field Force will presently advance against the Mohmands. The other branch prolongs the valley to the eastward. A few miles beyond Chakdara a long spur jutting from the southern mountains, blocks the valley. Round its base the river has cut a channel. The road passes along a narrow stone causeway between the river and the spur. Here is the Landakai position, or as the tribesmen have for centuries called it, the 'Gate of Swat'. Beyond this gate is Upper Swat, the ancient, beautiful and mysterious 'Udyana'.

The severe fighting at the Malakand and Chakdara had shown how formidable was the combination which had been raised against the British, among the hill tribes. The most distant and solitary valleys; the most remote villages had sent their armed men to join in the destruction of the infidel. All the Bajaur tribes had been well represented in the enemy's ranks. The Bunerwals, and the Utman Khels, had risen to a man. Instead of the two or three thousand men that had been estimated as the extreme number who would follow the Mad Fakir, it was now known that over 12,000 were in arms. In consequence of the serious aspect which the military and political situation had assumed, it was decided to mobilise a 3rd and Reserve Brigade under General J. H. Wodehouse.

The fighting of the preceding fortnight had left significant and terrible marks on the once smiling landscape. The rice crops were trampled down in all directions. The ruins of the villages which had been burned looked from a distance like blots of ink. In the attacks upon the Malakand position, about 700 tribesmen had perished. In the siege of Chakdara, where the open ground had afforded opportunity to the modern weapons, and Maxim guns, over 2,000 had been killed. Many others had fallen in the relief of Chakdara and in the cavalry pursuit. For days their bodies lay scattered about the country. In the standing crops, in the ruins of villages, among the rocks, festering bodies lay in the blazing sun, filling the valley with a dreadful smell. To devour these great numbers of vultures quickly assembled and disputed the abundant prey with the odious lizards.

Meanwhile the punishment that the tribesmen of the Swat Valley had received, and their heavy losses, had broken the spirit of many, and several deputations came to make their submission. The Lower Swatis surrendered unconditionally, and were allowed to return to their villages. Of this permission they at once availed themselves, and their figures could be seen moving about their ruined homes and endeavouring to repair the damage.

It is no exaggeration to say that perhaps half the tribesmen who attacked the Malakand, had thought that the soldiers there were the only troops that the Sirkar possessed. 'Kill these,' they had said, 'and all is done.' Little did they realise they had set the world humming; that military officers were hurrying 7,000 miles by sea and land from England, to the camps in the mountains; that long trains were carrying ammunition, material and supplies from distant depôts to the front. They only saw the forts and camps on the Malakand Pass and the swinging bridge across the river.

While the people of Lower Swat, deserted by the Mad Mullah, and confronted by the two brigades, were completely humbled and subdued, the Upper Swatis, encouraged by their priests, and, as they believed, safe behind their 'gate', assumed a much more independent air. They sent to inquire what terms the Government would offer, and said they would consider the matter. Their contumacious attitude induced the political officers to recommend the movement of troops through their country, to impress them with the determination and power of the Sirkar.

The expedition into the Upper Swat Valley was accordingly sanctioned; and Sir Bindon Blood began making the necessary prepara-

tions for the advance. He had concentrated a considerable force at
Amandara in view of a possible advance, and as soon as the movement
was sanctioned organised the column which amounted to an available
fighting strength of 3,500 rifles, and sabres, with eighteen guns. Supplies
for twelve days were carried, and the troops proceeded on 'the 80 lb.
scale' of baggage; which means, that they did not take tents, and a few
other comforts, and conveniences.

On August the 14th Sir Bindon Blood joined the special force, and
moved it on the 16th to Thana, a few miles further up the valley. At
the same time he ordered Brigadier-General Wodehouse to detach a
small force in the direction of the southern passes of Buner. The Highland Light Infantry, No. 3 Company Bombay Sappers and Miners, and
one squadron of the 10th Bengal Lancers accordingly marched from
Mardan, where the 3rd Brigade then was, to Rustum. By this move
they threatened the Bunerwals, and distracted their attention from the
Upper Swat Valley. Having thus weakened the enemy, Sir Bindon
Blood proceeded to force the 'Gate of Swat'.

At 6.30 a.m. on the 17th, the cavalry moved off, and soon came in
contact with the enemy, in some Buddhist ruins near a village called
Jalala. A skirmish ensued. The main position of the enemy was displayed. All along the crest of the spur of Landakai, could be seen a
fringe of standards, dark against the sky. Beneath them the sword-
blades of the tribesmen glinted in the sunlight. A long line of stone
sungars crowned the ridge, and behind the enemy clustered thickly. It
is estimated that over 5,000 were present.

It is not difficult to realise what a strong position this was. On the
left of the troops, was an unfordable river. On their right the mountains rose steeply. In front was the long ridge held by the enemy. The
only road up the valley was along the causeway, between the ridge
and the river. To advance further it was necessary to dislodge the
enemy from the ridge. Sir Bindon Blood rode forward, reconnoitred
the ground, and made his dispositions.

To capture the position by a frontal attack would involve heavy
loss. The enemy were strongly posted, and the troops would be exposed
to a heavy fire in advancing. On the other hand, if the ridge could
once be captured, the destruction of the tribesmen was assured. Their
position was good, but only as long as they held it. The moment of

defeat would be the moment of ruin. The reason was this. The ground behind the ridge was occupied by swampy rice fields, and the enemy could only retire very slowly over it. Their safe line of retreat lay up the spur, and on to the main line of hills. They were thus formed with their line of retreat in prolongation of their front. This is, of course, tactically one of the worst situations that people can get into.

Sir Bindon Blood, who knew what the ground behind the ridge was like, perceived at once how matters stood, and made his plans accordingly. He determined to strike at the enemy's left; thus not only turning their flank, but cutting off their one line of retreat. If once his troops held the point, where the long ridge ran into the main hills, all the tribesmen who had remained on the ridge would be caught. He accordingly issued orders as follows:

The Royal West Kent were to mask the front and occupy the attention of the enemy. The rest of the infantry, *viz.*, 24th and 31st Punjab Infantry and the 45th Sikhs, were to ascend the hills to the right, and deliver a flank attack, on the head of the ridge. The cavalry were to be held in readiness to dash forward along the causeway, as soon as the enemy were driven off the ridge which commanded it, and pursue them across the rice fields into the open country beyond. The whole of the powerful artillery was to come into action at once.

The troops then advanced. The Royal West Kent began the fight by driving some of the enemy from the Buddhist ruins, on a small spur in advance of the main position. The 10th Field Battery had been left in rear, in case the guns might stick in the narrow roads, near Thana village. It had, however, arrived safely, and now trotted up, and at 8.50 a.m. opened fire on the enemy's position, and at a stone fort which they occupied strongly. A few minutes later No. 7 Mountain Battery came into action from the spur which the Royal West Kent had taken. A heavy artillery fire thus prepared the way for the attack. The great shells of the Field Artillery astounded the tribesmen, who had never before witnessed the explosion of a twelve-pound projectile. The two mountain batteries added to their discomfiture. Many fled during the first quarter of an hour of the bombardment. All the rest took cover on the reverse slope and behind their *sungars*.

Meanwhile the flank attack was developing. General Meiklejohn and his infantry were climbing up the steep hillside, and moving steadily towards the junction of the ridge with the main hill. At length the tribesmen on the spur perceived the danger that was threatening them. They felt the grip on their line of retreat. They had imagined that the white troops would try and force their path along the causeway, and had massed considerable reserves at the lower end of the ridge. All these now realised that they were in great danger of being cut off. They were on a peninsula, as it were, while the soldiers were securing the isthmus. They accordingly began streaming along the ridge towards the left, at first with an idea of meeting the flank attack, but afterwards, as the fire grew hotter, only in the hopes of retreat. Owing to the great speed with which the mountaineers move about the hills, most of them were able to escape before the flank attack could cut them off. Many, however, were shot down as they fled, or were killed by the artillery fire.

Seeing the enemy in full flight, Sir Bindon Blood ordered the Royal West Kent to advance against the front of the now almost deserted ridge. The British infantry hurrying forward climbed the steep hill, and captured the stone *sungars*. From this position they established touch with the flank attack, and the whole force pursued the flying tribesmen with long-range fire.

The 'Gate of Swat' had been forced. It was now possible for troops to advance along the causeway. This had, however, been broken in various places by the enemy. The sappers and miners hastened forward to repair it. While this was being done, the cavalry had to wait in mad impatience, knowing that their chance lay in the plains beyond. As soon as the road was sufficiently repaired to allow them to pass, in single file, they began struggling along it, and emerged at the other end of the causeway in twos and threes.

An incident now ensued, which, though it afforded an opportunity for a splendid act of courage, yet involved an unnecessary loss of life, and must be called disastrous. As the cavalry got clear of the broken ground, the leading horsemen saw the tribesmen swiftly running towards the hills, about a mile distant.

Lieutenant-Colonel Adams, on entering into the plain, saw at once that if he could seize a small clump of trees near a cemetery, he would be able to bring effective dismounted fire to bear on the retreating tribesmen. He therefore collected as many men as possible, and with Lieutenant Maclean, and Lord Fincastle, the *Times* correspondent, rode in the direction of these points. Meanwhile Captain Palmer, who commanded the leading squadron, and Lieutenant Greaves of the Lancashire Fusiliers, who was acting war correspondent of the *Times of India*, galloped across the rice fields after the enemy. The squadron, unable to keep up, straggled out in a long string, in the swampy ground.

At the foot of the hills the ground was firmer, and reaching this, the two officers recklessly dashed in among the enemy. It is the spirit that loses the empire many lives, but has gained it many battles. But the tribesmen, who had been outmanœuvred rather than outfought, turned savagely on their pursuers. The whole scene was witnessed by the troops on the ridge. Captain Palmer cut down a standard-bearer. Another man attacked him. Raising his arm for another stroke, his wrist was smashed by a bullet. Another killed his horse. Lieutenant Greaves, shot through the body, fell at the same moment to the ground. The enemy closed around and began hacking him, as he lay, with their swords. Captain Palmer tried to draw his revolver. At this moment two Sowars got clear of the swampy rice fields, and at once galloped, shouting, to the rescue, cutting and slashing at the tribesmen. All would have been cut to pieces or shot down. The hillside was covered with the enemy. The wounded officers lay at the foot. They were surrounded. Seeing this Lieutenant-Colonel Adams and Lord Fincastle, with Lieutenant Maclean and two or three Sowars, dashed to their assistance. At their charge the tribesmen fell back a little way and opened a heavy fire. Lord Fincastle's horse was immediately shot, and he fell to the ground. Rising, he endeavoured to lift the wounded Greaves, on to Colonel Adams' saddle, but at this instant a second bullet struck that unfortunate officer, killing him instantly. Colonel Adams was slightly, and Lieutenant Maclean mortally, wounded while giving assistance, and all the horses but two were shot. In spite of the terrible fire, the body of Lieutenant Greaves and the other two wounded officers were rescued and carried to the little clump of trees.

The flight of the enemy terminated the action of Landakai. Thus in a few hours, and with hardly any loss, the 'Gate of Swat' which the tribesmen had regarded as impregnable, had been forced.

The next morning, the 18th, the force continued their march up the valley of the Upper Swat. The natives, thoroughly cowed, offered no further opposition, and sued for peace.

As the troops advanced up the fertile, and beautiful valley, all were struck by the numerous ruins of the ancient Buddhists. Here in former times were thriving cities, and civilised men. Here we learn from Fahien[1] were 'in all 500 Sangháramas', or monasteries. At these monasteries the law of hospitality was thus carried out: 'When stranger *bhikshees* (begging monks) arrive at one of them their wants are supplied for three days, after which they are told to find a resting-place for themselves'. All this is changed by time. The cities are but ruins. Savages have replaced the civilised, bland-looking Buddhists; and the traveller who should apply for hospitality, would be speedily shown 'a resting-place', which would relieve his hosts from further trouble concerning him.

On the 19th, the force reached Mingaora; and here for five days they waited in an agreeable camp, to enable Major Deane to receive the submission of the tribes. These appeared very humbled by their defeats; and sought to propitiate the troops by bringing in supplies of grain and forage. Over 800 arms of different descriptions, were surrendered during the halt. A few shots were fired into the camp on the night of the arrival at Mingaora, but the villagers, fearing lest they should suffer, turned out and drove the 'snipers' away. On the 21st a reconnaissance of the valley as far as the Kotke Pass afforded much valuable information as to the nature of the country.

While the troops rested at Barikot, Sir Bindon Blood personally reconnoitred the Karikar Pass, which leads from the Swat Valley into the country of the Bunerwals. The Bunerwals are a warlike and turbulent people. To their valley, after the suppression of the Indian Mutiny, many of the Sepoys and native officers who had been in revolt fled for refuge. Here, partly by force and partly by persuasion, they established themselves. They married women of the country, and made a settlement. In 1863 the Bunerwals came into collision with the British Government, and much severe fighting ensued, known to history as the Ambeyla Campaign. The refugees from India renewed their quarrel with the white troops with eagerness; and by their extraordinary courage and ferocity gained the name of the 'Hindustani Fanatics'. At the cost of thirty officers and 1,000 men Buner was subdued. The reputation the Bunerwals have enjoyed since their stout

[1] *Record of Buddhistic Kingdoms.* Translated by James Legge, M.A., LL.D.

resistance in 1863, has enabled them to take a leading position among the frontier tribes; and they have availed themselves of this to foment and aggravate several outbreaks against the British. Their black and dark-blue clothes had distinguished them from the other assailants of Malakand and Chakdara. They had now withdrawn to their valley and thence defied the Government and refused all terms.

As Sir Bindon Blood and his escort approached the top of the pass, a few shots were fired by the watchers there, but there was no opposition. All the Bunerwals had hurried over to defend the southern entrances to their country, which they conceived were in danger of attack from Brigadier-General Wodehouse's force at Rustum. The general reached the Kotal, and saw the whole valley beneath him. Great villages dotted the plains, and the aspect was fertile and prosperous.

The unguarded Karikar Pass was practicable for troops, and if the Government would give their consent, Buner might be reduced in a fortnight without difficulty, almost without fighting.

Telegrams were despatched to India on the subject, and after much delay and hesitation the Viceroy decided against the recommendation of his victorious general. Though the desirability of settling with the Bunerwals was fully admitted, the Government shrank from the risk. The Malakand Field Force thus remained idle for nearly a fortnight. The news that the Sirkar had feared to attack Buner spread like wildfire along the frontier, and revived the spirits of the tribes. They fancied they detected a sign of weakness. Nor were they altogether wrong. But the weakness was moral rather than physical.

CHAPTER VII

THE ADVANCE AGAINST THE MOHMANDS

The beginning of this chapter must mark a change in the standpoint from which the story is told. Hitherto the course of events has been recorded in the impersonal style of history. But henceforward I am able to rely on my own memory as well as on other people's evidence.[1] It may be doubtful whether an historical record gains or loses value when described by an eye-witness. What the narrative gains in accuracy of detail, it may lose in justness of proportion. In so nice a question I shall not pronounce.

The forthcoming chapter also introduces a new phase of the operations of the force. The Mohmands now become the enemy, and the scene is changed from Swat to Bajaur. Before marching into their country, it will be desirable to consider briefly those causes and events which induced the Government of India to despatch an expedition against this powerful and warlike tribe.

The tidal wave of fanaticism, which had swept the frontier, had influenced the Mohmands, as all other border peoples. Their situation was, however, in several important respects different from that of the natives of the Swat Valley. These Mohmands had neither been irritated, nor interfered with in any way. No military road ran through their territory. No fortified posts stirred their animosity, or threatened their independence. Had they respected in others, the isolation which they themselves have so long enjoyed, they might have remained for an

---

[1] I do not desire to bore the reader or depreciate the story by the introduction of personal matters. It will be sufficient, if, in the interests of coherency, I explain my connection with the Malakand Field Force. Having realized that if a British cavalry officer waits till he is ordered on active service, he is likely to wait a considerable time, I obtained six weeks' leave of absence from my regiment, and on the 2nd of September arrived at Malakand as Press correspondent of the *Pioneer* and *Daily Telegraph*, and in the hope of being sooner or later attached to the force in a military capacity.

indefinite period in that state of degraded barbarism which seems to appeal strongly to certain people in England.

In the heart of the wild and dismal mountain region in which these fierce tribesmen dwell, are the temple and village of Jarobi, the one a consecrated hovel, the other a fortified slum. This obscure and undisturbed retreat was the residence of a priest of great age and of peculiar holiness, known to fame as the Hadda Mullah. His name is Najim-ud-din. The Government of India have, however, had this man's personality brought vividly before them on several occasions. About thirteen years ago he quarrelled with the Amir of Afghanistan and raised the Mohmands against him. The Amir replied by summoning his rebellious subject – for Hadda, the Mullah's home and birthplace, is a village of Afghanistan – to answer for his conduct at Cabul. But the crafty priest declined the invitation, and retired to the independent Mohmand territory, where he has lived ever since.

The Amir was disposed to forget the offence. In a letter to his Commander-in-Chief, the 'Sipah Salar', a great friend of the Mullah, he described him as a 'light of Islam'. So powerful a light, indeed, he did not desire to have in his own dominions; but across the border it was fitting that respect should be shown to so holy a man. He therefore directed his officials to cherish and honour him. Thus he retained a powerful weapon – to be used when desirable. Whether by instigation or from personal motives, the Hadda Mullah has long been a bitter foe to the British power. In 1895 he sent the fighting men of the Mohmands to resist the Chitral Expeditionary Force. Since then he has been actively engaged, by preaching and by correspondence with other Mullahs, in raising a great combination against the advancing civilisation.

While the Mad Fakir was rousing Swat and Buner, this powerful priest incited the Mohmands. Though he was known to be a physical coward, his sanctity, the fact that he was their own particular holy man, not less than his eloquence, powerfully moved this savage tribe. A *Jehad* was proclaimed. How long should Islam be insulted? How long should its followers lurk in the barren lands of the north? He urged them to rise and join in the destruction of the white invaders. Those who fell should become saints; those who lived would be rich.

The combined allurements of plunder and paradise proved irresistible. On the 8th of August a great gathering, nearly 6,000 strong, crossed the frontier line, invaded British territory, burned the village of Shunkargarh, and attacked the fort of Shabkadr. This place is an advanced post in the defensive system of the frontier, and is situated some nineteen miles to the north-west of Peshawar. Its ordinary garrison consists of about fifty Border Police. It is strongly built, and is intended to attract the attention and delay the advance of a raiding-party, until the Peshawar Garrison has had time to take the field. Both of these objects it admirably fulfilled in this case.

As soon as the news of the incursion of the Mohmands was received in Peshawar, a flying column was mobilised and proceeded under the command of Lieut.-Colonel J. B. Woon, 20th Punjab Infantry, in the direction of the fort. At dawn on the 9th of August they found the tribesmen in force, in a strong position near Shabkadr. The force at Colonel Woon's disposal was small, about 750 men. The enemy numbered 6,000. Nevertheless it was decided to attack at once.

The infantry in advancing could only attack on a front of 600 yards. The enemy's line, being much longer, quickly turned both flanks. The fire became severe. Numerous casualties occurred. A retirement was ordered. At this point Brigadier-General Elles, commanding the Peshawar District, arrived on the field. He immediately ordered the squadrons of the 13th Bengal Lancers, to move well to the right flank, to charge across the front and check the enemy's advance. The 'cease fire' sounded as on a field day. Then there was a pause. The movements of the cavalry were concealed from most of the troops, but suddenly all noticed the slackening of the enemy's fire. Then the tribesmen were seen to be in retreat and disorder.

That the deliberate violation of British territory by these savages, should remain unpunished was of course impossible. Yet the vacillation and hesitancy which the Government of India had displayed in the matter of the Bunerwals, and the shocking and disgraceful desertion of the forts in the Khyber Pass, were so fresh in all men's minds, that the order to advance against the Mohmands was received with feelings of the greatest relief throughout the forces. The general plan of the operations as arranged by the Commander-in-Chief was as follows:

1. Sir Bindon Blood with two brigades of the Malakand Field Force and due proportions of cavalry and guns was to move through South Bajaur to

Nawagai, and on the 15th of September invade the Mohmand country from that place.

2. On the same date Major-General Elles with an equal force would leave Shabkadr, and entering the mountains march north-east to effect a junction.

3. This having been done, the combined forces under the supreme command of Sir Bindon Blood would be brought back through the Mohmands' territories to Shabkadr. Incidentally they would deal with the Hadda Mullah's village of Jarobi, and inflict such punishment on the tribesmen as might be necessary to ensure their submission. The troops would then be available for the Tirah Expedition, which it had by this time been decided to organise.

The fact that after leaving Nawagai, nothing was known of the configuration of the country, of which no maps existed; nor of the supplies of food, forage and water available by the way, made the preparations for, and the execution of, these operations somewhat difficult. Wide margins had to be allowed in the matter of rations, and in order to be prepared for all contingencies and obstructions of ground, Sir Bindon Blood equipped his 2nd Brigade entirely with mule transport. The 3rd Brigade with camels would follow if the road was passable.

For the sake of clearness, of brevity, I shall at once describe the whole of the marches, and manœuvres, by which Sir Bindon Blood moved his brigades across the Panjkora River, and after the Malakand Field Force is safely camped at Ghosam, the reader will be invited to return and remark the incidents of the way.

On the 2nd of September, definite orders to advance were received from Simla. In pursuance of these instructions, Sir Bindon Blood ordered Brigadier-General Wodehouse with the 3rd Brigade, which in anticipation had been moved from Uch a few days previously, to take over the bridge across the Panjkora from the Khan of Dir's Levies, and secure the passage. On the 6th, the 3rd Brigade marched from Sarai to Panjkora, and obtained possession of the bridge just in time to prevent it falling into the hands of the enemy, who had already gathered to seize it. The 12-pounder guns of the 10th Field Battery were placed in a strong position commanding the passage, and the brigade camped on the left bank. On the same day, Brigadier-General Jeffreys with Headquarters marched from Khar, to Chakdara. On the 7th he proceeded to Sarai, and on the 8th effected the passage of the Panjkora, and camped on the further bank at Kotkai. On the 10th, both brigades marched to Ghosam, where they concentrated. On the line of communications to the Malakand, stages were established at Chakdara and Sarai, with accommodation for sick and wounded. An advanced depôt was formed behind the Panjkora, to guard which, and to hold the passage, an additional force was moved from the Swat Valley.

This concentration at Ghosam, of which the details had worked out so mechanically, had been necessitated by the attitude of the tribesmen of Bajaur and the adjoining valleys. Great gatherings had collected, and up to the 7th of September, there had been every sign of determined opposition. The methodical, remorseless advance of powerful forces, filled the tribesmen with alarm. They made a half-hearted attempt to capture the Panjkora bridge, and finding themselves forestalled, fell again to discussing terms. And then suddenly the whole huge combination, which had been raised in our path, collapsed as an iceberg when southern waters have melted its base.

Having thus brought the brigades peacefully to Ghosam, I ask the reader to return to the Malakand and ride thence with the Headquarters Staff along the line of march. On the 5th of September, Sir Bindon Blood and his staff, which I had the pleasure to accompany, started from the Kotal Camp and proceeded across the plain of Khar to Chakdara. Here we halted for the night and continued without delay next morning. From Chakdara to Sarai, is a stage of twelve miles. The road runs steadily up the valley until the summit of the Catgalla Pass is reached.

The valley at Sarai is about two miles wide, and the mountains rise steeply from it. Five miles from Sarai the road dwindles to a mule track, and henceforward is not fit for wheeled traffic. In spite of this, the 10th Field Battery had succeeded in getting their guns along it, and had brought them safely to Panjkora. The scenery before the gorge of the river is reached is gloomy, but grand. Great cliffs tower up precipitously on the further bank, and the path is cut in the face of the rock. The river, which flows swiftly by, plunges into a narrow cleft about a mile below the bridge, and disappears among the mountains. It abounds in fish, but is rapid and dangerous, and, while the troops were encamped near it, two gunners lost their lives by falling in, and being carried down.

At length the bridge is reached. It is a frail structure, supported on wire ropes. At each end are gates, flanked by little mud towers. The battery was established on a knoll to the right, and the long muzzles of the guns peered through stone embrasures at the opposite hills. It was round the bases of these hills, that much hard fighting took place in the Chitral campaign.

The field telegraph stopped at the bridgehead, and a small tent with a half-dozen military operators, marked the breaking of the slender thread, that connected us across thousands of miles of sea and land, with London. Henceforward a line of signal stations with their flickering helios, would be the only links. We were at the end of the wire. I have often stood at the other, and watched the tape machine click off the news as it arrives. How different are the scenes. I can never doubt which is the right end to be at. It is better to be making the news than taking it; to be an actor rather than a critic.

To cross the bridge it was necessary to dismount and lead the horses over in single file. The passage of the transport under such conditions occupied the whole day. The staff passed quickly, however, and reached the camp at Kotkai about noon. Thence we proceeded on the following day to Ghosam.

At Ghosam the 2nd Brigade remained until joined by the 3rd, and pending negotiations between the political officers and the tribal Jirgahs. In this account I have zealously tried to avoid jargon and to minimise the use of native names. The term just employed has, however, been so freely used that it is perhaps as well to explain its meaning. A Jirgah is a deputation of tribesmen. It does not necessarily represent the tribe. It may present – and very often does – a minority report. Occasionally it expresses the opinion only of its own members. What has been settled one day is therefore very often overruled the next. The Jirgah may accept terms of peace in the morning, and the camp may be rushed that night. These were, however, genuine, and spoke in the name, and with the authority of the tribes. All day they kept arriving and squatting in rows before Major Deane's tent, to hear the Government terms. The chief condition imposed was the surrender of rifles. This method of punishment is peculiarly galling to a people whose life is so full of war. No other course was, however, open but submission; and promising that the terms should be complied with, the deputations departed. To stimulate their effort and zeal in collecting their arms, the combined movements were delayed for three days, and the forces remained encamped at Ghosam, near Manda.

I avail myself of this halt to touch, albeit with no little trepidation, the tangled and obscure subject of tribal politics in Dir and Bajaur. All the people, incited by their priests, are bitterly hostile to the British Government, except those benefited by the subsidies paid. They were now anxious to fight, and were only restrained by a fear, which fury or fanaticism, might at any moment overcome. Four principal khans exercise an authority which varies locally, from absolute dominion to a shadowy suzerainty, over the whole region. The Khan of Dir, the most important, is a Government nominee. He is supported by the British influence, and is, as I have already noticed, entrusted with the raising of Levies to protect and keep in repair the Chitral road. For these services he receives pay, and a certain allowance of arms, and ammunition. His own subjects are strongly opposed to his rule from dislike of his British sympathies, and he only maintains himself by the assistance which the Government gives him in arms and money.

The Khan of Nawagai is constrained by fear to display a friendly attitude towards the Sirkar. His subjects resent this, and his position is insecure. He receives some moral support from the British agents, and as his people are uncertain how far the Government would go to uphold him they have hitherto submitted sullenly to his rule.

The position and attitude of the Khan of Jar are similar, but he is a less influential chief. The fourth potentate, the Khan of Khar, is perhaps the most honest and trustworthy. He will appear in a later chapter, and the reader will have the opportunity of judging of his character from his conduct. Thus in these valleys, while the people are all hostile, their rulers find it expedient to preserve a friendly demeanour to the British, and for this they are hated by their subjects.

At this stage, the leader of the popular party claims attention. As is usual, he is out of office. After the Chitral expedition of 1895, Umra Khan was expelled from his territories, and escaped to Cabul. There he has remained. The Amir is under an obligation to the British Government to prevent his raising trouble in Bajaur. If the Amir desired war he would send Umra Khan back. This would create a strong faction throughout the whole country – but particularly in the Jandol, Salarzai and Mamund Valleys – hostile to the British and the friendly khans.

The Afghan sovereign is, however, well aware that he has at present nothing to gain, and many things to lose, by provoking a war with the great power which gave him his throne, and has since increased his revenue by subsidies. In the meanwhile, anxious to preserve his influence with the border tribes, and to impress the Indian Government with the fact that he could be a powerful foe, he keeps Umra Khan as a trump card, to be played when the occasion arises. That he may maintain his authority in Bajaur, the exiled khan is well supplied with funds, with which to arm and pay his retainers.

CHAPTER VIII

RECONNAISSANCE

While the infantry of both brigades remained halted at Ghosam near Manda, the cavalry made daily reconnaissances in all directions.

On the 10th, Major Deane visited the various chiefs in the Jandol Valley. I asked and obtained permission to accompany him. A party was formed, among whom were Major Beatson, Major Hobday, and Lord Fincastle. A squadron of the 11th Bengal Lancers acted as escort.

The valley of the Jandol, is about eight miles long, and perhaps half as broad. It runs out of the main valley which extends from the Panjkora to Nawagai, and is on all other sides surrounded by high and precipitous mountains. The bed of the river, although at the time of our visit occupied only by a small stream, is nearly half a mile broad and bordered by rice fields. The plain itself is arid and sandy, but at the winter season yields a moderate crop. The presence of water below the surface is attested by numerous groves of *chenar* trees.

This valley may, in natural and political features, be taken as typical of the Afghan valleys. Seven separate castles formed the strongholds of seven separate khans. Some of these potentates had been implicated in the attack on the Malakand and our visit to their fastnesses was not wholly of an amicable nature. They had all, four days before, been bound by the most sacred oaths, to fight to the death. The great tribal combination had, however, broken up, and at the last moment they had decided upon peace. But the Pathan does nothing by halves. No black looks, no sullen reserve, marred the geniality of their welcome. As we approached the first fortified village the sovereign and his army rode out to meet us, and with many protestations of fidelity, expressed his joy at our safe arrival. He was a fine-looking man and sat well on a stamping roan stallion. His dress was imposing. A waistcoat of gorgeous crimson, thickly covered with gold lace, displayed flowing sleeves of white linen, buttoned at the wrist. Long, loose, baggy, linen trousers,

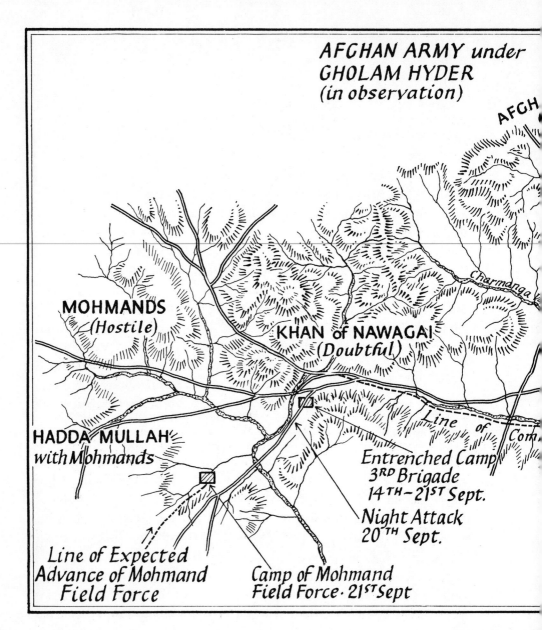

AFGHAN ARMY under
GHOLAM HYDER
(in observation)

AFGH

Charmanga

MOHMANDS
(Hostile)

KHAN of NAWAGAI
(Doubtful)

Line of Com

HADDA MULLAH
with Mohmands

Entrenched Camp
3ᴿᴰ Brigade
14ᵀᴴ–21ˢᵀ Sept.

Night Attack
20ᵀᴴ Sept.

Line of Expected
Advance of Mohmand
Field Force

Camp of Mohmand
Field Force · 21ˢᵀ Sept

THE OPERATI

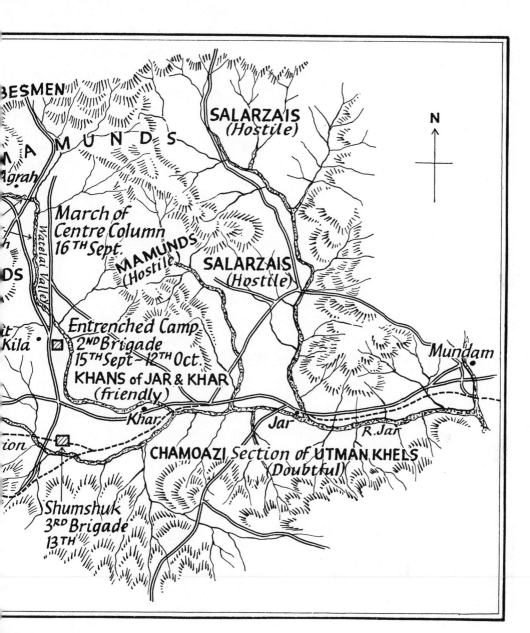

BESMEN

MAMUNDS

Agrah

SALARZAIS
(Hostile)

N

March of
Centre Column
16TH Sept.

MAMUNDS
(Hostile)

SALARZAIS
(Hostile)

Watelai Valley

Entrenched Camp
2ND Brigade
15TH Sept.–12TH Oct.

Kila

Mundam

KHANS of JAR & KHAR
(friendly)

Khar

Jar

R. Jar

tion

CHAMOAZI Section of UTMAN KHELS
(Doubtful)

Shumshuk
3RD Brigade
13TH

also fastened above the ankle, and curiously pointed shoes clothed his nether limbs. This striking costume was completed by a small skull-cap, richly embroidered, and an ornamental sabre.

He sprang from his horse with grace and agility, to offer his sword to Major Deane, who bade him mount and ride with him. The army, four or five rascally-looking men on shaggy ponies, each armed with rifles of widely different patterns, followed at a distance. The fort was an enclosure about a hundred yards square. Its walls were perhaps twenty feet high, and all along the top was a row of loopholes. At each corner a tall flanking tower enfiladed the approaches. At the gate of this warlike residence, some twenty or thirty tribesmen were gathered. All saluted us gravely. These matters of detail complied with, conversation began. It was conducted in Pushtu, and was naturally unintelligible to every one of our party except the two political officers.

They were asked where were the rifles they had been ordered to surrender. At this they looked blank. There were no rifles, there never had been any rifles. Let the soldiers search the fort, and see for themselves.

The Lancers, accustomed to the operation of hunting for arms, hurriedly searched the likely and usual places but without success; one thing, however, they noticed, which they immediately reported. There were no women and children in the fort. This had a sinister aspect. Our visit was unexpected and had taken them by surprise, but they were prepared for all emergencies. They had hidden their rifles and cleared for action.

The two chiefs smiled in superior virtue; of course there were no rifles; but matters took for them an unexpected turn. They had no rifles – said Major Deane – very well, they should come themselves. He turned to an officer of the Lancers; a section rode forward and surrounded both men. Resistance was useless. They behaved with oriental composure, ordered their ponies and, mounting, rode behind us under escort.

On returning to our camp, the political officers were pleased and the soldiers disappointed, to find that the tribesmen were determined to accept the Government terms. A hundred rifles from the Utman Khels had already been surrendered, and now lay outside Major Deane's tent, surrounded by a crowd of officers who were busily engaged in examining them.

It will now be convenient to make a digression into the question of the supply of arms to the frontier tribes, while a hundred rifles, probably a representative hundred, are piled in the main street of the camp at Ghosam.

The perpetual state of intestine war in which the border peoples live, naturally creates a keen demand for deadly weapons. A good Martini-Henry rifle will always command a price in these parts of Rs. 400 or about £25. As the actual value of such a rifle does not exceed Rs. 50, it is evident that a very large margin of profit accrues to the enterprising trader. All along the frontier, and from far down into India, rifles are stolen by expert and cunning thieves. One tribe, the Ut Khels, who live in the Khyber Pass, have made the traffic in arms their especial business. Their thieves are the most daring and their agents travel great distances. Some of their methods are highly ingenious.

Theft is not the only means by which the frontier tribes obtain weapons. Of a hundred rifles which the Utman Khels had surrendered, nearly a third were condemned Government Martinis, and displayed the Government stamp. Now no such rifles are supposed to exist. As soon as they are condemned the arsenal authorities are responsible that they are destroyed, and this is in every case carried out under European supervision. The fact that such rifles are not destroyed and are found in the possession of trans-frontier tribesmen, points to a very grave instance of dishonest and illegal traffic being carried on by some person connected with the arsenal.

Another point connected with these rifles is that even when they have been officially destroyed, by cutting them in three pieces, the fractions have a marketable value. Several were shown me, which had been rejointed, by the tribesmen. These were, of course, more dangerous to friend than enemy.

The next day, the 11th of September, the troops remained halted at Ghosam, and another squadron was ordered to escort the Intelligence Officer, Captain H. E. Stanton, o.s.o., while making a topographical reconnaissance of the passes into the Utman Khel country. The opportunity of making fresh maps, and of adding to and correcting the detail of the existing maps only occurs when troops are passing through them, and must not be neglected. The route lay up the main valley which leads to Nawagai. The landscape was one of the strangest I shall ever see. On the opposite bank of the river, were the dwellings of the Utman Khels, and in an area seven miles by three, I counted forty-six separate castles, with moats, towers and turrets. It almost seemed as if we had strayed into some strange domain of fancy, the resort of giants or ogres.

At length the steep ascent to the passes became visible. As there were two routes to be reconnoitred, the party was divided and after a hasty breakfast, we commenced the climb. For a considerable distance it was possible to ride. The head man of the village through which we had passed, had furnished a guide, a cheery, and amusing fellow who professed much solicitude for our safety. At length the horses and the greater part of the escort, had to be abandoned. I accompanied Captain Stanton, and Captain Cole, with a couple of troopers to the top of the pass. The day was intensely hot, and the arduous climb excited a thirst which there was nothing to allay. At length we gained the summit, and stood on the Kotal.

Far beneath was a valley upon which perhaps no white man had looked since Alexander crossed the mountains on his march to India. Numerous villages lay dotted about in its depths, while others nestled against the hills. Isolated forts were distinguishable, while large trees showed there was no lack of water. It was a view that repaid the exertions of the climb, for the thirsty spectators. While Captain Stanton was making his sketch, our guide squatted on the ground and pronounced the names of all the villages, as each one was pointed out. To make sure there was no mistake, the series of questions were repeated. This time he gave to each an entirely different name, with an appearance of great confidence and pride. However, one unpronounceable name is as good as another, and the villages of the valley will go down to official history, thus christened at the caprice of a peasant. Many records now accepted as beyond dispute, are derived from such slender authority.

The sketch finished, we commenced the descent and reached our horses without incident. The squadron returned and arrived at the camp at Ghosam, as the sun was setting.

CHAPTER IX

THE MARCH TO NAWAGAI

After considering such maps and information as to the nature of the country as were available, Sir Bindon Blood decided to enter the territories of the Mohmands by two routes. (1) The 3rd Brigade through the pass of Nawagai. (2) The 2nd Brigade over the Rambat Pass. As the 3rd Brigade had a greater distance to cover, it passed in front of the 2nd, and on the 12th of September, by a march of twelve miles, reached Shumshuk. The 2nd Brigade moved by an easy stage of seven miles to Jar, and there camped within supporting distance.

The Headquarters' staff was now transferred to the 3rd Brigade, and marched with them. The road lay for the first five or six miles, over the ground which the cavalry had reconnoitred the day before.

Another mile or so brought us to the Watelai River, a stream about thirty yards broad, which flows into the Jandol, and thence into the Panjkora. Crossing this and climbing the opposite bank, the great dimensions of the valley were displayed. Looking westward it was possible to see the hills behind the Panjkora, the sites of the former camps, and the entrance of the subsidiary valley of the Jandol. In front, at the further end, an opening in the mountain range showed the pass of Nawagai. Towering on the left was the great mass of the Koh-i-mohr, or 'Mountain of Peacocks' – a splendid peak, some 8,000 feet high. Arrian calls it Mount Meros. At its base the city of Nysa stood in former times, and among many others fell before the arms of Alexander. Its inhabitants, in begging for peace, boasted that they conducted their government 'with constitutional order', and that 'ivy which did not grow in the rest of India, grew among them'. City, ivy, and constitutional order have alike disappeared. The mountain alone remains. A little to the northward the Rambat Pass was distinguishable. On the right the smooth plain appeared to flow into the hill country, and a wide bay in the mountains, roughly circular in shape and nearly twelve miles across, opened out of the valley. The entrance was perhaps a mile broad. I remember that when I first looked into the valley, the black clouds of a passing storm hung gloomily over all, and filled it with a hazy half-light that contrasted with the brilliant sunshine outside. It was the Watelai, or as we got to call it later – the Mamund Valley.

The Khan of Khar met the general on the farther bank of the river. He was a tall, fine-looking man, with bright eyes, bushy black whiskers and white teeth, which his frequent smiles displayed. He was richly dressed, attended by a dozen horsemen, and mounted on a handsome though vicious dun horse. He saluted Sir Bindon Blood with great respect and ceremony. Some conversation took place, conducted, as the khan only spoke Pushtu, through the political officer. The khan asserted his loyalty and that of his neighbour the Khan of Jar. He would, he said do his utmost to secure the peaceful passage of the troops. Such supplies as they might need, he would provide, as far as his resources would go. He looked with some alarm at the long lines of marching men and animals. The general reassured him. If the forces were not interrupted or opposed, payment in cash would be made for all the grain and wood it was necessary to requisition.

The khan accepted this promise with gratitude and relief, and henceforth during the operations which took place at Nawagai, and in the Mamund Valley, he preserved a loyal and honourable behaviour.

The camel transport of the 3rd Brigade lagged on the road, and the troops, tired after their long march, had to wait in the blazing sun for a couple of hours without shelter, until the baggage came up.

At length it arrived, and we proceeded to camp as far as is possible without tents. Shelters were improvised from blankets, and with waterproof sheets supported on sticks; or from the green boughs of some adjacent trees. Beneath these scanty coverings, the soldiers lay, and waited for the evening.

Slowly the hours pass away. The heat is intense. The air glitters over the scorched plain, as over the funnel of an engine. The wind blows with a fierce warmth, and instead of bringing relief, raises only whirling dust devils, which scatter the shelters, and half-choke their occupants. The water is tepid, and fails to quench the thirst. At last the shadows begin to lengthen, as the sun sinks towards the western mountains.

Every one revives. Even the animals seem to share the general feeling of relief. The camp turns out to see the sunset and enjoy the twilight.

As there were still several days to spare before the Malakand Field Force was due to enter the Mohmand country, Sir Bindon Blood, ordered both brigades to remain halted on the 13th: the 3rd Brigade at Shumshuk; the 2nd at Jar.

Early next morning the 3rd Brigade, and three squadrons of the 11th Bengal Lancers, moved on to Nawagai and crossed the pass without opposition. The general and Headquarters' staff accompanied them, and we found ourselves in a wide and extensive valley, on the far side of which the Bedmanai Pass could be plainly seen. Here at last we got definite information of the Mohmands' intentions. The Hadda Mullah with 1,000 tribesmen, had gathered to oppose the further advance. After all there would be a fight. In the evening, Sir Bindon Blood, taking a squadron of cavalry, rode out to reconnoitre the approaches to the pass, and the general configuration of the ground. On his return he sent a despatch to the Government of India, that he would force it on the 18th.

It was already dusk when we returned from the reconnaissance. The evening was pleasant and we dined in the open air. All the valley was very dark. The mountains showed a velvet black. Presently the moon rose, and the valley was swiftly flooded with that mysterious light. She was gazing on a different scene eleven miles away, in the valley we had left.

The 2nd Brigade had marched that morning from Jar to the foot of the Rambat Pass, which it was intended to cross the next day. Brigadier-General Jeffreys, in anticipation of this movement, sent the Buffs up to hold the Kotal, and camped at the foot with the rest of his force. The situation of the camp, which had been adopted with a view to the advance at daybreak, favoured the approach of an enemy. The ground was broken, and intersected by numerous small and tortuous nullahs and strewn with rocks. Any other site, would, however, have necessitated a long march the next day, and no attack was thought likely.

At 8.15, as the officers were finishing dinner, three shots rang out in the silence. They were a signal. Instantly brisk firing broke out from the nullahs on the face of the square occupied by the Guides Infantry. Bullets whistled all about the camp, ripping through the tents, and killing and wounding the animals.

The Guides returned the fire with steadiness, and as the shelter trench they had dug in front of their section of the line was higher than at the other parts, no officers or men were hit. At ten o'clock a bugler among the enemy sounded the 'Retire', and the fire dwindled to a few dropping shots. All were congratulating themselves on a termination of the event, when at 10.30 the attack was renewed with vigour on the opposite side of the camp, occupied by the 38th Dogras. The enemy, who were largely armed with Martini-Henry rifles, crept up to within 100 yards of the trenches. These were only about eighteen inches high, but afforded sufficient cover to the soldiers. The officers, with a splendid disregard of the danger, exposed themselves freely. Walking coolly up and down in the brilliant moonlight, they were excellent targets. The brigadier proceeded himself to the threatened side of the camp, to control the firing and prevent the waste of ammunition. A good many thousand rounds were, however, fired away without much result. Several star shells were also fired by the battery. The ground was so broken that they revealed very little, but the tribesmen were much frightened by the smell they made, thinking it a poisonous gas. The officers were directed to take cover, but the necessity of sending messages and regulating the firing involved a great deal of exposure. And to all who showed above the trench, the danger was great. At 2.15 the firing ceased and the enemy drew off, taking their killed and wounded with them. They had no mind to be surprised by daylight, away from their hills.

Meanwhile, the 3rd Brigade had passed a tranquil night at Nawagai. Next morning, however, at about six o'clock, a message was heliographed from the Buffs on the Rambat Pass, to the effect that an attack had been made on General Jeffreys' camp; that heavy firing had continued all night, and that several officers were among the casualties. This news set everyone agog. While we were breakfasting, a native officer and ten Sowars of the 11th Bengal Lancers arrived at speed with full details: six hours' fighting with the Mamunds: three officers killed or mortally wounded; and nearly a hundred animals hit. In consequence of this information, Sir Bindon Blood cancelled the orders for the passage of the Rambat Pass, and instructed General Jeffreys to enter the Mamund Valley and thoroughly chastise the tribesmen.

CHAPTER X

THE ACTION OF THE MAMUND VALLEY
16th September

My story has now reached a point, which I cannot help regarding as its climax. The action of the Mamund Valley is recalled to me by so many vivid incidents and enduring memories that it assumes an importance which is perhaps beyond its true historic proportions. Throughout, the reader must make allowances for what I have called the personal perspective. Throughout he must remember how small is the scale of operations. The panorama is not filled with masses of troops. He will not hear the thunder of a hundred guns. No cavalry brigades whirl by with flashing swords. No infantry divisions are applied at critical points. The looker-on will see only the hillside, and may, if he watches with care, distinguish a few brown-clad men moving slowly about it, dwarfed almost to invisibility by the size of the landscape. I hope to take him close enough to see what these men are doing – and suffering, what their conduct is and what their fortunes are.

On the morning of the 16th, in pursuance of Sir Bindon Blood's orders, Brigadier-General Jeffreys moved out of his entrenched camp at Inayat Kila, and entered the Mamund Valley. His intentions were to chastise the tribesmen, by burning down and blowing up, all defensible villages, within reach of the troops. It was hoped that this might be accomplished in a single day, and that the brigade, having asserted its strength, would be able to march on the 17th to Nawagai and take part in the attack on the Bedmanai Pass, which had been fixed for the 18th. Up to that time no serious opposition had been offered by the tribesmen to the columns, and no news of any gathering had been reported to the general. The valley appeared deserted, the villages looked insignificant and defenceless. It was everywhere asserted that the enemy would not stand. In order to deal with the whole valley at once, the force was divided into three columns, to which were assigned the following tasks:

1. The right column, under Lieut.-Colonel Vivian, consisting of the 38th Dogras and some sappers, was ordered to attack the village of Domodoloh.

2. The centre column, under Colonel Goldney, consisting of six companies Buffs, six companies 35th Sikhs, a half-company Sappers, four guns of No. 8 Mountain Battery and the squadron of the 11th Bengal Lancers, was ordered to proceed to the head of the valley, and destroy the villages of Badelai and Shahi-Tangi (pronounced Shytungy).

3. The left column, under Major Campbell, consisting of five companies of the Guides Infantry, and some sappers, was directed against several villages at the western end of the valley. Two guns, and two companies from each battalion, were left to protect the camp, and a third company of the Guides was detached to protect the survey party. This reduced the strength of the infantry in the field to twenty-three companies, or slightly over 1,200 men. Deducting the 300 men of the 38th Dogras who were not engaged, the total force employed in the action was about 1,000 men of all arms.

It will be convenient to deal with the fortunes of the right column first. Lieut.-Colonel Vivian, after a march of six miles, arrived before the village of Domodoloh at about 9 a.m. He found it strongly held by the enemy, whose aspect was so formidable, that he did not consider himself strong enough to attack without artillery, and supports, and with prudence returned to camp, which he reached about 4 p.m. Two men were wounded by long-range fire.

The centre column advanced, covered by Captain Cole's squadron of Lancers, to which I attached myself. At about seven o'clock we observed the enemy on a conical hill on the northern slopes of the valley. Through the telescope, an instrument often far more useful to cavalry than field-glasses, it was possible to distinguish their figures. Long lines of men clad in blue or white, each with his weapon upright beside him, were squatting on the terraces. Information was immediately sent back to Colonel Goldney. For some time the tribesmen sat and watched the gradual deployment of the troops, which was developing in the plain below them. Then as the guns and infantry approached, they turned and began slowly to climb the face of the mountain.

In hopes of delaying them or inducing them to fight, the cavalry now trotted to within range, and dismounting, opened fire at 7.30 precisely. It was immediately returned. From high up the hillside, from the corn-fields at the base, and from the towers of the villages, little puffs of smoke darted. The skirmish continued for an hour without much damage to either side, as the enemy were well covered by the broken ground and the soldiers by the gravestones, and trees, of a cemetery. Then the infantry began to arrive. The Buffs had been detached from Colonel Goldney's column and were moving against the village of Badelai. The 35th Sikhs proceeded towards the long ridge, round the corner of which Shahi-Tangi stands. I followed the fortunes of the Sikhs. Very little opposition was encountered. A few daring sharp-shooters fired at the leading companies from the high corn. Others fired long-range shots from the mountains. Neither caused any loss. Colonel Goldney now ordered one and a half companies, under Captain Ryder, to clear the conical hill, and protect the right of the regiment, from the fire – from the mountains. These men, about seventy-five in number, began climbing the steep slope; nor did I see them again till much later in the day. Half a company was left with the dressing station near the cemetery, and two more were posted as supports at the bottom of the hills. The other two commenced the ascent of the long spur which leads to Shahi-Tangi.

It is impossible to realise without seeing it, how very slowly troops move on hillsides. It was eleven o'clock before the village was reached. The enemy fell back 'sniping', and doing hardly any damage. Part of the village and some stacks of *bhoosa*, a kind of chopped straw, were set on fire, and the companies prepared to return to camp.

But at about eight the cavalry patrols had reported the enemy in great strength at the north-west end of the valley. In consequence of this Brigadier-General Jeffreys ordered the Guides Infantry to join the main column. Major Campbell at once collected his men who were engaged in foraging, and hurried towards Colonel Goldney's column. After a march of five miles, he came in contact with the enemy in strength on his left front, and firing at once became heavy. At the sound of the musketry the Buffs were recalled from the village of Badelai, and also marched to support the 35th Sikhs.

While both these regiments were hurrying to the scene, the sound of firing first made us realise that our position at the head of the spur near

Shahi-Tangi, was one of increasing danger. The pressure on the left threatened the line of retreat, and no supports were available within a mile. A retirement was at once ordered. Up to this moment hardly any of the tribesmen had been seen. It appeared as if the retirement of the two companies was the signal for their attack. In any case the aspect of affairs immediately changed. From far up the hillsides men came running swiftly down, dropping from ledge to ledge, and dodging from rock to rock. The firing increased on every hand. Half a company was left to cover the withdrawal. The Sikhs made excellent practice on the advancing enemy, who approached by twos and threes, making little rushes from one patch of cover to another. At length a considerable number accumulated behind some rocks about a hundred yards away. The firing now became heavy, and the half-company finding its flank threatened, fell back to the next position.

A digression is necessary to explain the peculiar configuration of the ground. The spur at the top of which the village stands, consists of three rocky knolls, each one higher than the other, as the main hill is approached. These are connected by open necks of ground, which are commanded by fire from both flanks. In section the ground resembles a switchback railway.

The first of these knolls was evacuated without loss, and the open space to the next quickly traversed. I think a couple of men fell here, and were safely carried away. The second knoll was commanded by the first, on to which the enemy climbed, and from which they began firing. Again the companies retired. Lieutenant Cassells remained behind with about eight men, to hold the knoll, until the rest had crossed the open space. As soon as they were clear they shouted to him to retire. He gave the order.

Now suddenly black tragedy burst upon the scene. As Lieutenant Cassells rose to leave the knoll, he turned sharply and fell on the ground. Two Sepoys immediately caught hold of him. One fell shot through the leg. A soldier who had continued firing, sprang into the air, and, falling, began to bleed with strange and terrible rapidity from his mouth and chest. Another turned on his back kicking and twisting. A fourth lay quite still. Thus in the time it takes to write half the little party were killed or wounded. The enemy had worked round both flanks and had also the command. Their fire was accurate.

Two officers, the subadar major, by name Mangol Singh, and three or four Sepoys ran forward from the second knoll, to help in carrying the wounded off. Before they reached the spot two more men were hit. The subadar major seized Lieutenant Cassells, who was covered with blood and unable to stand, but anxious to remain in the firing line. The others caught hold of the injured and began dragging them roughly over the sharp rocks in spite of their screams and groans. Before we had gone thirty yards from the knoll, the enemy rushed on to it, and began firing. Lieutenant Hughes, the adjutant of the regiment, and one of the most popular officers on the frontier, was killed. The bullets passed in the air with a curious sucking noise, like that produced by drawing the air between the lips. Several men also fell. Lieut.-Colonel Bradshaw ordered two Sepoys to carry the officer's body away. This they began to do. Suddenly a scattered crowd of tribesmen rushed over the crest of the hill and charged, sword in hand, hurling great stones. It became impossible to remain an impassive spectator. Several of the wounded were dropped. The subadar major stuck to Lieutenant Cassells, and it is to him the lieutenant owes his life. The men carrying the other officer dropped him and fled. The body sprawled upon the ground. A tall man in dirty white linen pounced down upon it with curved sword. It was a horrible sight.

Had the swordsmen charged home, they would have cut everybody down. But they did not. These wild men of the mountains were afraid of closing. The retirement continued. Five or six times the two companies, now concentrated, endeavoured to stand. Each time the tribesmen pressed round both flanks. They had the whole advantage of ground, and commanded, as well as out-flanked the Sikhs. At length the bottom of the spur was reached, and the remainder of the two companies turned to bay in the nullah with fixed bayonets. The tribesmen came on impetuously, but stopped thirty yards away, howling, firing and waving their swords.

No other troops were in sight, except our cavalry, who could be seen retiring in loose squadron column – probably after their charge. They could give no assistance. The Buffs were nearly a mile away. Things looked grave. Colonel Goldney himself tried to re-form the men. The Sikhs, who now numbered perhaps sixty, were hard pressed, and fired without effect. Then someone – who it was is uncertain – ordered the bugler to sound the 'charge'. The shrill notes rang out not once but a dozen times. Everyone began to shout. The officers waved their swords frantically. Then the Sikhs commenced to move slowly forward, towards the enemy, cheering. It was a supreme moment. The tribesmen turned, and began to retreat. Instantly the soldiers opened a steady fire, shooting down their late persecutors, with savage energy.

During the retirement down the spur, I was unable to observe the general aspect of the action, and now in describing it, I have dealt only with the misadventures of one insignificant unit. While the two advanced companies were being driven down the hill, a general attack was made along the whole left front of the brigade, by at least 2,000 tribesmen, most of whom were armed with rifles. To resist the attack there were the cavalry, the two supporting companies of the 35th Sikhs and five of the Guides Infantry, who were arriving. All became engaged. Displaying their standards, the enemy advanced with great courage, in the face of a heavy fire. Many were killed and wounded, but they continued to advance in a long skirmish line, on the troops. One company of the 35th became seriously involved. Seeing this, Captain Cole moved his squadron forward, and though the ground was broken, charged. The enemy took refuge in the nullah, and opened a sharp fire on the cavalry at close range, hitting several horses and men. The squadron fell back. But the moral effect of their advance had been tremendous. The whole attack came to a standstill. The tribesmen began to retire, and they were finally repulsed at about twelve o'clock.

An opportunity was now presented of breaking off the action. The brigade had started from camp divided, and in expectation that no serious resistance would be offered. It had advanced incautiously. The leading troops had been roughly handled. That attack had been repulsed with slaughter, and the brigade was now concentrated. Considering the fatigues to which the infantry had been exposed, it would perhaps have been more prudent to return to camp, and begin again next morning. But Brigadier-General Jeffreys was determined to complete the destruction of Shahi-Tangi, and to recover the body of Lieutenant Hughes, which remained in the hands of the enemy.

A second attack was ordered. The Guides were to hold the enemy in check on the left. The Buffs, supported by the 35th Sikhs, were to take the village. Orders were signalled back to camp for troops to reinforce

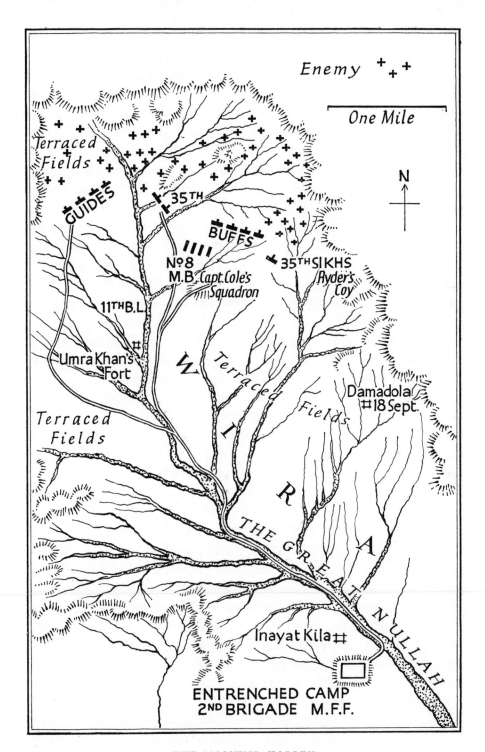

Enemy

One Mile

N

Terraced
Fields

GUIDES

35TH

BUFFS

Nº 8
M.B. Capt. Cole's
Squadron

35TH SIKHS
Ryder's
Coy

11TH B.L.

Umra Khan's
Fort

W
I
R
A

Terraced
Fields

Terraced
Fields

Damadola
⌗ 18 Sept.

THE GREAT NULLAH

Inayat Kila ⌗

ENTRENCHED CAMP
2ND BRIGADE M.F.F.

THE MAMUND VALLEY

the column in the field, and six fresh companies consequently started. At one o'clock the advance recommenced, the guns came into action on a ridge on the right of the brigade, and shelled the village continuously.

Again the enemy fell back 'sniping', and very few of them were to be seen. But to climb the hill alone took two hours. The village was occupied at three o'clock, and completely destroyed by the Buffs. At 3.30, orders reached them to return to camp, and the second withdrawal began. Again the enemy pressed with vigour, but this time there were ten companies on the spur instead of two, and the Buffs, who became rear-guard, held everything at a distance with their Lee-Metford rifles. At a quarter to five the troops were clear of the hills and we looked about us.

While this second attack was being carried out, the afternoon had slipped away. At about two o'clock Major Campbell and Captain Cole, both officers of great experience on the frontier, had realised the fact that the debate with the tribesmen could not be carried to a conclusion that day. At their suggestion a message was heliographed up to the general's staff officer, on the spur near the guns, as follows: 'It is now 2.30. Remember we shall have to fight our way home.' But the brigadier had already foreseen this possibility, and had, as described, issued orders for the return march. These orders did not reach Captain Ryder's company on the extreme right, until they had become hard pressed, by the increasing attack of the enemy. Their wounded delayed their retirement. They had pushed far up the mountain side, apparently with the idea they were to crown the heights, and we now saw them two miles away on the sky line hotly engaged.

We watched them through our glasses. Little figures running about confusedly, tiny puffs of smoke, a miniature officer silhouetted against the sky waving his sword. It seemed impossible to believe that they were fighting for their lives, or indeed in any danger. It all looked so small and unreal. They were, however, hard pressed, and had signalled that they were running out of cartridges. It was then five o'clock, and the approach of darkness was accelerated by heavy thunderclouds gathering over the northern mountains.

At about 3.30 the brigadier had ordered the Guides to proceed to Ryder's assistance and endeavour to extricate his company. He directed

Major Campbell to use his own discretion. It was a difficult problem, but the Guides and their leader were equal to it. They had begun the day on the extreme left. They had hurried to the centre. Now they were ordered to the extreme right. They had already marched sixteen miles, but they were still fresh. We watched them defiling across the front, with admiration. Meanwhile, the retirement of the brigade was delayed. It was necessary that all units should support each other.

Across the broad plain the whole of the brigade was in echelon. On the extreme right were Ryder's company and the Guides Infantry, both severely engaged. Half a mile away to the left rear the battery, the sappers and two companies of the 35th Sikhs were slowly retiring. Still farther to the left were the remainder of the 35th, and at the interval of half a mile were the Buffs. The cavalry were on the extreme left flank. This long line of troops, who were visible to each other but divided by the deep broad nullahs which intersected the whole plain, fell back slowly, halting frequently to keep touch. Seven hundred yards away were the enemy, coming on in a great half-moon nearly three miles long and firing continually. The darkness fell swiftly. The smoke puffs became fire flashes. Great black clouds overspread the valley and thunder began to roll. The daylight died away, and presently it was pitch dark. All communication, all mutual support, all general control now ceased. Each body of troops closed up and made the best of their way to the camp, which was about seven miles off.

The last two miles to camp were painful. After the cessation of the firing the fatigue of the soldiers asserted itself. The Buffs had been marching and fighting continuously for thirteen hours. They had had no food except their early morning biscuit since the preceding night. The older and more hardy amongst them laughed at their troubles. The younger ones collapsed in all directions.

The officers carried their rifles. Such ponies and mules as were available were laden with exhausted soldiers. Nor was this all. Other troops had passed before us, and more than a dozen native soldiers of different regiments were lying senseless by the roadside. All these were eventually carried in by the rear-guard, and the Buffs reached camp at nine o'clock. Meanwhile, the Guides had performed a brilliant feat of arms, and had rescued the remnants of the isolated company from the clutches of the enemy. After a hurried march they arrived at the foot of the hill down which Ryder's men were retiring. The Sikhs, utterly exhausted by the exertions of the day, were in disorder, and in many cases unable from extreme fatigue even to use their weapons. The tribesmen hung in a crowd on the flanks and rear of the straggling company, firing incessantly and even dashing in and cutting down individual soldiers.

Weary, outnumbered, surrounded on three sides, without un-wounded officers or cartridges, the end was only a matter of moments. But help was now at hand. The Guides formed line, fixed bayonets and advanced at the double towards the hill. At a short distance from its foot they halted and opened a terrible and crushing fire upon the exulting enemy. The loud detonations of their company volleys were heard, and the smoke seen all over the field, and on the left we wondered what was happening. The tribesmen, sharply checked, wavered. The company continued its retreat. Many brave deeds were done as the night closed in. Havildar Ali Gul of the Afridi Company of the Guides, seized a canvas cartridge carrier, a sort of loose jacket with large pockets, filled it with ammunition from his men's pouches, and rushing across the fire-swept space which separated the regiment from the Sikhs, distributed the precious packets to the struggling men. Returning he carried a wounded native officer on his back. Seeing this several Afridis in the Guides ran forward shouting and cheering to the rescue, and other wounded Sikhs were saved by their gallantry from a fearful fate. At last Ryder's company reached the bottom of the hill and the survivors re-formed under cover of the Guides.

These, thrown on their own resources, separated from the rest of the brigade by darkness and distance and assailed on three sides by the enemy, calmly proceeded to fight their way back. They reached camp at 9.30 in safety, and not without honour. The skill and experience of their officers, the endurance and spirit of the men, had enabled them to accomplish a task which many had believed impossible.

As the Buffs reached the camp the rain which had hitherto held off came down. It poured. The darkness was intense. The camp became a sea of mud. In expectation that the enemy would attack it, General Jeffreys had signalled in an order to reduce the perimeter. The camp was therefore closed up to half its original size.

Most of the tents had been struck and lay with the baggage piled in confused heaps on the ground. Many of the transport animals were loose and wandering about the crowded space. Dinner or shelter there was none. The soldiers, thoroughly exhausted, lay down supperless in the slush. The condition of the wounded was particularly painful. Among the tents which had been struck were several of the field hospitals. In the darkness and rain it was impossible to do more for the poor fellows than to improve the preliminary dressings and give morphia injections. After about an hour the rain stopped, and while the officers were bustling about making their men get some food before they went to sleep, it was realised that all the troops were not in camp.

The general, the battery, the sappers and four companies of infantry were still in the valley. Presently we heard the firing of guns. They were being attacked – overwhelmed perhaps. To send them assistance was to risk more troops being cut off. The Buffs who were dead beat, the Sikhs who had suffered most severe losses, and the Guides who had been marching and fighting all day, were not to be thought of. The 38th Dogras were, however, tolerably fresh, and Colonel Goldney, who commanded in the absence of the general, at once told off four companies to parade, and march to the relief. But the order was countermanded, and no troops left the camp that night.

Whether this decision was justified or not the reader shall decide. In the darkness and the broken ground it was probable the relief would never have found the general. It was possible that they would have been destroyed. The defenders of the camp itself were none too many. The numbers of the enemy were unknown. On the other hand it seemed unsoldierly, that we should try to sleep while the boom of the guns reminded us, that comrades were fighting for their lives only a few miles up in the valley.

CHAPTER XI

AT INAYAT KILA

Half an hour before dawn on the 17th, our men were mounted, and as soon as the light was strong enough to find a way through the broken ground, the squadron started in search of the missing troops. We had heard no more of their guns since about two o'clock. We therefore concluded they had beaten off the enemy. There might, of course, be a worse reason for their silence. As we drew near Bilot, it was possible to distinguish the figures of men moving about the walls and houses. The advanced files rode cautiously forward. Suddenly they cantered up to the wall and we knew some at least were alive. Captain Cole, turning to his squadron, lifted his hand. The Sowars, actuated by a common impulse, rose in their stirrups and began to cheer. But there was no response. Nor was this strange. The village was a shambles. In an angle of the outside wall, protected on the third side by a shallow trench, were the survivors of the fight. All around lay the corpses of men and mules. The bodies of five or six native soldiers were being buried in a hurriedly dug grave. It was thought that, as they were Mohammedans, their resting-place would be respected by the tribesmen.[1] Eighteen wounded men lay side by side in a roofless hut, and their faces drawn by pain and anxiety, looked ghastly in the pale light of the early morning. Two officers, one with his left hand smashed, the other shot through both legs, were patiently waiting for the moment when the improvised tourniquets could be removed and some relief afforded to their sufferings. The brigadier, his khaki coat stained with the blood from a wound on his head, was talking to his only staff-officer, whose helmet displayed a bullet-hole.

Gradually we learnt the story of the night. The battery, about thirty sappers and half the 35th Sikhs, were returning to camp. At about seven

[1] These bodies were afterwards dug up and mutilated by the natives: a foul act which excited the fury and indignation of soldiers of every creed in the force.

o'clock an order was sent for them to halt and remain out all night, to assist the Guides Infantry, whose firing could be heard and for whose safety the brigadier was above all things anxious. This order reached the battery and with the sappers as an escort they turned back, recrossed a nullah and met the general with two companies of Sikhs outside the village of Bilot. The half-battalion of the 35th did not apparently receive the order, for they continued their march. Lieutenant Wynter, R.A., was sent back to look for them. He did not find them but fell in with four fresh companies, two of the Guides and two of the 35th, who, under Major Worledge, had been sent from camp in response to the general's demand for reinforcements. Lieutenant Wynter brought these back, as an escort to the guns. On arrival at the village, the brigadier at once sent them to the assistance of the Guides. He counted on his own two companies of Sikhs. But when Worledge had moved off, and had already vanished in the night, it was found that these two companies had disappeared. They had lost touch in the darkness, and not perceiving that the general had halted, had gone on towards camp. Thus the battery was left with no other escort than thirty sappers.

A party of twelve men of the Buffs now arrived, and the circumstances which led them to the guns are worth recording. When the Buffs were retiring through the villages, they held a Mohammedan cemetery for a little while in order to check the enemy's advance. Whilst there, Lieutenant Byron, Orderly Officer to General Jeffreys, rode up and told Major Moody, who commanded the rear companies, that a wounded officer was lying in a dooly a hundred yards up the road, without any escort. He asked for a few men. Moody issued an order, and a dozen soldiers under a corporal started to look for the dooly. They missed it, but while searching, found the general and the battery outside the village. The presence of these twelve brave men – for they fully maintained the honour of their regiment – with their magazine rifles, just turned the scale.

The general now ordered the battery and sappers to go into the village, but it was so full of burning *bhoosa* that this was found to be impossible, and they set to work to entrench themselves outside. The village was soon full of the enemy. From the walls and houses, which on two sides commanded the space occupied by the battery, they began to fire at about thirty yards' range. The troops were as much exposed as if they had been in a racket court of which the enemy held the walls. They could not move, because they would have had to desert either the guns or the wounded. Fortunately, not many of the tribesmen, at this point, were armed with rifles. The others threw stones and burning *bhoosa* into the midst of the little garrison. By its light they took a good aim. Everybody got under such cover as was available. There was not much. Gunner Nihala, a gallant native soldier, repeatedly extinguished the burning *bhoosa* with his cloak at the imminent peril of his life. Lieutenants Watson and Colvin, with their sappers and the twelve men of the Buffs, forced their way into the village, and tried to expel the enemy with the bayonet. The village was too large for so small a party to clear. The tribesmen moved from one part to another, repeatedly firing. They killed and wounded several of the soldiers, and a bullet smashed Lieutenant Watson's hand. He however continued his efforts and did not cease until again shot, this time so severely as to be unable to stand. His men carried him from the village, and it was felt that it would be useless to try again.

At nine o'clock the rain stopped the firing, as the tribesmen were afraid of wetting their powder, but at about ten they opened again. They now made a great hole in the wall of the village, through which about a dozen men fired with terrible effect. Others began loopholing the walls. The guns fired case shot at twenty yards' range, at these fierce pioneers, smashing the walls to pieces and killing many. The enemy replied with bullets, burning *bhoosa* and showers of stones.

So the hours dragged away. The general and Captain Birch were both wounded, early in the night. Lieutenant Wynter, while behaving with distinguished gallantry, was shot through both legs at about 11.30. He was thus twice severely wounded within forty-five days. He now continued to command his guns, until he fainted from loss of blood. A native gunner then shielded him with his body, until he also was hit.

At length, at about 2.15, help arrived. Worledge's two companies had gone in search of the Guides, but had not found them. They now returned, and, hearing the firing at Bilot, sent an orderly of the 11th Bengal Lancers to ask if the general wanted assistance. This plucky boy – he was only a young recruit – rode coolly up to the village although the enemy were all around, and he stood an almost equal chance of being shot by our own men. He soon brought the four companies to the rescue, and the enemy, balked of their prey, presently drew off in the gloom. How much longer the battery and its defenders could have held out is uncertain. They were losing men steadily, and their numbers were so small that they might have been rushed at any moment.

No operations took place on the 17th. The soldiers rested, casualties were counted, wounds were dressed, confidence was restored, the funerals of the British officers and men killed the day before took place at noon. Everyone who could, attended; but all the pomp of military obsequies was omitted, and there were no Union Jacks to cover the bodies, nor were volleys fired over the graves lest the wounded should be disturbed.

The actual casualties were, in proportion to the numbers engaged, greater than in any action, of the British Army in India, for many years. Out of a force which at no time exceeded 1,000 men, nine British officers, four native officers and 136 soldiers were either killed or wounded.

The depression caused by the loss of amiable and gallant comrades was dispelled by the prospects of immediate action. Sir Bindon Blood, whose position at Nawagai was now one of danger, sent the brigadier, instead of reinforcements, orders to vigorously prosecute the operations against the tribesmen, and on the morning of the 18th the force moved to attack the village of Domodoloh; the same that the 38th had found so strongly occupied on the 16th.

The village lay in a re-entrant of the hills, from which two long spurs projected like the piers of a harbour. Behind, the mountains rose abruptly to a height of 5,000 feet. The ground embraced by the spurs, was filled with crops of maize and barley. A fort and watch-tower guarded the entrance. At 8.30 the advance was ordered. The enemy did not attempt to hold the fort, and it was promptly seized and blown up.

The enemy now opened fire from the spurs, both of which became crowned with little circles of white smoke. The 35th Sikhs advancing cleared the right ridge: the 38th Dogras the left. The Guides moved on the village, and up the main re-entrant itself. The Buffs were in reserve. The battery came into action on the left, and began shelling the crests of the opposite hills. Taking the range with their instruments, they fired two shots in rapid succession, each time at slightly different ranges. The little guns exploded with a loud report. Then, far up the mountain side, two balls of smoke appeared, one a little way above the other, and after a few seconds the noise of the bursting shells came faintly back. Gradually the spurs were cleared of the enemy and the Guides, passing through the village, climbed up the face of the mountain and established themselves among the great rocks of the steep water-course.

The sappers had now entered the village, and were engaged in preparing the hovels for destruction. Their flat roofs are covered with earth, and will not burn properly, unless a hole is made first in each. This took time. Meanwhile the troops held on to the positions they had seized, and maintained a dropping fire with the enemy. At about noon the place was lighted up, and a dense cloud of smoke rose in a high column into the still air. Then the withdrawal of the troops was ordered. Immediately the enemy began their counter attack; but the Guides were handled with much skill. The retirement of each company was covered by the fire of others, judiciously posted farther down the hill. No opportunity was offered to the enemy. By one o'clock all the troops were clear of the broken ground. The Buffs assumed the duty of rear-guard, and were delighted to have a brisk little skirmish – fortunately unattended with loss of life – with the tribesmen, who soon reoccupied the burning village. This continued for, perhaps, half an hour, and meanwhile the rest of the brigade returned to camp.

The casualties in this highly successful affair were small; two killed, six wounded.

The enemy's losses were considerable, but no reliable details could be obtained.

On the 19th the troops rested, and only foraging parties left the camp. On the 20th, fighting was renewed. From the position, at the entrance to the valley, it was possible to see all the villages that lay in the hollows of the hills, and to distinguish not only the scenes of past but also of future actions. The particular village which was selected for chastisement was never mentioned by name, and it was not until the brigade had marched some miles from the camp, that the objective became evident. The tribesmen therefore were unable to gather in really large numbers. At 5.30 the brigade started, and, preceded by the cavalry, marched up the valley – a long brown stream of men. Arrived nearly at the centre, the troops closed up into a more compact formation. Then suddenly the head wheeled to the left, and began marching on the village of Zagai. Immediately from high up on the face of the mountain, a long column of smoke shot into the air. It was a signal fire. Other hills answered it. The affair now became a question of time. If the village could be captured and destroyed before the clans had time to gather, then there would be little fighting. But if the force were delayed or became involved, it was impossible to say on what scale the action would be.

The village of Zagai stands in a similar situation to that of Domodoloh. On either side long spurs advance into the valley, and the houses are built in terraces on the sides of the hollow so formed. Great *chenar* trees growing in all their luxuriant beauty out of the rocky ground by the water-course, mark the hillside with a patch of green in contrast to the background of sombre brown. As the troops approached in fine array, the sound of incessant drumming was faintly heard, varied from time to time by the notes of a bugle. The cavalry reconnoitred, and trotted off to watch the flank, after reporting the place strongly occupied. The enemy displayed standards on the crests of the spurs. The advance continued: the Guides on the left, the 38th Dogras in the centre, the Buffs on the right, and the 35th Sikhs in reserve. Firing began on the left at about nine o'clock, and a quarter of an hour later the guns came into action near the centre. The Guides and Buffs now climbed the ridges to the right and left. The enemy fell back according to their custom, 'sniping'. Then the 38th pushed forward and occupied the village, which was handed over to the sappers to destroy. This they did most thoroughly, and at eleven o'clock a dense white smoke was rising from the houses and the stacks of *bhoosa*. Then the troops were ordered to withdraw. While the village was being destroyed, the enemy had been collecting. Their figures could be distinguished on the top of the mountain – a numerous line of dark dots against the sky; others had tried to come, from the adjoining valleys on the left and right.

As soon as the retirement was seen to be in progress, a general attack was made all along the line. On the left, the Guides were threatened by a force of about 500 men, who advanced displaying standards, and waving swords. They dispersed these and drove them away by a steady long-range fire, killing and wounding a large number. On the right, the Buffs were harassed by being commanded by another spur. From a point high up the mountain an accurate fire was directed upon them.

We tried to get the range of this point with the Lee-Metford rifles. It was, as nearly as could be determined, 1,400 yards. The tribesmen were only armed with Martini-Henrys. They nevertheless made excellent practice. Those who know the range and power of the Martini-Henry rifle will appreciate the skill and marksmanship which can inflict loss, even at so great a range.

As the retirement proceeded, the tribesmen came to closer quarters. The Buffs, however, used their formidable weapon with great effect. I witnessed one striking demonstration of its power. Lieutenant F. S. Reeves remained behind with a dozen men to cover the withdrawal of his company, and in hopes of bringing effective fire to bear on the enemy, who at this time were pressing forward boldly. Three hundred yards away was a nullah, and along this, they began running, in hopes of cutting off the small party. At one point, however, the line of their advance was commanded by our fire. Presently a man ran into the open. The section fired immediately. The great advantage of the rifle was that there was no difficulty about guessing the exact range, as the fixed sight could be used. The man dropped – a spot of white. Four others rushed forward. Again there was a volley. All four fell and remained motionless. After this we made good our retreat almost unmolested.

I shall make the reader no apology for having described at some length what was after all only a skirmish. The picture of the war on the frontier is essentially one of detail, and it is by the study of the details alone that a true impression can be obtained.

On the 22nd and 23rd the villages of Dag, and Tangi, were respectively captured, and destroyed, but as the resistance was slight and the operations were unmarked by any new features, I shall not weary the reader by further description.

By these operations the tribesmen of the Mamund Valley had been severely punished. Any exultation which they might have felt over the action of the 16th was completely effaced. The brigade had demonstrated its power to take and burn any village, that might be selected, and had inflicted severe loss on all who attempted to impede its action. The tribesmen were now thoroughly disheartened, and on the 21st began to sue for peace.

The situation was, however, complicated by the proximity of the

Afghan frontier. The western side of the Mamund Valley is bounded by the mountains of the Hindu Raj range, along the summits of which is the Durand line of demarcation with the Amir. On the farther side of this range Gholam Hyder, the Afghan commander-in-chief, lay with a powerful force, which, at the time of the actions I have described, amounted to nine battalions, six squadrons and fourteen mountain guns. During the attack upon Zagai, numerous figures in khaki uniform had been observed on the higher slopes of the hills, and it was alleged that one particular group appeared to be directing the movements of the tribesmen.

I am not in possession of sufficient evidence to pronounce on the question of the Amir's complicity in the frontier risings. It is certain that for many years, the Afghan policy has consistently been to forge and collect weapons, which might be used in raising a revolt among the Pathan tribes. But the advantages which the Amir would derive from a quarrel with the British are not apparent. It would seem more probable that he has only tried throughout to make his friendship, a matter of more importance to the Indian Government, with a view to the continuance or perhaps the increase of his subsidy. It is possible that he has this year desired to show us what a dangerous foe he might be, were he not so useful an ally. The question is a delicate and difficult one.

I do not see that the facts I have stated diminish or increase the probability of the Amir's complicity. It is no disparagement but rather to the honour of men, that they should be prepared to back with their lives, causes which claim their sympathy. It is indeed to such men that human advancement has been due. I allude to this matter only to explain the difficulties encountered in the Mamund Valley by the 2nd Brigade of the Malakand Field Force: to explain how it was that defenders of obscure villages were numbered by thousands, and why the weapons of poverty-stricken agriculturists, were excellent Martini-Henry rifles.

The Mamunds themselves were now genuinely anxious for peace. Their valley was in our hands; their villages and crops were at our mercy; but their allies, who suffered none of these things, were eager to continue the struggle. They had captured most of the rifles of the dead soldiers on the 16th, and they had no intention of giving them up. On the other hand, it was obvious that the British Raj could not afford

to be defied in this matter. We had insisted on the rifles being surrendered, and that expensive factor, Imperial prestige, demanded that
we should prosecute operations till we got them, no matter what the
cost might be. The rifles were worth little. The men and officers we
lost were worth a great deal. It was unsound economics, but Imperialism and economics clash as often as honesty and self-interest. Under
these unsatisfactory conditions the negotiations opened. They did not,
however, interfere with the military situation, and the troops continued
to forage daily in the valley, and the tribesmen to fire nightly into the
camp.

The reader must now accompany me to the camp of the 3rd Brigade,
twelve miles away, at Nawagai.

CHAPTER XII

NAWAGAI

The reader may have been struck, in the account of the fighting in the Mamund Valley, with the vigour with which the tribesmen follow up a retreating enemy, and press an isolated party. In war this is sound, practical policy. But the hillmen adopt it rather from a natural propensity, than from military knowledge. Their tactics are the outcome of their nature; all their actions, moral, political, strategic, are guided by the same principle. The powerful tribes who had watched the passage of the troops in sullen fear, only waited for a sign of weakness in order to rise behind them. As long as the brigades dominated the country, and appeared confident, and successful, their communications would be safe, and the risings localised; but a check, a reverse, a retreat would raise tremendous combinations on every side.

If the reader will bear this in mind, it will enable him to appreciate the position with which this chapter deals.

The strategic and political situation with which Sir Bindon Blood was confronted at Nawagai on the 17th of September was one of difficulty and danger. He had advanced into a hostile country. In his front the Mohmands had gathered at the Hadda Mullah's call to oppose his further progress. The single brigade he had with him was not strong enough to force the Bedmanai Pass, which the enemy held. The 2nd Brigade on which he had counted was fully employed twelve miles away in the Mamund Valley. The 1st Brigade, nearly four marches distant on the Panjkora River, had not sufficient transport to move. Meanwhile General Elles's division was toiling painfully through the difficult country north-east of Shabkadr, and could not arrive for several days. He was therefore isolated, and behind him was the 'network of ravines' through which a retirement would be a matter of the greatest danger and difficulty.

Besides this his line of communications, stretching away through sixty miles of hostile country, or country that at any moment might become hostile, was seriously threatened by the unexpected outbreak in the Mamund Valley. The Khan of Nawagai, a chief of great power and influence, was only kept loyal by the presence of Sir Bindon Blood's brigade. Had that brigade marched, as was advocated by the Government of India, back to join Brigadier-General Jeffreys in the Mamund Valley, this powerful chief would have thrown his whole weight against the British. The flame in the Mamund Valley, joining the flame in the Bedmanai Pass, would have produced a mighty conflagration. Bajaur would have risen to a man. Swat, in spite of its recent punishment, would have stirred ominously. Dir would have repudiated its ruler and joined the combination. The whole mountain region would have been ablaze.

Sir Bindon Blood decided to remain at Nawagai to cut the Hadda Mullah's gathering from the tribesmen in the Mamund Valley; to hold out a hand to General Elles; to keep the pass open and the khan loyal. Nawagai was the key of the situation. But that key could not be held without much danger. He therefore sent orders to Jeffreys to press operations against the Mamund tribesmen; assured the Khan of Nawagai of the confidence of the Government, and of their determination to 'protect' him from all enemies; heliographed to General Elles that he would meet him at Nawagai; entrenched his camp and waited.

He did not wait long in peace. The tribesmen, whose tactical instincts have been evolved by centuries of ceaseless war, were not slow to realise that the presence of the 3rd Brigade at Nawagai was fatal to their hopes. They accordingly resolved to attack it. The Suffi and Hadda Mullahs exerted the whole of their influence upon their credulous followers. The former appealed to the hopes of future happiness. Every Ghazi who fell fighting should sit above the Caaba, at the very footstool of the throne, and in that exalted situation should be solaced for his sufferings by the charms of a double allowance of celestial beauty. The Hadda Mullah used even more concrete inducements. The muzzles of the guns should be stopped for those who charged home. No bullet should harm them; they should be invulnerable. This promise appears to have carried more weight, as the Hadda Mullah's followers had three times as many killed and wounded as the candidates for the pleasures of the world to come.

A great gathering of the enemy, some 3,000 strong, now appeared in the plain. For about half an hour before sunset they danced, shouted and discharged their rifles. The mountain battery fired a few shells, but the distance was too great to do much good, or shall I say harm? Then it became dark. The whole brigade remained that night in the expectation of an attack, but only a very half-hearted attempt was made.

On the 20th, however, definite information was received from the political officer with the force, Mr Davis, that a determined assault would be made on the camp that night. The position of the camp was commanded by the surrounding heights. From these a searching rifle fire was now opened. All the tents were struck. The officers and men not employed in the trenches were directed to lie down. The majority of the bullets clearing the parapets of the entrenchment on one side, whizzed across without doing any harm to the prostrate figures; but all walking about was perilous, and besides this the dropping fire from the heights was galling to everyone.

Determined and vigorous sword charges were now delivered on all sides of the camp. The enemy, who numbered about 4,000, displayed the greatest valour. They rushed right up to the trenches and fell dead and dying, under the very bayonets of the troops.

The fire of the British was, however, crushing. The soldiers, confident in their power, were under perfect control. When the enemy charged, the order to employ magazine fire was passed along the ranks. The guns fired star shell. These great rockets, bursting into stars in the air, slowly fell to the ground shedding a pale and ghastly light, on swarming figures of the tribesmen, as they ran swiftly forward. Then the popping of the musketry became one intense roar as the ten cartridges, which the magazine of the rifle holds, were discharged almost instantaneously. Nothing could live in front of such a fire. At length the tribesmen sickened of the slaughter, and retired to their hills in gloom and disorder.

The situation was now cleared. The back of the Hadda Mullah's gathering was broken, and it dispersed rapidly. The Khan of Nawagai feverishly protested his unswerving loyalty to the Government. The Mamunds were disheartened. The next day General Elles' leading brigade appeared in the valley. Sir Bindon Blood rode out with his cavalry. The two generals met at Lakarai. It was decided that General

Elles should be reinforced by the 3rd Brigade of the Malakand Field Force, and should clear the Bedmanai Pass, and complete the discomfiture of the Hadda Mullah. Sir Bindon Blood with the cavalry would join Jeffreys' force in the Mamund Valley, and deal with the situation there. The original plan of taking two brigades from the Malakand to Peshawar, was thus discarded; and such troops of Sir Bindon Blood's force as were required for the Tirah expedition would, with the exception of the 3rd Brigade, reach their points of concentration *via* Nowshera.

The camp of the 3rd Brigade, was not attacked again. The tribesmen had learnt a bitter lesson from their experiences of the night before. The trenches were, however, lined at dark, and as small parties of the enemy were seen to be moving about across the front, occupied by the Queen's, there was some very excellent volley firing at intervals throughout the night. A few dropping shots came back out of the darkness, but no one was the worse, and the majority of the force made up for the sleep they had lost the night before.

The next morning Sir Bindon Blood, his staff and three squadrons of the 11th Bengal Lancers, rode back through the pass of Nawagai, and joined General Jeffreys at Inayat Kila. The 3rd Brigade now left the Malakand Field Force, and passed under the command of General Elles, and beyond the proper limits of this chronicle; but for the sake of completeness, and as the reader may be anxious to hear more of the fine regiment I shall briefly trace their further fortunes.

After General Wodehouse was wounded the command of the 3rd Brigade devolved upon Colonel Graves. They were present at the forcing of the Bedmanai Pass on the 29th of September, and at the subsequent capture and destruction of the Hadda Mullah's village of Jarobi, but as these actions were unattended by much loss of life, the whole brigade reached Shabkadr with only three casualties.

CHAPTER XIII

BACK TO THE MAMUND VALLEY

It is with a vague and undefined feeling of satisfaction, that I conduct the reader back to the entrenched camp of Inayat Kila, at the entrance of the Mamund Valley, where so much happened, and with which so many memories and experiences are associated.

When, on the afternoon of the 15th, the camp had first been pitched, only a small and hasty shelter-trench surrounded it. But as the weeks passed, the parapets grew higher, the ditches deeper, and the pits more numerous, until the whole place became a redoubt.

Since the action of the 16th of September the 2nd Brigade had been unable to move. Transport – the life and soul of an army – is an even more vital factor here than in less undeveloped countries. The mobility of a brigade depends entirely on its pack animals. On the 14th many mules were killed. On the 16th the field hospitals were filled with wounded. It now became impossible for the camp to move because the wounded could not be carried. It was impossible to leave them behind, because, deducting an adequate guard, the rest of the brigade would have been too few for fighting. The 2nd Brigade was therefore a fixture. Its striking power was limited to out and home marches. The first step taken by Sir Bindon Blood was to restore its mobility, by getting the wounded sent down to the base. Some changes in the constitution of the force were also made. The 11th Bengal Lancers, who now joined the Mohmand Field Force, were succeeded by the Guides Cavalry. The 35th Sikhs, who had suffered such severe losses, were replaced by the 31st Punjab Infantry from Panjkora. The Buffs who were full of fever, were exchanged for the Royal West Kent from the Malakand. No. 7 British Mountain Battery took the place of No. 8, which was now reduced to four guns, having lost in the week's fighting half its officers, a third of its mules, and a quarter of its men.

Camels to carry the wounded were sent up from Panjkora. The

Buffs escorted the long convoy down the line of communications. Everyone in camp was sorry to see the last of them. In the fighting of the week they had made it clear that the British Infantry battalion is the backbone of every mixed brigade, and they shared with the Guides Infantry one of those enviable reputations for steadiness which are so hard to gain, and so easy to lose on active service.

On the 24th of September Sir Bindon Blood received despatches appointing him to the command of the First Division of the Tirah Expeditionary Force, and as the negotiations with the Mamund Jirgahs were then in progress, and it seemed that a settlement might be reached, he proceeded with his staff to Panjkora. Mr Davis conducted the diplomatic relations with the Mamunds. On the 26th a Jirgah from the tribe came into camp. They deposited 4,000 rupees as a token of submission, and brought in fifty firearms. These, however, were of the oldest and most antiquated types, and were obviously not the weapons with which so many of our soldiers had been killed and wounded. This was pointed out to the tribal representatives. They protested they had no others. They were poor men, they said, and their property was at the mercy of the Government. But they had no other arms.

The political officer was firm, and his terms were explicit. Either they must give up the twenty-two rifles captured from the 35th Sikhs, on the 16th, or their villages would be destroyed. To this they replied that they had not got the rifles. They had all been taken, they said, and I think, with truth, by the Afghan tribesmen from the Kunar Valley. These would not give them up. Besides – this also with truth – they had been taken in 'fair war'.

One man, who had lived some years in Calcutta, was especially eloquent on the subject, and argued the case with much skill. He was, however, crushed by Mr Davis asking whether there were 'no grey-beards in the tribe', and why they were 'led by a Babri'. The discussion was extended to the whole question of their quarrel with the British power. They admitted having sent their young men to attack the Malakand and Chakdara. 'All the world was going *ghaza*,' they said They could not stay behind. They also owned to having gone five miles from their valley to attack the camp at Markhanai. Why had the Sirkar burnt their village? they asked. They had only tried to get even – for the sake of their honour. The matter reverted to the crucial point.

Would they give up their rifles or not? To this they replied evasively, that they would consult their fellow-tribesmen and return an answer on the next day. This practically amounted to a refusal, and as no reply was received on the 27th, the negotiations ceased.

In consequence of this and of the threatening attitude of the tribesmen throughout Dir and Bajaur, Sir Bindon Blood telegraphed to the Government of India and recommended the retention of a large force in these territories. By so doing he virtually resigned the command which awaited him of the Tirah expedition. The Government accepted the advice of their general. A force of eleven battalions, seven squadrons and three batteries was placed at Sir Bindon Blood's disposal, and he was directed to deal with the local situation as he should see fit. He immediately ordered General Jeffreys to resume the punitive operations against the Mamunds.

In pursuance of these orders, the 2nd Brigade on the 29th destroyed all the villages in the centre of the valley, some twelve or fourteen in number, and blew up with dynamite upwards of thirty towers and forts. The tribesmen, unable to contend with the troops in the open, remained sullenly on the hillsides, and contented themselves with firing from long range at the cavalry patrols.

I feel that this is a fitting moment to discuss the questions which village-burning raises. I have described with independent impartiality the progress of the quarrel between the British and the tribesmen. In a similar spirit I approach the examination of the methods of offence employed. Many misconceptions exist on this subject in England. One member of the House of Commons asked the Secretary of State whether, in the punishment of villages, care was taken that only the houses of the guilty parties should be destroyed. He was gravely told that great care was taken. The spectacle of troops, who have perhaps carried a village with the bayonet and are holding it against a vigorous counter-attack, when every moment means loss of life and increase of danger, going round and carefully discriminating which houses are occupied by 'guilty parties', and which by unoffending people, is ridiculous. Another member asked, 'Whether the villages were destroyed or only the fortifications'. 'Only the fortifications', replied the minister guilelessly. What is the actual fact? All along the Afghan border every man's house is his castle. The villages are the fortifications, the fortifications are the villages. Every house is loopholed, and whether it has a tower or not depends only on its owner's wealth. A third legislator, in the columns of his amusing weekly journal, discussed the question at some length, and commented on the barbarity of such tactics. They were not only barbarous, he affirmed, but senseless. Where did the inhabitants of the villages go? To the enemy of course! This reveals, perhaps, the most remarkable misconception of the actual facts. The writer seemed to imagine that the tribesmen consisted of a regular army who fought, and a peaceful, law-abiding population who remained at their business, and perhaps protested against the excessive military expenditure from time to time. Whereas in reality throughout these regions, every inhabitant is a soldier from the first day he is old enough to hurl a stone, till the last day he has strength to pull a trigger, after which he is probably murdered as an encumbrance to the community.

Equipped with these corrected facts, I invite the reader to examine the question of the legitimacy of village-burning for himself. A camp of a British brigade, moving at the order of the Indian Government and under the acquiescence of the people of the United Kingdom, is attacked at night. Several valuable and expensive officers, soldiers and transport animals are killed and wounded. The assailants retire to the hills. Thither it is impossible to follow them. They cannot be caught. They cannot be punished. Only one remedy remains – their property must be destroyed. Their villages are made hostages for their good behaviour. They are fully aware of this, and when they make an attack on a camp or convoy they do it because they have considered the cost and think it worth while. Of course, it is cruel and barbarous, as is much else in war, but it is only an unphilosophic mind that will hold it legitimate, to take a man's life, and illegitimate to destroy his property.

In official parlance the burning of villages is usually expressed euphemistically as 'So many villages were visited and punished', or, again, 'The fortifications were demolished'. I do not believe in all this circumlocution. The lack of confidence in the good sense of the British democracy, which the Indian Government displays, is one of its least admirable characteristics. The people of our islands only require to have the matter put fairly before them to arrive at sound, practical conclusions. If this were not so, we should not occupy our present position in the world.

To return to the Mamund Valley. On the 29th over a dozen villages in the plains were destroyed, without the loss of a single life. On the 30th the tale ran somewhat differently. The village of Agrah adjoins the village of Zagai, the capture of which has already been recorded. It stood in a broad re-entrant of the mountains, and amid ground so tangled and broken, that to move over it was difficult. On the steep face of the mountain great rocks, sometimes thirty feet high, lay tossed about: interspersed with these were huts or narrow terraces, covered with crops, and rising one above the other by great steps of ten or twelve feet each. The attack on such a place was further complicated by the fact that the same re-entrant contained another village called Gat, which had to be occupied at the same time. This compelled the brigade to attack on a broader front than their numbers allowed. It was evident as the Guides Cavalry approached the hills, that resistance was contemplated. Several red standards were visible to the naked eye, and the field-glasses disclosed numerous figures lining the ridges and spurs. The squadrons, advancing as far as the scrub would allow them, soon drew the fire of isolated skirmishers. The brigade now came into action, in the following formation. The cavalry on the extreme left covered the head of a considerable valley, from which our flank was threatened; the Guides Infantry and the Royal West Kent Regiment prolonged the line to the centre of attack; the 31st Punjab Infantry moved against the spurs to the right of the village, and the 38th Dogras were in reserve. The action was begun by the Guides Infantry storming the ridges to the left of the enemy's position. These were strongly held and fortified by *sungars*, behind which the defenders were sheltered. The tribesmen, shooting from excellent cover, maintained a hot fire. It was soon apparent that the enemy did not mean to abide the assault. When the troops got within 100 yards and fixed bayonets, a dozen determined men were still firing from the *sungars*. The Afridi and Pathan companies of the Guides, uttering shrill cries of exultation, culminating in an extraordinary yell, dashed forward, climbed the hill as only hillsmen can climb, and cleared the crest. On the side of the next hill the figures of the retreating tribesmen were visible, and many were shot down before they could find shelter.

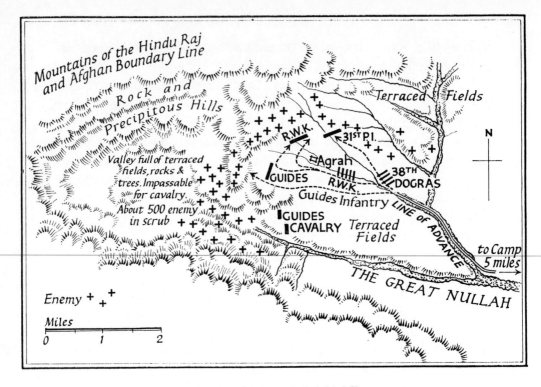

THE ATTACK UPON AGRAH

The West Kents had now come into line on the Guides' right, and while the latter held the long ridge they had taken, the British regiment moved upon the village. Here the resistance became very severe. The tangled and broken ground, rising in terraces, sometimes ten feet high, and covered with high crops, led to fighting at close quarters, with heavy loss on both sides. The 31st Punjab Infantry, who had ascended the spur on the right, soon joined hands with the West Kents, and both regiments became hotly engaged. It soon became evident that the troops were too few for the work. On the left the Guides Infantry were unable to leave the ridge they had captured, lest it should be reoccupied by the enemy. A gap opened in consequence, between the Guides and Royal West Kents, and this enabled the tribesmen to get round the left flank of the British regiment, while the 31st Punjab Infantry, on the right, were also turned by the enveloping enemy.

The British regiment forced its way through the village, and encountered the enemy strongly posted in *sungars* among the works above it. Here they were sharply checked. The leading company had stormed one of these fortifications, and the enemy at once retired higher up the hill. About fifteen men were inside the work, and perhaps thirty more just below it.

Of those inside, four or five were instantly killed or wounded. The *sungar* was a regular trap, and the company were ordered to retire. Lieutenant Browne–Clayton remained till the last, to watch the withdrawal, and in so doing was shot dead, the bullet severing the blood-vessels near the heart. The two or three men who remained, were handing down his body over the rock wall, when they were charged by about thirty Ghazis and driven down the hill. A hundred and fifty yards away Major Western had three companies of the West Kents in support. He immediately ordered Captain Styles to retake the *sungar*, and recover the body. The company charged. Captain Styles was the first to reach the stone wall, and with Lieutenant Jackson cleared it of such of the enemy as remained. Five or six men were wounded in the charge, and others fell in the *sungar*. The advanced position of this company was soon seen to be untenable, and they were ordered to fall back to the edge of the village, where the whole regiment was hotly engaged.

Meanwhile the 31st Punjab Infantry, who had advanced under Colonel O'Bryen on the right, were exposed to a severe fire from a rocky ridge on their flank. Their attack was directed against a great mass of boulders which were tenaciously held by the enemy. The fighting soon became close. The two advanced companies were engaged at a distance of under 100 yards. Besides this the cross fire from their right flank added to the difficulties.

Colonel O'Bryen moving swiftly from point to point directed the fire and animated the spirit of the men, who were devoted to him. It was not long before the enemy's marksmen began to take aim at this prominent figure. But for a considerable period, although bullets struck the ground everywhere around him, he remained unhurt. At last, however, he was shot through the body, and carried mortally wounded from the action.

The pressure now became so strong along the whole line that the brigadier, fearing that the troops might get seriously involved, ordered the withdrawal to commence. The village was, however, burning, and the enemy, who had also suffered severely from the close fighting, did not follow up with their usual vigour. The battery advanced to within 600 yards of the enemy's line, and opened a rapid fire of shrapnel to clear those spurs that commanded the line of retirement. The shells screamed over the heads of the West Kent Regiment, who were now clear of the hills and in front of the guns, and burst in little white puffs of smoke along the crest of the ridge, tearing up the ground into a thick cloud of dust by the hundreds of bullets they contained.

At length the withdrawal was completed, and the brigade returned to camp. The presence of the cavalry, who covered the rear, deterred the enemy from leaving the hills.

Riding back I observed a gruesome sight. At the head of the column of doolies and stretchers, were the bodies of the killed, each tied with cords upon a mule. Their heads dangled on one side and their legs on the other. The long black hair of the Sikhs, which streamed down to the ground, and was draggled with dust and blood, imparted a hideous aspect to these figures. There was no other way, however, and it was better than leaving their remains to be insulted, and defiled by the savages, with whom we were fighting.

As soon as Sir Bindon Blood, at his camp on the Panjkora, received the news of the severe fighting of the 30th,[1] he decided to proceed himself to Inayat Kila with reinforcements. He arrived on the 2nd of October, bringing No. 8 Mountain Battery; a wing of the 24th Punjab Infantry; and two troops of the Guides Cavalry; and having also sent orders to the Highland Light Infantry and four guns of the 10th Field Battery to follow him at once. He was determined to make a fresh attack on Agrah, and burn the village of Gat, which had only been partially destroyed; and this attack was fixed for the 5th. By that date the big 12-pounder guns of the Field Battery were to have arrived, and the fire of fourteen pieces would have been concentrated on the enemy's position. Everyone was anxious to carry matters to a conclusion with the tribesmen at all costs.

[1] After the action of the 30th of September, Lieut.-Colonel McRae, of the 45th Sikhs, was sent up to command the 31st Punjab Infantry in the place of Lieut.-Colonel O'Bryen, and I was myself attached as a temporary measure to fill another of the vacancies. This is, I believe, the first time a British officer has been attached to a native infantry regiment. After the kindness and courtesy with which I was treated, I can only hope it will not be the last.

On the 3rd, the force was ordered to take and burn the village of Badelai, against which the Buffs had advanced on the 16th, and from which they had been recalled in a hurry to support the 35th Sikhs. The attack and destruction of the village presented no new features; the tribesmen offered little resistance, and retired before the troops. But as soon as the brigade began its homeward march, they appeared in much larger numbers, than had hitherto been seen. As the cavalry could not work among the nullahs, and the broken ground, the enemy advanced boldly into the plain. In a great crescent, nearly four miles long, they followed the retiring troops. A brisk skirmish began at about 800 yards. Both batteries came into action, each firing about ninety shells. All the battalions of the brigade were engaged. The enemy, whose strength was estimated to be over 3,000, lost heavily, and drew off at 2.30, when the force returned to camp. Sir Bindon Blood and his staff watched the operations and reconnoitred the valley.

The next day the Highland Light Infantry and the field guns arrived. The former marched in over 700 strong, and made a fine appearance. They were nearly equal in numbers, to any two battalions in the brigade. The guns had accomplished a great feat in getting over the difficult and roadless country. They had had to make their own track, and in many places the guns had been drawn by hand. The 10th Field Battery had thus gone sixty miles further into the hill country, than any other wheeled traffic. They had quite a reception when they arrived. The whole camp turned out to look with satisfaction on the long polished tubes, which could throw twelve pounds a thousand yards further than the mountain guns could throw seven. They were, however, not destined to display their power. The Mamunds had again sued for peace. They were weary of the struggle. Their valley was desolate. The season of sowing the autumn crops approached. The arrival of reinforcements convinced them that the Government were determined to get their terms. Major Deane came up himself to conduct the negotiations. Meanwhile all important operations were suspended, though the foraging and 'sniping' continued as usual.

The force was now large enough for two brigades to be formed, and on the arrival of Brigadier-General Meiklejohn it was reconstituted.

I would that it were in my power to convey to the reader who has not had the fortune to live with troops on service, some just appreciation of the compensations of war. The healthy open-air life, the vivid incidents, the excitement, the generous and cheery friendships, the chances of distinction which are open to all, invest life with keener interests, and rarer pleasures. The uncertainty and importance of the present, reduce the past and future, to comparative insignificance, and clear the mind of minor worries. And when all is over, memories remain, which few men do not hold precious. As to the hardships, these though severe may be endured. Besides all this, the chances of learning about the next world, are infinitely greater. And yet we are confronted with a mournful but stubborn fact. In this contrary life, so prosaic is the mind of man, so material his soul, so poor his spirit, that there is no one who has been six months on active service, who is not delighted to get safe home again, to the comfortable monotonies of peace.

CHAPTER XIV

THE WORK OF THE CAVALRY

The negotiations of the Mamunds had this time opened under more propitious circumstances. The tribesmen were convinced by the arrival of the large reinforcements that the Government were in earnest. The return of 'the big general', as they called Sir Bindon Blood, to distinguish him from the brigadiers, impressed them with the fact that the operations would be at once renewed if they continued recalcitrant. They had still a few villages unburned, and they disliked the look of the long *topes*, or field guns, of whose powers they were uncertain. They therefore displayed a much more humble spirit.

On the other side every one in the force had realised that there were 'more kicks than ha'pence' to be got out of the Mamund Valley. There was no doubt as to the ability of the brigades to take and burn, any village they might select. At the same time it was certain that they would encounter relays of Afghan tribesmen, and regular soldiers from the Amir's army, and that they would lose officers and men in the operation. The matter had to be carried to a conclusion at whatever cost, but the sooner the end was reached the better.

But in spite of the auguries of peace, the foraging parties were usually fired upon, and this furnished several opportunities for the display of the value of the cavalry. I shall avail myself of the occasion to review the performances of the cavalry during the operations. As soon as the brigades entered Bajaur, the 11th Bengal Lancers were employed more and more in that legitimate duty of cavalry – reconnaissance. Major Beatson made daily expeditions towards the various valleys and passes, about which information was needed. This use of cavalry is an entirely new one on the frontier – it having been thought that it was dangerous to employ the army in this way. Though horsemen need good ground to fight to advantage on, they can easily move over any country, however broken, and where they are boldly used, can collect as much information as is necessary.

The task which is usually confided to cavalry in these mountain actions is to protect one of the flanks. The ground hardly ever admits of charging in any formation, and it is necessary for the men to use their carbines. On the 30th of September the cavalry were so employed. On the left of the hostile position was a wide valley full of scrubby trees, and stone walls, and occupied by large numbers of the enemy. Had these tribesmen been able to debouch from this valley, they would have fallen on the flank of the brigade, and the situation would have become one of danger. For five hours two weak squadrons of the Guides Cavalry were sufficient to hold them in check.

The methods they employed are worth noticing. On the 6th of October, I witnessed a squadron engaged in covering the operations of a foraging party. A line of patrols moving rapidly about presented difficult targets to the enemy's sharpshooters; I found the remainder of the squadron dismounted, in rear of a large bank of stones. Twenty Sowars with their carbines were engaged in firing at the enemy, who had occupied a *morcha* – a small stone fort – some 300 yards away. Desultory skirmishing continued for some time, shots being fired from the hills, which were half a mile away, as well as from the *morcha*. Bullets kept falling near the bank, but the cover it afforded was good and no one was hurt. At length word was brought that the foraging was finished and that the squadron was to retire under cover of the infantry. Now came a moment of some excitement. The officer in command knew well that the instant his men were mounted they would be fired at from every point which the enemy held. He ordered the first troop to mount, and the second to cover the retirement. The men scrambled into their saddles, and spreading out into an extended line cantered away towards a hollow about 300 yards distant. Immediately there was an outburst of firing. The dust rose in spurts near the horsemen, and the bullets whistled about their ears. No one was, however, hit. Meanwhile, the remaining troop had been keeping up a rapid fire on the enemy to cover their retirement. It now became their turn to go. Firing a parting volley the men ran to their horses, mounted, and followed the first troop at a hand-gallop, extending into a long line as they did so. Again the enemy opened fire, and again the dusty ground showed that the bullets were well directed. Again, however, nobody was hurt, and the Sowars reached the hollow laughing and talking in high glee. The morning's skirmish had, however, cost the squadron a man and horse, both severely wounded.

While I was with the Malakand Field Force I was a witness of the constant employment of the cavalry, and was several times informed by general officers that they would gladly have a larger number at their disposal. The reader may recall some of the numerous instances which these pages have recorded of cavalry work. On the morning of the 15th of September it was the cavalry who were able to catch up the enemy, before they could reach the hills, and take some revenge for the losses of the night. In the action of the 16th, the charge of Captain Cole's squadron, brought the whole attack of the enemy to a standstill, and enabled the infantry by their fire to convert the hesitation of the tribesmen into a retreat. Indeed, in every fight in the Mamund Valley, the cavalry were the first in, and the last out.

The fighting described in the last chapter, and the continual drain of disease, had again filled the field hospitals, and in order to preserve the mobility of the force it was decided to send all sick and wounded down to the base at once. The journey – over 100 miles by road – would take nearly a fortnight, and the jolting and heat make such an experience, a painful and weary one to injured men. But the stern necessities of war, render these things inevitable, and the desire of the men to get nearer home soothes much of their suffering. The convoy of sick and wounded was to be escorted as far as the Panjkora River by the Royal West Kent, who were themselves in need of some recuperation. To campaign in India without tents is always a trial to a British regiment; and when it is moved to the front from some unhealthy station like Peshawar, Delhi, or Mian Mir, and the men are saturated with fever and weakened by the summer heats, the sick list becomes long and serious. Typhoid from drinking surface water, and the other various kinds of fever which follow exposure to the heats of the day, or the chills of the night, soon take 100 men from the fighting strength, and the general of an Indian frontier force has to watch with equal care the movements of the enemy and the fluctuations of the hospital returns. As soon, therefore, as Sir Bindon Blood saw that the Mamunds were desirous of peace, and that no further operations against them were probable, he sent one of his British regiments to their tents near the Panjkora.

About sixty wounded men from the actions of 30th of September and 3rd of October, and the same number of sick, formed the bulk of the convoy. The slight cases are carried on camels, in cradles made by cutting a native bedstead in two, and called *cacolays*. The more serious cases are carried in doolies or litters, protected from the sun by white curtains, and borne by four natives. Those who are well enough ride on mules. The infantry escort is disposed along the line with every precaution that can be suggested, but the danger of an attack upon the long straggling string of doolies and animals on difficult and broken ground is a very real and terrible one.

Starting at six the column reached Jar, a march of eight miles, at about ten o'clock. Here we were joined by a wing of the 24th Punjab Infantry, who were coming up to relieve the Royal West Kents. The camp at Jar has the disadvantage of being commanded by a hill to the north, and the Salarzais, another pestilent tribe, whose name alone is an infliction, delight to show their valour by firing at the troops during the night. Of course this could be prevented by moving the camp out of range of this hill. But then, unfortunately, it would be commanded by another hill to the south, from which the Shamozai section of the Utman Khels – to whom my former remarks also apply – would be able to amuse themselves. The inconvenience of the situation had therefore to be faced.

We had not been long in camp before the eldest son of the Khan of Jar, who had been comparatively loyal during the operations, came to inform the colonel in command that there would be 'sniping' that night. Certain evil men, he said, had declared their intention of destroying the force, but he, the heir-apparent to the Khanate of Jar, and the ally of the Empress, would protect us. Four picquets of his own regular army should watch the camp – that our slumbers might not be disturbed – and when challenged by the sentries they would reply, '*chokidar*' (watchman). This all seemed very satisfactory, but we entrenched ourselves as usual, not, as we explained, because we doubted our protector's powers or inclinations, but merely as a matter of form.

At midnight precisely the camp was awakened by a dozen shots in rapid succession. The khan's picquets could be heard expostulating with the enemy, who replied by jeers and bitter remarks.

The firing continued for an hour, when the 'snipers', having satisfied their honour, relieved their feelings and expended their cartridges, went away rejoicing. The troops throughout remained silent,
and vouchsafed no reply.

It may seem difficult to believe that fifty bullets could fall in a camp,
only 100 yards square – crowded with animals and men – without
any other result than to hit a single mule in the tail. Such was, however,
the fact. This shows of what value a little active service is to the
soldier. The first time he is under fire, he imagines himself to be in
great danger. He thinks that every bullet is going to hit him, and that
every shot is aimed at him. Assuredly he will be killed in a moment.
If he goes through this ordeal once or twice, he begins to get some
idea of the odds in his favour. He has heard lots of bullets and they
have not hurt him. He will get home safely to his tent this evening,
just as he did the last time. He becomes a very much more effective
fighting machine.

Though the firing produced very little effect on the troops – most
of whom had been through the experience several times before – it
was a severe trial to the wounded, whose nerves, shattered by pain
and weakness, were unable to bear the strain. The surgeon in charge –
Major Tyrrell – told me that the poor fellows quivered at every shot
as if in anticipation of a blow. A bullet in the leg will make a brave
man a coward. A blow on the head will make a wise man a fool.
Indeed I have read that a sufficiency of absinthe can make a good man
a knave. The triumph of mind over matter does not seem to be quite
complete as yet.

I have devoted a good deal in this chapter to the account of the
'sniping' at Jar on the night of the 10th of October, and, perhaps, a
critic may inquire why so much should be written about so common
an incident. It is, however, because this night's firing is so common a
feature, that I feel no picture of the war on the Indian frontier would
be complete without some account of it.

The next day we crossed the Panjkora River, and I started to ride
down the line of communications to the base at Nowshera. At each
stage some of the comforts of civilisation, and peace reappeared. At
Panjkora we touched the telegraph wire; at Sarai were fresh potatoes;
ice was to be had at Chakdara; a comfortable bed at the Malakand;

and at length, at Nowshera, the railway. But how little these things matter after all. When they are at hand they seem indispensable, but when they cannot be obtained they are hardly missed. A little plain food, and a philosophic temperament, are the only necessities of life.

CHAPTER XV

SUBMISSION

At last the negotiations with the Mamunds began to reach a conclusion. The tribe were really desirous of peace, and prepared to make any sacrifices to induce the brigades to leave the valley. The Khan of Khar now proved of valuable assistance. He consistently urged them to make peace with the Sirkar, and assured them that the troops would not go away, until they had their rifles back. Finally the Mamunds said they would get the rifles. But the path of repentance was a stony one. On the very night that the tribesmen decided for peace at any price, a thousand warlike Afghans, spoiling for a fight, arrived from the Kunar Valley, on the other side of the mountains, and announced their intention of attacking the camp at once. The Mamunds expostulated with them. The retainers of the Khan of Khar implored them not to be so rash. In the end these unwelcome allies were persuaded to depart. But that night – the night of the 8th of October – the camp was warned that an attack was probable. The inlying picquets were accordingly doubled, and every man slept in his clothes, so as to be ready. The pathos of the situation was provided by the fact that the Mamunds were guarding us from our enemies. The wretched tribe, rather than face a renewal of hostilities, had posted picquets all round the camp to drive away 'snipers' and other assailants. Their sincerity was beyond suspicion.

The next day the first instalment of rifles was surrendered. Fifteen Martini-Henrys taken on the 16th from the 35th Sikhs were brought into camp, by the Khan of Khar's men, and deposited in front of the general's tent. Nearly all were hacked and marked by sword cuts, showing that their owners, the Sikhs, had perished fighting to the last. Perhaps these firearms had cost more in blood and treasure than any others ever made. The remainder of the twenty-one were promised later, and have since all been surrendered. But the rifles as they lay on the ground were a bitter comment on the economic aspect of the 'Forward Policy'. These tribes have nothing to surrender but their arms. To extort these few, had taken a month, had cost many lives, and thousands of pounds. It had been as bad a bargain as was ever made. People talk glibly of 'the total disarmament of the frontier tribes' as being the obvious policy. No doubt such a result would be most desirable. But to obtain it would be about as painful an undertaking as to extract the stings of a swarm of hornets, with naked fingers.

After the surrender of the rifles, the discussion of terms proceeded with smoothness. Full Jirgahs were sent to the camp from the tribe, and gradually a definite understanding was reached. The tribesmen bewailed the losses they had sustained. Why, they asked, had the Sirkar visited them so heavily? Why, replied Major Deane, had they broken the peace and attacked the camp? The elders of the tribe, following the practice of all communities, threw the blame on their 'young men'. These had done the evil, they declared. All had paid the penalty. At length definite terms were agreed to, and a full *durbar* was arranged for the 11th of the month for their ratification.

Accordingly on that date, at about one o'clock in the afternoon, a large and representative Jirgah of Mamunds, accompanied by the Khans of Khar, Jar and Nawagai, arrived at the village of Nawa Kila, about half a mile from the camp. At three o'clock Sir Bindon Blood, with Major Deane, Chief Political Officer; Mr Davis, Assistant Political Officer; most of the Headquarters Staff, and a few other officers, started, escorted by a troop of the Guides Cavalry, for the *durbar*. The general on arrival shook hands with the friendly khans, much to their satisfaction, and took a seat which had been provided. The tribesmen formed three sides of a square. The friendly khans were on the left with their retainers. The Mamund Jirgahs filled two other sides. Sir Bindon Blood, with Major Deane on his left and his officers around him, occupied the fourth side.

Then the Mamunds solemnly tendered their submission. They expressed their deep regret at their action, and deplored the disasters that had befallen them. They declared they had only fought because they feared annexation. They agreed to expel the followers of Umra Khan from the valley. They gave security for the rifles that had not yet been surrendered. They were then informed that as they had suffered severe punishment and had submitted the Sirkar would exact no fine or further penalty from them. At this they showed signs of gratification. The *durbar*, which had lasted fifteen minutes, was ended by the whole of the tribesmen swearing with uplifted hands to adhere to the terms and keep the peace. They were then dismissed.

Thus the episode of the Mamund Valley came to an end. On the morning of the 12th, the troops moved out of the camp at Inayat Kila for the last time, and the long line of men, guns and transport animals, trailed slowly away across the plain of Khar. The tribesmen gathered on the hills to watch the departure of their enemies, but whatever feelings of satisfaction they may have felt at the spectacle, were dissipated when they turned their eyes towards their valley. Not a tower, not a fort was to be seen. The villages were destroyed. The crops had been trampled down. They had lost heavily in killed and wounded, and the winter was at hand. No defiant shots pursued the retiring column. The ferocious Mamunds were weary of war.

And as the soldiers marched away, their reflections could not have been wholly triumphant. For a month they had held Inayat Kila, and during that month they had been constantly fighting. The Mamunds were crushed. The Imperial power had been asserted, but the cost was heavy. Thirty-three officers and 249 men had been killed and wounded, out of a fighting force that had on no occasion exceeded 1,200 men.

The main cause of these casualties was, as I have already written, the proximity of the Afghan border. But it would be unjust and ungenerous to deny to the people of the Mamund Valley, that reputation for courage, tactical skill and marksmanship, which they have so well deserved. During an indefinite period they had brawled and fought, in the unpenetrated gloom of barbarism. At length they struck a blow at civilisation, and civilisation will yet ungrudgingly admit, that they are a brave and warlike race.

The troops camped on the night of the 12th at Jar, and on the following day moved up the Salarzai Valley to Matashah. Here they remained for nearly a week. This tribe, terrified by the punishment of the Mamunds, made no regular opposition, though the camp was fired into regularly every night by a few hot-blooded 'snipers'. The reconnaissances in force, which were sent out daily to the farther end of the valley, were not resisted in any way, and the tribal Jirgahs used every effort to collect the rifles, which they had been ordered to surrender. By the 19th all were given up, and on the 20th the troops moved back to Jar. There Sir Bindon Blood received the submission of the Utman Khels, who brought in the weapons demanded from them, and paid a fine as an indemnity for attacking the Malakand and Chakdara.

All Indian military commanders, from Lord Clive and Lord Clive's times downwards, have inveighed against the practice of attaching civil officers to field forces. It has been said, frequently with truth, that they hamper the military operations, and infuse a spirit of vacillation into the plans. Although the political officers of the Malakand Field Force were always personally popular with their military comrades, there were many who disapproved of their presence. The duties of the civil officers, in a campaign, are twofold: firstly, to negotiate, and secondly, to collect information. It would seem that for the first of these duties they are indispensable. The difficult language, and peculiar characters of the tribesmen are the study of a lifetime. A knowledge of the local conditions, of the power and influence of the khans, or other rulers of the people; of the general history and traditions of the country, is a task which must be entirely specialised. Men are needed who understand the whole question, and all the details of the quarrel, between the natives and the Government, and who can in some measure appreciate both points of view. I do not believe that such are to be found in an army.

Respecting the second duty, it is difficult to believe that the collection of information as to the numbers and intentions of the enemy, would not be better carried out, by the Intelligence Department, and the cavalry. Civil officers should not be expected to understand what kind of military information a general requires. It is not their business. I am aware that Mr Davis procured the most correct intelligence about the great night attack at Nawagai, and thus gave ample warning to Sir Bindon Blood. But on the other hand the scanty information available about the Mamunds, previous to the action of the 16th, was the main cause of the severe loss sustained on that day. Civil officers should discharge diplomatic duties, and military officers the conduct of war.

After the Utman Khels had been induced to comply with our terms, the brigades recrossed the Panjkora River, and then marching by easy stages down the line of communications, returned to the Malakand. The Guides, moving back to Mardan, went into cantonments again, and turned in a moment from war to peace. The Buffs remained at Malakand in garrison. A considerable force was retained near Jelala to await the issue of the operations against the Afridis, and to be ready to move against the Bunerwals, should an expedition be necessary.

Here we leave the Malakand Field Force. It may be that there is yet another chapter of its history which remains to be written, and that the fine regiments of which it is composed, will, under their trusted commander, have other opportunities of playing the great game of war.

THE STORY OF

THE RIVER WAR

*An account of the re-conquest
of the Soudan*

INTRODUCTION[1]

Nearly thirty-five years have passed since this book was written, and I am very glad that it is now to take a renewed lease of life.

In those distant days the world was tranquil and our country relatively rich and powerful. The Royal Navy was more than equal to the next two or three navies put together. England was largely the world's manufacturer, and London was its unchallenged financial centre. With these great advantages we pursued a steady and modest policy of avoiding foreign entanglements, and only reluctantly accepted new possessions or responsibilities.

In spite, however, of the wishes of many of the statesmen of both political parties, England was drawn into Egypt. After the bombardment of Alexandria in 1881, when the French fleet sailed away before the action, we became to all intents and purposes the paramount power. The marvellous work of creating good government and prosperity for the Egyptians, which will for ever be linked with the name of Lord Cromer, was soon in full progress. A small band of first-class Englishmen, keeping themselves in the background, directed the whole process of reform and reconstruction with virtually sovereign power.

It was at this moment that the Rebellion of the Mahdi plunged the vast, remote provinces of the Soudan into bloodshed and confusion. Mr Gladstone's Government had no other wish than to escape from Egypt at the earliest possible moment. They viewed with horror being involved in the Soudan. The disturbances and disasters which befell the Egyptian armies and administration further stimulated their eagerness to quit the Nile valley. They unhesitatingly resolved to relinquish the Soudan to barbarism. General Gordon was sent to Khartoum to wind up affairs and bring away the surviving officials, soldiers and Egyptian colonists and traders.

Easier said than done! Once arrived at Khartoum, he made it a point of honour not to leave until he had safely evacuated all those committed to his charge. He was soon 'hemmed in' – the expression is

[1] Specially written for the Third Edition. See Publisher's Note, page 14.

Mr Gladstone's, who resented the word 'surrounded' – and the long blockade began. If General Gordon considered his honour involved in rescuing the Egyptians in the Soudan, Great Britain soon found an even stronger obligation to rescue *him*. Lord Hartington, the Liberal Secretary of State for War, moved very slowly; but when he considered his honour was involved, nothing could turn him from his path. Gordon must be rescued at all costs. Expeditions both by the winding Nile and by short-cuts across the desert were launched. After fierce fighting the Desert column reached Metemma, where Gordon's gunboats awaited them. The relievers arrived before Khartoum two days too late. The city was already in the hands of the Dervish mob. Gordon and nearly all the people he would not desert had been massacred. The evacuation of the Soudan was thus complete.

However, the story had sunk deeply into British hearts. The overthrow of Mr Gladstone on Home Rule in 1886 inaugurated what was practically twenty years of Conservative rule. Very slowly, patiently, cautiously and frugally the British Government set about the recovery of the ruined territory. The results achieved in Egypt were now so remarkable as to be the source of general pride. At the head of the Egyptian Army stood Kitchener, a British officer of exceptional capacity and growing repute. More than ten years after the sack of Khartoum, the first advance into the Dongola Province began, and two years later, in 1898, the armies of the savage Dervish empire were shattered and largely destroyed in the Battle of Omdurman. Thirteen years from General Gordon's death his countrymen resumed undisputed control over the city he had defended to the death.

The pacification, restoration and orderly development of the Soudan is a story in itself. It repeated in another form far to the southward the successes which our administrators had achieved along the lower Nile. The Soudan became an unbreakable link between Great Britain and Egypt. Neither can ever relinquish respective rights and interests there.

In these later times and in the moral exhaustion which followed victory in the Great War, successive British governments have adopted weak and unworthy policies in Egypt. Proposals have even been entertained to remove the British garrison from Cairo. Thus far their baseness and folly have fortunately been averted. It has therefore not been necessary to come to an issue with the Egyptian Government about the title-deeds of the Soudan.

I have always been in favour of preserving both the British relation with Egypt and the Egyptian relation with the Soudan. I trust both British and Egyptian statesmen and administrators will work together with goodwill and for the common advantage for centuries to come. These views are, however, highly controversial. A generation has grown up which knows little of why we are in Egypt and the Soudan, and what our work there has been. Uninstructed and ignorant impressions colour the decisions not only of parliaments but of cabinets. It is my hope that the story which these pages contain may be some help and encouragement to those young men and women who have still confidence in the destiny of Britain in the Orient. They may learn from it how much harder it is to build up and acquire, than to squander and cast away.

CHAPTER I

THE REBELLION OF THE MAHDI

The north-eastern quarter of the continent of Africa is drained and watered by the Nile. Among and about the headstreams and tributaries of this mighty river lie the wide and fertile provinces of the Egyptian Soudan. Situated in the very centre of the land, these remote regions are on every side divided from the seas by five hundred miles of mountain, swamp, or desert. The great river is their only means of growth, their only channel of progress. It is by the Nile alone that their commerce can reach the outer markets, or European civilisation can penetrate the inner darkness. The Soudan is joined to Egypt by the Nile, as a diver is connected with the surface by his air-pipe. Without it there is only suffocation.

The town of Khartoum,[1] at the confluence of the Blue and White Niles, is the great spout through which the merchandise collected from a wide area streams northwards to the Mediterranean shore. It marks the extreme northern limit of the fertile Soudan. Between Khartoum and Assuan the river flows for twelve hundred miles through deserts of surpassing desolation. At last the wilderness recedes and the living world broadens out again into Egypt and the Delta.

The real Soudan, known to the statesman and the explorer, lies far to the south – moist, undulating, and exuberant. But there is another Soudan, which some mistake for the true, whose solitudes oppress the Nile from the Egyptian frontier to Omdurman. This great tract, which may conveniently be called 'The Military Soudan', stretches with apparent indefiniteness over the face of the continent. Level plains of smooth sand are interrupted only by occasional peaks of rock – black, stark, and shapeless. Rainless storms dance tirelessly over the hot, crisp surface of the ground. The fine sand, driven by the wind, gathers into deep drifts, and silts among the dark rocks of the hills, exactly as snow

[1] Map, 'The Soudan', p. 181.

hangs about an Alpine summit; only it is a fiery snow, such as might fall in hell.

Through the desert flows the river – a thread of blue silk drawn across an enormous brown drugget; and even this thread is brown for half the year. Where the water laps the sand and soaks into the banks there grows an avenue of vegetation which seems very beautiful and luxuriant by contrast with what lies beyond. Yet the character of the vegetation is inhospitable. Thorn-bushes, bristling like hedgehogs, everywhere predominate and with their prickly tangles obstruct the path. Only the palms by the brink are kindly, and men journeying along the Nile must look often towards their bushy tops, where among the spreading foliage the red and yellow glint of date clusters proclaims the ripening of a generous crop.

There is life only by the Nile. If a man were to leave the river, he might journey westward and find no human habitation, nor the smoke of a cooking fire, except the lonely tent of a Kabbabish Arab or the encampment of a trader's caravan, till he reached the coast-line of America. Or he might go east and find nothing but sand and sea and sun until Bombay rose above the horizon. The thread of fresh water is itself solitary in regions where all living things lack company.

Through all the centuries the great river has performed the annual miracle of its flood. Every year when the rains fall and the mountain snows of Central Africa begin to melt, the headstreams become torrents and the great lakes are filled to the brim. A vast expanse of low, swampy lands, crossed by secondary channels and flooded for many miles, regulates the flow, and by a sponge-like action prevents the excess of one year from causing the deficiency of the next. Gradually the flood begins. The Bahr-el-Ghazal from a channel of stagnant pools and marshes becomes a broad and navigable stream. The Sobat and the Atbara from dry watercourses with occasional pools, in which the fish and crocodiles are crowded, turn to rushing rivers. After its confluence with the Atbara no drop of water reaches the Nile, and it flows for seven hundred miles through the sands or rushes in cataracts among the rocks of the Nubian Desert. Nevertheless, in spite of the tremendous diminution in volume caused by the dryness of the earth and air and the heat of the sun – all of which drink greedily – the river below Assuan is sufficiently great to supply nine millions of people with as much water as their utmost science and energies can draw, and yet to pour into the Mediterranean a low-water surplus current of 61,500 cubic feet per second. Nor is its water its only gift. As the Nile rises its complexion is changed. The clear blue river becomes thick and red, laden with the magic mud that can raise cities from the desert sand and make the wilderness a garden.

South of Khartoum and of 'The Military Soudan' the land becomes more fruitful. The tributaries of the Nile multiply the areas of riparian fertility. A considerable rainfall, increasing as the Equator is approached, enables the intervening spaces to support vegetation and consequently human life. The greater part of the country is feverish and unhealthy, nor can Europeans long sustain the attacks of its climate. Nevertheless it is by no means valueless. On the east the province of Sennar used to produce abundant grain, and might easily produce no less abundant cotton. Westward the vast territories of Kordofan and Darfur afford grazing-grounds to a multitude of cattle, and give means of livelihood to great numbers of Baggara or cow-herd Arabs, who may also pursue with activity and stratagem the fleet giraffe and the still fleeter ostrich. To the south-east lies Bahr-el-Ghazal, a great tract of country occupied by dense woods and plentifully watered. Further south and nearer the Equator the forests and marshes become exuberant with tropical growths, and the whole face of the land is moist and green. Amid groves of gigantic trees and through plains of high waving grass the stately elephant roams in herds which occasionally number four hundred, hardly ever disturbed by a well-armed hunter. The ivory of their tusks constitutes the wealth of the Equatorial Province. All other kinds of large beasts known to man inhabit these obscure retreats. The fierce rhinoceros crashes through the undergrowth. Among the reeds of melancholy swamps huge hippopotami, crocodiles, and buffaloes prosper and increase. Antelope of every known and many unclassified species; serpents of peculiar venom; countless millions of birds, butterflies, and beetles are among the offspring of prolific Nature.

The human inhabitants of the Soudan would not, but for their vices and misfortunes, be disproportioned in numbers to the *fauna* or less happy. War, slavery, and oppression have, however, afflicted them until the total population of the whole country does not exceed at the most liberal estimate three million souls. The Soudanese are of many tribes, but two main races can be clearly distinguished: the aboriginal natives, and the Arab settlers. The indigenous inhabitants of the country were negroes as black as coal. They displayed the virtues of barbarism. They were brave and honest. The smallness of their intelligence excused the degradation of their habits. Yet their eulogy must be short, for though their customs, language, and appearance vary, the history of all is a confused legend of strife and misery, and their condition is one of equal squalor and want.

Although the negroes are the more numerous, the Arabs exceed in power. During the second century of the Mohammedan era, when the inhabitants of Arabia went forth to conquer the world, one adventurous army struck south. The first pioneers were followed at intervals by continual immigrations of Arabs not only from Arabia but also across the deserts from Egypt and Morocco. The element thus introduced has spread and is spreading throughout the Soudan, as water soaks into a dry sponge. The aboriginals absorbed the invaders they could not repel. The stronger race imposed its customs and language on the negroes. The vigour of their blood sensibly altered the facial appearance of the Soudanese. For more than a thousand years the influence of Mohammedanism, which appears to possess a strange fascination for negroid races, has been permeating the Soudan, and the whole of the black race is gradually adopting the new religion and developing Arab characteristics. In the districts of the north, the evolution is complete, and the Arabs of the Soudan are a race formed by the interbreeding of negro and Arab, and yet distinct from both. In the more remote and inaccessible regions which lie to the south and west the negro race remains as yet unchanged by the Arab influence. And between these extremes every degree of mixture is to be found. In some tribes pure Arabic is spoken, and prior to the rise of the Mahdi the orthodox Moslem faith was practised. In others Arabic has merely modified the ancient dialects, and the Mohammedan religion has been adapted to the older superstitions.

The stronger race soon began to prey upon the simple aboriginals; some of the Arab tribes were camel-breeders; some were goat-herds; some were Baggaras or cow-herds. But all, without exception, were hunters of men. To the great slave-market at Jedda a continual stream of negro captives has flowed for hundreds of years. The invention of gunpowder and the adoption by the Arabs of firearms facilitated the traffic by placing the ignorant negroes at a further disadvantage. Thus the situation in the Soudan for several centuries may be summed up as follows: The dominant race of Arab invaders was unceasingly spreading its blood, religion, customs, and language among the black aboriginal population, and at the same time it harried and enslaved them.

All this was unheeded by the outer world, from which the Soudan is separated by the deserts. The impulse of conquest which hurried the French and English to Canada and the Indies, which sent the Dutch to the Cape and the Spaniards to Peru, spread to Africa and led the Egyptians to the Soudan. In the year 1819 Mohammed Ali, availing himself of the disorders alike as an excuse and an opportunity, sent his son Ismail up the Nile with a great army. The Arab tribes, torn by dissension, exhausted by thirty years of general war, and no longer inspired by their neglected religion, offered a weak resistance. Their slaves, having known the worst of life, were apathetic. The whole vast territory was conquered with very little fighting, and the victorious army, leaving garrisons, returned in triumph to the Delta.

From 1819 to 1883 Egypt ruled the Soudan. Her rule was not kindly, wise, or profitable. Its aim was to exploit, not to improve the local population. For the rough injustice of the sword there were substituted the intricacies of corruption and bribery. The land was undeveloped and poor. It barely sustained its inhabitants. The additional burden of a considerable foreign garrison and a crowd of rapacious officials increased the severity of the economic conditions. Famines were periodical. Corrupt and incapable Governors-General succeeded each other at Khartoum with bewildering rapidity. The success of their administration was measured by the Ministries in Egypt by the amount of money they could extort from the natives; among the officials in the Soudan, by the number of useless offices they could create. There were a few bright examples of honest men, but these, by providing a contrast, only increased the discontents.

The rule of Egypt was iniquitous: yet it preserved the magnificent appearance of Imperial dominion. The Egyptian Pro-consul lived in state at the confluence of the Niles. The representatives of foreign Powers established themselves in the city. The trade of the south converged upon Khartoum. Thither were sent the ivory of Equatoria, the ostrich feathers of Kordofan, gum from Darfur, grain from Sennar, and taxes collected from all the regions. Complex and imposing reports of revenue and expenditure were annually compiled. An elaborate and dignified correspondence was maintained between Egypt and its great dependency. Yet all was a hateful sham.[1] The arbitrary and excessive taxes were collected only at the point of the bayonet. If a petty chief fell into arrears, his neighbours were raised against him. If an Arab tribe were recalcitrant, a military expedition was despatched. Moreover, the ability of the Arabs to pay depended on their success as slave-hunters. When there had been a good catch, the revenue profited. The Egyptian Government had joined the International League against the slave trade. They continued, however, indirectly but deliberately, to make money out of it.[2]

The authority of a tyrannical Government was supported by the presence of a worthless army. Nearly forty thousand men were distributed among eight main and numerous minor garrisons. Isolated in a roadless country by enormous distances and natural obstacles, and living in the midst of large savage populations of fanatical character and warlike habits, the Viceregal forces might depend for their safety only on the skill of their officers, the excellence of their discipline, and the superiority of their weapons. But the Egyptian officers were at that time distinguished for nothing but their public incapacity and private misbehaviour. The evil reputation of the Soudan and its climate deterred the more educated or more wealthy from serving in such distant regions, and none went south who could avoid it. The officers remained for long periods, many all their lives, in the obscurity of the remote provinces. Some had been sent there in disgrace, others in disfavour. Many were hopeless and habitual drunkards. Nearly all were dishonest. All were indolent and incapable.

Under such leadership the finest soldiery would have soon degenerated. The Egyptians in the Soudan were not fine soldiers. Like their officers, they were the worst part of the Khedivial Army. Their training

---

[1] 'The government of the Egyptians in these far-off countries is nothing else but one of brigandage of the very worst description.' – Colonel Gordon in Central Africa, 11th April 1879.

[2] Egypt, No. 11, 1883.

was imperfect; their discipline was lax; their courage was low. Nor was even this all the weakness and peril of their position; for while the regular troops were thus demoralised, there existed a powerful local irregular force of Bazingers (Soudanese riflemen), as well armed as the soldiers, more numerous, more courageous, and who regarded the alien garrisons with fear that continually diminished and hate that continually grew. And behind regulars and irregulars alike the wild Arab tribes of the desert and the hardy blacks of the forests, goaded by suffering and injustice, thought the foreigners the cause of all their woes, and were delayed only by their inability to combine from sweeping them off the face of the earth. Never was there such a house of cards as the Egyptian dominion in the Soudan.

The names of two men of character and fame are for ever connected with the actual outburst. One was an English general, the other an Arab priest; yet, in spite of the great gulf and vivid contrast between their conditions, they resembled each other in many respects. Both were earnest and enthusiastic men of keen sympathies and passionate emotions. Both were powerfully swayed by religious fervour. Both exerted great personal influence on all who came in contact with them. Both were reformers. In the end they fought to the death, but for an important part of their lives their influence on the fortunes of the Soudan was exerted in the same direction. Mohammed Ahmed, 'The Mahdi', will be discussed in his own place. Charles Gordon needs little introduction.

It is impossible to study any part of Charles Gordon's career without being drawn to all the rest. As his wild and varied fortunes lead him from Sebastopol to Pekin, from Gravesend to South Africa, from Mauritius to the Soudan, the reader follows fascinated. Every scene is strange, terrible, or dramatic. Yet, remarkable as are the scenes, the actor is the more extraordinary. Potentates of many lands and different degree – the Emperor of China, the King of the Belgians, the Premier of Cape Colony, the Khedive of Egypt – competed to secure his services. The importance of his offices varied no less than their nature. One day he was a subaltern of sappers; on another he commanded the Chinese Army; the next he directed an orphanage; or was Governor-General of the Soudan, with supreme powers of life and death and peace and war. But in whatever capacity he laboured he was true to his reputation. Whether he is portrayed bitterly criticising to Graham the tactics of the assault on the Redan; or pulling the head of Lar Wang from under his bedstead and waving it in paroxysms of indignation before the astonished eyes of Sir Halliday Macartney; or riding alone into the camp of the rebel Suliman and receiving the respectful salutes of those who had meant to kill him; or telling the Khedive Ismail that he 'must have the whole Soudan to govern'; or reducing his salary to half the regulation amount because 'he thought it was too much'; we perceive a man careless alike of the frowns of men or the smiles of women, of life or comfort, wealth or fame.

It was a pity that one, thus gloriously free from the ordinary restraining influences of human society, should have found in his own character so little mental ballast. His moods were capricious and uncertain, his passions violent, his impulses sudden and inconsistent. The mortal enemy of the morning had become a trusted ally before the night. The friend he loved today he loathed tomorrow. Scheme after scheme formed in his fertile brain, and jostled confusingly together. All in succession were pressed with enthusiasm. All at times were rejected with disdain. His virtues are famous among men; his daring and resource might turn the tide of war; his energy would have animated a whole people; but it must also be set down that few more uncertain and impracticable forces than Gordon have ever been introduced into administration and diplomacy.

Although the Egyptian Government might loudly proclaim their detestation of slavery, their behaviour in the Soudan was viewed with suspicion by the European Powers, and particularly by Great Britain. To vindicate his sincerity the Khedive Ismail in 1874 appointed Gordon to be Governor of the Equatorial Province in succession to Sir Samuel Baker. The mission, which may have been originally instituted as a pretence, soon became in Gordon's energetic hands very real. The slave dealers had committed every variety of atrocity for which the most odious traffic in the world afforded occasion; but when, under the leadership of Zubehr Rahamna, they refused to pay their annual tribute, it was felt in Cairo that their crimes had cried aloud for chastisement.

Zubehr is sufficiently described when it has been said that he was the most notorious slave dealer Africa has ever produced. His infamy had spread beyond the limits of the continent which was the scene of his exploits to the distant nations of the north and west. In reality, his rule was a distinct advance on the anarchy which had preceded it, and certainly he was no worse than others of his vile trade. His scale of business was, however, more extended.

As early as 1869 he was practically the independent ruler of the Bahr-el-Ghazal. The Khedive resolved to assert his rights. A small Egyptian force was sent to subdue the rebel slaver who not only disgraced humanity but refused to pay tribute. Like most of the Khedivial expeditions they came, they saw, they ran away. Zubehr *apologised* for defeating the Viceregal soldiers and remained supreme in the Bahr-el-Ghazal. Thence he planned the conquest of Darfur, at that time an independent kingdom. The Egyptian Government were glad to join with him in the enterprise. The man they had been unable to conquer, they found it expedient to assist. The operations were successful. The King of Darfur, who was distinguished no less for his valour than for his folly, was killed. The whole country was subdued. The whole population available after the battles became slaves. Zubehr thus wielded a formidable power. The Khedivial Government, thinking to ensure his loyalty, created him a Pasha – a rank which he could scarcely disgrace; and the authority of the rebel was thus unwillingly recognised by the ruler. Such was the situation when Gordon first came to the Soudan.

It was beyond the power of the new Governor of the Equatorial Province at once to destroy the slave-hunting confederacy. Zubehr was enticed to Cairo, and, once there, the Government refused to allow their faithful ally and distinguished guest to go back to his happy-hunting grounds. Although the slave dealers were thus robbed of their great leader, they were still strong, and Zubehr's son, the brave Suliman, found a considerable following. Furious at his father's captivity, and alarmed lest his own should follow, he meditated revolt. But the Governor-General, mounted on a swift camel and attired in full uniform, rode alone into the rebel camp and compelled the submission of its chiefs before they could recover from their amazement. The confederacy was severely shaken, and when, in the following year, Suliman again revolted, the Egyptian troops under Gessi Pasha were able to disperse his forces and induce him to surrender on terms.

Towards the end of 1879 Gordon left the Soudan. With short

intervals he had spent five busy years in its provinces. His energy had stirred the country. He had struck at the root of the slave trade, he had attacked the system of slavery, and, as slavery was the greatest institution in the land, he had undermined the whole social system. He was, as he knew himself, the herald of the storm. Oppressed yet ferocious races had learned that they had rights; the misery of the Soudanese was lessened, but their knowledge had increased. The whole population was unsettled, and the wheels of change began slowly to revolve; nor did they stop until they had accomplished an enormous revolution.

Down to the year 1881 there was no fanatical movement in the Soudan. In their utter misery the hopeless inhabitants had neglected even the practices of religion. They were nevertheless prepared for any enterprise, however desperate, which might free them from the Egyptian yoke. All that delayed them was the want of some leader who could combine the tribes and restore their broken spirits, and in the summer of 1881 the leader appeared.

The man who was the proximate cause of the River War was born by the banks of the Nile, not very far from Dongola. His family were poor and of no account in the province. But as the Prophet had claimed a royal descent, and as a Sacred Example was sprung from David's line, Mohammed Ahmed asserted that he was of the 'Ashraf',[1] and the assertion, since it cannot be disproved, may be accepted. His father was a humble priest; yet he contrived to give his son some education in the practices of religion, the principles of the Koran, and the art of writing. Then he died while on a journey to Khartoum, and left the future Mahdi, still a child, to the mercies of the world. A boy deprived of a father's care often develops an independence and vigour of thought which may restore in after life the heavy loss of early days. It was so with Mohammed Ahmed. He looked around for an occupation and subsistence. A large proportion of the population of religious countries pass their lives at leisure, supported by the patient labour of the devout. The young man determined to follow the profession for which he felt his talents suited. He became a priest. He journeyed to Khartoum as soon as his religious education was completed, and became a disciple of the renowned and holy Sheikh, Mohammed Sherif.

[1] Descendants of the Prophet.

His devotion to his superior, to his studies and to the practice of austerities, and a strange personal influence he was already beginning to show, won him by degrees a few disciples of his own: and with them he retired to the island of Abba. Here by the waters of the White Nile Mohammed Ahmed lived for several years. His two brothers, who were boat-builders in the neighbourhood, supported him by their industry. We read that he 'hollowed out for himself a cave in the mud bank, and lived in almost entire seclusion, fasting often for days'[1].

This virtuous and frugal existence was disturbed and terminated by an untoward event. The renowned and holy Sheikh made a feast to celebrate the circumcision of his sons. Sherif, according to the lax practice of the time, granted a dispensation from any sins committed during the festivities, and proclaimed in God's name the suspension of the rules against singing and dancing by which the religious orders were bound. The ascetic of Abba island, with the recklessness of the reformer, protested against the demoralisation of the age, and loudly affirmed the doctrine that God alone could forgive sins. These things were speedily brought to the ears of the renowned Sheikh, and in all the righteous indignation that accompanies detected wrong-doing, he summoned Mohammed Ahmed before him. The latter obeyed. He respected his superior. He submissively entreated forgiveness; but in vain. Sherif felt that some sort of discipline must be maintained among his flock. Rising in anger, he drove the presumptuous disciple from his presence with bitter words, and expunged his name from the order of the elect.

Mohammed went home. He was greatly distressed. Placing a heavy wooden collar on his neck, clad in sackcloth and sprinkled with ashes, he again returned to his spiritual leader, and in this penitential guise implored pardon. He was ignominiously ejected. Nor did he venture to revisit the unforgiving Sheikh. But it happened that in a few weeks Sherif had occasion to journey to the island of Abba. His former disciple appeared suddenly before him, still clad in sackcloth and defiled by ashes. Careless of his plain misery, and unmoved by his loyalty,

---

[1] I take this passage from *Fire and Sword in the Soudan*, by Slatin. His account is the most graphic and trustworthy of all known records of the Mahdi. He had terrible opportunities of collecting information. I have followed his version (chapter iv) very closely on this subject.

which was the more remarkable since it was disinterested, the implacable Sheikh poured forth a stream of invective. Among the insults, one went home: 'Be off, you wretched Dongolawi.'

Abuse by class is a dangerous though effective practice. A man will perhaps tolerate an offensive word applied to himself, but will be infuriated if his nation, his rank, or his profession is insulted. Mohammed Ahmed rose. All that man could do to make amends he had done. Now he had been publicly called 'a wretched Dongolawi'. Reaching his house, he informed his disciples – for they had not abandoned him in all his trouble – that the Sheikh had finally cast him off, and that he would now take his discarded allegiance elsewhere. The rival, the Sheikh el Koreishi, lived near Mesalamia. He was jealous of Sherif and was therefore delighted to receive a letter from Mohammed Ahmed announcing his breach with his former superior and offering his most devoted services. He returned a cordial invitation, and the priest of Abba island made all preparation for the journey.

This new development seems to have startled the unforgiving Sherif. It was no part of his policy to alienate his followers, still less to add to those of his rival. After all, the quality of mercy was high and noble. He would at last graciously forgive the impulsive but repentant disciple. He wrote him a letter to this effect. But it was now too late. Mohammed replied with grave dignity that he had committed no crime, that he sought no forgiveness, and that 'a wretched Dongolawi' would not offend by his presence the renowned Sheikh el Sherif. After this indulgence he departed to Mesalamia.

But the fame of his doings spread far and wide throughout the land. Mohammed did not hesitate to declare that he had done what he had done as a protest against the decay of religious fervour and the torpor of the times. Rumour, loud-tongued, carried it about the land that a great Reformer was come to purify the faith and break the stony apathy which paralysed the hearts of Islam.

Throughout Nubia the Shukri belief prevails: some day, in a time of shame and trouble, a second great Prophet will arise – a *Mahdi* who shall lead the faithful nearer God and sustain the religion. The people of the Soudan always look inquiringly to any ascetic who rises to fame, and the question is often repeated, 'Art thou he that should come, or do we look for another?' Of this powerful element of disturbance

Mohammed Ahmed resolved to avail himself. He requested and obtained the permission of the Sheikh Koreishi to return to Abba, where he was well known, and with which island village his name was connected, and so came back in triumph to the scene of his disgrace. Thither many pilgrims began to resort. He journeyed preaching through Kordofan, and while he spoke of the purification of the religion, they thought that the burning words might be applied to the freedom of the soil. He supported his sermons by writings, which were widely read. When a few months later the Sheikh Koreishi died, the priest of Abba proceeded forthwith to erect a tomb to his memory, directing and controlling the voluntary labours of the reverent Arabs who carried the stones.

While Mohammed was thus occupied he received the support of a man, less virtuous than but nearly as famous as himself. Abdullah was one of four brothers, the sons of an obscure priest; but he inherited no great love of religion or devotion to its observances. He was a man of determination and capacity. He set before himself two distinct ambitions, both of which he accomplished: to free the Soudan of foreigners, and to rule it himself. So soon as he saw Mohammed Ahmed rising to fame and displaying qualities of courage and energy, he hastened to throw himself at his feet and assure him of his devotion.

Mohammed Ahmed received his new adherent kindly, but without enthusiasm. For some months Abdullah carried stones to build the tomb of the Sheikh el Koreishi. Gradually they got to know each other. 'But long before he entrusted me with his secret,' said Abdullah to Slatin, 'I knew that he was "the expected Guide".'[1] And though the world might think that the 'Messenger of God' was sent to lead men to happiness in heaven, Abdullah attached to the phrase a significance of his own, and knew that he should lead him to power on earth. The two formed a strong combination. The Mahdi – for such Mohammed Ahmed had already in secret announced himself – brought the wild enthusiasm of religion, the glamour of a stainless life, and the influence of superstition into the movement. But if he were the soul of the plot, Abdullah was the brain. He was the man of the world, the practical politician, the general.

There now commenced a great conspiracy against the Egyptian

[1] Slatin, *Fire and Sword*, p. 131.

Government. The Mahdi began to collect adherents and to extend his influence in all parts of the country. He made a second journey through Kordofan, and received everywhere promises of support from all classes. As the ramifications of the plot spread they were perceived by the renowned Sheikh Sherif, who warned the Egyptian Government. They, knowing his envy and hatred of his former disciple, discounted his evidence and for some time paid no attention to the gathering of the storm. But presently more trustworthy witnesses confirmed his statements, and Raouf Pasha, then Governor-General, finding himself confronted with a growing agitation, sent a messenger to the island of Abba, to summon Mohammed Ahmed to Khartoum to justify his behaviour and explain his intentions. The news of the despatch of the messenger was swiftly carried to the Mahdi. He consulted with his trusty lieutenant. They decided without further delay to defy the Government. When it is remembered how easily an organised army, even though it be in a bad condition, can stamp out the beginnings of revolt among a population, the courage of their resolve must be admired.

The messenger arrived. He was received with courtesy by Abdullah, and forthwith conducted before the Mahdi. He delivered his message, and urged Mohammed Ahmed to comply with the orders of the Governor-General. The Mahdi listened for some time in silence, but with increasing emotion; and when the messenger advised him, as he valued his own safety, to journey to Khartoum, if only to justify himself, his passion overcame him. 'What!' he shouted, rising suddenly and striking his breast with his hand. 'By the grace of God and his Prophet *I* am master of this country, and never shall I go to Khartoum to justify myself.'[1] The terrified messenger withdrew. The rebellion of the Mahdi had begun.

Both the priest and the Governor-General prepared for military enterprise. The Mahdi proclaimed a holy war against the foreigners, alike the enemies of God and the scourge of men. He roused the local tribes. He wrote letters to all parts of the Soudan, calling upon the people to fight for a purified religion, the freedom of the soil, and God's holy prophet 'the expected Mahdi'. He promised the honour of men to those who lived, the favour of God to those who fell, and lastly

[1] Slatin, *Fire and Sword*, p. 135.

that the land should be cleared of the miserable 'Turk'. 'Better,' he said, and it became the watchword of the revolt, 'thousands of graves than a dollar tax.'[1]

Nor was Raouf Pasha idle. He sent two companies of infantry each commanded by a Captain, with one gun by steamer to Abba to arrest the fanatic who disturbed the public peace. At sunset on an August evening in 1881 the steamer arrived at Abba. Both landed with their companies and proceeded by different routes under the cover of darkness to the village where the Mahdi dwelt. Arriving simultaneously from opposite directions, they fired into each other, and, in the midst of this mistaken combat, the Mahdi rushed upon them with his scanty following and destroyed them impartially. A few soldiers succeeded in reaching the bank of the river. But the captain of the steamer would run no risks, and those who could not swim out to the vessel were left to their fate. With such tidings the expedition returned to Khartoum.

The effect of the success was electrical. The news spread throughout the Soudan. Men with sticks had slain men with rifles. A priest had destroyed the soldiers of the Government. Surely this was the Expected One. Abdullah, however, had no illusions. More troops would be sent. They were too near to Khartoum. Prudence counselled flight to regions more remote. But before this new *Hegira* the Mahdi appointed his four Khalifas, in accordance with prophecy and precedent. The first was Abdullah. Of the others it is only necessary at this moment to notice Ali-Wad-Helu, the chief of one of the local tribes, and among the first to rally to the standard of revolt.

Then the retreat began; but it was more like a triumphal progress. Attended by a considerable following, and preceded by tales of the most wonderful miracles and prodigies, the Mahdi retired to a mountain in Kordofan to which he gave the name of Jebel Masa, that being the mountain whence 'the expected Guide' is declared in the Koran sooner or later to appear. He was now out of reach of Khartoum, but within reach of Fashoda. The Egyptian Governor of that town, Rishid Bey, a man of more enterprise and even less military knowledge than is usual in his race, determined to make an attempt to seize the rebel and disperse his following. Taking no precautions, he fell on the 9th of December into an ambush, was attacked unprepared, and was

[1] Ohrwalder, *Ten Years' Captivity in the Mahdi's Camp.*

himself, with fourteen hundred men, slaughtered by the ill-armed but valiant Arabs.

The Government, thoroughly alarmed by the serious aspect the revolt had assumed, organised a great expedition. Four thousand troops under Yusef, a Pasha of distinguished reputation, were sent against the rebels. Meanwhile the Mahdi and his followers suffered the extremes of want. Their cause was as yet too perilous for the rich to join. Only the poor flocked to the holy standard. All that Mohammed possessed he gave away, keeping nothing for himself, excepting only a horse to lead his followers in battle. Abdullah walked. Nevertheless the rebels were half-famished, and armed with scarcely any more deadly weapons than sticks and stones. The army of the Government anticipated an easy victory. Their contempt for the enemy was supreme. They did not even trouble themselves to post sentries by night, but slept calmly inside a slender thorn fence, unwatched save by their tireless foes. And so it came to pass that in the half-light of the early morning of the 7th of June the Mahdi, his ragged Khalifas, and his almost naked army rushed upon them, and slew them to a man.

The victory was decisive. Southern Kordofan was at the feet of the priest of Abba. Stores of arms and ammunition had fallen into his hands. Thousands of every class hastened to join his standard. No one doubted that he was the divine messenger sent to free them from their oppressors. The whole of the Arab tribes all over the Soudan rose at once. The smaller Egyptian posts, the tax-gatherers and local administrators, were massacred in every district. Only the larger garrisons maintained themselves in the principal towns. They were at once blockaded. All communications were interrupted. All legal authority was defied. Only the Mahdi was obeyed.

It is now necessary to look for a moment to Egypt. The misgovernment which in the Soudan had caused the rebellion of the Mahdi, in Egypt produced the revolt of Arabi Pasha. As the people of the Soudan longed to be rid of the foreign oppressors – the so-called 'Turks' – so those of the Delta were eager to free themselves from the foreign regulators and the real Turkish influence. While men who lived by the sources of the Nile asserted that tribes did not exist for officials to harry, others who dwelt at its mouth protested that nations were not made to be exploited by creditors or aliens. Mohammed Ahmed broke the Egyptian yoke; Arabi gave expression to the hatred of the Egyptians for the Turks. But although the hardy Arabs might scatter the effete Egyptians, the effete Egyptians were not likely to disturb the solid battalions of Europe. After much hesitation and many attempts at compromise, the Liberal Administration of Mr Gladstone sent a fleet which reduced the forts of Alexandria to silence and the city to anarchy. The bombardment of the fleet was followed by the invasion of a powerful army. Twenty-five thousand men were landed in Egypt. The Egyptian armies were slaughtered or captured. Their patriotic but commonplace leader was sentenced to death and condemned to exile, and Great Britain assumed the direction of Egyptian affairs.

The British soon restored law and order in Egypt, and the question of the revolt in the Soudan came before the English advisers of the Khedive. Notwithstanding the poverty and military misfortunes which depressed the people of the Delta, the desire to hold their southern provinces was evident. The British Government, which at that time was determined to pursue a policy of non-interference in the Soudan, gave a tacit consent, and another great expedition was prepared to suppress the False Prophet, as the English and Egyptians deemed him.

During the summer of 1883 the Egyptian troops gradually concentrated at Khartoum until a considerable army was formed. It was perhaps the worst army that has ever marched to war. One extract from General Hicks's letters will suffice. Writing on the 8th of June, 1883, to Sir E. Wood, he says incidentally: 'Fifty-one men of the Krupp battery deserted on the way here, although in chains.' The officers and men who had been defeated fighting for their own liberties at Tel-el-Kebir were sent to be destroyed, fighting to take away the liberties of others in the Soudan. They had no spirit, no discipline, hardly any training, and in a force of over eight thousand men there were scarcely a dozen capable officers. The two who were the most notable of these few – General Hicks, who commanded, and Colonel Farquhar, the Chief of the Staff – must be remarked.

El Obeid, the chief town of Kordofan, had fallen to the Mahdi before the ill-fated expedition left Khartoum; but the fact that Slatin Bey, an Austrian officer in the Egyptian service, was still maintaining himself in Darfur provided it with an object. On the 9th of September Hicks and his army (the actual strength of which was 7,000 infantry,

400 mounted Bashi Bazuks, 500 cavalry, 100 Circassians, 10 mounted guns, 4 Krupps, and 6 Nordenfeldt machine guns) left Omdurman and marched to Duem. Although the actual command of the expedition was vested in the English officer, Ala-ed-Din Pasha, the Governor-General who had succeeded Raouf Pasha, exercised an uncertain authority. Differences of opinion were frequent, though all the officers were agreed in taking the darkest views of their chances. The miserable host toiled slowly onward towards its destruction, marching in a south-westerly direction through Shat and Rahad.

On the approach of the Government troops the Mahdi had marched out of El Obeid and established himself in the open country. More than forty thousand men collected round his standard, and the Arabs were now armed with several thousand rifles and a few cannon, as well as a great number of swords and spears. To these proportions had the little band of followers who fought at Abba grown! The disparity of the forces was apparent before the battle. The Mahdi thereupon wrote to Hicks, calling on him to surrender and offering terms. His proposals were treated with disdain, although the probable result of an engagement was clear.

The collision took place on the 3rd of November. All through that day the Egyptians struggled slowly forward, in great want of water, losing continually from the fire of the Soudanese riflemen, and leaving several guns behind them. On the next morning they were confronted by the main body of the Arab Army, and their attempts to advance further were defeated with heavy loss. Scarcely five hundred Egyptians escaped death; hardly as many of the Arabs fell. The European officers perished fighting to the end; and the general met his fate sword in hand, his personal valour and physical strength exciting the admiration even of the fearless enemy, so that in chivalrous respect they buried his body with barbaric honours. Mohammed Ahmed celebrated his victory with a salute of one hundred guns; and well he might, for the Soudan was now his.

It is customary to lay to the charge of Mohammed Ahmed all the blood that was spilled. To my mind it seems that he may divide the responsibility with the unjust rulers who oppressed the land, with the incapable commanders who muddled away the lives of their men, with the vacillating Ministers who aggravated the misfortunes. But, whatever is set to the Mahdi's account, it should not be forgotten that he put life and soul into the hearts of his countrymen, and freed his native land of foreigners. The poor miserable natives, eating only a handful of grain, toiling half-naked and without hope, found a new, if terrible magnificence added to life. Within their humble breasts the spirit of the Mahdi roused the fires of patriotism and religion. There are many Christians who reverence the faith of Islam and yet regard the Mahdi merely as a commonplace religious impostor whom force of circumstances elevated to notoriety. In a certain sense, this may be true. But I know not how a genuine may be distinguished from a spurious Prophet, except by the measure of his success. The triumphs of the Mahdi were in his lifetime far greater than those of the founder of the Mohammedan faith; and the chief difference between orthodox Mohammedanism and Mahdism was that the original impulse was opposed only by decaying systems of government and society and the recent movement came in contact with civilisation and the machinery of science. Recognising this, I do not share the popular opinion, and I believe that if in future years prosperity should come to the peoples of the Upper Nile, and learning and happiness follow in its train, then the first Arab historian who shall investigate the early annals of that new nation will not forget, foremost among the heroes of his race, to write the name of Mohammed Ahmed.

CHAPTER II

THE FATE OF THE ENVOY

The triumph no less than the plunder which had rewarded the Mahdi's victories had called into existence a military spirit distinct from the warlike passions of the tribesmen – the spirit of the professional soldier.

The siege of Khartoum was carried on while this new influence was taking the place of the original forces of revolt. There was a period when a neutral point was obtained and the Mahdist power languished. But the invasion of the Eastern Soudan by the British troops in the spring and the necessary advance of the relieving columns in the winter of 1884 revived the patriotic element. The tribes who had made a great effort to free themselves from foreign domination saw in the operations of Sir Gerald Graham and Lord Wolseley an attempt to bring them again under the yoke. The impulse which was given to the Mahdi's cause was sufficient to raise a fierce opposition to the invading forces. The delay in the despatch of the relief expedition had sealed the fate of Khartoum, and the fall of the town established the supremacy of the military spirit on which the Dervish Empire was afterwards founded.

In order to describe conveniently the changing character of the revolt, I have anticipated the story and must revert to a period when the social and racial influences were already weakening and the military spirit was not yet grown strong. If the defeat of Yusef Pasha decided the whole people of the Soudan to rise in arms and strike for their liberties, the defeat of Hicks satisfied the British Government that those liberties were won. Had Egypt been left to herself, other desperate efforts would have been made. But the British Government had finally abandoned the policy of non-interference with Egyptian action in the Soudan. They 'advised' its abandonment. The Khedive bowed to superior authority. The Minister resigned. The policy of evacuation was firmly adopted. 'Let us,' said the Ministers, 'collect the garrisons and come away.' It was simple to decide on the course to be pursued, but almost impossible to follow it. Several of the Egyptian garrisons, as in Darfur and El Obeid, had already fallen. The others were either besieged, like Sennar, Tokar, and Sinkat, or cut off from the north, as in the case of the Equatorial Province, by the area of rebellion. The capital of the Soudan was, however, as yet unmolested; and as its Egyptian population exceeded the aggregate of the provincial towns, the first task of the Egyptian Government was obvious.

Mr Gladstone's Administration had repressed the revolt of Arabi Pasha. Through their policy the British were in armed occupation of Egypt. British officers were reorganising the army. A British official supervised the finances. A British plenipotentiary 'advised' the re-established Tewfik. A British fleet lay attentive before the ruins of Alexandria, and it was evident that Great Britain could annex the country in name as well as in fact. But Imperialism was not the object of the Radical Cabinet. As they were now determined that the Egyptians should evacuate the Soudan, so they had always been resolved that the British should evacuate Egypt.

The British Government watched with anxious solicitude the efforts of Egypt to evacuate the Soudan and bring the garrisons safely home. They utterly declined to assist with military force, but they were generous with their advice. Everybody at that time distrusted the capacities of the Egyptians, and it was thought the evacuation might be accomplished if it were entrusted to stronger and more honest men than were bred by the banks of the Nile. The Ministers looked about them, wondering how they could assist the Egyptian Government without risk or expense to themselves, and in an evil hour for their fame and fortunes someone whispered the word 'Gordon'. Forthwith they proceeded to telegraph to Cairo: 'Would General Charles Gordon be of any use to you or to the Egyptian Government; and, if so, in what capacity?' The Egyptian Government replied through Sir Evelyn Baring that as the movement in the Soudan was partly religious they were 'very much averse' from the appointment of a Christian in high command. The eyes of all those who possessed local knowledge were turned to a different person. There was one man who might stem the tide of Mahdism, who might perhaps restore the falling dominion of Egypt, who might at least save the garrisons of the Soudan. In their necessity and distress the Khedivial advisers and the British plenipotentiary looked as a desperate remedy to the man whose liberty they had curtailed, whose property they had confiscated, and whose son they had executed – Zubehr Pasha.

This was the agent for whom the Government of Egypt hankered. The idea was supported by all who were acquainted with the local conditions. A week after Sir Evelyn Baring had declined General Gordon's services he wrote: 'Whatever may be Zubehr's faults, he is said to be a man of great energy and resolution. The Egyptian Government considers that his services may be very useful. . . . Baker Pasha is anxious to avail himself of Zubehr Pasha's services.'[1] It is certain that had the Egyptian Government been a free agent, Zubehr would have been sent to the Soudan as its Sultan, and assisted by arms, money, and perhaps by men, to make head against the Mahdi. It is probable that at this particular period the Mahdi would have collapsed before a man whose fame was nearly equal to, and whose resources would have been much greater than, his own. But the British Ministry would countenance no dealings with such a man. They scouted the idea of Zubehr, and by so doing increased their obligation to suggest an alternative. Zubehr being rejected, Gordon remained.

It is known that from the very first Sir Evelyn Baring was bitterly opposed to General Gordon's appointment. No personal friendship existed between them, and the Administrator dreaded the return to the feverish complications of Egyptian politics of the man who had always been identified with unrest, improvisation, and disturbance. The pressure was, however, too strong for him to withstand. Nubar Pasha, the Foreign Office, the British public, everyone clamoured for the appointment. At length Baring yielded, and, as soon as his consent had been obtained, the Government turned with delight to Gordon. On the 17th of January Lord Wolseley requested him to come to England. On the 18th he met the Cabinet. That same night he started on the long journey from which he was never to return.

Gordon embarked on his mission in high spirits, sustained by that belief in personality which too often misleads great men and beautiful women. It was, he said, the greatest honour ever conferred upon him.

[1] Sir Evelyn Baring, letter of 9th December 1883.

The Ministers were intensely relieved. The most unbounded confidence
was reposed in the envoy. His interview with the Khedive was 'very
satisfactory'. His complete authority was proclaimed to all the notables
and natives of the Soudan.[1] He was assured of the support of the
Egyptian Government.[2] One hundred thousand pounds was placed
to his credit, and he was informed that further sums would be supplied
when this was exhausted. He was assured that no effort would be
wanting on the part of the Cairene authorities, whether English or
Egyptian, to afford him all the support and co-operation in their
power.[3] Under these propitious auguries the dismal and disastrous
enterprise began.

His task was clearly defined. 'You will bear in mind,' wrote Sir
Evelyn Baring, 'that the main end to be pursued is the evacuation of
the Soudan.' 'The object . . . of your mission to the Soudan,' declared
the Khedive, 'is to carry into execution the evacuation of those territories and to withdraw our troops, civil officials, and such of the
inhabitants . . . as may wish to leave for Egypt . . . and after the evacuation to take the necessary steps for establishing an organised Government in the different provinces.' Nor was he himself under any misconception. He drew up a memorandum when on board the *Tanjore*
in which he fully acquiesced in the evacuation of the Soudan. In a
sentence which breathes the same spirit as Mr Gladstone's famous
expression, 'a people rightly struggling to be free,' he wrote: 'I must
say that it would be an iniquity to conquer these peoples and then
hand them back to the Egyptians without guarantees of future good
government.' Finally, he unhesitatingly asserted: 'No one who has
ever lived in the Soudan can escape the reflection "What a useless
possession is this land!"' And Colonel Stewart, who accompanied
him and endorsed the memorandum, added: 'And what a huge encumbrance to Egypt!' Thus far there was complete agreement between
the British envoy and the Liberal Cabinet.

On the 22nd of February he arrived at Khartoum. He was received
with rejoicing by the whole population. Those who had been about to
fly for the north took fresh heart. They believed that behind the figure

[1] Proclamation of the Khedive, 26th January 1884.
[2] Sir Evelyn Baring to Major-General Gordon, 25th January 1884.
[3] Sir Evelyn Baring to Major-General Gordon, 25th January 1884.

of the envoy stood the resources of an Empire. The Mahdi and the gathering Dervishes were perplexed and alarmed. Gordon had come. The armies would follow.

Whatever confidence the General had felt in the power of his personal influence had been dispelled on the journey to Khartoum. He saw himself confronted with a tremendous racial movement. The people of the Soudan had risen against foreigners. His only troops were Soudanese. He was himself a foreigner. Foremost among the leaders of the revolt were the Arab slave dealers, furious at the attempted suppression of their trade. No one, not even Sir Samuel Baker, had tried harder to suppress it than Gordon. Lastly, the whole movement had assumed a fanatical character. Islam marched against the infidel. Gordon was a Christian. His own soldiers were under the spell they were to try to destroy. Every influence was hostile, and in particular hostile to his person. On the very day of his arrival at Khartoum, while the townsfolk were cheering his name in the streets and the batteries were firing joyful salutes, while the people of England thought his mission already accomplished, General Gordon sat himself down and telegraphed a formal request to Cairo for Zubehr Pasha.

The whole story of his relations with Zubehr is extremely characteristic. Zubehr's son, Suliman, had been executed, if not by Gordon's orders, at least during his administration of the Soudan and with his complete approval. He had hardly started from London on his new mission, when he telegraphed to Sir Evelyn Baring, telling him that Zubehr was a most dangerous man and requesting that he might be at once deported to Cyprus. The General arrived in Cairo like a whirlwind close behind his telegram, and was very angry to hear that Zubehr was still in Egypt. Before starting up the river he went to see Sherif Pasha. In the ex-Minister's ante-room he met the very man he had determined to avoid – Zubehr. He greeted him with effusion. They had a long talk about the Soudan, after which Gordon hurried to the Agency and informed Sir Evelyn Baring that Zubehr must accompany him to Khartoum at once. Baring did not himself disapprove of the plan. But he thought the change in Gordon's attitude too sudden to be relied on. Tomorrow he might change again. He begged the General to think more seriously of the matter. Gordon with his usual frankness admitted that his change of mind had been very sudden. He had been conscious, he said, of a 'mystic feeling' that Zubehr was necessary to save the situation in the Soudan.

Her Majesty's Government refused absolutely to have anything to do with Zubehr. They declined to allow the Egyptian Government to employ him. The historians of the future may occupy their leisure and exercise their wits in deciding whether the Ministers and the people were right or wrong.

But if the justice of the decision is doubtful, its consequences were obvious. Either the British Government were concerned with the Soudan, or they were not. If they were not, then they had no reason or right to prohibit the appointment of Zubehr. If they were, they were bound to see that the garrisons were rescued. England had not misgoverned the Soudan, had not raised the revolt or planted the garrisons. All that Egypt had a right to expect was commiseration. But the moment Zubehr was prohibited the situation was changed. The refusal to permit his employment was tantamount to an admission that affairs in the Soudan involved the honour of England as well as the honour of Egypt. When the British people – for this was not merely the act of the Government – adopted a high moral attitude with regard to Zubehr, they bound themselves to rescue the garrisons, peaceably if possible, forcibly if necessary.

Gordon considered that he was personally pledged to effect the evacuation of Khartoum by the garrison and civil servants. He had appointed some of the inhabitants to positions of trust, thus compromising them with the Mahdi. Others had undoubtedly been encouraged to delay their departure by his arrival. He therefore considered that his honour was involved in their safety. Henceforward he was inflexible. Neither rewards nor threats could move him. Nothing that men could offer would induce him to leave Khartoum till its inhabitants were rescued. The Government on their side were equally stubborn. Nothing, however sacred, should induce them to send troops to Khartoum.

The deadlock was complete. To some men the Foreign Office might have suggested lines of retreat, covered by the highest official praise. Others would have welcomed an order to leave so perilous a post. But the man they had sent was the one man of all others who was beyond their control, who cared nothing for what they could give or take away. So events dragged on their wretched course. Gordon's proposals became more and more impracticable as the best courses he could devise were successively vetoed by the Government. He had asked for Zubehr. Zubehr was refused. He had requested Turkish troops. Turkish troops were refused. He had asked for Mohammedan regiments from India. The Government regretted their inability to comply. He asked for a *Firman* from the Sultan to strengthen his position. It was 'peremptorily refused'. He proposed to go south in his steamers to Equatoria. The Government forbade him to proceed beyond Khartoum. He asked that 200 British troops might be sent to Berber. They were refused. He begged that a few might be sent to Assuan. None were sent. He proposed to visit the Mahdi himself and try to arrange matters with him personally. Perhaps he recognised a kindred spirit. The Government in this case very naturally forbade him.

At last the quarrel is open. He makes no effort to conceal his disgust. 'I leave you,' he says, 'the indelible disgrace of abandoning the garrisons.'[1] He reiterates his determination to abide with the garrison of Khartoum. 'I will not leave these people after all they have gone through.'[2] He tosses his commission contemptuously from him: 'I would also ask her Majesty's Government to accept the resignation of my commission.'[3] The Government 'trust that he will not resign',[4] and his offer remains in abeyance. Finally, in bitterness and vexation, thinking himself abandoned and disavowed, he appeals to Sir Evelyn Baring personally: 'I feel sure, whatever you may feel diplomatically, I have your support – and that of every man professing himself a gentleman – in private';[5] and as a last hope he begs Sir Samuel Baker to appeal to 'British and American millionaires' to subscribe two hundred thousand pounds to enable him to carry out the evacuation without, and even in spite of, the Governments of Cairo and London;

[1] Major-General Gordon to Sir Evelyn Baring (telegraphic), received at Cairo, 16th April.
[2] Major-General Gordon to Sir Evelyn Baring, Khartoum, 30th July; received at Cairo, 15th October.
[3] Major-General Gordon to Sir Evelyn Baring (telegraphic), Khartoum, 9th March.
[4] Earl Granville to Sir Evelyn Baring, Foreign Office, 13th March.
[5] Major-General Gordon to Sir Evelyn Baring (telegraphic), received at Cairo, 16th April.

and Sir Samuel Baker writes a long letter to *The Times* in passionate protest and entreaty.

But meanwhile other and still more stirring events were passing outside the world of paper and ink. The arrival of Gordon at Khartoum had seriously perplexed and alarmed Mohammed Ahmed and his Khalifas. They feared lest the General should be the herald of armies. As the weeks passed without reinforcements arriving, the Mahdi and Abdullah determined to put a brave face on the matter and blockade Khartoum itself. They were assisted in this enterprise by a revival of the patriotic impulse throughout the country and a consequent stimulus to the revolt. To discover the cause it is necessary to look to the Eastern Soudan, where the next tragedy, after the defeat of Hicks, is laid.

The Hadendoa tribe, infuriated by oppression and misgovernment, had joined the rebellion under the leadership of the celebrated Osman Digna. The Egyptian garrisons of Tokar and Sinkat were beleaguered and hard pressed. Her Majesty's Government disclaimed all responsibility. Yet, since these towns were not far from the coast, they did not prohibit an attempt on the part of the Egyptian Government to rescue the besieged soldiers. Accordingly an Egyptian force 3,500 strong marched from Suakin in February 1884 to relieve Tokar, under the command of General Baker, once the gallant colonel of the 10th Hussars. Hard by the wells of Teb they were, on the 5th of February, attacked by about a thousand Arabs.

'On the square being only threatened by a small force of the enemy ... the Egyptian troops threw down their arms and ran, carrying away the black troops with them, and allowing themselves to be killed without the slightest resistance.'[1] The British and European officers in vain endeavoured to rally them. The single Soudanese battalion fired impartially on friend and foe. The General, with that unshaken courage and high military skill which had already on the Danube gained him a continental reputation, collected some fifteen hundred men, mostly unarmed, and so returned to Suakin. Ninety-six officers and 2,250 men were killed. Krupp guns, machine guns, rifles, and a large supply of ammunition fell to the victorious Arabs. Success inflamed their ardour to the point of madness. The attack of the towns was pressed with

[1] General Baker to Sir Evelyn Baring, 6th February (official despatch), telegraphic.

redoubled vigour. The garrison of Sinkat, 800 strong, sallied out and attempted to fight their way to Suakin. The garrison of Tokar surrendered. Both were destroyed.

The garrisons they had refused to rescue the British Government now determined to avenge. In spite of their philanthropic professions, and in spite of the advice of General Gordon, who felt that his position at Khartoum would be still further compromised by operations on his only line of retreat,[1] a considerable military expedition consisting of one cavalry and two infantry brigades, was sent to Suakin. The command was entrusted to General Graham. Troops were hurriedly concentrated. The 10th Hussars, returning from India, were stopped and mounted on the horses of the *gendarmerie*. With admirable celerity the force took the field. Within a month of the defeat at Teb they engaged the enemy almost on the very scene of the disaster. On the 4th of March they slew 3,000 Hadendoa and drove the rest in disorder from the ground. Four weeks later a second action was fought at Tamai. Again the success of the British troops was complete; again the slaughter of the Arabs was enormous. But neither victory was bloodless. El Teb cost 24 officers and 168 men; Tamai, 13 officers and 208 men. The effect of these operations was the dispersal of Osman Digna's gathering. That astute man, not for the first or last time, made a good retreat.

Ten thousand men had thus been killed in the space of three months in the Eastern Soudan. By the discipline of their armies the Government were triumphant. The tribes of the Red Sea shore cowered before them. But as they fought without reason, so they conquered without profit.

Gordon's mission was an admitted failure. After that the only question was how to bring him away as quickly as possible. It was certain that he would not come willingly. Force was necessary. Yet it was difficult to know how to apply it. After the victories in the Eastern Soudan the opportunity presented itself. The road was open. The local tribes were crushed. Berber had not then fallen. The Mahdi was himself still on the road from El Obeid to Khartoum. Sir Evelyn Baring saw the chance. With all his influence he urged the despatch of a small flying column to Khartoum. His idea was simple. One thousand or twelve hundred men were to mount on camels and ride thither via Berber. Those who fell ill or whose camels broke down would

[1] Sir Evelyn Baring to Earl Granville, Cairo, 23rd February.

have to take their chance by the roadside. The plan, however, broke down in the military detail. Only one honourable course remained – a regular expedition. This the British Agent at once began to urge. This the Government obstinately refused to admit; and meanwhile time was passing.

While the British Government was indulging in vengeful operations in the Eastern Soudan, the Mahdi advanced slowly but steadily upon Khartoum with a following variously estimated at from fifteen to twenty thousand men. On the 7th of March Colonel Stewart telegraphed from Khartoum: 'The Mahdi has attempted to raise the people of Shendi by an emissary. . . . We may be cut off;'[1] and on the 11th Gordon himself reported: 'The rebels are four hours distant on the Blue Nile.'[2] Thereafter no more telegrams came. for on the 15th the wire was cut between Shendi and Berber, and the blockade had commenced.

The long and glorious defence of the town of Khartoum will always fascinate attention. That one man, a European among Africans, a Christian among Mohammedans, should by his genius have inspired the efforts of 7,000 soldiers of inferior race, and by his courage have sustained the hearts of 30,000 inhabitants of notorious timidity, and with such materials and encumbrances have offered a vigorous resistance to the increasing attacks of an enemy who, though cruel, would yet accept surrender, during a period of 317 days, is an event perhaps without parallel in history. But it may safely be predicted that no one will ever write an account which will compare in interest with that set forth by the man himself in the famous 'Journals at Khartoum'.

Perhaps it is because he is careless of the sympathy of men that Charles Gordon so readily wins it. Before the first of the six parts into which the Journals were divided is finished, the reader has been won. Henceforth he sees the world through Gordon's eyes. With him he scoffs at the diplomatists; despises the Government; becomes impatient – unreasonably, perhaps – with a certain Major Kitchener in the Intelligence Branch, whose information miscarried or was not despatched; is wearied by the impracticable Shaiggia Irregulars; takes

[1] Lieut.-Colonel Stewart to Sir Evelyn Baring, 7th March 1884.
[2] Major-General Gordon to Sir Evelyn Baring, 11th March 1884.

interest in the turkey-cock and his harem of four wives; laughs at the
'black sluts' seeing their faces for the first time in the mirror. When the
end of the account is reached, no man of British birth can read the
last words, 'Now mark this, if the Expeditionary Force – and I ask
for no more than two hundred men – does not come within ten days,
the town may fall; and I have done my best for the honour of our
country. Goodbye', without being thrilled with vain regrets and
futile resolutions. And then the account stops short. Henceforward
Gordon's perils were unrecorded.

I would select one episode only from the Journals as an example of
the peculiarity and the sternness of Charles Gordon's character – his
behaviour towards Slatin. This Austrian officer had been Governor of
Darfur with the rank in the Egyptian service of Bey. For four years he
had struggled vainly against the rebellion. He had fought numerous
engagements with varied success. He had been several times wounded.
Throughout his province and even beyond its limits he bore the reputation of a brave and capable soldier, a man of feeling and of honour.
He had, however, committed an act which deprived him of Gordon's
sympathy and respect. During the fighting in Darfur, after several
defeats, his Mohammedan soldiers were discouraged and attributed
their evil fortune to the fact that their commander was an infidel under
the curse of the Almighty. Slatin therefore proclaimed himself a
follower of the Prophet, and outwardly at least adopted the faith of
Islam. The troops, delighted at his conversion and cheered by the hope
of success, renewed their efforts, and the resistance of the Governor
of Darfur was prolonged. The end, however, was deferred, not averted.
After the destruction of General Hicks's Army Slatin was compelled
to surrender to the Dervishes. The religion he had assumed to secure
victory he observed to escape death. The Arab leaders, who admired
his courage, treated him at first with respect and kindness, and he was
conducted to the Mahdi in his encampment before Khartoum. There
during the siege he remained, closely watched but not imprisoned.
Thence he wrote letters to Gordon explaining his surrender, excusing
his apostasy, and begging that he might be allowed – not even assisted –
to escape to Khartoum. The letters are extant, and scarcely anyone
who reads them, reflecting on the twelve years of danger and degradation that lay before this man, will refuse their compassion.

Gordon was inflexible. This is the uncompromising minute in the Journals: 'Oct. 16. The letters of Slatin have arrived. I have no remarks to make on them, and cannot make out why he wrote them.'[1]

Slatin's position, it should be observed, was not that of an officer released on parole, but of a prisoner of war in durance in the enemy's camp. In such circumstances he was clearly entitled to escape at his own proper risk. If his captors gave him the chance, they had only themselves to blame.

Slatin was, however, in no position to argue his case. His correspondence with Gordon was discovered. For some days his life hung on a thread. For several months he was heavily chained and fed on a daily handful of uncooked *doura*, such as is given to horses and mules. Tidings of these things were carried to Gordon. 'Slatin,' he observes icily, 'is still in chains.' He never doubted the righteousness of the course he had adopted, never for an instant.

Gordon's responsibility was undivided. There was no one to whom he could talk as an equal. There was no one to whom he could reveal his doubts. To some minds the exercise of power is pleasant, but few sensations are more painful than responsibility without control. The General could not supervise the defence. The officers robbed the soldiers of their rations. The sentries slumbered at their posts. The townspeople bewailed their misfortunes, and all ranks and classes intrigued with the enemy in the hope of securing safety when the town should fall. Spies of all kinds pervaded the town. The Egyptian Pashas, despairing, meditated treason. Once an attempt was made to fire the magazine. Once no less than eighty thousand *ardebs* of grain was stolen from the arsenal. From time to time the restless and ceaseless activity of the commander might discover some plot and arrest the conspirators; or, checking some account, might detect some robbery; but he was fully aware that what he found out was scarcely a tithe of what he could not hope to know. The Egyptian officers were untrustworthy. Yet he had to trust them. The inhabitants were thoroughly broken by war, and many were disloyal. He had to feed and inspirit them. The town itself was scarcely defensible. It must be defended to the end. From the flat roof of his palace his telescope commanded a view of the forts and lines. Here he would spend the greater part of

[1] *Journals at Khartoum.*

each day, scrutinising the defences and the surrounding country with his powerful glass. The Journals, the only receptacle of his confidences, display the bitterness of his sufferings no less than the greatness of his character. 'There is no contagion,' he writes, 'equal to that of fear. I have been rendered furious when from anxiety I could not eat, I would find those at the same table were in like manner affected.'

To the military anxieties was added every kind of worry which may weary a man's soul. The belief that he was abandoned and discredited, that history would make light of his efforts, would perhaps never know of them, filled his mind with a sense of wrong and injustice which preyed upon his spirits. The miseries of the townsfolk wrung his noble, generous heart. The utter loneliness depressed him. And over all lay the shadow of uncertainty. To the very end the possibility that 'all might be well' mocked him with false hopes. The first light of any morning might reveal the longed-for steamers of relief and the uniforms of British soldiers. He was denied even the numbing anaesthetic of despair.

Yet he was sustained by two great moral and mental stimulants: his honour as a man, his faith as a Christian. The first had put all courses which he did not think right once and for all out of the question, and so allayed many doubts and prevented many vain regrets. But the second was the real source of his strength. He was sure that beyond this hazardous existence, with all its wrongs and inequalities, another life awaited him – a life which, if he had been faithful and true here upon earth, would afford him greater faculties for good and wider opportunities for their use. 'Look at me now,' he once said to a fellow-traveller, 'with small armies to command and no cities to govern. I hope that death will set me free from pain and that great armies will be given me, and that I shall have vast cities under my command.'[1]

As the severity of military operations increases, so also must the sternness of discipline. When fortune is dubious or adverse; when supplies fail, arrangements miscarry, and disasters impend, the ugly truth is revealed that fear is the foundation of obedience. It is certain that the influence of General Gordon upon the garrison and townspeople of Khartoum owed its greatest strength to that sinister element.

[1] Lieut.-Colonel N. Newnham Davis, 'Some Gordon Reminiscences', published in *The Man of the World* newspaper, 14th December 1898.

'It is quite painful,' he writes in his Journals in September, 'to see men tremble so, when they come and see me, that they cannot hold the match to their cigarette.' As the winter drew on, the sufferings of the besieged increased and their faith in their commander and his promises of relief diminished. To preserve their hopes – and, by their hopes, their courage and loyalty – was beyond the power of man. But what a great man in the utmost exercise of his faculties and authority might do, Gordon did.

His extraordinary spirit never burned more brightly than in these last, gloomy days. The money to pay the troops was exhausted. He issued notes, signing them with his own name. The citizens groaned under the triple scourge of scarcity, disease, and war. He ordered the bands to play merrily and discharged rockets. It was said that they were abandoned, that help would never come, that the expedition was a myth – the lie of a General who was disavowed by his Government. Forthwith he placarded the walls with the news of victories and of the advance of a triumphant British Army; or hired all the best houses by the river's bank for the accommodation of the officers of the relieving force. A Dervish shell crashed through his palace. He ordered the date of its arrival to be inscribed above the hole. For those who served him faithfully he struck medals and presented them with pomp and circumstance. Others less laudable he shot. And by all these means and expedients the defence of the city was prolonged through the summer, autumn, and winter of 1884 and on into the year 1885.

All this time the public anxiety in England had been steadily growing. If Gordon was abandoned, he was by no means forgotten. As his mission had been followed with intense interest throughout the whole country, so its failure had caused general despondency. Disappointment soon gave place to alarm. The subject of the personal safety of the distinguished envoy was first raised in the House of Commons on the 16th of March by Lord Randolph Churchill.

'Colonel Coetlogon has stated that Khartoum may be easily captured; we know that General Gordon is surrounded by hostile tribes and cut off from communications with Cairo and London; and under these circumstances the House has a right to ask her Majesty's Government whether they are going to do anything to relieve him. Are they going to remain indifferent to the fate of the one man on whom they have counted to extricate them from their dilemmas, to leave him to shift for himself, and not make a single effort on his behalf?'[1]

The Government remained impassive. But the subject, once raised, was not allowed to drop. The Opposition were continually growing stronger. Almost every night Ministers were invited to declare whether they would rescue their envoy or leave him to his fate. Mr Gladstone returned evasive answers. The agitation became intense. Even among the supporters of the Government there was dissatisfaction. But the Prime Minister was obdurate and unflinching.

It is usual to look upon Mr Gladstone's conduct in the matter of the relief of Gordon as dictated by benevolent weakness. History may take another view. Strong and stubborn as was the character of the General, that of the Minister was its equal. If Gordon was the better man, Gladstone was incomparably the greater. Few men have feared responsibility less than Gladstone. On the other hand, the expressed desire of the nation was a force to which he had always bowed – to which, indeed, he owed his political existence. Yet, in spite of the growing agitation throughout the land, he remained stern and silent. Most men do what is right, or what they persuade themselves is right; nor is it difficult to believe that Mr Gladstone did not feel justified in involving the nation in operations in the heart of the Soudan for the purpose, not of saving the life of the envoy – for Gordon had but to embark on his steamers and come home – but simply in order to vindicate the personal honour of a man. And it is possible that a feeling of resentment against the officer whose intractable nature was bringing such odium upon the Government may have coloured his resolution with a darker tinge.

But for all his power and influence he was forced to give way. The Government which had long ignored the call of honour abroad, was driven to the Soudan by the cries of shame at home. Lord Hartington, at that time Secretary of State for War, must be dissociated from the general censure which his principal colleagues have incurred. He was the first to recognise the obligation which lay upon the Cabinet, and through the Cabinet upon the nation, and it was to his influence that the despatch of the relieving expedition was mainly due. The Commander-in-Chief and the Adjutant-General, who were fully alive to the

[1] *Hansard's Parliamentary Debates*, 16th March 1884.

critical position at Khartoum, added their recommendations. But even at the last moment Mr Gladstone was induced to sanction the advance only by the belief that the scale of the operations would be small, and that only a single brigade would be necessary. The decision was taken forthwith by the Ministry and announced to the nation. The Adjutant-General, however, asked for a very different force from what the Government had anticipated, and the single brigade was expanded into an expedition of ten thousand men, selected from the whole army.

To reverse the decision was now, however, impossible, and the 'Gordon Relief Expedition' began. The commander to whom the conduct of the operations had been entrusted reviewed the situation. He saw himself confronted with a task which was easy and safe if it were undertaken at leisure, and which was doubtful and perilous if begun in haste. Shrewdly estimating the military difficulties, he made his plans for a methodical and deliberate advance which would leave nothing to luck.

Troops and stores were steadily collected at Wady Halfa and along the Nile. The new Camel Corps, consisting of four regiments, practised their drills and evolutions. To pilot the boats up the Cataracts *voyageurs* were brought from Canada. At length, when all preparations were complete, the expedition started. The plan was simple. A strong column of infantry in boats was to work up the river. In case that should not arrive in time, the Camel Corps was to strike across the Bayuda Desert from Korti to Metemma. Having arrived there, a small detachment was to be thrown into Khartoum by Gordon's steamers to sustain the defence until the arrival of the main body in March or even April of 1885, when the town could be regularly relieved.

The Desert Column started from Korti on the 30th of December. Their strength did not exceed 1,100 officers and men, but they were the flower of the army. Dropping their communications, they set forth along the caravan route towards Metemma. The knowledge which we have since gained of the resources of the Mahdists enables the peril of their desperate venture to be fully appreciated. Although the Dervishes were neither so well armed nor trained as at a later date, they were nearly as numerous and equally devoid of fear. Their tactics were more in accordance with modern conditions: their fanaticism was at its height. The British force, on the other hand, was equipped with weapons scarcely comparable with those employed in the concluding campaigns. Instead of the powerful Lee-Metford rifle, with its smokeless powder, its magazine action, and its absence of recoil, they were armed with the Martini-Henry, which possessed none of these advantages. In place of the deadly Maxim there was the Gardner gun – the very gun that jammed at Tamai, and that jammed again at Abu Klea. The artillery was also in every respect inferior to that now in general use. Besides all this, the principles of fire-discipline and of scientific musketry were new, little understood, and hardly admitted. Nevertheless, the Camel Corps went boldly forward, and engaged an enemy whose destruction ultimately required the strength of a better-armed and better-instructed army twelve times as strong.

On the 3rd of January they reached Gakdul Wells. A hundred miles of their march was accomplished. But they were now delayed by the necessity of escorting a second column of supplies to Gakdul, and after that until the arrival of reinforcements which raised their strength to 1,800 of all ranks. The interval was employed in building two small forts and establishing an advanced depôt; nor was it until the 13th that the march was resumed. The number of camels was not sufficient for the necessities of the transport. The food of the camels was too poor for the work they had to perform. By the 16th, however, they had made fifty miles, and approached the wells of Abu Klea. Here their further advance was disputed by the enemy.

The news of the advance of the Desert Column had been duly reported to the Mahdi and his Arab generals. A small party of English, it was said, with camels and some cavalry, were coming swiftly to the rescue of the accursed city. Their numbers were few, scarce 2,000 men. How should they hope to prevail against 'the expected Mahdi' and the conquering Ansar who had destroyed Hicks? They were mad; yet they should die; not one should escape. The delay in the advance offered ample opportunity. A great force of Arabs was concentrated. Several thousand men under important Emirs were·detached from the army before Khartoum and marched northward eager for the slaughter of the 'enemies of God'. With the reinforcements from Omdurman the total force of the Arabs actually at hand was not less than 10,000, and behind were many thousands more. They permitted the little column to advance until their retreat, if defeated, was impossible, and then, confident of victory, offered battle near the wells of Abu Klea.

The Camel Corps remained halted during the morning of the 16th, and built a small fort, in which they placed their reserve of stores, and made some arrangement for the reception of wounded. At one o'clock they moved leisurely forward, passed through the rocky defile which led into the valley of Abu Klea and bivouacked. Early the next morning the force moved out in square formation and advanced upon the enemy. The most savage and bloody action ever fought in the Soudan by British troops followed. Notwithstanding the numbers and the valour of the Arabs, that they penetrated the square, and that they inflicted on the troops a loss of nine officers and sixty-five men killed and nine officers and eighty-five men wounded – 10 per cent of the entire force – they were driven from the field with great slaughter, and the Desert Column camped at the wells.

On the morning of the 18th they rested, placed their wounded in the small fort they had built, and buried their dead. In the afternoon they continued their advance, marched all through the night, and, having covered twenty-three miles, halted exhausted, almost within sight of the river, at daylight on the 19th. Meanwhile the enemy had again collected in great strength, and an effective rifle fire was opened on the column. Sir Herbert Stewart received the wound of which a few weeks later he died. The command devolved upon Sir Charles Wilson. The position was desperate. Water was running short. The Nile was only four miles away; but the column were impeded by their wounded and stores, and between the river and the thirsty men lay the Dervish Army, infuriated by their losses and fully aware of the sore straits to which their astonishing enemy was now reduced.

It now became necessary to divide the small force. Some must remain to guard the baggage and the wounded; the others must fight their way to the water. At three o'clock in the afternoon of the 19th, 900 men left the hastily made *zeriba* and marched towards the river. Without their camels or those of the transport they appeared insignificant, a mere speck on the broad plain of Metemma. The Dervishes hastened to clinch the matter.

The square advances slowly and painfully over the stony ground, with frequent jerky halts to preserve order and to pick up the wounded.

Little puffs of white smoke dot the distant sandhills. Here and there a gaudy flag waves defiantly. In front the green tops of the palm-trees by the Nile tantalise but stimulate the soldiers. On the left the great mud labyrinth of Metemma stretches indefinitely. Suddenly the firing stops. The low scrub in front is alive with the swarming figures of the enemy. All the flags dance forward together. Ragged white figures spring up in hundreds. Emirs on horses appear as if by magic. Everywhere are men running swiftly forward, waving their spears and calling upon the Prophet of God to speed their enterprise. The square halts. The weary men begin to fire with thoughtful care. The Dervishes drop thickly. On then, children of the desert! you are so many, they are so few. One rush will trample the accursed under the feet of the faithful. The charge continues. A bugle sounds in the waiting square. The firing stops. What is this? They lose heart. Their ammunition is exhausted. On then, and make an end. Again the smoke ripples along the line of bayonets and fire is re-opened, this time at closer range and with far greater effect. The stubborn grandeur of the British soldier is displayed by desperate circumstances. The men shoot to hit. The attack crumples. The Emirs – horse and man – collapse. The others turn and walk – for they will not run – sullenly back towards the town. The square starts forward. The road to the river is open. With dusk the water is reached, and never have victors gained a more longed-for prize. The Nile is won. Gordon remains.

Sir Charles Wilson, having collected his force, remained three days by the bank of the Nile before attempting any further advance on Khartoum. He has explained why this delay was necessary, to the satisfaction of most military critics. On the fourth day he embarked on two of Gordon's steamers, which awaited the relieving column, and taking with him twenty British soldiers and a few blue-jackets set forth towards the Shabluka Gorge and the town that lay beyond. On the 27th of January the rescuers came in sight of Khartoum and under the fire of the enemy. Many of their perilous adventures seem to belong to romance rather than to reality. But the scene that appeals to the imagination above all the others is that where with both banks ablaze with musketry and artillery, the black smoke pouring through the shot-holes in the funnels, the water rising in spurts from the bullets, the men who had come so far and braved so much stared at the palace roof and, seeing no flag flying, knew that all was over and that they had come too late.

The news of the Dervish defeats at Abu Klea and Abu Kru impelled the Mahdi to a desperate venture. The English were but 120 miles away. They were few, but victorious. In spite of the wrath of the true God and the valour of Islam they might prevail. The Mahdi depended on success for existence. The tremendous forces of fanaticism are exerted only in a forward direction. Retreat meant ruin. All must be staked on an immediate assault. Thus the night of the 25th of January arrived.

The band played as usual in the evening. Gradually the shadows fell and it became dark. The hungry inhabitants betook themselves to bed. The anxious but indomitable commander knew that the crisis impended, and knew also that he was powerless to avert it. Perhaps he slept, satisfied that he had done his duty; and in the silence of the night the savage enemy crawled stealthily towards the town. On a sudden the loud explosion of musketry broke the stillness of the night and the slumbers of the people; and with a continual shouting thousands of Dervishes swarmed through the unprotected space and entered Khartoum.

One mob of assailants made their way to the palace. Gordon came out to meet them. The whole courtyard was filled with wild, harlequin figures and sharp, glittering blades. He attempted a parley. 'Where is your master, the Mahdi?' He knew his influence over native races. Perhaps he hoped to save the lives of some of the inhabitants. Perhaps in that supreme moment imagination flashed another picture before his eyes; and he saw himself facing that savage circle with a fanaticism equal to, and a courage greater than, their own; marching in all the pride of faith 'and with retorted scorn' to a martyr's death.

It was not to be. Mad with the joy of victory and religious frenzy, they rushed upon him and, while he disdained even to fire his revolver, stabbed him in many places. The body fell down the steps and lay – a twisted heap – at the foot. There it was decapitated. The head was carried to the Mahdi. The trunk was stabbed again and again by the infuriated creatures, till nothing but a shapeless bundle of torn flesh and bloody rags remained of what had been a great and famous man and the envoy of her Britannic Majesty. The blood soaked into the ground, and left a dark stain which was not immediately effaced. Slatin mentions that the Arabs used often to visit the place.

With the capture of the city and the death of the envoy the reason for the expedition disappeared. It remained only to withdraw the troops. The stores which had been brought across the desert at a terrible cost were thrown hastily into the Nile. The battered steamers which had waited so long at Metemma were hurriedly dismantled. The Camel Corps, their extraordinary efforts futile and their camels killed, marched back on foot to Korti. Their retreat was pressed by the exultant enemy. The River Column, whose boats after months of labour had just cleared the Cataracts, and who had gained a success at Kirbekan, were carried back swiftly by the strong current against which they had hopefully struggled. The whole Expeditionary Force – Guards, Highlanders, sailors, Hussars, Indian soldiers, Canadian *voyageurs*, mules, camels, and artillery – trooped back forlornly over the desert sands, and behind them the rising tide of barbarism followed swiftly, until the whole vast region was submerged. For several months the garrison of Kassala under a gallant Egyptian maintained a desperate resistance, but at last famine forced them to surrender. The evacuation of the Soudan was thus complete.

THE DERVISH EMPIRE

It might seem at first a great advantage that the peoples of the Soudan, instead of being a multitude of wild, discordant tribes, should unite of their own accord into one strong community, living under fixed laws, and ruled by a single sovereign. But there is one form of centralised government which is almost entirely unprogressive and beyond all other forms costly and tyrannical – the rule of an army. History records many such dominations, ancient and modern, civilised or barbaric; and though education and culture may modify, they cannot change their predominant characteristics. The evil qualities of military hierarchies are always the same. The results of their rule are universally unfortunate. The degree may vary with time and place, but the political supremacy of an army always leads to the formation of a great centralised capital, to the consequent impoverishment of the provinces, to the degradation of the peaceful inhabitants through oppression and want, to the ruin of commerce, the decay of learning, and the ultimate demoralisation even of the military order through overbearing pride and sensual indulgence.

After the fall of Khartoum and the retreat of the British Armies the Mahdi became the absolute master of the Soudan. Whatever pleasures he desired he could command, and, following the example of the founder of the Mohammedan faith, he indulged in what would seem to Western minds gross excesses. He established an extensive harem for his own peculiar use, and immured therein the fairest captives of the war. The conduct of the ruler was imitated by his subjects. The presence of women increased the vanity of the warriors: and it was not very long before the patched smock which had vaunted the holy poverty of the rebels developed into the gaudy *jibba* of the conquerors. Since the unhealthy situation of Khartoum amid swamps and marshes did not commend itself to the now luxurious Arabs, the Mahdi began to build on the western bank of the White Nile a new capital, which, from the detached fort which had stood there in Egyptian days, was called Omdurman.[1] Among the first buildings which he set his subjects to construct were a mosque for the services of religion, an arsenal for the storage of military material, and a house for himself.

In the middle of the month of June, scarcely five months after the completion of his victorious campaigns, the Mahdi fell sick. For a few days he did not appear at the mosque. The people were filled with alarm. They were reassured by remembering the prophecy that their liberator should not perish till he had conquered the earth. Mohammed, however, grew worse. Presently those who attended him could doubt no longer that he was attacked by typhus fever. The Khalifa Abdullah watched by his couch continually. On the sixth day the inhabitants and the soldiers were informed of the serious nature of their ruler's illness, and public prayers were offered by all classes for his recovery. On the seventh day it was evident that he was dying. All those who had shared his fortunes crowded the small room. For some hours he lay unconscious or in delirium, but as the end approached he rallied a little, and, collecting his faculties by a great effort, declared his faithful follower and friend the Khalifa Abdullah his successor, and adjured the rest to show him honour. 'He is of me, and I am of him; as you have obeyed me, so you should deal with him. May God have mercy upon me!'[2] Then he immediately expired.

Grief and dismay filled the city. In spite of the emphatic prohibition by law of all loud lamentations, the sound of 'weeping and wailing arose from almost every house'. The whole people, deprived at once of their acknowledged sovereign and spiritual guide, were shocked and affrighted. Only the Mahdi's wives, if we may credit Slatin, 're-joiced secretly in their hearts at the death of their husband and master,' and, since they were henceforth to be doomed to an enforced and inviolable chastity, the cause of their satisfaction is as obscure as its manifestation was unnatural. The body of the Mahdi, wrapped in linen, was reverently interred in a deep grave dug in the floor of the room in which he had died, nor was it disturbed until after the capture of Omdurman by the British forces in 1898, when by the orders of

[1] Map 'The Soudan and the Dervish Empire', p. 181.
[2] Slatin, *Fire and Sword*.

Sir H. Kitchener the sepulchre was opened and the corpse exhumed.

The Khalifa Abdullah had been declared by the Mahdi's latest breath his successor. He determined to have the choice ratified once for all by the popular vote. Hurrying to the pulpit in the courtyard of the mosque, he addressed the assembled multitude in a voice which trembled with intense excitement and emotion. His oratory, his reputation as a warrior, and the Mahdi's expressed desire aroused the enthusiasm of his hearers, and the oath of allegiance was at once sworn by thousands.

As the various provinces had been cleared of the Egyptians, the new Executive had appointed military governors by whom the country was ruled and taxed, subject to the pleasure of Mohammed Ahmed. His death was the signal for a long series of revolts of all kinds – military, political, and religious. Garrisons mutinied; Emirs plotted; prophets preached. Nor was the land torn only by internal struggles. On the east the tremendous power of Abyssinia loomed terrible and menacing. There was war in the north with Egypt and around Suakin with England. The Italians must be confronted from the direction of Massowa. Far to the south Emin Pasha still maintained a troublesome resistance. Yet the Khalifa triumphed over nearly all his enemies; and the greatest spectacle which the Soudan presented from 1885 to 1898 was of this strong, capable ruler bearing up against all reverses, and offering a firm front to every foe.

During the thirteen years of his reign Abdullah tried nearly every device by which Oriental rulers have sought to fortify their perilous sovereignty. The general massacre of all possible claimants usually follows the accession of a usurper to an Oriental throne. The Khalifa was able to avoid this extreme measure. Nevertheless he took precautions. Availing himself of the grief and terror that had followed Mohammed Ahmed's death, he had extorted the oath of allegiance from the two other Khalifas and from the 'Ashraf' or relations of the Prophet.[1] But these complaisant men soon repented of their submission. Both the unsuccessful Khalifas combined against Abdullah. But that sagacious ruler had secured the loyalty of the Baggara tribe, to a section of which he belonged, and of a considerable force of black riflemen.

[1] The Mahdi had superseded the original Mohammed as 'the Prophet'. His relations consequently became the 'Ashraf'.

Both parties prepared for war. Abdullah drew up his array without the city, and challenged his rivals to the utmost proof. The combined forces of the ousted Khalifas were the more numerous. But the fierce Baggara waved their swords, and the Soudanese riflemen were famous for their valour. For some hours a bloody struggle appeared imminent. Eventually both bowed to the superior force of the ruler and the superior courage of his followers. Once they had submitted, their power was gone, and they became for the future the useful supporters of a Government they were unable to subvert.

Abdullah knew that to rule the Soudan he must have a great army. To make the great army obedient he must have another separate force; for the influences which keep European armies in subjection were not present among the Dervishes. For some years, indeed, he was compelled to leave much to chance or the loyalty of his officers. But latterly, when he had perfected his organisation, he became quite independent and had no need to trust anyone.

He invited his own tribe, the Taaisha section of the Baggara Arabs, to come and live in Omdurman. Allured by the hopes of wealth and wives and the promise of power, the savage herdsmen came to the number of 7,000 warriors. Their path was made smooth and easy. Granaries were erected along the route. Steamers and sailing-vessels waited on the Nile. Arrived at the capital, all were newly clothed at the expense of the State. An entire district of the city was forcibly cleared of its inhabitants for the accommodation of the strangers. What the generosity of the Khalifa forgot or refused, the predatory habits of his clansmen procured; and they robbed, plundered, and swindled with all the arrogance and impunity of royal favourites. The populace of the city returned a bitter hatred for these injuries; and the Khalifa's object was attained. He had created a class in Omdurman who were indissolubly attached to him. Like him, they were detested by the local tribes. Like him, they were foreigners in the land. But, like him, they were fierce and brave and strong. Their lives depended on their loyalty.

Here was the motor muscle which animated the rest. The Taaisha Baggara controlled the black Jehadia, once the irregular troops of the Egyptians, now become the regulars of the Khalifa. The black Jehadia overawed the Arab Army in the capital. The army in the capital dominated the forces in the provinces. The forces in the provinces subdued the inhabitants. The centralisation of power was assured by the concentration of military material. Cannon, rifles, stores of ammunition, all the necessities of war were accumulated in the arsenal. Rifles were issued to the Soudanese whenever safe and necessary; cartridges only when they were about to be used. Thus several millions of warlike and savage people were brought into the firm grip of a single man.

The third principle of government which the Khalifa was compelled to adopt was to keep the relative power of the various tribes and classes conveniently proportioned. If an Emir rose to great influence and wealth, he became a possible rival, and suffered forthwith death, imprisonment, or spoliation. If a tribe threatened the supremacy of the Taaisha it was struck down while its menace was yet a menace. Such was the statecraft of a savage from Kordofan.

His greatest triumph was the Abyssinian war. For some time a harassing and desultory warfare disturbed the border. At length in 1885 a Dervish – half-trader, half-brigand – sacked an Abyssinian church. Ras Adal, the Governor of the Amhara province, demanded that this sacrilegious robber should be surrendered to justice. The Arabs haughtily refused. The response was swift. Collecting an army which may have amounted to 30,000 men, the Abyssinians invaded the district of Gallabat and marched on the town. Against this host the Emir Wad Arbab could muster no more than 6,000 soldiers. But, encouraged by the victories of the previous four years, the Dervishes accepted battle, in spite of the disparity of numbers. Neither valour nor discipline could withstand such odds. The Moslems, broken by the fierce onset and surrounded by the overwhelming numbers of their enemies, were destroyed, together with their intrepid leader. The Abyssinians indulged in all the triumphs of savagery. The wounded were massacred: the slain were mutilated: the town of Gallabat was sacked and burnt. All these tidings came to Omdurman. Under this heavy and unexpected blow the Khalifa acted with prudence. He opened negotiations with King John of Abyssinia for the ransom of the captured wives and children, and at the same time he sent the Emir Yunes with a large force to Gallabat. The immediate necessities having thus been dealt with, Abdullah prepared for revenge.

Of all the Arab leaders which fifteen years of continual war and

tumult throughout the Soudan produced, none displayed higher
ability, none obtained greater successes, and none were more honourable, than the man whom the Khalifa selected to avenge the destruction
of the Gallabat Army. Abu Anga had been a slave in Abdullah's
family long before the Mahdi had preached at Abba island and while
Egypt yet oppressed the country. After the revolt had broken out, his
adventurous master summoned him from the distant Kordofan home
to attend him in the war, and Abu Anga came with that ready obedience and strange devotion for which he was always distinguished.
Nominally as a slave, really as a comrade, he fought by Abdullah's
side in all the earlier battles of the rebellion. The Khalifa was a judge
of men. He saw very clearly that the black Soudanese troops, who
were surrendering as town after town was taken, might be welded
into a powerful weapon. And in Abu Anga he knew a man who could
not only fashion the blade, but would hold it ever loyally at his
master's disposal. The former slave threw himself into the duties of
his command with extraordinary energy. More than any other Emir,
Abu Anga contributed to the destruction of Hicks's army. The
Jehadia, as his soldiers were called – because they had joined in the
Jehad, or Holy War – became famous throughout the land for their
weapons, their courage, and their cruelty.

At the end of June Abu Anga reached Omdurman with an army
variously estimated at from 22,000 to 31,000 men, of whom at least
10,000 were armed with Remington rifles. The Khalifa received him
with the utmost honour. After a private interview, which lasted for
several hours, a formal entry into the town was arranged. At daybreak
on the following morning the whole force marched into the city and
camped along the northern suburbs, applauded and welcomed alike
by the population and their ruler. A few days after this a great review
was held under the Kerreri hills. The whole plain was filled with the
throng. Banners of every hue and shape waved gaily in the breeze,
and the sunlight glinted from innumerable spear-points. The swarming
Dervishes displayed their bright parti-coloured *jibbas*. The wild
Baggara cavalry circled on the flanks of the array. The brown dome of
the Mahdi's tomb, rising above the city, seemed to assure the warriors
of supernatural aid. Abdullah was at the summit of his power. The
Khalifa had embarked on a great venture in planning the invasion of

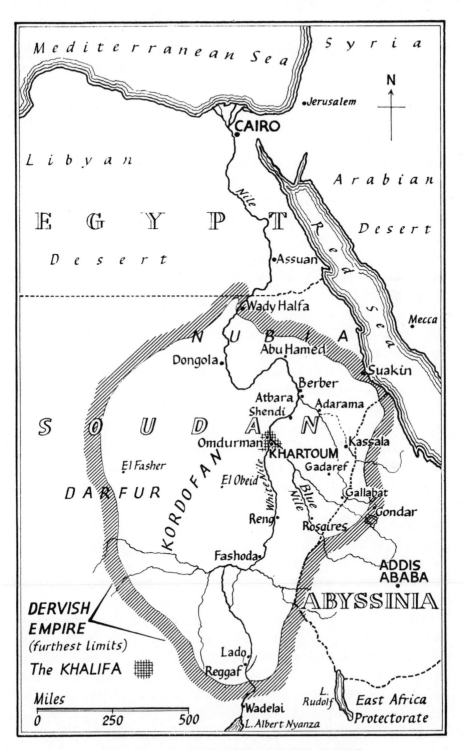

THE SOUDAN AND THE DERVISH EMPIRE

Abyssinia. The vast strength of the Negus was known to the Dervishes, and the Mahdi had forbidden such a war. An ill-omened prophecy further declared that the King of Abyssinia would tether his horse to a solitary tree by Khartoum, while his cavalry should ride through the city fetlock deep in blood. But Abdullah feared neither God nor man.

The Abyssinians had not watched the extensive hostile preparations apathetically. Ras Adal had collected an army which in numbers actually exceeded that of the Dervishes. But the latter were far superior in rifles, and the black infantry were of invincible valour. Nevertheless, confident in his strength and relying on his powerful cavalry, the Abyssinian general allowed the Arabs to toil through all the mountainous country, to traverse the Mintik Pass, and to debouch unmolested on to the plain of Debra Sin. Abu Anga neglected no precaution. He knew that since he must fight in the heart of Abyssinia, with the mountains behind him, a defeat would involve annihilation. He drew up his army swiftly and with skill. Then the Abyssinians attacked. The rifle fire of the Soudanese repulsed them. The onset was renewed with desperate gallantry. It was resisted with equal valour and superior weapons. After frightful losses the Abyssinians wavered, and the wise Arab seized the moment for a counterstroke. In spite of the devotion of his cavalry Ras Adal was driven from the field. Great numbers of his army were drowned in the river in front of which he had recklessly elected to fight. His camp was captured, and a valuable spoil rewarded the victors, who also gratified their passions with a wholesale slaughter of the wounded – a practice commonly followed by savages. The effect of the victory was great. The whole of the Amhara province submitted to the invaders, and in the spring of 1887 Abu Anga was able to advance without further fighting to the capture and sack of Gondar, the ancient capital of Abyssinia.

The Dervishes did not long remain in Abyssinia, as they suffered from the climate. In December the army returned to Gallabat, which they commenced to fortify, and their victorious general followed to Omdurman, where he received the usual welcome accorded by warlike peoples to military heroes. But the famous and faithful slave may have been more gratified by the tears of joy which his master and sovereign shed on beholding him again safe and successful.

The greater struggle was still to come. The whole of Abyssinia was convulsed with fury, and King John in person prepared to take the field and settle the quarrel for ever. He assembled a mighty host, which is said to have amounted to 130,000 foot and 20,000 horsemen. The rumours of this formidable concentration reached Gallabat and Omdurman, and in spite of the recent victory caused deep alarm. The Khalifa saw his frontiers – even his existence – menaced, for King John had declared that he would sweep the Dervishes from off the face of the earth: and in the hour of need the general on whom so much depended died of some poisonous medicine with which he had endeavoured to cure himself of indigestion. Abu Anga was buried in his red-brick house at Gallabat amid the lamentations of his brave black soldiers, and gloom pervaded the whole army. The Khalifa appointed Zeki Tummal, one of Anga's lieutenants, to the command of the forces at Gallabat, which by strenuous exertions he brought up to a total of 85,000 men.

At dawn on the 9th of March 1889, the Abyssinians came within sight of their enemies, and early the next morning the battle began. The Abyssinians, undaunted by the rifle fire of the Soudanese, succeeded in setting the *zeriba* alight. Then, concentrating all their force on one part of the defence, they burst into the enclosure and town. The division of Wad Ali, a fourth part of the entire Dervish Army, which bore the brunt of this attack, was almost completely destroyed. The interior of the *zeriba* was crowded with women and children, who were ruthlessly butchered by the exultant Abyssinians. The assailants scattered in all directions in search of plunder, and they even had time to begin to disinter the body of Abu Anga, which they were eager to insult in revenge for Gondar. The Dervishes already wavered when suddenly a rumour spread about among the Abyssinians that the King was killed. Seizing what booty they could snatch, the victorious army began a general retreat, and the *zeriba* was soon cleared. The Arabs were too exhausted to pursue, but when on the following day the attack was not renewed they learned, to their surprise, that they were the victors and that their enemy was falling back towards the Atbara River. Zeki Tummal resolved to pursue. Two days after the battle the Dervishes overtook the enemy's rearguard, and, surprising their camp, inflicted severe loss and captured much booty. The temporary Negus who had been appointed to fill the vacancy caused by the death of King John was among the killed. The body of that courageous monarch fell into the hands of the Dervishes, who struck off the head and sent it – a tangible proof of victory – to Omdurman.

The arrival in Omdurman of King John's head intoxicated the Khalifa with joy. Abyssinia was regarded throughout the Soudan as a far greater power than Egypt, and here was its mighty ruler slain and decapitated. But the victory had been dearly purchased. The two great battles had been fought with indescribable ferocity by both sides, and the slaughter was appalling. The flower of the Dervish Army, the heroic blacks of Abu Anga, were almost destroyed. The Khalifa had won a Pyrrhic triumph. Never again was he able to put so great a force in the field.

During the progress of the struggle with Abyssinia the war against Egypt languished. The Mahdi, counting upon the support of the population, had always declared that he would free the Delta from 'the Turks', and was already planning its invasion when he and his schemes were interrupted by death. His successor inherited all the quarrel, but not all the power. The success of the Abyssinian war encouraged and enabled the Khalifa to resume the offensive on his northern frontier, and he immediately ordered Wad-el-Nejumi, who commanded in Dongola, to march with his scanty force to the invasion of Egypt. The mad enterprise ended, as might have been foreseen, in the destruction of both Emir and army at Toski. The Khalifa received the news with apparent grief, but it is difficult to avoid suspecting him of dark schemes. He was far too clever to believe that Egypt could be conquered by five thousand men. He knew that besides the Egyptians there was a strange white tribe of men, the same that had so nearly saved Khartoum. 'But for the English,' he exclaimed on several occasions, 'I would have conquered Egypt.' Yet, knowing of the British occupation, he deliberately sent an army to its inevitable ruin. It is difficult to reconcile such conduct with the character for sagacity and intelligence which Abdullah has deserved.

The terrible slaughter of the Abyssinian war had fallen mainly on the Jehadia and the eastern Arabs. The jealous tribes in the north had not suffered. The balance of power was in need of re-adjustment. The Jaalin and Barabra were fast becoming dangerous. Nejumi's army was recruited almost entirely from these sources. The reinforcements sent from Omdurman consisted of men selected from the flag of the Khalifa Sherif, who was growing too powerful, and of the Batahin tribe, who had shown a mutinous spirit.[1] The success of such an army in Egypt would be glorious. Its destruction anywhere would be convenient. Whatever Abdullah's motives may have been, his advantage was certain.

Other forces were soon added to the work of exhaustion. The year following the end of the Abyssinian war was marked by a fearful famine. Slatin and Ohrwalder vie with each other in relating its horrors – men eating the raw entrails of donkeys; mothers devouring their babies; scores dying in the streets, all the more ghastly in the bright sunlight; hundreds of corpses floating down the Nile. The depopulation caused by the scarcity was even greater than that produced by the fighting. The famine area extended over the whole Soudan and ran along the banks of the river as far as Lower Egypt. Entire districts between Omdurman and Berber became wholly depopulated. The camel-breeding tribes ate their she-camels. The riverain peoples devoured their seed-corn. The population of Gallabat, Gedaref, and Kassala was reduced by nine-tenths, and the frightful mortality, general throughout the whole country, may be gauged by the fact that Zeki Tummal's army, which before the famine numbered not fewer than 87,000, could scarcely muster 10,000 men in the spring of 1890.

The new harvest came only in time to save the inhabitants of the Soudan from becoming extinct. The remnant were preserved for further misfortunes. In 1890 innumerable swarms of locusts descended on the impoverished soil. The multitude of their red or yellow bodies veiled the sun and darkened the air, and although their flesh, tasting when roasted like fried shrimps, might afford a delicate meal to the natives, they took so heavy a toll of the crops that the famine was prolonged and scarcity became constant. Since their first appearance the locusts are said to have returned annually.[2] Their destructive efforts were aided by millions of little red mice, who destroyed the seeds before they could grow. So vast and immeasurable was the number

[1] Ohrwalder, *Ten Years' Captivity.*
[2] Ohrwalder, *Ten Years' Captivity.*

of these tiny pests that after a heavy rain the whole country was strewn with, and almost tinted by, the squirrel-coloured corpses of the drowned.

Yet, in spite of all the strokes of fate, the Khalifa maintained his authority unshaken. The centralisation which always occurs in military States was accelerated by the famine. The provincial towns dwindled; thousands and tens of thousands perished; but Omdurman continually grew, and its ruler still directed the energies of a powerful army. Thus for the present we leave the Dervish Empire.

CHAPTER IV

THE YEARS OF PREPARATION

In the summer of 1886, when all the troops had retreated to Wady Halfa and all the Soudan garrisons had been massacred, the British people averted their eyes in shame and vexation from the valley of the Nile. Besides the pain produced by the death of General Gordon, the heavy losses in officers and men, and the serious expenditure of public money, the nation smarted under failure and disappointment, and were, moreover, deeply sensible that they had been humiliated before the whole world. The situation in Egypt was scarcely more pleasing. The reforms initiated by the British Administrators had as yet only caused unpopularity. Baring's interference galled the Khedive and his Ministers. Vincent's parsimony excited contempt. Moncrieff's energy had convulsed the Irrigation Department. Wood's army was the laughing-stock of Europe. Among and beneath the rotten weeds and garbage of old systems and abuses the new seed was being sown. But England saw no signs of the crop; saw only the stubborn husbandmen begrimed with the dust and dirt, and herself hopelessly involved in the Egyptian muddle: and so in utter weariness and disgust, stopping her ears to the gibes and cat-calls of the Powers, she turned towards other lands and other matters.

The regeneration of Egypt is not a theme which would fall within the limits of this account. But the reorganisation of the Egyptian Army, the forging of the weapon of reconquest, is an essential feature. On the 20th of December 1882, the old Egyptian Army – or, rather, such parts as had escaped destruction – was disbanded by a single sentence of a British decree, and it was evident that some military body must replace that which had been swept away. All sorts of schemes for the employment of foreign legions or Turkish janissaries were devised. But Lord Dufferin adhered firmly to the principle of entrusting the defence of a country to its inhabitants, and it was determined to form a new

Egyptian Army. The force was intended only for the preservation of internal order and the defence of the southern and western frontiers of Egypt against the Bedouin Arabs. Six thousand men was the number originally drawn by conscription – for there are no volunteers in Egypt – from a population of more than 6,000,000. Twenty-six British officers – either poor men attracted by the high rates of pay, or ambitious allured by the increased authority – and a score of excellent drill-sergeants undertook the duty of teaching the recruits to fight. Sir Evelyn Wood directed the enterprise, and became the first British Sirdar of the Egyptian Army. The work began and immediately prospered. Within three months of its formation the army had its first review. The whole 6,000 paraded in their battalions and marched past the Khedive and their country's flag. Their bearing and their drill extorted the half-contemptuous praise of the indifferent spectators. Indeed, the new army differed greatly from the old. In the first place, it was paid. The recruits were treated with justice. Their rations were not stolen by the officers. The men were given leave to go to their villages from time to time. When they fell sick, they were sent to hospital instead of being flogged. In short, the European system was substituted for the Oriental.

It was hardly possible that the fertile soil and enervating climate of the Delta would have evolved a warrior race. Ages of oppression and poverty rarely produce proud and warlike spirits. The *fellah* soldier lacks the desire to kill. Even the Mohammedan religion has failed to excite his ferocity. He may be cruel. He is never fierce. Yet he is not without courage – a courage which bears pain and hardship in patience, which confronts ill-fortune with indifference, and which looks on death with apathetic composure. He has other military virtues. He is obedient, honest, sober, well-behaved, quick to learn, and, above all, physically strong. Generations of toiling ancestors, though they could not brace his nerves, have braced his muscles. Under the pressure of local circumstances there has been developed a creature who can work with little food, with little incentive, very hard for long hours under a merciless sun.

Such was the material out of which the British officers have formed the new Egyptian Army. At first, indeed, their task was embittered by the ridicule of their comrades in the British and Indian Services; but as the drill and bearing of the force improved, the thoughtless scorn would have been diverted from the Englishmen to fall only upon the Egyptian soldiers. But the British officers identified themselves with their men. Those who abused the *fellah* soldier were reminded that they insulted English gentlemen. Thus a strange bond of union was established between the officers and soldiers of the Egyptian Service; and although material forces may have accomplished much, without this moral factor the extraordinary results would never have been achieved.

The numbers of the army grew with its responsibilities. Up to the end of 1883 the infantry still consisted of eight *fellahin* battalions. In 1884 the first Soudanese battalion was raised. The black soldier was of a very different type from the *fellahin*. The Egyptian was strong, patient, healthy, and docile. The negro was in all these respects his inferior. His delicate lungs, slim legs, and loosely knit figure contrasted unfavourably with the massive frame and iron constitution of the peasant of the Delta. Always excitable and often insubordinate, he required the strictest discipline. But he possessed two tremendous military virtues. To the faithful loyalty of a dog he added the heart of a lion. He loved his officer, and feared nothing in the world. With the introduction of this element the Egyptian Army became a formidable military machine. In Lord Kitchener's campaigns on the Nile the losses in the six Soudanese battalions exceeded the aggregate of the whole of the rest of the army.

The service was hard and continual. Though the operations were petty, an untiring vigilance was imperative. A pitiless economy was everywhere enforced. The British officer was deprived of his leave and the Egyptian private of his rations, that a few pounds might be saved to the Egyptian Treasury. The clothing of the battalions wore thin and threadbare, and sometimes their boots were so bad that the soldiers' feet bled from the cutting edges of the rocks, and the convoy escorts left their trails behind them. But the army improved in efficiency, and the constant warfare began to produce, even among the *fellahin* infantry, experienced soldiers. The sword of reconquest was gradually sharpened; and when the process was almost complete, the man who was to wield it presented himself.

Horatio Herbert Kitchener, the eldest son of a lieutenant-colonel, was born in 1850, and, entered in 1869 the Royal Military Academy at

Woolwich as a cadet of the Royal Engineers. In the spring of 1871 he obtained his commission, and for the first ten years of his military service remained an obscure officer, performing his duties with regularity, but giving no promise of the talents and character which he was afterwards to display. One powerful weapon, however, he acquired in this time of waiting. In 1874 accident or instinct led him to seek employment in the surveys that were being made of Cyprus and Palestine, and in the latter country he learned Arabic. For six years the advantage of knowing a language with which few British officers were familiar brought him no profit. For procuring military preferment Arabic was in 1874 as valueless as Patagonian. All this was swiftly changed by the unexpected course of events. The year 1882 brought the British fleet to Alexandria, and the connection between England and Egypt began to be apparent. Kitchener did not neglect his opportunity. Securing leave of absence, he hurried to the scene of crisis. Alexandria was bombarded. Detachments from the fleet were landed to restore order. The British Government decided to send an army to Egypt.

Lord Wolseley soon found employment for the active officer who could speak Arabic. Kitchener served through the campaign of 1882 as a major. He joined the new army which was formed at the conclusion of the war, as one of the original twenty-six officers. In the Nile expedition of 1885 Arabic again led him to the front, and in the service of the Intelligence Department he found ample opportunity for his daring and energy. His efforts to communicate with Gordon in Khartoum did not, however, meet with much success, and the Journals bristle with so many sarcastic comments that their editor has been at pains to explain in his preface that there was really no cause for complaint. Major Kitchener, however, gave satisfaction to his superiors in Cairo, if not to the exacting General at Khartoum, and in 1886 he was appointed Governor of Suakin. This post, always one of responsibility and danger, did not satisfy Kitchener. Eager for more responsibility and more danger, he harried and raided the surrounding tribes; he restricted and almost destroyed the slender trade which was again springing up, and in consequence of his measures the neighbourhood of Suakin was soon in even greater ferment than usual. This culminated at the end of 1887 in the reappearance and advance of Osman Digna. The defences of the town had been greatly strengthened and improved by the skill and activity of its new Governor.[1] Osman Digna retreated. The 'friendlies' were incited to follow, and Kitchener, although he had been instructed not to employ British officers or Egyptian regulars in offensive operations, went out in support. At Handub on the morning of the 17th of January 1888, the friendlies attacked the camp of Osman Digna. They were at first successful; but while they dispersed to plunder the enemy rallied and, returning, drove them back with loss. Kitchener arrived on the field with the support, to find a defeat instead of a victory awaiting him. He bravely endeavoured to cover the retreat of the friendlies, and in so doing was severely – as it first seemed dangerously – wounded in the jaw. The loss among the friendlies and the support amounted to twenty men killed and two British officers and twenty-eight men wounded. The Governor returned in great pain and some discomfiture to Suakin. In spite of his wound and his reverse he was impatient to renew the conflict, but this was definitely forbidden by the British Government. 'The policy which it is desirable to follow . . . in the Eastern Soudan,' wrote Sir Evelyn Baring on the 17th of March, in measured rebuke, 'should consist in standing purely on the defensive against any hostile movement or combination of the Arab tribes, in avoiding any course of action which might involve the ultimate necessity of offensive action, and in encouraging legitimate trade by every means in our power.'[2]

The Governor could scarcely be expected to carry out a policy so much at variance with his views and inclinations, and in the summer of 1888 he was transferred to a purely military appointment and became Adjutant-General of the Egyptian Army. For the next four years he worked busily in the War Office at Cairo, effecting many useful reforms and hard economies, and revealing powers of organisation which were noticed by one vigilant eye. In 1892 Sir F. Grenfell resigned the post of Sirdar, and the chief command of the Egyptian Army was vacant. Two men stood out prominently as candidates – Colonel Wodehouse, who held the command of the Halfa Field Force, and the Adjutant-General. Colonel Wodehouse had undoubtedly the greater claims. He

[1] See despatch from Major-General Dormer to War Office, Cairo, 22nd April 1888: 'With regard to the military works and defences of the town, I was much struck with the great improvement that has been effected by Colonel Kitchener since my last visit to Suakin in the autumn of 1884.'

[2] Sir Evelyn Baring to Consul Cameron, 14th March 1888.

had been for several years in command of a large force in continual contact with the enemy. He had conducted the civil administration of the
frontier province with conspicuous success, and he was popular with all
ranks of the Egyptian Army. Kitchener had little to set against this. He had
shown himself a brave and active soldier. He was known to be a good
official. But he had not been in accord with the Government in his civil
administration, and was, moreover, little known to his brother officers.
Sir Evelyn Baring's influence, however, turned the scale. Somewhat,
therefore, to the astonishment of the Egyptian Army, Kitchener was
promoted Sirdar. Lord Cromer had found the military officer whom he
considered capable of reconquering the Soudan when the opportunity
should come.

The years of preparation, wasted by no one in Egypt, were employed
by no department better than by the Intelligence Branch. The greatest
disadvantage from which Lord Wolseley had suffered was the general
ignorance of the Soudan and its peoples. The Intelligence Branch of the
Egyptian Army rose under the direction of Colonel (now Sir Reginald) Wingate to an extraordinary efficiency. For ten years the history,
climate, geography, and inhabitants of the Soudan were the objects
of a ceaseless scrutiny. The sharp line between civilisation and savagery
was drawn at Wady Halfa; but beyond that line, up the great river,
within the great wall of Omdurman, into the arsenal, into the treasury,
into the mosque, into the Khalifa's house itself, the spies and secret
agents of the Government – disguised as traders, as warriors, or as
women – worked their stealthy way. By whatever route it came, information – whispered at Halfa, catalogued at Cairo – steadily accumulated, and the diaries of the Intelligence Department grew in weight
and number, until at last every important Emir was watched and located,
every garrison estimated, and even the endless intrigues and brawls
in Omdurman were carefully recorded.

The reports of the spies were at length confirmed and amplified by
two most important witnesses. At the end of 1891 Father Ohrwalder
made his escape from Omdurman and reached the Egyptian territory.
Besides giving the Intelligence Department much valuable information,
he published a thrilling account of his captivity,[1] which created a wide
and profound impression in England. In 1895 a still more welcome

[1] Ohrwalder, *Ten Years' Captivity*.

fugitive reached Assuan. Early on the 16th of March a weary, travel-stained Arab, in a tattered *jibba* and mounted on a lame and emaciated camel, presented himself to the Commandant. He was received with delighted wonder, and forthwith conducted to the best bathroom available. Two hours later a little Austrian gentleman stepped forth, and the telegraph hastened to tell the news that Slatin, sometime Governor of Darfur, had escaped from the Khalifa's clutches. Here at last was a man who knew everything that concerned the Dervish Empire. Slatin, the Khalifa's trusted and confidential servant, almost his friend, who had lived with him, who was even permitted to dine with him alone, who had heard all his counsels, who knew all his Emirs, and moreover Slatin, the soldier and administrator, who could appreciate all he had learned, was added with the rank of Pasha to the Staff of the Intelligence Department. While his accurate knowledge confirmed the belief of the Egyptian authorities that the Dervish power was declining, his tale of 'Fire and Sword in the Soudan' increased the horror and anger of thoughtful people in England at the cruelties of the Khalifa. Public opinion began to veer towards the policy of re-conquest.

The year 1895 brought in a Conservative and Unionist Administra-tion, supported by a majority which was so strong that there seemed little reason to expect a transference of power for five or six years. Ministers belonged chiefly to that party in the State which had con-sistently assailed Mr Gladstone's Egyptian policy. Here was an oppor-tunity of repairing the damage done by their opponents. The idea of reconquering the Soudan presented itself indefinitely, but not un-pleasingly, alike to the Government and the people of Great Britain. The unforeseen course of events crystallised the idea into a policy.

On the 1st of March 1896, the Battle of Adowa was fought, and Italy at the hands of Abyssinia sustained a crushing defeat. Two results followed. First, a great blow had been struck at European prestige in North Africa. It seemed probable that the Abyssinian success would encourage the Dervishes to attack the Italians at Kassala. It was possible that they might also attack the Egyptians at Suakin or on the Wady Halfa frontier. Secondly, the value of Italy as a factor in European politics was depreciated. The fact that her defeat had been assisted by the arms and munitions of war which had been supplied to the

Abyssinians from French and Russian sources complicated the situation. The Triple Alliance was concerned. The third partner had been weakened. The balance might be restored if Great Britain would make some open sign of sympathy.

In these circumstances the British Government determined to assist Italy by making a demonstration on the Wady Halfa frontier. They turned to Egypt. It had always been recognised that the recovery of the lost provinces was a natural and legitimate aspiration. 'The doubtful point was to decide the time when the military and financial resources of the country were sufficiently developed to justify an assumption of the offensive.'[1] From a purely Egyptian point of view the best possible moment had not yet arrived. A few more years of recuperation were needed. The country would fight the Soudan campaigns more easily if first refreshed by the great reservoirs which were projected. For more than two years both projects had been pressed upon the Government of his Highness the Khedive – or, to write definitely, upon Lord Cromer. At regular intervals Sir Herbert Kitchener and Sir William Garstin would successively visit the British Agency (it would be treason to call it 'Government House') – the one to urge the case for a war, the other to plead for a reservoir. The reservoir had won. Only a few weeks before the advance to Dongola was ordered Garstin met Kitchener returning from the Agency. 'I'm beaten,' said Kitchener abruptly; 'you've got your dam' – and Garstin went on his way rejoicing.

The decision of the British Government came therefore as a complete surprise to the Cairene authorities. The season of the year was unfavourable to military operations. The hot weather was at hand. The Nile was low. With the exception of a small raid on a village in the Wady Halfa district and an insignificant incursion into the Tokar Delta the Dervish forces had during the year maintained 'a strictly defensive attitude'.[2] Lord Cromer, however, realised that while the case for the reservoirs would always claim attention, the re-conquest of the Soudan might not receive the support of a Liberal Government. The increasing possibility of French intrigues upon the Upper Nile had also to be considered. All politics are series of compromises and bargains, and while the historian may easily mark what would have been the best possible

[1] Lord Cromer's Reports: Egypt, No. 2, 1896.
[2] Egypt, No. 1, 1896.

moment for any great undertaking, a good moment must content the administrator.

It will be convenient, before embarking upon the actual chronicle of the military operations, to explain how the money was obtained to pay for the war. About half the revenue of Egypt is devoted to the development and government of the country, and the other half to the payment of the interest on the debt and other external charges; and the London Convention in 1885 prescribed that the annual expenditure of Egypt shall not exceed a certain sum. When the expenditure exceeds this amount, for every pound that is spent on the government or development of Egypt another pound must be paid to the Commissioners of the Debt; so that, after the limit is reached, for every pound that is required to promote Egyptian interests two pounds must be raised by taxation from an already heavily taxed community. But the working of the law was found to be so severe that, like all laws which exceed the human conception of justice, it has been somewhat modified. By an arrangement which was effected in 1888, the Caisse de la Dette are empowered, instead of devoting *their* surplus pound to the sinking fund, to pay it into a general reserve fund, from which the Commissioners may make grants to meet 'extraordinary expenses'; those expenses, that is to say, which may be considered 'once for all' (capital) expenditure and not ordinary annual charges.

The Dongola expedition was begun, as has been said, without reference to the immediate internal condition of Egypt. It was obviously impossible for Egypt to provide for the extraordinary expenses of the military operations out of revenue. The Ministry of Finance therefore appealed to the Caisse de la Dette for a grant from the general reserve fund. Here was an obvious case of 'extraordinary expenses'. The Egyptian Government asked for £E500,000.

The Caisse met in council. Six Commissioners – representing England, France, Russia, Germany, Austria, and Italy – duly discussed the application. Four Commissioners considered that the grant should be made. Two Commissioners, those representing France and Russia, voted against it. The majority decided. The grant was made. The money was handed to the Egyptian Government and devoted to the prosecution of the war.

Egypt as a sovereign power had already humbly begged to be allowed to devote part of the surplus of her own revenues to her own objects. A greater humiliation remained. The Commissioners of France and Russia, who had been out-voted, brought an action against their colleagues on the grounds that the grant was *ultra vires*; and against the Egyptian Government for the return of the money thus wrongly obtained. Other actions were brought at French instigation by various people purporting to represent the bondholders, who declared that their interests were threatened. The case was tried before the Mixed Tribunals, an institution which exists in Egypt superior to and independent of the sovereign rights of that country.

The Mixed Tribunals, an international institution, delivered its judgement on strictly political grounds, the judges taking their orders from the different countries they represented. It was solemnly pronounced that war expenses were not 'extraordinary expenses'. A state of war was apparently regarded as usual in Egypt. On this wise and sensible ground the Egyptian Government were condemned to pay back £E500,000, together with interest and costs. After a momentary hesitation as to whether the hour had not come to join issue on the whole subject of the financial restrictions of Egypt, it was decided to bow to this iniquitous decision. The money had now to be refunded. It had already been spent. More than that, other sums were needed for the carrying on of the war. It was impossible to stop; yet without money it seemed impossible to go on; and, besides, it appeared that Egypt would be unable to repay the £E500,000 which she had been granted, and of which she was now deprived.

At this period France still exercised a considerable force on Egyptian politics. One Egyptian party, the weaker, but still by no means insignificant, looked towards her for support. The news of the French success cheered their hearts and raised their spirits. Orientals appreciate results. The result was a distinct reverse to the British. The conclusion to the native mind was obvious. Great Britain had been weighed in the European balances and found wanting.

But meanwhile the Consul-General telegraphed to Lord Salisbury, asking that he might be 'authorised to state directly that her Majesty's Government will be prepared to advance the money on conditions to be hereafter arranged'. The reply was prompt, though guarded. 'You are authorised,' said Lord Salisbury, 'by the Chancellor of the Exchequer to state that though of course the primary liability for the payment of the £E500,000 rests with the Egyptian Government, her Majesty's Government will hold themselves prepared to advance, on conditions to be decided hereafter, such a sum as they feel satisfied that the Egyptian Treasury is powerless to provide.'[1] This obvious development does not seem to have been foreseen by the French diplomatists, and when, on the 3rd of December, it was rumoured in Cairo that Great Britain was prepared to pay the money, a great feeling of astonishment and of uncertainty was created. But the chances of the French interference proving effective still seemed good. It was believed that the English Government would not be in a position to make an advance to the Egyptian Government until funds had been voted by Parliament for the purpose. It was also thought that Egypt would be utterly unable to find the money immediately. A complete disillusionment, however, awaited the French Government. The taxes in Egypt, as in other countries, are not collected evenly over the whole year. During some months there is a large cash balance in the Exchequer. In others the money drains in slowly. It happened at this period of the year, after the cotton crop had been gathered, that a considerable balance had accumulated in the Treasury, and on the guarantee of the English Government being received, to the effect that they would ultimately assist Egypt with regard to the expenses of the expedition, Lord Cromer determined to repay the money at once.

On the 5th of December the Egyptian Council of Ministers, presided over by the Khedive in person, decided on their own initiative to despatch an official letter expressing in warm terms their gratitude for the financial help offered them by her Majesty's Government.

On the 6th of December £E500,000, together with £E15,600 interest and costs, in gold, was conveyed in boxes in a cart from the Egyptian Treasury to the offices of the Caisse de la Dette. The effect was tremendous. The reverse of the French diplomacy was far greater even than its success had appeared.

---

[1] The original £500,000 was afterwards increased to £800,000; which sum was paid by the British Exchequer to the Egyptian Government, at first as a loan, and later as a gift.

CHAPTER V

THE BEGINNING OF THE WAR

Shortly before midnight on the 12th of March 1896, the Sirdar received instructions from Lord Cromer authorising an expedition into the Dongola province and directing him to occupy Akasha. The next morning the news was published in *The Times*, ostensibly as coming from its correspondent in Cairo: and the Egyptian Cabinet was convened to give a formal assent by voting the decree.

On Sunday, the 15th of March, three days after the Sirdar had received his orders, and before the first reinforcements had started from Cairo, Colonel Hunter, who commanded on the frontier, formed a small column of all arms to seize and hold Akasha. At dawn on the 18th the column started, and the actual invasion of the territory which for ten years had been abandoned to the Dervishes began. The route lay through a wild and rocky country – the debatable ground, desolated by years of war – and the troops straggled into a long procession, and had several times for more than an hour to move in single file over passes and through narrow defiles strewn with the innumerable boulders from which the 'Belly of Stones' has derived its name. The right of their line of march was protected by the Nile, and although it was occasionally necessary to leave the bank, to avoid difficult ground, the column camped each night by the river. The cavalry and the Camel Corps searched the country to the south and east; for it was expected that the Dervishes would resist the advance. Creeping along the bank, and prepared at a moment's notice to stand at bay at the water's edge, the small force proceeded on its way. Wady Atira was reached on the 18th, Tanjore on the 19th, and on the 20th the column marched into Akasha.

Akasha was now converted into a strong entrenched camp, in which an advanced base was formed. Its garrison of three battalions, a battery, and the mounted troops, drew their supplies by camel transport from

Sarras. The country to the south and east was continually patrolled, and the communications were further strengthened by the establishment of fortified posts at Semna, Wady Atira, and Tanjore. The friendly Arab tribes – Bedouin, Kabbabish, and Foggara – ranged still more widely in the deserts and occupied the scattered wells. All this time the Dervishes watched supinely from their position at Firket, and made no attempt to disturb the operations.

Meanwhile the concentration of the Egyptian Army on the frontier was proceeding. The line of communications from Cairo, the permanent base, to the advanced post at Akasha was 825 miles in length. But of this distance only the section lying south of Assuan could be considered as within the theatre of war. The ordinary broad-gauge railway ran from Cairo to Balliana, where a river base was established. From Balliana to Assuan reinforcements and supplies were forwarded by Messrs Cook's fleet of steamers, by barges towed by small tugs, and by a number of native sailing craft. A stretch of seven miles of railway avoids the First Cataract, and joins Assuan and Shellal. Above Shellal a second flotilla of gunboats, steamers, barges, and Nile boats was collected to ply between Shellal and Halfa. The military railway ran from Halfa to Sarras. South of Sarras supplies were forwarded by camels. To meet the increased demands of transport, 4,500 camels were purchased in Egypt and forwarded in boats to Assuan, whence they marched via Korosko to the front. The British Government had authorised the reconstruction of the military railway to Akasha, and a special railway battalion was collected at Assuan, through which place sleepers and other material at once began to pass to Sarras. The strategic railway construction will form the subject of a later chapter.

By the 1st of April, less than three weeks from the commencement of the advance, the whole line of communications had been organised and was working efficiently, although still crowded with the concentrating troops.

As soon as the 16th Battalion of reservists arrived at Suakin, the IXth Soudanese were conveyed by transports to Kossier, and marched thence across the desert to Kena. The distance was 120 miles, and the fact that in spite of two heavy thunderstorms – rare phenomena in Egypt – it was covered in four days is a notable example of the marching powers of the black soldiers. It had been determined that the Xth

Soudanese should follow at once, but circumstances occurred which detained them on the Red Sea littoral and must draw the attention of the reader thither.

The aspect and history of the town and port of Suakin might afford a useful instance to a cynical politician. Most of the houses stand on a small barren island which is connected with the mainland by a narrow causeway. At a distance the tall buildings of white coral present an imposing appearance, and the prominent chimneys of the condensing machinery – for there is scarcely any fresh water – seem to suggest manufacturing activity. But a nearer view reveals the melancholy squalor of the scene. A large part of the town is deserted. The narrow streets wind among the tumbled-down and neglected houses. The soil exhales an odour of stagnation and decay. The traveller who lands on Quarantine Island is first confronted with the débris of the projected Suakin–Berber Railway. Huge piles of railway material rot, unguarded and neglected, on the shore. Rolling stock of all kinds – carriages, trucks, vans, and ballast wagons – are strewn or heaped near the sheds. The Christian cemetery alone shows a decided progress, and the long lines of white crosses which mark the graves of British soldiers and sailors increase the depression of the visitor. The numerous graves of Greek traders protest that the climate of the island is pestilential.

The island on which the town stands is joined to the mainland by a causeway, at the further end of which is an arched gateway of curious design called 'the Gate of the Soudan'. Upon the mainland stands the crescent-shaped suburb of El Kaff. It comprises a few mean coral-built houses, a large area covered with mud huts inhabited by Arabs and fishermen, and all the barracks and military buildings. The whole is surrounded by a strong wall a mile and a half long, fifteen feet high, six feet thick, with a parapet pierced for musketry and strengthened at intervals by bastions armed with Krupp guns.

Three strong detached posts complete the defences of Suakin. Ten miles to the northward, on the scene of Sir H. Kitchener's unfortunate enterprise, is the fort of Handub. Tambuk is twenty-five miles inland and situate upon a high rock, and consisting only of a store, a formidable blockhouse, and a lookout tower, is safe from any enemy unprovided with artillery. Both Handub and Tambuk were at the outset of the campaign provisioned for four months. The third post, Tokar Fort, lies fifty miles along the coast to the south. Its function is to deprive the Arabs of a base in the fertile delta of the Tokar River. The fort is strong, defended by artillery, and requires for its garrison an entire battalion of infantry.

No description of Suakin would be complete without some allusion to the man to whom it owes its fame. Osman Digna had been for many years a most successful and enterprising Arab slave dealer. The attempted suppression of his trade by the Egyptian Government drove him naturally into opposition. He joined in the revolt of the Mahdi, and by his influence roused the whole of the Hadendoa and other powerful tribes of the Red Sea shore. Year after year, at a horrid sacrifice of men and money, the Imperial Government and the old slaver fought like wolves over the dry bone of Suakin. Often defeated, but never crushed, the wily Arab might justly boast to have run further and fought more than any Emir in the Dervish armies.

It had scarcely seemed possible that the advance on Dongola could influence the situation around Kassala, yet the course of events encouraged the belief that the British diversion in favour of Italy had been effective; for at the end of March – as soon, that is to say, as the news of the occupation of Akasha reached him – Osman Digna separated himself from the army threatening Kassala, and marched with 300 cavalry, 70 camelry, and 2,500 foot towards his old base in the Tokar Delta.

The state of affairs in the Eastern Soudan has always been turbulent. The Hadendoa and other tribes who lived under the walls of Suakin professed loyalty to the Egyptian Government, not from any conviction that their rule was preferable to that of Osman Digna, but simply for the sake of a quiet life. As their distance from Suakin increased, the loyalty of the tribesmen became even less pronounced, and at a radius of twenty miles all the Sheikhs oscillated alternately between Osman Digna and the Egyptian Government, and tried to avoid open hostilities with either. Omar Tita, Sheikh of the district round about Erkowit, found himself situated on this fringe of intriguing neutrality. Although he was known to have dealings with Osman, it was believed that if he had the power to choose he would side with the Egyptian Government. Early in April Omar Tita reported that Osman Digna was in the neighbourhood of Erkowit with a small force, and that he, the faithful ally of the Government, had on the 3rd of the month defeated him with a loss of four camels. He also said that if the Egyptian Government would send up a force to fight Osman, he, the aforesaid ally, would keep him in play until it arrived.

After a few days of hesitation and telegraphic communication with the Sirdar, Colonel Lloyd, the Governor of Suakin, who was then in very bad health, decided that he had not enough troops to justify him in taking the risk of going up to Erkowit to fight Osman. Around Suakin, as along the Indian frontier, a battle was always procurable on the shortest notice. In the present instance it was determined to have only a small-scale operation. The Governor therefore arranged a plan for a demonstration at the foot of the hills near Khor Wintri by means of combined movements from Suakin and Tokar. The garrison of Suakin consisted of the 1st and half the 5th Egyptian Battalions; the 16th Egyptian Reservists, who had just replaced the IXth Soudanese, and were as yet hardly formed into a military body; one squadron of cavalry, one company of Camel Corps, and some detachments of artillery. The garrison of Tokar consisted of the Xth Soudanese and a few gunners. From these troops there was organised in the second week in April, with all due ceremony, a 'Suakin Field Force'.

The plan of campaign was simple. Colonel Lloyd was to march out from Suakin and effect a junction with the 'Tokar Column' at Khor Wintri, where the Erkowit road enters the hills. It was then hoped that Osman Digna would descend and fight a battle of the required dimensions in the open; after which, if victorious, the force would return to Suakin and Tokar.

In order to make the Suakin Column as mobile as possible, the whole force was mounted on camels, of which more than 1,000 were requisitioned, as well as 60 mules and 120 donkeys. Six days' forage and rations, one day's reserve of water, 200 rounds per man, and 100 shell per gun were carried. At five o'clock on the afternoon of Tuesday, the 14th of April, the troops paraded outside the walls of Suakin, and bivouacked in the open ready to march at daylight.

The next morning the column, which numbered about 1,200 men of all arms, started. After marching for four or five hours in the direction of Khor Wintri the cavalry, who covered the advance, came in contact with the Dervish scouts. The force thereupon assumed an oblong formation: the mixed Soudanese company and the two guns in front, three Egyptian companies on each flank, the Camel Corps company in the rear, and the transport in the centre. The pace was slow, and, since few of the camels had ever been saddled or ridden, progress was often interrupted by their behaviour and by the broken and difficult nature of the country. Nevertheless at about four o'clock in the afternoon, Teroi Wells, eight miles from Khor Wintri, were reached; and here, having marched nineteen miles, Colonel Lloyd determined to halt. While the infantry were making the *zeriba*, the cavalry were sent on under Captain Fenwick (an infantry officer employed on the Staff) to gain touch with the Tokar force, who were expected to have already reached the rendezvous. Apparently under the belief that Omar Tita and his Arabs would give timely notice of an attack, the cavalry seem to have neglected many of the usual precautions, and in consequence at about five o'clock, when approaching Khor Wintri, they found themselves suddenly confronted with a force of about 200 Dervish horsemen supported by a large body of infantry. The squadron wheeled about with promptitude, and began to retire at a trot. The Dervish horsemen immediately pursued. The result was that the Egyptians began a disorderly flight at a gallop through the thick and treacherous scrub and over broken, dangerous ground. Sixteen horses fell; their riders were instantly speared by the pursuers. Rallying thirty-eight troopers, Captain Fenwick seized a rocky hillock, and dismounting with the natural instinct of an infantry soldier, prepared to defend himself to the last. The remainder of the squadron continued their flight, and thirty-two troopers, under an Egyptian officer (whose horse is said to have bolted), arrived at the Teroi *zeriba* with the news that their comrades had been destroyed, or had perhaps 'returned to Suakin', and that they themselves had been closely followed by the enemy. The news caused the gravest anxiety, which was aggravated towards midnight, when the Dervishes began to approach the *zeriba*. In the darkness what was thought to be a body of horsemen was seen moving along a shallow *khor* opposite the right face of the defence. At the same moment a loud yell was raised by the enemy on the other side. An uncontrolled musketry fire immediately broke out. The guns fired blindly up the valley;

the infantry wildly on all sides. The fusillade continued furiously for some time, and when by the efforts of the British officers the troops were restrained, it was found that the Dervishes had retired, leaving behind them a single wounded man.

Meanwhile Captain Fenwick maintained his solitary and perilous position on the hillock. He was soon surrounded by considerable bodies of the enemy, and as soon as it became dark he was sharply attacked. But the Dervishes fortunately possessed few rifles, and the officers and troopers, by firing steady volleys, succeeded in holding their ground and repulsing them. The sound of the guns at Teroi encouraged the Egyptians and revealed the direction of their friends. With the daylight the Dervishes, who seem throughout the affair to have been poor-spirited fellows, drew off, and the detachment, remounting, made haste to rejoin the main body.

The force, again united, pursued their way to Khor Wintri, where they found the column from Tokar already arrived. Marching early on the 15th, Major Sidney with 250 men of the Xth Soudanese, the only really trustworthy troops in the force, had reached Khor Wintri the same afternoon.

Up to this point Colonel Lloyd's plan had been successfully carried out. The columns from Suakin and Tokar had effected a junction at Khor Wintri on the Erkowit road. It now remained to await the attack of Osman Digna, and inflict a heavy blow upon him. It was decided, however, in view of what had occurred, to omit this part of the scheme, and both forces returned together without delay to Suakin, which they reached on the 18th, having lost in the operations eighteen Egyptian soldiers killed and three wounded.

After the affair of Khor Wintri it was evident that it would not be possible to leave Suakin to the defence only of the 16th Battalion of Reservists. On the other hand, Sir H. Kitchener required every soldier the Egyptian Army could muster to carry out the operations on the Nile. It was therefore determined to send Indian troops to Suakin to garrison the town and forts, and thus release the Xth Soudanese and the Egyptian battalions for the Dongola Expedition. Accordingly early in the month of May the Indian Army authorities were ordered to prepare a brigade of all arms for service in Egypt.

The troops selected were as follows: 26th Bengal Infantry, 35th

Sikhs, 1st Bombay Lancers, 5th Bombay Mountain Battery, two Maxim guns, one section Queen's Own (Madras) Sappers and Miners – in all about 4,000 men. The command was entrusted to Colonel Egerton, of the Corps of Guides.

On the 30th of May the dreary town of Suakin was enlivened by the arrival of the first detachments, and during the following week the whole force disembarked at the rotten piers and assumed the duties of the defence.

The Indian contingent landed in the full expectation of being immediately employed against the enemy. After a week, when all the stores had been landed, officers and men spent their time speculating when the order to march would come. It was true that there was no transport in Suakin, but that difficulty was easily overcome by rumours that 5,000 camels were on their way from the Somali coast to enable the force to move on Kassala or Berber. As these did not arrive, General Egerton sent in a proposed scheme to the Sirdar, in which he undertook to hold all the advanced posts up to the Kokreb range, if he were supplied with 1,000 camels for transport. A characteristic answer was returned, to the effect that it was not intended to use the Indian contingent as a mobile force. They had come as a garrison for Suakin, and a garrison for Suakin they should remain. This information was not, however, communicated to the troops, who continued to hope for orders to advance until the fall of Dongola.

The heat when the contingent arrived was not great, but as the months wore on the temperature rose steadily, until in August and September the thermometer rarely fell below 103° during the night, and often rose to 115° by day. Dust storms were frequent. A veritable plague of flies tormented the unhappy soldiers. The unhealthy climate, the depressing inactivity, and the scantiness of fresh meat or the use of condensed water, provoked an outbreak of scurvy. At one time nearly all the followers and 50 per cent of the troops were affected. Several large drafts were invalided to India. All the Europeans suffered acutely from prickly heat. Malarial fever was common. There were numerous cases of abscess on the liver. Twenty-five per cent of the British officers were invalided to England or India, and only six escaped a stay in hospital. The experiences of the battalion holding Tokar Fort were even worse than those of the troops in Suakin. At length the longed-for time of departure arrived. With feelings of relief and delight the Indian contingent shook the dust of Suakin off their feet and returned to India. It is a satisfaction to pass from the dismal narrative of events in the Eastern Soudan to the successful campaign on the Nile.

By the middle of April the concentration on the frontier was completed. Eleven thousand troops had been massed at and beyond Wady Halfa. But no serious operations could take place until a strong reserve of stores had been accumulated at the front. Meanwhile the army waited, and the railway grew steadily. The battalions were distributed in three principal fortified camps – Halfa, Sarras, and Akasha – and detachments held the chain of small posts which linked them together.

Including the North Staffordshire Regiment, the garrison of Wady Halfa numbered about 3,000 men. The town and cantonment, nowhere more than 400 yards in width, straggle along the river-bank, squeezed in between the water and the desert, for nearly three miles. The houses, offices, and barracks are all built of mud, and the aspect of the place is brown and squalid. The whole town is protected towards the deserts by a ditch and mud wall; and heavy Krupp field-pieces are mounted on little bastions where the ends of the rampart rest upon the river. Five small detached forts strengthen the land front, and the futility of an Arab attack at this time was evident. Halfa had now become the terminus of a railway, which was rapidly extending; and the continual arrival and despatch of tons of material, the building of sheds, workshops, and storehouses lent the African slum the bustle and activity of a civilised city.

Sarras Fort is an extensive building, perched on a crag of black rock rising on the banks of the Nile about thirty miles south of Halfa. During the long years of preparation it had been Egypt's most advanced outpost and the southern terminus of the military railway. The beginning of the expedition swelled it into an entrenched camp, holding nearly 6,000 men. From each end of the black rock on which the fort stood a strong stone wall and wire entanglement ran back to the river. The space thus enclosed was crowded with rows of tents and lines of animals and horses; and in the fort Colonel Hunter, commanding the district known as 'Sarras and the South', had his headquarters.

The railway reconstruction followed the old track which had been prepared through the desert in 1885. The convoy route wound along by the river. Both were protected from attack. The 7th Egyptians guarded Railhead, while the chain of small posts secured the road by the Nile to Akasha. The advanced base grew during the months of April and May into a strong position.

The Sirdar, accompanied by Colonel Rundle, his Chief of Staff, had left Cairo on the 22nd of March, and after a short stay at Assuan reached Wady Halfa on the 29th. Here he remained during the month of April, superintending and pressing the extension of the railroad and the accumulation of supplies. On the 1st of May he arrived at Akasha, with a squadron of cavalry, under Major Burn-Murdoch, as his escort.

During May the preparations for the advance on the Dervish position at Firket continued, and towards the end of the month it became evident that they were nearly complete. The steady accumulation of stores at Akasha had turned that post into a convenient base from which the force might operate for a month without drawing supplies of any kind from the north. The railway, which had progressed at the rate of about half a mile a day, had reached and was working to Ambigole Wells, where a four-gun fort and entrenchment had been built. The distance over which convoys must plod was reduced by half, and the business of supply was doubly accelerated. By degrees the battalions and squadrons began to move forward towards Akasha. Sarras, deprived of its short-lived glory, became again the solitary fort on a crag. Wady Halfa was also deserted, and, except for the British battalion in garrison, could scarcely boast a soldier. Both the Egyptian battalions from Suakin had arrived on the Nile. The Xth Soudanese were on their way. The country beyond Akasha had been thoroughly reconnoitred and mapped to within three miles of the Dervish position. Everything was ready.

The actual concentration may be said to have begun on the 1st of June. Construction work on the railway came to a full stop. The railway battalions, dropping their picks and shovels, shouldered their Remington rifles and became the garrisons of the posts on the line of communications. On the 2nd of June the correspondents were permitted to proceed to Akasha. On the 3rd the Xth Soudanese passed through Ambigole and marched south. The Horse battery from Halfa followed. The Egyptian battalions and squadrons which had been camped along the river at convenient spots from Ambigole to Akasha marched to a point opposite Okma. Between this place and the advanced post an extensive camp, stretching three miles along the Nile bank, arose with magic swiftness. On the 4th the 7th Egyptians moved from Railhead, and with these the last battalion reached the front. Nine thousand men, with ample supplies, were collected within striking distance of the enemy.

CHAPTER VI

FIRKET

7th June 1896

Since the end of 1895 the Dervish force in Firket had been under the command of the Emir Hammuda, and it was through the indolence and neglect of this dissipated Arab that the Egyptian Army had been able to make good its position at Akasha without any fighting. Week after week the convoys had straggled unmolested through the difficult country between Sarras and the advanced base. No attack had been made upon the brigade at Akasha. No enterprise was directed against its communications. This fatal inactivity did not pass unnoticed by Wad Bishara, the Governor of Dongola; but although he was nominally in supreme command of all the Dervish forces in the province he had hardly any means of enforcing his authority. His rebukes and exhortations, however, gradually roused Hammuda, and during May two or three minor raids were planned and executed, and the Egyptian position at Akasha was several times reconnoitred.

Bishara remained unsatisfied, and at length, despairing of infusing energy into Hammuda, he ordered his subordinate Osman Azrak to supersede him. Osman was a Dervish of very different type. He was a fanatical and devoted believer in the Mahdi and a loyal follower of the Khalifa. For many years he had served on the northern frontier of the Dervish Empire, and his name was well known to the Egyptian Government as the contriver of the most daring and the most brutal raids. His cruelty to the wretched inhabitants of the border villages had excluded him from all hope of mercy should he ever fall into the hands of the enemy. Among the Emirs gathered at Firket there was none whose death would have given greater satisfaction to the military authorities than the man who was now to replace Hammuda.

The force which the Sirdar had concentrated for the capture of

Firket amounted to about nine thousand men, and was organised as follows:

Commander-in-Chief: THE SIRDAR
The Infantry Division: COLONEL HUNTER Commanding

1st Brigade	2nd Brigade	3rd Brigade
MAJOR LEWIS	MAJOR MACDONALD	MAJOR MAXWELL
3rd Egyptians	IXth Soudanese	2nd Egyptians
4th ,,	XIth ,,	7th ,,
Xth Soudanese	XIIth ,,	8th ,,
	XIIIth ,,	

Mounted Forces: MAJOR BURN-MURDOCH

Egyptian Cavalry	7 squadrons
Camel Corps	8 companies

Artillery

Horse Artillery	1 battery
Field Artillery	2 batteries
Maxim Guns	1 battery

Two roads led from Akasha to Firket – one by the bank of the river, the other inland and along the projected railway line. The Sirdar determined to avail himself of both. The force was therefore divided into two columns. The main column, under command of the Sirdar, was to move by the river road, and consisted of the infantry division, the Field Artillery, and the Maxim guns. The Desert Column, under command of Major Burn-Murdoch, consisted of the mounted forces, the Horse Artillery, and one battalion of infantry (the XIIth Soudanese) drawn from MacDonald's brigade and mounted upon camels: in all about two thousand men.

The infantry column began to march out of Akasha at 3.30 in the afternoon of the 6th, and trailed southwards along the track by the river in the following order: Lewis's brigade, with the Xth Soudanese leading; two Maxim guns and the artillery; MacDonald's brigade; Maxwell's brigade; and lastly, the field hospitals and a half-battalion forming rearguard. The Sirdar marched behind the artillery. The rear of the long column was clear of the camp by 4.30, and about two hours later the mounted force started by the desert road. The River Column made good progress till dark, but thereafter the advance was slow and tedious. The track was so narrow that it nowhere allowed a larger front to be formed than of four men abreast. In some places the sharp rocks and crumbling heaps of stone almost stopped the gun-mules altogether, while the infantry tripped and stumbled painfully. The moon had not risen, and the darkness was intense. Still the long procession of men, winding like a whiplash between the jagged hills, toiled onward through the night, with no sound except the tramping of feet and the rattle of accoutrements. At half past ten the head of Lewis's brigade debouched into a smooth sandy plain about a mile to the north of Sarkamatto village. This was the spot – scarcely three miles from the enemy's position – where the Sirdar had decided to halt and bivouac.

Meanwhile the mounted force were also on their way. Like the River Column, they were disordered by the broken ground, and the XIIth Soudanese, who were unused to camel riding and mounted only on transport saddles, were soon wearied. After one o'clock many men, both in the Camel Corps and in the battalion, fell asleep on their camels, and the officers had great difficulty in keeping them awake. However, the force reached their point of concentration – about three miles to the south-east of Firket – at a quarter to three.

The Sirdar moved on again with the infantry at 2.30. The moon had risen over the rocks, but it was only a thin crescent and did not give much light. The very worst part of the whole track was encountered immediately the bivouac was left, and the column of nearly six thousand men had to trickle through one narrow place in single file. There were already signs of the approach of dawn; the Dervish camp was near; the Sirdar and his Staff began to look anxious. He sent many messages to the leading battalions to hurry; and the soldiers, although now very weary, ran and scrambled through the difficult passage like sheep crowding through a gate. By four o'clock the leading brigade had cleared the obstacle, and the most critical moment seemed to have passed.

The great mass of Firket mountain, still dark in the half-light, now rose up on the left of the line of march. Between it and the river stretched a narrow strip of scrub-covered ground; and here, though obstructed by the long grass, bushes, palm-trees, and holes, the leading brigade was ordered to deploy. There was, however, as yet only room for the Xth Soudanese to form line, and the 3rd and 4th Egyptians contented themselves with widening to column of companies – the 3rd in rear of the right of the Xth, the 4th in rear of the centre. The force now began to emerge from the narrow space between the hills and the river, and debouch into open country. As the space widened No. 1 Field battery came into line on the left, and No. 2 on the right of the Xth Soudanese. A swell of ground hid Firket village, though it was known to be within a mile, and it was now daylight. Still there was no sign that the Dervishes were prepared. It seemed scarcely possible to believe that the advance had not yet been discovered. The silence seemed to forbode some unexpected attack. The leading brigade and guns halted for a few minutes to allow MacDonald to form his battalions from 'fours' into column of companies. Then at five o'clock the advance was resumed, and at this moment from the shoulder of Firket mountain there rang out a solitary shot. The Dervish outposts had at last learned their danger. Several other shots followed in quick succession, and were answered by a volley from the Xth, and then from far away to the south-east came the report of a field-gun. The Horse Artillery battery had come into action. The operation of the two columns was simultaneous: the surprise of the enemy was complete.

The great object was now to push on and deploy as fast as possible. The popping of musketry broke out from many points, and the repeated explosions of the Horse battery added to the eager excitement of the troops. The Xth Soudanese had now reached the top of the rise which had hidden Firket, and the whole scene came into view. To the right front the village of Firket stretched by the side of the river – a confusion of mud houses nearly a mile in length and perhaps 300 yards broad. On the landward side the tents and straw shelters of the Dervish force showed white and yellow. A system of mud walls and loopholed houses strengthened the northern end of the village. Behind it as a background stood lines and clusters of palm-trees, through which the broad river and the masts of the Arab boats might be seen. In front of the troops, but a little to their left, rose a low rocky ridge surmounted with flags and defended by a stone breastwork running along its base. Across the open space between the village and the hill hundreds of Dervishes on horse and on foot were hurrying to man their defences, and others scrambled up the rocks to see for themselves the numbers of the enemy.

The attack developed very rapidly. The narrow passage between the mountain and the river poured forth its brigades and battalions, and the firing-line stretched away to the right and left with extra-ordinary speed. The Xth Soudanese opened fire on the village as soon as they topped the rise. The 3rd and 4th Egyptians deployed on the right and left of the leading regiment, two companies of the 4th extending down on to the foreshore below the steep river-bank. Peake's battery (No. 1) and the Maxim guns, coming into action from a spur of Firket mountain, began to fire over the heads of the advancing infantry.

The whole of Lewis's brigade now swung to the right and attacked the village; MacDonald's, coming up at the double in line of battalion columns, deployed to the left, inland, round the shoulder of the mountain, and, bearing away still more to the left, advanced swiftly upon the rocky ridge. The ground in MacDonald's front was much broken by boulders and scrub, and a deep *khor* delayed the advance. The enemy, though taken at obvious disadvantage, maintained an irregular fire; but the Soudanese, greatly excited, pressed on eagerly towards the breastworks. When the brigade was still 200 yards from the ridge, about fifty Dervish horsemen dashed out from among the rocks and charged the left flank. All were immediately shot down by a wild but heavy independent fire. With joyful yells the blacks broke into a run and carried the breastworks at the bayonet. The Dervishes did not await the shock. As soon as they saw their horsemen – among whom was the Emir Hammuda himself and Yusef Angar, Emir of the Jehadia – swept away, they abandoned the first ridge and fell back on another which lay behind. The Soudanese followed closely, and pursued the outnumbered enemy until at last the hills were cleared of all except the dead, and the fugitives were running towards the river-bank.

While MacDonald's brigade was storming the hills, Lewis's had advanced on the village and the Dervish camp. The Arabs made a stubborn resistance, and the 4th battalion by the river-bank were sharply engaged. Encouraged by their enormous superiority in number and weapons, the Egyptians showed considerable zeal in the attack, and their conduct on this occasion was regarded as a very happy augury for the war.

As Lewis's brigade had swung to its right, and MacDonald's had borne away to the left, a wide gap had opened in the centre of the attack. This was immediately filled by Maxwell's brigade, so that the whole force was now formed in one line, which curved and wheeled continually to the right until, by the time the rocky hills had been taken, all three brigades practically faced west and were advancing together towards the Nile. The Dervishes – penned between the river and the enemy, and unable to prevent the remorseless advance – now thought only of flight, and they could be seen galloping hither and thither seeking for some means of escape. The position of the Desert Column would have enabled the XIIth Soudanese, by moving down to the river, to cut off this line of retreat; but the foreshore of the river at the southern end of Firket is concealed from a landward view by the steep bank, and by this sandy path the greater number of the fugitives found safety.

The three brigades now closed upon the village and, clearing it step by step, advanced to the water's edge. MacDonald's brigade did not indeed stop until they had crossed the swampy isthmus and occupied the island. The Arabs, many of whom refused quarter, resisted desperately, and more than eighty corpses were afterwards found in one group of buildings. By 7.20 all firing had ceased; the entire Dervish camp was in the hands of the Egyptian troops, and the engagement of Firket was over.

The local inhabitants, tired of the ceaseless war which had desolated the frontier province for so long, welcomed their new masters with an appearance of enthusiasm. The main pursuit stopped at Suarda, but a week later two squadrons and sixteen men of the Camel Corps, under Captain Mahon, were pushed out twenty miles further south, and an Arab store of grain was captured.

The Dervish loss in action was severe. More than 800 dead were left on the field, and there were besides 500 wounded and 600 prisoners. The casualties in the Egyptian Army were 1 British officer – Captain Legge – wounded, 20 native soldiers killed and 83 wounded.

Firket is officially classed as a general action: special despatches were written, and a special clasp struck. The whole operation was well and carefully planned, and its success in execution was complete. The affair caused great satisfaction in England, and the further prosecution of the campaign was looked for with increasing interest.

CHAPTER VII

THE RECOVERY OF THE DONGOLA PROVINCE

Countless and inestimable are the chances of war. Those who read the story, and still more those who share the dangers, of a campaign feel that every incident is surrounded with a host of possibilities, any one of which, had it become real, would have changed the whole course of events.

The 'Sirdar's luck' became almost proverbial in the Soudan. As the account progresses numerous instances will suggest themselves. But after Firket all things were contrary. One unexpected misfortune succeeded another. Difficulties were replaced by others as soon as they had been overcome. The autumn of 1896 was marked by delay and disappointment. The state of the Nile, the storms, the floods, the cholera, and many minor obstacles, vexed but did not weary the commander. The army had made one spring forward; it must now gather energy for another. A strong camp was formed at Firket. MacDonald's brigade occupied Suarda two days after the fight, and this place now became the advanced post, just as Akasha had been in the first phase of the campaign. The accumulation of stores at Firket and Suarda began forthwith. Owing to the arrangements which had been made before the engagement it was possible to collect within one week of the action two months' supplies at Suarda for the garrison of 2,000 men, and one month's at Firket for the 7,000 troops encamped there. Thereafter, however, the necessity of hurrying the railway construction and the considerable daily demands of 9,000 men only allowed this margin to be increased very gradually.

The army had now passed beyond the scope of a pack-animal system of supply, except for very short distances, and it was obvious that they could only advance in future along either the railway or a navigable reach of the river, and preferably along both. From the Dal Cataract near Kosheh there is a clear waterway at high Nile to Merawi. To Kosheh, therefore, the railway must be extended before active operations could recommence. A third condition had also to be observed. For the expulsion of the Dervishes from Kerma and Dongola it was desirable that a flotilla of gunboats should co-operate with the land forces. Four of these vessels – the *Tamai*, *El Teb*, the *Metemma*, and the *Abu Klea*; and three steamers – the *Kaibar*, *Dal*, and *Akasha*, which it was proposed to arm – had, since 1885, patrolled the river from Assuan to Wady Halfa, and assisted in protecting the frontier from Dervish raids. All seven were now collected at the foot of the Second Cataract, and awaited the rise of the river to attempt the passage. To strengthen the flotilla three new and very powerful gunboats had been ordered in England. These were to be brought in sections over the railway to a point above the Second Cataract, and be fitted together there. It was thus necessary to wait, firstly, for the railway to reach Kosheh; secondly, for the Nile to rise; thirdly, for the old gunboats to ascend the Cataract; fourthly, for the new gunboats to be launched on the clear waterway; and, fifthly, for the accumulation of supplies. With all these matters the Sirdar now busied himelf.

The reconstruction of the railway to Akasha and its extension beyond this place towards Kosheh was pressed forward. Kosheh is six miles south of Firket, and consists, like most places in the 'Military Soudan', of little more than a name and a few ruined mud-huts which were once a village. On the 5th of July the whole camp was moved thither from the scene of the action. The reasons were clear and apparent. Kosheh is a point on the river above the Dal Cataract whence a clear waterway runs at high Nile to beyond Dongola. The camp at Firket had become foul and insanitary. The dysentery which had broken out was probably due to the 'green' water of the Nile; for during the early period of the flood what is known as 'the false rise' washes the filth and sewage off the foreshore all along the river, and brings down the green and rotting vegetation from the spongy swamps of Equatoria. The water is then dangerous and impure. There was nothing else for the army to drink; but it was undesirable to aggravate the evil by keeping the troops in a dirty camp.

The earliest freight which the railway carried to Kosheh was the first

of the new stern-wheel gunboats. Train after train arrived with its load
of steel and iron, or with the cumbrous sections of the hull, and a war-
ship in pieces – engines, armaments, fittings, and stores – soon lay
stacked by the side of the river. An improvised dockyard, equipped with
powerful twenty-ton shears and other appliances, was established, and
the work of fitting and riveting together the hundreds of various parts
proceeded swiftly. The new gunboats were in every way remarkable.
The old vessels had been 90 feet long. These were 140 feet. Their
breadth was 24 feet. They steamed twelve miles an hour. They had a
command of 30 feet. Their decks were all protected by steel plates, and
prepared by loopholed shields for musketry. Their armament was
formidable. Each carried one twelve-pounder quick-firing gun forward,
two six-pounder quick-firing guns in the central battery, and four
Maxim guns. Every modern improvement – such as ammunition hoists,
telegraphs, search-lights, and steam-winches – was added. Yet with all
this they drew only thirty-nine inches of water.

The vessels and machinery had been constructed and erected in the
works in London; they were then marked, numbered, and taken to
pieces, and after being transported to the front were finally put together
at Kosheh. Although in a journey of 4,000 miles they were seven times
transhipped, not a single important piece was lost.

The convenience of Kosheh on the clear waterway, and the dirty
condition of Firket, were in themselves sufficient reasons for the change
of camp; but another and graver cause lay behind. During the month of
June an epidemic of cholera began to creep up the Nile from Cairo.
On the 29th there were some cases at Assuan. On the 30th it reached
Wady Halfa. In consequence of this the North Staffordshire Regiment
marched into camp at Gemai. During the sixteen-mile march along the
railway track to Gemai the first fatal case occurred, and thereafter the
sickness clung to the regiment until the middle of August, causing continual deaths.

The cholera spread steadily southward up the river, claiming successive victims in each camp. In the second week of July it reached the
new camp at Kosheh, whence all possible precautions to exclude it had
proved vain. The epidemic was at first of a virulent form. Of the first
thousand cases between Assuan and Suarda nearly eight hundred
proved fatal. Nor were the lives thus lost to be altogether measured by

the number.[1] To all, the time was one of trial, almost of terror. The Egyptians, in spite of their fatalistic creed, manifested profound depression. The English soldiers were moody and ill-tempered. Even the light-hearted Soudanese lost their spirits.

At length the epidemic was stamped out, and by the middle of August it had practically ceased to be a serious danger. But the necessity of enforcing quarantine and other precautions had hampered movement up and down the line of communications, and so delayed the progress of the preparations for an advance.

Other unexpected hindrances arose. Sir H. Kitchener had clearly recognised that the railway, equipped as it then was, would be at the best a doubtful means for the continual supply of a large force many miles ahead of it. He therefore organised an auxiliary boat service and passed *gyassas* and *nuggurs*[2] freely up the Second Cataract. During the summer months, in the Soudan, a strong north wind prevails, which not only drives the sailing-boats up against the stream – sometimes at the rate of twenty miles a day – but also gratefully cools the air. This year, for forty consecutive days, at the critical period of the campaign, the wind blew hot and adverse from the south. The whole auxiliary boat service was thus practically arrested. But in spite of these aggravating obstacles the preparations for the advance were forced onwards, and it soon became necessary for the gunboats and steamers to be brought on to the upper reach of the river.

The Second Cataract has a total descent of sixty feet, and is about nine miles long. For this distance the Nile flows down a rugged stairway formed by successive ledges of black granite. The flood river deeply submerges these steps, and rushes along above them with tremendous force, but with a smooth though swirling surface. As the Nile subsides, the steps begin to show, until the river tumbles violently from ledge to ledge, its whole surface for miles churned to the white foam of broken water, and thickly studded with black rocks. At the

---

[1] The attacks and deaths from cholera in the Dongola Expeditionary Force were as follows:

	Attacks	Deaths
British troops	24	19
Native troops	406	260
Followers	788	640

[2] Native sailing craft.

Second Cataract, moreover, the only deep channel of the Nile is choked
between narrow limits, and the stream struggles furiously between
stern walls of rock. These dark gorges present many perils to the
navigator. The most formidable, the Bab-el-Kebir, is only thirty-five
feet wide. The river here takes a plunge of ten feet in seventy yards, and
drops five feet at a single bound. An extensive pool above, formed by
the junction of two arms of the river, increases the volume of the water
and the force of the stream, so that the 'Gate' constitutes an obstacle of
difficulty and danger.

Everything depended upon the rise of the river, and in the perversity
of circumstances the river this year rose much later and slower than
usual. By the middle of August, however, the attempt appeared
possible. On the 14th the first gunboat, the *Metemma*, approached the
Cataract. The North Staffordshire Regiment from Gemai, and the 6th
and 7th Egyptian Battalions from Kosheh, marched to the 'Gate' to
draw the vessel bodily up in spite of the current. The best native pilots
had been procured. Colonel Hunter and the naval officers under Commander Colville directed the work. The boat had been carefully prepared for the ordeal. To reduce, by raising the free-board, the risk of
swamping, the bows were heightened and strengthened, and stout
wooden bulwarks were built running from bow to stern. Guns and
ammunition were then removed, and the vessel lightened by every
possible means. A strop of wire rope was passed completely round the
hull, and to this strong belt the five cables were fastened – two on each
side and one at the bow. So steep was the *slope of the water* that it was
found necessary to draw all the fires, and the steamer was thus dependent entirely upon external force. It was luckily possible to obtain
a direct pull, for a crag of black rock rose above the surface of the
pool opposite the 'Gate'. On this a steel block was fixed, and the
hawser was led away at right angles until it reached the east bank,
where a smooth stretch of sand afforded a convenient place for the
hauling parties. Two thousand men were then set to pull at the cables,
yet such was the extraordinary force of the current that, although the
actual distance in which these great efforts were necessary was scarcely
one hundred yards, the passage of each steamer occupied an hour and
a half, and required the most strenuous exertions of the soldiers. No
accident, however, occurred, and the six other vessels accomplished

the ascent on successive days. In a week the whole flotilla steamed safely in the open water of the upper reach.

And now for a moment it seemed that the luck of the expedition had returned. The cholera was practically extinct. All the seven steamers which had passed the Cataract arrived in a stately procession opposite the camp. Almost at the same time the wind changed to the north, and a cool and delicious breeze refreshed the weary men and bore southward to Suarda a whole fleet of sailing boats laden with supplies, which had been lying weather-bound during the previous six weeks at the head of the rapids. At last the miserable delay was over.

From Kosheh to Kerma, the first Dervish position, the distance by river is 127 miles. By land marches this can be shortened by nearly forty-one miles; thirty miles being saved by cutting across the great loop of the Nile from Kosheh to Sadin Fanti, and eleven miles by avoiding the angle from Fereig to Abu Fatmeh. From Kerma to Dongola, which latter town was the objective of the expedition, a further distance of thirty-five miles must be traversed, making a total of 120 miles by land or 161 by river. The long desert march from Kosheh to Sadin Fanti was the only natural difficulty by land. Although the river from Kosheh to Kerma is broken by continual rapids, it is, with one interval, freely navigable at half Nile. At Hannek the three miles of islands, rocks, rapids, and broken water which are called the Third Cataract are, except at high Nile, a formidable barrier. Once this is passed, there is open water for more than 200 miles at all seasons to Merawi. The banks of the river, except near Sadin Fanti, where the hills close in, are flat and low. The eastern bank is lined with a fringe of palm-trees and a thin strip of cultivation, which constitutes what is called 'the fertile province of Dongola'. On the other side the desert reaches the water's edge. Along the right bank of this part of the river the army was now to move.

The first act of the advance was the occupation of Absarat, and on the 23rd of August MacDonald's brigade marched thither from Suarda, cutting across the desert to Sadin Fanti, and then following the bank of the Nile. The occupation of Absarat covered the next movement. On the 26th Lewis's brigade was ordered to march across the loop from Kosheh to Sadin Fanti, and reinforce the brigade at Absarat. The distance of thirty-seven miles was far too great to be

accomplished without a system of watering-places. This the Sirdar
rapidly organised. Water-depôts were formed by carrying tanks and
water-skins on camels to two points in the desert, and replenishing
them by daily convoys. But now a heavy calamity descended on the
arrangements of the General and the hopes of the troops.

During the afternoon of the 25th the wind veered suddenly to the
south, and thereupon a terrific storm of sand and rain, accompanied by
thunder and lightning, burst over the whole of the Nubian desert, and
swept along the line of communications from Suarda to Halfa. On
the next day a second deluge delayed the march of Lewis's brigade.
Late on the 27th they started. Before they had reached the first watering-
place a third tempest, preceded by its choking sandstorm, overtook
them. Nearly 300 men fell out during the early part of the night, and
crawled and staggered back to Kosheh. Before the column reached
Sadin Fanti 1,700 more sank exhausted to the ground. Out of one
battalion 700 strong, only sixty men marched in. Nine deaths and
eighty serious cases of prostration occurred, and the movement of the
brigade from Kosheh to Absarat was grimly called 'The Death March'.

The violent rains produced floods such as had not been seen in the
Soudan for fifty years. The water, pouring down the broad valleys,
formed furious torrents in the narrower gorges. More than twelve
miles of the railway was washed away. The rails were twisted and
bent; the formation entirely destroyed. The telegraph wires were
broken. The work of weeks was lost in a few hours. The advance
was stopped as soon as it had been begun.

In this time of crisis the success of the whole campaign hung in the
balance. Public opinion was still undecided on the general question of
the war. All the croakers were ready. 'A Jingo Government' – 'An
incapable general' – 'Another disaster in the Soudan' – such were the
whispers. A check would be the signal for an outcry. The accounts of
'The Death March' had not yet reached England; but the correspondents, irritated at being 'chained to headquarters', were going to see
about that. And, besides all this, there were the army to feed and the
Dervishes to fight. In this serious emergency, which threatened to
wreck his schemes, the Sirdar's organising talents shone more brilliantly
than at any other moment in this account. Travelling swiftly to Mogh-
rat, he possessed himself of the telephone, which luckily still worked.

He knew the exact position of every soldier, coolie, camel, or donkey at his disposal. In a few hours, in spite of his crippled transport, he concentrated 5,000 men on the damaged sections of the line, and thereafter fed them until the work was finished. In seven days traffic was resumed. The advance had been delayed, but it was not prevented.

On the 5th of September the 1st (Lewis) and 2nd (MacDonald) Brigades moved to Dulgo, and at the same time the remainder of the army began to march across the loop from Kosheh by Sadin Fanti to Absarat. Every available soldier had been collected for the final operation of the campaign.

The Expeditionary Force was organised as follows:

Commander-in-Chief: THE SIRDAR
The Infantry Division: COLONEL HUNTER *Commanding*

1st Brigade	2nd Brigade	3rd Brigade	4th Brigade
MAJOR LEWIS	MAJOR MACDONALD	MAJOR MAXWELL	MAJOR DAVID
3rd Egyptians	XIth Soudanese	2nd Egyptians	1st Egyptians
4th ,,	XIIth ,,	7th ,,	5th ,,
IXth Soudanese	XIIIth ,,	8th ,,	15th ,,
Xth ,,			

Cavalry Brigade and Mounted Forces: MAJOR BURN-MURDOCH

Cavalry	8 squadrons
Camel Corps	6 companies
Horse Artillery	1 battery

Artillery: MAJOR PARSONS

Field Artillery	2 batteries
Maxims	1 battery (British)

Divisional Troops: MAJOR CURRIE
North Staffordshire Regiment   1st Battalion

The Flotilla: COMMANDER COLVILLE

Gunboats	*Zafir, Tamai, Abu Klea, Metemma, El Teb*
Armed Steamers	*Kaibar, Dal, Akasha*

Total: 15,000 men, 8 war-vessels, and 36 guns

Thus thirteen of the sixteen battalions of the Egyptian Army were employed at the front. Two others, the 6th and XIVth, were disposed along the line of communication, holding the various fortified posts. The 16th Battalion of Reservists remained at Suakin. The whole native army was engaged in the war, and the preservation of domestic order in the capital and throughout the Khedive's dominions was left entirely to the police and to the British Army of Occupation. By the 9th all four brigades had reached the rendezvous at Dulgo; on the 10th the British regiment, which it was determined to send up in the steamers, was moved to Kosheh by rail from Sarras and Gemai. The Sirdar prepared to start with the flotilla on the 12th.

But a culminating disappointment remained. By tremendous exertions the gunboat *Zafir* had been finished at Kosheh in time. On the afternoon of the 11th of September many officers and men came to witness her trial trip. The bank was lined with spectators. Colville took command. The Sirdar and his Staff embarked. Flags were hoisted and amid general cheering the moorings were cast off. But the stern paddle had hardly revolved twice when there was a loud report, like that of a heavy gun, clouds of steam rushed up from the boilers, and the engines stopped. Sir H. Kitchener and Commander Colville were on the upper deck. The latter rushed below to learn what had happened, and found that she had burst her low-pressure cylinder, a misfortune impossible to repair until a new one could be obtained from Halfa and fitted.

In spite of this, however, the advance was not delayed. On the 13th the 1st, 2nd, and 3rd Brigades occupied Kaderma. Here the flotilla overtook them, and henceforward the boats on the river kept pace with the army on the bank. Fareig was reached on the 14th, and on the 16th the 4th Brigade arrived, and the concentration of the force was then complete.

After the annihilation of his strong advanced post at Firket, the Dervish Emir, Wad Bishara, concentrated his remaining forces in Dongola. Here during the summer he had waited, and in the middle of August some small reinforcements under one Emir of low rank reached him from Omdurman. The Khalifa, indeed, promised that many more should follow, but his promises long remained unfulfilled, and the greatest strength that Bishara could muster was 900 Jehadia, 800 Baggara Arabs, 2,800 spearmen, 450 camelmen, 650 cavalry – in all 5,600 men, with six small brass cannon and one mitrailleuse gun.

The first sign that the forces were drawing closer was the cutting of the telegraph-wire by a Dervish patrol on the 6th of September.

On the 10th the Sirdar heard that Kerma was strongly held. On the 15th of September the Egyptian cavalry first established contact with the Dervish scouts, and a slight skirmish took place. On the 18th the whole force advanced to Sardek, and as Bishara still held his position at Kerma it looked as if an action was imminent. It was resolved to attack the Dervish position at Kerma at dawn. With the first light the army began to move, and when the sun rose the spectacle of the moving masses of men and artillery, with the gunboats on the right, was inspiring. The soldiers braced themselves for the expected action. But no sooner were the village and fort of Kerma visible than the report passed along the ranks that they were deserted. On reaching Kerma it was found that the Dervishes had evacuated the place, and only the strong, well-built mud fort attested the recent presence of Bishara. Whither had he gone?

Half a mile to the southward, on the opposite bank of the river, ran a long and continuous line of shelter trenches and loopholed walls. The flanks of this new position rested on the deep morasses which extend from the river both on the north and south sides of Hafir. A small steamer, a fleet of large *gyassas* and other sailing vessels moored to the further shore explained what had happened. Conscious of his weakness, the prudent Emir had adroitly transported himself across the river, and had thus placed that broad flood between his troops and their destruction.

The Dervish position was about half a mile in length. As the gunboats approached the northern end they opened fire with their guns, striking the mud entrenchments at every shot, and driving clouds of dust and splinters into the air. Now, as on other occasions throughout the war, the Dervishes by their military behaviour excited the admiration of their enemies. Encouraged by the arrival in the morning of a reinforcement from Omdurman of 1,000 Black Jehadia and 500 spearmen under Abdel Baki, the Dervish gunners stood to their guns and the riflemen to their trenches, and, although suffering severely, maintained a formidable fire.

The gunboats continued to advance, beating up slowly against the strong current. As they came opposite Hafir, where the channel narrows to about 600 yards, they were received by a very heavy fire from guns placed in cleverly screened batteries, and from the riflemen

sheltered in deep pits by the water's edge or concealed amid the foliage
of the tops of the palm-trees. These aerial skirmishers commanded the
decks of the vessels, and the shields of the guns were thus rendered of
little protection. All the water round the gunboats was torn into foam
by the projectiles. The bullets pattered against their sides, and, except
where they were protected by steel plates, penetrated. So hot was the
fire that it was thought doubtful whether to proceed with the bombardment, and the *Tamai* swung round, and hurried down the river
with the current and at full steam to report to the Sirdar. The other
gunboats remained in action, and continued to shell the Dervish
defences. The *Tamai* soon returned to the fight, and, steaming again up
the river, was immediately hotly re-engaged.

The sight which the army witnessed was thrilling. Beyond the flood
waters of the river, backed against a sky of staring blue and in the
blazing sunlight, the whole of the enemy's position was plainly visible.
Behind the entrenchments and among the mud houses and enclosures
strong bodies of the *jibba*-clad Arabs were arrayed. Still further back
in the plain a large force of cavalry – conspicuous by the gleams of
light reflected from their broad-bladed spears – wheeled and manœuvred.
By the Nile all the tops of the palm-trees were crowded with daring
riflemen, whose positions were indicated by the smoke-puffs of their
rifles, or when some tiny black figure fell, like a shot rook, to the
ground. In the foreground the gunboats, panting and puffing up the
river, were surrounded on all sides by spouts and spurts of water, thrown
up by the shells and bullets. Again the flotilla drew near the narrow
channel; again the watching army held their breath; and again they
saw the leading boat, the *Metemma*, turn and run down stream towards
safety, pursued by the wild cheers of the Arabs. It was evident that the
gunboats were not strong enough to silence the Dervish fire.

The firing had lasted two hours and a half, and the Sirdar saw that
his flotilla could not hope to silence the Dervishes. He therefore ordered
De Rougemont – who had assumed the command after Colville was
wounded – to run past the entrenchments without trying to crush
their fire, and steam on to Dongola. To support and cover the movement, the three batteries of artillery under Major Parsons were brought
into action from the swampy island of Artagasha, which was connected
at this season with the right bank by a shoal. At the same time three

battalions of infantry were moved along the river until opposite the Arab position. At 9 a.m. the eighteen guns on the island opened a tremendous bombardment at 1,200 yards range on the entrenchments, and at the same time the infantry and a rocket detachment concentrated their fire on the tops of the palm-trees. The artillery now succeeded in silencing three of the five Dervish guns and in sinking the little Dervish steamer *Tahra*, while the infantry by a tremendous long-range fire drove the riflemen out of the palms. Profiting by this, the gunboats at ten o'clock moved up the river in line, and, disregarding the fusillade which the Arabs still stubbornly maintained, passed by the entrenchment and steamed on towards Dongola. After this the fight may be said to have ended.

It is doubtful whether Bishara would have retreated, if he had not feared being cut off. He seems to have believed that the Sirdar would march along the right bank at once to Dongola, and cross there under cover of his gunboats. Like all Moslem soldiers, he was nervous about his line of retreat. Nor, considering the overwhelming force against him, can we wonder. There was, besides this strategic reason for retiring, a more concrete cause. All his supplies of grain were accumulated in the *gyassas* which lay moored to the west bank. These vessels were under the close and accurate fire of the artillery and Maxim guns on Artagasha island. Several times during the night the hungry Dervishes attempted to reach their store; but the moon was bright and the gunners watchful. Each time they were driven back. When morning dawned, it was found that Hafir was evacuated, and that the enemy had retreated on Dongola.

Wad Bishara's anxiety about his line of retreat was unnecessary, for the Sirdar could not advance on Dongola with a strong Dervish force on his line of communications: and it was not desirable to divide the army and mask Hafir with a covering force. But as soon as the Dervishes had left their entrenchments the situation was simplified. At daybreak all the Arab boats were brought over to the right bank by the villagers, who reported that Bishara and his soldiers had abandoned the defence and were retreating to Dongola. Thereupon the Sirdar, relieved of the necessity of forcing the passage, transported his army peacefully to the other bank.

The casualties on the 19th were not numerous, and in a force of nearly 15,000 men they appear insignificant. The total – fourteen – amounted to less than one per thousand of the troops engaged. Nevertheless this picturesque and bloodless affair has been solemnly called the 'Battle of Hafir'. It is officially counted in records of service as a 'general action'. Telegrams of congratulation were received from her Majesty and the Khedive. A special clasp was struck. Of all the instances of cheaply bought glory which the military history of recent years affords, Hafir is the most remarkable.

Bishara continued his retreat during the 20th, and, marching all day, reached Dongola in the evening. Wounded as he was, he re-occupied the town and began forthwith to make preparations for the defence of its considerable fortifications.

Notwithstanding that the army did not finish crossing the river until the afternoon of the 21st, the Sirdar determined to continue his advance without delay, and the force accordingly marched twelve miles further south and camped opposite the middle of the large island of Argo. At daybreak the troops started again, and before the sun had attained its greatest power reached Zowarat. This place was scarcely six miles from Dongola, and, as it was expected that an action would be fought the next day, the rest of eighteen hours was welcomed by the weary soldiers. All day long the army remained halted by the palms of the Nile bank. Looking through their glasses up the river, the officers might watch the gunboats methodically bombarding Dongola, and the sound of the guns was clearly heard. At intervals during the day odd parties of Dervishes, both horse and foot, approached the outpost line and shots were exchanged.

All these things, together with the consciousness that the culmination of the campaign was now at hand, raised the excitement of the army to a high pitch. An atmosphere of unrest hung over the bivouac, and few slept soundly. At three o'clock the troops were aroused, and at half past four the final advance on Dongola had begun.

It was still night. The full moon, shining with tropical brilliancy in a cloudless sky, vaguely revealed the rolling plains of sand and the huge moving mass of the army. Presently the warmer, yellower light of dawn began to grow across the river and through the palms, and gradually, as the sun rose and it became daylight, the dense formation of the army was extended to an array more than two miles long. On the left, nearest the river, marched Lewis's brigade – three battalions in line and the fourth in column as a reserve. Next in order Maxwell's three battalions prolonged the line. The artillery were in the centre, supported by the North Staffordshire Regiment. MacDonald's brigade was on the right. David's brigade followed in rear of the centre as a reserve. The cavalry, the Camel Corps, and the Horse Artillery watched the right flank; and on the left the gunboats steamed along the river.

For two hours the army were the only living things visible on the smooth sand, but at seven o'clock a large body of Dervish horse appeared on the right flank. The further advance of half a mile discovered the Arab forces. Their numbers were less than those of the Egyptians, but their white uniforms, conspicuous on the sand, and the rows of flags of many colours lent an imposing appearance to their array. Their determined aspect, no less than the reputation of Bishara, encouraged the belief that they were about to charge.

The disparity of the forces was, however, too great; and as the Egyptian Army steadily advanced, the Dervishes slowly retired. Their retreat was cleverly covered by the Baggara horse, who, by continually threatening the desert flank, delayed the progress of the troops. Bishara did not attempt to re-enter the town, on which the gunboats were now concentrating their fire, but continued to retire in excellent order towards the south and Debba.

The Egyptian infantry halted in Dongola, which when they arrived they found already in the hands of detachments from the flotilla. The red flag with the crescent and star waved once again from the roof of the Mudiria. The garrison of 400 Black Jehadia had capitulated, and were already fraternising with their Soudanese captors, whose comrades in arms they were soon to be. While the infantry occupied the town the cavalry and Camel Corps were despatched in pursuit. Wad Bishara, Osman Azrak, and the Baggara horse made good their flight across the desert to Metemma, and, in spite of terrible sufferings from thirst, retained sufficient discipline to detach a force to hold Abu Klea Wells in case the retreat was followed. The Dervish infantry made their way along the river to Abu Hamed, and were much harassed by the gunboats until they reached the Fourth Cataract, when the pursuit was brought to an end.

The Egyptian losses in the capture of Dongola and in the subsequent pursuit were: British, *nil*. Native ranks: killed, 1; wounded 25. Total, 26.

The occupation of Dongola terminated the campaign of 1896. About 900 prisoners, mostly the Black Jehadia, all the six brass cannon, large stores of grain, and a great quantity of flags, spears, and swords fell to the victors, and the whole of the province, said to be the most fertile in the Soudan, was restored to the Egyptian authority. The existence of a perpetual clear waterway from the head of the Third Cataract to Merawi enabled the gunboats at once to steam up the river for more than 200 miles, and in the course of the following month the greater part of the army was established in Merawi below the Fourth Cataract, at Debba, or at Korti, drawing supplies along the railway, and from Railhead by a boat service on the long reach of open water. The position of a strong force at Merawi – only 120 miles along the river bank from Abu Hamed, the northern Dervish post – was, as will be seen, convenient to the continuance of the campaign whenever the time should arrive. But a long delay in the advance was now inevitable, and nearly a year was destined to pass without any collision between the forces of the Khedive and those of the Khalifa.

CHAPTER VIII

THE DESERT RAILWAY

It often happens that in prosperous public enterprises the applause of the nation and the rewards of the sovereign are bestowed on those whose offices are splendid and whose duties have been dramatic. Others whose labours were no less difficult, responsible, and vital to success are unnoticed. If this be true of men, it is also true of things.

It cannot be denied that a battle, the climax to which all military operations tend, is an event which is not controlled by strategy or organisation. In savage warfare in a flat country the power of modern machinery is such that flesh and blood can scarcely prevail, and the chances of battle are reduced to a minimum. Fighting the Dervishes was primarily a matter of transport. The Khalifa was conquered on the railway.

Throughout the Dongola campaign in 1896 the Nile was the main channel of communication between the Expeditionary Force and its base in Egypt. All supplies were brought to the front as far as possible by water transport. Wherever the Nile was navigable, it was used. But the Nile is not always available. Frequent cataracts obstruct its course for many miles. Other long reaches are only navigable when the river is in flood. To join the navigable reaches, and thus preserve the continuity of the communications, a complex system of railways and caravans was necessary.

In the expedition to Dongola a line of railway was required to connect the two navigable reaches of the Nile which extend from Assuan to Wady Halfa, and from Kerma to Merawi. Before the capture of Dongola, however, this distance was shortened by the fact that the river at high Nile is navigable between the Third Cataract and Kerma. In consequence it was at first only necessary to construct the stretch of 108 miles between Wady Halfa and Kosheh. During the years when Wady Halfa was the southernmost garrison of the Egyptian forces a strong post had been maintained at Sarras. In the Nile expeditions of 1885 the railway from Halfa had been completed through Sarras and as far as Akasha, a distance of eighty-six miles. After the abandonment of the Soudan the Dervishes destroyed the line as far north as Sarras. The position in 1896 may, in fact, be summed up as follows: The section of thirty-three miles from Wady Halfa to Sarras was immediately available and in working order. The section of fifty-three miles from Sarras to Akasha required partial reconstruction. The section of thirty-two miles from Akasha to Kosheh must, with the exception of ten miles of embankment completed in 1885, at once be newly made. And, finally, the section from Kosheh to Kerma must be completed before the Nile flood subsided.

The first duty, therefore, which the Engineer officers had to perform was the reconstruction of the line from Sarras to Akasha. The lack of men with technical knowledge was doubtfully supplied by the enlistment of a 'Railway Battalion' 800 strong. These men were drawn from many tribes and classes. Their only qualification was capacity and willingness for work. They presented a motley appearance. Dervish prisoners, released but still wearing their *jibbas*, assisted stalwart Egyptians in unloading rails and sleepers. Dinkas, Shillooks, Jaalin, and Barabras shovelled contentedly together at the embankments. One hundred civilian Soudanese – chiefly time-expired soldiers – were also employed; and these, since they were trustworthy and took an especial pride in their work, soon learned the arts of spiking rails and sleepers, fishing rails together, and straightening. To direct and control the labours of these men of varied race and language, but of equal inexperience, some civilian foremen platelayers were obtained at high rates of pay from Lower Egypt. These, however, with very few exceptions were not satisfactory, and they were gradually replaced by intelligent men of the 'Railway Battalion', who had learned their trade as the line progressed. The projection, direction, and execution of the whole work were entrusted to a few subalterns of Engineers, of whom the best known was Edouard Girouard.

As the line grew longer, native officers and non-commissioned officers from the active and reserve lists of the Egyptian Army were appointed stationmasters. Intelligent non-commissioned officers and men were converted into shunters, guards, and pointsmen. Traffic was controlled by telephone. To work the telephone, men were discovered who could read and write – very often who could read and write only their own names, and even that with such difficulty that they usually preferred a seal. To improve their education, and to train a staff in the office work of a railway, two schools were instituted at Halfa. In these establishments, which were formed by the shade of two palm-trees, twenty pupils received the beginnings of knowledge.

The rolling stock of the Halfa-Sarras line was in good order and sufficient quantity but the eight locomotives were out of all repair, and had to be patched up again and again with painful repetition. The regularity of their breaks-down prevented the regularity of the road, and the Soudan military railway gained a doubtful reputation during the Dongola expedition and in its early days. Nevertheless the work went on continually.

The initial difficulties of the task were aggravated by an unexpected calamity. On the 26th of August the violent cyclonic rain-storm of which some account has been given in the last chapter broke over the Dongola province.

A writer on the earlier phases of the war[1] has forcibly explained why the consequences were so serious:

'In a country where rain is an ordinary event the engineer lays his railway line, not in the bottom of a valley, but at a higher level on one slope or the other. Where he passes across branching side valleys, he takes care to leave in all his embankments large culverts to carry off flood-water. But here, in what was thought to be the rainless Soudan, the line south of Sarras followed for mile after mile the bottom of the long valley of Khor Ahrusa, and no provision had been made, or had been thought necessary, for culverts in the embankments where minor hollows were crossed. Thus, when the flood came, it was not merely that the railway was cut through here and there by the rushing deluge. It was covered deep in water, the ballast was swept away, and some of the banks so destroyed that in places rails and sleepers were left hanging in the air across a wide gap.'

Nearly fourteen miles of track were destroyed. The camp of the construction gangs was wrecked and flooded. Some of the rifles of the escort – for the conditions of war were never absent – were

[1] A. Hilliard Atteridge, *Towards Khartoum.*

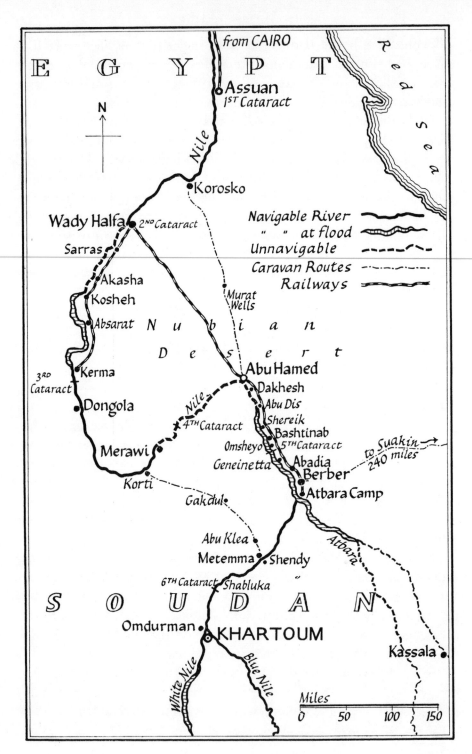

RAIL AND RIVER

afterwards recovered from a depth of three feet of sand. In one place, where the embankment had partly withstood the deluge, a great lake several miles square appeared. By extraordinary exertions the damage was repaired in a week.

As soon as the line as far as Kosheh was completed, the advance towards Dongola began. After the army had been victorious at Hafir the whole province was cleared of Dervishes, and the Egyptian forces pushed on to Merawi. Here they were dependent on river transport. But the Nile was falling rapidly, and the army were soon in danger of being stranded by the interruption of river traffic between the Third Cataract and Kerma. The extension of the line from Kosheh to Kerma was therefore of vital importance. Of the ninety-five miles of extended track, fifty-six were through the desert, and the constructors here gained the experience which was afterwards of value on the great Desert Railway from Wady Halfa to the Atbara. Track-laying commenced south of Kosheh on the 9th of October, and the whole work was carried forward with feverish energy. As it progressed, and before it was completed, the reach of the river from the Third Cataract to Kerma ceased to be navigable. The army were now dependent for their existence on the partly finished railway, from the head of which supplies were conveyed by an elaborate system of camel transport. Every week the line grew. Railhead moved forward, and the strain upon the pack animals diminished. The carrying capacity of the line was strictly limited. The worn-out engines frequently broke down. Three times the construction had to be suspended to allow the army to be revictualled. Every difficulty was, however, overcome. By the beginning of May the line to Kerma was finished.

In the first week in December the Sirdar returned from England with permission to continue the advance towards Khartoum, and the momentous question of the route to be followed arose. It may at first seem that the plain course was to continue to work along the Nile, connecting its navigable reaches by sections of railway. But from Merawi to Abu Hamed the river is broken by continual cataracts, and the broken ground of both banks made a railway nearly an impossibility. The movements of the French expeditions towards the Upper Nile counselled speed. The poverty of Egypt compelled economy. The Nile route, though sure, would be slow and very expensive. A short cut must be found. Three daring and ambitious schemes presented themselves: (1) the line followed by the Desert Column in 1884 from Korti to Metemma; (2) the celebrated, if not notorious, route from Suakin to Berber; (3) across the Nubian desert from Korosko or Wady Halfa to Abu Hamed.

The question involved the whole strategy of the war. The known strength of the Khalifa made it evident that a powerful force would be required for the destruction of his army and the capture of his capital. The use of railway transport to some point on the Nile whence there was a clear waterway was therefore imperative. Berber and Metemma were known, and Abu Hamed was believed, to fulfil this condition. But both Berber and Metemma were important strategic points. It was improbable that the Dervishes would abandon these keys to Khartoum and the Soudan without severe resistance. It seemed likely, indeed, that the Khalifa would strongly reinforce both towns, and desperately contest their possession. The deserts between Korti and Metemma, and between Suakin and Berber, contained scattered wells, and small raiding parties might have cut the railway and perhaps have starved the army at its head. It was therefore too dangerous to project the railway towards either Berber or Metemma until they were actually in our hands. The argument is circular. The towns could not be taken without a strong force; so strong a force could not advance until the railway was made; and the railway could not be made till the towns were taken.

Both the Korti–Metemma and the Suakin–Berber routes were therefore rejected. The resolution to exclude the latter was further strengthened by the fact that the labour of building a railway over the hills behind Suakin would have been very great.

The route *via* Abu Hamed was selected by the exclusion of the alternatives. But it had distinct and apparent advantages. Abu Hamed was within striking distance of the army at Merawi. It was not a point essential to the Dervish defences, and not, therefore, likely to be so strongly garrisoned as Berber or Metemma. It might, therefore, be captured by a column marching along the river, and sufficiently small to be equipped with only camel transport. The deserts through which the railway to Abu Hamed would pass contain few wells, and therefore it would be difficult for small raiding parties to cut the line or attack the construction gangs; and before the line got within reach of the Dervish garrison at Abu Hamed, that garrison would be dislodged and the place seized.

The plan was perfect, and the argument in its favour conclusive. It turned, however, on one point: Was the Desert Railway a possibility? The General appealed to expert opinion. Eminent railway engineers in England were consulted. They replied with unanimity that, having due regard to the circumstances, and remembering the conditions of war under which the work must be executed, it was impossible to construct such a line. Distinguished soldiers were approached on the subject. They replied that the scheme was not only impossible, but absurd. Having received this advice, and reflected on it duly, the Sirdar ordered the railway to be constructed, without more delay.

A further question immediately arose: Should the railway to Abu Hamed start from Korosko or from Wady Halfa? There were arguments on both sides. The adoption of the Korosko line would reduce the river stage from Assuan by forty-eight hours up stream. The old caravan route, by which General Gordon had travelled to Khartoum on his last journey, had been from Korosko *via* Murat Wells to Abu Hamed. On the other hand, many workshops and appliances for construction were already existing at Wady Halfa. It was the northern terminus of the Dongola railway. This was an enormous advantage. Both routes were reconnoitred: that from Wady Halfa was selected. The decision having been taken, the enterprise was at once begun.

Lieutenant Girouard, to whom everything was entrusted, was told to make the necessary estimates. Sitting in his hut at Wady Halfa, he drew up a comprehensive list. Nothing was forgotten. Every want was provided for; every difficulty was foreseen; every requisite was noted. The questions to be decided were numerous and involved. The answers to all these questions were set forth by Lieutenant Girouard in a ponderous volume several inches thick; and such was the comprehensive accuracy of the estimate that the working parties were never delayed by the want even of a piece of brass wire.

In any circumstances the task would have been enormous. It was, however, complicated by five important considerations: It had to be executed with military precautions. There was apparently no water

along the line. The feeding of 2,000 platelayers in a barren desert was
a problem in itself. The work had to be completed before the winter.
And, finally, the money voted was not to be outrun. The Sirdar
attended to the last condition.

Girouard was sent to England to buy the plant and rolling stock.
Fifteen new engines and two hundred trucks were ordered. The
necessary new workshops were commenced at Halfa. Experienced
mechanics were procured to direct them. Fifteen hundred additional
men were enlisted in the Railway Battalion and trained. Then the
water question was dealt with. The reconnoitring surveys had reported
that though the line was certainly 'good and easy' for 110 miles – and,
according to Arab accounts, for the remaining 120 miles – no drop of
water was to be found, and only two likely spots for wells were noted.
Camel transport was, of course, out of the question. Each engine must
first of all haul enough water to carry it to Railhead and back, besides
a reserve against accidents. It was evident that the quantity of water
required by any locomotive would continually increase as the work
progressed and the distance grew greater, until finally the material
trains would have one-third of their carrying power absorbed in
transporting the water for their own consumption. The amount of
water necessary is largely dependent on the grades of the line. The
'flat desert' proved to be a steady slope up to a height of 1,600 feet
above Halfa, and the calculations were further complicated. The
difficulty had, however, to be faced, and a hundred 1,500-gallon tanks
were procured. These were mounted on trucks and connected by
hose; and the most striking characteristic of the trains of the Soudan
military railway was the long succession of enormous boxes on wheels,
on which the motive power of the engine and the lives of the passengers
depended.

The first spadeful of sand of the Desert Railway was turned on the
first day of 1897; but until May, when the line to Kerma was finished,
no great efforts were made, and only forty miles of track had been
laid. In the meanwhile the men of the new Railway Battalion were
being trained; the plant was steadily accumulating; engines, rolling
stock, and material of all sorts had arrived from England. All this was
preparation; nor was it until the 8th of May that track-laying into the
desert was begun in earnest. The whole of the construction gangs

and railroad staff were brought from Kerma to Wady Halfa, and the daring pioneers of modern war started on their long march through the wilderness, dragging their railway behind them.

It is scarcely within the power of words to describe the savage desolation of the regions into which the line and its constructors plunged. A smooth ocean of bright-coloured sand spread far and wide to distant horizons. The tropical sun beat with senseless perseverance upon the level surface until it could scarcely be touched with a naked hand, and the filmy air glittered and shimmered as over a furnace. Here and there huge masses of crumbling rock rose from the plain, like islands of cinders in a sea of fire. Alone in this vast expanse stood Railhead – a canvas town of 2,500 inhabitants, complete with station, stores, post office, telegraph office, and canteen, and only connected with the living world of men and ideas by two parallel iron streaks, three feet six inches apart, growing dim and narrower in a long perspective until they were twisted and blurred by the mirage and vanished in the indefinite distance.

Every morning in the remote nothingness there appeared a black speck growing larger and clearer, until with a whistle and a welcome clatter, amid the aching silence of ages, the 'material' train arrived, carrying its own water and 2,500 yards of rails, sleepers, and accessories. At noon came another speck, developing in a similar manner into a supply train, also carrying its own water, food and water for the half-battalion of the escort and the 2,000 artificers and platelayers, and the letters, newspapers, sausages, jam, whisky, soda-water, and cigarettes which enable the Briton to conquer the world without discomfort. And presently the empty trains would depart, reversing the process of their arrival, and vanishing gradually along a line which appeared at last to turn up into the air and run at a tangent into an unreal world.

So, week in, week out, the work went on. Every few days saw a further advance into the wilderness. As Wady Halfa became more remote and Abu Hamed grew near, an element of danger, the more appalling since it was peculiar, was added to the strange conditions under which the inhabitants of Railhead lived. What if the Dervishes should cut the line behind them? They had three days' reserve of water. After that, unless the obstruction were removed and traffic restored, all must wither and die in the sand, and only their bones and their cooking-pots would attest the folly of their undertaking.

By the 20th of July a hundred and thirty miles of line had been finished, and it became too dangerous to advance further until Abu Hamed had been cleared of the Dervish force. They were still a hundred miles away, but camels travel fast and far, and the resources of the enemy were uncertain. It appeared that progress would be checked, but on the 7th of August General Hunter, marching from Merawi along the river bank, attacked and took Abu Hamed – an operation which will be described hereafter. Work was at once resumed with renewed energy. The pace of construction now became remarkable. As much as 5,300 yards of track was surveyed, embanked, and laid in a single day. On the 1st of November Abu Hamed was reached, and by the banks of the Nile the men who had fought their way across the desert joined hands with those who had fought their way along the river.

The strain and hardship had not, however, been without effect on the constructors. Two of the Engineer subalterns – Polwhele and Cator – out of the eight concerned in the laying of the Dongola and the Desert railways had died. Their places were eagerly filled by others.

The completion of the line was accelerated by nearly a month through the fortunate discovery of water. At the beginning of July a well was sunk in what was thought to be a likely place at 'No. 4 Station', seventy-seven miles from Halfa. After five weeks' work water was found in abundance at a depth of 90 feet. A steam-pump was erected, and the well yielded a continual supply. In October a second well was sunk at 'No. 6 Station', 55 miles further on, whence water was obtained in still greater quantity. These discoveries modified, though they did not solve, the water question. They substantially increased the carrying capacity of the line, and reduced the danger to which the construction gangs were exposed.

As the railway had been made, the telegraph-wire had, of course, followed it. Every consignment of rails and sleepers had been accompanied by its proportion of telegraph-poles, insulators, and wire. Another subaltern of Engineers, Lieutenant Manifold, who managed this part of the military operations against the Arabs, had also laid a line from Merawi to Abu Hamed, so that immediate correspondence was effected round the entire circle of rail and river.

The labours of the Railway Battalion and its officers did not end with the completion of the line to Abu Hamed. The Desert Railway was made. It had now to be maintained, worked, and rapidly extended. The terminus at Halfa had become a busy town. A mud village was transformed into a miniature Crewe. The great workshops that had grown with the line were equipped with diverse and elaborate machines. Plant of all kinds purchased in Cairo or requisitioned from England, with odds and ends collected from Ismail's scrap heaps, filled the depôts with an extraordinary variety of stores. Foundries, lathes, dynamos, steam-hammers, hydraulic presses, cupola furnaces, screw-cutting machines, and drills had been set up and were in continual work. They needed constant attention. Every appliance for repairing each must be provided. To haul the tonnage necessary to supply the army and extend the line nearly forty engines were eventually required. Purchased at different times and from different countries, they included ten distinct patterns; each pattern needed a special reserve of spare parts. Some of the engines were old and already worn out. These broke down periodically. The frictional parts of all were affected by the desert sand, and needed ceaseless attention and repair. The workshops were busy night and day for seven days a week.

To the complication of machinery was added the confusion of tongues. Natives of various races were employed as operatives. Foremen had been obtained from Europe. No fewer than seven separate languages were spoken in the shops. Wady Halfa became a second Babel. Yet the undertaking prospered. The Engineer officers displayed qualities of tact and temper: their director was cool and indefatigable. Over all the Sirdar exercised a regular control. The sympathy of common labour won him the affection of the subalterns. Nowhere in the Soudan was he better known than on the railroad. Nowhere was he so ardently believed in.

It is now necessary to anticipate the course of events. As soon as the railway reached Abu Hamed, General Hunter's force, which was holding that place, dropped its slender camel communications with Merawi and drew its supplies along the new line direct from Wady Halfa. After the completion of the desert line there was still left

17 miles of material for construction, and the railway was consequently at once extended to Dakhesh, 16 miles south of Abu Hamed. Meanwhile Berber was seized, and military considerations compelled the concentration of a larger force to maintain that town. The four battalions which had remained at Merawi were floated down stream to Kerma, and, there entraining, were carried by Halfa and Abu Hamed to Dakhesh – a journey of 450 miles.

When the railway had been begun across the desert, it was believed that the Nile was always navigable above Abu Hamed. In former campaigns it had been reconnoitred and the waterway declared clear. But as the river fell it became evident that this was untrue. With the subsidence of the waters cataracts began to appear, and to avoid these it became necessary first of all to extend the railway to Bashtinab, later on to Abadia, and finally to the Atbara. To do this more money had to be obtained, and the usual financial difficulties presented themselves. Finally, however, the matter was settled, and the extension began at the rate of about a mile a day. From Bashtinab to Abadia another desert section of 50 miles was necessary to avoid some very difficult ground by the Nile bank. From Abadia to the Atbara the last stretch of the line runs across a broad alluvial expanse from whose surface plane-trees of mean appearance, but affording welcome shade, rise, watered by the autumn rains. The fact that the railway was approaching regions where rain is not an almost unknown phenomenon increased the labour of construction. To prevent the embankments from being washed away in the watercourses, ten bridges and sixty culverts had to be made; and this involved the transport over the railway of more than 1,000 tons of material in addition to the ordinary plant.

By the arrival of the reinforcements at Berber the fighting force at the front was doubled: doubled also was the business of supply. The task of providing the food of an army in a desert, a thousand miles from their base, and with no apparent means of subsistence at the end of the day's march, is less picturesque, though not less important, than the building of railways along which that nourishment is drawn to the front. Supply and transport stand or fall together; history depends on both. The Sirdar exercised a direct and personal supervision over the whole department of supply, but his action was restricted almost entirely to the distribution of the rations. Their accumulation and regular supply were the task of Colonel Rogers, and this officer, by three years of exact calculation and unfailing allowance for the unforeseen, has well deserved his high reputation as a feeder of armies.

The first military necessity of the war was, as has been described, to place the bulk of the Egyptian Army at Akasha. In ordinary circumstances this would not have been a serious commissariat problem. The frontier reserves of food were calculated to meet such an emergency. But in 1895 the crops in Egypt had been much below the average. At the beginning of 1896 there was a great scarcity of grain. When the order for the advance was issued, the frontier grain stores were nearly exhausted. The new crops could not be garnered until the end of April. Thus while the world regarded Egypt as a vast granary, her soldiers were obliged to purchase 4,000 tons of *doura* and 1,000 tons of barley from India and Russia on which to begin the campaign.

The chief item of a soldier's diet in most armies is bread. In several of our wars the health, and consequently the efficiency, of the troops has been impaired by bad bread or by the too frequent substitution of hard biscuit. For more than a year the army up the river ate 20 tons of flour daily, and it is easy to imagine how bitter amid ordinary circumstances would have been the battle between the commissariat officers, whose duty it was to insist on proper quality, and the contractors – often, I fear, meriting the epithet 'rascally' – intent only upon profit. But the War Department had in 1892 converted one of Ismail Pasha's gun factories near Cairo into a victualling-yard. Here were set up their own mills for grinding flour, machinery for manufacturing biscuit to the extent of 60,000 rations daily, and even for making soap. Three great advantages sprang from this wise arrangement. Firstly, the good quality of the supply was assured. Secondly, all risk of contractors failing to deliver in time was avoided. Lastly, the funds resulting from the economy had been utilised to form a useful corps of 150 bakers. And thus, although the purchase of foreign grain added to the expense, the beginning of the war found the commissariat of the Egyptian Army in a thoroughly efficient state.

Vast reserves of stores were quickly accumulated at Assuan. From these not an ounce of food was issued without the Sirdar's direct sanction. At the subsidiary depôt, formed at Wady Halfa, the same rule prevailed. The man who was responsible to no one took all the responsibility; and the system whereby a Chief of the Staff is subjected to the continual bombardment of heads of departments was happily avoided. Sufficient supplies having been accumulated at Akasha to allow of a forward movement, Firket was fought. After Firket the situation became difficult, and the problem of the supply officers was to keep the troops alive without delaying the progress of the railway with the carriage of their food. A small quantity of provisions was painfully dragged, with an average loss of 50 per cent from theft and water damage, up the succession of cataracts which obstruct the river-way from Halfa to Kosheh. Camel convoys from Railhead carried the rest. But until the line reached Kosheh the resources of the transport were terribly strained, and at one time it was even necessary to send the mounted troops north to avoid actual famine. The apparent inadequacy of the means to the end reached a climax when the army moved southward from Dulgo. The marches and halts to Dongola were estimated to take ten days, which was the utmost capacity of camel and steam transport. A few boat-loads of grain might be captured; a few handfuls of dates might be plucked; but scarcely any local supplies would be available. The sailing-boats, which were the only regular means of transport, were all delayed by the adverse winds. Fortune returned at the critical moment. By good luck on the first day of the march the north wind began to blow, and twelve days' supplies, over and above those moved by camel and steamer, reached Dongola with the troops. With this reserve in hand, the occupation of the province was completed, and although the army only existed from hand to mouth until the railway reached Kerma, no further serious difficulty was experienced in supplying them.

The line continued to grow rapidly, and as it grew the weight was shifted from the backs of the camels and the bottoms of the sailing-boats to the trucks of the iron road. The strong hands of steam were directed to the prosecution of the war, and the swiftness of the train replaced the toilsome plodding of the caravan. The advance of the Dervishes towards Berber checked the progress of the railway. Military precautions were imperative. Construction was delayed by the passage of the 1st British Brigade from Cairo to the front, and by the consequently increased volume of daily supplies. By the 10th of March, however, the line was completed to Bashtinab. On the 5th of May it had reached Abadia. On the 3rd of July the whole railway from Wady Halfa to the Atbara was finished, and the southern terminus was established in the great entrenched camp at the confluence of the rivers. The question of supply was then settled once and for all. In less than a week stores sufficient for three months were poured along the line, and the exhausting labours of the commissariat officers ended. Their relief and achievement were merged in the greater triumph of the Railway Staff. The director and his subalterns had laboured long, and their efforts were crowned with complete success. On the day that the first troop train steamed into the fortified camp at the confluence of the Nile and the Atbara rivers the doom of the Dervishes was sealed.

CHAPTER IX

ABU HAMED

The news of the fall of Dongola created a panic in Omdurman. Great numbers of Arabs, believing that the Khalifa's power was about to collapse, fled from the city. All business was at a standstill. For several days there were no executions. Abdullah himself kept his house. On the fifth day, he proceeded to the mosque, and after the morning prayer ascended his small wooden pulpit and addressed the assembled worshippers. After admitting the retreat of the Dervishes under Wad Bishara, he enlarged on the losses the 'Turks' had sustained and described their miserable condition. He bewailed the lack of faith in God which had allowed even the meanest of the Ansar to abandon the *Jehad* against the infidel. But he proclaimed his confidence in the loyalty of his subjects and his enjoyment of the favour of God and the counsels of the late Mahdi; and having by his oratory raised the fanatical multitude to a high pitch of excitement, he thus concluded: 'It is true that our chiefs have retired from Dongola. Yet they are not defeated. Only they that disobeyed me have perished. I instructed the faithful to refrain from fighting and return to Metemma. For the angel of the Lord and the spirit of the Mahdi have warned me in a vision that the souls of the accursed Egyptians and of the miserable English shall leave their bodies between Dongola and Omdurman, at some spot which their bones shall whiten. Thus shall the infidels be conquered.' Then, drawing his sword, he cried with a loud voice: '*Ed din mansur!* The religion is victorious! Islam shall triumph!' Whereupon the worshippers, who to the number of 20,000 filled the great quadrangle, saw his sword flashing in the sunlight, and with one accord imitated him, waving their swords and spears, and raising a mighty shout of fury and defiance.

In order that the divine favour might be assisted by human effort, Abdullah adopted every measure or precaution that energy or prudence could suggest. At first he seems to have apprehended that the Sirdar's army would advance at once upon Omdurman, following the route of the Desert Column in 1885 from Korti to Metemma. He therefore ordered Osman Azrak – in spite of his severe wound – to hold Abu Klea Wells with the survivors of his flag. Bishara, who had rallied and reorganised the remains of the Dongola army, was instructed to occupy Metemma, the headquarters of the Jaalin. Emir Ibrahim Khalil was recalled from the Ghezira, or the land between the Blue and White Niles, and with his force of about 4,000 Jehadia and Baggara soon reached the city. Another chief, Ahmed Fedil, who was actually on his way to Gedaref, was ordered to return to the capital. Thither also Osman Digna repaired from Adarama. But it appears that the Khalifa only required the advice of that wily councillor, for he did not reduce the number of Dervishes in the small forts along the line of the Atbara – Ed Damer, Adarama, Asubri, El Fasher – and after a short visit and a long consultation Osman Digna returned to his post at Adarama. Last of all Mahmud, who commanded the 'Army of the West', was ordered to leave very reduced garrisons in Kordofan and Darfur, and march with his whole remaining force, which may have numbered 10,000 fighting men, to the Nile, and so to Omdurman. Mahmud, who was as daring and ambitious as he was conceited and incapable, received the summons with delight, and began forthwith to collect his troops.

The Khalifa saw very clearly that he could not trust the riverain tribes. The Jaalin and Barabra were weary of his rule and of war. In proportion as the Egyptian Army advanced, so their loyalty and the taxes they paid decreased. He therefore abandoned all idea of making a stand at Berber. The Emir Yunes – who, since he had been transferred from Dongola in 1895, had ruled the district – was directed to collect all the camels, boats, grain, and other things that might assist an invading army and send them to Metemma. The duty was most thoroughly performed. The inhabitants were soon relieved of all their property and of most of their means of livelihood.

The power of the gunboats and their effect in the Dongola campaign were fully appreciated by the Arabs; and the Khalifa, in the hopes of closing the Sixth Cataract, began to construct several forts at the northern end of the Shabluka gorge. But the prophecy of the

Mahdi exercised a powerful effect on the Khalifa's mind, and while he neglected no detail he based his hopes on the issue of a great battle on the plains of Kerreri, when the invaders should come to the walls of the city.

But after a while it became apparent that the 'Turks' were not advancing. They tarried on the lands they had won. The steamers went no further than Merawi. The iron road stopped at Kerma. Why had they not followed up their success? Obviously because they feared the army that awaited them at Omdurman. At this the Khalifa took fresh courage, and in January 1897 he began to evolve schemes for taking the offensive and expelling the invaders from the Dongola province. The army drilled and manœuvred continually on the plains of Kerreri; great numbers of camels were collected at Omdurman; large stores of dried *kisru* or 'Soudan biscuit', the food of Dervishes on expeditions, were prepared.

At the end of May, Mahmud with his army arrived at Omdurman. The Khalifa received him with delight, and several imposing reviews were held outside the city. Mahmud himself was eager to march against the 'Turks'. He had no experience of modern rifles, and felt confident that he could easily destroy or at least roll back the invading forces. Partly persuaded by the zeal of his lieutenant, and partly by the wavering and doubtful attitude of the Jaalin, the Khalifa determined early in June to send the Kordofan army to occupy Metemma, and thereby either to awe the tribe into loyalty, or force them to revolt while the Egyptian troops were still too distant to assist them. He summoned the chief of the Jaalin, Abdalla-Wad-Saad, to Omdurman, and informed him that the Jaalin territories were threatened by the Turks. In the goodness of his heart, therefore, and because he knew that they loved the Mahdi and practised the true religion, he was resolved to protect them from their enemies. The trusty Mahmud with his army would be sent for that purpose; Abdalla might show his loyalty in furnishing them with all supplies and accommodation. But the Jaalin chief had the temerity to protest. He assured the Khalifa of his loyalty, and of the ability of his tribe to repel the enemy. He implored him not to impose the burden of an army upon them. He exaggerated the poverty of Metemma; he lamented the misfortunes of the times. Finally he begged forgiveness for making his protest.

The Khalifa was infuriated. Forgetting his usual self-control and
the forms of public utterance, he broke out into a long and abusive
harangue. Abdalla-Wad-Saad crept from the presence, and returned
in fury and disgust to Metemma. Having collected the head men of
his tribe, he informed them of his reception and the Khalifa's intent.
They did not need to be told that the quartering upon them of Mahmud's army meant the plunder of their goods, the ruin of their homes,
and the rape of their women. It was resolved to revolt and join the
Egyptian forces. As a result of the council the Jaalin chief wrote two
letters. The first was addressed to the Sirdar, and reached General
Rundle at Merawi by messenger on the 24th of June. It declared the
Jaalin submission to the Government, and begged for help, if possible
in men, or, failing that, in arms. The second letter – a mad and fatal
letter – carried defiance to the Khalifa.

Rundle, who was at Merawi when the Jaalin messenger found him,
lost no time. A large amount of ammunition and 1,100 Remington
rifles were speedily collected and hurried on camels across the desert
by the Korti-Metemma route, escorted by a strong detachment of
the Camel Corps. The Khalifa did not receive his letter until the
27th of June. But he acted with even greater promptitude. Part of
Mahmud's army had already started for the north. Mahmud and the
rest followed on the 28th. On the 30th the advanced guard arrived
before Metemma. The Jaalin prepared to resist desperately. Nearly
the whole tribe had responded to the summons of their chief, and
more than 2,500 men were collected behind the walls of the town.
But in all this force there were only eighty serviceable rifles, and
only fifteen rounds of ammunition each.

On the morning of the 1st of July, Mahmud, with a force variously
estimated at 10,000 or 12,000 men, began his assault. The first attack
fell, as the chief had anticipated, on the southern face. It was repulsed
with severe loss by the Jaalin riflemen. A second attack followed
immediately. The enemy had meanwhile surrounded the whole town,
and just as the Jaalin ammunition was exhausted a strong force of the
Dervishes penetrated the northern face of their defences, which was
held only by spearmen. The whole of Mahmud's army poured in
through the gap, and the garrison, after a stubborn resistance, were
methodically exterminated. An inhuman butchery of the children

and some of the women followed. Abdalla-Wad-Saad was among the killed.

But while the attention of the Khalifa was directed to these matters, a far more serious menace offered from another quarter. Unnoticed by the Dervishes, or, if noticed, unappreciated, the railway was stretching farther and farther into the desert. By the middle of July it had reached the 130th mile. The Nile was rising fast. Very soon steamers would be able to pass the Fourth Cataract. It should have been evident that the next movement in the advance of the 'Turks' impended. The Khalifa seems, indeed, to have understood that the rise of the river increased his peril, for throughout July he continued to send orders to the Emir in Berber – Yunes – that he should advance into the Monassir district, harry such villages as existed, and obstruct the frequent reconnaissances from Merawi. Yunes, however, preferred to do otherwise, and remained on the left bank opposite Berber until, at length, his master recalled him to Omdurman to explain his conduct.

At the end of July preparations were made, as secretly as possible, to despatch a flying column against Abu Hamed. The Dervish garrison, under Mohammed-ez-Zein, was not believed to exceed 600 men, but in order that there should be no doubt as to the result it was determined to employ a strong force.

A brigade of all arms was formed as follows:

Commanding: MAJOR-GENERAL HUNTER

Cavalry	One troop
Artillery	No. 2 Field Battery[1]
Infantry MACDONALD's Brigade	3rd Egyptians IXth Soudanese Xth ,, XIth ,,

Major-General Sir Archibald Hunter, the officer to whom the operation was entrusted, was from many points of view the most imposing figure in the Egyptian Army. He had served through the Nile Expedition of 1884–85, with some distinction, in the Khedive's service. Thenceforward his rise was rapid, even for an Egyptian officer,

---

[1] This battery consisted of six Krupp guns, two Maxims, one Gardner gun, and one Nordenfeldt – an effective medley.

and in ten years he passed through all the grades from Captain to Major-General. Foremost in every action, twice wounded – once at the head of his brigade – always distinguished for valour and conduct, Hunter won the admiration of his comrades and superiors. During the River War he became, in spite of his hard severity, the darling of the Egyptian Army. All the personal popularity which great success might have brought to the Sirdar focused itself on his daring, good-humoured subordinate, and it was to Hunter that the soldiers looked whenever there was fighting to be done. The force now placed under his command for the attack upon Abu Hamed amounted to about 3,600 men. Until that place was taken all other operations were delayed. The Sirdar awaited the issue at Merawi. The railway paused in mid-desert.

The troops composing the 'flying column' concentrated at Kassingar, a small village a few miles above Merawi, on the right (or Abu Hamed) bank of the Nile. General Hunter began his march on the 29th of July. The total distance from Kassingar to Abu Hamed is 146 miles. Speed was essential; for if the Dervish garrison in Abu Hamed were reinforced from Berber, the flying column might not be strong enough to take the village. On the other hand, the great heat and the certainty that the troops would have to fight an action at the end of the march imposed opposite considerations on the commander. To avoid the sun, the greater part of the distance was covered at night.

Throughout the whole length of the course of the Nile there is no more miserable wilderness than the Monassir Desert. The stream of the river is broken and its channel obstructed by a great confusion of boulders, among which the water rushes in dangerous cataracts. The line of advance lay along the river; but no road relieved the labour of the march. Sometimes trailing across a broad stretch of white sand, in which the soldiers sank to their ankles; sometimes winding over a pass or through a gorge of sharp-cut rocks – always in a long, jerky, and interrupted procession of men and camels, often in single file – the column toiled painfully like the serpent to whom it was said, 'On thy belly shalt thou go, and dust shalt thou eat.'

The column started at 5.30 in the evening, and by a march of sixteen and a half miles reached Mushra-el-Obiad at about midnight. Here a convenient watering-place, not commanded by the opposite bank, and the shade of eight or ten thorny bushes afforded the first suitable bivouac. At 3.30 p.m. on the 30th the march was continued eight and a half miles to a spot some little distance beyond Shebabit. It was after dark when the halting-place was reached. General Hunter had proposed to push on the next day to Hosh-el-Geref, but the fatigues of his troops in the two night marches had already been severe, and as, after Abu Haraz, the track twisted away from the river so that there was no water for five miles, he resolved to halt for the day and rest. Hosh-el-Geref was therefore not reached until the 1st of August – a day later than had been expected; but the rest had proved of such benefit to the troops that the subsequent acceleration of progress fully compensated for the delay.

On the 5th, the force reached Khula. Here they were joined by Sheikh Abdel-Azim with 150 Ababda camel-men from Murat Wells. Up to this point three Egyptians had died and fifty-eight men had been left behind exhausted in depôts. A double ration of meat was issued to the whole force. The column moved on during the night, and arrived at Ginnifab at eight in the morning of the 6th. Here startling news of the enemy was received. It was known that Moham-med-ez-Zein was determined to fight, and a trustworthy report was now received that a large force was coming down from Berber to support the Abu Hamed garrison. In spite of the long marches and the fatigues of the troops, General Hunter resolved to hurry on. He had already made up the day spent at Abu Haraz. He now decided to im-prove on the prescribed itinerary, accelerate his own arrival and antici-pate that of the Dervish reinforcements. Accordingly the troops marched all through the night of the 6–7th with only a short halt of an hour and a half, so as to attack Abu Hamed at dawn.

The village of Abu Hamed straggles along the bank of the Nile, and consists of a central mass of mud houses, intersected by a network of winding lanes and alleys, about 500 yards long by perhaps 100 yards wide. To the north and south are detached clusters of ruined huts, and to the south there rises a large, ragged pile of rocks. The ground slopes gradually up from the river, so that at a distance of 300 yards the village is surrounded on three sides by a low plateau. Upon this plateau stand three stone watch-towers, which were erected by General Gordon. The Dervish garrison were strongly posted in shelter trenches and loopholed houses along the eastern face of the village. The towers were held by their outposts.

Making a wide circuit to their left, and then swinging round to the right, so as to front facing the river, the brigade silently moved towards the enemy's position, and at a quarter past six occupied the plateau in a crescent-shaped formation; the XIth Soudanese on the right, opposite the north-east corner of the village; the battery, escorted by the remaining half-battalion of the 3rd Egyptians, next; then the IXth in the centre, and the Xth Soudanese on the left flank. As the troops approached the watch-towers the Dervish outposts fell back, and the force continued to advance until the edge of the plateau was reached.

The day was just breaking, and the mist hung low and white over the steel-grey surface of the river. The Dervish riflemen crouched in the shelter trench that ran round the village. Their cavalry, perhaps a hundred strong, were falling in hurriedly on the sandy ground to the south near the ragged rocks.

At half past six the battery came into action, and after a few shells had been fired at the loopholed houses in the left centre of the position, a general advance was ordered. In excellent order the three Soudanese battalions, with General Hunter, Lieut.-Colonel MacDonald, and the other British officers on horseback in front of their line, advanced slowly down the hill, opening a destructive fire on the entrenchment. The distance was scarcely three hundred yards; but the crescent formation of the attack made the lines of advance converge, and before half the distance was covered the Xth were compelled to halt, lest the XIth Soudanese on the right flank should fire into them. The Dervishes remained silent until the troops were within a hundred yards, when they discharged two tremendous volleys, which were chiefly effective upon the halted battalion. Major Sidney, Lieutenant Fitzclarence, and a dozen men were shot dead. More than fifty men were wounded. All the Soudanese thereupon with a loud shout rushed upon the entrenchment, stormed it, and hunted the Dervishes into the houses. In the street-fighting which followed, the numbers of the troops prevailed. The advance scarcely paused until the river bank was reached, and by 7.30 Abu Hamed was in the possession of the Egyptian forces.

The Dervish horsemen, who had remained spectators near the

southern crag during the attack, fled towards Berber as soon as they saw the attack successful. Scarcely any of the infantry escaped.

In this action, besides the two British officers, Major H. M. Sidney and Lieutenant E. Fitzclarence, 21 native soldiers were killed; 61 native soldiers were wounded.

The news of the capture of Abu Hamed was carried swiftly by camel and wire. The Sirdar, anticipating the result, had already ordered the gunboats to commence the passage of the Fourth Cataract. The Dervishes who were hurrying from Berber were only twenty miles from Abu Hamed when they met the fugitives. They immediately turned back, and retired to the foot of the Fifth Cataract, whence after a few days' halt they continued their retreat. Their proximity to the captured village shows how little time the column had to spare, and that General Hunter was wise to press his marches. The Emir who commanded at Berber heard of the loss of the outpost on the 9th. He sent the messenger on to Metemma. Mahmud replied on the 11th that he was starting at once with his whole army to reinforce Berber. Apparently, however, he did not dare to move without the Khalifa's permission.

On the 4th of August the gunboats *El Teb* and *Tamai* approached the Fourth Cataract to ascend to the Abu Hamed–Berber reach of the river. Major David was in charge of the operation. Lieutenants Hood and Beatty (Royal Navy) commanded the vessels. Two hundred men of the 7th Egyptians were towed in barges to assist in hauling the steamers in the difficult places. The current was, however, too strong, and it was found necessary to leave three barges, containing 160 soldiers, at the foot of the rapids. Nevertheless, as the cataract was not considered a very formidable barrier, Major David determined to make the attempt. Early on the 5th, therefore, the *Tamai* tried the ascent. The steamer, with her engines working at full speed, succeeded in mounting half the distance. But the rush of water was then so great that her bows were swept round, and, after a narrow escape of capsizing, she was carried swiftly down the stream.

The officers thought that this failure was due to the accidental fouling of a rope at a critical moment, and to the fact that there were not enough local tribesmen pulling at the hawsers. Four hundred more Shaiggia were therefore collected from the neighbouring villages, and in the afternoon *El Teb* attempted the passage. Her fortunes were far worse than those of the *Tamai*. Owing to the lack of co-operation and discipline among the local tribesmen, and the want of proper supervision, the hauling power was again too weak. Again the bows of the steamer were swept round, and, as the hawsers held, a great rush of water poured over the bulwarks. In ten seconds *El Teb* heeled over and turned bottom upwards. The hawsers parted under this new strain, and she was swept down stream with only her keel showing. Lieutenant Beatty and most of the crew were thrown, or glad to jump, into the foaming water of the cataract, and, being carried down the river, were picked up below the rapids by the *Tamai*, which was luckily under steam. Their escape was extraordinary, for of the score who were flung into the water only one Egyptian was drowned.

Search was now made for another passage. This was found on the 6th, nearer the right bank of the river. On the 8th the *Metemma* arrived with 300 more men of the 7th Egyptians. Three days were spent in preparations and to allow the Nile to rise a little more. On the 13th, elaborate precautions being observed, the *Metemma* passed the cataract safely, and was tied up to the bank on the higher reach. The *Tamai* followed the next day. On the 19th and 20th the new gunboats *Fateh*, *Naser* and *Zafir*, the most powerful vessels on the river, accomplished the passage. Meanwhile the *Metemma* and *Tamai* had already proceeded up stream. On the 23rd the unarmed steamer *Dal* made the ascent, and by the 29th the whole flotilla reached Abu Hamed safely.

The sudden dart upon Abu Hamed had caused the utmost consternation among the Dervishes. Finding that Mahmud was not going to reinforce him, and fearing the treachery of the local tribes, Zeki Osman, the Emir in Berber, decided to fall back, and on the 24th he evacuated Berber and marched south. On the 27th General Hunter at Abu Hamed heard that the Dervish garrison had left the town. The next day he despatched Abdel-Azim, the chief of Irregulars, and Ahmed Bey Khalifa, his brother, with forty Ababda tribesmen, to reconnoitre. These bold fellows pushed on recklessly, and found the inhabitants everywhere terrified or acquiescent. Spreading extraordinary tales of the strength of the army who were following them, they created a panic all along the river, and, in spite of a sharp fight with a Dervish patrol, reached Berber on the 31st. As there was no

armed force in the town, the enterprising allies rode into the streets
and occupied the grain store – the only public building – in the name
of the Government. They then sent word back to Abu Hamed of what
they had done, and sat down in the town, thus audaciously captured,
to await developments.

The astonishing news of the fall of Berber reached General Hunter
on the 2nd of September. He immediately telegraphed to Merawi.
Sir Herbert Kitchener was confronted with a momentous question:
should Berber be occupied or not? It may at first seem that there could
be little doubt about the matter. The objective of the expedition was
Omdurman. The occupation of Berber by an Egyptian garrison would
settle at once the difficulties near Suakin. The moral effect of its capture
upon the riverain tribes and throughout the Soudan would be enormous. Berber was, in fact, the most important strategic point on the
whole line of advance.

The opposite considerations were, however, tremendous. Abu
Hamed marked a definite stage in the advance. As long as Merawi
and the other posts in Dongola were strongly held, the line from Abu
Hamed to Debba was capable of easy defence. Abu Hamed could
soon be made impregnable to Dervish attack. The forces in Dongola
could be quickly concentrated on any threatened point. At this moment
in the campaign it was possible to stop and wait with perfect safety.
In the meantime the Khalifa would steadily weaken and the railway
might steadily grow. When the line reached the angle of the river, it
would be time to continue the systematic and cautious advance. Until
then to occupy Berber was to risk much. Mahmud, with a large and
victorious army, lay at Metemma. Osman Digna, with 2,000 men,
held Adarama almost within striking distance. The railway still lagged
in the desert. The Dongola garrisons must be weakened to provide a
force for Berber. The Dervishes had the advantage of occupying the
interior of the angle which the Nile forms at Abu Hamed. The troops
in Berber would have to draw their supplies by a long and slender
line of camel communication, winding along all the way from Merawi,
and exposed throughout its whole length to attack. More than all this:
to advance to Berber must inevitably force the development of the
whole war.

The Sirdar and the Consul-General faced the responsibility together.

On the 3rd of September General Hunter received orders to occupy Berber. He started at once with 350 men of the IXth Soudanese on board the gunboats *Tamai*, *Zafir*, *Naser*, and *Fateh*. Shortly after daybreak on the 5th the Egyptian flag was hoisted over the town. Having disembarked the infantry detachment, the flotilla steamed south to try to harass the retreating Emir. On the next day they caught him, moving along the bank in considerable disorder, and, opening a heavy fire, soon drove the mixed crowd of fugitives, horse and foot, away from the river into the desert. Meanwhile the Sirdar had started for the front himself, and reached Berber on the 10th of September. Having inspected the immediate arrangements for defence, he withdrew to Abu Hamed, and there busily prepared to meet the developments which he knew must follow.

CHAPTER X

BERBER

The town of Berber stands at a little distance from the Nile, on the right bank of a channel which is full only when the river is in flood. Between this occasional stream and the regular waterway there runs a long strip of rich alluvial soil, covered during the greater part of the year with the abundant crops which result from its annual submersion and the thick coating of Nile mud which it then receives. The situation of Berber is fixed by this fertile tract, and the houses stretch for more than seven miles along it and the channel by which it is caused. The town, as is usual on the Nile, is comparatively narrow, and in all its length it is only at one point broader than three-quarters of a mile. The Berber of Egyptian days lies in ruins at the southern end of the main road. The new town built by the Dervishes stands at the north. Both are foul and unhealthy. The houses of both were constructed by a simple method. A hole was dug in the ground. The excavated mud formed the walls of the building. The roof consisted of palm-leaves and thorn-bushes. The hole became a convenient cesspool. Such was Berber, and it contained at the time of its recapture by the Egyptian forces a miserable population of 5,000 males and 7,000 females, as destitute of property as their dwellings were of elegance.

The Egyptian garrison of Berber at first consisted only of the 350 men of the IXth Soudanese, and two companies of the Camel Corps, who arrived on the 16th of September, having marched across the desert from Merawi. But the proximity of Osman Digna at Adarama made it necessary speedily to strengthen the force.

The effect of the occupation of Berber upon the tribes around Suakin was decisive. Osman Digna's influence was destroyed. The friendly villages were no longer raided. The Governor of the town became in reality, as well as in name, the Governor of the Red Sea Littoral. The route from Suakin to Berber was opened; and a Camel

Corps patrol, several small caravans of traders, and a party of war correspondents – the first Europeans to make the journey for thirteen years – passed safely along it.

It is now necessary to look to the enemy. Had the Khalifa allowed the Emir Mahmud to march north immediately after the destruction of the Dervish outpost in Abu Hamed, the course of the operations would have been very different. Mahmud would certainly have defended Berber with his whole army. But, as the last chapter has described, the sudden seizure of Abu Hamed, the defection of the riverain tribes, and the appearance of the gunboats above the Fourth Cataract persuaded Abdullah that the climax of the war approached, and that he was about to be attacked in his capital. He accordingly devoted himself to his preparations for defence, and forbade his lieutenant to advance north of Metemma or attempt any offensive operations. An elaborate system of forts armed with artillery was constructed outside the great wall of Omdurman along the river-bank. The concentration of Arab and black soldiery from Gedraef, Kordofan, and Darfur continued. Large quantities of grain, of camels and other supplies, were requisitioned from the people of the Ghezira (the country lying between the Blue and White Niles) and stored or stabled in the city. The Khalifa Sherif, who had been suspected of sympathising with the Jaalin, was made a prisoner at large. The direst penalties attended the appearance of sedition, and the Khalifa was able to muster all the remaining force of the Dervish Empire to meet the expected onslaught of his enemies.

As soon as Berber had been strongly occupied by the Egyptian troops, Osman Digna realised that his position at Adarama was not only useless but very dangerous. Mahmud had long been imperiously summoning him to join the forces at Metemma; and although he hated the Kordofan general, and resented his superior authority, the wary and cunning Osman decided that in this case it would be convenient to obey. Accordingly he withdrew with his two thousand Hadendoa from Adarama, moved along the left bank of the Atbara until the tongue of desert between the rivers became sufficiently narrow for it to be crossed in a day, and so made his way by easy stages to Shendi.

When the Sirdar heard of the evacuation of Adarama he immediately determined to assure himself of the fact, to reconnoitre the unmapped country in that region, and to destroy any property that Osman might have left behind him. On the 23rd of October, therefore, a flying column started from Berber under the command of General Hunter. The report that Osman Digna had returned to the Nile proved to be correct. His former headquarters were deserted, and although a patrol of sixty of the Camel Corps and the Arab irregulars scouted for forty miles further up the river, not a single Dervish was to be seen.

It was now November. The Nile was falling fast, and an impassable rapid began to appear at Um Tiur, four miles north of the confluence. The Sirdar had a few days in which to make up his mind whether he would keep his gunboats on the upper or lower reach. As in the latter case their patrolling limits would have been restricted, and they would no longer have been able to watch the army at Metemma, he determined to leave them on the enemy's side of the obstruction. This involved the formation of a depôt at Dakhila, where simple repairs could be executed and wood and other necessities stored. To guard this little dockyard half the 3rd Egyptian battalion was moved from Berber and posted in a small entrenchment. The other half-battalion followed in a few weeks. The post at the confluence was gradually growing into the great camp of a few months later.

A regular system of gunboat patrolling was established on the upper reach, and on the 1st of November the *Zafir*, *Naser*, and *Metemma*, under Commander Keppel, again steamed south to reconnoitre Mahmud's position. The next day they were joined by the *Fateh*, and on the 3rd the three larger boats ran the gauntlet of the forts. A brisk artillery duel ensued, but the Dervish aim was, as usual, erratic, and the vessels received no injury. It was observed that the position of the Dervish force was unchanged, but that three new forts had been constructed to the south of the town.

No other incident enlivened the monotony of November. The Khalifa continued his defensive preparations. Mahmud remained motionless at Metemma; and although he repeatedly begged to be allowed to advance against the force near Berber he was steadily refused, and had to content himself with sending raiding parties along the left bank of the Nile, and collecting large stores of grain from all the villages within his reach. Meanwhile the railway was stretching further and further to the south, and the great strain which the sudden occupation of Berber had thrown upon the transport was to some extent relieved. The Sirdar, delighted that he was neither attacked nor harassed in any way, journeyed to Kassala to arrange the details of its retrocession.

The convenient situation of Kassala – almost equally distant from Omdurman, Berber, Suakin, Massowa, and Rosaires – and the fertility of the surrounding region raise it to the dignity of the most important place in the Eastern Soudan. The soil is rich; the climate, except in the rainy season, not unhealthy. A cool night breeze relieves the heat of the day, and the presence of abundant water at the depth of a few feet below the surface supplies the deficiency of a river. In the year 1883 the population is said to have numbered more than 60,000. The Egyptians considered the town of sufficient value to require a garrison of 3,900 soldiers. A cotton mill adequately fitted with machinery and a factory chimney gave promise of the future development of manufacture. But in 1885, after a long siege and a stubborn resistance, Kassala was taken by the Dervishes. The garrison were massacred, enslaved, or incorporated in the Mahdi's army. The town was plundered and the trade destroyed. For nearly ten years an Arab force occupied the ruins and a camp outside them. Kassala became a frontier post of the Dervish Empire. Its population perished or fled to the Italian territory. This situation might have remained unaltered until after the Battle of Omdurman if the Dervishes had been content with the possession of Kassala. But in 1893 the Emir in command of the garrison, being anxious to distinguish himself, disobeyed the Khalifa's instructions to remain on the defensive and attacked the Europeans at Agordat. The Arab force of about 8,000 men were confronted by 2,300 Italian troops, protected by strong entrenchments, under Colonel Arimondi. After a fierce but hopeless attack the Dervishes were repulsed with a loss of 3,000 men, among whom was their rash leader. The engagement was, however, as disastrous to Italy as to the Khalifa. The fatal African policy of Signor Crispi received a decided impetus, and in the next year, agreeably to their aspirations in Abyssinia, the Italians under General Baratieri advanced from Agordat and captured Kassala. The occupation was provisionally recognised by Egypt without prejudice to her sovereign rights, and 900 Italian regulars and irregulars established themselves in a well-built fort.

The severe defeat at Adowa in 1896, the disgrace of Baratieri, the destruction of his army, and the fall of the Crispi Cabinet rudely dispelled the African ambitions of Italy. Kassala became an encumbrance. Nor was that all. The Dervishes, encouraged by the victory of the Abyssinians, invested the fort, and the garrison were compelled to fight hard to hold what their countrymen were anxious to abandon. In these circumstances the Italian Government offered to retrocede Kassala to Egypt. The offer was accepted, and an arrangement made. The advance of the Khedivial forces into the Dongola province relieved, as has been described, the pressure of the Dervish attacks. The Arabs occupied various small posts along the Atbara and contented themselves with raiding. The Italians remained entirely on the defensive, waiting for the moment when the fort could be handed over to the Egyptian troops.

The Sirdar had no difficulty in coming to a satisfactory arrangement with General Caneva, the Italian commander. The fort was to be occupied by an Egyptian force, the stores and armament to be purchased at a valuation, and a force of Italian Arab irregulars to be transferred to the Egyptian service. Kitchener then returned to the Nile, where the situation had suddenly become acute. During November Colonel Parsons, the 16th Egyptian Battalion, and a few native gunners marched from Suakin, and on the 20th of December arrived at Kassala. The Italian irregulars – henceforth to be known as the Arab battalion – were at once despatched to the attack of the small Dervish posts at El Fasher and Asubri, and on the next day these places were surprised and taken with scarcely any loss. The Italian officers, although a little disgusted at the turn of events, treated the Egyptian representatives with the most perfect courtesy, and the formal transference of Kassala fort was arranged to take place on Christmas Day.

Here, then, for a year we leave Colonel Parsons and his small force to swelter in the mud fort. The reader, like the Sirdar, must return in a hurry to the Upper Nile.

Towards the end of November the Khalifa had begun to realise that the 'Turks' did not mean to advance any further till the next flood of the river. As soon as he had come to this conclusion, he no longer turned a deaf ear to Mahmud's solicitations. He knew that the falling Nile would restrict the movements of the gunboats. He knew that

there were only 2,000 men in Berber – a mere handful. He did not
realise the tremendous power of rapid concentration which the railway
had given his enemies; and he began to think of offensive operations.
But Mahmud should not go alone. The whole strength of the Dervish
Army should be exerted to drive back the invaders. All the troops in
Omdurman were ordered north. A great camp was again formed
near Kerreri. At the beginning of December he sent his own secretary
to Mahmud to explain the plan, and to assure him of early reinforcements and supplies. Lastly, Abdullah preached a new *Jehad*, and it is
remarkable that, while all former exhortations had been directed
against 'the infidel' – i.e. those who did not believe in the Mahdi –
his letters and sermons on this occasion summoned the tribes to destroy
not the Egyptians but the Christians. There were at this time scarcely
150 Europeans in the Soudan; but they had made their presence felt.

Kitchener's reply to the Khalifa's open intent was to order a general
concentration of the available Egyptian Army towards Berber, to
telegraph to Lord Cromer asking for a British brigade, and to close
the Suakin–Berber route.

The gunboat depôt at the confluence, with only a half-battalion
escort, was now in an extremely exposed position. The gunboats
could not steam north, for the cataract four miles below the confluence was already impassable. Since they must remain on the enemy's
side, so must their depôt; and the depôt must be held by a much stronger
force. Although the Sirdar felt too weak to maintain himself even on
the defensive without reinforcements, he was now compelled to push
still further south. On the 22nd of December Lewis's brigade of four
battalions and a battery were hurried along the Nile to its junction
with the Atbara, and began busily entrenching themselves in an angle
formed by the rivers. The Atbara fort sprang into existence.

Meanwhile the concentration was proceeding. All the troops in
Dongola, with the exception of scanty garrisons in Merawi, Korti,
and Debba, were massed at Berber. The infantry and guns, dropping
down the river in boats, entrained at Kerma, were carried back to
Halfa, then hustled across the invaluable Desert Railway, past Abu
Hamed, and finally deposited at Railhead, which then (1st January)
stood at Dakhesh. The whole journey by rail from Merawi to Dakhesh
occupied four days, whereas General Hunter with his flying column

had taken eight. The Egyptian cavalry at Merawi received their orders on the 25th of December, and the British officers hurried from their Christmas dinners to prepare for their long march across the bend of the Nile to Berber. Of the eight squadrons, three were pushed on to join Lewis's force at the position which will hereinafter be called 'the Atbara encampment', or more familiarly 'the Atbara'; three swelled the gathering forces at Berber; and two remained for the present in the Dongola province, looking anxiously out towards Gakdul Wells and Metemma.

The War Office, who had been nervous about the situation in the Soudan since the hasty occupation of Berber, and who had a very lively recollection of the events of 1884 and 1885, lost no time in the despatch of British troops. The 1st Battalions of the Royal Warwickshire Regiment, of the Lincoln Regiment, and of the Cameron Highlanders were formed into a brigade and moved from Cairo into the Soudan. The 1st Battalion of the Seaforth Highlanders was brought from Malta to Egypt, and held in immediate readiness to reinforce the troops at the front.

The officer selected for the command of the British brigade was a man of high character and ability. General Gatacre had already led a brigade in the Chitral expedition. He left India, leaving behind him golden opinions, just before the outbreak of the great Frontier rising, and was appointed to a brigade at Aldershot. Thence we now find him hurried to the Soudan – a spare, middle-sized man, of great physical strength and energy, of marked capacity and unquestioned courage, but disturbed by a restless irritation, which often left him the exhausted victim of his own vitality.

By the end of January a powerful force lay encamped along the river from Abu Hamed to the Atbara. Meanwhile the Dervishes made no forward movement. Their army was collected at Kerreri; supplies were plentiful; all preparations had been made. Yet they tarried. The burning question of the command had arisen. When the whole army was regularly assembled, the Khalifa announced publicly that he would lead the faithful in person; but at the same time he arranged privately that many Emirs and notables should beg him not to expose his sacred person. After proper solicitation, therefore, he yielded to their appeals. Then he looked round for a subordinate. The Khalifa Ali-Wad-Helu

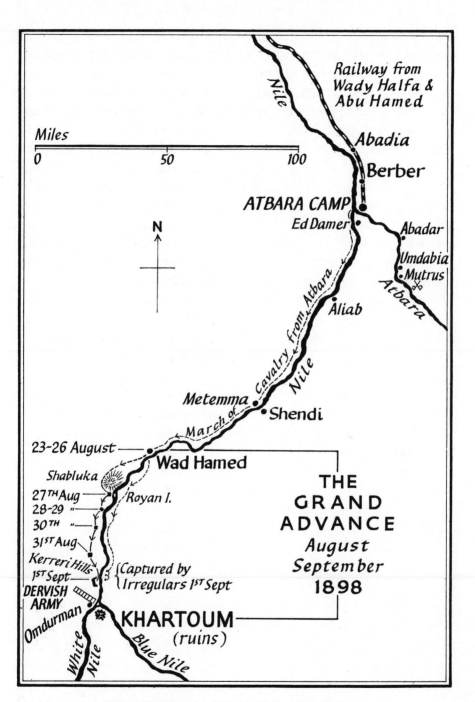

THE NILE FROM ATBARA TO KHARTOUM

presented himself. In the Soudan every advantage and honour accrues to the possessor of an army, and the rival chief saw a chance of regaining his lost power. This consideration was not, however, lost upon Abdullah. He accepted the offer with apparent delight, but he professed himself unable to spare any rifles for the army which Ali-Wad-Helu aspired to lead. 'Alas!' he cried, 'there are none. But that will make no difference to so famous a warrior.' Ali-Wad-Helu, however, considered that it would make a great deal of difference, and declined the command. Osman Sheikh-ed-Din offered to lead the army, if he might arm the riverain tribes and use them as auxiliaries to swell his force. This roused the disapproval of Yakub. Such a policy, he declared, was fatal. The riverain tribes were traitors – dogs – worthy only of being destroyed. The squabble continued, until at last the Khalifa, despairing of any agreement, decided merely to reinforce Mahmud, and accordingly ordered the Emir Yunes to march to Metemma with about 5,000 men. But it was then discovered that Mahmud hated Yunes, and would have none of him. At this the Khalifa broke up his camp, and the Dervish Army marched back for a second time, in disgust, to the city.

It seemed to those who were acquainted with the Dervish movements that the break-up of the Kerreri camp was the end of the Khalifa's determination to move north. There would be a hot and uneventful summer, and with the Nile flood the expedition would begin its final advance. The news which was received on the 15th of February came as a great and pleasant surprise. Mahmud was crossing the Nile and proposed to advance on Berber without reinforcements of any kind. The Sirdar, highly satisfied at this astounding piece of good fortune, immediately began to mass his force nearer the confluence. The Seaforths began their journey from Cairo, and the various battalions of the Egyptian Army pressed forward towards Berber and Atbara fort. On the 25th, Mahmud being reported as having crossed to the right bank, the general concentration was ordered.

CHAPTER XI

RECONNAISSANCE

The hazards which were courted by the daring occupation of Berber have been discussed in the last chapter. From October to December the situation was threatening. In December it suddenly became critical. Had the Emir Mahmud advanced with the Dervishes at Metemma even as late as the middle of January, he might possibly have re-captured Berber. If the great Omdurman army had taken the field, the possibility would have become a certainty. But it was not until the Khalifa had sent his own army back into the city that, being very badly informed of the numbers and disposition of the Egyptian force, he allowed the Metemma Dervishes to move.

Mahmud received permission to advance at the end of January. He eagerly obeyed the longed-for order. But the whole situation was now changed. The Egyptian Army was concentrated; the British brigade had arrived; the railway had reached Geneinetti; the miserable hamlet of Dakhila, at the confluence, had grown from a small depôt to an entrenched camp, against which neither Dervish science nor strength could by any possibility prevail. Perhaps Mahmud did not realise the amazing power of movement that the railway had given his foes; perhaps he still believed, with the Khalifa, that Berber was held only by 2,000 Egyptians; or else – and this is the most probable – he was reckless of danger and strong in his own conceit. At any rate, during the second week in February he began to transport himself across the Nile, with the plain design of an advance north. With all the procrastination of an Arab he crawled leisurely forward towards the confluence of the rivers. At El Aliab some idea of the strength of the Atbara entrenchment seems to have dawned upon him. A council was held. Mahmud was for a continued advance and for making a direct attack on the enemy's position. Osman Digna urged a more prudent course. Many years of hard fighting against disciplined troops had taught the wily Hadendoa slaver the power of modern rifles, and much sound tactics besides. He pressed his case with jealous enthusiasm upon the commander he detested and despised. An insurmountable obstacle confronted them. Yet what could not be overcome might be avoided. The hardy Dervishes could endure privations which would destroy the soldiers of civilisation. Barren and inhospitable as was the desert, they might move round the army at the Atbara fort and once they were behind the Egyptians, these accursed ones were lost. The railway – that mysterious source of strength – could be cut. The host that drew its life along it must fight at a fearful disadvantage or perish miserably. Besides, he reminded Mahmud, they could count on help in Berber itself.

The agreement of the Emirs, called to the council, decided the Dervish leader. His confidence in himself was weakened, his hatred of Osman Digna increased. Nevertheless, following the older man's advice, he left Aliab on the 18th of March, and struck north-east into the desert towards the village and ford of Hudi on the Atbara River. Thence by a long desert march he might reach the Nile and Berber. But while his information of the Sirdar's force and movements was uncertain, the British General was better served. As soon, therefore, as Kitchener learned that the Dervishes had left the Nile and were making a detour around his left flank, he marched up the Atbara River to Hudi. This offered Mahmud the alternative of attacking him in a strong position or of making a still longer detour. He chose the latter, and, deflecting his march still more to the east, reached the Atbara at Nakheila. But from this point the distance to Berber was far too great for him to cover. He could not carry enough water in his skins. The wells were few, and held against him. Further advance was impossible. So he waited and entrenched himself, uncertain what to do. Supplies were running short. His magazines at Shendi had been destroyed as soon as he had left the Nile. The Dervishes might exist, but they did not thrive, on the nuts of the dôm palms. Soldiers began to desert. Osman Digna, although his advice had been followed, was at open enmity.

And all this time his terrible antagonist watched him as a tiger gloats on a helpless and certain prey – silent, merciless, inexorable. The tiger crept forward two measured strides – from Ras-el-Hudi to

Abadar, from Abadar to Umdabia – crouched for a moment, and
then bounded with irresistible fury upon its prey and tore it to pieces.
At daybreak on the morning of the 6th of April the whole army
broke camp at Abadar and marched to the deserted village of Umdabia,
where they bivouacked close by a convenient pool of the Atbara and
seven miles nearer the Dervish camp. The camp at Umdabia lay in the
scrub which grows by the banks of the Atbara, as by those of the
Nile, and in order to profit by the open, level ground the four infantry
brigades moved by parallel routes into the desert, and then formed
facing south-east in column of brigade squares, the British brigade
leading. The mounted forces, with four batteries of artillery, waited
in camp until two o'clock the next morning, and did not break their
march. The distance from the river-bank to the open plain was perhaps
a mile and a half, and the whole infantry force had cleared the scrub
by six o'clock. The sun was setting, and the red glow, brightening
the sandy hillocks, made the western horizon indefinite, so that it was
hard to tell where the desert ended and the sky began. On the great
plain 12,000 infantry, conscious of their strength and eager to encounter the enemy, were beautifully arranged in four solid masses.
Then the march began. The actual distance from the camp to the
Dervish position was scarcely seven miles, but the circle necessary to
avoid the bushes and the gradual bends of the river added perhaps
another five to the length of the road. The pace of the advance was
slow, and the troops had not gone far when the sun sank and, with
hardly an interval of twilight, darkness enveloped everything.

No operation of a war is more critical than a night-march. Over
and over again in every country frightful disaster has overtaken the
force that has attempted it. In the gloom the shape and aspect of the
ground are altered. Places well known by daylight appear strange and
unrecognisable. The smallest obstacle impedes the column, which
can only crawl sluggishly forward with continual checks and halts.
The effect of the gloom upon the nerves of the soldiers is not less than
on the features of the country. Each man tries to walk quietly, and
hence all are listening for the slightest sound. Every eye seeks to pierce
the darkness. In such hours doubts and fears come unbidden to the
brain, and the marching men wonder whether they themselves will
survive the event. And if suddenly out of the black silence there burst

the jagged glare of rifles and the crash of a volley followed by the yell of an attacking foe, the steadiest troops may be thrown into confusion, and a panic, once afoot, stops only with the destruction or dispersal of the whole force.

For more than two hours the force advanced, moving across smooth swells of sand broken by rocks and with occasional small bushes. Several shallow *khors* traversed the road, and these rocky ditches, filled with a strange, sweet-scented grass, delayed the brigades until the pace was hardly two miles an hour.

At nine o'clock the army halted in a previously selected space, near the deserted village of Mutrus and about two miles from the river. Nearly half the distance to Mahmud's *zeriba* was accomplished, and barely four miles in the direct line divided the combatants; but since it was not desirable to arrive before the dawn, the soldiers, still formed in their squares, lay down upon the ground.

During the halt the moon had risen, and when at one o'clock the advance was resumed, the white beams revealed a wider prospect and, glinting on the fixed bayonets, crowned the squares with a sinister glitter. For three hours the army toiled onwards at the same slow and interrupted crawl. Strict silence was now enforced, and all smoking was forbidden. The cavalry, the Camel Corps, and the five batteries had overtaken the infantry, so that the whole attacking force was concentrated. Meanwhile the Dervishes slept.

At three o'clock the glare of fires became visible to the south, and, thus arrived before the Dervish position, the squares, with the exception of the reserve brigade, were unlocked, and the whole force, assuming formation of attack, now advanced in one long line through the scattered bush and scrub, presently to emerge upon a large plateau which overlooked Mahmud's *zeriba* from a distance of about 900 yards.

It was still dark, and the haze that shrouded the Dervish camp was broken only by the glare of the watch-fires. The silence was profound. It seemed impossible to believe that more than 25,000 men were ready to join battle at scarcely the distance of half a mile. Yet the advance had not been unperceived, and the Arabs knew that their terrible antagonists crouched on the ridge waiting for the morning. At last, after what seemed an interminable period, the uniform blackness of the horizon was broken by the first glimmer of the dawn. Gradually the

light grew stronger until, as a theatre curtain is pulled up, the darkness rolled away, the vague outlines in the haze became definite, and
the whole scene was revealed.

The British and Egyptian Army lay along the low ridge in the form
of a great bow – the British brigade on the left, MacDonald in the
centre, Maxwell curving forward on the right. The whole crest of
the swell of ground was crowned with a bristle of bayonets and the
tiny figures of thousands of men sitting or lying down and gazing
curiously before them. Behind them, in a solid square, was the transport, guarded by Lewis's brigade. The leading squadrons of the cavalry
were forming leisurely towards the left flank. The four batteries and
a rocket detachment, moving between the infantry, ranged themselves
on two convenient positions about a hundred yards in front of the
line of battalions. All was ready.

Half a mile away, at the foot of the ridge, a long irregular black
line of thorn bushes enclosed the Dervish defences. Behind this *zeriba*
low palisades and entrenchments bent back to the scrub by the river.
Odd shapeless mounds indicated the positions of the gun-emplace-
ments, and various casemates could be seen in the middle of the enclosure. Without, the bushes had been cleared away, and the smooth
sand stretched in a gentle slope to where the army waited. Within
were crowds of little straw huts and scattered bushes, growing thicker
to the southward. Such was Mahmud's famous *zeriba*, which for more
than a month had been the predominant thought in the minds of the
troops. It was scarcely imposing, and at first the soldiers thought it
deserted. Only a dozen stray horsemen sat silently on their horses
outside the entrenchment, watching their enemies, and inside a few
dirty-white figures appeared and disappeared behind the parapets.
Yet, insignificant as the *zeriba* looked, the smoke of many fires cooking
the morning meal showed that it was occupied by men; and gay
banners of varied colour and device, flaunting along the entrenchments
or within the enclosure, declared that some at least were prepared to
die in its defence.

The hush of the hour and the suspense of the army were broken
by the bang of a gun. Everyone on the ridge jumped up and looked
towards the sound. A battery of Krupps a little to the right of the
Cameron Highlanders had opened fire. Another gun further to the

right was fired. Another shell burst over the straw huts among the palm-trees. The two Maxim-Nordenfeldt batteries had come into action. The officers looked at their watches. It was a quarter past six. The bombardment had begun.

Explosion followed explosion in quick succession until all four batteries were busily engaged. The cannonade grew loud and continuous. The rocket detachment began to fire, and the strange projectiles hissed and screamed as they left the troughs and jerked erratically towards the *zeriba*. At the very first shot all the dirty-white figures disappeared, bobbing down into their pits and shelters; but a few solitary horsemen remained motionless for a while in the middle of the enclosure, watching the effect of the fire, as if it had no concern with them.

After the bombardment had lasted about ten minutes a great cloud of dust sprang up in the *zeriba*, and hundreds of horsemen were seen scrambling into their saddles and galloping through a gap in the rear face out into the open sand to the right. To meet the possibility of an attempt to turn the left flank of the attack, the eight squadrons of cavalry and two Maxim guns jingled and clattered off in the direction of the danger. The dust, which the swift passage of so many horsemen raised, shut the scene from the eyes of the infantry, but continual dust-clouds above the scrub to the left and the noise of the Maxims seemed to indicate a cavalry fight. The Baggara horse, however, declined an unequal combat. Twice they showed some sort of front, and the squadrons thought they might find opportunity to charge; but a few rounds from the Maxims effectually checked the enemy. With the exception of one squadron detached on the right, the Egyptian cavalry force, however, remained on the left flank, and shielded the operations of the assaulting infantry.

Meanwhile the bombardment continued with accuracy and precision. The batteries searched the interior of the *zeriba*, threshing out one section after another, and working the whole ground regularly from front to rear. The *zeriba* and palisades were knocked about in many places, and at a quarter to seven a cluster of straw huts caught fire and began to burn briskly. At a quarter past seven the infantry were ordered to form in column for assault.

The plan of the attack for the army was simple. The long, deployed

line were to advance steadily against the entrenchments, subduing
by their continual fire that of the enemy. They were then to tear the
zeriba to pieces. Covered by their musketry, the dense columns of
assault which had followed the line were to enter the defences through
the gaps, deploy to the right, and march through the enclosure,
clearing it with the bayonet and by fire.

At twenty minutes to eight the Sirdar ordered his bugles to sound
the general advance. The call was repeated by all the brigades, and the
clear notes rang out above the noise of the artillery. The superior
officers – with the exception of Hunter, Maxwell, and MacDonald –
dismounted and placed themselves at the head of their commands.
The whole mass of the infantry, numbering nearly eleven thousand
men, immediately began to move forward upon the *zeriba*. The scene
as this great force crested the ridge and advanced down the slope was
magnificent and tremendous. Large solid columns of men, preceded
by a long double line, with the sunlight flashing on their bayonets
and displaying their ensigns, marched to the assault in regular and
precise array. The pipes of the Highlanders, the bands of the Soudanese,
and the drums and fifes of the English regiments added a wild and
thrilling accompaniment. As soon as the advance masked the batteries,
the guns were run forward with the firing line, in order effectually to
support the attack. The deployed battalions opened a ceaseless and
crushing fire on the entrenchment, and as the necessity of firing
delayed the advance of the attacking columns, the pace did not exceed
a slow march.

The Dervishes remained silent until the troops were within 300 yards.
Then the smoke-puffs spurted out all along the stockades, and a sharp
fusillade began, gradually and continually growing in intensity until
the assaulting troops were exposed to a furious and effective fire.
From 250 yards up to the position losses began to occur. The whole
entrenchment was rimmed with flame and smoke, amid which the
active figures of the Dervish riflemen were momentarily visible, and
behind the filmy curtain solid masses of swordsmen and spearmen
appeared. The fortunate interposition of a small knoll in some degree
protected the advance of the Lincoln Regiment, but in both Highland
battalions soldiers began to drop. The whole air was full of a strange
chirping whistle. Numerous explosive bullets, fired by the Arabs,

made queer startling reports. All the deployed battalions began to suffer. But they and the assaulting columns, regardless of the fire, bore down on the *zeriba* in all the majesty of war – an avalanche of men, stern, unflinching, utterly irresistible.

The loss during the passage of the *zeriba* and in the assault of the entrenchments was severe. Captain Findlay and Major Urquhart, of the Cameron Highlanders, were both mortally wounded in the fight at the stockades, and expired still cheering on their men. Major Napier, of the same regiment, and Captain Baillie, of the Seaforth Highlanders, received the wounds, of which they subsequently died, a few yards further on. At all points the troops broke into the enclosure. Behind the stockade there ran a treble trench. The whole interior was honey-combed with pits and holes. From these there now sprang thousands of Dervishes, desperately endeavouring to show a front to the attack. Many soldiers were killed and wounded in the narrow space. In the five minutes which were occupied in the passage of the obstruction about four hundred casualties occurred.

The British brigade had struck the extremity of the north front of the *zeriba*, and thus took the whole of the eastern face in *enfilade*, sweeping it with their terrible musketry from end to end, and strewing the ground with corpses. Although, owing to the lines of advance having converged, there was not room for more than half the force to deploy, the brigades pushed on. The conduct of the attack passed to the company commanders. All these officers kept their heads, and brought their companies up into the general lines as the front gradually widened and gaps appeared. So the whole force – companies, battalions, even brigades – mixed up together and formed in one dense, ragged, but triumphant line, marched on unchecked towards the river bed, driving their enemies in hopeless confusion before them. Yet, although the Dervishes were unable to make head against the attack, they disdained to run. Many hundreds held their ground, firing their rifles valiantly till the end. Others charged with spear and sword. The greater part retired in skirmishing order, jumping over the numerous pits, walking across the open spaces, and repeatedly turning round to shoot. The XIth Soudanese encountered the most severe resistance after the defences were penetrated. As their three deployed companies pressed on through the enclosure, they were confronted by a small

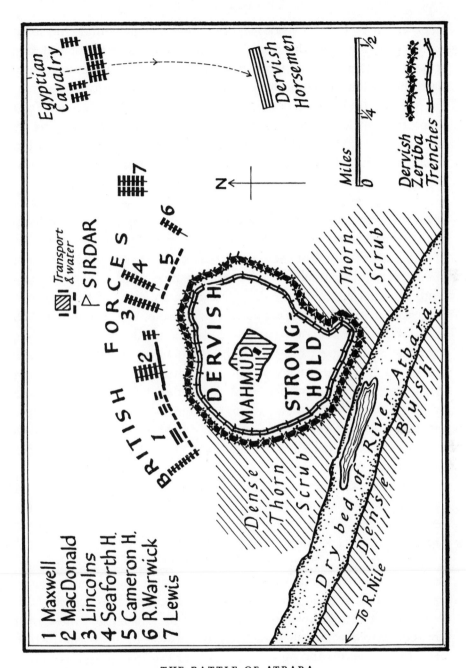

1 Maxwell
2 MacDonald
3 Lincolns
4 Seaforth H.
5 Cameron H.
6 R.Warwick
7 Lewis

Egyptian Cavalry

Dervish Horsemen

Transport & water

SIRDAR

BRITISH FORCES

DERVISH STRONG-HOLD

MAHMUD

Thorn Scrub

Dense Thorn Scrub

Dense Thorn Scrub

Dry bed of River Atbara

Dense Bush

To R.Nile

Miles

Dervish Zeriba Trenches

N

THE BATTLE OF ATBARA

inner *zeriba* stubbornly defended by the Emir Mahmud's personal bodyguard. These poured a sudden volley into the centre company at close range, and so deadly was the effect that nearly all the company were shot, falling to the ground still in their ranks. Notwithstanding this severe check the regiment, gallantly led by their colonel and supported by the Xth Soudanese, rushed this last defence and slew its last defenders. Mahmud was himself captured, and, on his being recognised, the intervention of a British officer alone saved him from the fury of the excited Soudanese.

At about twenty minutes past eight the whole force, with the Seaforth Highlanders well forward on the left, arrived at the bank of the Atbara, having marched completely through the position, and shot or bayoneted all in their path. Hundreds of Dervishes were still visible retiring across the dry bed of the river, and making for the scrub on the opposite bank. The leading companies of the Seaforth Highlanders and Lincolns, with such odd parties of Camerons as had been carried on with the attack, opened a murderous fire on these fugitives. Since they would not run their loss was heavy, and it was a strange sight – the last vivid impression of the day – to watch them struggling through the deep sand, with the dust knocked up into clouds by the bullets which struck all round them. Very few escaped, and the bodies of the killed lay thickly dotting the river-bed with heaps of dirty-white. Then at 8.25 the 'Cease fire' sounded, and the battle of the Atbara ended.

The losses had been severe. In the assault – a period not exceeding half an hour – eighteen British, sixteen native officers and 525 men had been killed or wounded, the greater part during the passage of the *zeriba*.

The actual pursuit was abortive. Colonel Lewis, with his two battalions, followed a line of advance which led south of the *zeriba*, and just before reaching the river bank found and fired upon a few Dervishes retreating through the scrub. All the cavalry and the Camel Corps crossed the Atbara and plunged into the bush on the further side. But so dense and tangled was the country that after three miles of peril and perplexity they abandoned the attempt, and the routed Arabs fled unmolested. The Baggara horse had ridden off during the action, headed by the prudent Osman Digna, and under that careful leadership suffered little loss. The rest of the army was, however, destroyed or dispersed. Of the powerful force of 12,000 fighting men which Mahmud had gathered at Metemma, scarcely 4,000 reached Gedaref in safety. These survivors were added to the army of Ahmed Fedil, and thus prevented from spreading their evil tidings among the populace at Omdurman. Osman Digna, Wad Bishara, and other important Emirs whose devotion and discretion were undoubted, alone returned to the capital.

As soon as the troops were re-formed, the *zeriba* was evacuated and the army drew up in line along the neighbouring ridge. It was then only nine o'clock, and the air was still cool and fresh. The soldiers lit fires, made some tea, and ate their rations of biscuits and meat. Gradually, as the hours passed, the sun became powerful. There was no shade, and only a few thin, leafless bushes rose from the sand. The hours of a day, peculiarly hot, even for the country and season, dragged wearily away. The water in the *fantasses* and bottles was hot and scarce. The pool of the Atbara was foul and tainted. In spite of the devoted efforts of the few medical officers who had been allowed to accompany the force, the wounded officers and soldiers endured the greatest miseries, and it is certain that several died of their wounds who might in happier circumstances have been saved.

Several hundred prisoners were taken. They were mostly negroes – for the Arabs refused to surrender, and fought to the last or tried to escape. The captive blacks, who fight with equal willingness on either side, were content to be enlisted in the Soudanese regiments; so that many of those who served the Khalifa on the Atbara helped to destroy him at Omdurman. The most notable prisoner was the Emir Mahmud – a tall, strong Arab, about thirty years old. Immediately after his capture he was dragged before the Sirdar. 'Why,' inquired the General, 'have you come into my country to burn and kill?' 'I have to obey my orders, and so have you,' retorted the captive sullenly, yet not without a certain dignity. He was removed in custody – a fine specimen of proud brutality, worthy perhaps of some better fate than to linger indefinitely in the gaol at Rosetta.

As the Battle of the Atbara had been decisive, the whole Expeditionary Force went into summer quarters. The Egyptian Army was distributed into three principal garrisons – four battalions at Atbara camp, six battalions and the cavalry at Berber, three battalions at Abadia. The artillery and transport were proportionately divided. The British brigade encamped with two battalions at Darmali and two at the village of Selim, about a mile and a half distant.

For the final phase of the campaign three new gunboats had been ordered from England. These were now sent in sections over the Desert Railway. Sir H. Kitchener himself proceeded to Abadia to accelerate the construction of the vessels on which so much depended. Here during the heat of the summer he remained, maturing his plans, and waiting only for the rise of the river to complete the downfall of his foes.

CHAPTER XII

THE GRAND ADVANCE

All through the early months of the summer the preparations for the final advance were steadily proceeding. A second British brigade was ordered to the Soudan. A new battery of Howitzer artillery – the 37th – firing enormous shells charged with lyddite, was despatched from England. Two large 40-pounder guns were sent from Cairo. Another British Maxim battery of four guns was formed in Cairo from men of the Royal Irish Fusiliers. Three new screw gunboats of the largest size and most formidable pattern had been passed over the indefatigable railway in sections, and were now launched on the clear waterway south of the Atbara encampment; and last, but not least, the 21st Lancers[1] were ordered up the Nile. Events now began to move rapidly. There was no delay at the Atbara encampment. Even before the whole of the second brigade had arrived, some of its battalions were being despatched to Wad Hamed, the new point of concentration. This place was a few miles north of Shabluka, and only fifty-eight miles from Omdurman. It was evident, therefore, that the decisive moment of the three years' war approached. The Staff, the British infantry, one squadron, the guns, and the stores were carried south in steamers and barges. The Egyptian division marched to Wad Hamed by brigades. The horses of the batteries, the transport animals of the British division (about 1,400 in number), the chargers of the officers, some cattle, and most of the war correspondents were sent along the left bank of the river escorted by two squadrons of the 21st Lancers and two Maxim guns.

All the thirteen squadrons of cavalry remained three days at Wad Hamed. After the fatigues of the march we were glad to have an opportunity of looking about, of visiting regiments known in other

[1] The author led a troop in this regiment during the final advance to Omdurman; and it is from this standpoint that the ensuing chapters are to some extent conceived.

279

circumstances, and of writing a few letters. This last was the most important, for it was now known that after leaving Wad Hamed there would be no post or communication with Cairo and Europe until the action had been fought and all was over. The halt was welcome for another reason. The camp itself was well worth looking at. It lay lengthways along the river-bank, and was nearly two miles from end to end. The Nile secured it from attack towards the east. On the western and southern sides were strong lines of thorn bushes, staked down and forming a *zeriba*; and the north face was protected by a deep artificial watercourse which allowed the waters of the river to make a considerable inundation. Far away to the southward the white tents of the British division; a little nearer rows and rows of grass huts and blanket shelters, the bivouacs of the Egyptian and Soudanese brigades; the Sirdar's large white tent, with the red flag of Egypt flying from a high staff, on a small eminence; and to the right the grove of palm-trees in which the officers of the Egyptian cavalry had established themselves. The whole riverside was filled by a forest of masts; *gyassas*, barges, and steamers were moored closely together.

The road to the next camp was a long one; for though Royan island, opposite to which the site had been selected, was only seven miles in the direct line, it was necessary to march eight miles into the desert to avoid the Shabluka heights, and then to turn back to the Nile. The infantry were therefore provided with camel transport to carry sufficient water in small iron tanks for one night; and they were thus able to bivouac half-way, and to complete the journey on the next morning, thus making a two days' march. The mounted troops, who remained at Wad Hamed till all had gone south, were ordered to move on the 27th of August, and by a double march catch up the rest of the army.

Wad Hamed then ceased for the time being to exist except in name. All the stores and transport were moved by land or water to the south of Shabluka, and an advanced base was formed upon Royan island. Communications with the Atbara encampment and with Cairo were dropped, and the army carried with them in their boats sufficient supplies to last until after the capture of Omdurman. It was calculated that the scope of this operation would not be greater than three weeks, and on the 27th the army were equipped with twenty-one days' supplies, of which two were carried by the troops, five by the regimental barges, and fourteen in the army transport sailing-vessels. All surplus stores were deposited at Royan island, where a field hospital was also formed.

The total strength of the Expeditionary Force supplied for the culminating moment of the River War amounted to 8,200 British and 17,600 Egyptian soldiers, with 44 guns and 20 Maxims on land, with 36 guns and 24 Maxims on the river, and with 2,469 horses, 896 mules, 3,524 camels, and 229 donkeys, besides followers and private animals.

While the army were to move along the west bank of the river – the Omdurman side – a force of Arab irregulars, formed from the friendly tribes, would march along the east bank and clear it of any Dervishes. All the debris which the Egyptian advance had broken off the Dervish Empire was thus to be hurled against that falling State. Eager for plunder, anxious to be on the winning side, Sheikhs and Emirs from every tribe in the Military Soudan had hurried, with what following the years of war had left them, to Wad Hamed. On the 26th of August the force of irregulars numbered about 2,500 men, principally Jaalin survivors, but also comprising bands and individuals of Bisharin; of Hadendoa from Suakin; of Shukria, the camel-breeders; of Batahin, who had suffered a bloody diminution at the Khalifa's hands; of Shaiggia, Gordon's vexatious allies; and lastly some Gemilab Arabs under a reputed son of Zubehr Pasha. The command of the whole motley force was given to Major Stuart-Wortley, Lieutenant Wood accompanying him as Staff Officer; and the position of these officers among the cowed and untrustworthy Arabs was one of considerable peril.

While the infantry divisions were marching round the heights of Shabluka to the camp opposite Royan island, the steamers and gunboats ascended the stream and passed through the gorge, dragging up with them the whole fleet of barges and *gyassas*. The northern end of the narrow passage had been guarded by the five Dervish forts, which now stood deserted and dismantled. They were well built, and formed nearly a straight line – four on one bank and one on the other. Each fort had three embrasures, and might, when occupied, have been a formidable defence to the cataract.

The mounted forces marched from Wad Hamed at dawn on the 27th and, striking out into the desert, skirted the rocky hills. Besides the 21st Lancers and nine squadrons of Egyptian cavalry, the column included the Camel Corps, 800 strong, and a battery of Horse Artillery; and it was a fine sight to see all these horsemen and camel-men trotting swiftly across the sand by squadrons and companies, with a great cloud of dust rising from each and drifting away to the northward.

The *zeriba* of the camp at Royan had been already made and much of the ground cleared by the energy of the Soudanese division, which had been the first to arrive. An advanced depôt was established at Royan island, which was covered with white hospital tents, near which there was a forest of masts and sails. The barges and boats containing the stores and kits awaited the troops, and they had only to bivouac along the river-bank and shelter themselves as quickly as possible from the fierce heat of the sun. The eternal Nile flowed swiftly by the tents and shelters, and disappeared mysteriously in the gloom of the gorge; and on the further bank there rose a great mountain – Jebel Royan – from the top of which it was said that men might see Khartoum.

The whole army broke camp at Royan on the 28th of August at four o'clock in the afternoon, and marched to Wady el Abid, six miles further south. We now moved on a broad front, which could immediately be converted into a fighting formation. This was the first time that it had been possible to see the whole force – infantry, cavalry, and guns – on the march at once. In the clear air the amazing detail of the picture was striking. There were six brigades of infantry, composed of twenty-four battalions; yet every battalion showed that it was made up of tiny figures, all perfectly defined on the plain. A Soudanese brigade had been sent on to hold the ground with pickets until the troops had constructed a *zeriba*. But a single Dervish horseman managed to evade these and, just as the light faded, rode up to the Warwickshire Regiment and flung his broad-bladed spear in token of defiance. So great was the astonishment which this unexpected apparition created that the bold man actually made good his escape uninjured.

On the 29th the forces remained halted opposite Um Teref, and only the Egyptian cavalry went out to reconnoitre. They searched the country for eight or nine miles, and Colonel Broadwood returned in the afternoon, having found a convenient camping-ground, but nothing else. During the day the news of two river disasters arrived – the first to ourselves, the second to our foes. On the 28th the gunboat *Zafir* was steaming from the Atbara to Wad Hamed, intending thereafter to ascend the Shabluka Cataract. Suddenly – overtaken now, as on the eve of the advance on Dongola, by misfortune – she sprang a leak, and, in spite of every effort to run her ashore, foundered by the head in deep water near Metemma. The Sirdar received the news at Royan. His calculations were disturbed by the loss of a powerful vessel; but the days of struggling warfare were over, and the General knew that he had a safe margin of strength.

The other catastrophe afflicted the Khalifa, and its tale was brought to the advancing army by the Intelligence spies, who to the last – even when the forces were closing – tried to pass between them. Not content with building batteries along the banks, Abdullah, fearing the gunboats, had resolved to mine the river. An old officer of the old Egyptian Army, long a prisoner in Omdurman, was brought from his chains and ordered to construct mines. Two iron boilers were filled with gunpowder, and it was arranged that these should be sunk in the Nile at convenient spots. Buried in the powder of each was a loaded pistol with a string attached to the trigger. On pulling the string the pistol, and consequently the mine, would be exploded. So the Khalifa argued; nor was he wrong. It was resolved to lay one mine first. On the 17th of August the Dervish steamer *Ismailia* moved out into the middle of the Nile, carrying one of the boilers fully charged and equipped with pistol detonator. Arrived at the selected spot, the great cylinder of powder was dropped over the side. Its efficiency as a destructive engine was immediately demonstrated, for, on the string being pulled by accident, the pistol discharged itself, the powder exploded, and the *Ismailia* and all on board were blown to pieces.

Undeterred by the loss of life, and encouraged by the manifest power of the contrivance, the Khalifa immediately ordered the second of the two boilers to be sunk in the stream. As the old Egyptian officer had been killed by the explosion, the Emir in charge of the arsenal was entrusted with the perilous business. He rose, however, to the occasion, and, having first taken the precaution of letting the water into the boiler so as to damp the powder, he succeeded in laying the second mine in mid-stream, to the joy and delight of Abdullah, who, not understanding that it was now useless, overwhelmed him with praise and presents.

Beguiled with such stories and diversions, the day of rest at Wady el Abid passed swiftly. Night brought beetles, bugs, and ants, and several men were stung by scorpions – a most painful though not dangerous affair. Towards morning it began to rain, and everyone was drenched and chilled when the sun rose across the river from behind a great conical hill and dispersed the clouds into wisps of creamy flame. Then we mounted and set out.

When we had advanced a little further, there arose above the scrub the dark outlines of a rocky peak, the hill of Merreh. The whole of the 21st Lancers now concentrated, and, trotting quickly forward, occupied this position, whence a considerable tract of country was visible. We were hardly twenty-five miles from Khartoum, and of that distance at least ten miles were displayed. Yet there were no enemy. Had they all fled? Should we find Omdurman deserted or submissive? These were questions which occurred to everyone, and many answered them affirmatively. Colonel Martin had meanwhile heliographed back to the Sirdar that all the ground was up to this point clear, and that there were no Dervishes to be seen. After some delay orders were signalled back for one squadron to remain till sunset in observation on the hill and for the rest to return to camp.

With two troops thrown out a mile in front we waited watching on the hill. Time passed slowly, for the sun was hot. Suddenly it became evident that one of the advanced troops was signalling energetically. The message was spelt out. The officer with the troop perceived Dervishes in his front. We looked through our glasses. It was true. There, on a white patch of sand among the bushes of the plain, were a lot of little brown spots, moving slowly across the front of the cavalry outposts towards an Egyptian squadron, which was watching far out to the westward. There may have been seventy horsemen altogether. We could not take our eyes off those distant specks we had travelled so far, if possible, to destroy. Presently the Dervish patrol approached our right troop, and apparently came nearer than they imagined, for the officer who commanded opened fire on them with carbines, and we saw them turn and ride back, but without hurrying.

The camp to which we returned was a very different place from the one we had left in the morning. Instead of lying along the river-bank, it was pitched in the thinner scrub. The bushes had on all sides been cut down, the ground cleared, and an immense oblong *zeriba* was built, around which the six brigades were drawn up, and into which cavalry, guns, and transport were closely packed.

Very early next morning the advance was continued. The army paraded by starlight, and with the first streak of the dawn the cavalry were again flung far out in advance. Secure behind the screen of horse-men and Camel Corps, the infantry advanced in regular array. Up to the 27th of August the force marched by divisions; but on and after the 30th of August the whole force commenced to march in fighting formation. The British division was on the left, the Egyptian Army on the right. All the brigades marched in line, or in a slight echelon. The flank brigades kept their flank battalions in column or in fours. Other British battalions had six companies in the front line (in company column of fours) and two companies in support. The Egyptian brigades usually marched with three battalions in the front line and one in reserve, each of the three in the front line having four companies in front and two in support.

Day after day and hour after hour the advance was maintained. Arrived at the camping-ground, the *zeriba* had to be built; and this involved a long afternoon of fatigue. In the evening, when the dusty, tired out squadrons returned, the troopers attended to their horses, and so went to sleep in peace. It was then that the dusty tired-out infantry provided sentries and pickets, who in a ceaseless succession paced the *zeriba* and guarded its occupants.

The position of the next camp was a strong one, on a high swell of open ground which afforded a clear field of fire in every direction. Everyone that night lay down to sleep with a feeling of keen expec-tancy. One way or the other all doubts would be settled the next day. The cavalry would ride over the Kerreri Hills if they were not occupied by the enemy, and right up to the walls of Omdurman. If the Dervishes had any army – if there was to be any battle – we should know within a few hours. The telegrams which were despatched that evening were the last to reach England before the event. During the night heavy rain fell, and all the country was drenched. The telegraph-wire had been laid along the ground, as there had been no time to pole it. The sand when dry is a sufficient insulator, but when wet its non-conductivity is destroyed. Hence all communications ceased, and those at home who had husbands, sons, brothers, or friends in the Expeditionary Force were left in an uncertainty as great as that in which we slept – and far more painful.

CHAPTER XIII

THE OPERATIONS OF THE
FIRST OF SEPTEMBER

The British and Egyptian cavalry, supported by the Camel Corps and Horse Artillery, trotted out rapidly, and soon interposed a distance of eight miles between them and the army. As before, the 21st Lancers were on the left nearest the river, and the Khedivial squadrons curved backwards in a wide half-moon to protect the right flank. Meanwhile the gunboat flotilla was seen to be in motion. The white boats began to ascend the stream leisurely. The orders of the cavalry were to reconnoitre Omdurman; of the gunboats to bombard it.

As soon as the squadrons of the 21st Lancers had turned the shoulder of the steep Kerreri Hills, we saw in the distance a yellow-brown pointed dome rising above the blurred horizon. It was the Mahdi's Tomb, standing in the very heart of Omdurman. From the high ground the field-glass disclosed rows and rows of mud houses, making a dark patch on the brown of the plain. To the left the river, steel-grey in the morning light, forked into two channels, and on the tongue of land between them the gleam of a white building showed among the trees. Before us were the ruins of Khartoum and the confluence of the Blue and White Niles.

A black, solitary hill rose between the Kerreri position and Omdurman. A long, low ridge running from it concealed the ground beyond. For the rest there was a wide-rolling, sandy plain of great extent, surrounded on three sides by rocky hills and ridges, and patched with coarse, starveling grass or occasional bushes. By the banks of the river which framed the picture on the left stood a straggling mud village, and this, though we did not know it, was to be the field of Omdurman. It was deserted. Not a living creature could be seen. And now there were many who said once and for all that there would be no fight; for here we were arrived at the very walls of Omdurman, and never an enemy to bar our path.

It was about three miles to the last ridge which lay between us and the city. If there was a Dervish Army, if there was to be a battle, much must be visible from that ridge. We looked over. At first nothing was apparent except the walls and houses of Omdurman and the sandy plain sloping up from the river to distant hills. Then four miles away on our right front emerged a long black line with white spots. It was the enemy. It seemed to us, as we looked, that there might be 3,000 men behind a high dense *zeriba* of thorn-bushes. That, said the officers, was better than nothing. It is scarcely necessary to describe our tortuous movements towards the Dervish position. Always edging nearer, the cavalry slowly approached, and halted in the plain about three miles away – three great serpents of men – the light-coloured one, the 21st Lancers; a much longer and a blacker one, the Egyptian squadrons; a mottled one, the Camel Corps and Horse Artillery.

It was now nearly eleven o'clock. Suddenly the whole black line which seemed to be *zeriba* began to move. It was made of men, not bushes. Behind it other immense masses and lines of men appeared over the crest; and while we watched, amazed by the wonder of the sight, the whole face of the slope became black with swarming savages. Four miles from end to end, and, as it seemed, in five great divisions, this mighty army advanced – swiftly. The whole side of the hill seemed to move. Between the masses horsemen galloped continually; before them many patrols dotted the plain; above them waved hundreds of banners, and the sun, glinting on many thousand hostile spear-points, spread a sparkling cloud.

It is now known that the Khalifa had succeeded in concentrating at Omdurman an army of more than 60,000 men. He remembered that all the former victories over the Egyptians had been won by the Dervishes attacking. He knew that in all the recent defeats they had stood on the defensive. He therefore determined not to oppose the advance at the Shabluka or on the march thence to Omdurman. All was to be staked on the issue of a great battle on the plains of Kerreri. The Mahdi's prophecy was propitious. When the 'Turks' arrived, they should be driven into the river. Accordingly the Khalifa had only watched the advance of the Expeditionary Force from Wad

Hamed with a patrol of cavalry about 200 strong. On the 30th he was informed that the enemy drew near, and on the 31st he assembled his bodyguard and regular army, with the exception of the men needed for the river batteries, on the Omdurman parade ground. The next day all the male population of the city were compelled to join the army in the field, and only the gunners and garrisons on the river-face remained within. In spite, however, of his utmost vigilance, nearly 6,000 men deserted during the nights of the 31st of August and the 1st of September. This and the detachments in the forts reduced the force actually engaged in the battle to 52,000 men. The host that now advanced towards the British and Egyptian cavalry was perhaps 4,000 stronger.

Their array was regular and precise, and, facing north-east, stretched for more than four miles from flank to flank. A strong detachment of the *mulazemin* or guard was extended in front of the centre. Ali-Wad-Helu, with his bright green flag, prolonged the line to the left; and his 5,000 warriors, chiefly of the Degheim and Kenana tribes, soon began to reach out towards the Egyptian cavalry. The centre and main force of the army was composed of the regular troops, formed in squares under Osman Sheikh-ed-Din and Osman Azrak. This great body comprised 12,000 black riflemen and about 13,000 black and Arab spearmen. In their midst rose the large, dark green flag which the Sheikh-ed-Din had adopted to annoy Ali-Wad-Helu, of whose distinctive emblem he was inordinately jealous. The Khalifa with his own bodyguard, about 2,000 strong, followed the centre. In rear of all marched Yakub with the Black Flag and 13,000 men – nearly all swordsmen and spearmen, who with those extended in front of the army constituted the guard. The right wing was formed by the brigade of the Khalifa Sherif, consisting of 2,000 Danagla tribesmen, whose principal ensign was a broad red flag. Osman Digna, with about 1,700 Hadendoa, guarded the extreme right and the flank nearest Omdurman, and his fame needed no flag. Such was the great army which now moved swiftly towards the watching squadrons; and these, pausing on the sandy ridge, pushed out a fringe of tentative patrols, as if to assure themselves that what they saw was real.

The Egyptian cavalry had meanwhile a somewhat different view of the spectacle. Working on the right of the 21st Lancers, and keeping further from the river, the leading squadrons had reached the extreme western end of the Kerreri ridge at about seven o'clock. From here the Mahdi's Tomb was visible, and, since the rocks of Surgham did not obstruct the view from this point, the British officers, looking through their field-glasses, saw what appeared to be a long column of brown spots moving south-westwards across the wide plain which stretches away to the west of Omdurman. The telescope, an invaluable aid to reconnaissance, developed the picture. The brown objects proved to be troops of horses grazing; and beyond, to the southward, camels and white flapping tents could be distinguished. There were no signs that a retreat was in progress; but from such a distance – nearly four miles – no certain information could be obtained. Colonel Broadwood accordingly led his whole command south-westward towards a round-topped hill which rose about four miles from the end of the Kerreri ridge and was one of the more distant hill features bounding the plain on the western side. The Egyptian cavalry moved slowly across the desert to this new point of observation, and at half past eleven began to climb the lower slopes of the round-topped hill. Here the whole scene burst suddenly upon them. Scarcely three miles away the Dervish Army was advancing with the regularity of parade. The south wind carried the martial sound of horns and drums and – far more menacing – the deep murmur of a multitude to the astonished officers. Like the 21st Lancers – three miles away to their left, at the end of the long sandy ridge which runs westward from Surgham – the soldiers remained for a space spell-bound. But all eyes were soon drawn from the thrilling spectacle of the Dervish advance by the sound of guns on the river.

At about eleven o'clock the gunboats had ascended the Nile, and now engaged the enemy's batteries on both banks. Throughout the day the loud reports of their guns could be heard, and, looking from our position on the ridge, we could see the white vessels steaming slowly forward against the current, under clouds of black smoke from their furnaces and amid other clouds of white smoke from the artillery. The forts, which mounted nearly fifty guns, replied vigorously; but the British aim was accurate and their fire crushing. Despite the tenacity and courage of the Dervish gunners, they were driven from their defences and took refuge among the streets of the city. The great wall of Omdurman was breached in many places, and a large number of unfortunate non-combatants were killed and wounded.

Meanwhile the Arab irregulars, under Major Wortley, had been sharply engaged. That officer's orders were to co-operate with the flotilla by taking in rear the forts and fortified villages on the east bank of the river. As soon as the gunboats had silenced the lower forts, Major Wortley ordered the irregulars to advance on them and on the houses. He placed the Jaalin, who were practically the only trustworthy men in his force, in reserve, and formed the tribes according to their capabilities and prejudices. On the order to attack being given, the whole force, some 3,000 strong, advanced on the buildings, from which the Dervishes at once opened fire. Arrived within 500 yards they halted, and began to discharge their rifles in the air; they also indulged in frantic dances expressive of their fury and valour, but declined to advance any further.

Major Wortley then ordered the Jaalin to attack. These – formed in a long column, animated by the desire for vengeance, and being besides brave men – moved upon the village at a slow pace, and, surrounding one house after another, captured it and slew all its defenders, including the Dervish Emir and 350 of his followers. The Jaalin themselves suffered a loss of about sixty killed and wounded.

The village being captured, and the enemy on the east bank killed or dispersed, the gunboats proceeded to engage the batteries higher up the river. The howitzer battery was now landed, and at 1.30 began to bombard the Mahdi's Tomb. This part of the proceedings was plainly visible to us, waiting and watching on the ridge, and its interest even distracted attention from the Dervish Army. The dome of the tomb rose tall and prominent above the mud houses of the city. A lyddite shell burst over it – a great flash, a white ball of smoke, and, after a pause, the dull thud of the distant explosion. Another followed. At the third shot, instead of the white smoke, there was a prodigious cloud of red dust, in which the whole tomb disappeared. When this cleared away we saw that, instead of being pointed, it was now flat-topped. Other shells continued to strike it with like effect, some breaking holes in the dome, others smashing off the cupolas, all enveloping it in dust.

All this time the Dervishes were coming nearer, and the steady and

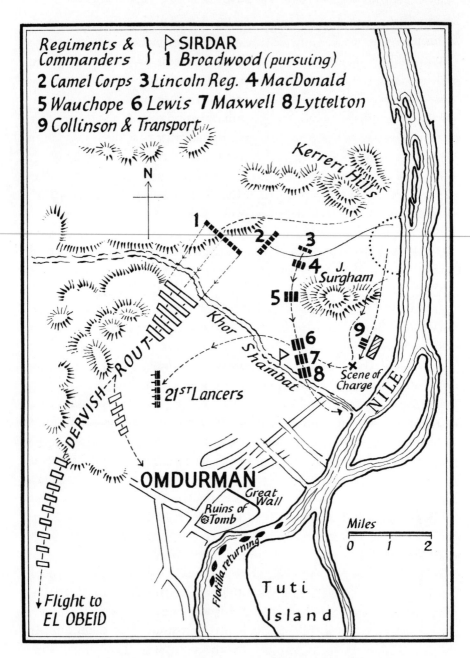

THE BATTLE OF OMDURMAN—THE FIRST ATTACK

continuous advance of the great army compelled the Egyptian cavalry to mount their horses and trot off to some safer point of view. Colonel Broadwood conceived his direct line of retreat to camp threatened, and shortly after one o'clock he began a regular retirement. The Dervish horsemen contented themselves with firing occasional shots, and the boggy ground of the Khor Shambat was recrossed in safety.

When the Arab horsemen saw all the cavalry retiring they became very bold, and numerous small groups of fives and sixes began to draw nearer at a trot. Accordingly, whenever the ground was favourable, the squadrons halted in turn for a few minutes to fire on them. In this way perhaps half a dozen were killed or wounded. The great army, however, still advanced majestically, pressing the cavalry back before it; and it was evident that if the Khalifa's movement continued, in spite of it being nearly one o'clock, there would be a collision between the main forces before the night.

The British and Egyptian Army had been ordered to stand to arms at two o'clock in formation to resist the attack which it seemed the Dervishes were about to deliver. But at a quarter to two the Dervish Army halted. Their drill was excellent, and they all stopped as by a single command. Then suddenly their riflemen discharged their rifles in the air with a great roar – a barbaric *feu de joie*. The smoke sprang up along the whole front of their array, running from one end to the other. After this they lay down on the ground, and it became certain that the matter would not be settled that day. We remained in our position among the sandhills of the ridge until the approach of darkness. As the light failed, we returned to the river to water and encamp, passing into the *zeriba* through the ranks of the British division, where officers and men, looking out steadfastly over the fading plain, asked us whether the enemy were coming – and, if so, when.

When the gunboats had completed their bombardment, had sunk a Dervish steamer, had silenced all the hostile batteries, and had sorely battered the Mahdi's Tomb, they returned leisurely to the camp, and lay moored close to the bank to lend the assistance of their guns in case of attack. As the darkness became complete they threw their powerful searchlights over the front of the *zeriba* and on to the distant hills. The wheeling beams of dazzling light swept across the desolate, yet not deserted, plain. The Dervish Army lay for the night along the eastern slope of the Shambat depression. All the 50,000 faithful warriors rested in their companies near the flags of their Emirs. The Khalifa slept in rear of the centre of his host, surrounded by his generals. Suddenly the whole scene was lit by a pale glare. Abdullah and the chiefs sprang up. Everything around them was bathed in an awful white illumination. Far away by the river there gleamed a brilliant circle of light – the cold, pitiless eye of a demon. The Khalifa put his hand on Osman Azrak's shoulder – Osman, who was to lead the frontal attack at dawn – and whispered, 'What is this strange thing?' 'Sire,' replied Osman, 'they are looking at us.' Thereat a great fear filled all their minds. The Khalifa had a small tent, which showed conspicuously in the searchlight. He had it hurriedly pulled down. Some of the Emirs covered their faces, lest the baleful rays should blind them. All feared that some terrible projectile would follow in the path of the light. And then suddenly it passed on – for the sapper who worked the lens could see nothing at that distance but the brown plain – and swept along the ranks of the sleeping army, rousing up the startled warriors, as a wind sweeps over a field of standing corn.

The moonlit camp, with its anxious generals, its weary soldiers, its fearful machinery of destruction, all strewn along the bank of the great river, remained plunged in silence, as if brooding over the chances of the morrow and the failures of the past. And hardly four miles away another army – twice as numerous, equally confident, equally brave – were waiting impatiently for the morning and the final settlement of the long quarrel.

CHAPTER XIV

THE BATTLE OF OMDURMAN

2nd September 1898

The bugles all over the camp by the river began to sound at half-past four. Then it grew gradually lighter, and cavalry mounted their horses, the infantry stood to their arms, and the gunners went to their batteries; while the sun, rising over the Nile, revealed the wide plain, the dark rocky hills, and the waiting army.

Even before it became light several squadrons of British and Egyptian cavalry were pushed swiftly forward to gain contact with the enemy and learn his intentions. The first of these, under Captain Baring, occupied Surgham Hill, and waited in the gloom until the whereabouts of the Dervishes should be disclosed by the dawn. It was a perilous undertaking, for he might have found them unexpectedly near. As the sun rose, the 21st Lancers trotted out of the *zeriba* and threw out a spray of officers' patrols. As there had been no night attack, it was expected that the Dervish Army would have retired to their original position or entered the town. It was hardly conceivable that they would advance across the open ground to attack the *zeriba* by daylight. But these anticipations were immediately dispelled by the scene which was visible from the crest of the ridge.

It was a quarter to six. The light was dim, but growing stronger every minute. There in the plain lay the enemy, their numbers unaltered, their confidence and intentions apparently unshaken. Their front was now nearly five miles long, and composed of great masses of men joined together by thinner lines. Behind and near to the flanks were large reserves. From the ridge they looked dark blurs and streaks, relieved and diversified with an odd-looking shimmer of light from the spear-points. At about ten minutes to six it was evident that the masses were in motion and advancing swiftly. Their Emirs galloped about and before their ranks. Scouts and patrols scattered themselves all over the front. Then they began to cheer. They were still a mile away from the hill, and were concealed from the Sirdar's army by the folds of the ground. The noise of the shouting was heard, albeit faintly, by the troops down by the river. But to those watching on the hill a tremendous roar came up in waves of intense sound, like the tumult of the rising wind and sea before a storm.

The British and Egyptian forces were arranged in line, with their back to the river. The flanks were secured by the gunboats lying moored in the stream. Before them was the rolling sandy plain, looking from the slight elevation of the ridge smooth and flat as a table. To the right rose the rocky hills of the Kerreri position, near which the Egyptian cavalry were drawn up – a dark solid mass of men and horses. On the left the 21st Lancers, with a single squadron thrown out in advance, were halted watching their patrols, who climbed about Surgham Hill, stretched forward beyond it, or perched, as we did, on the ridge.

Although the Dervishes were steadily advancing, a belief that their musketry was inferior encouraged a nearer view, and we trotted round the south-west slopes of Surgham Hill until we reached the sandhills on the enemy's side, among which the regiment had waited the day before. Thence the whole array was visible in minute detail. It seemed that every single man of all the thousands could be examined separately. The pace of their march was fast and steady, and it was evident that it would not be safe to wait long among the sandhills. Yet the wonder of the scene exercised a dangerous fascination, and for a while we tarried.

The emblems of the more famous Emirs were easily distinguishable. On the extreme left the chiefs and soldiers of the bright green flag gathered under Ali-Wad-Helu; between this and the centre the large dark green flag of Osman Sheikh-ed-Din rose above a dense mass of spearmen, preceded by long lines of warriors armed presumably with rifles; over the centre, commanded by Yakub, the sacred black banner of the Khalifa floated high and remarkable; while on the right a great square of Dervishes was arrayed under an extraordinary number of white flags, amid which the red ensign of Sherif was almost hidden. All the pride and might of the Dervish Empire were massed on this last great day of its existence. Riflemen who had helped to destroy

Hicks, spearmen who had charged at Abu Klea, Emirs who saw the sack of Gondar, Baggara fresh from raiding the Shillooks, warriors who had besieged Khartoum – all marched, inspired by the memories of former triumphs and embittered by the knowledge of late defeats, to chastise the impudent and accursed invaders.

The advance continued. The Dervish left began to stretch out across the plain towards Kerreri – as I thought, to turn our right flank. Their centre, under the Black Flag, moved directly towards Surgham. The right pursued a line of advance south of that hill. This mass of men were the most striking of all. They could not have mustered fewer than 6,000. Their array was perfect. They displayed a great number of flags – perhaps 500 – which looked at the distance white, though they were really covered with texts from the Koran, and which by their admirable alignment made this division of the Khalifa's army look like the old representations of the Crusaders in the Bayeux tapestry.

If there was one arm in which the Arabs were beyond all comparison inferior to their adversaries, it was in guns. Yet it was with this arm that they opened their attack. In the middle of the Dervish line now marching in frontal assault were two puffs of smoke. About fifty yards short of the thorn fence two red clouds of sand and dust sprang up, where the projectiles had struck. It looked like a challenge. It was immediately answered. Great clouds of smoke appeared all along the front of the British and Soudanese brigades. One after another four batteries opened on the enemy at a range of about 3,000 yards. The sound of the cannonade rolled up to us on the ridge, and was re-echoed by the hills. Above the heads of the moving masses shells began to burst, dotting the air with smoke-balls and the ground with bodies. But a nearer tragedy impended. The 'White Flags' were nearly over the crest. In another minute they would become visible to the batteries. Did they realise what would come to meet them? They were in a dense mass, 2,800 yards from the 32nd Field Battery and the gunboats. The ranges were known. It was a matter of machinery. The more distant slaughter passed unnoticed, as the mind was fasci-nated by the approaching horror. In a few seconds swift destruction would rush on these brave men. They topped the crest and drew out into full view of the whole army. Their white banners made them conspicuous above all. As they saw the camp of their enemies, they discharged their rifles with a great roar of musketry and quickened their pace. For a moment the white flags advanced in regular order, and the whole division crossed the crest and were exposed. Forthwith the gunboats, the 32nd British Field Battery, and other guns from the *zeriba* opened on them. About twenty shells struck them in the first minute. Some burst high in the air, others exactly in their faces. Others, again, plunged into the sand and, exploding, dashed clouds of red dust, splinters, and bullets amid their ranks. The white banners toppled over in all directions. Yet they rose again immediately, as other men pressed forward to die for the Mahdi's sacred cause and in the defence of the successor of the True Prophet. It was a terrible sight, for as yet they had not hurt us at all, and it seemed an unfair advantage to strike thus cruelly when they could not reply. Under the influence of the shells the mass of the 'White Flags' dissolved into thin lines of spearmen and skirmishers, and came on in altered formation and diminished numbers, but with unabated enthusiasm. And now, the whole attack being thoroughly exposed, it became the duty of the cavalry to clear the front as quickly as possible, and leave the further conduct of the debate to the infantry and the Maxim guns. All the patrols trotted or cantered back to their squadrons, and the regiment retired swiftly into the *zeriba*, while the shells from the gunboats screamed overhead and the whole length of the position began to burst into flame and smoke.

The tumult grew louder and more intense, until even the flickering stutter of the Maxims could scarcely be heard above the continuous din. Eighty yards away, and perhaps twenty feet above us, the 32nd Field Battery was in action. The officers, some standing on biscuit-boxes, peered through their glasses and studied the effect. Of this I had one glimpse. Eight hundred yards away a ragged line of men were coming on desperately, struggling forward in the face of the pitiless fire – white banners tossing and collapsing; white figures subsiding in dozens to the ground; little white puffs from their rifles, larger white puffs spreading in a row all along their front from the bursting shrapnel.

The infantry fired steadily and stolidly, without hurry or excitement, for the enemy were far away and the officers careful. Besides, the soldiers were interested in the work and took great pains. But presently the mere physical act became tedious. The tiny figures seen over the slide of the back-sight seemed a little larger, but also fewer at each successive volley. The rifles grew hot – so hot that they had to be changed for those of the reserve companies. And all the time out on the plain on the other side bullets were shearing through flesh, smashing and splintering bone; valiant men were struggling on through a hell of whistling metal, exploding shells, and spurting dust – suffering, despairing, dying. Such was the first phase of the Battle of Omdurman.

The Khalifa's plan of attack appears to have been complex and ingenious. It was, however, based on an extraordinary miscalculation of the power of modern weapons. He first ordered about 15,000 men, drawn chiefly from the army of Osman Sheikh-ed-Din and placed under the command of Osman Azrak, to deliver a frontal attack. He himself waited with an equal force near Surgham Hill to watch the result. If it succeeded, he would move forward with his bodyguard, the flower of the Arab Army, and complete the victory. If it failed, there was yet another chance. The Dervishes who were first launched against the *zeriba*, were not by any means his best or most reliable troops. Their destruction might be a heavy loss, but it would not end the struggle. While the attack was proceeding, the valiant left, consisting of the rest of the army of Osman Sheikh-ed-Din, might move unnoticed to the northern flank and curve round on to the front of the *zeriba* held by the Egyptian brigade. Ali-Wad-Helu was meanwhile to march to the Kerreri Hills, and remain out of range and, if possible, out of sight among them. Should the frontal and flank attacks be unhappily repulsed, the 'enemies of God', exulting in their easy victory, would leave their strong place and march to the capture of the city. Then, while they were yet dispersed on the plain, with no *zeriba* to protect them, the chosen warriors of the True Religion would abandon all concealment, and hasten in their thousands to the utter destruction of the accursed – the Khalifa with 15,000 falling upon them from behind Surgham; Ali-Wad Helu and all that remained of Osman's army assailing them from Kerreri. Attacked at once from the north and south, and encompassed on every side, the infidels would abandon hope and order, and Kitchener might share the fate of Hicks and Gordon. Two circumstances prevented the accomplishment of this plan. The second attack was not executed simultaneously by the two divisions of the Dervish Army; and even had it been, the power of the musketry would have triumphed, and though the Expeditionary Force might have sustained heavier losses the main result could not have been affected. The last hopes of barbarism had passed with the shades of night.

Colonel Broadwood, with nine squadrons of cavalry, the Camel Corps, and the Horse Artillery, had been ordered to check the Dervish left, and prevent it enveloping the down-stream flank of the *zeriba*, as this was held by the Egyptian brigade, which it was not thought desirable to expose to the full weight of an attack. With this object he had occupied the Kerreri ridge with the Horse battery and the Camel Corps, holding his cavalry in reserve in rear of the centre.

The Kerreri ridge, to which reference has so frequently been made, consists of two main features, which rise to the height of about 300 feet above the plain, are each above a mile long, and run nearly east and west, with a dip or trough about 1,000 yards wide between them. The eastern ends of these main ridges are perhaps 1,000 yards from the river, and in this intervening space there are several rocky under-features and knolls. The Kerreri Hills, the spaces between them, and the smaller features are covered with rough boulders and angular stones of volcanic origin, which render the movements of horses and camels difficult and painful.

The cavalry horses and camels were in the dip between the two ridges; and the dismounted men of the Camel Corps were deployed along the crest of the most southerly of the ridges, with their right at the desert end. Next in order to the Camel Corps, the centre of the ridge was occupied by the dismounted cavalry. The Horse Artillery were on the left. The remainder of the cavalry waited in the hollow behind the guns.

The tempestuous advance of Osman soon brought him into contact with the mounted force. His real intentions are still a matter of conjecture. Whether he had been ordered to attack the Egyptian brigade, or to drive back the cavalry, or to disappear behind the Kerreri Hills in conformity with Ali-Wad-Helu, is impossible to pronounce. His action was, however, clear. He could not safely assail the Egyptians with a powerful cavalry force threatening his left rear. He therefore continued his move across the front of the *zeriba*. Keeping out of the range of infantry fire, bringing up his right, and marching along due north, he fell upon Broadwood. This officer, who had expected to have to deal with small bodies on the Dervish flank, found himself suddenly exposed to the attack of nearly 15,000 men, many of whom were riflemen. The Sirdar, seeing the situation from the *zeriba*, sent him an order to withdraw within the lines of infantry. Colonel Broadwood, however, preferred to retire through the Kerreri Hills to the northward, drawing Osman after him. He replied to that effect.

The Dervishes, advancing in a north-easterly direction, attacked the Kerreri Hills obliquely. They immediately enveloped the right flank of the mounted troops holding them. As soon as the Dervish riflemen gained a point west and in prolongation of the trough between the two ridges, they not only turned the right flank, but also threatened the retreat of the defenders of the southerly ridge; for they were able to sweep the trough from end to end with their fire. As soon as it became certain that the southerly ridge could not be held any longer, Colonel Broadwood retired the battery to the east end of the second or northern ridge. This was scarcely accomplished when the dip was enfiladed, and the cavalry and Camel Corps who followed lost about fifty men and many horses and camels killed and wounded. It was now painfully evident that in rocky ground the Dervishes could go faster on their feet than the soldiers on their camels. Pressing on impetuously at a pace of nearly seven miles an hour, and unchecked by artillery fire from the *zeriba* and from the Horse battery, the Arabs rapidly diminished the distance between themselves and their enemies. In these circumstances Colonel Broadwood decided to send the Camel Corps back to the *zeriba* under cover of a gunboat, which, observing the progress of the fight, was coming down stream to assist. The distance which divided the combatants was scarcely 400 yards and decreasing every minute. The cavalry were drawn up across the eastern or river end of the trough. The guns of the Horse battery fired steadily from their new position on the northern ridge. But the Camel Corps were still struggling in the broken ground, and it was clear that their position was one of great peril.

The Dervishes already carpeted the rocks of the southern ridge with dull yellow swarms, and, heedless of the shells which still assailed them in reverse from the *zeriba*, continued to push their attack home. On the very instant that they saw the Camel Corps make for the river they realised that those they had deemed their prey were trying, like a hunted animal, to run to ground within the lines of infantry. With that instinctive knowledge of war which is the heritage of savage peoples, the whole attack swung to the right, changed direction from north to east, and rushed down the trough and along the southern ridge towards the Nile, with the plain intention of cutting off the Camel Corps and driving them into the river.

The moment was critical. It appeared to the cavalry commander that the Dervishes would actually succeed, and their success must involve the total destruction of the Camel Corps. The whole nine squadrons of cavalry assumed a preparatory formation. The British officers believed that a terrible charge impended. They would meet in direct collision the swarms of men who were hurrying down the trough. The diversion might enable the Camel Corps to escape. But the ground was bad; the enemy's force was overwhelming; the Egyptian troopers were prepared to obey – but that was all. There was no exalted enthusiasm such as at these moments carries sterner breeds to victory. Nevertheless, the operation appeared inevitable. The Camel Corps were already close to the river. But thousands of Dervishes were running swiftly towards them at right angles to their line of retreat, and their only hope lay in maintaining themselves by their fire near the river-bank until help could reach them, and, in order to delay and weaken the Dervish attack the cavalry would have to make a desperate charge.

But at the critical moment the gunboat arrived on the scene and began suddenly to blaze and flame from Maxim guns, quick-firing guns, and rifles. The range was short; the effect tremendous. The terrible machine, floating gracefully on the waters – a beautiful white devil – wreathed itself in smoke. The river slopes of the Kerreri Hills, crowded with the advancing thousands, sprang up into clouds of dust and splinters of rock. The charging Dervishes sank down in tangled heaps. The masses in rear paused, irresolute. The approach of another gunboat completed their discomfiture. The Camel Corps, hurrying along the shore, slipped past the fatal point of interception, and saw safety and the *zeriba* before them.

Exasperated by their disappointment, the soldiers of Osman Sheikh-ed-Din turned again upon the cavalry, and, forgetting in their anger the mobile nature of their foe, pursued the elusive squadrons three long miles to the north. The cavalry, intensely relieved by the escape of the Camel Corps, played with their powerful antagonist, as the *banderillo* teases the bull. Colonel Broadwood thus succeeded in luring this division of the Dervish Army far away from the field of battle, where they were sorely needed.

Both gunboats, having watched the Camel Corps safely into the *zeriba*, now returned with the current and renewed their attack upon the Arabs. Opening a heavy and accurate fire upon the river flank, they drove them westward and away from the Nile. Through the gap thus opened Broadwood and his squadrons trotted to rejoin the main body.

While these things were passing on the northern flank, the frontal attack was in progress. The debris of the 'White Flags' joined the centre, and the whole 14,000 pressed forward against the *zeriba*, spreading out by degrees and abandoning their dense formations, and gradually slowing down. At about 800 yards from the British division the advance ceased, and they could make no headway. Opposite the Soudanese, who were armed only with the Martini-Henry rifle, the assailants came within 300 yards; and one brave old man, carrying a flag, fell at 150 paces from the shelter trench. But the attack was shattered. The leader, clad in his new *jibba* of many colours, rode on steadfastly towards the inexorable firing line, until, pierced by several bullets, he fell lifeless. Such was the end of that stubborn warrior of many fights – wicked Osman Azrak, faithful unto death. The surviving Dervishes lay down on the ground. Unable to advance, they were unwilling to retire; and their riflemen, taking advantage of the folds of the plain, opened and maintained an unequal combat. By eight o'clock it was evident that the whole attack had failed.

The Sirdar and his generals were all agreed on one point. They must occupy Omdurman before the Dervish Army could get back there. They could fight as many Dervishes as cared to come in the plain; among the houses it was different. The Arabs were out in the desert.

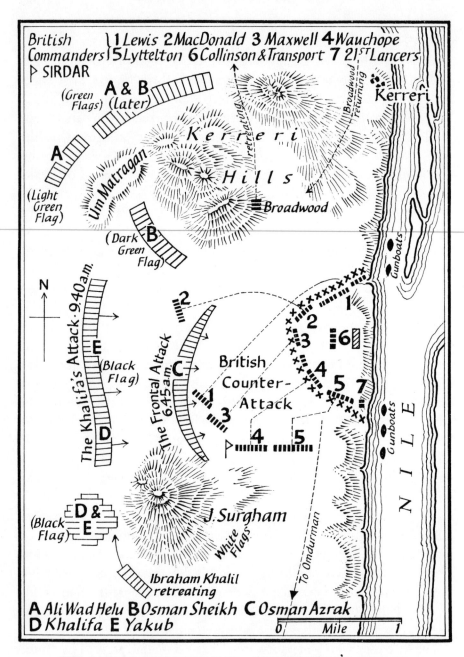

THE BATTLE OF OMDURMAN – THE KHALIFA'S ATTACK

A great part of their army was even as far away as Kerreri. The troops could move on interior lines. They were bound to reach Omdurman first. The order was therefore given to march on the city at once. But first the Surgham ridge must be reconnoitred, and the ground between the *zeriba* and Omdurman cleared of the Dervishes – with infantry if necessary, but with cavalry if possible, because that would be quicker. The 21st Lancers were again called upon to act.

As the fusillade slackened, the Lancers stood to their horses. Then General Gatacre, with Captain Brooke and the rest of his Staff, came galloping along the rear of the line of infantry and guns, and shouted for Colonel Martin. There was a brief conversation, an order, and we were all scrambling into our saddles and straightening the ranks in high expectation. We started at a trot, two or three patrols galloping out in front, towards the high ground, while the regiment followed in mass – a great square block of ungainly brown figures and little horses, hung all over with water-bottles, saddle-bags, picketing-gear; the polish of peace gone; but still a regiment of light cavalry in active operation against the enemy.

The crest of the ridge was only half a mile away. It was found un-occupied. The rocky mass of Surgham obstructed the view and con-cealed the great reserve collected around the Black Flag. But southward, between us and Omdurman, the whole plain was exposed. It was infested with small parties of Dervishes, moving about, mounted and on foot, in tens and twenties. Three miles away a broad stream of fugitives, of wounded, and of deserters flowed from the Khalifa's army to the city. The sight was sufficient to excite the fiercest instincts of cavalry. Only the scattered parties in the plain appeared to prevent a glorious pursuit. The signalling officer was set to heliograph back to the Sirdar that the ridge was unoccupied and that several thousand Dervishes could be seen flying into Omdurman. Pending the answer, we waited; and looking back northwards, across the front of the *zeriba*, where the first attack had been stopped, perceived a greyish-white smudge, perhaps a mile long. The glass disclosed details – hundreds of tiny white figures heaped or scattered; dozens hopping, crawling, staggering away; a few horses standing stolidly among the corpses; a few unwounded men dragging off their comrades. Then the heliograph in the *zeriba* began to talk in flashes of light that opened and shut capriciously. The actual order is important. 'Advance,' said the helio, 'and clear the left flank, and use every effort to prevent the enemy re-entering Omdurman.' That was all, but it was sufficient. In the distance the enemy could be seen re-entering Omdurman in hundreds. They must be stopped, and incidentally these small parties in the plain might be brushed away. We remounted; the ground looked smooth and unbroken; yet it was desirable to reconnoitre. Two patrols were sent out. The first struck out towards Omdurman, and began to push in between the scattered Dervishes, who fired their rifles and showed great excitement. The other patrol, under Lieutenant Grenfell, were sent to see what the ground looked like from further along the ridge and on the lower slopes of Surgham. They, too, had had good fortune in their adventurous ride. They reported that in a shallow and apparently practicable *khor* about three-quarters of a mile to the south-west, and between the regiment and the fugitives, there was drawn up a formed body of Dervishes about 1,000 strong. Colonel Martin decided on this information to advance and attack this force, which alone interposed between him and the Arab line of retreat. Then we started.

But all this time the enemy had been busy. At the beginning of the battle the Khalifa had posted a small force of 700 men on his extreme right, to prevent his line of retreat to Omdurman being harassed. This detachment was composed entirely of the Hadendoa tribesmen of Osman Digna's flag, and was commanded by one of his subordinate Emirs, who selected a suitable position in the shallow *khor*. As soon as the 21st Lancers left the *zeriba* the Dervish scouts on the top of Surgham carried the news to the Khalifa. It was said that the English cavalry were coming to cut him off from Omdurman. Abdullah thereupon determined to strengthen his extreme right; and he immediately ordered four regiments, each 500 strong, drawn from the force around the Black Flag and under the Emir Ibrahim Khalil, to reinforce the Hadendoa in the *khor*. While we were waiting for orders on the ridge these men were hurrying southwards along the depression, and concealed by a spur of Surgham Hill. The Lancer patrol reconnoitred the *khor*, at the imminent risk of their lives, while it was only occupied by the original 700 Hadendoa. Galloping back, they reported that it was held by about 1,000 men. Before they reached the regiment this number was increased to 2,700. This, however, we had no means of knowing. The Khalifa, having despatched his reinforcement, rode on his donkey with a scanty escort nearly half a mile from the Black Flag towards the *khor*, in order to watch the event, and in consequence he was within 500 yards of the scene.

We advanced at a walk in mass for about 300 yards. The scattered parties of Dervishes fell back and melted away, and only one straggling line of men in dark blue waited motionless a quarter of a mile to the left front. They were scarcely a hundred strong. The regiment formed into line of squadron columns, and continued at a walk until within 300 yards of this small body of Dervishes. There was complete silence, intensified by the recent tumult. Far beyond the thin blue row of Dervishes the fugitives were visible streaming into Omdurman. And should these few devoted men impede a regiment? Yet it were wiser to examine their position from the other flank before slipping a squadron at them. The heads of the squadrons wheeled slowly to the left, and the Lancers, breaking into a trot, began to cross the Dervish front in column of troops. Thereupon and with one accord the blue-clad men dropped on their knees, and there burst out a loud crackling fire of musketry. It was hardly possible to miss such a target at such a range. Horses and men fell at once. The only course was plain and welcome to all. The Colonel, nearer than his regiment, already saw what lay behind the skirmishers. He ordered 'Right wheel into line' to be sounded. The trumpet jerked out a shrill note, heard faintly above the trampling of the horses and the noise of the rifles. On the instant all the sixteen troops swung round and locked up into a long galloping line, and the 21st Lancers were committed to their first charge in war.

Two hundred and fifty yards away the dark-blue men were firing madly in a thin film of light-blue smoke. Their bullets struck the hard gravel into the air, and the troopers, to shield their faces from the stinging dust, bowed their helmets forward, like the Cuirassiers at Waterloo. The pace was fast and the distance short. Yet, before it was half covered, the whole aspect of the affair changed. A deep crease in the ground – a dry watercourse, a *khor* – appeared where all had seemed smooth, level plain; and from it there sprang, with the suddenness of a pantomime effect and a high-pitched yell, a dense white

mass of men nearly as long as our front and about twelve deep. A
score of horsemen and a dozen bright flags rose as if by magic from the
earth. Eager warriors sprang forward to anticipate the shock. The
rest stood firm to meet it. The Lancers acknowledged the apparition
only by an increase of pace. Each man wanted sufficient momentum
to drive through such a solid line. The flank troops, seeing that they
overlapped, curved inwards like the horns of a moon. But the whole
event was a matter of seconds. The riflemen, firing bravely to the last,
were swept head over heels into the *khor*, and jumping down with
them, at full gallop and in the closest order, the British squadrons
struck the fierce brigade with one loud furious shout. The collision
was prodigious. Nearly thirty Lancers, men and horses, and at least
two hundred Arabs were overthrown. The shock was stunning to
both sides, and for perhaps ten wonderful seconds no man heeded his
enemy. Terrified horses wedged in the crowd, bruised and shaken
men, sprawling in heaps, struggled, dazed and stupid, to their feet,
panted, and looked about them. Several fallen Lancers had even time
to remount. Meanwhile the impetus of the cavalry carried them on.

Stubborn and unshaken infantry hardly ever meet stubborn and
unshaken cavalry. Either the infantry run away and are cut down in
flight, or they keep their heads and destroy nearly all the horsemen by
their musketry. On this occasion two living walls had actually crashed
together. The Dervishes fought manfully. They tried to hamstring
the horses. They fired their rifles, pressing the muzzles into the very
bodies of their opponents. They cut reins and stirrup-leathers. They
flung their throwing-spears with great dexterity. They tried every
device of cool, determined men practised in war and familiar with
cavalry; and, besides, they swung sharp, heavy swords which bit
deep. The hand-to-hand fighting on the further side of the *khor* lasted
for perhaps one minute. Then the horses got into their stride again,
the pace increased, and the Lancers drew out from among their antagonists. Within two minutes of the collision every living man was
clear of the Dervish mass. All who had fallen were cut at with swords
till they stopped quivering.

Two hundred yards away the regiment halted, rallied, faced about,
and in less than five minutes were re-formed and ready for a second
charge. The men were anxious to cut their way back through their

enemies. We were alone together – the cavalry regiment and the Dervish brigade. The ridge hung like a curtain between us and the army. The general battle was forgotten, as it was unseen. This was a private quarrel. The other might have been a massacre; but here the fight was fair, for we too fought with sword and spear. Indeed the advantage of ground and numbers lay with them. All prepared to settle the debate at once and for ever. But some realisation of the cost of our wild ride began to come to those who were responsible. Riderless horses galloped across the plain. Men, clinging to their saddles, lurched helplessly about, covered with blood from perhaps a dozen wounds. Horses, streaming from tremendous gashes, limped and staggered with their riders. In 120 seconds five officers, 65 men, and 119 horses out of fewer than 400 had been killed or wounded.

The Dervish line, broken by the charge, began to re-form at once. They closed up, shook themselves together, and prepared with constancy and courage for another shock. But on military considerations it was desirable to turn them out of the *khor* first and thus deprive them of their vantage-ground. The regiment again drawn up, three squadrons in line and the fourth in column, now wheeled to the right, and, galloping round the Dervish flank, dismounted and opened a heavy fire with their magazine carbines. Under the pressure of this fire the enemy changed front to meet the new attack, so that both sides were formed at right angles to their original lines. When the Dervish change of front was completed, they began to advance against the dismounted men. But the fire was accurate, and there can be little doubt that the moral effect of the charge had been very great, and that these brave enemies were no longer unshaken. Be this as it may, the fact remains that they retreated swiftly, though in good order, towards the ridge of Surgham Hill, where the Khalifa's Black Flag still waved, and the 21st Lancers remained in possession of the ground – and of their dead.

Such is the true and literal account of the charge. An officer was despatched with the news to the Sirdar, and on the instant both cannonade and fusillade broke out again behind the ridge, and grew in a crashing crescendo until the whole landscape seemed to vibrate with the sound of explosions. The second phase of the battle had begun.

Even before the 21st Lancers had reconnoitred Surgham ridge, the

Sirdar had set his brigades in motion towards Omdurman. He was determined, even at a very great risk, to occupy the city before the army in the plain could return to defend it. The advantage might be tremendous. Nevertheless the movement was premature. The Khalifa still remained undefeated west of Surgham Hill; Ali-Wad-Helu lurked behind Kerreri; Osman was rapidly re-forming. There were still at least 35,000 men on the field. Nor, as the event proved, was it possible to enter Omdurman until they had been beaten.

As soon as the infantry had replenished their ammunition, they wheeled to the left in echelon of brigades, and began to march towards Surgham ridge. The movements of a great force are slow. It was not desirable that the British division, which led the echelon, should remain in the low ground north of Surgham – where they were commanded, had no field of fire, and could see nothing – and accordingly both these brigades moved forward almost together to occupy the crest of the ridge. Thus two steps of the ladder were run into one, and Maxwell's brigade, which followed Wauchope's, was 600 yards further south than it would have been had the regular echelon been observed. In the *zeriba* MacDonald had been next to Maxwell. But a very significant change in the order was now made. General Hunter evidently conceived the rear of the echelon threatened from the direction of Kerreri. Had the earth swallowed all the thousands who had moved across the plain towards the hills? At any rate, he would have his best brigade and his most experienced general in the post of possible danger. He therefore ordered Lewis's brigade to follow Maxwell, and left MacDonald last of all, strengthening him with three batteries of artillery and eight Maxim guns. Collinson marched with the transport. MacDonald moved out westward into the desert to take his place in the echelon, and also to allow Lewis to pass him as ordered. Lewis hurried on after Maxwell, and, taking his distance from him, was thus also 600 yards further south than the regular echelon admitted. The step which had been absorbed when both British brigades moved off – advisedly – together, caused a double gap between MacDonald and the rest of the army. And this distance was further increased by the fact that while he was moving west, to assume his place in correct echelon, the other five brigades were drawing off to the southward. Hence MacDonald's isolation.

At 9.15 the whole army was marching south in echelon, with the rear brigade at rather more than double distance. Collinson had already started with the transport, but the field hospitals still remained in the deserted *zeriba*, busily packing up. The medical staff had about 150 wounded on their hands. The Sirdar's orders had been that these were to be placed on the hospital barges, and that the field hospitals were to follow the transport. But the moving of wounded men is a painful and delicate affair, and by a stupid and grievous mistake the three regular hospital barges, duly prepared for the reception of the wounded, had been towed across to the right bank. It was necessary to use three ammunition barges, which, although in no way arranged for the reception of wounded, were luckily at hand. Meanwhile time was passing, and the doctors, who worked with devoted energy, became suddenly aware that, with the exception of a few detachments from the British division and three Egyptian companies, there were no troops within half a mile, and none between them and the dark Kerreri Hills. The two gunboats which could have guarded them from the river were down stream, helping the cavalry; MacDonald with the rear brigade was out in the plain; Collinson was hurrying along the bank with his transport. They were alone and unprotected. The army and the river together formed a huge V pointing south. The northern extremity – the gorge of the redan, as it were – gaped open towards Kerreri; and from Kerreri there now began to come, like the first warning drops before a storm of rain, small straggling parties of Dervish cavalry. The interior of the V was soon actually invaded by these predatory patrols, and one troop of perhaps a score of Baggara horse watered their ponies within 300 yards of the unprotected hospitals. Behind, in the distance, the banners of an army began to re-appear. The situation was alarming. The wounded were bundled on to the barges, although, since there was no steamer to tow them, they were scarcely any safer when embarked. While some of the medical officers were thus busied, Colonel Sloggett galloped off, and, running the gauntlet of the Baggara horsemen, hurried to claim protection for the hospitals and their helpless occupants. In the midst of this excitement and confusion the wounded from the cavalry charge began to trickle in.

When the British division had moved out of the *zeriba*, a few skirmishers among the crags of Surgham Hill alone suggested the presence of an enemy. Each brigade, formed in four parallel columns of route, which closed in until they were scarcely forty paces apart, and both at deploying interval – the second brigade nearer the river, the first almost in line with it and on its right – hurried on, eager to see what lay beyond the ridge. All was quiet, except for a few 'sniping' shots from the top of Surgham. But gradually as Maxwell's brigade – the third in the echelon – approached the hill, these shots became more numerous, until the summit of the peak was spotted with smoke-puffs. The British division moved on steadily, and, leaving these bold skirmishers to the Soudanese, soon reached the crest of the ridge. At once and for the first time the whole panorama of Omdurman – the brown and battered dome of the Mahdi's Tomb, the multitude of mud houses, the glittering fork of water which marked the confluence of the rivers – burst on their vision. For a moment they stared entranced. Then their attention was distracted; for trotting, galloping, or halting and gazing stupidly about them, terrified and bewildered, a dozen riderless troop-horses appeared over the further crest – for the ridge was flat-topped – coming from the plain, as yet invisible, below. It was the first news of the Lancers' charge. Details soon followed in the shape of the wounded, who in twos and threes began to make their way between the battalions, all covered with blood and many displaying most terrible injuries – faces cut to rags, bowels protruding, fishhook spears still stuck in their bodies – realistic pictures from the darker side of war. Thus absorbed, the soldiers hardly noticed the growing musketry fire from the peak. But suddenly the bang of a field-gun set all eyes looking backward. A battery had unlimbered in the plain between the *zeriba* and the ridge, and was beginning to shell the summit of the hill. The report of the guns seemed to be the signal for the whole battle to reopen. From far away to the right rear there came the sound of loud and continuous infantry firing, and immediately Gatacre halted his division.

Almost before the British had topped the crest of the ridge, before the battery had opened from the plain, while Colonel Sloggett was still spurring across the dangerous ground between the river and the army, the Sirdar knew that his enemy was again upon him. Looking back from the slopes of Surgham, he saw that MacDonald, instead of continuing his march in echelon, had halted and deployed. The veteran brigadier had seen the Dervish formations on the ridge to the west of Surgham, realised that he was about to be attacked, and, resolving to anticipate the enemy, immediately brought his three batteries into action at 1,200 yards. Five minutes later the whole of the Khalifa's reserve, 15,000 strong, led by Yakub with the Black Flag, the body-guard and 'all the glories' of the Dervish Empire, surged into view from behind the hill and advanced on the solitary brigade with the vigour of the first attack and thrice its chances of success. Thereupon Sir Herbert Kitchener ordered Maxwell to change front to the right and storm Surgham Hill. He sent Major Sandbach to tell Lewis to conform and come into line on Maxwell's right. He galloped himself to the British division – conveniently halted by General Gatacre on the northern crest of the ridge – and ordered Lyttelton with the 2nd Brigade to form facing west on Maxwell's left south of Surgham, and Wauchope with the 1st Brigade to hurry back to fill the wide gap between Lewis and MacDonald. Last of all he sent an officer to Collinson and the Camel Corps with orders that they should swing round to their right rear and close the open part of the V. By these movements the army, instead of facing south in echelon, with its left on the river and its right in the desert, was made to face west in line, with its left in the desert and its right reaching back to the river. It had turned nearly a complete somersault.

In obedience to these orders Lyttelton's brigade brought up their left shoulders, deployed into line, and advanced west; Maxwell's Soudanese scrambled up the Surgham rocks, and, in spite of a sharp fire, cleared the peak with the bayonet and pressed on down the further side; Lewis began to come into action on Maxwell's right; MacDonald, against whom the Khalifa's attack was at first entirely directed, remained facing south-west, and was soon shrouded in the smoke of his own musketry and artillery fire. The three brigades which were now moving west and away from the Nile attacked the right flank of the Dervishes assailing MacDonald, and, compelling them to form front towards the river, undoubtedly took much of the weight of the attack off the isolated brigade. There remained the gap between Lewis and MacDonald. But Wauchope's brigade – still in four parallel columns of route – had shouldered completely round to the north,

and was now doubling swiftly across the plain to fill the unguarded
space. With the exception of Wauchope's brigade and of Collinson's
Egyptians, the whole infantry and artillery force were at once furiously
engaged.

The firing became again tremendous, and as each fresh battalion
was brought into line the tumult steadily increased. The three leading
brigades continued to advance westward in one long line looped up
over Surgham Hill, and with the right battalion held back in column.
As the forces gradually drew nearer, the possibility of the Dervishes
penetrating the gap between Lewis and MacDonald presented itself,
and the flank battalion was wheeled into line so as to protect the right
flank. The aspect of the Dervish attack was at this moment most
formidable. Enormous masses of men were hurrying towards the
smoke-clouds that almost hid MacDonald. Other masses turned to
meet the attack which was developing on their right. Within the angle
formed by the three brigades facing west and MacDonald facing
nearly south a great army of not fewer than 15,000 men was enclosed,
like a flock of sheep in a fold, by the thin brown lines of the British
and Egyptian brigades. As the 7th Egyptians, the right battalion of
Lewis's brigade and nearest the gap between that unit and MacDonald,
deployed to protect the flank, they became unsteady, began to bunch
and waver, and actually made several retrograde movements. There
was a moment of danger; but General Hunter, who was on the spot,
himself ordered the two reserve companies of the 15th Egyptians
under Major Hickman to march up behind them with fixed bayonets.
Their morale was thus restored and the peril averted. The advance
of the three brigades continued.

Yakub found himself utterly unable to withstand the attack from
the river. His own attack on MacDonald languished. The musketry
was producing terrible losses in his crowded ranks. The valiant Wad
Bishara and many other less famous Emirs fell dead. Gradually
he began to give ground. It was evident that the civilised troops were
the stronger. But even before the attack was repulsed, the Khalifa,
who watched from a close position, must have known that the day
was lost.

The three brigades advancing drove the Khalifa's Dervishes back
into the desert. Along a mile of front an intense and destructive fire

flared and crackled. The Maxim guns pulsated feverishly. Two were even dragged by the enterprise of a subaltern to the very summit of Surgham, and from this elevated position intervened with bloody effect. Thus the long line moved forward in irresistible strength. In the centre, under the red Egyptian flag, careless of the bullets which that conspicuous emblem drew, and which inflicted some loss among those around him, rode the Sirdar, stern and sullen, equally unmoved by fear or enthusiasm. Before that terrible line the Khalifa's division began to break up. The whole ground was strewn with dead and wounded, among whose bodies the soldiers picked their steps with the customary Soudan precautions. Surviving thousands struggled away towards Omdurman and swelled the broad stream of fugitives upon whose flank the 21st Lancers already hung vengefully. Yakub and the defenders of the Black Flag disdained to fly, and perished where they stood, beneath the holy ensign, so that when their conquerors reached the spot the dark folds of the banner waved only over the dead.

While all this was taking place – for events were moving at speed – the 1st British Brigade were still doubling across the rear of Maxwell and Lewis to fill the gap between the latter and MacDonald. As they had wheeled round, the regiments gained on each other according to their proximity to the pivot flank. The brigade assumed a formation which may be described as an echelon of columns of route, with the Lincolns, who were actually the pivot regiment, leading. By the time that the right of Lewis's brigade was reached and the British had begun to deploy, it was evident that the Khalifa's attack was broken and that his force was in full retreat. In the near foreground the Arab dead lay thick. Crowds of fugitives were trooping off in the distance. The Black Flag alone waved defiantly over the corpses of its defenders. In the front of the brigade the fight was over. But those who looked away to the right saw a different spectacle. What appeared to be an entirely new army was coming down from the Kerreri Hills. While the soldiers looked and wondered, fresh orders arrived. A mounted officer galloped up. There was a report that terrible events were happening in the dust and smoke to the northward. The spearmen had closed with MacDonald's brigade; were crumpling his line from the flank; had already broken it. Such were the rumours. The orders were more precise. The nearest regiment – the Lincolnshire – was to hurry to MacDonald's threatened flank to meet the attack. The rest of the brigade was to change front half right, and remain in support. The Lincolnshires, breathless but elated, forthwith started off again at the double. They began to traverse the rear of MacDonald's brigade, dimly conscious of rapid movements by its battalions, and to the sound of tremendous independent firing, which did not, however, prevent them from hearing the venomous hiss of bullets.

Had the Khalifa's attack been simultaneous with that which was now developed, the position of MacDonald's brigade must have been almost hopeless. In the actual event it was one of extreme peril. The attack in his front was weakening every minute, but the far more formidable attack on his right rear grew stronger and nearer in inverse ratio. Both attacks must be met. The moment was critical; the danger near. All depended on MacDonald, and that officer, who by valour and conduct in war had won his way from the rank of a private soldier to the command of a brigade, was equal to the emergency.

To meet the Khalifa's attack he had arranged his force facing south-west, with three battalions in line and the fourth held back in column of companies in rear of the right flank – an inverted L-shaped formation. As the attack from the south-west gradually weakened and the attack from the north-west continually increased, he broke off his battalions and batteries from the longer side of the L and transferred them to the shorter. He timed these movements so accurately that each face of his brigade was able to exactly sustain the attacks of the enemy. As soon as the Khalifa's force began to waver he ordered the XIth Soudanese and a battery on his left to move across the angle in which the brigade was formed, and deploy along the shorter face to meet the impending onslaught of Ali-Wad-Helu. Perceiving this, the IXth Soudanese, who were the regiment in column on the right of the original front, wheeled to the right from column into line without waiting for orders, so that two battalions faced towards the Khalifa and two towards the fresh attack. By this time it was clear that the Khalifa was practically repulsed, and MacDonald ordered the Xth Soudanese and another battery to change front and prolong the line of the IXth and XIth. He then moved the 2nd Egyptians diagonally to their right front, so as to close the gap at the angle between their line and that of the three other battalions. These difficult manœuvres were carried out under a heavy fire, which in twenty minutes caused over 120 casualties in the four battalions – exclusive of the losses in the artillery batteries – and in the face of the determined attacks of an enemy who outnumbered the troops by seven to one and had only to close with them to be victorious. Amid the roar of the firing and the dust, smoke, and confusion of the change of front, the general found time to summon the officers of the IXth Soudanese around him, rebuked them for having wheeled into line in anticipation of his order, and requested them to drill more steadily in brigade.

The three Soudanese battalions were now confronted with the whole fury of the Dervish attack from Kerreri. The bravery of the blacks was no less conspicuous than the wildness of their musketry. They evinced an extraordinary excitement – firing their rifles without any attempt to sight or aim, and only anxious to pull the trigger, re-load, and pull it again. In vain the British officers strove to calm their impulsive soldiers. In vain they called upon them by name, or, taking their rifles from them, adjusted the sights themselves. The independent firing was utterly beyond control. Soon the ammunition began to be exhausted, and the soldiers turned round clamouring for more cartridges, which their officers doled out to them by twos and threes in the hopes of steadying them. It was useless. They fired them all off and clamoured for more. Meanwhile, although suffering fearfully from the close and accurate fire of the three artillery batteries and eight Maxim guns, and to a less extent from the random firing of the Soudanese, the Dervishes drew nearer in thousands, and it seemed certain that there would be an actual collision. The valiant blacks prepared themselves with delight to meet the shock, notwithstanding the overwhelming numbers of the enemy. Scarcely three rounds per man remained throughout the brigade. The batteries opened a rapid fire of case-shot. Still the Dervishes advanced, and the survivors of their first wave of assault were scarcely 100 yards away. Behind them both green flags pressed forward over enormous masses of armed humanity, rolling on as they now believed to victory.

At this moment the Lincoln Regiment began to come up. As soon as the leading company cleared the right of MacDonald's brigade, they formed line, and opened an independent fire obliquely across the front of the Soudanese. Groups of Dervishes in twos and threes were then within 100 yards. The great masses were within 300 yards. The independent firing lasted two minutes, during which the whole regiment deployed. Its effect was to clear away the leading groups of Arabs. The deployment having been accomplished with the loss of a dozen men, including Colonel Sloggett, who fell shot through the breast while attending to the wounded, section volleys were ordered. With excellent discipline the independent firing was instantly stopped, and the battalion began with machine-like regularity to carry out the principles of modern musketry, for which their training had efficiently prepared them and their rifles were admirably suited. They fired on an average sixty rounds per man, and finally repulsed the attack.

The Dervishes were weak in cavalry, and had scarcely 2,000 horsemen on the field. About 400 of these, mostly the personal retainers of the various Emirs, were formed into an irregular regiment and attached to the flag of Ali-Wad-Helu. Now when these horsemen perceived that there was no more hope of victory, they arranged themselves in a solid mass and charged the left of MacDonald's brigade. The distance was about 500 yards, and, wild as was the firing of the Soudanese, it was evident that they could not possibly succeed. Nevertheless, many carrying no weapon in their hands, and all urging their horses to their utmost speed, they rode unflinchingly to certain death. All were killed and fell as they entered the zone of fire – three, twenty, fifty, two hundred, sixty, thirty, five and one out beyond them all – a brown smear across the sandy plain. A few riderless horses alone broke through the ranks of the infantry.

After the failure of the attack from Kerreri the whole Anglo-Egyptian army advanced westward, in a line of bayonets and artillery nearly two miles long, and drove the Dervishes before them into the desert, so that they could by no means rally or re-form. At half past eleven Sir H. Kitchener shut up his glasses, and, remarking that he thought the enemy had been given 'a good dusting', gave the order for the brigades to resume their interrupted march on Omdurman.

Meanwhile the great Dervish Army, who had advanced at sunrise in hope and courage, fled in utter rout, pursued by the Egyptian cavalry, harried by the 21st Lancers, and leaving more than 9,000 warriors dead and even greater numbers wounded behind them.

Thus ended the Battle of Omdurman – the most signal triumph ever gained by the arms of science over barbarians.

CHAPTER XV

THE FALL OF THE CITY

Now, when the Khalifa Abdullah saw that the last army that remained to him was broken, that all his attacks had failed, and that thousands of his bravest warriors were slain, he rode from the field of battle in haste, and, regaining the city, proceeded like a brave and stubborn soldier to make preparations for its defence, and, like a prudent man, to arrange for his own flight should further resistance be impossible. He ordered his great war-drum to be beaten and the *ombya* to be blown, and for the last time those dismal notes boomed through the streets of Omdurman. They were not heeded. The Arabs recognised that all was lost. Besides, to return to the city was difficult and dangerous.

As soon as it was apparent that the surrender of individuals was accepted, the Dervishes began to come in and lay down their arms – at first by twos and threes, then by dozens, and finally by scores. Meanwhile those who were still intent on flight made a wide detour to avoid the cavalry, and streamed past our front at a mile's distance in uninterrupted succession. The disarming and escorting of the prisoners delayed our advance, and many thousands of Dervishes escaped from the field. But the position of the cavalry and the pressure they exerted shouldered the routed army out into the desert, so that retiring they missed the city of Omdurman altogether, and, disregarding the Khalifa's summons to defend it and the orders of their Emirs, continued their flight to the south. To harry and annoy the fugitives a few troops were dismounted with carbines, and a constant fire was made on such as did not attempt to come in and surrender. Yet the crowds continued to run the gauntlet, and at least 20,000 men made good their escape. Many of these were still vicious, and replied to our fire with bullets, fortunately at very long range. It would have been madness for 300 Lancers to gallop in among such masses, and we had to be content with the results of the carbine fire.

While all this had been going on, the advance of the army on Omdurman was continuing. Nor was it long before we saw the imposing array of infantry topping the sandhills near Surgham and flooding out into the plain which lay between them and the city. High over the centre brigade flew the Black Flag of the Khalifa, and underneath a smaller flash of red marked the position of the Headquarters Staff. The black masses of men continued to move slowly across the open ground while we fired at the flying Arabs, and at twelve o'clock we saw them halt near the river about three miles from the city. Orders now reached us to join them, and as the sun was hot, the day dragged, all were tired and hungry, and the horses needed water, we were not long in complying, and the remnants of the Dervish Army made good their retreat unmolested.

It was not until four o'clock that the cavalry received orders to ride round the outside of the city and harry such as should seek to escape. The Egyptian squadrons and the 21st Lancers started forthwith, and, keeping about a mile from the houses of the suburbs, proceeded to make the circle of the town. The infantry had already entered it, as was evident from a continual patter of shots and an occasional rattle of the Maxim guns. The leading Soudanese brigade – Maxwell's – had moved from Khor Shambat at 2.30, formed in line of company columns and in the following order:

Direction of Advance

XIVth Soudanese	XIIth Soudanese	↑ ↗	Maxims	8th Egyptians	32nd Field Battery	XIIIth Soudanese

The Sirdar, attended by his whole Staff, with the Black Flag of the Khalifa carried behind him and accompanied by the band of the XIth Soudanese, rode in front of the XIVth battalion. The regiments were soon enveloped by the numberless houses of the suburbs and divided by the twisting streets; but the whole brigade pressed forward on a broad front. Behind followed the rest of the army – battalion after battalion, brigade after brigade – until all, swallowed up by the maze of mud houses, were filling the open spaces and blocking and choking the streets and alleys with solid masses of armed men, who marched or pushed their way up to the great wall.

For two miles the progress through the suburbs continued, and the

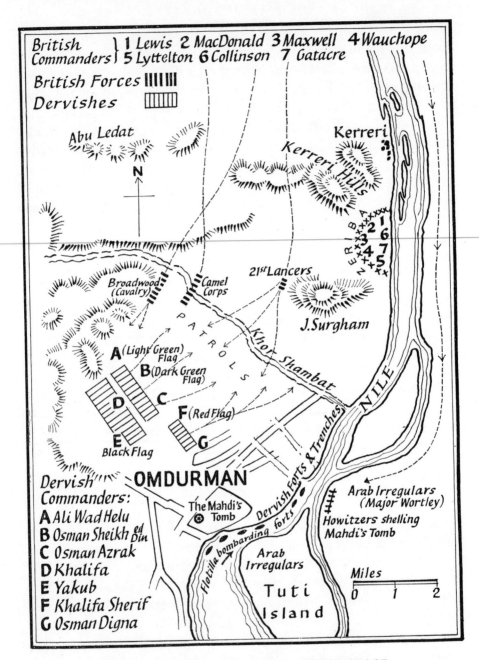

British Commanders } 1 Lewis 2 MacDonald 3 Maxwell 4 Wauchope 5 Lyttelton 6 Collinson 7 Gatacre

British Forces IIIIII

Dervishes

Abu Ledat

N

Kerreri

Kerreri Hills

KERREBA

X X X
2 1
3 6
4 7
5

Broadwood (Cavalry)

Camel Corps

21st Lancers

PATROLS

J. Surgham

A (Light Green) Flag

B (Dark Green Flag)

D   C

F (Red Flag)

E   G

Black Flag

Khor Shambat

NILE

Dervish Forts & Trenches

OMDURMAN

The Mahdi's Tomb

Flotilla bombarding forts

Arab Irregulars (Major Wortley)

Howitzers shelling Mahdi's Tomb

Arab Irregulars

Tuti Island

Miles
0   1   2

Dervish Commanders:
A Ali Wad Helu
B Osman Sheikh ed Din
C Osman Azrak
D Khalifa
E Yakub
F Khalifa Sherif
G Osman Digna

THE BATTLE OF OMDURMAN – FINAL STAGE

General, hurrying on with his Staff, soon found himself, with the band, the Maxims, and the artillery, at the foot of the great wall. Several hundred Dervishes had gathered for its defence; but the fact that no *banquette* had been made on which they could stand to fire prevented their resistance from being effective. A few ill-aimed shots were, however, fired, to which the Maxim guns replied with vigour. In a quarter of an hour the wall was cleared. The Sirdar then posted two guns of the 32nd Field Battery at its northern angle, and then, accompanied by the remaining four guns and the XIVth Soudanese, turned eastwards and rode along the foot of the wall towards the river, seeking some means of entry into the inner city. The breach made by the gunboats was found temporarily blocked by wooden doors, but the main gate was open, and through this the General passed into the heart of Omdurman. Within the wall the scenes were more terrible than in the suburbs. The effects of the bombardment were evident on every side. Women and children lay frightfully mangled in the roadway. Dead Dervishes, already in the fierce heat beginning to decompose, dotted the ground. The houses were crammed with wounded. Hundreds of decaying carcasses of animals filled the air with a sickening smell. Here, as without the wall, the anxious inhabitants renewed their protestations of loyalty and welcome; and interpreters, riding down the narrow alleys, proclaimed the merciful conditions of the conquerors and called on the people to lay down their arms. Great piles of surrendered weapons rose in the streets, guarded by Soudanese soldiers. All Dervishes who did not immediately surrender were shot or bayoneted, and bullets whistled at random along or across the streets. But while women crowded round his horse, while sullen men fired carefully from houses, while beaten warriors cast their spears on the ground and others, still resisting, were despatched in corners, the Sirdar rode steadily onward through the confusion, the stench, and the danger, until he reached the Mahdi's Tomb.

At the mosque two fanatics charged the Soudanese escort, and each killed or badly wounded a soldier before he was shot. The day was now far spent, and it was dusk when the prison was reached. The General was the first to enter that foul and gloomy den. Charles Neufeld and some thirty heavily shackled prisoners were released.

Neufeld, who was placed on a pony, seemed nearly mad with delight, and talked and gesticulated with queer animation. 'Thirteen years,' he said to his rescuer, 'have I waited for this day.' From the prison, as it was now dark, the Sirdar rode to the great square in front of the mosque, in which his headquarters were established, and where both British brigades were already bivouacking. The rest of the army settled down along the roadways through the suburbs, and only Maxwell's brigade remained in the city to complete the establishment of law and order – a business which was fortunately hidden by the shades of night.

While the Sirdar with the infantry of the army was taking possession of Omdurman, the British and Egyptian cavalry had moved round to the west of the city. There for nearly two hours we waited, listening to the dropping fusillade which could be heard within the great wall and wondering what was happening. Large numbers of Dervishes and Arabs, who, laying aside their *jibbas*, had ceased to be Dervishes, appeared among the houses at the edge of the suburbs. Several hundreds of these, with two or three Emirs, came out to make their submission; and we were presently so loaded with spears and swords that it was impossible to carry them, and many interesting trophies had to be destroyed. It was just getting dark when suddenly Colonel Slatin galloped up. The Khalifa had fled! The Egyptian cavalry were at once to pursue him. The 21st Lancers must await further orders. Slatin appeared very much in earnest. He talked with animated manner to Colonel Broadwood, questioned two of the surrendered Emirs closely, and hurried off into the dusk, while the Egyptian squadrons, mounting, also rode away at a trot.

It was not for some hours after he had left the field of battle that Abdullah realised that his army had not obeyed his summons, but were continuing their retreat, and that only a few hundred Dervishes remained for the defence of the city. He seems, if we judge from the accounts of his personal servant, an Abyssinian boy, to have faced the disasters that had overtaken him with singular composure. He rested until two o'clock, when he ate some food. Thereafter he repaired to the Tomb, and in that ruined shrine, amid the wreckage of the shellfire, the defeated sovereign appealed to the spirit of Mohammed Ahmed to help him in his sore distress. It was the last prayer ever

offered over the Mahdi's grave. The celestial counsels seem to have
been in accord with the dictates of common-sense, and at four o'clock
the Khalifa, hearing that the Sirdar was already entering the city, and
that the English cavalry were on the parade ground to the west,
mounted a small donkey, and, accompanied by his principal wife, a
Greek nun, as a hostage, and a few attendants, rode leisurely off towards
the south. Eight miles from Omdurman a score of swift camels awaited
him, and on these he soon reached the main body of his routed army.
Here he found many disheartened friends; but the fact that, in this
evil plight, he found any friends at all must be recorded in his favour
and in that of his subjects. When he arrived he had no escort – was,
indeed, unarmed. The fugitives had good reason to be savage. Their
leaders had led them only to their ruin. To cut the throat of this one
man who was the cause of all their sufferings was as easy as they
would have thought it innocent. Yet none assailed him. The tyrant,
the oppressor, the scourge of the Soudan, the hypocrite, the abomi-
nated Khalifa; the embodiment, as he has been depicted to European
eyes, of all the vices; the object, as he was believed in England, of his
people's bitter hatred, found safety and welcome among his flying
soldiers. The surviving Emirs hurried to his side. Many had gone down
on the fatal plain. Osman Azrak, the valiant Bishara, Yakub, and scores
whose strange names have not obscured these pages, but who were,
nevertheless, great men of war, lay staring up at the stars. Yet those
who remained never wavered in their allegiance. Ali-Wad-Helu,
whose leg had been shattered by a shell splinter, was senseless with
pain; but the Sheikh-ed-Din, the astute Osman Digna, Ibrahim
Khalil, who withstood the charge of the 21st Lancers, and others of
less note rallied to the side of the appointed successor of Mohammed
Ahmed, and did not, even in this extremity, abandon his cause. And
so all hurried on through the gathering darkness, a confused and
miserable multitude – dejected warriors still preserving their trashy
rifles, and wounded men hobbling pitifully along; camels and donkeys
laden with household goods; women crying, panting, dragging
little children; all in thousands – nearly 30,000 altogether; with little
food and less water to sustain them; the desert before them, the gunboats on the Nile, and behind the rumours of pursuit and a broad
trail of dead and dying to mark the path of flight.

In the battle and capture of Omdurman the losses of the Expeditionary Force were as follows: 20 officers, 462 men.

The Dervish losses were, from computations made on the field and corrected at a later date, ascertained to be 9,700 killed, and wounded variously estimated at from 10,000 to 16,000. There were, besides, 5,000 prisoners.

CHAPTER XVI

'THE FASHODA INCIDENT'

The long succession of events, of which I have attempted to give some account, has not hitherto affected to any great extent other countries than those which are drained by the Nile. But this chapter demands a wider view, since it must describe an incident which might easily have convulsed Europe, and from which far-reaching consequences have arisen.

The undisputed facts are few. Towards the end of 1896 a French expedition was despatched from the Atlantic into the heart of Africa under the command of Major Marchand. The re-occupation of Dongola was then practically complete, and the British Government were earnestly considering the desirability of a further advance. In the beginning of 1897 a British expedition, under Colonel Macdonald, and comprising a dozen carefully selected officers, set out from England to Uganda, landed at Mombasa, and struck inland. The misfortunes which fell upon this enterprise are beyond the scope of this account, and I shall not dwell upon the local jealousies and disputes which marred it. It is sufficient to observe that Colonel Macdonald was provided with Soudanese troops who were practically in a state of mutiny and actually mutinied two days after he assumed command. The officers were compelled to fight for their lives. Several were killed. A year was consumed in suppressing the mutiny and the revolt which arose out of it. If the object of the expedition was to reach the Upper Nile, it was soon obviously unattainable, and the Government were glad to employ the officers in making geographical surveys.

At the beginning of 1898 it was clear to those who, with the fullest information, directed the foreign policy of Great Britain that no results affecting the situation in the Soudan could be expected from the Macdonald Expedition. The advance to Khartoum and the reconquest of the lost provinces had been irrevocably undertaken. An Anglo-

Egyptian force was already concentrating at Berber. Lastly, the Marchand Mission was known to be moving towards the Upper Nile, and it was a probable contingency that it would arrive at its destination within a few months. It was therefore evident that the line of advance of the powerful army moving south from the Mediterranean and of the tiny expedition moving east from the Atlantic must intersect before the end of the year, and that intersection would involve a collision between the Powers of Great Britain and France.

With these introductory reflections we may return to the theatre of war.

On the 7th of September, five days after the battle and capture of Omdurman, the *Tewfikia*, a small Dervish steamer – one of those formerly used by General Gordon – came drifting and paddling down the river. Her Arab crew soon perceived by the Egyptian flags which were hoisted on the principal buildings, and by the battered condition of the Mahdi's Tomb, that all was not well in the city; and then, drifting a little further, they found themselves surrounded by the white gunboats of the 'Turks', and so incontinently surrendered. The story they told their captors was a strange one. They had left Omdurman a month earlier, in company with the steamer *Safia*, carrying a force of 500 men, with the Khalifa's orders to go up the White Nile and collect grain. For some time all had been well; but on approaching the old Government station of Fashoda they had been fired on by black troops commanded by white officers under a strange flag – and fired on with such effect that they had lost some forty men killed and wounded. Doubting who these formidable enemies might be, the foraging expedition had turned back, and the Emir in command, having disembarked and formed a camp at a place on the east bank called Reng, had sent the *Tewfikia* back to ask the Khalifa for instructions and reinforcements. The story was carried to the Sirdar and ran like wildfire through the camp. Many officers made their way to the river, where the steamer lay, to test for themselves the truth of the report. The woodwork of the hull was marked with many newly made holes, and cutting into these with their penknives the officers extracted bullets – not the roughly cast leaden balls, the bits of telegraph wire, or old iron which savages use, but the conical nickel-covered bullets of small-bore rifles such as are fired by civilised forces alone. Here was positive proof. A European Power was on the Upper Nile: which? Some said it was the Belgians from the Congo; some that an Italian expedition had arrived; others thought that the strangers were French; others, again, believed in the Foreign Office – it was a British expedition, after all. The Arab crew were cross-examined as to the flag they had seen. Their replies were inconclusive. It had bright colours, they declared; but what those colours were and what their arrangement might be they could not tell.

The camp for the most part received the news with a shrug. After their easy victory the soldiers walked delicately. They knew that they belonged to the most powerful force that had ever penetrated the heart of Africa. If there was to be more war, the Government had but to give the word, and the Grand Army of the Nile would do by these newcomers as they had done by the Dervishes.

On the 8th the Sirdar started up the White Nile for Fashoda with five steamers, the XIth and XIIIth Battalions of Soudanese, two companies of the Cameron Highlanders, Peake's battery of artillery, and four Maxim guns. Three days later he arrived at Reng, and there found, as the crew of the *Tewfikia* had declared, some 500 Dervishes encamped on the bank, and the *Safia* steamer moored to it. These stupid fellows had the temerity to open fire on the vessels. Whereat the *Sultan*, steaming towards their *dêm*, replied with a fierce shell fire which soon put them to flight. The *Safia*, being under steam, made some attempt to escape – whither, it is impossible to say – and Commander Keppel by a well-directed shell in her boilers blew her up, much to the disgust of the Sirdar, who wanted to add her to his flotilla.

After this incident the expedition continued its progress up the White Nile. The *sudd* which was met with two days' journey south of Khartoum did not in this part of the Nile offer any obstacle to navigation, as the strong current of the river clears the waterway; but on either side of the channel a belt of the tangled weed, varying from twelve to twelve hundred yards in breadth, very often prevented the steamers from approaching the bank to tie up. The banks themselves depressed the explorers by their melancholy inhospitality. At times the river flowed past miles of long grey grass and swamp-land, inhabited only by hippopotami. At times a vast expanse of dreary mud

flats stretched as far as the eye could see. At others the forest, dense
with an impenetrable undergrowth of thorn-bushes, approached the
water, and the active forms of monkeys and even of leopards darted
among the trees. Whether forest, mud-flat, or prairie it was a wet
land steaming under a burning sun and humming with mosquitoes
and all kinds of insect life.

Onward and southward toiled the flotilla, splashing the brown
water into foam and startling the strange creatures on the banks, until
on the 18th of September they approached Fashoda. The gunboats
waited, moored to the bank for some hours of the afternoon, to allow
a message which had been sent by the Sirdar to the mysterious Europeans, to precede his arrival, and early in the morning of the 19th a
small steel rowing-boat was observed coming down stream to meet
the expedition. It contained a Senegalese sergeant and two men, with
a letter from Major Marchand announcing the arrival of the French
troops and their formal occupation of the Soudan. It, moreover,
congratulated the Sirdar on his victory, and welcomed him to Fashoda
in the name of France.

A few miles' further progress brought the gunboats to their destination, and they made fast to the bank near the old Government buildings
of the town. Major Marchand's party consisted of eight French officers
or non-commissioned officers, and 120 black soldiers drawn from the
Niger district. They possessed three steel boats fitted for sail or oars,
and a small steam launch, the *Faidherbe*, which latter had, however,
been sent south for reinforcements. They had six months' supplies
of provisions for the French officers, and about three months' rations
for the men; but they had no artillery, and were in great want of small-
arm ammunition. Their position was indeed precarious. The little
force was stranded, without communications of any sort, and with no
means of either withstanding an attack or of making a retreat. They
had fired away most of their cartridges at the Dervish foraging party,
and were daily expecting a renewed attack. Indeed, it was with consternation that they had heard of the approach of the flotilla. The
natives had carried the news swiftly up the river that the Dervishes
were coming back with five steamers, and for three nights the French
had been sleeplessly awaiting the assault of a powerful enemy.

Their joy and relief at the arrival of a European force were undisguised. The Sirdar and his officers on their part were thrilled with admiration at the wonderful achievements of this small band of heroic men. Two years had passed since they left the Atlantic coast. For four months they had been absolutely lost from human ken. They had fought with savages; they had struggled with fever; they had climbed mountains and pierced the most gloomy forests. Five days and five nights they had stood up to their necks in swamp and water. A fifth of their number had perished; yet at last they had carried out their mission and, arriving at Fashoda on the 10th of July, had planted the tricolour upon the Upper Nile.

Moved by such reflections the British officers disembarked. Major Marchand, with a guard of honour, came to meet the General. They shook hands warmly. 'I congratulate you,' said the Sirdar, 'on all you have accomplished.' 'No,' replied the Frenchman, pointing to his troops; 'it is not I, but these soldiers who have done it.' And Kitchener, telling the story afterwards, remarked, 'Then I knew he was a gentleman.'

Into the diplomatic discussions that followed, it is not necessary to plunge. The Sirdar politely ignored the French flag, and, without interfering with the Marchand Expedition and the fort it occupied, hoisted the British and Egyptian colours with all due ceremony, amid musical honours and the salutes of the gunboats. A garrison was established at Fashoda, consisting of the XIth Soudanese, four guns of Peake's battery, and two Maxims, the whole under the command of Colonel Jackson, who was appointed military and civil commandant of the Fashoda district.

At three o'clock on the same afternoon the Sirdar and the gunboats resumed their journey to the south, and the next day reached the mouth of the Sobat, sixty-two miles from Fashoda. Here other flags were hoisted and another post formed with a garrison of half the XIIIth Soudanese battalion and the remaining two guns of Peake's battery. The expedition then turned northwards, leaving two gunboats – the *Sultan* and the *Abu Klea* – at the disposal of Colonel Jackson.

I do not attempt to describe the international negotiations and discussions that followed the receipt of the news in Europe, but it is pleasing to remember that a great crisis found England united. The determination of the Government was approved by the loyalty of the Opposition, supported by the calm resolve of the people, and armed with the efficiency of the fleet. At first indeed, while the Sirdar was still steaming southward, wonder and suspense filled all minds; but when suspense ended in the certainty that eight French adventurers were in occupation of Fashoda and claimed a territory twice as large as France, it gave place to a deep and bitter anger. They should go. They should evacuate Fashoda, or else all the might, majesty, dominion, and power of everything that could by any stretch of the imagination be called 'British' should be employed to make them go.

Those who find it difficult to account for the hot, almost petulant, flush of resolve that stirred the nation must look back over the long history of the Soudan drama. It had always been a duty to reconquer the abandoned territory. When it was found that this might be safely done, the duty became a pleasure. The operations were watched, with extravagant attention, and while they progressed the earnestness of the nation increased. As the tides of barbarism were gradually driven back, the old sea-marks came one after another into view. Names of towns that were half forgotten – or remembered only with sadness – reappeared on the posters, in the gazettes, and in the newspapers. We were going back. 'Dongola', 'Berber', 'Metemma' – who had not heard of them before? Now they were associated with victory.

When the final triumph, long expected, came in all its completeness it was hailed with a shout of exultation, and the people of Great Britain, moved far beyond their wont, sat themselves down to give thanks to their God, their Government, and their General. Suddenly, on the chorus of their rejoicing there broke a discordant note. They were confronted with the fact that a 'friendly Power' had, unprovoked, endeavoured to rob them of the fruits of their victories. They now realised that while they had been devoting themselves to great military operations, in broad daylight and the eye of the world, and prosecuting an enterprise on which they had set their hearts, other operations – covert and deceitful – had been in progress in the heart of the Dark Continent, designed solely for the mischievous and spiteful object of depriving them of the produce of their labours.

Great Britain was determined to have Fashoda or fight; and as soon as this was made clear, the French were willing to give way. Fashoda was a miserable swamp, of no particular value to them. Marchand, Lord Salisbury's 'explorer in difficulties upon the Upper Nile', was

admitted by the French Minister to be merely an 'emissary of civilisation'. It was not worth their while to embark on the hazards and
convulsions of a mighty war for either swamp or emissary. Besides,
the plot had failed. The negro tribes gazed with wonder on the
strangers, but had no intention of fighting for them. The pride and
barbarism of the Khalifa rejected all overtures and disdained to dis-
criminate between the various breeds of the accursed 'Turks'. Finally,
the victory of Omdurman and its forerunner – the Desert Railway –
had revolutionised the whole situation in the Nile valley. After some
weeks of tension, the French Government consented to withdraw
their expedition from the region of the Upper Nile.

Meanwhile events were passing at Fashoda. The town, the site of
which had been carefully selected by the old Egyptian Government, is
situated on the left bank of the river, on a gentle slope of ground which
rises about four feet above the level of the Nile at full flood. During
the rainy season, which lasts from the end of June until the end of
October, the surrounding country is one vast swamp, and Fashoda
itself becomes an island. It is not, however, without its importance;
for it is the only spot on the west shore for very many miles where
landing from the river is possible. All the roads – mere camel-tracks –
from Lower Kordofan meet at the Government post, but are only
passable in the dry season. The soil is fertile, and, since there is a super-
abundance of sun and water, almost any crop or plant can be grown.
The French officers, with the adaptive thrift of their nation, had already,
in spite of the ravages of the water-rats, created a good vegetable
garden, from which they were able to supplement their monotonous
fare. The natives, however – aboriginal negroes of the Dinka and Shil-
look tribes – are unwilling to work, except to provide themselves
with the necessaries of life; and since these are easily obtained, there
is very little cultivation, and the fertility of the soil may be said to
increase the poverty of the country. At all seasons of the year the
climate of Fashoda is pestilential, and the malarial fever attacks every
European or Egyptian, breaking down the strongest constitutions,
and in many cases causing death.[1]

---

[1] The place is most unhealthy, and in March 1899 (the driest season of the year)
out of a garrison of 317 men only 37 were fit for duty. – *Sir William Garstin's Report:
Egypt, No. 5, 1899.*

On this dismal island, far from civilisation, health, or comfort, the Marchand Mission and the Egyptian garrison lived in polite antagonism for nearly three months. The French fort stood at the northern end. The Egyptian camp lay outside the ruins of the town. Civilities were constantly exchanged between the forces, and the British officers repaid the welcome gifts of fresh vegetables by newspapers and other conveniences. The Senegalese riflemen were smart and well-conducted soldiers, and the blacks of the Soudanese battalion soon imitated their officers in reciprocating courtesies. A feeling of mutual respect sprang up between Colonel Jackson and Major Marchand. The dashing commandant of the XIth Soudanese, whose Egyptian medals bear no fewer than fourteen clasps, was filled with a generous admiration for the French explorer. Realising the difficulties, he appreciated the magnificence of the achievement; and as he spoke excellent French a good and almost cordial understanding was established, and no serious disagreement occurred. But, notwithstanding the polite relations, the greatest vigilance was exercised by both sides, and whatever civilities were exchanged were of a formal nature.

The Dinkas and Shillooks had on the first arrival of the French made submission, and had supplied them with provisions. They knew that white men were said to be coming, and they did not realise that there were different races among the whites. Marchand was regarded as the advance guard of the Sirdar's army. But when the negroes gradually perceived that these bands of white men were at enmity with each other – were, in fact, of rival tribes – they immediately transferred their allegiance to the stronger force, and, although their dread of the Egyptian flag was at first very marked, boycotted the French entirely.

In the middle of October despatches from France arrived for Marchand by steamer; and that officer, after reading them, determined to proceed to Cairo. Jackson, who was most anxious that no disagreement should arise, begged him to give positive orders to his subordinate to maintain the *status quo*, as had been agreed. Marchand gladly consented, and departed for Omdurman, where he visited the battlefield, and found in the heaps of slain a grim witness of the destruction from which he had been saved, and so on to Cairo, where he was moved

to tears and speeches. But in his absence Captain Germain, who succeeded to the command, diverged from his orders. No sooner had
Marchand left than Germain, anxious to win distinction, embarked
upon a most aggressive policy. He occupied the Dinka country on
the right bank of the river, pushed reconnoitring parties into the
interior, prevented the Dinka Sheikhs from coming to make their
submission at Fashoda, and sent his boats and the *Faidherbe* steam
launch, which had returned from the south, beyond the northern
limits which the Sirdar had prescribed and Marchand had agreed to
recognise.

Colonel Jackson protested again and again. Germain sent haughty
replies, and persisted in his provoking policy. At last the British
officer was compelled to declare that if any more patrols were sent
into the Dinka country, he would not allow them to return to the
French post. Whereat Germain rejoined that he would meet force
with force. All tempers were worn by fever, heat, discomfort, and
monotony. The situation became very difficult, and the tact and
patience of Colonel Jackson alone averted a conflict which would
have resounded in all parts of the world. He confined his troops
strictly to their lines, and moved as far from the French camp as
was possible. But there was one dark day when the French officers
worked in their shirts with their faithful Senegalese to strengthen
the entrenchments, and busily prepared for a desperate struggle. On
the other side little activity was noticeable. The Egyptian garrison,
although under arms, kept out of sight, but a wisp of steam above the
funnels of the redoubtable gunboats showed that all was ready.

At length in a fortunate hour Marchand returned, reproved his
subordinate, and expressed his regrets to Colonel Jackson. Then it
became known that the French Government had ordered the evacuation of Fashoda. Some weeks were spent in making preparations for the
journey, but at length the day of departure arrived. At 8.20 on the
morning of the 11th of December the French lowered their flag with
salute and flourish of bugle. The British officers, who remained in
their own camp and did not obtrude themselves, were distant but
interested spectators. On the flag ceasing to fly, a *sous-officier* rushed
up to the flagstaff and hurled it to the ground, shaking his fists and
tearing his hair in a bitterness and vexation from which it is impossible

to withhold sympathy, in view of what these men had suffered uselessly and what they had done. The French then embarked, and at 9.30 steamed southward, the *Faidherbe* towing one oblong steel barge and one old steel boat, the other three boats sailing, all full of men. As the little flotilla passed the Egyptian camp a guard of honour of the XIth Soudanese saluted them and the band struck up their national anthem. The French acknowledged the compliment by dipping their flag, and in return the British and Egyptian flags were also lowered. The boats then continued their journey until they had rounded the bend of the river, when they came to land, and, honour being duly satisfied, Marchand and his officers returned to breakfast with Colonel Jackson. The meeting was very friendly. Jackson and Germain exchanged most elaborate compliments, and the commandant, in the name of the XIth Soudanese, presented the expedition with the banner of the Emir who had attacked them, which had been captured at Reng. Marchand shook hands all round, and the British officers bade their gallant opponents a final farewell.

Once again the eight Frenchmen, who had come so far and accomplished so much, set out upon their travels, to make a safe though tedious journey through Abyssinia to the coast, and thence home to the country they had served faithfully and well, and which was not unmindful of their services.

It only remains to discuss the settlement made between the conquerors of the Soudan. Great Britain and Egypt had moved hand in hand up the great river, sharing, though unequally, the cost of the war in men and money. The prize belonged to both. The direct annexation of the Soudan by Great Britain would have been an injustice to Egypt. Moreover, the claim of the conquerors to Fashoda and other territories rested solely on the former rights of Egypt. On the other hand, if the Soudan became Egyptian again, it must wear the fetters of that imprisoned country. Mixed Tribunals, Ottoman Suzerainty, and other vexatious burdens would be added to the difficulties of Soudan administration. To free the new country from the curse of internationalism was a paramount object. The Soudan Agreement by Great Britain and Egypt, published on the 7th of March 1899, achieves this. Like most of the best work done in Egypt by the British Agency, the Agreement was slipped through without attracting much notice. Under its authority a State has been created in the Nile Valley which is neither British nor Ottoman, nor anything else so far known to the law of Europe. International jurists are confronted with an entirely new political status. A diplomatic 'Fourth Dimension' has been discovered. Great Britain and Egypt rule the country together. The allied conquerors have become the joint-possessors. 'What does this Soudan Agreement mean?' the Austrian Consul-General asked Lord Cromer; and the British Agent, whom twenty-two years' acquaintance with Egyptian affairs had accustomed to anomalies, replied, 'It means simply this'; and handed him the inexplicable document, under which the conquered country may some day march to Peace and Plenty.

CHAPTER XVII

ON THE BLUE NILE

The authority of the Khalifa and the strength of his army were for ever broken on the 2nd of September, and the Battle of Omdurman is the natural climax of this tale of war. After the victory the public interest was no longer centred in the Soudan. The last British battalion had been carried north of Assuan; the last Press correspondent had hurried back to Cairo or London. But the military operations were by no means over.

The enemy had been defeated. It remained to reconquer the territory. The Dervishes of the provincial garrisons still preserved their allegiance to the Khalifa. Several strong Arab forces kept the field. Distant Kordofan and even more distant Darfur were as yet quite unaffected by the great battle at the confluence of the Niles. There were rumours of Europeans in the Far South.

The unquestioned command of the waterways which the Sirdar enjoyed enabled the greater part of the Egyptian Soudan to be at once formally re-occupied. All towns or stations on the main rivers and their tributaries were at the mercy of the gunboats. It was only necessary to send troops to occupy them and to hoist the British and Egyptian flags. Two expeditions were forthwith sent up the White and Blue Niles to establish garrisons, and as far as possible to subdue the country. The first, under the personal command of the Sirdar, left Omdurman on the 8th of September, and steamed up the White Nile towards Fashoda. The events which followed that momentous journey have already been related. The second expedition consisted of the gunboats *Sheikh* and *Hafir*, together with two companies and the brass band of the Xth Soudanese and a Maxim battery, all under the command of General Hunter. Leaving Omdurman on the 19th of September, they started up the Blue Nile to Abu Haraz.

On the 22nd of September a considerable part of the army of Osman

Digna, which had not been present at the Battle of Omdurman, was found encamped on the Ghezira, a few miles north of Rufaa. The Sheikhs and Emirs, on being summoned by General Hunter, surrendered, and a force of about 2,000 men laid down their arms.

But there was one Dervish force which had no intention of surrendering to the invaders. Ahmed Fedil, a zealous and devoted adherent of the Khalifa, had been sent, after the defeat on the Atbara, to collect all the Dervishes and bring them to join the growing army at Omdurman. The Emir was hurrying to his master's assistance with a strong and well disciplined force of no fewer than 8,000 men when, while yet sixty miles from the city, he received the news of 'the stricken field'. He immediately halted, and sought to hide the disaster from his soldiers by announcing that the Khalifa had been victorious and no longer needed their assistance. The truth was not, however, long concealed; for a few days later two emissaries despatched by Slatin arrived at the Dervish camp and announced the destruction of the Omdurman army, the flight of the Khalifa, and the fall of the city. The messengers were authorised to offer Ahmed terms; but that implacable Dervish flew into a rage, and, having shot one, sent the other, covered with insults and stripes, to tell the 'Turks' that he would fight to the bitter end. His Dervishes, whose families and women had been left with large stores of grain and ammunition in Gedaref, under a strong garrison of 3,000 men, urged their commander to return and collect these possessions.

On the 7th of September Colonel Parsons, in command of the forces at Kassala, in conformity with previous instructions, set out for Gedaref. It was known that Ahmed Fedil had marched towards Omdurman. It was believed that Gedaref was only weakly held, and the opportunity of cutting the most powerful remaining Dervish Army from its base was too precious to be neglected. But the whole available strength of the Kassala garrison was 1,350 motley soldiers, untried, little disciplined, worn with waiting and wasted by disease, without cavalry, artillery, or machine guns, and with only seven British officers.

During the night of the 21st, when the column was within twelve miles of Gedaref, startling news arrived. A deserter from the Dervishes made his way into the camp and informed Colonel Parsons that the Emir Saadalla awaited him with 3,500 men two miles before the town. The situation was grave. A retreat through the broken country in the face of a powerful enemy seemed impossible. There was no alternative but to attack.

Very early on the morning of the 22nd – the same day on which General Hunter on the Blue Nile was compelling Musa Digna and his followers to surrender – Colonel Parsons and the Kassala column set forth to march into Gedaref and to fight whatever force it might contain. At half past seven, and about three miles from Gedaref, the enemy's scouts were encountered. At eight o'clock the column halted, and Colonel Parsons and his officers ascended a small knoll to reconnoitre.

A most menacing spectacle confronted them. Four lines of white figures rising out of the grass showed by their length the number, and by their regularity, the discipline of the enemy. Subsequent investigation has shown that the Emir Saadalla marched out of Gedaref with 1,700 riflemen, 1,600 spearmen, and 300 horse.

The valley was rocky, and overgrown; but to the right of the track there rose a high saddleback hill, the surface of which looked more open, and which appeared to command the approaches from Gedaref. The troops knew nothing of the country; the Dervishes understood it thoroughly. The high ground gave at least advantage of view. Colonel Parsons resolved to occupy it.

The order was given, and the column began to double across the valley towards the saddleback. The Dervishes, perceiving the nature of the movement, hurried their advance in the hope of catching the troops on the move, but they were too late. Colonel Parsons and his force reached the saddleback safely, and advanced along it in column in the direction of Gedaref.

The Dervishes, seeing that the troops had already reached the hill, swung to their left and advanced to the attack. Thereupon at half past eight the column wheeled into line to meet them, and standing in the long grass, which even on the summit of the hill was nearly breast-high, opened a heavy and destructive fire. The enemy, although suffering severe loss, continued to struggle bravely onward, replying vigorously to the musketry of the soldiers. At nine o'clock, while the frontal attack was still undecided, Colonel Parsons became aware that a strong force of Dervishes had moved round the left rear and were about to attack the hospital and transport. He at once sent to warn Captain Fleming, R.A.M.C., who combined the duties of medical officer and commander of the baggage column, of the impending assault. The Arab Sheikhs, who in the absence of officers were acting as orderlies, had scarcely brought the news to Fleming, when the enemy, some 300 strong, rushed with great determination upon the baggage, and the escort of 120 Arab irregulars at once broke and fled. The situation became desperate; but Ruthven with thirty-four Slavery Department camel-men hastened to meet the exultant enemy and protect the baggage column. In spite of all their efforts the rear of the baggage column was broken and cut up. The survivors fell back towards their main body, hotly pressed by the enemy.

At this moment Captain Ruthven observed one of his native officers, lying wounded on the ground, about to fall into the hands of the Dervishes and perish miserably. He immediately went back and, being a man of great physical strength, carried the body off in his arms. The enemy were, however, so close that he was three times compelled to set his burden down and defend himself with his revolver. Meanwhile the retirement towards the main body continued and accelerated.

Colonel Parsons and his force were now between two fires. The frontal attack was within 200 yards. The rear attack, flushed with success, were hurrying impetuously forward. The defeat and consequent total destruction of the Kassala column appeared certain. But in the nick of time the Dervish frontal attack, which had been suffering heavily from the fire of the troops, wavered; and when the Arab battalion and the 16th Egyptians advanced upon them, they broke and fled. Colonel Parsons at once endeavoured to meet the rear attack. The 16th Egyptians, on being called upon by their commanding officer, Captain McKerrell, faced steadily about to encounter the fresh attack.

The heavy fire of the regular battalion checked the Dervish advance, and Captain Fleming, the rest of the dismounted camel-men, and Ruthven, still carrying his native officer,[1] found safety in their ranks. A short fierce musketry combat followed at a range of less than a hundred yards, at the end of which the assailants of the baggage

[1] For his gallantry on this occasion Captain Ruthven received the Victoria Cross.

convoy were completely repulsed. The action was now practically over and success was won.

The town of Gedaref surrendered at noon. The Dervish Emir, Nur Angara, who with 200 black riflemen and two brass guns had been left in command of the garrison, made haste to submit. The remainder of the Dervishes, continuing their flight under the Emir Saadalla, hurried to tell the tale of defeat to Ahmed Fedil.

The victory had been won, the enemy were routed, and the town was taken: it had now to be defended. The position was good and adaptable. It consisted of three large enclosures, capable of holding the entire force, situated in echelon, so as to protect each other by their fire, and with strong brick walls six feet high. All were at once set to work to clear the approaches, to level the mud houses without, and to build ramparts or *banquettes* within the walls. While the infantry were thus engaged, Ruthven and his camel-men made daily reconnaissances of the surrounding country.

By great good fortune a convoy of ammunition from Mugatta reached Gedaref on the afternoon of the 27th. At dawn the next day Ruthven reported that the advance guard of Ahmed Fedil was approaching the town. The attack began at half past eight. The Dervishes, who fought with their customary gallantry, simultaneously assaulted the north, south, and west faces of the defences. Creeping forward through the high *doura*, they were able to get within 300 yards of the enclosures. But the intervening space had been carefully cleared of cover, and was swept by the musketry of the defenders. All attempts to cross this ground – even the most determined rushes – proved vain. After an hour's heavy fusillade the attack weakened, and presently ceased altogether.

The Dervishes remained for two days in the palm grove two miles to the west of the town, but on the 1st of October Ahmed Fedil was forced to retire to a more convenient camp eight miles to the southward. Here for the next three weeks he remained, savage and sulky; until the arrival of a relief expedition to the Kassala column forced him to realise that he had no chance of recapturing the town.

After his defeat before Gedaref, Ahmed Fedil reverted to his intention of joining the Khalifa in Kordofan, and he withdrew southwards towards the Dinder river with a following that still numbered more than 5,000. To pass the Nile in the face of the gunboats appeared impossible. He did not, however, believe that steamers could navigate the higher reaches of the rivers, and in the hopes of finding a safe crossing-place he directed his march so as to strike the Blue Nile south of Karkoj. Moving leisurely, and with frequent delays to pillage the inhabitants, he arrived on the Dinder, twenty-five miles to the east of Karkoj, on the 7th of November. Here he found two powerful vessels already patrolling it. Again frustrated, he turned southwards, meaning to cross above the Rosaires Cataract, which was without doubt impassable to steamers.

During the end of November the Sheikh Bakr, who had deserted the Dervishes after their retreat from Gedaref, arrived at Karkoj where Colonel Lewis, who had been marching through the centre of the Ghezira to re-establish the Egyptian authority, had halted, with 350 irregulars. He claimed to have defeated his former chief many times, and produced a sack of heads as evidence of his success. His loyalty being thus placed beyond doubt, he was sent to keep contact with the Dervishes and encouraged by the permission to appropriate whatever spoils of war he could capture.

Meanwhile Ahmed Fedil was working his way slowly southward along a deep *khor* which runs almost parallel to the Blue Nile and is perhaps twenty miles from it. As soon as the position of the Dervish Emir was definitely known, Colonel Lewis moved his force from Karkoj to Rosaires. On the 20th of December, information was received that on the 18th Ahmed Fedil had reached the village of Dakhila, about twenty miles south of the Rosaires post; that he himself had immediately crossed with his advanced guard, and was busily passing the women and children across the river on rafts.

On the 22nd, therefore, Colonel Lewis hurried the Sheikh Bakr up the west bank to cut off their flocks and harass the Dervishes who had already crossed the river. The irregulars accordingly departed; and the next day news was brought that the Dervish force was almost equally divided by the Blue Nile, half being on one bank and half on the other.

Colonel Lewis determined to attack what part of Ahmed Fedil's force still remained on the east bank of the river, and on Christmas Day, at five o'clock in the afternoon, he marched with every man he could muster in the direction of Dakhila.

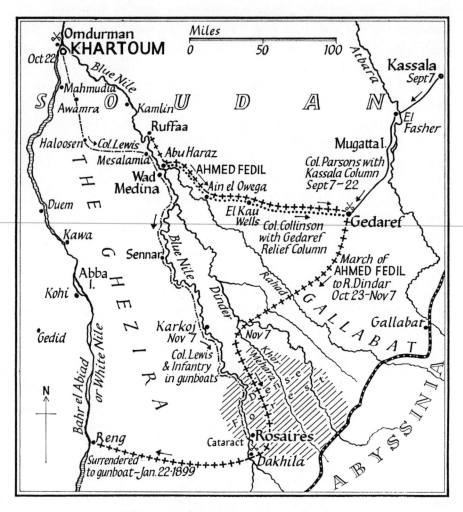

THE CAMPAIGN ON THE BLUE NILE

Moving in single file along a track which led through a dense forest of thorny trees, the column reached Abu Zogholi, a village thought to be half, but really not one-third, of the way to Dakhila, at eleven o'clock on Christmas night. Here they bivouacked until 3 a.m. on the 26th, when the march was resumed in the same straggling order through the same tangled scrub. Daylight found them still several miles from the Dervish position, and it was not until eight o'clock that the enemy's outposts were discovered. After a few shots the Arab picquet fell back, and the advance guard, hurrying after them, emerged from the forest upon the open ground of the river-bank. Into this space the whole column gradually debouched.

The Dervish position was well chosen and of great defensive strength. A little to the north of Dakhila the Blue Nile bifurcates – one rapid but shallow stream flowing fairly straight under the east bank; another very deep stream running in a wide curve under the west bank, cutting into it so that it is precipitous. These two branches of the river enclose an island a mile and a quarter long by 1,400 yards wide, and on this island, surrounded by a natural moat of swiftly flowing water, was the Dervish *dêm*. The western side of the island rose into a line of low sandhills covered with scrub and grass, with a steep reverse slope towards the foreshore of the river-bank; and here, in this excellent cover, what eventually proved to be three-quarters of the force of Ahmed Fedil were drawn up. Backed against the deep arm of the river they had no choice, nor indeed any other wish, but to fight. Before them stretched a bare slope of heavy shingle, 1,000 yards wide, over which their enemies must advance to the attack. Behind them the high precipitous west bank of the river, which rose in some places to a height of fifty feet, was lined with the 300 riflemen who had already crossed; and from this secure position Ahmed Fedil and four of his Emirs were able to watch, assist, and direct the defence of the island. The force on the island was under the sole command of the Emir Saadalla, of Gedaref repute.

The prospect was uninviting. Colonel Lewis discovered that he had absurdly under-rated the strength and discipline of the Dervish force. It had been continually reported that the defeats at Gedaref had demoralised them, and that their numbers did not exceed 2,000 men. Moreover, he had marched to the attack in the belief that they were equally divided on both sides of the river. Retreat was, however, impossible. Strong as was the position of the enemy, the direct assault was actually safer than a retirement through the nineteen miles of gloomy forest which lay between the adventurous column and Rosaires. At nine o'clock the two Maxims, which represented the artillery of the little force, came into action in good positions, while the Xth Soudanese and most of the irregulars lined the east bank. Musketry and Maxim fire was now opened at long range. The Dervishes

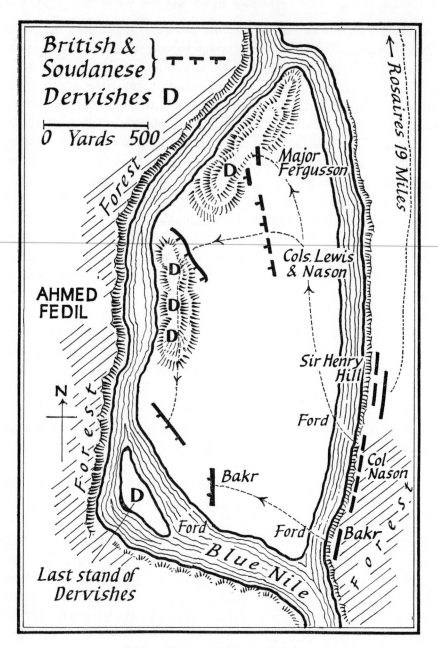

THE ACTION NEAR ROSAIRES

replied, and it soon became evident that no long-range fire could dislodge them; and Colonel Lewis resolved, in spite of the great disparity of force and disadvantage of ground, to attack them with the bayonet. Some time was spent in finding fords across the interposing arm of the river, and it was not until past ten o'clock that Bakr's men crossed on to the island, and, supported by a company of the Xth Soudanese, advanced towards the enemy's right and took up a position at about 800 yards from their line, to cover the rest of the passage.

Colonel Lewis now determined to turn the enemy's left from the north, attack them in flank, and roll them into the deep part of the river. With the Xth Soudanese, under Colonel Nason and Major Fergusson, he marched northwards along the river's edge, sheltering as far as possible under the curve of the bank from the fire. Having reached the position from which it was determined to deliver the attack, the battalion deployed into line, and, changing front half left, advanced obliquely by alternate companies across the bare shingle towards the sandhills. As they advanced, a galling fire was opened upon the left flank by two hundred Dervishes admirably placed on a knoll.

The Dervish musketry now became intense. The Soudanese began to drop on all sides, and the ground was soon dotted with the bodies of the killed and wounded. But undaunted by fire and cross-fire, the heroic black soldiers pressed forward without the slightest check or hesitation, and, increasing their pace to a swift run, reached the first sandhills and found cover beneath them.

The rapidity of their advance had exhausted the Soudanese, and Lewis ordered Nason to halt under cover of the sandhills for a few minutes, so that the soldiers might get their breath before the final effort. Thereupon the Dervishes, seeing that the troops were no longer advancing, and believing that the attack was repulsed, resolved to clinch the matter. Ahmed Fedil from the west bank sounded the charge on drum and bugle, and with loud shouts of triumph and enthusiasm the whole force on the island rose from among the upper sandhills, and, waving their banners, advanced impetuously in counter-attack. But the Xth Soudanese, panting yet unconquerable, responded to the call of their two white officers, and, crowning the little dunes behind which they had sheltered, met the exultant enemy with a withering fire and a responding shout.

The range was short and the fire effective. The astonished Arabs wavered and broke; and then the soldiers, nobly led, swept forward in a long scattered line and drove the enemy from one sandy ridge to another, until all who were not killed or wounded were penned at the extreme southern end of the island, with the deep unfordable arm of the river behind them and the fierce black soldiers, roused to fury by their losses, in front.

The Sheikh Bakr, with his men and the rest of the irregulars, joined the victorious Soudanese, and from the cover of the sandhills, now in the hands of the troops, a terrible fire was opened upon the Dervishes crowded together on the bare and narrow promontory and on the foreshore. Some tried to swim across the rushing river to their friends on the west bank. Many were drowned – among them Saadalla, who sank horse and man beneath the flood. Others took refuge from the fire by standing up to their necks in the stream. The greater part, however, escaped to a smaller island a little further up the river. But the cover was bad, and, after being exposed for an hour and a half to the musketry of two companies, the survivors – 300 strong – surrendered.

By 11.30 the whole island was in the possession of the troops.

Ahmed Fedil escaped with scarcely a dozen followers to join the Khalifa.

CHAPTER XVIII

THE END OF THE KHALIFA

The Khalifa still remained in Kordofan. After he had made good his escape from the battlefield of Omdurman, Abdullah had hurried in the direction of El Obeid. In the beginning of November he moved westward to Aigailla. Here he was joined by the Emir El Khatem with the El Obeid garrison. This chief and his followers had never been engaged with the 'Turks', and were consequently fresh and valiant. Their arrival greatly encouraged the force which the Khalifa had rallied. A large *dêm* was formed at Aigailla, and here, since the water was plentiful during December, Abdullah abode quietly, sending his raiding parties to collect grain and other supplies.

As soon as the Sirdar, who had returned from England, received the news he determined to make an attempt to capture the Khalifa; and on the 29th of December sent for Colonel Kitchener, to whom he had decided to entrust this honourable enterprise. The colonel was directed to take a small mixed force into Kordofan and to reconnoitre the enemy's position. If possible, he was to attack and capture Abdullah, whose followers were believed not to exceed 1,000 ill-armed men.

The prime difficulty of the operation was the want of water. The Khalifa's position was nearly 125 miles from the river. The intervening country is, in the wet season, dotted with shallow lakes, but by January these are reduced to mud puddles and only occasional pools remain. All the water needed by the men, horses, and mules of the column must therefore be carried. The camels must go thirsty until one of the rare pools might be found. Now, the capacity of a camel for endurance without drinking is famous; but it has its limits. It was thought that, partly by the water carried in skins, partly by the drying-up pools, and partly by the camel's power of endurance, it might be just possible for a force of about 1,200 men to strike out

349

125 miles into the desert, to have three days to do their business in, and to come back to the Nile. The force were supplied with food up till the 9th of February, and their radius of action, except as restricted by water, was nineteen days. This was further extended five days by the arrangement of a convoy which was to set out on the 30th of January to meet them as they returned.

The column – numbering 1,604 officers and men and 1,624 camels and other beasts of burden – started from Kohi at 3 p.m. on the 23rd of January. The country through which their route lay was of barren and miserable aspect. Ten miles from the river all vestiges of animal life disappeared. The land was a vast unprofitable thicket, whose interlacing thorn bushes, unable to yield the slightest nourishment to living creatures, could yet obstruct their path.

Through this the straggling column, headed in the daylight by the red Egyptian flag and at night by a lantern on a pole, wound its weary way, the advanced guard cutting a path with axes and marking the track with strips of calico. Three long marches brought them on the 25th to Gedid.

The march was resumed on the 26th. The trees were now larger; the scrub became a forest; the sandy soil changed to a dark red colour; but otherwise the character of the country was unaltered. The column rested at Abu Rokba. A few starving inhabitants who occupied the huts pointed out the grave of the Khalifa's father and the little straw house in which Abdullah was wont to pray during his visits.

At the end of the next march, which was made by day, the guides discovered a large pool of good water, and all drank deeply in thankful joy. A small but strong *zeriba* was built near this precious pool, and the reserve food and a few sick men were left with a small garrison under an Egyptian officer. The column resumed their journey. On the 29th they reached Aigailla, and here, with feelings of astonishment scarcely less than Robinson Crusoe experienced at seeing the footprint in the sand, they came upon the Khalifa's abandoned camp. A wide space had been cleared of bush, and beyond stood the encampment – a great multitude of yellow spear-grass dwellings, perfectly clean, neatly arranged in streets and squares, and stretching for miles. The aspect of this strange deserted town, rising, silent as a cemetery, out of the awful scrub, chilled everyone who saw it. Its size might

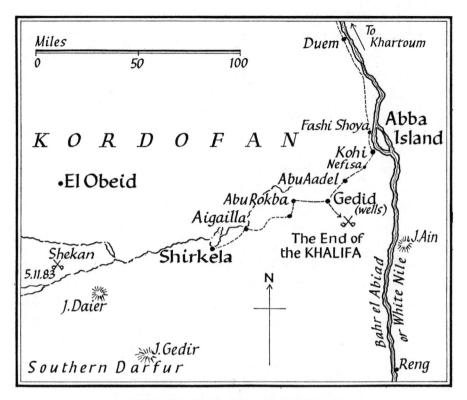

Miles
0   50   100

Duem   To Khartoum

K O R D O F A N

Fashi Shoya   **Abba Island**

Kohi
Nefisa
AbuAadel
AbuRokba   Gedid
(wells)
•El Obeid

Aigailla

The End of
the KHALIFA   J.Ain

Shekan   Shirkela
5.11.83   N

J.Daier   Bahr el Abiad or White Nile

J.Gedir
Southern Darfur   Reng

THE SHIRKELA RECONNAISSANCE

indeed concern their leader. At the very lowest computation it had contained 20,000 people. How many of these were fighting men? Certainly not fewer than 8,000 or 9,000. Yet the expedition had been sent on the assumption that there were scarcely 1,000 warriors with the Khalifa!

Observing every precaution of war, the column crawled forward, and the cavalry and Camel Corps, who covered the advance, soon came in contact with the enemy's scouts. Shots were exchanged and the Arabs retreated. The column halted three miles to the east of this position, and, forming a strong *zeriba*, passed the night in expectation of an attack. Nothing, however, happened, and at dawn Mitford was sent out with some mounted 'friendlies' to reconnoitre. At ten o'clock he returned, and his report was startling. He estimated not fewer than 2,000 Arab riflemen in the front line.

The small force were 125 miles from their base; behind them lay an almost waterless country, and in front was a powerful enemy. An informal council of war was held. The Sirdar had distinctly ordered that there was to be no waiting; the troops were either to attack or retire. Colonel Kitchener decided to retire. The homeward march was not less long and trying than the advance, and neither hopes of distinction nor glamour of excitement cheered the weary soldiers.

Towards the end of the journey the camels, terribly strained by their privation of water, began to die, and it was evident that the force would have no time to spare. On the 5th of February the column reached Kohi, and the Kordofan Field Force, having overcome many difficulties and suffered many hardships, was broken up.

For nearly a year no further operations were undertaken against the Khalifa, and he remained all through the spring and summer of 1899 supreme in Kordofan, reorganising his adherents and plundering the country – a most serious element of unrest. The barren and almost waterless regions into which he had withdrawn presented very difficult obstacles to any military expedition, and although powerful forces were still concentrated at Khartoum, the dry season and the uncertain whereabouts of the enemy prevented action. But towards the end of August trustworthy information was received by the Intelligence Department, that the Khalifa, with all his army, was encamped at Jebel Gedir – that same mountain in Southern Kordofan to which nearly twenty years before he and the Mahdi had retreated after the flight from Abba island. Here among old memories which his presence revived he became at once a centre of fanaticism. Night after night he slept upon the Mahdi's stone; and day after day tales of his dreams were carried by secret emissaries not only throughout the Western Soudan, but into the Ghezira and even to Khartoum. And now, his position being definite and his action highly dangerous, it was decided to move against him.

It was at first universally believed that the Khalifa's intention was to retire to an almost inaccessible distance – to El Obeid or Southern Darfur. But soon strange rumours began to run about the bazaars of Omdurman of buried weapons and whispers of revolt. For a few days a vague feeling of unrest pervaded the native city, and then suddenly on the 12th of November came precise and surprising news. The Khalifa was not retreating to the south or to the west, but advanc-

ing northward with Omdurman, not El Obeid, as his object. He
had resolved to stake all that yet remained to him in one last desperate
attempt to recapture his former capital; and so, upon the 12th of
November, his advanced guard, under the Emir Ahmed Fedil, struck
the Nile opposite Abba island.

The name of Abba island may perhaps carry the reader back to the
very beginning of this story. Here, eighteen years before, the Mahdi
had lived and prayed after his quarrel with the haughty Sheikh; here
Abdullah had joined him; here the flag of the revolt had been set up,
and the first defeat had been inflicted upon the Egyptian troops. It
is a curious instance of the occasional symmetry of history that final
destruction should have befallen the last remains of the Mahdist
movement so close to the scene of its origin!

The news which had reached Khartoum set all wheels in motion.
Kitchener hurried south from Cairo, and arrived in Khartoum on the
18th. A field force of some 2,300 troops – one troop of cavalry, the
2nd Field Battery, the 1st Maxim Battery, the Camel Corps, IXth
Soudanese, XIIIth Soudanese, and one company 2nd Egyptians –
was immediately formed, and the command entrusted to Sir Reginald
Wingate. There were besides some 900 Arab riflemen and a few irregular mounted scouts. On the 20th these troops were concentrated
at Fashi Shoya, whence Colonel Lewis had obliged Ahmed Fedil to
withdraw, and at 3.30 on the afternoon of the 21st the expedition
started in a south-westerly direction upon the track of the enemy.

The troops bivouacked some ten miles south-west of Fashi Shoya,
and then marched in bright moonlight to Nefisa, encountering only
a Dervish patrol of about ten men. At Nefisa was found the evacuated
camp of Ahmed Fedil, containing a quantity of grain which he had
collected from the riverain district, and, what was of more value, a
sick but intelligent Dervish who stated that the Emir had just moved
to Abu Aadel, five miles further on.

Accordingly cavalry, Camel Corps, Maxims, and irregulars set off
at their best pace: and after them at 9.15 hurried the infantry, refreshed
by a drink at the water tanks and a hasty meal. As they advanced the
scrub became denser, and all were in broken and obstructed ground
when, at about ten o'clock, the sound of Maxim firing and the patter
of musketry proclaimed that the cavalry under Colonel Mahon had

come into contact. The firing soon became more rapid, and as the infantry approached it was evident that the mounted troops were briskly engaged. The position which they occupied was a low ridge comparatively bare of scrub; from this it was possible at a distance of 800 yards to overlook the Dervish encampment huddled around the water pools. It was immediately evident that the infantry and the battery were arriving none too soon. The Dervishes, who had hitherto contented themselves with maintaining a ragged and desultory fire from the scrub, now sallied forth into the open and delivered a most bold and determined charge upon the guns. The intervening space was little more than 200 yards, and for a moment the attack looked as if it might succeed. But upon the instant the IXth and XIIIth Soudanese, who had been doubled steadily for upwards of two miles, came into line, filling the gap between Mahon's guns and dismounted Camel Corps and the irregular riflemen; and so the converging fire of the whole force was brought to bear upon the enemy – now completely beaten and demoralised. Three hundred and twenty corpses were counted, and at least an equal number must have been wounded. Ahmed Fedil and one or two of his principal Emirs escaped to the southward and to the Khalifa.

It was learned from the prisoners that the Khalifa, with about 5,000 fighting men, was moving northwards towards the wells of Gedid, of which we have already heard in the Shirkela reconnaissance, and which were some twenty-five miles from the scene of the fight. The troops were already fatigued by their severe exertions. The water pool was so foul that even the thirsty camels refused to drink of it, and moreover scarcely any water remained in the tanks. It was therefore of vital importance to reach the wells of Gedid. But supposing exhausted troops famishing for water reached them only to be confronted by a powerful Dervish force already in possession! Sir Reginald Wingate decided, however, to face the risk, and at a few minutes before midnight the column set out again on its road. The ground was broken; the night was sultry: and as the hours passed by the sufferings of the infantry began to be most acute. Many men fell exhausted to the ground; and it was with a feeling of immense relief that at nine o'clock on the morning of the 24th news was received from the cavalry that the wells had been occupied by them without opposition.

All the water in the tanks was at once distributed, and thus refreshed the infantry struggled on and settled down at midday around a fine pool of comparatively pure water.

At Gedid, as at Nefisa, a single Dervish was captured, and from him it was learned that the Khalifa's army was encamped seven miles to the south-east. It was now clear that his position was strategically most unfavourable. His route to the north lay barred; his retreat to the south lay through waterless and densely wooded districts; and as the seizure of the grain supplies which had resulted from Fedil's foraging excursions rendered his advance or retirement a matter of difficulty, it seemed probable he would stand. Wingate, therefore, decided to attack him at dawn.

Leaving the transport under guard by the water with instructions to follow at four o'clock, the troops moved off at midnight. At three o'clock, when about three miles from the enemy's position, the force was deployed into fighting formation. The irregular riflemen covered the front; behind them the XIIIth and IXth Soudanese; and behind these, again, the Maxims and the artillery were disposed. Cautiously and silently the advance was resumed, and now in the distance the beating of war drums and the long booming note of the Khalifa's horn broke on the stillness, proclaiming that the enemy were not unprepared. At a few minutes before four o'clock another low ridge, also comparatively bare of scrub, was reached and occupied as a position. The cavalry were now withdrawn from the front, a few infantry picquets were thrown out, and the rest of the force lay down in the long grass of the little ridge and waited for daylight.

After about an hour the sky to the eastward began to grow paler with the promise of the morning and in the indistinct light the picquets could be seen creeping gradually in; while behind them along the line of the trees faint white figures, barely distinguishable, began to accumulate. Sir Reginald Wingate, fearing lest a sudden rush should be made upon him, now ordered the whole force to stand up and open fire; and forthwith a loud crackling fusillade began. It was immediately answered. The enemy's fire flickered along a wide half-circle and developed continually with greater vigour opposite the Egyptian left, which was consequently reinforced. As the light improved, large bodies of shouting Dervishes were seen advancing; but the fire was too hot, and their Emirs were unable to lead them far beyond the edge of the wood. So soon as this was perceived Wingate ordered a general advance; and the whole force, moving at a rapid pace down the gentle slope, drove the enemy through the trees into the camp about a mile and a half away. Here, huddled together under their straw shelters, 6,000 women and children were collected, all of whom, with many unwounded combatants, made signals of surrender and appeals for mercy. The 'cease fire' was sounded at half past six. Then, and not till then, was it discovered how severe the loss of the Dervishes had been. In one space not much more than a score of yards square lay all the most famous Emirs of the once far-reaching Dervish domination. The Khalifa Abdullah, pierced by several balls, was stretched dead on his sheepskin; on his right lay Ali-Wad-Helu, on his left Ahmed Fedil. Before them was a line of lifeless bodyguards; behind them a score of less important chiefs; and behind these, again, a litter of killed and wounded horses. Such was the grim spectacle which in the first light of the morning met the eyes of the British officers, to some of whom it meant the conclusion of a perilous task prolonged over many years. And while they looked in astonishment not unmingled with awe, there scrambled unhurt from under a heap of bodies the little Emir Yunes, of Dongola, who added the few links necessary to complete the chain.

At Omdurman Abdullah had remained mounted behind the hill of Surgham, but in this his last fight he had set himself in the forefront of the battle. Almost at the first discharge, his son Osman, the Sheikh-ed-Din, was wounded, and as he was carried away he urged the Khalifa to save himself by flight; but the latter, with a dramatic dignity sometimes denied to more civilised warriors, refused. Dismounting from his horse, and ordering his Emirs to imitate him, he seated himself on his sheepskin and there determined to await the worst of fortune. And so it came to pass that in this last scene in the struggle with Mahdism the stage was cleared of all its striking characters, and Osman Digna alone purchased by flight a brief ignoble liberty, soon to be followed by a long ignoble servitude.

Twenty-nine Emirs, 3,000 fighting men, 6,000 women and children surrendered themselves prisoners. The Egyptian losses were three killed and twenty-three wounded.

The long story now approaches its conclusion. The River War is over. In its varied course, which extended over fourteen years and involved the untimely destruction of perhaps 300,000 lives, many extremes and contrasts have been displayed. But the result is at length achieved, and the flags of England and Egypt wave unchallenged over the valley of the Nile.

THE STORY OF

LONDON TO LADYSMITH

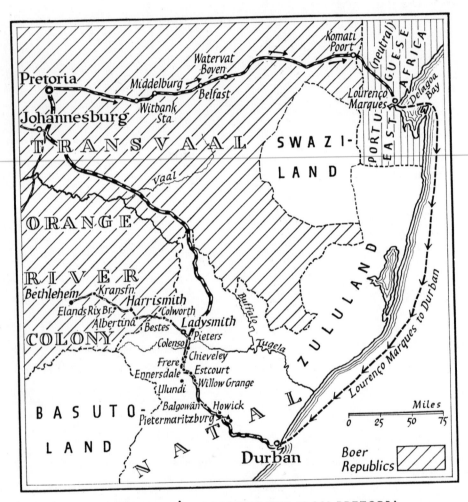

MR CHURCHILL'S ESCAPE ROUTE FROM PRETORIA

R.M.S. 'Dunottar Castle,' at sea: 26th October 1899

The last cry of 'Any more for the shore?' had sounded, the last good-bye had been said, the latest pressman or photographer had scrambled ashore, and all Southampton was cheering wildly along a mile of pier and promontory when at 6 p.m., on 14th October, the Royal Mail steamer *Dunottar Castle* left her moorings and sailed with Sir Redvers Buller for the Cape.

We left London amid rumours of all kinds. Terrible disasters had occurred and had been contradicted; great battles were raging – unconfirmed; and beneath all this froth the tide of war was really flowing, and no man could shut his eyes to grave possibilities. Then the ship sailed, and all was silence – a heaving silence.

Monotony is the characteristic of a modern voyage, and who shall describe it? Yet even monotony is not without its secret joy. Here during a period which is too long while it lasts, too short when it is over, we may placidly reflect on the busy world that lies behind and the tumult that is before us.

Inoculation against enteric fever proceeds daily. The doctors lecture in the saloon. One injection of serum protects; a second secures the subject against attacks. Wonderful statistics are quoted in support of the experiment. Nearly everyone is convinced. The operations take place forthwith, and the next day sees haggard forms crawling about the deck in extreme discomfort and high fever. The day after, however, all have recovered and rise gloriously immune. Others, like myself, remembering that we still stand only on the threshold of pathology, remain unconvinced, resolved to trust to 'health and the laws of health'. But if they will invent a system of inoculation against bullet wounds I will hasten to submit myself.

29th October

News at last! This morning we sighted a sail – a large homeward-bound steamer, spreading her canvas to catch the trades, and with who should say what tidings on board. We crowded the decks, and from every point of view telescopes, field glasses, and cameras were directed towards the stranger. She passed us at scarcely two hundred yards, and as she did so her crew and company, giving three hearty cheers, displayed a long black board, on which was written in white paint: 'Boers defeated; three battles; Penn Symons killed'. There was a little gasp of excitement. A dozen groups were formed, a hum of conversation arose, and meanwhile the vessels separated and in a few moments the homeward bound lay far in our wake.

So Sir Penn Symons is killed! Well, no one would have laid down his life more gladly in such a cause. Twenty years ago the merest chance saved him from the massacre at Isandhlwana, and Death promoted him in an afternoon from subaltern to senior captain. May the State in her necessities find others like him!

Cape Town: 1st November 1899

On the afternoon of 30th October we sighted land, and looking westward I perceived what looked like a dark wave of water breaking the smooth rim of the horizon. A short time developed the wave into the rocks and slopes of Robben Island – a barren spot inhabited by lepers, poisonous serpents, and dogs undergoing quarantine. Then with the darkness we entered Table Bay, and, steaming slowly, reached the anchorage at ten o'clock. Another hour of waiting followed until the tugboat obeyed the signal; but at last she ran alongside, and there stepped on board a Man Who Knew. Others with despatches pushed roughly through the crowd of soldiers, officers, passengers, and war correspondents to the General's cabin. We caught the Man Who Knew – I think he was a passage agent, or something like that – and, setting him half-way up the ladder to the hurricane deck, required him forthwith to tell us of the war.

The crowd of brown uniforms under the electric clusters broke up into loud-voiced groups; some hastened to search for newspapers, some to repeat what they had heard to others; only a few leaned against the bulwarks and looked long and silently towards the land, where the lights of Cape Town, its streets, its quays, and its houses gleamed from the night like diamonds on black velvet.

Next morning Sir Redvers Buller landed in state. The ship was decked out in bunting from end to end. A guard of honour lined the quay; a mounted escort attended the carriage; an enormous crowd gathered outside the docks. At nine o'clock precisely the General stepped on to the gangway. The crew and stokers of the *Dunottar Castle* gave three hearty cheers; the cinematograph buzzed loudly; forty cameras clicked; the guard presented arms, and the harbour batteries thundered the salute. So Sir Redvers Buller came back again to South Africa, the land where his first military reputation was made, where he won his Victoria Cross, the land which – let us pray – he will leave having successfully discharged the heavy task confided to him by the Imperial Government.

Now, what is the situation which confronts the General and the army? In their dealing with the military republics which had become so formidable a power throughout the Cape, the Ministers who were responsible for the security of our South African possessions were compelled to reckon with two volumes of public opinion – British and colonial. The colonial opinion was at its best (from our point of view) about three months ago. The attempts to satisfy the conscientious British public by giving the republics every possible opportunity to accept our terms and the delays in the despatch of troops, have been misinterpreted in South Africa. The situation in the Cape Colony has become much graver. We have always been told of the wonderful loyalty of the Dutch. It is possible that had war broken out three months ago that loyalty would have been demonstrated for all time. War after three months of hesitation – for such it was considered – has proved too severe a test, and it is no exaggeration to say that a considerable part of the Colony trembles on the verge of rebellion. On such a state of public opinion the effect of any important military reverse would be lamentable.

Nor is the military position such as to exclude anxiety. The swift flame of war ran in a few days around the whole circle of the republican frontiers. Far away to the north there was a skirmish at Tuli. On the west Khama's territories are threatened with invasion. Mafeking is surrounded, isolated, and manfully defending itself against continual attack. Vryburg has been treacherously surrendered by its rebel inhabitants to the enemy. Kimberley offers a serene front to a hesitating attack, and even retaliates with armoured trains and other enterprises. The southern frontier is armed, and menaced, and the expectation of collision is strong. But it is on the eastern side that the Boers have concentrated their greatest energies. They have gone Nap on Natal. The configuration of the country favours an invader. The long tongue of plain running up into the mountains could be entered from both sides. The communications of the advanced garrisons would be assailed: their retreat imperilled. The Boers seemed bound to clear northern Natal of the troops. If, on the other hand, they were, or should now be, suddenly driven back on their own country, they have only to retire up the tongue of plain, with their exposed front narrowing every mile between the mountains, and await their pursuers on the almost inexpungable position of Laing's Nek. Appreciating all this, their leaders have wisely resolved to put forth their main strength against the force in Natal, and by crushing it to rouse their sympathisers within the Cape Colony.

A democratic Government cannot go to war unless the country is behind it, and until it has general support must not place itself in a position whence, without fighting, there is no retreat. The difficulty of rallying public opinion in the face of the efforts of Mr Morley, Mr Courtney, Sir William Harcourt, and others has caused a most dangerous delay in the despatch of reinforcements.

For the last three months the Imperial Government has been in the unpleasant position of watching its adversaries grow continually stronger without being able to make adequate counter-preparations.

The Boers had the advantage of drawing first blood, and the destruction of the armoured train near Mafeking was magnified by them, as by the sensational Press in Great Britain, into a serious disaster. But a few days later another armoured train ran out from Kimberley, and its Maxim guns killed five Boers without any loss to the troops. The magnifying process was also applied to this incident with equal though opposite results. Then came the news of the battle of Glencoe. The first accounts, which were very properly controlled – for we are at war with the pen as well as the sword – told only of the bravery of the troops, of the storming of the Boer position, and of the capture of prisoners. That the troops had suffered the heavier loss, that the Boers had retired to further positions in rear of the first, drawing their artillery with them, and that General Yule had retreated by forced marches to Ladysmith after the victory – for tactical victory it undoubtedly was – leaked into Cape Colony very gradually; nor was it until a week later that it was known that the wounded had been left behind, and that the camp with all stores and baggage, except ammunition, had fallen into the enemy's hands. Before that happened the news of Elands Laagte had arrived, and this brilliant action dazzled all eyes, so that the sequel to Glencoe was unnoticed, or at any rate produced little effect on public opinion.

The Natal Field Force is now concentrated at Ladysmith, and confronts in daily opposition the bulk of the Boer Army. Though the numbers of the enemy are superior and their courage claims the respect of their professional antagonists, it is difficult to believe that any serious reverse can take place in that quarter, and meanwhile many thousand soldiers are on the seas. But the fact is now abundantly plain to those who are acquainted with the local conditions and with the Boer character, that a fierce, certainly bloody, possibly prolonged struggle lies before the army of South Africa.

East London: 5th November 1899

Last night I started by rail for East London, whence a small ship carries the weekly English mail to Natal, and so by this circuitous route I hope to reach Ladysmith on Sunday morning.

Railway travelling in South Africa is more expensive but just as comfortable as in India. Lying-down accommodation is provided for all, and meals can be obtained at convenient stopping places. The train, which is built on the corridor system, runs smoothly over the rails – so smoothly, indeed, that I found no difficulty in writing. The sun is warm, and the air keen and delicious. But the scenery would depress the most buoyant spirits. We climbed up the mountains during the night, and with the daylight the train was in the middle of the Great

Karroo. Wherefore was this miserable land of stone and scrub created? Huge mounds of crumbling rock, fashioned by the rains into the most curious and unexpected shapes, rise from the gloomy desert of the plain. Yet, though the Karroo looks a hopeless wilderness, flocks of sheep at distant intervals manage to subsist; and now and again the traveller sees some far-off farm.

We look about eagerly for signs of war. Little is as yet to be seen, but all along the southern frontier of the Free State the expectation of early collision grows.

Beyond Matjesfontein every bridge, and even every culvert, is watched by a Kaffir with a flag, so that the train runs no risk of coming on unexpected demolitions. On the road to De Aar we passed the second half of the Brigade Division of Artillery, the gunners hurrying to the front in three long trains, each taking half a battery complete with guns, horses, and men.

At Beaufort West grave news awaited the mail, and we learned of the capitulation of twelve hundred soldiers near Ladysmith. It is generally believed that this will precipitate a rising of the Dutch throughout this part of the colony and an invasion by the commandos now gathered along the Orange River. The Dutch farmers talk loudly and confidently of 'our victories', meaning those of the Boers, and the racial feeling runs high. But the British colonists have an implicit faith – marvellous when the past is remembered – in the resolve of the Imperial Government never to abandon them again.

At De Aar the stage of our journey which may be said to have been uncertain began. Armoured trains patrol the line; small parties of armed police guard the bridges; infantry and artillery detachments occupy the towns. De Aar, Colesberg, and Stormberg are garrisoned as strongly as the present limited means allow, but the reports of Boer movements seem to indicate that a hostile advance is imminent. The Colesberg bridge across the Orange River has been seized by the enemy, the line between Bethulie and Colesberg has just been cut, and each train from De Aar to Stormberg is expected to be the last to pass unassailed. We, however, slept peacefully through the night, and, passing Colesberg safely, arrived at Stormberg Junction.

Here we found the confirmation of many rumours. The news of a Boer advance on Burghersdorp, twenty-five miles away, is, it seems,

well founded, and when our train arrived the evacuation of Stormberg
by its garrison, a half-battalion of the Berkshire Regiment, 350 men
of the Naval Brigade, a company of mounted infantry, and a few guns,
was busily proceeding.

Stormberg is itself an important railway junction. For more than a
week the troops have been working night and day to put it in a state of
defence. Little redoubts have been built on the kopjes, entrenchments
have been dug, and the few houses near the station are already strongly
fortified. I was shown one of these by the young officer in charge. The
approaches were cleared of everything except wire fences and entanglements; the massive walls were loopholed, the windows barricaded with
sandbags, and the rooms inside broken one into the other for convenience in moving about.

Then suddenly had come the message to evacuate and retreat. The
train with the naval detachment and its guns steamed off, and we gave
it a feeble cheer. Another train awaited the Berkshires. The mounted
infantry were already on the march. 'Mayn't we even blow up this lot?'
said a soldier, pointing to the house he had helped to fortify. But there
was no such order, only this one which seemed to pervade the air: 'The
enemy are coming. Retreat – retreat – retreat!' The stationmaster –
one of the best types of Englishmen to be found on a long journey –
was calm and cheerful.

'No more traffic north of this,' he said. 'Yours was the last train
through from De Aar. I shall send away all my men by the special
tonight. And that's the end as far as Stormberg goes.'

'And you?'

'Oh, I shall stay. I have lived here for twelve years, and am well
known. Perhaps I may be able to protect the company's property.'

So we left Stormberg in much anger and some humiliation, and
jolted away towards the open sea, where British supremacy is not yet
contested by the Boer.

Estcourt: 6th November 1899

The reader may remember that we started post haste from Cape Town, and, having the good fortune to pass along the southern frontier from De Aar to Stormberg by the last train before the interruption of traffic, had every hope of reaching Ladysmith while its investment was incomplete. I had looked forward to writing an account of our voyage from East London to Durban while on board the vessel; but the weather was so tempestuous, and the little steamer of scarcely 100 tons burthen so buffeted by the waves, that I lay prostrate in all the anguish of seasickness, and had no thought for anything else. Moreover, we were delayed some twenty hours by contrary winds; nor was it until we had passed St John's that the gale, as if repenting, veered suddenly to the south-west and added as much to our speed as it had formerly delayed us.

The little steamer reached Durban safely at midnight on 4th November, and we passed an impatient six hours waiting for daylight and news. Both came in their turn. The sun rose, and we learned that Ladysmith was cut off. Still, 'As far as you can as quickly as you can' must be the motto of the war correspondent, and seven o'clock found us speeding inland in the extra coach of a special train carrying the mails.

Pietermaritzburg is sixty miles from Durban, but as the railway zigzags up and down hill and contorts itself into curves that would horrify the domestic engineer, the journey occupies four hours. It is a sleepy, dead-alive place. Even the fact that Colonel Knowle, the military engineer, was busily putting it into a state of defence, digging up its hills, piercing its walls, and encircling it with wire obstructions did not break its apathy. But the composure of the civil population is a useful factor in war, and I wish it were within the power of my poor pen to bring home to the people of England how excellently the colonists of Natal have deserved of the State.

The colonists have had many dealings with the Boers. They knew their strength, they feared their animosity. But they have never for one moment lost sight of their obligations as a British colony. Their loyalty has been splendid. From the very beginning they warned the Imperial

Government that their territories would be invaded. Throughout the course of the long negotiations they knew that if war should come, on them would fall the first fury of the storm. Now at last there is war. It means a good deal to all of us, but more than to any it comes home to the Natalian. He is invaded; his cattle have been seized by the Boer; his towns are shelled or captured; the most powerful force on which he relies for protection is isolated in Ladysmith; his capital is being loop-holed and entrenched; Newcastle has been abandoned, Colenso has fallen, Estcourt is threatened; the possibility that the whole province will be overrun stares him in the face. From the beginning he asked for protection. From the beginning he was promised complete protection; but scarcely a word of complaint is heard. The townsfolk are calm and orderly, the Press dignified and sober. The men capable of bearing arms have responded nobly. Boys of sixteen march with men of fifty to war – to no light easy war. All the volunteers are in the field bearing their full share of the fighting like men.

Estcourt: 9th November 1899

Sir George White's headquarters are scarcely forty miles away, but between them and Estcourt stretches the hostile army. Let us review the situation. On Wednesday last, on 1st November, the Boer lines of investment drew round Ladysmith. On Thursday the last train passed down the railway under the fire of artillery. That night the line was cut about four miles north of Colenso. Telegraphic communication also ceased. On Friday Colenso was itself attacked. A heavy gun came into action from the hills which dominate the town, and the slender garrison of infantry volunteers and naval brigade evacuated in a hurry, and, covered to some extent by the armoured train, fell back on Est-court.

Estcourt is a South African town – that is to say, it is a collection of about three hundred detached stone or corrugated iron houses, nearly all one-storied, arranged along two broad streets – for space is plentiful – or straggling away towards the country. The little place lies in a cup of the hills, which rise in green undulations on all sides. For this reason it will be a very difficult place to defend if the invaders should come upon it. It is, besides, of mean and insignificant aspect; but, like all these towns in Natal, it is the centre of a large agricultural district. Indeed, it was a surprise to find on entering the shops how great a variety and quantity of goods these unpretentious shanties contained.

Estcourt now calls itself 'The Front'. Colonel Wolfe Murray, the officer who commands the lines of communication of the Natal Field Force, hastened up as soon as the news of the attack on Colenso was received to make preparation to check the enemy's advance.

The force at his disposal is not, however, large – two British battalions – the Dublin Fusiliers, who were hurried out of Ladysmith to strengthen the communications when it became evident that a blockade impended, and the Border Regiment from Malta, a squadron of the Imperial Light Horse, 300 Natal volunteers with twenty-five cyclists, and a volunteer battery of 9-pounder guns – perhaps 2,000 men in all. With so few it would be quite impossible to hold the long line of hills necessary for the protection of the town, but a position has been selected and fortified, where the troops can maintain themselves – at any rate for several days. But the confidence of the military authorities in the strength of Estcourt may be gauged by the frantic efforts they are making to strengthen Pietermaritzburg, seventy-six miles, and even Durban, 130 miles further back, by earthworks and naval guns.

It seems, however, certain that a considerable force will be moved here soon to restore the situation and to relieve Ladysmith. Meanwhile we wait, not without anxiety or impatience. The Imperial Horse, a few mounted infantry, the volunteer cyclists, and the armoured train, patrol daily towards Colenso and the north, always expecting to see the approaching Boer commandos. Yesterday I travelled with the armoured train. This armoured train is a very puny specimen, having neither gun nor Maxims, with no roof to its trucks and no shutters to its loopholes, and being in every way inferior to the powerful machines I saw working along the southern frontier. Nevertheless it is a useful means of reconnaissance, nor is a journey in it devoid of interest. We started at one o'clock. A company of the Dublin Fusiliers formed the garrison. Half were in the car in front of the engine, half in that behind. Three empty trucks, with a platelaying gang and spare rails to mend the line, followed. The train maintained a good speed; and, though it stopped repeatedly to question Kaffirs or country folk, and to communicate with the cyclists and other patrols who were scouring the country on the flanks, reached Chieveley, five miles from Colenso, by about three o'clock; and from here the Ladysmith balloon, a brown speck floating above and beyond the distant hills, was plainly visible.

Beyond Chieveley it was necessary to observe more caution. The speed was reduced – the engine walked warily. The railway officials scanned the track, and often before a culvert or bridge was traversed we disembarked and examined it from the ground. At other times long halts were made while the officers swept the horizon and the distant hills with field glasses and telescopes. But the country was clear and the line undamaged, and we continued our slow advance. Presently Colenso came into view – a hundred tin-pot houses under the high hills to the northward. We inspected it deliberately. On a mound beyond the village rose the outline of the sandbag fort constructed by the Naval Brigade. The flagstaff, without the flag, still stood up boldly. But, so far as we could tell, the whole place was deserted.

There followed a discussion. Perhaps the Boers were lying in wait for the armoured train; perhaps they had trained a gun on some telegraph post, and would fire the moment the engine passed it; or perhaps, again, they were even now breaking the line behind us. Some Kaffirs approached respectfully, saluting. A Natal volunteer – one of the cyclists – came forward to interrogate. He questioned the natives, and reported their answers. The Kaffirs said that the Dutchmen were assuredly in the neighbourhood. They had been seen only that morning. 'How many?' The reply was vague – twelve, or seventeen, or one thousand; also they had a gun – or five guns – mounted in the old fort, or on the platform of the station, or on the hill behind the town. At daylight they had shelled Colenso. 'But why,' we asked, 'should they shell Colenso?' Evidently to make sure of the range of some telegraph post. 'It only takes one shell to do the trick with the engine,' said the captain who commanded. 'Got to hit us first, though,' he added. 'Well, let's get a little bit nearer.'

The electric bell rang three times, and we crept forward – halted – looked around, forward again – halt again – another look round; and so, yard by yard, we approached Colenso. Half a mile away we stopped finally. The officer, taking a sergeant with him, went on towards the village on foot. I followed. We soon reached the trenches that had been made by the British troops before they evacuated the place. 'Awful rot giving this place up,' said the officer. 'These lines took us a week to dig.' From here Colenso lay exposed about 200 yards away – a silent, desolate village. The streets were littered with the belongings of the inhabitants. Two or three houses had been burned. A dead horse lay in the road, his four legs sticking stiffly up in the air, his belly swollen. The whole place had evidently been ransacked and plundered by the Boers and the Kaffirs. A few natives loitered near the far end of the street, and one, alarmed at the aspect of the train, waved a white rag on a stick steadily to and fro. But no Dutchmen were to be seen. We made our way back to the railway line and struck it at the spot where it was cut. Two lengths of rails had been lifted up, and, with the sleepers attached to them, flung over the embankment. The broken telegraph wires trailed untidily on the ground. Several of the posts were twisted. But the bridge across the Tugela was uninjured, and the damage to the lines was such as could be easily repaired. The Boers realise the advantage of the railway. At this moment, with their trains all labelled 'To Durban', they are drawing supplies along it from Pretoria to within six miles of Ladysmith. They had resolved to use it in their further advance, and their confidence in the ultimate issue is shown by the care with which they avoid seriously damaging the permanent way. We had learned all that there was to learn – where the line was broken, that the village was deserted, that the bridge was safe, and we made haste to rejoin the train. Then the engine was reversed, and we withdrew out of range of the hills beyond Colenso at full speed.

Estcourt: 10th November 1899

When I awoke yesterday morning there was a strange tremor in the air, a silent thudding, a vibration which scarcely seemed to constitute what is called sound, yet which left an intense impression on the ear. I went outside the tent to listen. Morning had just broken, and the air was still and clear. What little wind there was came from the north-wards, from the direction of Ladysmith, and I knew that it carried to Estcourt the sound of distant cannon.

Later in the day we rode out to find some nearer listening point. The whole force was making a reconnaissance towards Colenso. Galloping over the beautiful grassy hills to the north of the town, I soon reached a spot whence the column could be seen. First of all came a cyclist – a Natal volunteer pedalling leisurely along with his rifle slung across his back – then two more, then about twenty. Next, after an interval of a quarter of a mile, rode the cavalry – the squadron of the Imperial Light Horse, sixty Natal Carabineers, a company of mounted infantry, and about forty of the Natal mounted police. That is the total cavalry force in Natal, all the rest is bottled up in Ladysmith, and scarcely 300 horse-men are available for the defence of the colony against a hostile army entirely composed of mounted men. After the horse the foot: the Dublin Fusiliers, a fine regiment which distinguished itself at Glencoe, and the Border Regiment – which had yet their spurs to win. The volunteer battery was sandwiched between the two British battalions, and the rear of the column was brought up by the Durban volunteers. The force, when it had thus passed in review, looked painfully small, and this impression was aggravated by the knowledge of all that depended on it.

A high, flat-topped hill to the north-west promised a wide field of vision and a nearer listening point for the Ladysmith cannonade. With my two companions I rode towards it, and after an hour's climb reached the summit. The land lay spread before us like a map. Estcourt, indeed, was hidden by its engulfing hills, but Colenso was plainly visible. Far away to the east the dark serrated range of the Drakensberg rose in a mighty wall. But it was not on these features that we turned our glasses. To the right of Colenso the hills were lower and more broken, and the country behind, though misty and indistinct, was exposed to view. First there was a region of low rocky hills rising in strange confusion and falling away on the further side to a hollow. Above this extensive depression clouds of smoke from grass and other fires hung and drifted, like steam over a cauldron. At the bottom – invisible in spite of our great elevation – stood the town and camp of Ladysmith.

The owner of the nearest farm joined us while we were thus engaged – a tall, red-bearded man of grave and intelligent mien. 'They've had heavy fighting this morning,' he said. 'Not since Monday week' (the Black Monday of the war) 'has there been such firing. But they are nearly finished now for the day.' Absorbed by the distant drama, all the more thrilling since its meaning was doubtful and mysterious, we had shown ourselves against the skyline, and our conversation was now suddenly interrupted. Over the crest of the hill to the rear, two horsemen trotted swiftly into view. A hundred yards away to the left three or four more were dismounting among the rocks. Three other figures appeared on the other side. We were surrounded – but by the Natal Carabineers. 'Got you, I think,' said the sergeant, who now arrived. 'Will you kindly tell us all about who you are?' We produced our passes and satisfied the patrol that we were not eligible for capture. The sergeant looked disappointed but was appeased by being photographed 'for the London papers', and we hastened to accept the farmer's invitation to lunch. 'Only plain fare,' said he, 'but perhaps you are used to roughing it.'

The farm stood in a sheltered angle of the hill at no great distance from its summit. It was a good-sized house, with stone walls and a corrugated iron roof. A few sheds and outhouses surrounded it, four or five blue gums afforded a little shade from the sun and a little relief to the grassy smoothness of the landscape. Two women met us at the door, one the wife, the other, I think, the sister of our host. Over a most excellent luncheon we discussed many things with these kind people, and spoke of how the nation was this time resolved to make an end of the long quarrel with the Boers. 'We have always known,' said the farmer, 'that it must end in war, and I cannot say I am sorry it has come at last. But it falls heavily on us. I am the only man for twenty miles who has not left his farm. Of course we are defenceless here. Any day the Dutchmen may come. They wouldn't kill us, but they would burn or plunder everything, and it's all I've got in the world. Fifteen years have I worked at this place, and I said to myself we may as well stay and face it out, whatever happens.'

We started on our long ride home, for the afternoon was wearing away and picket lines are dangerous at dusk. The military situation is without doubt at this moment most grave and critical. We have been at war three weeks. The army that was to have defended Natal, and was indeed expected to repulse the invaders with terrible loss, is blockaded and bombarded in its fortified camp. At nearly every point along the circle of the frontiers the Boers have advanced and the British retreated. Wherever we have stood we have been surrounded. The Boers hold more than 1,200 unwounded British prisoners, a number that bears a disgraceful proportion to the casualty lists, and a very unsatisfactory relation to the number of Dutchmen that we have taken. All this is mainly the result of being unready. That we are unready is largely due to those in England who have endeavoured by every means in their power to hamper and obstruct the Government, who have scoffed at the possibility of the Boers becoming the aggressors, and who have represented every precaution for the defence of the colonies as a deliberate provocation to the Transvaal State. It is also due to an extraordinary under-estimation of the strength of the Boers. These military republics have been for ten years cherishing vast ambitions, and for five years, enriched by the gold mines, they have been arming and preparing for the struggle. It is a very remarkable fact that these ignorant peasant communities have had the wisdom and the enterprise to possess themselves of good advisers, and to utilise the best expert opinion in all matters of armament and war.

Their artillery is inferior in numbers, but in nothing else, to ours. Yesterday I visited Colenso in the armoured train. In one of the deserted British-built redoubts I found two boxes of shrapnel shells and charges. The Boers had not troubled to touch them. Their guns were of a later pattern, and fired powder and shell made up together like a great rifle cartridge. The combination, made for the first time in the history of war, of heavy artillery and swarms of mounted infantry is formidable and effective. The enduring courage and confident spirit of the enemy must also excite surprise. In short, we have grossly underrated their fighting powers.

To return to Estcourt. The garrison is utterly insufficient to resist the Boers; the position wholly indefensible. If the enemy attack, the troops must fall back on Pietermaritzburg, if for no other reason because they are the only force available for the defence of the strong lines now being formed around the chief town. There are so few cavalry outside Ladysmith that the Boers could raid in all directions. As I write the situation is saved only by what seems to me the over-confidence of the enemy. They are concentrating all their efforts on Ladysmith, and evidently hope to compel its surrender. It may, however, be said with absolute certainty that the place can hold out for a month at the least. The reinforcements are on the seas. The railway works regularly with the coast. Even now sidings are being constructed and troop trains prepared. It is with all this that they should interfere, and they are perfectly competent to do so. They could compel us to retreat on Pietermaritzburg, they could tear up the railway, they could blow up the bridges; and by all these means they could delay the arrival of a relieving army, and so have a better chance of making Ladysmith a second Saratoga. Since Saturday last that has been our fear. Nearly a week has passed and they have done nothing. Why? To some extent I think they have been influenced by the fear of the Tugela River rising behind their raiding parties, and cutting their line of retreat; to some extent by the serene and confident way in which General Wolfe Murray has handled his force and maintained by frequent reconnaissance the appearance of actual strength; but when all has been said on these grounds, the fact will remain that the enemy have not destroyed the railway because they do not fear the reinforcements that are coming, because they do not believe that many will come, and because they are sure that, however many may come, they will defeat them. To this end they preserve the line, and watch the bridges as carefully as we do. It is by the railway that they are to be supplied in their march through Natal to the sea. After what they have accomplished it would be foolish to laugh at any of their ambitions.

Pretoria: 20th November 1899

A week ago I described to you a reconnoitring expedition in the Est-court armoured train, and I pointed out the many defects in the construction and the great dangers in the employment of that forlorn military machine. So patent were these to all who concerned themselves in the matter that the train was nicknamed in the camp 'Wilson's death trap'.

On Tuesday the 14th, the mounted infantry patrols reported that the Boers in small parties were approaching Estcourt from the directions of Weenen and Colenso, and Colonel Long made a reconnaissance in force to ascertain what strength lay behind the advanced scouts. The reconnaissance revealed little, but it was generally believed that a considerable portion of the army investing Ladysmith was moving, or was about to move, southwards to attack Estcourt, and endeavour to strike Pietermaritzburg. The movement that we had awaited for ten days impended. Accordingly certain military preparations were made to guard against all contingencies, and at daylight on Wednesday morning another spray of patrols was flung out towards the north and northwest, and the Estcourt armoured train was ordered to reconnoitre towards Chieveley. The train was composed as follows: an ordinary truck, in which was a 7-pounder muzzle-loading gun, served by four sailors from the *Tartar*; an armoured car fitted with loopholes and held by three sections of a company of the Dublin Fusiliers; the engine and tender; two more armoured cars containing the fourth section of the Fusilier company, one company of the Durban Light Infantry (volunteers), and a small civilian breakdown gang; lastly, another ordinary truck with the tools and materials for repairing the road; in all five wagons, the locomotive, one small gun, and 120 men. Captain Haldane, D.S.O., whom I had formerly known, commanded.

We started at half past five and reached Frere Station in about an hour. Here a small patrol of the Natal police reported that there were no enemy within the next few miles, and that all seemed quiet. Captain Haldane decided to push on cautiously as far as Chieveley, near which place an extensive view of the country could be obtained. Not a sign of the Boers could be seen. The rolling grassy country looked as peaceful and deserted as on former occasions.

All was clear as far as Chieveley, but as the train reached the station I saw about a hundred Boer horsemen cantering southwards about a mile from the railway. Beyond Chieveley a long hill was lined with a row of black spots, showing that our further advance would be disputed. The telegraphist who accompanied the train wired back to Estcourt reporting our safe arrival, and that parties of Boers were to be seen at no great distance, and Colonel Long replied by ordering the train to return to Frere and remain there in observation during the day, watching its safe retreat at nightfall. We proceeded to obey, and were about a mile and three-quarters from Frere when on rounding a corner we saw that a hill which commanded the line at a distance of 600 yards was occupied by the enemy. So after all there would be a fight, for we could not pass this point without coming under fire. The four sailors loaded their gun – an antiquated toy – the soldiers charged their magazines, and the train, which was now in the reverse of the order in which it had started, moved slowly towards the hill.

The moment approached: but no one was much concerned, for the cars were proof against rifle fire, and this ridge could at the worst be occupied only by some daring patrol of perhaps a score of men. 'Besides,' we said to ourselves, 'they little think we have a gun on board. That will be a nice surprise.'

The Boers held their fire until the train reached that part of the track nearest to their position. Standing on a box in the rear armoured truck I had an excellent view through my glasses. The long brown rattling serpent with the rifles bristling from its spotted sides crawled closer to the rocky hillock on which the scattered black figures of the enemy showed clearly. Suddenly three wheeled things appeared on the crest, and within a second a bright flash of light – like a heliograph, but much yellower – opened and shut ten or twelve times. Then two much larger flashes; no smoke nor yet any sound, and a bustle and stir among the little figures. So much for the hill. Immediately over the rear truck of the train a huge white ball of smoke sprang into being and tore out into a cone like a comet. Then came the explosions of the near guns and the nearer shell. The iron sides of the truck tanged with a patter of bullets. There was a crash from the front of the train and half a dozen sharp reports. The Boers had opened fire on us at 600 yards with two large field guns, a Maxim firing small shells in a stream, and from riflemen lying on the ridge. I got down from my box into the cover of the armoured sides of the car without forming any clear thought. Equally involuntarily, it seems that the driver put on full steam, as the enemy had intended. The train leapt forward, ran the gauntlet of the guns, which now filled the air with explosions, swung round the curve of the hill, ran down a steep gradient, and dashed into a huge stone which awaited it on the line at a convenient spot.

To those who were in the rear truck there was only a tremendous shock, a tremendous crash, and a sudden full stop. What happened to the trucks in front of the engine is more interesting. The first, which contained the materials and tools of the breakdown gang and the guard who was watching the line, was flung into the air and fell bottom upwards on the embankment. (I do not know what befell the guard, but it seems probable that he was killed.) The next, an armoured car crowded with the Durban Light Infantry, was carried on twenty yards and thrown over on its side, scattering its occupants in a shower on the ground. The third wedged itself across the track, half on and half off the rails. The rest of the train kept to the metals.

We were not long left in the comparative peace and safety of a railway accident. The Boer guns, swiftly changing their position, re-opened from a distance of 1,300 yards before anyone had got out of the stage of exclamations. The tapping rifle fire spread along the hillside, until it encircled the wreckage on three sides, and a third field gun came into action from some high ground on the opposite side of the line.

To all of this our own poor little gun endeavoured to reply, and the sailors, though exposed in an open truck, succeeded in letting off three rounds before the barrel was struck by a shell, and the trunnions, being smashed, fell altogether out of the carriage.

The armoured truck gave some protection from the bullets, but since any direct shell must pierce it like paper and kill everyone, it seemed almost safer outside, and, wishing to see the extent and nature of the damage, I clambered over the iron shield, and, dropping to the ground, ran along the line to the front of the train. As I passed the engine another shrapnel shell burst immediately, as it seemed, overhead, hurling its contents with a rasping rush through the air. The driver at once sprang out of the cab and ran to the shelter of the overturned trucks. His face was cut open by a splinter, and he complained in bitter futile indignation. He was a civilian. What did they think he was paid for? To be killed by bombshells? Not he. He would not stay another minute. It looked as if his excitement and misery – he was dazed by the blow on his head – would prevent him from working the engine further, and as only he understood the machinery all chances of escape seemed to be cut off. Yet when I told this man that if he continued to stay at his post he would be mentioned for distinguished gallantry in action, he pulled himself together, wiped the blood off his face, climbed back into the cab of his engine, and thereafter during the one-sided combat did his duty bravely and faithfully.

I reached the overturned portion of the train uninjured. The volunteers who, though severely shaken, were mostly unhurt, were lying down under such cover as the damaged cars and the gutters of the railway line afforded. Having seen this much, I ran along the train to the rear armoured truck and told Captain Haldane that in my opinion the line might be cleared. We then agreed that he with musketry should keep the enemy's artillery from destroying us, and that I should try to throw the wreckage off the line, so that the engine and the two cars which still remained on the rails might escape.

The task of clearing the line would not, perhaps, in ordinary circumstances have been a very difficult one. But the breakdown gang and their tools were scattered to the winds, and several had fled along the track or across the fields. Moreover, the enemy's artillery fire was pitiless, continuous, and distracting.

The first thing to be done was to detach the truck half off the rails from the one completely so. To do this the engine had to be moved to slacken the strain on the twisted couplings. When these had been released, the next step was to drag the partly derailed truck backwards along the line until it was clear of the other wreckage, and then to throw it bodily off the rails. This may seem very simple, but the dead weight of the iron truck half on the sleepers was enormous, and the engine wheels skidded vainly several times before any hauling power was obtained. At last the truck was drawn sufficiently far back, and I called for volunteers to overturn it from the side while the engine pushed it from the end. It was very evident that these men would be exposed to considerable danger. Twenty were called for, and there was an immediate response. But only nine, including the major of volunteers and four or five of the Dublin Fusiliers, actually stepped out into the open. The attempt was nevertheless successful. The truck heeled further over under their pushing, and, the engine giving a shove at the right moment, it fell off the line and the track was clear. Safety and success appeared in sight together, but disappointment overtook them.

The engine was about six inches wider than the tender, and the corner of its footplate would not pass the corner of the newly overturned truck. It did not seem safe to push very hard, lest the engine should itself be derailed. So time after time the engine moved back a yard or two and shoved forward at the obstruction, and each time moved it a little. But soon it was evident that complications had set in. The newly derailed truck became jammed with that originally off the line, and the more the engine pushed the greater became the block. Volunteers were again called on to assist, but though seven men, two of whom, I think, were wounded, did their best, the attempt was a failure.

Perseverance, however, is a virtue. If the trucks only jammed the tighter for the forward pushing they might be loosened by pulling backwards. Now, however, a new difficulty arose. The coupling chains of the engine would not reach by five or six inches those of the overturned truck. Search was made for a spare link. By a solitary gleam of good luck one was found. The engine hauled at the wreckage, and before the chains parted pulled it about a yard backwards. Now, certainly, the line was clear at last. But again the corner of the footplate jammed with the corner of the truck, and again we came to a jarring halt.

Nothing remained but to continue pounding at the obstructing corner in the hopes that the iron work would gradually be twisted and torn, and thus give free passage. As we pounded so did the enemy. I adjured the driver to be patient and to push gently, for it did not seem right to imperil the slender chance of escape by running the risk of throwing the engine off the line. But after a dozen pushes had been given with apparently little result a shell struck the front of the engine, setting fire to the woodwork, and the driver thereupon turned on more steam, and with considerable momentum we struck the obstacle once more. There was a grinding crash; the engine staggered, checked, shore forward again, until with a clanging, tearing sound it broke past the point of interception, and nothing but the smooth line lay between us and home.

Brilliant success now seemed won, for I thought that the rear and gun trucks were following the locomotive, and that all might squeeze into them, and so make an honourable escape. But looking backward, I saw that the couplings had parted or had been severed by a shell, and that the trucks still lay on the wrong side of the obstruction, separated by it from the engine. No one dared to risk imprisoning the engine again by making it go back for the trucks, so an attempt was made to drag the trucks up to the engine. Owing chiefly to the fire of the enemy this failed completely, and Captain Haldane determined to be content with saving the locomotive. He accordingly permitted the driver to retire along the line slowly, so that the infantry might get as much shelter from the ironwork of the engine as possible, and the further idea was to get into some houses near the station, about 800 yards away, and there hold out while the engine went for assistance.

As many wounded as possible were piled on to the engine, standing in the cab, lying on the tender, or clinging to the cowcatcher. And all this time the shells fell into the wet earth throwing up white clouds, burst with terrifying detonations overhead, or actually struck the engine and the iron wreckage. Besides the three field guns, which proved to be 15-pounders, the shell-firing Maxim continued its work, and its little shells, discharged with an ugly thud, thud, thud, exploded with startling bangs on all sides. One I remember struck the footplate of the engine scarcely a yard from my face, lit up into a bright yellow flash, and left me wondering why I was still alive. Another hit the coals in the tender, hurling a black shower into the air. A third – this also I saw – struck the arm of a private in the Dublin Fusiliers. The whole arm was smashed to a horrid pulp – bones, muscle, blood, and uniform all mixed together. At the bottom hung the hand, unhurt, but swelled instantly to three times its ordinary size. The engine was soon crowded and began to steam homewards – a mournful, sorely battered loco-motive – with the woodwork of the firebox in flames and the water spouting from its pierced tanks. The infantrymen straggled along beside it at the double.

Seeing the engine escaping the Boers increased their fire, and the troops, hitherto somewhat protected by the iron trucks, began to suffer. The major of volunteers fell, shot through the thigh. Here and there men dropped on the ground, several screamed – this is very rare in war – and cried for help. About a quarter of the force was very soon killed or wounded. The shells which pursued the retreating soldiers scattered them all along the track. Order and control vanished. The engine, increasing its pace, drew out from the thin crowd of fugitives and was soon in safety. The infantry continued to run down the line in the direction of the houses, and, in spite of their disorder, I honestly consider that they were capable of making a further resistance when some shelter should be reached. But at this moment one of those miserable incidents – much too frequent in this war – occurred.

A private soldier who was wounded, in direct disobedience of the positive orders that no surrender was to be made, took it on himself to wave a pocket-handkerchief. The Boers immediately ceased firing, and with equal daring and humanity a dozen horsemen galloped from the hills into the scattered fugitives, scarcely any of whom had seen the white flag, and several of whom were still firing, and called loudly on them to surrender. Most of the soldiers, uncertain what to do, then halted, gave up their arms, and became prisoners of war. Those further away from the horsemen continued to run and were shot or hunted down in twos and threes, and some made good their escape.

For my part I found myself on the engine when the obstruction was at last passed and remained there jammed in the cab next to the man with the shattered arm. In this way I travelled some 500 yards, and passed through the fugitives, noticing particularly a young officer, Lieutenant Frankland, who with a happy, confident smile on his face was endeavouring to rally his men. When I approached the houses where we had resolved to make a stand, I jumped on to the line, in order to collect the men as they arrived, and hence the address from which this letter is written, for scarcely had the locomotive left me than I found myself alone in a shallow cutting and none of our soldiers, who had all surrendered on the way, to be seen. Then suddenly there appeared on the line at the end of the cutting two men not in uniform. 'Platelayers,' I said to myself, and then, with a surge of realisation, 'Boers.' My mind retains a momentary impression of these tall figures, full of animated movement, clad in dark flapping clothes, with slouch, storm-driven hats poising on their rifles hardly a hundred yards away. I turned and ran between the rails of the track, and the only thought I achieved was this, 'Boer marksmanship.' Two bullets passed, both within a foot, one on either side. I flung myself against the banks of the cutting. But they gave no cover. Another glance at the figures; one was now kneeling to aim. Again I darted forward. Movement seemed the only chance. Again two soft kisses sucked in the air, but nothing struck me. This could not endure. I must get out of the cutting – that damnable corridor. I scrambled up the bank. The earth sprang up beside me, and something touched my hand, but outside the cutting was a tiny depression. I crouched in this, struggling to get my wind. On the other side of the railway a horseman galloped up, shouting to me and waving his hand. He was scarcely forty yards off. With a rifle I could have killed him easily. I knew nothing of white flags, and the bullets had made me savage. I reached down for my Mauser pistol. 'This one at least,' I said, and indeed it was a certainty; but alas! I had left the weapon in the cab of the engine in order to be free to work at the wreckage. What then? There was a wire fence between me and the horseman. Should I continue to fly? The idea of another shot at such a short range decided me. Death stood before me, grim sullen Death without his light-hearted companion, Chance. So I held up my hand, and like Mr Jorrocks's foxes, cried 'Capivy'. Then I was herded with the other prisoners in a miserable group, and about the same time I noticed that my hand was bleeding, and it began to pour with rain.

Two days before I had written to an officer in high command at home, whose friendship I have the honour to enjoy: 'There has been a great deal too much surrendering in this war, and I hope people who do so will not be encouraged.' Fate had intervened, yet though her tone was full of irony she seemed to say, as I think Ruskin once said, 'It matters very little whether your judgements of people are true or untrue, and very much whether they are kind or unkind,' and repeating that I will make an end.

Pretoria: 24th November 1899

When the prisoners captured after the destruction of the armoured train had been disarmed and collected in a group we found that there were fifty-six unwounded or slightly wounded men, besides the more serious cases lying on the scene of the fight. The Boers crowded round, looking curiously at their prize, and we ate a little chocolate that by good fortune – for we had had no breakfast – was in our pockets, and sat down on the muddy ground to think. The rain streamed down from a dark leaden sky, and the coats of the horses steamed in the damp.

'Voorwärts,' said a voice, and, forming in a miserable procession, two wretched officers, a bare-headed, tattered Correspondent, four sailors with straw hats and 'H.M.S. *Tartar*' in gold letters on the ribbons – ill-timed jauntiness – some fifty soldiers and volunteers, and two or three railwaymen, we started, surrounded by the active Boer horsemen. Yet, as we climbed the low hills that surrounded the place of combat I looked back and saw the engine steaming swiftly away beyond Frere Station. Something at least was saved from the ruin.

'You need not walk fast,' said a Boer in excellent English; 'take your time.' Then another, seeing me hatless in the downpour, threw me a soldier's cap – one of the Irish Fusilier caps, taken, probably, near Lady-smith. So they were not cruel men, these enemy. That was a great surprise to me, for I had read much of the literature of this land of lies, and fully expected every hardship and indignity. At length we reached the guns which had played on us for so many minutes – two strangely long barrels sitting very low on carriages of four wheels, like a brake in which horses are exercised. They looked offensively modern, and I wondered why our Army had not got field artillery with fixed am-munition and 8,000 yards range. Some officers and men of the Staats Artillerie, dressed in a drab uniform with blue facings, approached us. The commander, Adjutant Roos – as he introduced himself – made a polite salute. He regretted the unfortunate circumstances of our meet-ing; he complimented the officers on their defence – of course, it was hopeless from the first; he trusted his fire had not annoyed us; we should, he thought, understand the necessity for them to continue; above all he wanted to know how the engine had been able to get away, and how the line could have been cleared of wreckage under his guns. In fact, he behaved as a good professional soldier should, and his manner impressed me.

We waited here near the guns for half an hour, and meanwhile the Boers searched amid the wreckage for dead and wounded. A few of the wounded were brought to where we were, and laid on the ground, but most of them were placed in the shelter of one of the overturned trucks.

After a while we were ordered to march on, and looking over the crest of the hill a strange and impressive sight met the eye. Only about 300 men had attacked the train, and I had thought that this was the enterprise of a separate detachment, but as the view extended I saw that this was only a small part of a large, powerful force marching south, under the personal direction of General Joubert, to attack Estcourt. Behind every hill, thinly veiled by the driving rain, masses of mounted men, arranged in an orderly disorder, were halted, and from the rear long columns of horsemen rode steadily forward. Certainly I did not see less than 3,000, and I did not see nearly all. Evidently this was the long expected advance.

Our captors conducted us to a rough tent which had been set up in a hollow in one of the hills, and which we concluded was General Joubert's headquarters. Here we were formed in a line, and soon surrounded by a bearded crowd of Boers cloaked in mackintosh. I explained that I was a Special Correspondent, and asked to see General Joubert. My credentials were taken from me by a man who said he was a Field Cornet, and who promised that they should be laid before the General forthwith. Meanwhile we waited in the rain, and the Boers questioned us. My certificate as a correspondent bore a name better known than liked in the Transvaal. Moreover, some of the private soldiers had been talking. 'You are the son of Lord Randolph Churchill?' said a Scottish Boer, abruptly. I did not deny the fact. Immediately there was much talking, and all crowded round me, looking and pointing, while I heard my name repeated on every side. 'I am a newspaper correspondent,' I said, 'and you ought not to hold me prisoner.' The Scottish Boer laughed. 'Oh,' he said, 'we do not catch lords' sons every day.'

All this time I was expecting to be brought before General Joubert, from whom I had some hopes I should obtain assurances that my character as a press correspondent would be respected. But suddenly a mounted man rode up and ordered the prisoners to march away towards Colenso. The escort, twenty horsemen, closed round us. I addressed their leader, and demanded either that I should be taken before the General, or that my credentials should be given back. But the so-called Field Cornet was not to be seen. The only response was, 'Voorwärts,' and as it seemed useless to discuss the matter further I turned and marched off with the rest.

We tramped for six hours across sloppy fields and along tracks deep and slippery with mud, while the rain fell in a steady downpour and

soaked everyone to the skin. The Boer escort told us several times not
to hurry and to go our own pace, and once they allowed us to halt for
a few moments. But we had had neither food nor water, and it was
with a feeling of utter weariness that I saw the tin roofs of Colenso rise
in the distance. We were put into a corrugated iron shed near the
station, the floors of which were four inches deep with torn railway
forms and account books. Here we flung ourselves down exhausted,
and what with the shame, the disappointment, the excitement of the
morning, the misery of the present, and physical weakness, it seemed
that love of life was gone.

After the Boers had lit two fires they opened one of the doors of the
shed and told us we might come forth and dry ourselves. A newly
slaughtered ox lay on the ground, and strips of his flesh were given to
us. These we toasted on sticks over the fire and ate greedily, though
since the animal had been alive five minutes before one felt a kind of
cannibal. Other Boers not of our escort who were occupying Colenso
came to look at us. With two of these who were brothers, English by
race, Afrikanders by birth, Boers by choice, I had some conversation.
The war, they said, was going well. Of course, it was a great matter to
face the power and might of the British Empire, still they were resolved. They would drive the English out of South Africa for ever, or
else fight to the last man. I said:

'You attempt the impossible. Pretoria will be taken by the middle of
March. What hope have you of withstanding a hundred thousand
soldiers?'

'If I thought,' said the younger of the two brothers vehemently, 'that
the Dutchmen would give in because Pretoria was taken, I would smash
my rifle on those metals this very moment. We will fight for ever.' I
could only reply:

'Wait and see how you feel when the tide is running the other way.
It does not seem so easy to die when death is near.' The man said:

'I will wait.'

Then we made friends. I told him that I hoped he would come safely
through the war, and live to see a happier and a nobler South Africa
under the flag which had been good enough for his forefathers; and he
took off his blanket – which he was wearing with a hole in the middle
like a cloak – and gave it to me to sleep in. So we parted, and presently,

as night fell, the Field Cornet who had us in charge bade us carry a little forage into the shed to sleep on, and then locked us up in the dark.

I could not sleep. The rights and wrongs of the quarrel, the fortunes and chances of the war, forced themselves on the mind. What men they were, these Boers! I thought of them as I had seen them in the morning riding forward through the rain – thousands of independent riflemen, thinking for themselves, possessed of beautiful weapons, led with skill, living as they rode without commissariat or transport or ammunition column, moving like the wind, and supported by iron constitutions and a stern, hard Old Testament God who should surely smite the Amalekites hip and thigh. And then, above the rain storm that beat loudly on the corrugated iron, I heard the sound of a chaunt. The Boers were singing their evening psalm, and the menacing notes – more full of indignant war than love and mercy – struck a chill into my heart, so that I thought after all that the war was unjust, that the Boers were better men than we, that Heaven was against us, that Ladysmith, Mafeking, and Kimberley would fall, that foreign Powers would intervene, that we should lose South Africa, and that that would be the beginning of the end. Nor was it till the morning sun – all the brighter after the rain storms, all the warmer after the chills – struck in through the windows that things reassumed their true colours and proportions.

Pretoria: 30th November 1899

The first light of dawn was just peering in through the skylight of the corrugated iron shed. The soldiers lay in a brown litter about the floor, several snoring horribly. The meaning of it came home with a slap. Imprisoned; not able to come and go at will; about to be dragged off and put in some secluded place while others fought the great quarrel to the end; out of it all – like a pawn taken early in the game and flung aside into the box. I groaned with vexation, and, sitting up, aroused Frankland, who shared my blanket. Then the Boers unlocked the doors and ordered us to get ready to march at once.

The forage which we had spread on the floor rustled, and the first idea of escape crossed my mind. Why not lie buried underneath this litter until prisoners and escort had marched away together? Would they count? Would they notice? I did not think so. They would reason – we know they all went in; it is certain none could have escaped during the night: therefore all must be here this morning. The scheme pleased my fancy exceedingly, and I was just resolving to conceal myself, when one of the guards entered and ordered everyone to file out forthwith.

We chewed a little more of the ox, slain and toasted the night before, and drank some rainwater from a large puddle. Then we set out – a sorry gang of dirty, tramping prisoners. We marched across the wagon bridge of the Tugela, and following the road, soon entered the hills. Among these we journeyed for several hours, wading across the gullies which the heavy rains had turned into considerable streams and persecuted by the slanting rays of the sun.

We passed through Pieters without a check at the same toilsome plod and on to Nelthorpe. The advance of half an hour brought us to a very strong picket, where we were ordered to halt and rest. Nearly two hundred Boers swarmed round in a circle and began at once – for they are all keen politicians and as curious as children – to ask questions of every sort. What did we think of South Africa? How long would the English go on fighting? When would the war end? and the reply, 'When you are beaten,' was received with shouts of laughter.

Very soon after this we were ordered to march again, and we began to move to the eastward in the direction of the Bulwana Hill, descending as we did so into the valley of the Klip River. The report of the intermittent guns engaged in the bombardment of Ladysmith seemed very loud and near, and the sound of the British artillery making occasional reply could be plainly distinguished. After we had crossed the railway line beyond Nelthorpe I caught sight of another evidence of the proximity of friends. High above the hills, to the left of the path, hung a speck of gold-beater's skin. It was the Ladysmith balloon. There, scarcely two miles away, were safety and honour. The soldiers noticed the balloon too. 'Those are our blokes,' they said. 'We ain't all finished yet,' and so they comforted themselves.

We kept our eyes on the balloon till it was hidden by the hills, and I thought of all that lay at the bottom of its rope. Beleaguered

Ladysmith, with its shells, its flies, its fever, and its filth seemed a glorious paradise to me.

We forded the Klip River breast high, and, still surrounded by our escort, trudged on towards the laagers behind Bulwana. But it was just three o'clock, after about ten hours' marching, that we reached the camp where we were to remain for the night. I was so utterly worn out on arrival that at first I cared for nothing but to lie down under the shade of a bush. But after the Field Cornet had given us some tea and bully beef, and courteously bidden us to share the shelter of his tent, I felt equal to further argument.

The Boers were delighted and crowded into the small tent.

'Will you tell us why there is this war?'

I said that it was because they wanted to beat us out of South Africa and we did not like the idea.

'Oh no, that is not the reason. I will tell you what is the real cause of this war. It's all those damned capitalists. They want to steal our country, and they have bought Chamberlain, and now these three, Rhodes, Beit, and Chamberlain, think they will have the Rand to divide between them afterwards.'

'Don't you know that the gold mines are the property of the share-holders, many of whom are foreigners – Frenchmen and Germans and others? After the war, whatever government rules, they will still belong to these people.'

'What are we fighting for then?'

'Because you hate us bitterly, and have armed yourselves in order to attack us.'

'Don't you think it wicked to try to steal our country?'

'We only want to protect ourselves and our own interests. We didn't want your country.'

'No, but the damned capitalists do.'

'If you had tried to keep on friendly terms with us there would have been no war. But you want to drive us out of South Africa. Think of a great Afrikander Republic – all South Africa speaking Dutch – a United States under your President and your Flag, sovereign and international.'

Their eyes glittered. 'That's what we want,' said one. 'Yaw, yaw,' said the others, 'and that's what we're going to have.'

'Well, that's the reason of the war.'

'No, no. You know it's those damned capitalists and Jews who have caused the war.' And the argument recommenced its orbit.

As the evening fell the Commandant required us to withdraw to some tents which had been pitched at the corner of the laager. A special tent was provided for the officers, and now, for the first time, they found themselves separated from their men. I had a moment in which to decide whether I would rank as officer or private, and chose the former, a choice I was soon to regret. Gradually it became night.

In the morning, before the sun was up, the Commandant Davel came to rouse us. The prisoners were to march at once to Elands Laagte Station. 'How far?' we asked, anxiously, for all were very footsore. 'Only a very little way – five hours' slow walking.' We stood up – for we had slept in our clothes and cared nothing for washing – and said that we were ready. The Commandant then departed, to return in a few minutes bringing some tea and bully beef, which he presented to us with an apology for the plainness of the fare. He asked an English-speaking Boer to explain that they had nothing better themselves. After we had eaten and were about to set forth, Davel said, through his interpreter, that he would like to know from us that we were satisfied with the treatment we met with at his laager. We gladly gave him the assurance, and with much respect bade goodbye to this digni-fied and honourable enemy. Then we were marched away over the hills towards the north, skirting the picket line round Ladysmith to the left.

It was about eleven o'clock when we reached Elands Laagte Station. A train awaited the prisoners. There were six or seven closed vans for the men and a first carriage for the officers. Two Boers with rifles sat themselves between us, and the doors were locked. I was desperately hungry, and asked for both food and water. 'Plenty is coming,' they said, so we waited patiently, and sure enough, in a few minutes a railway official came along the platform, opened the door, and thrust before us in generous profusion two tins of preserved mutton, two tins of preserved fish, four or five loaves, half a dozen pots of jam, and a large can of tea. As far as I could see the soldiers fared no worse. While we ate our first satisfying meal for three days, a great crowd of Boers gathered around the train and peered curiously in at the windows. One of them was a doctor, who, noticing my hand was bound up, inquired whether I were wounded. The cut caused by the splinter of bullet was insignificant, but since it was ragged and had received no attention for two days it had begun to fester. I therefore showed him my hand, and he immediately bustled off to get bandages and hot water and what not, with which he soon bound me up very correctly.

I noticed about a hundred Boers embarking with their horses in a dozen large cattle trucks behind the engine. At or about noon we steamed off, moving slowly along the line.

Two stations beyond Elands Laagte the Boer commando, or portion of commando, left the train, and the care and thought that had been lavished on the military arrangements were very evident. All the stations on the line were fitted with special platforms 300 or 400 yards long, consisting of earth embankments revetted with wood towards the line and sloping to the ground on the other side. The horsemen were thereby enabled to ride their horses out of the trucks, and in a few minutes all were cantering away across the plain. One of the Boer guards noticed the attention I paid to these arrangements. 'It is in case we have to go back quickly to the Biggarsberg or Laing's Nek,' he explained. As we travelled on I gradually fell into conversation with this man. His name, he told me, was Spaarwater, which he pronounced *Spare*-water. He was a farmer from the Ermolo district. In times of peace he paid little or no taxes. For the last four years he had escaped altogether. But for such advantages he lay under the obligation to serve without pay in war-time, providing horse, forage, and provisions. He was a polite little man, very anxious in all the discussion to say nothing that could hurt the feelings of his prisoners, and I took a great liking to him.

A little further on the ticket collector came to join in the conversation. He was a Hollander, and very eloquent.

'Why should you English take this country away from us?' he asked, and the silent Boer chimed in in broken English: 'Are not our farms our own? Why must we fight for them?'

I endeavoured to explain the ground of our quarrel. 'After all British government is not a tyranny.'

'It's no good for a working-man,' said the ticket collector; 'look at

Kimberley. Kimberley was a good place to live in before the capitalists collared it. Look at it now. Look at me. What are my wages?'

I forget what he said they were, but they were extraordinary wages for a ticket collector.

'Do you suppose I should get such wages under the English Government?'

I said 'No'.

'There you are,' he said. 'No English Government for me,' and added inconsequently, 'We fight for our freedom.'

Now I thought I had an argument that would tell. I turned to the farmer, who had been listening approvingly:

'Those are very good wages.'

'Ah, yes.'

'Where does the money come from?'

'Oh, from the taxes . . . and from the railroad.'

'Well, now, you send a good deal of your produce by rail, I suppose?'

'Ya' (an occasional lapse into Dutch).

'Don't you find the rates very high?'

'Ya, ya,' said both the Boers together; 'very high.'

'That is because he' (pointing to the ticket collector) 'is getting such good wages. You are paying them.' At this they both laughed heartily, and said that that was quite true, and that the rates were too high.

'Under the English Government,' I said, 'he will not get such high wages; you will not have to pay such high rates.'

They received the conclusion in silence. Then Spaarwater said, 'We want to be left alone. We are free, you are not free.'

'How do you mean "not free"?'

'Well, is it right that a dirty Kaffir should walk on the pavement – without a pass too? That's what they do in your British Colonies. Brother! Equal! Ugh! Free! Not a bit. We know how to treat Kaffirs.'

I had touched a very sensitive nerve. We had got down from underneath the political and reached the social. What is the true and original root of Dutch aversion to British rule? It is not Slagters Nek, nor Broomplatz, nor Majuba, nor the Jameson Raid. It is the abiding fear and hatred of the movement that seeks to place the native on a level with the white man. British government is associated in the Boer farmer's mind with violent social revolution. Black is to be proclaimed the same as white. The servant is to be raised against the master; the Kaffir is to be declared the brother of the European, to be constituted his legal equal, to be armed with political rights.

This Boer farmer was a very typical character, and represented to my mind all that was best and noblest in the African Dutch character. The spectacle of this citizen soldier, called reluctant, yet not unwilling, from the quiet life of his farm to fight bravely in defence of the soil on which he lived, which his fathers had won by all manner of suffering and peril, and to preserve the independence which was his pride and joy, against great enemies of regulars – surely that would have drawn the most earnest sympathy of the idealist. And then suddenly a change, a jarring note in the duet of agreement.

'*We* know how to treat Kaffirs in *this* country. Fancy letting the black filth walk on the pavement!'

And after that no more agreement: but a gulf widening every moment.

'Educate a Kaffir! Ah, that's you English all over. We educate 'em with a stick. Treat 'em with humanity and consideration – I like that. They were put here by the God Almighty to work for us. We'll stand no damned nonsense from them. We'll keep them in their proper places. What do you think? Insist on their proper treatment will you? Ah, that's what we're going to see about now. We'll settle whether you English are to interfere with us before this war is over.'

The afternoon dragged away before the train passed near Dundee. After Talana Hill was lost to view we began to search for Majuba, and saw it just as night closed in – a great dark mountain with memories as sad and gloomy as its appearance. The Boer guards pointed out to us where they had mounted their big cannons to defend Laing's Nek, and remarked that the pass was now impregnable.

We now approached the frontier. I had indulged in hopes of leaving the train while in the Volksrust Tunnel by climbing out of the window. The possibility had, however, presented itself to Spaarwater, for he shut both windows, and just before we reached the entrance opened the breech of his Mauser to show me that it was fully loaded. So prudence again imposed patience. It was quite dark when the train reached Volksrust, and we knew ourselves actually in the enemy's country. The platform was densely crowded with armed Boers. It appeared that two new commandos had been called out, and were waiting for trains to take them to the front. The windows were soon blocked with the bearded faces of men who gazed stolidly and commented freely to each other on our appearance.

Before the train left Volksrust we changed our guards. The honest burghers who had captured us had to return to the front, and we were to be handed over to the police. The leader of the escort – a dear old gentleman – I am ignorant of his official rank – approached and explained through Spaarwater that it was he who had placed the stone and so caused our misfortunes. He said he hoped we bore no malice. We replied by no means, and that we would do the same for him with pleasure any day.

Then we said 'goodbye', and I gave him, and also Spaarwater, a little slip of paper setting forth that they had shown kindness and courtesy to British prisoners of war, and personally requesting anyone into whose hands the papers might come to treat them well, should they themselves be taken by the Imperial forces.

We were then handed to a rather dilapidated policeman of a gendarme type, who spat copiously on the floor of the carriage and informed us that we should be shot if we attempted to escape. Having no desire to speak to this fellow, we let down the sleeping shelves of the compartment and, as the train steamed out of Volksrust, turned to sleep.

Pretoria: 3rd December 1899

It was, as nearly as I can remember, midday when the train-load of prisoners reached Pretoria. We pulled up in a sort of siding with an earth platform on the right side which opened into the streets of the town. The day was fine, and the sun shone brightly. There was a considerable crowd of people to receive us. Someone unlocked the door of the railway carriage and told us to come out; and out we came – a very ragged and tattered group of officers. About a dozen cameras were clicking busily, establishing an imperishable record of our shame. Then they loosed the men and bade them form in rank. The soldiers came out of the dark vans, in which they had been confined, with some eagerness, and began at once to chirp and joke, which seemed to me most ill-timed good humour. We waited altogether for about twenty minutes. Now for the first time since my capture I hated the enemy. The simple, valiant burghers at the front, fighting bravely as they had been told 'for their farms', claimed respect, if not sympathy. But here in Pretoria I seemed to smell corruption in the air. Here were the creatures who had fattened on the spoils. There in the field were the heroes who won them.

At last, when the crowd had thoroughly satisfied their patriotic curiosity, we were marched off; the soldiers to the enclosed camp on the racecourse, the officers to the States Model Schools prison.

The distance was short, so far as we were concerned, and surrounded by an escort of three armed policemen to each officer, we swiftly reached our destination; a long, low, red brick building with a slated veranda and a row of iron railings before it. The veranda was crowded with bearded men in khaki uniforms or brown suits of flannel – smoking, reading, or talking. They looked up as we arrived. The iron gate was opened, and passing in we joined sixty British officers 'held by the enemy'; and the iron gate was then shut again.

The States Model Schools is a one-storied building of considerable size and solid structure, which occupies a corner formed by two roads through Pretoria. It consists of twelve large classrooms, seven or eight of which were used by the British officers as dormitories and one as a dining-room; a large lecture hall, which served as an improvised fives court; and a well-fitted gymnasium. It stood in a quadrangular playground about 120 yards square, in which were a dozen tents for the police guards, a cookhouse, two tents for the soldier servants, and a newly set-up bathshed. At the time of my coming into the prison, there was room enough for everyone.

The Transvaal Government provided a daily ration of bully beef and groceries, and the prisoners were allowed to purchase from the local storekeeper, a Mr Boshof, practically everything they cared to order, except alcoholic liquors. During the first week of my detention we requested that this last prohibition might be withdrawn, and after profound reflection and much doubtings, the President consented to countenance the buying of bottled beer. Until this concession was obtained our liquid refreshment would have satisfied the most immoderate advocate of temperance, and the only relief was found when the Secretary of State for War, a kind-hearted Portuguese, would smuggle in a bottle of whisky hidden in his tail-coat pocket or amid a basket of fruit. In spite of the high prices prevailing in Pretoria – prices which were certainly not lowered for our benefit – the somewhat meagre rations which the Government allowed were supplemented, until we lived, for three shillings a day, quite as well as any regiment on service.

On arrival, every officer was given a new suit of clothes, bedding, towels, and toilet necessaries, and the indispensable Mr Boshof was prepared to add to this wardrobe whatever might be required on payment either in money or by a cheque on Messrs Cox & Co., whose accommodating fame had spread even to this distant hostile town. I took an early opportunity to buy a suit of tweeds of a dark neutral colour, and as unlike the suits of clothes issued by the Government as possible. I would also have purchased a hat, but another officer told me that he had asked for one and had been refused. After all, what use could I find for a hat, when there were plenty of helmets to spare if I wanted to walk in the courtyard? And yet my taste ran towards a slouch hat.

The case of the soldiers was less comfortable than ours. Their rations were very scanty: only one pound of bully beef once a week and two pounds of bread; the rest was made up with mealies, potatoes, and such-like – and not very much of them. Moreover, since they had no money of their own, and since prisoners of war received no pay, they were unable to buy even so much as a pound of tobacco.

The custody and regulating of the officers were entrusted to a board of management, four of whose members visited us frequently and listened to any complaints or requests. M. de Souza, the Secretary of War, was perhaps the most friendly and obliging of these, and I think we owed most of the indulgences to his representations. He was a farseeing little man who had travelled to Europe, and had a very clear conception of the relative strengths of Britain and the Transvaal. He enjoyed a lucrative and influential position under the Government, and was therefore devoted to its interests, but he was nevertheless suspected by the Inner Ring of Hollanders of having some sympathy for the British. He had therefore to be very careful. Commandant Opperman, who was directly responsible for our safe custody, was in times of peace a Landrost or Justice. He was too fat to go and fight, but he was an honest and patriotic Boer. Dr Gunning was an amiable little Hollander, fat, rubicund, and well educated. He was a keen politician, and much attached to the Boer Government, which paid him an excellent salary for looking after the State Museum. He had a wonderful collection of postage stamps, and was also engaged in forming a Zoological Garden. This last ambition had just before the war led him into most serious trouble, for he was unable to resist the lion which Mr Rhodes had offered him. He confided to me that the President had spoken 'most harshly' to him in consequence, and had peremptorily ordered the immediate return of the beast under threats of instant dismissal. My private impression is that he will acquiesce in any political settlement which leaves him to enlarge his museum undisturbed.

The fourth member of the Board, Mr Malan, was a foul and objectionable brute. His personal courage was better suited to insulting the prisoners in Pretoria than to fighting the enemy at the front. He was closely related to the President, but not even this advantage could altogether protect him from taunts of cowardice, which were made even in the Executive Council, and somehow filtered down to us. On one occasion he favoured me with some of his impertinence; but I reminded him that in war either side may win, and asked whether he was wise to place himself in a separate category as regards behaviour to the prisoners. 'Because,' quoth I, 'it might be so convenient to the British Government to be able to make one or two examples.' He never came near me again.

Although, as I have frequently stated, there were no legitimate grounds of complaint against the treatment of British regular officers while prisoners of war, the days I passed at Pretoria were the most monotonous and among the most miserable of my life. I could not write, for the ink seemed to dry upon the pen. I could not read with any perseverance. When at last the sun sank behind the fort upon the hill and twilight marked the end of another wretched day, I used to walk up and down the courtyard looking reflectively at the dirty, unkempt 'zarps' who stood on guard, racking my brains to find some way, by force or fraud, by steel or gold, of regaining my freedom.

About ten days after my arrival at Pretoria I received a visit from the American Consul, Mr Macrum. It seems that some uncertainty prevailed at home as to whether I was alive, wounded or unwounded, and in what light I was regarded by the Transvaal authorities. Mr Bourke Cockran, an American Senator who had long been a friend of mine, telegraphed from New York to the United States representative in Pretoria, hoping by this neutral channel to learn how the case stood. I had not, however, talked with Mr Macrum for very long before I realised that neither I nor any other British prisoner was likely to be the better for any efforts which he might make on our behalf. His sympathies were plainly so much with the Transvaal Government that he even found it difficult to discharge his diplomatic duties. However, he so far sank his political opinions as to telegraph to Mr Bourke Cockran, and the anxiety which my relations were suffering on my account was thereby terminated.

No sooner had I reached Pretoria than I demanded my release from the Government, on the grounds that I was a press correspondent and a non-combatant. So many people have found it difficult to reconcile this position with the accounts which have been published of what transpired during the defence of the armoured train, that I am compelled to explain. Besides the soldiers of the Dublin Fusiliers and Durban Light Infantry who had been captured, there were also eight or ten civilians, including a fireman, a telegraphist, and several men of the breakdown gang. Now it seems to me that according to international practice and the customs of war, the Transvaal Government were perfectly justified in regarding all persons connected with a military train as actual combatants; indeed, the fact that they were not soldiers was, if anything, an aggravation of their case. But the Boers were at that time overstocked with prisoners whom they had to feed and guard, and they therefore announced that the civilians would be released as soon as their identity was established, and only the military retained as prisoners.

In my case, however, General Joubert directed that since I had taken part in the fighting I was to be treated as a combatant officer.

Now, as it happened, I had confined myself strictly to the business of clearing the line, which was entrusted to me, and although I do not pretend that I considered the matter in its legal aspect at the time, the fact remains that I did not give a shot, nor was I armed when captured. I therefore claimed to be included in the same category as the civilian railway officials and men of the breakdown gang, whose declared duty it was to clear the line, pointing out that though my action might differ in degree from theirs, it was of precisely the same character, and that if they were regarded as non-combatants I had a right to be considered a non-combatant too.

To this effect I wrote two letters, one to the Secretary of War and one to General Joubert; but, needless to say, I did not indulge in much hope of the result, for I was firmly convinced that the Boer authorities regarded me as a kind of hostage. I therefore continued to search for a path of escape; and indeed it was just as well that I did so, for I never received any answer to either of my applications while I was a prisoner, although I have since heard that one arrived by a curious coincidence the very day *after* I had departed.

While I was looking about for means, and awaiting an opportunity to break out of the Model Schools, I made every preparation to make a graceful exit when the moment should arrive. I gave full instructions to my friends as to what was to be done with my clothes and the effects I had accumulated during my stay; I paid my account to date with the excellent Boshof; cashed a cheque on him for 20*l*.; changed some of the notes I had always concealed on my person since my capture into gold; and lastly, that there might be no unnecessary unpleasantness, I wrote the following letter to the Secretary of State:

States Model Schools Prison,
10th December 1899.

Sir, – I have the honour to inform you that as I do not consider that your Government have any right to detain me as a military prisoner, I have decided to escape from your custody. I have every confidence in the arrangements I have made with my friends outside, and I do not therefore expect to have another opportunity of seeing you. I therefore take this occasion to observe that I consider your treatment of prisoners is correct and humane, and that I see no grounds for complaint. When I return to the British lines I will make a public statement to this effect. I have also to thank you personally for your civility to me, and to express the hope that we may meet again at Pretoria before very long, and under different circumstances. Regretting that I am unable to bid you a more ceremonious or a personal farewell.

I have the honour, to be, Sir,

Your most obedient servant,

Winston Churchill.

To Mr de Souza,
Secretary of War, South African Republic.

I arranged that this letter, which I took great pleasure in writing, should be left on my bed, and discovered so soon as my flight was known.

It only remained now to find a hat. Luckily for me Mr Adrian Hofmeyr, a Dutch clergyman and pastor of Zeerust, had ventured before the war to express opinions contrary to those which the Boers thought befitting for a Dutchman to hold. They had therefore seized him on the outbreak of hostilities, and after much ill-treatment and many indignities on the western border, brought him to the States Schools. He knew most of the officials, and could, I think, easily have obtained his liberty had he pretended to be in sympathy with the Republics. He was, however, a true man, and after the clergyman of the Church of England, who was rather a poor creature, omitted to read the prayer for the Queen one Sunday, it was to Hofmeyr's evening services alone that most of the officers would go. I borrowed his hat.

Lourenço Marques: 22nd December 1899

All the news we heard in Pretoria was derived from Boer sources. Every day we read in the *Volksstem* – probably the most astounding tissue of lies ever presented to the public under the name of a newspaper – of Boer victories and of the huge slaughters and shameful flights of the British. However much one might doubt and discount these tales, they made a deep impression. A month's feeding on such literary garbage weakens the constitution of the mind. We wretched prisoners lost heart. I do not pretend that impatience at being locked up was not the foundation of my determination; but I should never have screwed up my courage to make the attempt without the earnest desire to do something, however small, to help the British cause. Of course, I am a man of peace. I did not then contemplate becoming an officer of Irregular Horse. But swords are not the only weapons in the world. Something may be done with a pen. So I determined to take all hazards; and, indeed, the affair was one of very great danger and difficulty.

The States Model Schools stand in the midst of a quadrangle, and are surrounded on two sides by an iron grille and on two by a corrugated iron fence about ten feet high. These boundaries offered little obstacle to anyone who possessed the activity of youth, but the fact that they were guarded on the inside by sentries, fifty yards apart, armed with rifle and revolver, made them a well-nigh insuperable barrier. No walls are so hard to pierce as living walls. I thought of the penetrating power of gold, and the sentries were sounded. They were incorruptible. I seek not to deprive them of the credit, but the truth is that the bribery market in the Transvaal has been spoiled by the millionaires. I could not afford with my slender resources to insult them heavily enough. So nothing remained but to break out in spite of them. With another officer who may for the present – since he is still a prisoner – remain nameless, I formed a scheme.

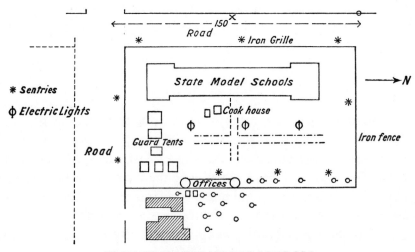

PLAN OF STATES MODEL SCHOOLS

After continual watching, it was discovered that when the sentries near the offices walked about on their beats they were at certain moments unable to see the top of a few yards of the wall. The electric lights in the middle of the quadrangle brilliantly lighted the whole place but cut off the sentries beyond them from looking at the eastern wall, for from behind the lights all seemed darkness by contrast. The first thing was therefore to pass the two sentries near the offices. It was necessary to hit off the exact moment when both their backs should be turned together. After the wall was scaled we should be in the garden of the villa next door. There our plan came to an end. Everything after this was vague and uncertain. How to get out of the garden, how to pass unnoticed through the streets, how to evade the patrols that surrounded the town, and above all how to cover the 280 miles to the Portuguese frontiers, were questions which would arise at a later stage. All attempts to communicate with friends outside had failed. We cherished the hope that with chocolate, a little Kaffir knowledge, and a great deal of luck, we might march the distance in a fortnight, buying mealies at the native kraals and lying hidden by day. But it did not look a very promising prospect.

We determined to try on the night of the 11th of December. I passed the afternoon in positive terror. Nothing, since my schooldays, has ever disturbed me so much as this. There is something appalling in the idea of stealing secretly off in the night like a guilty thief. The fear of detection has a pang of its own. Besides, we knew quite well that on occasion, even on excuse, the sentries would fire. Fifteen yards is a short range. And beyond the immediate danger lay a prospect of severe hardship and suffering, only faint hopes of success, and the probability at the best of five months in Pretoria Gaol.

The afternoon dragged tediously away. I tried to read; I played chess and was hopelessly beaten. At last it grew dark. At seven o'clock the bell for dinner rang and the officers trooped off. Now was the time. But the sentries gave us no chance. They did not walk about. One of them stood exactly opposite the only practicable part of the wall. We waited for two hours, but the attempt was plainly impossible, and so with a most unsatisfactory feeling of relief to bed.

Tuesday, the 12th! Another day of fear, but fear crystallising more and more into desperation. Anything was better than further suspense.

Night came again. Again the dinner bell sounded. Choosing my opportunity I strolled across the quadrangle and secreted myself in one of the offices. Through a chink I watched the sentries. For half an hour they remained stolid and obstructive. Then all of a sudden one turned and walked up to his comrade and they began to talk. Their backs were turned. Now or never. I darted out of my hiding place and ran to the wall, seized the top with my hands and drew myself up. Twice I let myself down again in sickly hesitation, and then with a third resolve scrambled up. The top was flat. Lying on it I had one parting glimpse of the sentries, still talking, still with their backs turned; but, I repeat, fifteen yards away. Then I lowered myself silently down into the adjoining garden and crouched among the shrubs. I was free.

It now remained to await the arrival of my comrade. The bushes of the garden gave a good deal of cover, and in the moonlight their shadows lay black on the ground. Twenty yards away was the house, and I had not been five minutes in hiding before I perceived that it was full of people; the windows revealed brightly lighted rooms, and within I could see figures moving about. This was a fresh complication. We had always thought the house unoccupied. Presently – how long afterwards I do not know, for the ordinary measures of time, hours, minutes, and seconds are quite meaningless on such occasions – a man came out of the door and walked across the garden in my direction. Scarcely ten yards away he stopped and stood still, looking steadily towards me. I cannot describe the surge of panic which nearly overwhelmed me. I dared not stir an inch. My heart beat so violently that I felt sick. But amid a tumult of emotion, reason, seated firmly on her throne, whispered, 'Trust to the dark background.' I remained absolutely motionless. For a long time the man and I remained opposite each other, and every instant I expected him to spring forward. After a spell another man came out of the house, lighted a cigar, and both he and the other walked off together. No sooner had they turned than a cat pursued by a dog rushed into the bushes and collided with me. The startled animal uttered a 'miaul' of alarm and darted back again, making a horrible rustling. Both men stopped at once. But it was only the cat, as they doubtless observed, and they passed out of the garden gate into the town.

I looked at my watch. An hour had passed since I climbed the wall. Where was my comrade? Suddenly I heard a voice from within the quadrangle say, quite loud, 'All up.' I crawled back to the wall. Two officers were walking up and down the other side jabbering Latin words, laughing and talking all manner of nonsense – amid which I caught my name. I risked a cough. One of the officers immediately began to chatter alone. The other said slowly and clearly, '. . . cannot get out. The sentry suspects. It's all up. Can you get back again?' But now all my fears fell from me at once. To go back was impossible. I said to the officers, 'I shall go on alone.'

Now I was in the right mood for these undertakings – that is to say that, thinking failure almost certain, no odds against success affected me. A glance at the plan (p. 402) will show that the gate which led into the road was only a few yards from another sentry. I said to myself, 'Toujours de l'audace': put my hat on my head, strode into the middle of the garden, walked past the windows of the house without any attempt at concealment, and so went through the gate and turned to the left. I passed the sentry at less than five yards. Most of them knew me by sight. Whether he looked at me or not I do not know, for I never turned my head. But after walking a hundred yards and hearing no challenge, I knew that the second obstacle had been surmounted. I was at large in Pretoria.

I walked on leisurely through the night humming a tune and choosing the middle of the road. The streets were full of burghers, but they paid no attention to me. Gradually I reached the suburbs, and on a little bridge I sat down to reflect and consider. I was in the heart of the enemy's country. I knew no one to whom I could apply for succour. Nearly 300 miles stretched between me and Delagoa Bay. My escape must be known at dawn. Pursuit would be immediate. Yet all exits were barred. The town was picketed, the country was patrolled, the trains were searched, the line was guarded. I had 75*l.* in my pocket and four slabs of chocolate, but the compass and the map which might have guided me, the opium tablets and meat lozenges which should have sustained me, were in my friend's pockets in the States Model Schools. Worst of all, I could not speak a word of Dutch or Kaffir, and how was I to get food or direction?

But when hope had departed, fear had gone as well. I formed a plan. I would find the Delagoa Bay Railway. Without map or compass I must follow that in spite of the pickets. I looked at the stars. Orion shone brightly. Scarcely a year ago he had guided me when lost in the desert to the banks of the Nile. He had given me water. Now he should lead me to freedom.

After walking south for half a mile, I struck the railroad. Was it the line to Delagoa Bay or the Pietersburg branch? If it were the former it should run east. But so far as I could see this line ran northwards. Still, it might be only winding its way out among the hills. I resolved to follow it. The night was delicious. A cool breeze fanned my face and a wild feeling of exhilaration took hold of me. At any rate, I was free, if only for an hour. That was something. The fascination of the adventure grew. Unless the stars in their courses fought for me I could not escape. Where, then, was the need of caution? I marched briskly along the line. Here and there the lights of a picket fire gleamed. Every bridge had its watchers. But I passed them all, making very short detours at the dangerous places, and really taking scarcely any precautions. Perhaps that was the reason I succeeded.

As I walked I extended my plan. I could not march 300 miles to the frontier. I would board a train in motion and hide under the seats, on the roof, on the couplings – anywhere. What train should I take? The first, of course. After walking for two hours I perceived the signal lights of a station. I left the line, and, circling round it, hid in the ditch by the track about 200 yards beyond it. I argued that the train would stop at the station and that it would not have got up too much speed by the time it reached me. An hour passed. I began to grow impatient. Suddenly I heard the whistle and the approaching rattle. Then the great yellow head lights of the engine flashed into view. The train waited five minutes at the station and started again with much noise and steaming. I crouched by the track. I rehearsed the act in my mind. I must wait until the engine had passed, otherwise I should be seen. Then I must make a dash for the carriages.

The train started slowly, but gathered speed sooner than I had expected. The flaring lights drew swiftly near. The rattle grew into a roar. The dark mass hung for a second above me. The engine-driver silhouetted against his furnace glow, the black profile of the engine, the clouds of steam rushed past. Then I hurled myself on the trucks, clutched at something, missed, clutched again, missed again, grasped some sort of hand-hold, was swung off my feet – my toes bumping on the line, and with a struggle seated myself on the couplings of the fifth truck from the front of the train. It was a goods train, and the trucks were full of sacks, soft sacks covered with coal dust. I crawled on top and burrowed in among them. In five minutes I was completely buried. The sacks were warm and comfortable. Perhaps the engine-driver had seen me rush up to the train and would give the alarm at the next station: on the other hand, perhaps not. Where was the train going to? Where would it be unloaded? Would it be searched? Was it on the Delagoa Bay line? What should I do in the morning? Ah, never mind that. Sufficient for the day was the luck thereof. I resolved to sleep, nor can I imagine a more pleasing lullaby than the clatter of the train that carries you at twenty miles an hour away from the enemy's capital.

How long I slept I do not know, but I woke up suddenly with all feelings of exhilaration gone, and only the consciousness of oppressive difficulties heavy on me. I must leave the train before daybreak, so that I could drink at a pool and find some hiding place while it was still dark. Another night I would board another train. I crawled from my cosy hiding place among the sacks and sat again on the couplings. The train was running at a fair speed, but I felt it was time to leave it. I took hold of the iron handle at the back of the truck, pulled strongly with my left hand, and sprang. My feet struck the ground in two gigantic strides, and the next instant I was sprawling in the ditch, considerably shaken but unhurt. The train, my faithful ally of the night, hurried on its journey.

It was still dark. I was in the middle of a wide valley, surrounded by low hills, and carpeted with high grass drenched in dew. I searched for water in the nearest gully, and soon found a clear pool.

Presently the dawn began to break, and the sky to the east grew yellow and red, slashed across with heavy black clouds. I saw with relief that the railway ran steadily towards the sunrise. I had taken the right line, after all.

Having drunk my fill, I set out for the hills, among which I hoped to find some hiding place, and as it became broad daylight I entered a small grove of trees which grew on the side of a deep ravine. Here I resolved to wait till dusk. I had one consolation: no one in the world knew where I was – I did not know myself. It was now four o'clock. Fourteen hours lay between me and the night. My impatience to proceed, while I was still strong, doubled their length. At first it was terribly cold, but by degrees the sun gained power, and by ten o'clock the heat was oppressive. My sole companion was a gigantic vulture, who manifested an extravagant interest in my condition, and made hideous and ominous gurglings from time to time. From my lofty position I commanded a view of the whole valley. The railway ran through the middle of the valley, and I could watch the passage of the various trains. I counted four passing each way, and from this I drew the conclusion that the same number would run by night. I marked a steep gradient up which they climbed very slowly, and determined at nightfall to make another attempt to board one of these. During the day I ate one slab of chocolate, which, with the heat, produced a violent thirst. The pool was hardly half a mile away, but I dared not leave the shelter of the little wood, for I could see the figures of white men riding or walking occasionally across the valley, and once a Boer came and fired two shots at birds close to my hiding place.

The elation and the excitement of the previous night had burnt away, and a chilling reaction followed. I was very hungry, for I had had no dinner before starting, and chocolate, though it sustains, does not satisfy. I had scarcely slept, but yet my heart beat so fiercely that I could not rest. I thought of all the chances that lay against me; I dreaded and detested more than words can express the prospect of being caught and dragged back to Pretoria. I found no comfort in any of the philosophical ideas which some men parade in their hours of ease and strength and safety. I realised with awful force that no exercise of my own feeble wit and strength could save me from my enemies, and that without the assistance of that High Power which interferes in the eternal sequence of causes and effects more often than we are always prone to admit, I could never succeed. I prayed long and earnestly for help and guidance. My prayer, as it seems to me, was swiftly and wonderfully answered. I cannot now relate the strange circumstances which followed, and which changed my nearly hopeless position into one of superior advantage. But after the war is over I shall hope to lengthen this account.[1]

[1] In a full account of his escape, published many years later (*My Early Life*, 1930) the writer tells how he made his way towards some distant fires, hoping they might be from a native *kraal*, which might befriend him. They turned out to be those of a coal mine. The manager, though a naturalised burgher, was of British birth, and with the complicity of two Scottish miners, he hid the fugitive in the mine shaft until he could be conveyed in a coal truck on the train to Lourenço Marques.

The long day reached its close at last. The western clouds flushed into fire; the shadows of the hills stretched out across the valley. The daylight died, and soon it was quite dark. Then, and not till then, I set forth. I hurried to the railway line, pausing on my way to drink at a stream of sweet, cold water. I waited for some time at the top of the steep gradient in the hope of catching a train. But none came, and I have since found that I guessed right, that the train I had already travelled in was the only one that ran at night. At last I resolved to walk on. I walked for about six hours. How far I travelled I do not know, but I do not think that it was very many miles in the direct line. Every bridge was guarded by armed men; every few miles were gangers' huts; at intervals there were stations with villages clustering round them. All the veldt was bathed in the bright rays of the full moon, and to avoid these dangerous places I had to make wide circuits and often to creep along the ground. Leaving the railroad I fell into bogs and swamps, so that I was drenched to the waist. I felt very miserable when I looked around and saw here and there the lights of houses, and thought of the warmth and comfort within them, but knew that they only meant danger to me. After six or seven hours of walking I thought it unwise to go further lest I should exhaust myself, so I lay down in a ditch to sleep. I was nearly at the end of my tether. Nevertheless, by the will of God, I was enabled to sustain myself during the next few days, obtaining food at great risk here and there, resting in concealment by day and walking only at night. On the fifth day I was beyond Middelburg, so far as I could tell, for I dared not inquire nor as yet approach the stations near enough to read the names. In a secure hiding place I waited for a suitable train, knowing that there is a through service between Middelburg and Lourenço Marques.

Meanwhile there had been excitement in the States Model Schools, temporarily converted into a military prison. Early on Wednesday morning – barely twelve hours after I had escaped – my absence was discovered. The alarm was given. Telegrams with my description at great length were despatched along all the railways. Three thousand photographs were printed. A warrant was issued for my immediate arrest. Every train was strictly searched. Everyone was on the watch. The worthy Boshof, who knew my face well, was hurried off to Komati Poort to examine all and sundry people 'with red hair' travelling towards the frontier. It was certain, said the *Standard and Diggers' News*, that I had escaped disguised as a woman. The next day I was reported captured at Komati Poort dressed as a Transvaal policeman. Other telegrams said that I had been arrested at Brugsbank, at Middelburg, and at Bronkerspruit. But the captives proved to be harmless people after all. Finally it was agreed that I had never left Pretoria. I had – it appeared – changed clothes with a waiter, and was now in hiding at the house of some British sympathiser in the capital. On the strength of this all the houses of suspected persons were searched from top to bottom, and these unfortunate people were, I fear, put to a great deal of inconvenience.

All these things may provoke a smile after the danger is past; but during the days when I was lying up in holes and corners, waiting for a good chance to board a train, the causes that had led to them preyed more than I knew on my nerves. To be an outcast, to be hunted, to lie under a warrant for arrest, to fear every man, to have imprisonment – not necessarily military confinement either – hanging overhead, to fly the light, to doubt the shadows – all these things ate into my soul and have left an impression that will not perhaps be easily effaced.

On the sixth day the chance I had patiently waited for came. I found a convenient train duly labelled to Lourenço Marques standing in a siding. I withdrew to a suitable spot for boarding it – for I dared not make the attempt in the station – and, filling a bottle with water to drink on the way, I prepared for the last stage of my journey.

The truck in which I ensconced myself was laden with great sacks of some soft merchandise, and I found among them holes and crevices by means of which I managed to work my way to the inmost recess. The hard floor was littered with gritty coal dust, and made a most uncomfortable bed. The heat was almost stifling. I was resolved, however, that nothing should lure or compel me from my hiding place until I reached Portuguese territory. I expected the journey to take thirty-six hours; it dragged out into two and a half days. I hardly dared sleep for fear of snoring.

I dreaded lest the trucks should be searched at Komati Poort, and my anxiety as the train approached this neighbourhood was very great. To prolong it we were shunted on to a siding for eighteen hours either at Komati Poort or the station beyond it. Once indeed they began to search my truck, and I heard the tarpaulin rustle as they pulled at it, but luckily they did not search deep enough, so that, providentially protected, I reached Delagoa Bay at last, and crawled forth from my place of refuge and of punishment, weary, dirty, hungry, but free once more.

Thereafter everything smiled. I found my way to the British Consul, Mr Ross, who at first mistook me for a fireman off one of the ships in the harbour, but soon welcomed me with enthusiasm. I bought clothes, I washed, I sat down to dinner with a real tablecloth and real glasses; and fortune, determined not to overlook the smallest detail, had arranged that the steamer *Induna* should leave that very night for Durban. It is from the cabin of this little vessel, as she coasts along the sandy shores of Africa, that I write the concluding lines of this letter, and the reader will perhaps understand why I write them with a feeling of triumph, and better than triumph, a feeling of pure joy.

Frere: 24th December 1899

The voyage of the *Induna* from Delagoa Bay to Durban was speedy and prosperous, and on the afternoon of the 23rd we approached our port, and saw the bold headland that shields it rising above the horizon to the southward. An hour's steaming brought us to the roads. More than twenty great transports and supply vessels lay at anchor, while three others, crowded from end to end with soldiery, circled impatiently as they waited for pilots to take them into the harbour. Our small vessel was not long in reaching the jetty, and I perceived that a very considerable crowd had gathered to receive us. But it was not until I stepped on shore that I realised that I was myself the object of this honourable welcome.

After an hour of turmoil, which I frankly admit I enjoyed extremely, I escaped to the train, and the journey to Pietermaritzburg passed very quickly in the absorbing occupation of devouring a month's newspapers and clearing my palate from the evil taste of the exaggerations of Pretoria by a liberal antidote of our own versions.

I received then and have since been receiving a great number of

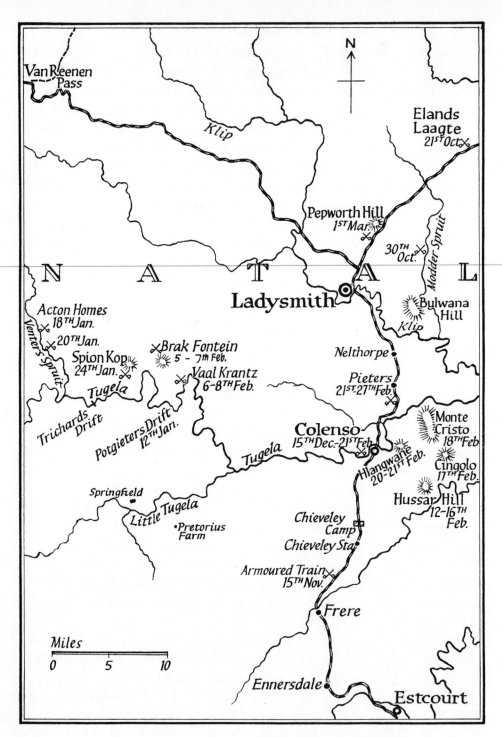

THE THEATRE OF OPERATIONS IN NATAL

telegrams and messages from all kinds of people and from all countries of the earth. One gentleman invited me to shoot with him in Central Asia. Another favoured me with a poem which he had written in my honour, and desired me to have it set to music and published. A third – an American – wanted me to plan a raid into Transvaal territory along the Delagoa Bay line to arm the prisoners and seize the President.

The correspondence varied vastly in tone as well as in character, and I cannot help quoting a couple of telegrams as specimens. The first was from a worthy gentleman who, besides being a substantial farmer, is also a member of the Natal Parliament. He wrote: 'My heartiest congratulations on your wonderful and glorious deeds, which will send such a thrill of pride and enthusiasm through Great Britain and the United States of America, that the Anglo-Saxon race will be irresistible.'

The intention of the other, although his message was shorter, was equally plain.

'*London, December 30th.* – Best friends here hope you won't go making further ass of yourself. – M'Neill.'

I found time to visit the hospitals – long barracks which before the war were full of healthy men, and are now crammed with sick and wounded. Everything seemed beautifully arranged, and what money could buy and care provide was at the service of those who had sustained hurt in the public contention. But for all that I was not sorry to hasten away by the night mail northwards to the camps. Morning had broken when the train reached Frere, and I got out and walked along the line inquiring for my tent, and found it pitched by the side of the very same cutting down which I had fled for my life from the Boer marksmen, and only fifty yards from the spot on which I had surrendered myself prisoner. So after much trouble and adventure I came safely home again to the wars. Six weeks had passed since the armoured train had been destroyed. The hills which I had last seen black with the figures of the Boer riflemen were crowned with British pickets. The valley in which we had lain exposed to their artillery fire was crowded with the white tents of a numerous army. The iron bridge across the Blue Krantz River lay in a tangle of crimson-painted wreckage across the bottom of the ravine, and the railway ran over an unpretentious but substantial wooden structure. All along the line near the station fresh sidings had been built, and many trains concerned in the business of supply occupied them. When I had last looked on the landscape it meant fierce and overpowering danger, with the enemy on all sides. Now   was in the midst of a friendly host. But though much was altered some things remained the same. The Boers still held Colenso. Their forces still occupied the free soil of Natal. Ladysmith was still locked in the strong grip of the invader, and as I listened I heard the distant booming of the same bombardment which I had heard two months before.

Looking backward over the events of the last two months, it is impossible not to admire the Boer strategy. From the beginning they have aimed at two main objects: to exclude the war from their own territories, and to confine it to rocky and broken regions suited to their tactics. No part of the earth's surface is better adapted to Boer tactics than Northern Natal, yet observe how we have been gradually but steadily drawn into it, until the mountains have swallowed up the greater part of the whole Army Corps. Before the war began men said: 'Let them come into Natal and attack us if they dare. They would go back quicker than they would come.' So the Boers came and fierce fighting took place, but it was the British who retired. Then it was said: 'Never mind. The forces were not concentrated. Now that all the Natal Field Force is massed at Ladysmith, there will be no mistake.' But still the Dutch advance continued. The concentrated Ladysmith force, 20 squadrons, 6 batteries, and 11 battalions, sallied out to meet them. The Staff said: 'By tomorrow night there will not be a Boer within twenty miles of Ladysmith.' By the evening of 30th October the whole of Sir George White's command had been flung back into the town with 300 men killed and wounded, and nearly 1,000 prisoners. Then everyone said: 'But now we have touched bottom. The Ladysmith position is the *ne plus ultra*. So far they have gone; but no further!' Then it appeared that the Boers were reaching out round the flanks. What was their design? To blockade Ladysmith? Ridiculous and impossible! However, send a battalion to Colenso to keep the communications open, and make assurance doubly sure. So the Dublin Fusiliers were railed southwards, and entrenched themselves at Colenso. Two days later the Boers cut the railway south of Ladysmith at Pieters, shelled the small garrison out of Colenso, shut and locked the gate on the Ladysmith force, and established themselves in the almost impregnable positions north of the Tugela. Still there was no realisation of the meaning of the investment. It would last a week, they said. Two months have passed. But all the time we have said: 'Never mind; wait till our army comes. We will soon put a stop to the siege of Ladysmith.'

Then the army began to come. Its commander, knowing the disadvantageous nature of the country, would have preferred to strike northwards through the Free State and relieve Ladysmith at Bloemfontein. But the pressure from home was strong. First 2 brigades, then 4, the artillery of 2 divisions, and a large mounted force were diverted from the Cape Colony and drawn into Natal. Finally, Sir Redvers Buller had to follow the bulk of his army. Then the action of Colenso was fought, and in that unsatisfactory engagement the British leaders learned that the blockade of Ladysmith was no unstable curtain that could be brushed aside, but a solid wall.

Whoever selected Ladysmith as a military centre must sleep uneasily at nights. Tactically it may be strongly defensible, politically it has become invested with much importance, but for strategic purposes it is absolutely worthless. It is worse. It is a regular trap. The town and cantonment stand in a huge circle of hills which enclasp it on all sides like the arms of a giant, and once an enemy has established himself on these heights it is beyond the power of the garrison to dislodge him, or even to break out. Not only do the surrounding hills keep the garrison in, but they also form a formidable barrier to the advance of a relieving force. Thus it is that the 10,000 troops in Ladysmith are at this moment actually an encumbrance. To extricate them – I write advisedly, to endeavour to extricate them – brigades and divisions must be diverted from all the other easy lines of advance, and Sir Redvers Buller, who had always deprecated any attempt to hold Natal north of the Tugela, is compelled to attack the enemy on their own terms and their own ground.

What are those terms? The northern side of the Tugela River at nearly every point commands the southern bank. Ranges of high hills strewn with boulders and dotted with trees rise abruptly from the water, forming a mighty rampart for the enemy. Before this the river, a broad torrent with few and narrow fords and often precipitous banks, flows rapidly – a great moat. And before the river again, on our side stretches a smooth, undulating, grassy country – a regular glacis. To defend the rampart and sweep the glacis are gathered, according to my information derived in Pretoria, 12,000, according to the Intelligence Branch 15,000, of the best riflemen in the world armed with beautiful magazine rifles, supplied with an inexhaustible store of ammunition, and supported by 15 or 20 excellent quick-firing guns, all artfully entrenched and concealed. The drifts of the river across which our columns must force their way are all surrounded with trenches and rifle pits, from which a converging fire may be directed, and the actual bottom of the river is doubtless obstructed by entanglements of barbed wire and other devices. But when all these difficulties have been overcome the task is by no means finished. Nearly twenty miles of broken country, ridge rising beyond ridge, kopje above kopje, all probably already prepared for defence, intervene between the relieving army and the besieged garrison.

Ladysmith has stood two months' siege and bombardment. Food and ammunition stores are dwindling. Disease is daily increasing. The strain on the garrison has been, in spite of their pluck and stamina, a severe one. How long can they hold out? It is difficult to say precisely, but another month must be the limit of their endurance, and then if no help comes Sir George White will have to fire off all his ammunition, blow up his heavy guns, burn wagons and equipment, and sally out with his whole force in a fierce endeavour to escape southwards. Perhaps half the garrison might succeed in reaching our lines, but the rest, less the killed and wounded, would be sent to occupy the new camp at Waterfall, which has been already laid out for their accommodation. So we are going to try to force the Tugela within the week, and I dare say my next letter will give you some account of our fortunes.

Frere: 4th January 1900

25th December – Christmas Day! So no great shells were fired into the Boer entrenchments at dawn, and the hostile camps remained tranquil throughout the day. Even the pickets forbore to 'snipe' each other, and both armies attended divine service in the morning and implored

Heaven's blessing on their righteous causes. In the afternoon the British held athletic sports, and the Boers profited by the cessation of the shell fire to shovel away at their trenches. In the evening there were Christmas dinners in our camp – roast beef, plum pudding, a quart of beer for everyone, and various smoking concerts afterwards.

Perhaps 1900 is to mark the beginning of a century of good luck and good sense in British policy in Africa. When I was a prisoner at Pretoria the Boers showed me a large green pamphlet Mr Reitz had written. It was intended to be an account of the Dutch grounds of quarrel with the English, and was called *A Century of Wrong*. Much was distortion and exaggeration, but a considerable part dealt with acknowledged facts. Wrong in plenty there has been on both sides, but latterly more on theirs than on ours; and the result is war – bitter, bloody war tearing the land in twain; dividing brother from brother, friend from friend, and opening a terrible chasm between the two white races who must live side by side as long as South Africa stands above the ocean, and by whose friendly co-operation alone it can enjoy the fullest measure of prosperity. We have done with 'a century of wrong'. God send us now 'a century of right'.

Spearman's Hill: 13th January 1900

Secrets usually leak out in a camp, no matter how many people are employed to keep them. For two days before 10th January rumours of an impending move circulated freely. On the 6th we heard that orders had been given to clear the Pietermaritzburg hospitals of all patients, evidently because new inmates were expected. On the 7th it was reported that the hospitals were all clear. On the 8th an ambulance train emptied the field hospitals at Frere, and that same evening there arrived 700 civilian stretcher-bearers – brave men who had volunteered to carry wounded under fire, and whom the army somewhat ungratefully nicknames the 'Body-snatchers'. The commissariat told tales of accumulations of supplies, meaningless by themselves, but full of significance when viewed side by side with other circumstances.

Accordingly I was scarcely surprised when, chancing to ride from Chieveley to Frere on the afternoon of the 10th, I discovered the whole of Sir Charles Warren's division added to the already extensive camp.

This was the first move of the complicated operations by which Sir Redvers Buller designed to seize the passage of the Tugela at Potgieter's Ferry. When I got back to Chieveley all was bustle in the camp. Orders to march at dawn had arrived.

So far as Chieveley was concerned, the following was the programme: Barton's Brigade to entrench itself strongly and to remain before Colenso, covering the head of the line of communications, and demonstrating against the position; Hildyard's Brigade to move westward at daylight on the 11th to Pretorius's Farm; cavalry, guns, and baggage (miles of it) to take a more circuitous route to the same place. Thither also Hart was to move from Frere, joining Hildyard and forming Clery's division. Warren was to rest until the next day. The force for the relief of Ladysmith, exclusive of Barton's Brigade and communication troops, was briefly, 19,000 infantry, 3,000 cavalry, and 60 guns.

All were busy with their various tasks – Barton's Brigade entrenching, making redoubts and shelter pits, or block-houses of railway iron; the other brigades packing up ready for the march as night closed in. In the morning we started. And here let me make an unpleasant digression. The vast amount of baggage this army takes with it on the march hampers its movements and utterly precludes all possibility of surprising the enemy. I have never before seen even officers accommodated with tents on service, though both the Indian frontier and the Soudan lie under a hotter sun than South Africa. But here today, within striking distance of a mobile enemy, every private soldier has canvas shelter, and the other arrangements are on an equally elaborate scale. The consequence is that roads are crowded, drifts are blocked, marching troops are delayed, and all rapidity of movement is out of the question. Meanwhile, the enemy completes the fortification of his positions, and the cost of capturing them rises. It is a poor economy to let a soldier live well for three days at the price of killing him on the fourth.[1]

[1] This complaint was not in one respect justified by what followed, for after we left Spearman's we only saw our tents for a day or two, and at rare intervals, until Ladysmith was relieved.

After marching about three miles we reached the point where the track from Frere joined the track from Chieveley, and here two streams of wagons flowed into one another like the confluence of rivers. Shortly after this all the mounted forces with the baggage were directed to concentrate at the head of the column, and we trotted swiftly forward. Pretorius's Farm was reached at noon – a tin-roofed house, a few sheds, a dozen trees, and an artificial pond filled to the brim by the recent rains. Here drawn up in the spacious plain were the Royal Dragoons, one squadron of the already famous Imperial Light Horse, and Bethune's Mounted Infantry. The Dragoons remained at the farm, which was that night to be the camping place of Clery's division. But all the rest of the mounted forces, about 1,000 men, and a battery of artillery were hurried forward to seize the bridge across the Little Tugela at Springfield.

Now we approached Springfield, and perhaps at Springfield we should find the enemy. Surely if they did not oppose the passage they would blow up the bridge. Tiny patrols – beetles on a green baize carpet – scoured the plain – and before we reached the crease, scarcely perceptible at a mile's distance, in which the Little Tugela flows – word was brought that no Dutchmen were anywhere to be seen. 'Perhaps we can seize Potgieter's tonight. They don't like having a flooded river behind them.' So we came safely to Springfield – three houses, a long wooden bridge 'erected by public subscription, at a cost of 4,300l.' – half a dozen farms with their tin roofs – and no Boers. Orders were to seize the bridge: seized accordingly; and after all had crossed and watered in the Little Tugela – swollen by the rains to quite a considerable Tugela, eighty yards wide – we looked about for something else to do.

Meanwhile more patrols came in; all told the same tale: no Boers anywhere. Well, then, let us push on. Why not seize the heights above Potgieter's? If held, they would cost a thousand men to storm; now, perhaps, they might be had for nothing. Again, why not? Orders said, 'Go to Springfield'; nothing about Potgieter's at all. Never mind – if cavalry had never done more than obey their orders how different English history would have been! All and sundry were eager to get on. It is very easy to see what to do in the field of war until you put on the thick blue goggles of responsibility. Lord Dundonald reflected, reflected

again, and finally resolved. *Voorwärts!* So on we went accordingly.
300 men and 2 guns were left to hold the Springfield bridge, 700 men
and 4 guns hurried on through the afternoon to Potgieter's Ferry,
or, more properly speaking, the heights commanding it, and reached
them safely at six o'clock, finding a strong position strengthened by loopholed stone walls, unguarded and unoccupied. The whole force climbed
to the top of the hills, and with great labour succeeded in dragging the
guns with them before night. Then we sent back to announce what we
had done and to ask for reinforcements.

The necessity for reinforcements seemed very real to me, for I have a
wholesome respect for Boer military enterprise. 'No Boers this side of
the Tugela.' How did we know? We had not seen any, but the deep
valleys along the river might easily conceal 2,000 horsemen. I said to
myself, the Boer has always a reason for everything he does. He left the
Springfield bridge standing. It would have cost him nothing to blow it
up. Why, then, had he neglected this obvious precaution? Again, the
position we had seized had actually been fortified by the enemy. Why,
then, had they abandoned it to a parcel of horsemen without a shot
fired? I could quite understand that the flooded Tugela was not a
satisfactory feature to fight in front of, but the uninjured bridge
appeared to me a trap: the unguarded position a bait. Suppose they
were, we should be attacked at daylight. The line we had to hold to
cover the approaches to our hill-top was far greater than 700 men could
occupy. Had we been only cavalry and mounted men we could have
fallen back after the position became untenable, but we were encum-
bered with 4 field guns – a source of anxiety, not of strength. 2,000 good
infantry would make everything absolutely secure. And ten miles away
were infantry by thousands.

We passed a wet and watchful night without food or sleep, and were
glad to find the break of day unbroken by the musketry of a heavy
attack. From our lofty position on the heights the whole country
beyond the Tugela was spread like a map. I sat on a great rock which
overhung the valley, and searched the landscape inch by inch with
field glasses. After an hour's study it was no longer difficult to understand why the Springfield bridge had been spared and the heights
abandoned.

The ground fell almost sheer 600 feet to the flat bottom of the valley.

Beneath, the Tugela curled along like a brown and very sinuous serpent. Never have I seen such violent twists and bends in a river. At times the waters seemed to loop back on themselves. One great loop bent towards us, and at the arch of this the little ferry of Potgieter's floated, moored to ropes which looked through the field glasses like a spider's web. The ford, approached by roads cut down through the steep bank, was beside it, but closed for the time being by the flood. The loop of river enclosed a great tongue of land which jutted from the hills on the enemy's side almost to our feet. A thousand yards from the tip of

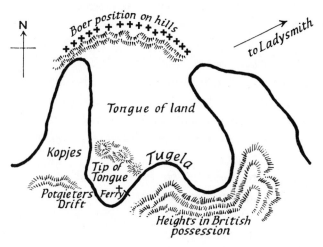

POTGIETER'S FERRY

this tongue rose a line of low kopjes crowned with reddish stones. The whole tongue was virtually ours. Our guns on the heights or on the bank could sweep it from flank to flank, enfilade and cross fire. Therefore the passage of the river was assured. We had obtained what amounted to a practical bridgehead, and could cross whenever we thought fit. But the explanation of many things lay beyond. At the base of the tongue, where it sprang from the Boer side of the valley, the ground rose in a series of gentle grassy slopes to a long horseshoe of hills, and along this, both flanks resting securely on unfordable reaches of the river, out of range from our heights of any but the heaviest guns, approachable by a smooth grass glacis, which was exposed to two or three tiers of cross fire and converging fire, ran the enemy's position. Please look at the sketch on p. 421.

It will be seen that there is no difficulty in shelling the Boers out of the little kopjes, of fortifying them, and of passing the army on to the tip of the tongue; but to get off the tongue on to the smooth plateau that runs to Ladysmith it was necessary to force the tremendous Boer position enclosing the tongue. In technical language the possession of the heights virtually gave us a bridgehead on the Tugela, but the debouches from that bridgehead were barred by an exterior line of hills fortified and occupied by the enemy.

What will Sir Redvers Buller do? To cross and deliver a frontal attack will cost at least 3,000 men. Is a flank attack possible? Can the position be turned? Fords few and far between, steep banks, mighty positions on the further banks: such are some of the difficulties. But Buller's personality impresses everyone with the idea of some great reserve of force. Certainly he has something up his sleeve.

But some part of the army will certainly cross at Potgieter's; and as I looked down on the smooth smiling landscape it seemed very strange to think that in a few days it would blaze into a veritable hell. Yet the dark lines of shelter trenches, the redoubts crowning the hills, the bristle of tiny black figures busily entrenching against the sky line, hundreds of horses grazing in the plain, all promised a fierce and stubborn defence. I turned about. The country to the southward was also visible. What looked to the naked eye like an endless thin rope lay streaked across the spacious veldt, and when I looked through the glass I saw that it was ten or twelve miles of marching men and baggage. The armies were approaching.

The falling of the Tugela increased the danger of our position, and I was delighted when I woke up the next morning, the second of our adventurous occupation, to find Colonel Sandbach, to whom I had confided my doubts, outside my tent, saying 'I suppose you'll be happy now. Two battalions have arrived.' And, sure enough, when I looked southwards, I saw a steady rivulet of infantry trickling through the gorge, and forming a comfortable brown inundation in the hollow where our camp lay. A few minutes later Sir Redvers Buller and his staff rode up to see things for themselves, and then we knew that all was well.

The General made his way to the great stone we call the observatory, and lying down on his back peered through a telescope in silence for the best part of an hour. Then he went off to breakfast with the Cavalry Brigade staff. A few officers remained behind to take a still more exhaustive view. 'There'll be some wigs on that green before long.' Two artillerymen were loitering near. Said one: 'We ought to have the Queen up here, in her little donkey carriage.' 'Ah, we'd do it all right then,' replied his comrade. But when I looked at the peaceful plain and reflected on the storm and tumult presently to burst upon it, I could not help being glad that no gentle eye would view that bloody panorama.

Venter's Spruit: 22nd January 1900

On Thursday 11th January Sir Redvers Buller began his operations for forcing the Tugela and relieving Ladysmith. Barton's Brigade entrenched itself at Chieveley, guarding the line of railway communication. Hildyard's Brigade marched westward six miles to Pretorius's Farm, where they were joined by the cavalry, the naval guns, three batteries Field Artillery, and Hart's Brigade from Frere. The infantry and two batteries remained and encamped, making Clery's division, while the mounted forces under Dundonald moved forward to take the bridge across the Little Tugela at Springfield, and, finding this unoccupied, pushed on and seized the heights overlooking Potgieter's Drift on the Tugela. On the 12th Warren's division, comprising the brigades of Lyttelton and Woodgate, with three batteries, marched to Springfield, where they camped. On the 13th the mounted troops, holding the heights above Potgieter's Drift, were strengthened by the arrival of two battalions of Lyttelton's Brigade from Springfield. Sir Redvers Buller established his headquarters in this camp. On the 14th the rest of the brigade followed, and the same day the corps troops, consisting of Coke's Brigade, one howitzer, and one field battery, reached Springfield. On the 15th Coke moved to the position before Potgieter's, and the naval guns were established on the heights commanding the ford. All this while the Boers contented themselves with

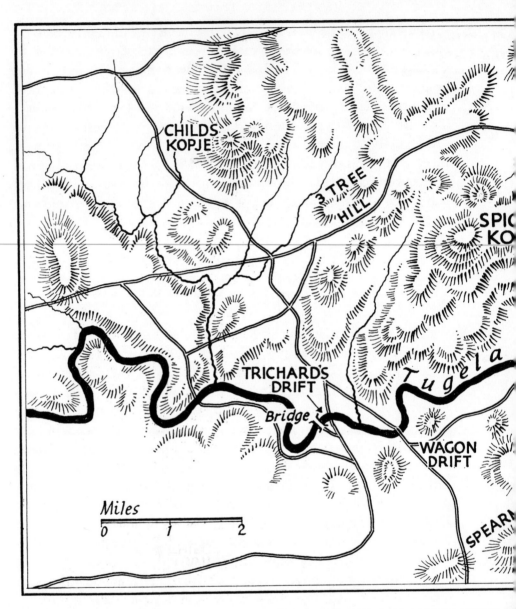

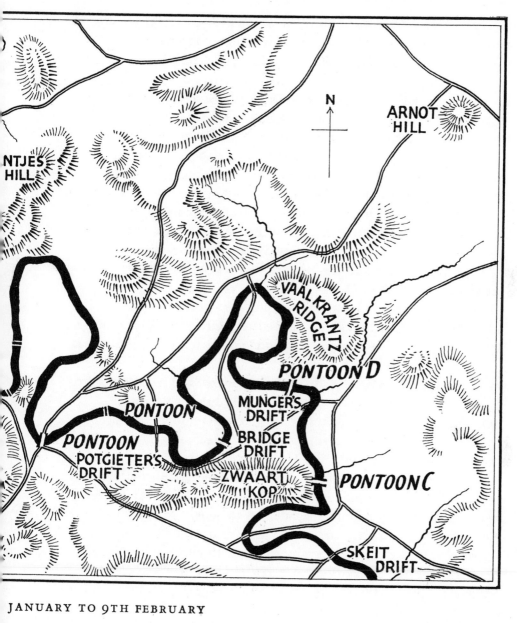

JANUARY TO 9TH FEBRUARY

fortifying their horseshoe position which enclosed the debouches from Potgieter's Drift, and only picket firing disturbed the general peace.

Such was the situation when I wrote my last letter. It was soon to develop, though in a most leisurely and deliberate manner. Daily we watched the enemy fortifying his position, and observed the long lines of trenches which grew and spread along the face of the opposite hills. Daily we made reconnoitring expeditions both east and west along the Tugela, expeditions always attended with incident, sometimes with adventure. Nightly the cavalry camp went to sleep in the belief that a general attack would open on the enemy's position at dawn. Day after day the expected did not happen. Buller had other resources than to butt his head against the tremendous entrenchments which were springing up before him. Everyone discussed every conceivable alternative, and in the meanwhile it was always 'battle tomorrow', but never 'battle today'.

But though there has been but little powder burned the situation has materially altered, and its alteration has been entirely to our advantage. We have crossed the Tugela. The river which for two months has barred the advance of the relieving army lies behind us now. With hardly any loss Sir Redvers Buller has gained a splendid advantage. Let me describe the steps by which this result has been obtained.

On the afternoon of the 16th, as we were sitting down to luncheon, we noticed a change in the appearance of the infantry camps on the reverse slopes of Spearman's Hill. There was a busy bustling of men; the tents began to look baggy, then they all subsided together; the white disappeared, and the camping grounds became simply brown patches of moving soldiery. Lyttelton's Brigade had received orders to march at once. They were to cross the river and seize the near kopjes beyond Potgieter's Drift. Orders for cavalry and guns to move arrived in quick succession; the entire cavalry force, excepting only Bethune's Mounted Infantry, to march at 5.30 p.m., with five days' rations, 150 rounds per man, and what they stood up in – tents, blankets, waterproof sheets, picketing gear, all to be left behind. Our camp was to remain standing. The infantry had struck theirs. I puzzled over this for some time, in fact until an officer pointed out that our camp was in full view of the Boer outposts on Spion Kop, while the infantry camps were hidden by a turn of the hill.

As the darkness fell the cavalry column started. On all sides men were marching through the night: much important business was toward, which the reader may easily understand by studying the map, but cannot without such attention.

Having placed his army within striking distance of the various passages across the Tugela, Sir Redvers Buller's next object was to cross and debouch. To this end his plan appears to have been something as follows: Lyttelton's Brigade, the corps troops forming Coke's Brigade, the ten naval guns, the battery of howitzers, one field battery, and Bethune's Mounted Infantry to demonstrate in front of the Potgieter position, keeping the Boers holding the horseshoe in expectation of a frontal attack, and masking their main position; Sir Charles Warren to march by night from Springfield with the brigades of Hart, Woodgate, and Hildyard, the Royal Dragoons, six batteries of artillery, and the pontoon train to a point about five miles west of Spearman's Hill, and opposite Trichard's Drift on the Tugela. Here he was to meet the mounted forces from Spearman's Hill, and with these troops he was next day, the 17th, to throw bridges, force the passage of the river, and operate at leisure and discretion against the right flank of the enemy's horseshoe before Potgieter's, resting on Spion Kop, a commanding mountain, ultimately joining hands with the frontal force from Spearman's Hill at a point on the Acton Homes–Ladysmith road.

After about two hours' easy marching the cavalry reached the point of rendezvous among the hills opposite Trichard's Drift, and here we halted and awaited developments in the blackness. An hour passed. Then there arrived Sir Charles Warren and staff. 'Move the cavalry out of the way – 15,000 men marching along this road tonight.' So we moved accordingly and waited again. Presently the army began to come. It was not possible to stand unmoved and watch the ceaseless living stream – miles of stern-looking men marching in fours so quickly that they often had to run to keep up, of artillery, ammunition columns, supply columns, baggage, slaughter cattle, thirty great pontoons, white-hooded, red-crossed ambulance wagons, all the accessories of an army hurrying forward under the cover of night – and before them a guiding star, the red gleam of war.

At about eight o'clock next morning the passage of the river began. Two battalions of Hildyard's Brigade, the West Yorkshires and the

Devons, moved towards the drift in the usual open formation, occupied the houses, and began to entrench themselves in the fields. Six batteries came into action from the wooded heights commanding the passage. The pontoons advanced. Two were launched, and in them the West Yorkshire Regiment began to cross, accumulating gradually in the shelter of the further bank. Then the sappers began to build the bridges. The batteries opened on the farms, woods, and kopjes beyond the river, shelling them assiduously, though there was not an enemy to be seen, and searching out the ground with great thoroughness. I watched this proceeding of making 'sicker' from the heights. The drift was approached from the ground where we had bivouacked by a long, steep, descending valley. At nine o'clock the whole of Hart's Brigade poured down this great gutter and extended near the water. The bridge was growing fast – span after span of pontoons sprang out at the ends as it lay along the bank. Very soon it would be long enough to tow into position across the flood. Moreover, the infantry of the West Yorks and Devons had mostly been ferried across, and were already occupying the lately well-shelled farms and woods. At eleven o'clock the bridge was finished, the transported infantry were spreading up the hills, and Woodgate's Brigade moved forward down the valley.

It soon became time for the cavalry to cross, but they were not accommodated, as were the infantry, with a convenient bridge. About a quarter of a mile down stream from Trichard's Drift there is a deep and rather dangerous ford, called the Wagon Drift. Across this at noon the mounted men began to make their way, and what with the uneven bottom and the strong current there were a good many duckings. The Royal Dragoons mounted on their great horses, indeed, passed without much difficulty, but the ponies of the Light Horse and Mounted Infantry were often swept off their feet, and the ridiculous spectacle of officers and men floundering in the torrent provided a large crowd of spectators – who had crossed by the bridge – with a comedy.

During the afternoon the busy Engineers built a second bridge across the river, and by this and the first the artillery, the ammunition columns, and the rest of the mass of wheeled transport defiled. All that day and through the night this monotonous business of passing the wagons across continued. The cavalry had bivouacked – all tents and even waterproofs were now left behind – within the infantry picket lines, and we awoke at the break of day expecting to hear the boom of the first gun. But no guns fired near Trichard's Drift, and only the frontal force at Potgieter's began its usual bombardment. Sir Charles Warren, moreover, said that his artillery had not finished crossing – one battery still to cross – and that there was no hurry. So again everyone was puzzled, and not a few were critical, for even a native camp follower has his views on tactics and strategy.

All that Warren did with his infantry on this day, the 18th, was to creep cautiously forward about two miles towards the Boer position, which with its left resting on Spion Kop stretched along the edge and crest of a lofty plateau, from which long gently sloping spurs and *arêtes* ran down to the river. For us, however, there was more diverting employment. 'The mounted brigade will guard the left flank of the infantry.' Such was the order; and is not offence the surest defence? Accordingly all the irregular cavalry moved in a considerable column westward across the front of the Boer position, endeavouring to find where its flank rested.

There were many halts, and no one hurried, so that at two o'clock the whole cavalry formed a line of observation along the lower kopjes by the river about five miles long. The composite regiment was not, however, to be seen. Major Graham, who commanded it, had been observed trotting swiftly off to the westward. 200 Boers had also been reported moving in that direction. Presently came the sound of distant musketry – not so very distant either. Two miles away to the left was a green hill broken by rocky kopjes. Looking through my glasses I could see ten or twelve riderless horses grazing. A mile further on a group of Boers sheltering behind a kopje from the continual fire was visible. Suddenly one galloped away madly, and even at the distance it was possible to see the cloud of dust from pursuing bullets. A straggling column of Boers was trekking away across the plain back to their main position. Then came reports and rumours. Behind the rumours Barnes, adjutant of the Imperial Light Horse, joyful, with a breathless horse, explained how they had seen 200 Boers moving towards distant hills, to make sure of their line of retreat by the Acton Homes road into the Free State; galloped to cut them off; reached the hills first, with just five minutes to spare; dismounted, commanding the road, and waited.

The Boers admitted afterwards that they thought that the squadrons visible on the other hills two miles back were the head of our column, and they also blamed their scouts, particularly one, an Austrian. 'If we had only had a *veldt* Boer out we should never have been caught.' Caught, however, they undoubtedly were. The Carabineers and the Imperial Light Horse held their fire until the scouts walked into their midst, and then let drive at the main body, 300 yards range, mounted men, smooth open grass plain. There was a sudden furious, snapping fusillade. The Boer column stopped paralysed; then they broke and rushed for cover. The greater number galloped fast from the field; some remained on the ground dead or wounded. Others took refuge among the rocks of the kopjes and apparently proposed to hold out until dark, and hence the arrival of Lieutenant Barnes demanding reinforcements, 60th Rifles, Mounted Infantry, and anything else, so as to attack these fellows in flank and 'bag the lot'. I arrived in time to see the end. The Boers – how many we could not tell – were tenaciously holding the black rocks of a kopje and were quite invisible. The British riflemen curved round them in a half-moon, firing continually at the rocks. The squadron of South African Light Horse had worked almost behind the enemy, and every Dutchman who dared make a dash for liberty ran a terrible gauntlet. Still the surrender did not come. The white flag flickered for a moment above the rocks, but neither side stopped firing. Evidently a difference of opinion among the enemy. Night is coming on. Let us rush them with the bayonet and settle the matter. This from the Rifles – nobody else had bayonets. So a section pushed forward against the rocks, crawling along the ground. Anxious to see the surrender, I followed on my pony, but on the instant there broke out a savage fire from the kopje, and with difficulty I found shelter in a donga. Here were two of the Natal Carabineers – one a bearded man of the well-to-do farmer class, the other a young fair-haired gentleman – both privates, both as cool as ice. We lay still on the grass slope and awaited developments. I peered cautiously. A hundred yards away the Mounted Infantry section were extended. The dust spurts rose around the men, who remained pinned to the earth, scarcely able to raise their heads to fire. Whatever passed over them came whizzing in our direction. The line of riflemen was certainly retiring, wriggling backwards slowly on their bellies. Two brown forms lay still and hunched in the abandoned position. Then suddenly the retiring riflemen sprang up and ran for shelter in our donga. One lad jumped right in among us laughing and panting, and the whole party turned at once and lined the bank. 'We got to within fifty yards of the Dutchmen,' they said; 'but it was too hot to go further.' Eventually we all retired to the main position on the ridge above us. Lord Dundonald and his staff had just arrived.

'There! there's the white flag again. Shoot the devils!' cried a soldier, and the musketry crashed out fiercely. 'What's to be done, sir?' said the Captain, turning to the Brigadier; 'the white flag has been up off and on for the last half hour, but they don't stop firing, and they've just killed two of my men.'

'Give them one more chance.' 'Cease fire – cease fire there, will you?' for the men were very angry, and so at last the musketry died away, and there was silence. Then from among the rocks three dark figures stood up holding up their hands, and at this tangible evidence of surrender we got on our horses and galloped towards them waving pocket handkerchiefs and signalling flags to show them that their surrender was accepted. Altogether there were twenty-four prisoners – all Boers of the most formidable type – a splendid haul, and I thought with delight of my poor friends the prisoners at Pretoria. This might redeem a few. Then we searched the ground, finding ten dead or dying and twenty loose horses, ten dead and eight badly wounded men. The soldiers crowded round these last, covering them up with blankets or mackintoshes, propping their heads with saddles for pillows, and giving them water and biscuits from their bottles and haversacks. Anger had turned to pity in an instant. The desire to kill was gone. The desire to comfort replaced it.

So the soldiers succoured the Boer wounded, and we told the prisoners that they would be shown courtesy and kindness worthy of brave men and a famous quarrel. The Boer dead were collected and a flag of truce was sent to the enemy's lines to invite a burying and identification party at dawn. I have often seen dead men, killed in war – thousands at Omdurman – scores elsewhere, black and white, but the Boer dead aroused the most painful emotions. Here by the rock under which he had fought lay the Field Cornet of Heilbron, Mr de Mentz – a grey-haired man of over sixty years, with firm aquiline features and a short beard. The stony face was grimly calm, but it bore the stamp of unalterable resolve; the look of a man who had thought it all out, and was quite certain that his cause was just, and such as a sober citizen might give his life for. Nor was I surprised when the Boer prisoners told me that Mentz had refused all suggestions of surrender, and that when his left leg was smashed by a bullet he had continued to load and fire until he bled to death; and they found him, pale and bloodless, holding his wife's letter in his hand. Beside him was a boy of about seventeen shot through the heart. Further on lay our own two poor riflemen with their heads smashed like egg-shells. Ah, horrible war, amazing medley of the glorious and the squalid, the pitiful and the sublime, if modern men of light and leading saw your face closer, simple folk would see it hardly ever.

Venter's Spruit: 25th January 1900

When Buller had arrived at Potgieter's he found himself confronted by a horseshoe position of great strength, enclosing and closing the debouches from the ford where he had secured a practical bridgehead. He therefore masked Potgieter's with seven battalions and twenty-four guns, and sent Warren with twelve battalions and thirty-six guns to turn the right, which rested on the lofty hill – almost mountain – of Spion Kop. The Boers, to meet this turning movement, extended their line westwards along the heights of the Tugela valley almost as far as Acton Homes. Their whole position was, therefore, shaped like a note of interrogation laid on its side, – the curve in front of General Lyttelton, the straight line before Sir Charles Warren. At the angle formed by the junction of the curve and the line stands Spion Kop – 'look-out hill'. These letters have completed the chronicle down to the evening of the 18th, when the successful cavalry action was fought on the extreme left.

On the 20th Warren began his attack. The brigades of Generals Woodgate and Hart pushed forward on the right, and the Lancashire and Irish regiments, fighting with the usual gallantry of her Majesty's troops, succeeded, in spite of a heavy fire of rifles and artillery, in effecting lodgments at various points along the edge of the plateau, capturing some portions of the enemy's first line of entrenchments. On the extreme left the cavalry under Lord Dundonald demonstrated effectively, and the South African Light Horse under Colonel Byng actually took and held without artillery support of any kind a high hill, called henceforward 'Bastion Hill', between the Dutch right and centre. In the evening infantry reinforcements of Hildyard's Brigade arrived, and at dawn the cavalry handed over the hill to their charge.

On the 21st the action was renewed. Hart's and Woodgate's brigades on the right made good and extended their lodgments, capturing all the Boer trenches of their first defensive line along the edge of the plateau. To the east of 'Bastion Hill' there runs a deep re-entrant, which appeared to open a cleft between the right and centre of the Boer position. The tendency of General Hildyard's action, with five battalions and two batteries, on the British left this day was to drive a wedge of infantry into this cleft and so split the Boer position in two. But as the action developed, the great strength of the second line of defence gradually revealed itself. It ran along the crest of the plateau, which rises about a thousand yards from the edge in a series of beautiful smooth grassy slopes of concave surface, forming veritable glacis for the musketry of the defence to sweep; and it consisted of a line of low rock and earth redoubts and shelter trenches, apparently provided with overhead cover, and cleverly arranged to command all approaches with fire – often with cross fire, sometimes with converging fire. Throughout the 21st, as during the 20th, the British artillery consisting of six field batteries and four howitzers, bombarded the whole Boer position ceaselessly, firing on each occasion nearly 3,000 shells. They claim to have inflicted considerable loss on the enemy, and must have inflicted some, but failed utterly and painfully to silence the musketry, to clear the trenches, or reach and overpower the Dutch artillery, which did not number more than seven or eight guns and two Maxim shell-guns, but which were better served and manœuvred and of superior quality.

During the 22nd and 23rd the troops held the positions they had won, and the infantry were subjected to a harassing shell fire from the Boer guns, which, playing from either flank, searched the re-entrants in which the battalions sheltered, and which, though they did not cause a greater loss than forty men on the 22nd and twenty-five on the 23rd, nevertheless made their position extremely uncomfortable. It was quite evident that the troops could not be fairly required to endure this bombardment, against which there was no protection, indefinitely.

Three alternatives presented themselves to the council of war held on the 22nd. First, to attack the second Boer position frontally along the crest by moonlight. This would involve a great slaughter and a terrible risk. Secondly, to withdraw again, beyond the Tugela, and look elsewhere for a passage: a moral defeat and a further delay in the relief of Ladysmith; and thirdly, to attack by night the mountain of Spion Kop, and thence to enfilade and command the Boer entrenchments.

It was decided to attack Spion Kop by night, rush the Boer trenches with the bayonet, entrench as far as possible before dawn, hold on during the day, drag guns up at night, and thus dominate the Boer lines. There is, of course, no possible doubt that Spion Kop is the key of the whole position, and the reader has only to think of the horizontal note of interrogation, and remember that the mountain at the angle divides, commands, and enfilades the enemy's lines, to appreciate this fact.

General Woodgate was entrusted with the command, and Colonel Thorneycroft with much of the arrangement and direction of the night attack. Thorneycroft declined to attack on the night of the 22nd because the ground had not been reconnoitred, and the infantry therefore had another day's shelling on the 23rd. Good reconnaissances were, however, made, Lyttelton was strengthened by two Fusilier battalions from Chieveley, Warren was reinforced by Talbot Coke's Brigade and the Imperial Light Infantry, and at one o'clock on the morning of 24th January, General Woodgate started from his camp with the Lancashire Fusiliers, the Royal Lancaster Regiment, two companies of the South Lancashires, and Thorneycroft's Mounted Infantry. Guided by Colonel Thorneycroft the force made its way successfully up the southern spur of the mountain, over most difficult and dangerous ground, and surprised the Boers guarding the entrenchments on the summit. At three o'clock those listening in the plain heard the sudden outburst of musketry, followed by the loud cheers of the troops, and knew that the position had been carried. Ten soldiers were killed and wounded in the firing. Six Boers perished by the bayonet. The force then proceeded to fortify itself, but the surface of the hill was extremely unsuited to defence. The rocks which covered the summit made digging an impossibility, and were themselves mostly too large to be built into sangars.

Morning broke, and with it the attack. A fierce and furious shell fire was opened forthwith on the summit, causing immediate and continual loss. General Woodgate was wounded, and the command devolved on a regimental officer, who, at half past six, applied for reinforcements in a letter which scarcely displayed that composure and determination necessary in such a bloody debate.

Sir Redvers Buller then took the extreme step of appointing Major Thorneycroft – local Brigadier-General commanding on the summit of Spion Kop. The Imperial Light Infantry, the Middlesex Regiment, and a little later the Somersets, from General Talbot Coke's Brigade, were ordered to reinforce the defence, but General Coke was directed to remain below the summit of the hill, so that the fight might still be conducted by the best fighting man.

The Boers followed, and accompanied their shells by a vigorous rifle attack on the hill, and about half past eight the position became most critical. The troops were driven almost entirely off the main plateau and the Boers succeeded in reoccupying some of their trenches. A frightful disaster was narrowly averted. About twenty men in one of the captured trenches abandoned their resistance, threw up their hands, and called out that they would surrender. Colonel Thorneycroft, whose great stature made him everywhere conspicuous, and who was from dawn till dusk in the first firing line, rushed to the spot. The Boers advancing to take the prisoners – as at Nicholson's Nek – were scarcely thirty yards away. Thorneycroft shouted to the Boer leader: 'You may go to hell. I command on this hill and allow no surrender. Go on with your firing.' Which latter they did with terrible effect, killing many. The survivors, with the rest of the firing line, fled 200 yards, were rallied by their indomitable commander, and, being reinforced by two brave companies of the Middlesex Regiment, charged back, recovering all lost ground, and the position was maintained until nightfall. No words in these days of extravagant expression can do justice to the glorious endurance which the English regiments – for they were all English – displayed throughout the long dragging hours of hell fire. Thirst tormented the soldiers, for though water was at hand the fight was too close and furious to give even a moment's breathing space. But nothing could weaken the stubborn vigour of the defence, and night closed in with the British still in possession of the hill.

It drove us all mad to watch idly in camp the horrible shelling that was directed on the captured position, and at about four o'clock I rode with Captain R. Brooke, 7th Hussars, to Spion Kop, to find out what the true situation was. I had seen some service and Captain Brooke has been through more fighting than any other officer of late years. We were so profoundly impressed by the situation that we resolved to go and tell Sir Charles Warren what we had seen. The fight had been so close that no proper reports had been sent to the General, so he listened with great patience and attention. One thing was quite clear – unless good and efficient cover could be made during the night, and unless guns could be dragged to the summit of the hill to match the Boer artillery, the infantry could not endure another day.

The questions were, could guns be brought up the hill; and, if so, could the troops maintain themselves? The artillery officers had examined the track. They said 'No', and that even if they could reach the top of the hill they would only be shot out of action.

Another informal council of war was called. Sir Charles Warren wanted to know Colonel Thorneycroft's views. I was sent to obtain them. The darkness was intense. The track stony and uneven. It was hopelessly congested with ambulances, stragglers, and wounded men. I soon had to leave my horse, and then toiled upwards, finding everywhere streams of men winding about the almost precipitous sides of the mountain, and an intermittent crackle of musketry at the top. Only one solid battalion remained – the Dorsets. All the others were intermingled. Officers had collected little parties, companies and half-companies; here and there larger bodies had formed, but there was no possibility, in the darkness, of gripping anybody or anything. The darkness and the broken ground paralysed everyone.

I found Colonel Thorneycroft at the top of the mountain. He was sitting on the ground surrounded by the remnants of the regiment he had raised, who had fought for him like lions and followed him like dogs. I explained the situation as I had been told and as I thought. Naval guns were prepared to try, sappers and working parties were already on the road with thousands of sandbags. What did he think? But the decision had already been taken. He had never received any messages from the

General, had not had time to write any. The fight had been too hot, too close. So, having heard nothing and expecting no guns, he had decided to retire. As he put it tersely: 'Better six good battalions safely down the hill than a mop up in the morning.' Then we came home, drawing down our rearguard after us very slowly and carefully, and as the ground grew more level the regiments began to form again into their old solid blocks.

Such was the fifth of the series of actions called the Battle of Spion Kop. It redounds to the honour of the soldiers, though not greatly to that of the generals. But when all that will be written about this has been written, and all the bitter words have been said by the people who never do anything themselves, the wise and just citizen will remember that these same generals are, after all, brave, capable, noble English gentlemen, trying their best to carry through a task which may prove to be impossible.

We will have another try, and, if it pleases God, do better next time.

Spearman's Hill: 4th February 1900

We awoke on the morning of 25th January in most gloomy spirits. I had seen the evacuation of Spion Kop during the night, and I did not doubt that it would be followed by the abandonment of all efforts to turn the Boer left from the passages of the Tugela at and near Trichard's Drift. Nor were these forebodings wrong. Before the sun was fairly risen orders arrived, 'All baggage to move east of Venter's Spruit immediately. Troops to be ready to turn out at thirty minutes' notice.' General retreat, that was their meaning. Buller was withdrawing his train as a preliminary to disengaging, if he could, the fighting brigades, and retiring across the river. Buller! So it was no longer Warren! The Commander-in-Chief had arrived.

The army was puzzled and disappointed by failure which it did not admit nor understand. The enemy were flushed with success. The opposing lines in many places were scarcely a thousand yards apart. As the infantry retired the enemy would have commanding ground from which to assail them at every point. Behind flowed the Tugela, a deep, rapid, only occasionally fordable river, eighty-five yards broad, with precipitous banks. We all prepared ourselves for a bloody and even disastrous rearguard action. But now, I repeat, when things had come to this pass, Buller took personal command. He arrived on the field calm, cheerful, inscrutable as ever, rode hither and thither with a weary staff and a huge notebook, gripped the whole business in his strong hands, and so shook it into shape that we crossed the river in safety, comfort, and good order, with most remarkable mechanical precision, and without the loss of a single man or a pound of stores.

A successful retreat is a poor thing for a relieving army to boast of when their gallant friends are hard pressed and worn out. But this withdrawal showed that this force possesses both a leader and machinery of organisation, and it is this, and this alone, that has preserved our confidence. We believe that Buller gauged the capacity of one subordinate at Colenso, of another at Spion Kop, and that now he will do things himself.

We have waited a week in the camp behind Spearman's Hill. To replace the 1,600 killed and wounded in the late actions, drafts of 2,400 men have arrived. A mountain battery, A Battery R.H.A., and two great fortress guns have strengthened the artillery. Two squadrons of the 14th Hussars have been added to the cavalry, so that we are actually today numerically stronger by more than 1,000 men than when we fought at Spion Kop, while the Boers are at least 500 weaker. Everyone has been well fed, reinforced and inspirited, and all are prepared for a supreme effort, in which we shall either reach Ladysmith or be flung back truly beaten with a loss of 6,000 or 7,000 men.

It is generally believed that we fight tomorrow at dawn, and as I write this letter seventy guns are drawing up in line on the hills to open the preparatory bombardment.

It is a solemn Sunday, and the camp, with its white tents looking snug and peaceful in the sunlight, holds its breath that the beating of its heart may not be heard. I attended a church parade this morning. On every side were drawn up deep masses of soldiery, rank behind rank – perhaps, in all, 5,000. In the hollow square stood the General, the man on whom everything depended. All around were men who within the week had been face to face with Death, and were going to face him again in a few hours. Life seemed very precarious, in spite of the sunlit landscape. What was it all for? What was the good of human effort? How should it befall a man who died in a quarrel he did not understand? All the anxious questionings of weak spirits. It was one of those occasions when a fine preacher might have given comfort and strength where both were sorely needed. But the Church had her lamp untrimmed. A chaplain with a raucous voice discoursed on the details of 'The siege and surrender of Jericho'. The soldiers froze into apathy, and after a while the formal perfunctory service reached its welcome conclusion.

General Buller's Headquarters: 9th February 1900

On the afternoon of 4th February the superior officers were made acquainted with the outlines of the plan of action to be followed. The reader will, perhaps, remember the description in a former letter of the Boer position before Potgieter's and Trichard's Drift as a horizontal note of interrogation, of which Spion Kop formed the centre angle ⌒. The fighting of the previous week had been directed towards the straight line, and on the angle. The new operation was aimed at the curve. The general scheme was to seize the hills which formed the left of the enemy's position and roll him up from left to right. It was known that the Boers were massed mainly in their central camp behind Spion Kop, and that, as no demonstration was intended against the position in front of Trichard's Drift, their whole force would be occupying the curve and guarding its right flank. The details of the plan were well conceived.

The battle would begin by a demonstration against the Brak Fontein position, which the Boers had fortified by four tiers of trenches, with bombproof casemates, barbed wire entanglements, and a line of redoubts, so that it was obviously too strong to be carried frontally. This demonstration would be made by Wynne's Brigade supported by six batteries of artillery, the Howitzer Battery, and the two 4·7 naval guns. These troops crossed the river by the pontoon bridge at

Potgieter's on the 3rd and 4th, relieving Lyttelton's Brigade which had been in occupation of the advanced position on the low kopjes.

A new pontoon bridge was thrown at the angle of the river a mile below Potgieter's, the purpose of which seemed to be to enable the frontal attack to be fully supported. While the Artillery preparation of the advance against Brak Fontein and Wynne's advance were going on, Clery's division (consisting of Hart's Brigade and Hildyard's) and Lyttelton's Brigade were to mass near the new pontoon bridge (No. 2), as if about to support the frontal movement. When the bombardment had been in progress for two hours these three brigades were to move, not towards the Brak Fontein position, but eastwards to Munger's Drift, throw a pontoon bridge covered first by one battery of Field Artillery withdrawn from the demonstration, secondly by the fire of guns which had been dragged to the summit of Zwaart Kop, and which formed a powerful battery of fourteen pieces. As soon as the bridge was complete Lyttelton's Brigade would cross, and, ignoring the fire from the Boer left, extended along the Doornkloof heights, attack the Vaal Krantz ridge, which formed the left of the horseshoe curve around the debouches of Potgieter's. This attack was to be covered on its right by the guns already specified on Zwaart Kop and the 64th Field Battery, and prepared by the six artillery batteries employed in the demonstration, which were to withdraw one by one at intervals of ten minutes, cross No. 2 pontoon bridge, and take up new positions opposite to the Vaal Krantz ridge.

If and when Vaal Krantz was captured all six batteries were to move across No. 3 bridge and take up positions on the hill, whence they could prepare and support the further advance of Clery's division, which, having crossed, was to move past Vaal Krantz, pivot to the left on it, and attack the Brak Fontein position from its left flank. The 1st Cavalry Brigade under Burn-Murdoch would also cross and run the gauntlet of Doornkloof and break out on to the plateau beyond Clery's division. The 2nd Cavalry Brigade were to guard the right and rear of the attacking troops from any attack coming from Doornkloof. Wynne was to co-operate as opportunity offered. Talbot Coke was to remain in reserve. Such was the plan, and it seemed to all who heard it good and clear.

On Sunday afternoon the Infantry Brigades began to move to their respective positions, and at daylight on the 5th the Cavalry Division broke its camp behind Spearman's. At nine minutes past seven the bombardment of the Brak Fontein position began, and by half past seven all the artillery except the Zwaart Kop guns were firing in a leisurely fashion at the Boer redoubts and entrenchments. At the same time Wynne's Brigade moved forward in dispersed formation towards the enemy, and the Cavalry began to defile across the front and to mass near the three Infantry Brigades collected near No. 2 pontoon bridge. For some time the Boers made no reply, but at about ten o'clock their Vickers-Maxim opened on the batteries firing from the Potgieter's plain, and the fire gradually increased as other guns, some of great range, joined in, until the artillery was sharply engaged in an unsatisfactory duel – fifty guns exposed in the open against six or seven guns concealed and impossible to find. But though the artillery apparently produced no impression on the Boer guns, they did not suffer as severely as might have been expected, losing no more than fifteen officers and men altogether. At intervals of ten minutes the batteries withdrew in beautiful order and defiled across the second pontoon bridge. Meanwhile Wynne's Brigade had advanced to within 1,200 yards of the Brak Fontein position and retired, drawing the enemy's heavy fire; the three brigades under Clery had moved to the right near Munger's Drift; the cavalry were massed in the hollows at the foot of Zwaart Kop; and the engineers had constructed the third pontoon bridge, with excellent method and despatch under a sharp fire from Boer skirmishers and a Maxim.

The six batteries and the howitzers now took up positions opposite Vaal Krantz, and seventy guns began to shell this ridge to reply to three Boer guns which had now opened from Doornkloof and our extreme right. At midday the Durham Light Infantry of Lyttelton's Brigade crossed the third pontoon bridge and advanced briskly along the opposite bank on the Vaal Krantz ridge. They were supported by the 3rd King's Royal Rifles, and behind these the other two battalions of the Brigade strengthened the attack. The troops moved across the open in fine style, paying no attention to the enemy's guns on Doornkloof, which burst their shrapnel at 7,000 yards with remarkable accuracy. In an hour the leading companies had reached the foot of the ridge, and the active riflemen could be seen clambering swiftly up.

The Durham Light Infantry carried the hill at the point of the bayonet, losing seven officers and sixty or seventy men, and capturing five Boer prisoners, besides ten horses and some wounded. Most of the enemy, however, had retired before the attack, unable to endure the appalling concentration of artillery which had prepared it.

By nightfall the whole of General Lyttelton's Brigade had occupied Vaal Krantz, and were entrenching themselves. The losses in the day's fighting were not severe, and though no detailed statement has yet been compiled, I do not think they exceeded 150. Part of Sir Redvers Buller's plan had been successfully executed. The fact that the action had not been opened until 7 a.m. and had been conducted in a most leisurely manner left the programme only half completed. It remained to pass Clery's division across the third bridge, to plant the batteries in their new position on Vaal Krantz, to set free the 1st Cavalry Brigade in the plain beyond, and to begin the main attack on Brak Fontein. It remained and it still remains.

During the night of the 5th Lyttelton's Brigade made shelters and traverses of stones, and secured the possession of the hill; but it was now reported that field guns could not occupy the ridge because, first, it was too steep and rocky – though this condition does not apparently prevent the Boers dragging their heaviest guns to the tops of the highest hills – and, secondly, because the enemy's long-range rifle fire was too heavy. The hill, therefore, which had been successfully captured, proved of no value whatever. Beyond it was a second position which was of great strength, and which if it was ever to be taken must be taken by the infantry without artillery support. This was considered impossible or at any rate too costly and too dangerous to attempt.

During the next day the Boers continued to bombard the captured ridge, and also maintained a harassing long-range musketry fire. A great gun firing a hundred-pound 6-in. shell came into action from the top of Doornkloof, throwing its huge projectiles on Vaal Krantz and about the bivouacs generally; one of them exploded within a few yards of Sir Redvers Buller. Two Vickers-Maxims from either side of the Boer position fired at brief intervals, and other guns burst shrapnel effectively from very long range on the solitary brigade which held Vaal Krantz. To this bombardment the Field Artillery and the naval guns – seventy-two pieces in all, both big and little – made a noisy but futile response. The infantry of Lyttelton's Brigade, however, endured patiently throughout the day, in spite of the galling crossfire and severe losses. At about four in the afternoon the Boers made a sudden attack on the hill, creeping to within short range, and then opened a quick fire. The Vickers-Maxim guns supported this vigorously. The pickets at the western end of the hill were driven back with loss, and for a few minutes it appeared that the hill would be retaken. But General Lyttelton ordered half a battalion of the Durham Light Infantry, supported by the King's Royal Rifles, to clear the hill, and these fine troops, led by Colonel Fitzgerald, rose up from their shelters and, giving three rousing cheers – the thin, distant sound of which came back to the anxious, watching army – swept the Boers back at the point of the bayonet. Colonel Fitzgerald was, however, severely wounded.

While these things were passing a new pontoon bridge was being constructed at a bend of the Tugela immediately under the Vaal Krantz ridge, and by five o'clock this was finished. Nothing else was done during the day, but at nightfall Lyttelton's Brigade was relieved by Hildyard's, which marched across the new pontoon (No. 4) under a desultory shell fire from an extreme range. Lyttelton's Brigade returned under cover of darkness to a bivouac underneath the Zwaart Kop guns. Their losses in the two days' operations had been 225 officers and men.

At midnight the Boers made a fresh effort to regain the position, and the sudden roar of musketry awakened the sleeping army. The attack, however, was easily repulsed. At daybreak the shelling began again, only now the Boers had brought up several new guns, and the bombardment was much heavier. Owing, however, to the excellent cover which had been arranged the casualties during the day did not exceed 40.

In the evening Sir Redvers Buller, who throughout these two days had been sitting under a tree in a somewhat exposed position, and who had bivouacked with the troops, consulted with his generals. There was a general consensus of opinion that it was impossible to advance further along this line. At eleven at night Hildyard's Brigade was withdrawn from Vaal Krantz, evacuating the position in good order, and carrying with them their wounded, whom till dark it had been impossible to collect. Orders were issued for the general retirement of the army to Springfield and Spearman's, and by ten o'clock on the 8th this operation was in full progress.

Thus the fourth attempt to relieve Ladysmith, which had been begun with such hopes and enthusiasm, fizzled out into failure.

What I have written is a plain record of facts, and I am so deeply conscious of their significance that I shall attempt some explanation.

The Boer covering army numbers at least 12,000 men, with perhaps a dozen excellent guns. They hold along the line of the Tugela what is practically a continuous position of vast strength. Their superior mobility, and the fact that they occupy the chord, while we must move along the arc of the circle, enables them to forefront us with nearly their whole force wherever an attack is aimed, however it may be disguised. Therefore there is no way of avoiding a direct assault. Now, according to Continental experience the attacking force should outnumber the defence by three to one. Therefore Sir Redvers Buller should have 36,000 men. Instead of this he has only 22,000. Moreover, behind the first row of positions, which practically runs along the edge of an unbroken line of steep flat-topped hills, there is a second row standing back from the edge at no great distance. Any attack on this second row the Artillery cannot support, because from the plain below they are too far off to find the Boer guns, and from the edge they are too close to the enemy's riflemen. Therefore the attacking infantry of insufficient strength must face unaided the fire of cool, entrenched riflemen, armed with magazine weapons and using smokeless powder.

Sir Redvers Buller has to remember that his army, besides being the Ladysmith Relief Column, is also the only force which can be spared to protect South Natal. Is he, therefore, justified in running the greatest risks? On the other hand, how can we let Ladysmith and all its gallant defenders fall into the hands of the enemy? It is agonising to contemplate such a conclusion to all the efforts and sacrifices that have been made. I believe and trust we shall try again.

General Buller's Headquarters: 15th February 1900

The army has moved from Spearman's and Springfield to Chieveley, General Lyttelton, who had succeeded Sir Francis Clery, in command of the 2nd Division and 4th Brigade, marching via Pretorius's Farm on the 9th and 10th, Sir Charles Warren covering the withdrawal of the supplies and transport and following on the 10th and 11th. The regular Cavalry Brigade, under Burn-Murdoch, was left with two battalions to hold the bridge at Springfield, beyond which place the Boers, who had crossed the Tugela in some strength at Potgieter's, were reported to be showing considerable activity.

On the 12th orders were issued to reconnoitre Hussar Hill, a grassy and wooded eminence four miles to the east of Chieveley, and the direction of the next attack was revealed. The reader of the accounts of this war is probably familiar with the Colenso position, the proper left of which rests on the rocky, scrub-covered hill of Hlangwane, which rises on the British side of the Tugela. If this hill can be captured and secured from cross fire, then all the trenches of Fort Wylie and along the river bank will be completely enfiladed, and the Colenso position will become untenable, so that Hlangwane is the key of the Colenso position. In order, however, to guard this key carefully the Boers have extended their left – as at Trichard's Drift they extended their right – until it occupies a very lofty range of mountains four or five miles to the east of Hlangwane. The long delays have given ample time to the enemy to complete his fortifications, and the trenches here are provided with overhead cover against shells and carefully made loopholes. In front of them stretches a bare slope, on either side rise formidable hills from which long-range guns can make a continual cross fire.

We are to make – at least in spite of disappointments we hope and believe we are to make – a supreme effort to relieve Ladysmith. At the same time we are the army for the defence of South Natal. If we had put the matter to the test at Potgieter's and failed, our line of communications might have been cut behind us, and the whole army might have been captured or dispersed. Here we have the railway behind us. We are not as we were at Potgieter's 'formed to a flank'. We derive an accession of strength from the fact that the troops holding Railhead are now available for the general action.

At eight o'clock – we never get up early in this war – Lord Dundonald started from the cavalry camp. The Irregular Horse were familiar with the ground, and we soon occupied Hussar Hill, driving back a small Boer patrol and wounding two of the enemy. At noon Sir

Redvers Buller arrived, and made a prolonged reconnaissance of the ground with his telescope. At one o'clock we were ordered to withdraw, and the difficult task of extricating the advanced pickets from close contact with the enemy was performed under a sharp fire.

After you leave Hussar Hill on the way back to Chieveley camp it is necessary to cross a wide dip of ground. We had withdrawn several miles in careful rearguard fashion, and the last two squadrons were walking across this dip towards the ridge on the homeward side. Perhaps we had not curled in our tail quite quick enough, or perhaps the enemy has grown more enterprising of late, in any case just as we were reaching the ridge a single shot was fired from Hussar Hill, and then without more ado a loud crackle of musketry burst forth. The distance was nearly 2,000 yards, but the squadrons in close formation were a good target. I chanced to be riding with Colonel Byng in rear, and looking round saw that we had good luck. For though bullets fell among the troopers quite thickly enough, the ground 200 yards further back was all alive with jumping dust, as it was very dry weather. The Boers were shooting short.

We reached the ridge and cover in a minute, and as soon as the front was clear the four little pink guns of Captain Hill's Colt Battery began spluttering furiously. The South African Light Horse dismounted and, lining the ridge, opened fire with their rifles. Thorneycroft's Mounted Infantry came into line on our left flank, and Major Gough's Regiment and the Royal Welsh Fusiliers, who had almost reached cover, turned round of their own accord and hurried eagerly in the direction of the firing.

There now ensued a strange little skirmish. Not less than 400 men on either side were firing as fast as modern rifles will allow. Between us stretched the smooth green dip of ground. Beyond there rose the sharper outlines of Hussar Hill, two or three sheds, and a few trees. That was where the Boers were. But they were quite invisible to the naked eye, and no smoke betrayed their positions. With a telescope they could be seen – a long row of heads above the grass. We were equally hidden. Still their bullets – a proportion of their bullets – found us, and I earnestly trust that some of ours found them.

I happened to pass along the line on some duty or other when I noticed my younger brother, whose keen desire to take some part in the public quarrel had led me, in spite of misgivings, to procure him a lieutenancy, lying on the ground, with his troop. As I approached I saw him start in the quick, peculiar manner of a stricken man. I asked him at once whether he was hurt, and he said something – he thought it must be a bullet – had hit him on the gaiter and numbed his leg. He was quite sure it had not gone in, but when we had carried him away we found – as I expected – that he was shot through the leg. The wound was not serious, but the doctors declared he would be a month in hospital. It was his baptism of fire, and I have since wondered at the strange caprice which strikes down one man in his first skirmish and protects another time after time.

It was neither our business nor our pleasure to remain and continue this long-range duel with the Boers. Our work for the day was over, and all were anxious to get home to luncheon. Accordingly, as soon as the battery had come into action to cover our withdrawal we commenced withdrawing squadron by squadron and finally broke off the engagement, for the Boers were not inclined to follow further.

Cingolo Neck: 19th February 1900

Not since I wrote the tale of my escape from Pretoria have I taken up my pen with such feelings of satisfaction and contentment as I do to-night. There is really good hope that Sir Redvers Buller has solved the Riddle of the Tugela – at last. At last! I expect there will be some who will inquire – 'Why not "at first"?' All I can answer is this: knowing the General and the difficulties, I am inclined to ask, not whether he might have succeeded sooner, but rather whether anyone else would have succeeded at all.

Anyone who stands on Gun Hill near Chieveley can see the whole of the Boer position about Colenso sweeping before him in a wide curve. The mountain wall looks perfectly unbroken. The river lies everywhere buried in its gorge, and is quite invisible. To the observer there is only a smooth green bay of land sloping gently downward, and embraced by the rocky, scrub-covered hills. Along this crescent of high ground runs – or rather, by God's grace, ran – the Boer line, strong in its natural features, and entrenched from end to end. When the map on page 455 is consulted, however, it is seen that the Tugela does not flow uniformly along the foot of the hills as might be expected, but that after passing Colenso village it plunges into the mountainous country, and bends sharply northward; so that, though the left of the Boer line might appear as strong as the right, there was this difference, that the Boer right had the river on its front, the Boer left had it in its rear.

The attack of the 15th of December had been directed against the Boer right, because after reconnaissance Sir Redvers Buller deemed that, in spite of the river advantage, the right was actually the weaker of the two flanks. The attack of the 15th was repulsed with heavy loss. It might, therefore, seem that little promise of success attended an attack on the Boer left. The situation, however, was entirely altered by the great reinforcements in heavy artillery which had reached the army.

Let us now consider the Boer left by itself. It ran in a chain of sangars, trenches, and rifle pits, from Colenso village, through the scrub by the river, over the rugged hill of Hlangwane, along a smooth grass ridge we called 'The Green Hill', and was extended to guard against a turning movement on to the lofty wooded ridges of Monte Cristo and Cingolo and the neck joining these two features. Sir Redvers Buller's determination was to turn this widely extended position on its extreme left, and to endeavour to crumple it from left to right. As it were, a gigantic right arm was to reach out to the eastward, its shoulder at Gun Hill, its elbow on Hussar Hill, its hand on Cingolo, its fingers, the Irregular Cavalry Brigade, actually behind Cingolo.

On 12th February a reconnaissance in force of Hussar Hill was made by Lord Dundonald. On the 14th the army moved east from Chieveley to occupy this ground. General Hart with one brigade held Gun Hill and Railhead. The First Cavalry Brigade watched the left flank at Springfield, but with these exceptions the whole force marched for Hussar Hill. The Irregular Cavalry covered the front, and the South African Light Horse, thrown out far in advance, secured the position by half past eight, just in time to forestall a force of Boers which had been despatched, so soon as the general movement of the British was evident, to resist the capture of the hill. A short sharp skirmish followed, which was terminated after half an hour by the arrival of the leading Infantry battalion – the Royal Welsh Fusiliers. During the day the occupation was completed, and the brigades of Generals Wynne, Coke, and Barton, then joining Warren's division with the artillery, entrenched themselves strongly and bivouacked on the hill. Meanwhile Lyttelton's division marched from its camp in the Blue Krantz Valley, east of Chieveley, along the valley to a position short of the eastern spurs of Hussar Hill.

On the afternoon of the 16th Sir Redvers Buller resolved to plunge, and orders were issued for a general advance at dawn. Two hours before dawn the army was on the move. Hart's Brigade, the 6-in. and other great guns at Chieveley, guarded Railhead. Hlangwane Hill, and the long line of entrenchments rimming the Green Hill, were masked and fronted by the display of the field and siege batteries which were also able to prepare and support the attack on Cingolo Neck and Monte Cristo Ridge. Lyttelton's division with Wynne's Fusilier Brigade was to stretch out to the eastward and, by a wide turning movement pivoting on the guns and Barton's Brigade, attack the Cingolo Ridge. Dundonald's Cavalry Brigade was to make a far wider detour and climb up the end of the ridge, thus making absolutely certain of finding the enemy's left flank at last.

By daybreak all were moving, and as the Irregular Cavalry forded the Blue Krantz stream on their enveloping march we heard the boom of the first gun. The Cavalry Brigade marched ten miles eastward through most broken and difficult country, which made it imperative to move in single file, and the sound of the general action grew fainter and fainter. Gradually, however, we began to turn again towards it. The slope of the ground rose against us. The scrub became more dense. We dismounted and led our horses, who scrambled and blundered painfully among the trees and boulders. So scattered was our formation that I did not care to imagine what would have happened had the enemy put in an appearance. But our safety lay in these same natural difficulties.

At length we reached the foot of the hill and halted to reconnoitre the slopes as far as was possible. After half an hour, since nothing could be seen, the advance was resumed up the side of a precipice and through a jungle so thick that we had to cut our road. It was eleven o'clock before we reached the summit of the ridge and emerged on to more or less open plateau, diversified with patches of wood and heaps of great boulders. Two squadrons had re-formed on the top and had deployed to cover the others. The troopers of the remaining seven squadrons were working their way up about four to the minute. It would take at least two hours before the command was complete: and meanwhile! Suddenly there was a rifle shot. Then another, then a regular splutter of musketry. Bullets began to whizz overhead. The Boers had discovered us.

Now came the crisis. There might be a hundred Boers on the hill, in which case all was well. On the other hand there might be a thousand, in which case——! and retreat down the precipice was, of course, quite out of the question. Luckily there were only about a hundred, and after a skirmish, they fell back and we completed our deployment on the top of the hill.

The squadron of Imperial Light Horse and the Natal Carabineers now advanced slowly along the ridge, clearing it of the enemy. Half-way along the Queen's, the right battalion of Hildyard's attack, which had now rushed the top, came into line and supported the dismounted men. The rest of the cavalry descended into the plain on the other side of the ridge, outflanking and even threatening the retreat of its defenders, so that in the end the Boers, who were very weak in numbers, were hunted off the ridge altogether, and Cingolo was ours. Cingolo and Monte Cristo are joined together by a neck of ground from which both heights rise steeply. On either side of Monte Cristo and Cingolo long spurs run at right angles to the main hill.

By the operations of the 17th the Boer line had been twisted off Cingolo, and turned back along the subsidiary spurs of Monte Cristo, and the British forces had placed themselves diagonally across the left of the Boer position thus:

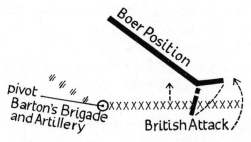

BOER POSITION AT MONTE CRISTO, 17TH FEBRUARY

The advantages of this situation were to be enjoyed on the morrow.

Finding our further advance barred by the turned-back position the enemy had adopted, and which we could only attack frontally, the cavalry threw out a line of outposts and prepared to bivouac for the night.

At dawn the artillery began on both sides, and we were ourselves awakened by Creusot shells bursting in our bivouac. The enemy's fire was chiefly directed on the company of the Queen's which was holding the top of Cingolo, and only the good cover which the great rocks afforded prevented serious losses. But we knew that we held the best cards; and so did the Boers. At eight o'clock Hildyard's Brigade advanced against the peak of the Monte Cristo ridge which lay beyond the neck. The West Yorks led, the Queen's and East Surrey supported. The musketry swelled into a constant crackle like the noise of a good fire roaring up the chimney, but, in spite of more than a hundred casualties, the advance never checked for an instant, and by half past ten the bayonets of the attacking infantry began to glitter among the trees of the summit. The Boers, who were lining a hastily-dug trench half-way along the ridge, threatened in front with an overwhelming force and assailed in flank by the long-range fire of the cavalry, began to fall back. By eleven o'clock the fight on the part of the enemy resolved itself into a rearguard action.

Under the pressure of the advancing and enveloping army this degenerated very rapidly. When the Dutchman makes up his mind to go he throws all dignity to the winds, and I have never seen an enemy leave the field in such a hurry as did these valiant Boers who found their flank turned, and remembered for the first time that there was a deep river behind them. Shortly after twelve o'clock the summit of the ridge of Monte Cristo was in our hands. The spurs which started at right angles from it were, of course, now enfiladed and commanded. The Boers evacuated both in great haste.

The spur on the Colenso or western side was none other than the Green Hill itself, and judging rightly that its frowning entrenchments were now empty of defenders Sir Redvers Buller ordered a general advance frontally against it. Two miles of trenches were taken with scarcely any loss. The enemy fled in disorder across the river. A few prisoners, some wounded, several cartloads of ammunition and stores,

five camps with all kinds of Boer material, and last of all, and compared
to which all else was insignificant, the dominating Monte Cristo ridge
stretching northward to within an easy spring of Bulwana Hill, were
the prize of victory.

From the captured ridge we could look right down into Ladysmith,
and at the first opportunity I climbed up to see it for myself. Only eight
miles away stood the poor little persecuted town – a twenty-acre patch
of tin houses and blue gum trees, but famous to the uttermost ends of
the earth.

The victory of Monte Cristo has laid open a practicable road to Ladysmith. Great difficulties and heavy opposition have yet to be encountered and overcome, but the word 'impossible' must no longer be
– should, perhaps, never have been used.

Hospital Ship 'Maine': 4th March 1900

Since I finished my last letter, on the 21st February, I have found no
time to sit down to write until now, because we have passed through a
period of ceaseless struggle and emotion, and I have been seeing so
many things that I could not pause to record anything. Now the great
event is over, and I take a few days' leisure on the good ship *Maine*,
where everyone is busy getting well, to think about it all and set down
some things on paper.

First and foremost there was the Monte Cristo ridge, that we had
captured on the 18th, which gave us the Green Hill, Hlangwane Hill,
and, when we chose to take it, the whole of the Hlangwane plateau.
The Monte Cristo ridge is the centrepiece to the whole of this battle.
As soon as we had won it I telegraphed to the *Morning Post* that now
at last success was a distinct possibility. With this important feature
in our possession it was certain that we held the key to Ladysmith, and
though we might fumble a little with the lock, sooner or later, barring
the accidents of war, we should open the door.

On the 19th General Buller made good his position on Green Hill,
occupied Hlangwane with Barton's Brigade, built or improved his

roads and communications from Hussar Hill across the Gomba Valley, and brought up his heavy guns. On the 20th the south side of the Tugela was entirely cleared of the enemy, who retired across the bridge they had built, and, moreover, a heavy battery was established on the spurs of Hlangwane to drive them out of Colenso. In the afternoon Hart's Brigade advanced from Chieveley, and his leading battalion, under Major Stuart-Wortley, occupied Colenso village without any resistance.

The question now arose – Where should the river be crossed? Sir Redvers Buller possessed the whole of the Hlangwane plateau, which fills up the re-entrant angle made opposite Pieters by the Tugela after it leaves Colenso. From this Hlangwane plateau he could either cross the river where it ran north and south or where it ran east and west. Sir Redvers Buller determined to cross the former reach beyond Colenso village. To do this he had to let go his hold on the Monte Cristo ridge and resign all the advantages which its possession had given him, and had besides to descend into the low ground, where his army must be cramped between the high hills on its left and the river on its right.

There was, of course, something to be said for the other plan, which was advocated strongly by Sir Charles Warren. The crossing, it was urged, was absolutely safe, being commanded on all sides by our guns, and the enemy could make no opposition except with artillery. Moreover, the army would get on its line of railway and could 'advance along the railroad'. This last was a purely imaginary advantage, to be sure, because the railway had no rolling-stock, and was disconnected from the rest of the line by the destruction of the Tugela bridge. But what weighed with the Commander-in-Chief much more was the accumulating evidence that the enemy were in full retreat. The Intelligence reports all pointed to this situation. Boers had ridden off in all directions. Wagons were seen trekking along every road to the north and west. The camps between us and Ladysmith began to break up. Everyone said, 'This is the result of Lord Roberts's advance: the Boers find themselves now too weak to hold us off. They have raised the siege.'

Undoubtedly the Boers had been reduced in strength by about 5,000 men, who had been sent into the Free State for its defence against Lord Roberts's advance. Until the Monte Cristo ridge was lost to them they deemed themselves quite strong enough to maintain the siege.

When, however, this position was captured, the situation was revolutionised. They saw that we had found their flank, and thoroughly appreciated the significance and value of the long high wedge of ground, which cut right across the left of their positions, and seemed to stretch away almost to Bulwana Mountain. They knew perfectly well that if we advanced by our right along the line of this ridge, which they called 'the Bush Kop', supporting ourselves by it as a man might rest his hand on a balustrade, we could turn their Pieters position just as we had already turned their entrenchments at Colenso.

Therein lay the true reason of their retirement, and in attributing it either to Lord Roberts's operations or to the beating we had given them on the 18th we made a mistake, which was not repaired until much blood had been shed.

In the belief, however, that the enemy were in retreat the General resolved to cross the river by a pontoon bridge and follow the railway line. On the 21st, therefore, he moved his army westward across the Hlangwane plateau, threw his bridge, and during the afternoon passed his two leading infantry brigades over it. As soon as the Boers perceived that he had chosen this line of advance their hopes revived. They returned to the number of about 9,000 burghers, and manned the trenches of the Pieters position, with the result that Wynne's Lancashire Brigade, which was the first to cross, soon found itself engaged in a sharp action among the low kopjes, and suffered 150 casualties, including its General, before dark. Musketry fire was continuous throughout the night. The 1st Cavalry Brigade had been brought in from Springfield on the 20th, and on the morning of the 22nd both the Regular and Irregular Cavalry were to have crossed the river. We accordingly marched from our camp at the neck between Cingolo and Monte Cristo and met the 1st Cavalry Brigade, which had come from Chieveley, at the pontoon bridge. A brisk action was crackling away beyond the river, and it looked as if the ground scarcely admitted of our intervention. Indeed, we had hardly arrived when a Staff Officer came up, and brought us orders to camp near Hlangwane Hill, as we should not cross that day.

Presently I talked to the Staff Officer, who chanced to be a man with a capacity for sustained thought, an eye for country, and some imagination. He said: 'I don't like the situation; there are more of them than we

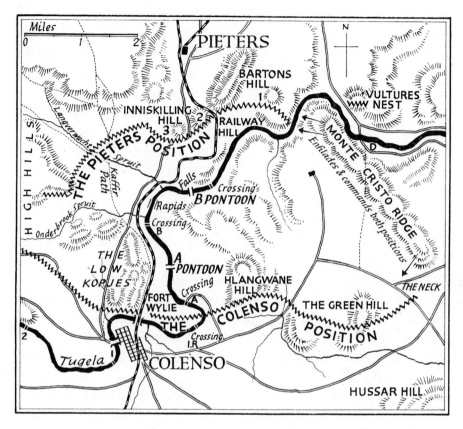

OPERATIONS OF THE NATAL FIELD ARMY, 14TH TO 28TH FEBRUARY

expected. We have come down off our high ground. We have taken all the big guns off the big hills. We are getting ourselves cramped up among these kopjes in the valley of the Tugela. It will be like being in the Coliseum and shot at by every row of seats.'

Sir Redvers Buller, however, still believing he had only a rearguard in front of him, was determined to persevere. He moved the whole of his infantry, with the exception of Barton's Brigade, and nearly all the artillery, heavy and field, across the river, and in the afternoon sent two battalions forward against the low kopjes. By nightfall a good deal of this low, rolling ground was in our possession, though at some cost in men and officers.

At dusk the Boers made a fierce and furious counter-attack. I was watching the operations from Hlangwane Hill through a powerful telescope. As the light died my companions climbed down the rocks to the cavalry camp and left me alone staring at the bright flashes of the guns which stabbed the obscurity on all sides. Suddenly, above the booming of the cannon, there arose the harsh rattling roar of a tremendous fusillade. Without a single intermission this continued for several hours. The Howitzer Battery, in spite of the darkness, evidently considered the situation demanded its efforts, and fired salvoes of lyddite shells, which, bursting in the direction of the Boer position, lit up the whole scene with flaring explosions. I went anxiously to bed that night, wondering what was passing beyond the river.

There was still a steady splutter of musketry at dawn on the 23rd, and before the light was full grown the guns joined in the din. We eagerly sought for news of what had passed. Apparently the result was not unfavourable to the army. 'Push for Ladysmith today, horse, foot, and artillery' was the order; 'Both cavalry brigades to cross the river at once.'

At eight o'clock the cavalry crossed the river under shell fire directed on the bridge, and were massed at Fort Wylie, near Colenso. I rode along the railway line to watch the action from one of the low kopjes. A capricious shell fire annoyed the whole army as it sheltered behind the rocky hills, and an unceasing stream of stretchers from the front bore true witness to the serious nature of the conflict, for this was the third and bloodiest day of the seven days' fighting called the Battle of Pieters.

I must now describe the main Pieters position, one hill of which was about to be attacked. It ran from the high and, so far as we were concerned, inaccessible hills on the west to the angle of the river, and then along the three hills.

Sir Redvers Buller's plan was as follows: On the 22nd he had taken the low kopjes, and his powerful artillery gave him complete command of the river gorge. Behind the kopjes, which acted as a kind of shield, and along the river gorge he proposed to advance his infantry until the angle of the river was passed and there was room to stretch out his, till then, cramped right arm and reach round the enemy's left on Inniskilling Hill, and so crumple it.

This perilous and difficult task was entrusted to the Irish Brigade, which comprised the Dublin Fusiliers, the Inniskilling Fusiliers, the Connaught Rangers, and the Imperial Light Infantry, in all about 3,000 men, supported by 2,000 more. Their commander, General Hart, was one of the bravest officers in the army, and it was generally felt that such a leader and such troops could carry the business through if success lay within the scope of human efforts.

The account of the ensuing operation is so tragic and full of mournful interest that I must leave it to another letter.

Hospital Ship 'Maine': 5th March 1900

At half past twelve on the 23rd General Hart ordered his brigade to advance. The battalions, which were sheltering among hastily constructed cover on the reverse slope of the kopje immediately in front of that on which we stood, rose up one by one and formed in rank. They then moved off in single file along the railroad, the Inniskilling Fusiliers leading, the Connaught Rangers, Dublin Fusiliers, and the Imperial Light Infantry following in succession. At the same time the Durham Light Infantry and the 2nd Rifle Brigade began to march to take the place of the assaulting brigade on the advanced kopje.

Wishing to have a nearer view of the attack, I descended the wooded hill, cantered along the railway and, dismounting, climbed the rocky sides of the advanced kopje. On the top, in a little half-circle of stones, I found General Lyttelton, who received me kindly, and together we watched the development of the operation. Nearly a mile of the railway line was visible, and along it the stream of infantry flowed steadily. Thus far, at least, they were not under fire. The low kopjes which were held by the other brigades shielded the movement. A mile away the river and railway turned sharply to the right; the river plunged into a steep gorge, and the railway was lost in a cutting. There was certainly plenty of cover; but just before the cutting was reached the iron bridge across the Onderbrook Spruit had to be crossed, and this was evidently commanded by the enemy's riflemen. Beyond the railway and the moving trickle of men the brown dark face of Inniskilling Hill, crowned with sangars and entrenchments, rose up gloomy and, as yet, silent.

The head of the column reached the exposed ground, and the soldiers began to walk across it. Then at once above the average fusillade and cannonade rose the extraordinary rattling roll of Mauser musketry in great volume. I turned my telescope on the Dutch defences. All along the rim of the trenches, clear cut and jet black against the sky, stood a crowded line of slouch-hatted men, visible as far as their shoulders, and wielding what looked like thin sticks.

Far below by the red ironwork of the railway bridge – 2,000 yards, at least, from the trenches – the infantry were still moving, but no longer slowly – they were running for their lives. Man after man emerged from the sheltered railroad, which ran like a covered way across the enemy's front, into the open and the driving hail of bullets, ran the gauntlet and dropped down the embankment on the further side of the bridge into safety again. The range was great, but a good many soldiers were hit and lay scattered about the ironwork of the bridge. But the advancing infantry never hesitated for a moment, and continued to scamper across the dangerous ground, paying their toll accordingly. More than sixty men were shot in this short space.

The enemy's shells, which occasionally burst on the advanced kopje, and a whistle of stray bullets from the left, advised us to change our position, and we moved a little further down the slope towards the river. Here the bridge was no longer visible. I looked towards the hilltop, whence the roar of musketry was ceaselessly proceeding.

Meanwhile the afternoon had been passing. The infantry had filed steadily across the front, and the two leading battalions had already accumulated on the eastern spurs of Inniskilling Hill. At four o'clock General Hart ordered the attack, and the troops forthwith began to climb the slopes. The broken ground delayed their progress, and it was nearly sunset by the time they had reached the furthest position which could be gained under cover. The Boer entrenchments were about 400 yards away. The *arête* by which the Inniskillings had advanced was bare, and swept by a dreadful frontal fire from the works on the summit and a still more terrible flanking fire from the other hills. It was so narrow that, though only four companies were arranged in the firing line, there was scarcely room for two to deploy. There was not, however, the slightest hesitation, and as we watched with straining eyes we could see the leading companies rise up together and run swiftly forward on the enemy's works with inspiring dash and enthusiasm.

But if the attack was superb, the defence was magnificent; nor could the devoted heroism of the Irish soldiers surpass the stout endurance of the Dutch. The artillery redoubled their efforts. The whole summit of the hill was alive with shell. Shrapnel flashed into being above the crests, and the ground sprang up into dust whipped by the showers of bullets and splinters. Again and again whole sections of the entrenchments vanished in an awful uprush of black earth and smoke. The cannonade grew to a tremendous thundering hum. But the musketry was never subdued for an instant. Amid the smoke and the dust the slouch hats could still be seen. The Dutch, firm and undaunted, stood to their parapets and plied their rifles with deadly effect.

The terrible power of the Mauser rifle was displayed. As the charging companies met the storm of bullets they were swept away. Officers and men fell by scores on the narrow ridge. Though assailed in front and flank by the hideous whispering Death, the survivors hurried obstinately onward, until their own artillery were forced to cease firing, and it seemed that, in spite of bullets, flesh and blood would prevail. But at the last supreme moment the weakness of the attack was shown. The Inniskillings were too few to effect their purpose; and when the Boers saw that the attack had withered they shot all the straighter, and several of the boldest leapt out from their trenches and, running forward to meet the soldiers, discharged their magazines at the closest range. It was a frantic scene of blood and fury.

Thus confronted, the Irish perished rather than retire. A few men indeed ran back down the slope to the nearest cover, and there savagely turned to bay, but the greater part of the front line was shot down. Other companies, some from the Connaught Rangers, some from the Dublin Fusiliers, advanced to renew – it was already too late to support – the attack, and as the light faded another fierce and bloody assault was delivered and was repulsed. Yet the Irish soldiers would not leave the hill, and, persuaded at length that they could not advance further, they lay down on the ground they had won, and began to build walls and shelters, from behind which they opened a revengeful fire on the exulting Boers. In the two attacks both colonels, three majors, twenty officers, and 600 men had fallen out of an engaged force of scarcely 1,200. Then darkness pulled down the curtain, and the tragedy came to an end for the day.

As soon as it was daylight I rode out with Captain Brooke to learn what had happened in the night. We knew that the hill had not been carried before dusk, but hoped, since the combatants were so close together, that in the darkness the bayonet would have settled the matter.

We had just reached the hollow behind the advanced kopje from which I had watched the attack on the previous evening, when suddenly a shrapnel shell burst in the air above our heads with a sharp, startling bang. The hollow and slope of the hill were crowded with infantry battalions lying down in quarter column. The bullets and splinters of the shell smote the ground on all sides. We were both mounted and in the centre of the cone of dispersion. I was immediately conscious that nothing had happened to me, though the dust around my horse was flicked up, and I concluded that everyone had enjoyed equally good fortune. Indeed, I turned to Brooke, and was about to elaborate my theory that shrapnel is comparatively harmless, when I saw some stir and turmoil and no less than eight men were picked up killed or wounded by this explosion. I have only once before seen in war such a successful shell, and on that occasion I was studying the effect from the other side.

My respect for modern artillery was mightily increased by this example of its power. Two more shells followed in quick succession. The first struck down four men, and broke in two the leg of an infantry officer's charger, so that the poor beast galloped about in a circle, preventing his rider from dismounting for some time; the second shore along the Howitzer Battery, killing one soldier and wounding an officer, five soldiers, and three horses. All this occurred in a space of about two minutes, and the three shells between them accounted for nineteen men and four horses.

We climbed on to the top of the kopje, which was sprinkled with staff officers and others. Inniskilling Hill was still crowned with the enemy. Its slopes were scored with numerous brown lines, the stone walls built by the attacking brigade during the night, and behind these the telescope showed the infantry clustering thickly. The Boers on their part had made some new trenches in advance of those on the crest of the hill, so that the opposing firing lines were scarcely 300 yards apart, which meant that everyone in them must lie still or run grave risks. Thus they remained all day, firing at each other continually, while on the bare ground between them the dead and wounded lay thickly scattered, the dead mixed with the living, the wounded untended, without dressings, food, or water, and harassed by the fire from both sides and from our artillery. It was a very painful thing to watch these poor fellows moving about feebly and trying to wriggle themselves into some position of safety.

During the 24th there was heavy firing on both sides, but no movement of infantry on either.

Sir Redvers Buller now saw that his plan of filing his army round the angle of the river and across the enemy's front would, in any case, be very costly, and was perhaps impossible. He, therefore, determined to get back to the Hlangwane plateau, and try the extreme left of the enemy's position. He had the strategic advantage of being on interior lines, and was consequently able to move his troops with great ease from one flank to the other. His new plan was to pass the brigades of his left and centre across the pontoon bridge from the left to the right, so that Hart, who was formerly the extreme right, would now become almost the extreme left, and, having thus extended his right arm, to cross the river where it flowed east and west, and make a still wider swoop on the enemy's flank.

The first thing to do was to move the heavy guns, and this, with certain redistributions of the cavalry, occupied the whole day. A long-range four-gun naval battery was established on the western slopes of the Monte Cristo ridge. Another similar battery was placed on the spurs of Hlangwane. The 4·7-in. naval guns and the 5-in. fortress battery were brought into line in the centre of the Hlangwane plateau. All this was good. The big guns were getting back on to the big hills.

The battalions, who were attacked frontally, lay down with fixed bayonets and prayed that the Boers might be encouraged by their silence to make an assault. The latter, however, kept their distance. The firing on both sides was unaimed, and very little harm was done. No one, however, had much sleep. The condition of the wounded, still lying sore and thirsty on the bare hillside, was now so shocking that Sir Redvers Buller was forced, much against his inclination, at dawn on the 25th, to send in a flag of truce to the Boer commander and ask for an armistice. This the Boers formally refused, but agreed that if we would not fire on their positions during the day they would not prevent our bearer companies from removing the wounded and burying the dead.

The arrangement worked well; the enemy were polite to our medical officers, and by noon all the wounded had been brought down and the dead buried. The neglect and exposure for forty-eight hours had much aggravated the case of the former, and the bodies of the dead, swollen, blackened, and torn by the terrible wounds of the expansive bullets, now so generally used by the enemy, were ugly things to see.

At dawn on the 26th the artillery reopened on both sides, and during the day a constant bombardment was maintained, in which we, having more guns, fired the greater number of shells, and the Dutch, having larger targets, hit a greater number of men. The losses were not, however, severe.

Considerable movements of troops were made. Colenso and the kopjes about Fort Wylie were converted into a bridge-head, garrisoned by Talbot Coke's Brigade. A new line of communications was opened around the foot of Hlangwane. A pontoon bridge was arranged ready to be thrown below the falls of the river, not far from the still intact Boer bridge. Hildyard's English Brigade stood fast on the advanced low kopjes forming the extreme left of the line. Hart's command held its position about the slopes of Inniskilling Hill and in the gorge of the river. Barton's Fusilier Brigade, Kitchener's Lancashire Brigade, and the two remaining battalions of Norcott's (formerly

Lyttelton's) Brigade crossed the old bridge to the Hlangwane plateau.

All was now ready for the final attack on the left of the Pieters position, and it was generally recognised throughout the army that the fate of Ladysmith must depend on the success of the next day's operations.

Since 11th January, a period of more than six weeks, the troops had been continuously fighting and bivouacking. The peaceful intervals of a few days had merely been in order to replenish stores and ammunition. During this time the only reinforcements to reach the army had been a few drafts, a cavalry regiment, a horse battery, and some heavy guns. Exclusive of the 1,100 casualties suffered at Colenso in December, the force, rarely more than 20,000 men, had had over 3,500 killed and wounded, had never had a single gleam of success, and had hardly seen the enemy who hit them so hard.

Colenso, Spion Kop, Vaal Krantz, and the third day at Pieters were not inspiring memories, and it was felt that the attempt to be made on the morrow would be the last effort the Natal Field Army would be asked or allowed to make.

Commandant's Office, Durban: 6th March 1900

Day broke behind a cloudy sky, and the bang of an early gun reminded us that a great business was on hand. We arose – all had slept in their boots and had no need to dress – drank some coffee and rejoiced that the day promised to be cool. It would help the infantry, and on the infantry all depended.

At half past six Dundonald's Brigade marched towards the northern end of the Hlangwane plateau, where we were to take up positions on the spurs of Monte Cristo and along the bluffs of the south bank of the Tugela, from which we might assist the infantry attack, and particularly the attack of Barton's Brigade, by long-range rifle fire, and by our Colt battery and Maxim guns.

The position which had been assigned to the South African Light Horse afforded a close yet extensive view of the whole scene. Deep in its gorge below our feet flowed the Tugela, with the new pontoon bridge visible to the left, just below a fine waterfall. Behind us, on a rounded spur of Monte Cristo, one of the long-range batteries was firing away busily. Before us, across the river, there rose from the water's edge first a yellow strip of sandy foreshore, then steep, scrub-covered banks, and then smooth, brown slopes, terminating in the three hills which were to be successively assaulted, and which were sur-mounted by the dark lines of the Boer forts and trenches.

It was like a stage scene viewed from the dress circle. Moreover, we were very comfortable. There were large convenient rocks to sit behind in case of bullets, or to rest a telescope on, and the small trees which sparsely covered the ridge gave a partial shade from the sun. Opposite our front a considerable valley, thickly wooded, ran back from the river, and it was our easy and pleasant task to 'fan' this, as an American officer would say, by scattering a ceaseless shower of rifle and machine-gun bullets throughout its length. Under these satisfactory circumstances I watched the battle.

It developed with the deliberation which characterises all our manœuvres. The guns gradually worked themselves into a state of excitement, and what with our musketry and the machine-guns puffing like steam engines, we soon had a capital loud noise, which I think is a most invigorating element in an attack.

The spectacle of 2,000 men firing for half a day at nothing may pro-voke the comment 'shocking waste of ammunition'. Very likely there was waste. But all war is waste, and cartridges are the cheapest item in the bill. At any rate, we made it too hot for the 'snipers' to show their heads, which was certainly worth fifty men to the assaulting brigades.

While we were thus occupied the infantry of Barton's Brigade were marching across the pontoon bridge, turning to their right and filing along the sandy foreshore. The plan of attack to which Sir Redvers Buller had finally committed himself was as follows: Hildyard's Brigade to hold its position on the low kopjes; Barton's Brigade to cross the new pontoon bridge opposite to the left of the enemy's position, and assault the hill called Barton's Hill. Next Kitchener's Brigade was to cross, covered by Barton's fire, to assault the centre hill marked '2', and called Railway Hill. Lastly, Norcott's two untouched battalions were to join the rest of their brigade, and, supported by General Hart's Brigade, attack Inniskilling Hill.

In brief, we were to stretch out our right arm, reach round the enemy's flank, and pivoting on Hildyard's Brigade crumple him from (his) left to right. It was the same plan as before, only that we now had our right hand on the Monte Cristo ridge, from which commanding position our long-range guns could enfilade and even take in reverse some of the enemy's trenches.

The leading brigade was across the river by nine o'clock, and by ten had reached its position ready for attacking at the foot of Barton's Hill. The advance began forthwith and the figures of the infantry could be seen swarming up the steep slopes of the river gorge. The Boers did very little to stop the attack. They knew their weakness. One side of Barton's Hill was swept and commanded by the guns on Monte Cristo. The other side, at the back of which was the donga we were 'fanning', was raked by the heavy artillery on the Hlangwane spur and by the field batteries arranged along the south side of the river. Observe the influence of the Monte Cristo ridge! It made Barton's Hill untenable by the Boer; he could not hold this all-important feature once he had lost the Monte Cristo ridge.

As soon as Barton had occupied this hill (which proved, moreover, far more extensive than had been expected), he was heavily attacked by rifle fire from its under features and from a network of dongas to the eastward, and as the artillery were busy preparing the attack on Railway Hill, the brigade, particularly the Scots and Irish Fusiliers, soon became severely engaged and suffered grievous loss.

The fact that Barton's Hill was in our possession made the Boers on Railway and Inniskilling Hills very insecure. A powerful infantry force was holding the left of their position, and though it was itself being actively attacked on the eastern face, it could spare at least a battalion to assail their flank and threaten their rear. Covered by this flanking fire, by the long-range musketry, and by a tremendous bombardment, in which every gun, from the lumbering 5-in. siege guns to the little 9-pounder mountain battery, joined, the main attack was now launched. It proceeded simultaneously against Railway Hill, Inniskilling Hill, and the neck between them, but as the general line was placed obliquely across the Boer front, the attack fell first on Railway Hill and the neck.

The right battalions drew up in many long lines on the sides of the river gorge. Then men began gradually to work their way upwards, until all the dead patches of ground and every scrap of cover sheltered a fierce little group. Behind the railway embankment, among the rocks, in the scrub, in a cutting, near a ruined house, clusters of men eagerly awaited the decisive moment: and all this time more than seventy guns concentrated their fire on the entrenchments. Then, suddenly, shortly after four o'clock, all further attempts at advancing under cover were abandoned, and the Lancashire Brigade marched proudly into the open ground and on the enemy's works. The Mauser musketry burst forth at once, and the bullets, humming through the assaulting waves of infantry, reached us on our hillside and wounded a trooper in spite of the distance. But, bullets or no bullets, we could not take our eyes off the scene.

The Lancashire Brigade advanced on a wide front. Norcott's Riflemen were already prolonging their line to the right. The Boer fire was dispersed along the whole front of attack, instead of converging on one narrow column. The assault was going to succeed. We stood up on our rocks. Bayonets began to glitter on the distant slope. The moving lines increased their pace. The heads of the Boers bobbing up and down in their trenches grew fewer and fewer. They knew the tide was running too strongly. Then the sky line of Railway Hill bristled with men, who dropped on their knees forthwith and fired in particular haste at something that was running away down the other side. There was the sound of cheering. Railway Hill was ours. I looked to the left.

The neck between the hills was lined with trenches. The South Lancashire Regiment had halted, pinned to the ground by the Boer fire. Were they going to lose the day for us when it was already won? The question was soon answered. In an instant there appeared on the left of the Boer trench a dozen – only a dozen – violent forms rushing forward. A small party had worked their way to the flank, and were at close quarters with cold steel. And then – by contrast to their former courage – the valiant burghers fled in all directions, and others held out their rifles and bandoliers and begged for mercy, so that by the time the whole attack had charged forward into the trenches there was a nice string of thirty-two prisoners winding down the hill: at which token of certain victory we shouted loudly.

Inniskilling Hill alone remained, and that was almost in our hands. Its slopes were on three sides alive with the active figures of the Light Brigade, and the bayonets sparkled. The hill ran into a peak. Many of the trenches were already deserted, but the stone breastwork at the summit still contained defenders. There, painted against the evening sky, were the slouch hats and moving rifles. Shell after shell exploded among them: overhead, in their faces, in the trench itself, behind them, before them, around them. Showers of rock and splinters fell on all sides.

Yet they held their ground. But the Infantry were drawing very near. At last the Dutchmen fled. One, a huge fellow in a brown jersey, tarried to spring on the parapet and empty his magazine once more into the approaching ranks, and while he did so a 50 lb. lyddite shell burst, as it seemed, in the midst of him, and the last defender of Inniskilling Hill vanished.

Forthwith came orders for the Cavalry to cross the river, and we mounted in high expectation, knowing that behind the captured hill lay an open plain stretching almost to the foot of Bulwana. We galloped swiftly down to the pontoon bridge, and were about to pass over it, when the General-in-Chief met us. The Boer artillery were firing heavily to cover the retreat of their riflemen. He would not allow us to go across that night lest we should lose heavily in horses. So the brigade returned disappointed to its former position, watered horses, and selected a bivouac. I was sent to warn the Naval Battery that a heavy counter-stroke would probably be made on the right of Barton's Brigade during the night.

On the way I passed through Sir Charles Warren's camp, and there found a gang of prisoners – forty-eight of them – all in a row, almost the same number that the Boers had taken in the armoured train. Looking at these very ordinary people, who might, from their appearance, have been a knot of loafers round a public-house, it was difficult to understand what qualities made them such a terrible foe.

We got neither food nor blankets that night, and slept in our waterproofs on the ground; but we had at last that which was better than feast or couch, for which we had hungered and longed through many weary weeks – Victory.

Commandant's Office, Durban: 9th March 1900

The successful action of the 27th had given Sir Redvers Buller possession of the whole of the left and centre of the Pieters position, and in consequence of these large sections of their entrenchments having fallen into British hands, the Boers evacuated the remainder and retreated westward on to the high hills and northward towards Bulwana Mountain.

But we were not prepared for the complete results that followed the operations of the 27th. Neither the General nor his army expected to enter Ladysmith without another action. Before us a smooth plain, apparently unobstructed, ran to the foot of Bulwana, but from this forbidding eminence a line of ridges and kopjes was drawn to the high hills of Doornkloof, and seemed to interpose another serious barrier. It was true that this last position was within range, or almost within range, of Sir George White's guns, so that its defenders might be caught between two fires, but we knew, and thought the Boers knew, that the Ladysmith garrison was too feeble from want of food and other privations to count for very much. So Sir Redvers Buller, facing the least satisfactory assumption, determined to rest his army on the 28th, and attack Bulwana Hill on 1st March.

He accordingly sent a message by heliograph into Ladysmith to say that he had beaten the enemy thoroughly, and was sending on his cavalry to reconnoitre. Ladysmith had informed herself, however, of the state of the game. Captain Tilney, from his balloon, observed all that passed in the enemy's lines on the morning of the 28th. At first, when he heard no artillery fire, he was depressed, and feared lest the relieving army had retreated again. Then, as it became day, he was sure that this was not so, for the infantry in crowds were occupying the Boer position, and the mounted patrols pricked forward into the plain. Presently he saw the Boers rounding up their cattle and driving them off to the north. Next they caught and began to saddle their horses. The great white tilted wagons of the various laagers filed along the road around the eastern end of Bulwana. Lastly, up went a pair of shears over 'Long Tom',[1] and at this he descended to the earth with the good news that the enemy were off at last.

Meanwhile, since there was no fire from the enemy's side, our cavalry and artillery were rapidly and safely crossing the river.

As we filed on to the floating roadway we were amused to see a large fingerpost at the entrance, on which the engineers had neatly painted, 'To Ladysmith'. The brigade passed over the neck between Railway and Inniskilling Hills, and we massed in a suitable place on the descending slopes beyond. Ladysmith was still hidden by the remaining ridges, but we thought that somehow we might have a look at it before night.

Under Bulwana the wagons of the Boers and several hundred horsemen could be seen hurrying away. Patrols were sent out in all directions, and while this reconnaissance was going on I climbed up Inniskilling Hill to examine the trenches.

The trench was cut deep in the ground, and, unlike our trenches, there was scarcely any parapet. A few great stones had been laid in front, but evidently the Boer believed in getting well into the ground. The bottom was knee deep in cartridge cases, and every few yards there was an enormous heap of Mauser ammunition, thousands of rounds, all fastened neatly, five at a time, in clips. A large proportion were covered with bright green slime, which the soldiers declared was poison, but which on analysis may prove to be wax, used to preserve the bullet.

The Boers, however, were not so guiltless of other charges. A field officer of the East Surreys, recognising me, came up and showed me an expansive bullet of a particularly cruel pattern. The tip had been cut off, exposing the soft core, and four slits were scored down the side. Whole boxes of this ammunition had been found. An officer who had been making calculations told me that the proportion of illegal bullets was nearly one in five. I should not myself have thought it was so large, but certainly the improper bullets were very numerous. I have a specimen of this particular kind by me as I write, and I am informed by people who shoot big game that it is the most severe bullet of its kind yet invented. Five other sorts have been collected by the medical officers, who have also tried to classify the wounds they respectively produce.

[1] The famous Boer cannon which shelled Ladysmith.

I have tried to do justice to the patriotic virtues of the Boers, and it is now necessary to observe that the character of these people reveals, in stress, a dark and spiteful underside. A man – I use the word in its fullest sense – does not wish to lacerate his foe, however earnestly he may desire his life.

The popping of musketry made me hasten to rejoin my regiment. The squadron of mounted infantry had reached Pieters Railway Station, only to be heavily fired on from a low hill to the westward; and they now came scampering back with half a dozen riderless horses. Happily, the riders mostly arrived on foot after a few minutes. But it was evidently necessary to push forward very carefully.

In a little while – to revert to the narrative – the horse artillery battery came up, and the offending hill was conscientiously shelled for an hour. Then the patrols crept forward again, but progress was necessarily slow. We were still six miles from Ladysmith at three o'clock.

At this hour the Boer ambulances had been invited to come for such of their wounded as could be moved, for since the enemy returned our wounded from Spion Kop we have followed the practice of sending back theirs on all occasions should they prefer it.

Anxious to find out the impression produced on the Boers by the late actions, I hastened to meet the ambulances, which, preceded by three horsemen carrying a large white flag, were now coming from the direction of Bulwana. Their leader was a fine old fellow of the genuine veldt Boer type. He spoke English fluently, and we were soon in conversation.

Cronje's surrender had been officially announced to us on the previous day, and I inquired whether he had heard of it. He replied that he knew Cronje was in difficulties, but understood he had managed to escape with his army. As for the surrender, it might be true or it might be false. 'We are told so many lies that we believe nothing.'

When I rejoined the South African Light Horse the Irregular Brigade had begun to advance again. Major Gough's Composite Regiment had scouted the distant ridge and found it unoccupied. Now Dundonald moved his whole command thither, and with his staff climbed to the top. But to our disappointment Ladysmith was not to be seen. Two or three other ridges hung like curtains before us. The afternoon had passed, and it was already after six o'clock. The Boer artillery was still firing, and it seemed rash to attempt to reconnoitre further when the ground was broken and the light fading.

The order was given to retire and the movement had actually begun when a messenger came back from Gough with the news that the last ridge between us and the town was unoccupied by the enemy, that he could see Ladysmith, and that there was, for the moment, a clear run in. Dundonald immediately determined to go on himself into the town with the two squadrons who were scouting in front, and to send the rest of the brigade back to camp. He invited me to accompany him, and without delay we started at a gallop.

Never shall I forget that ride. The evening was deliciously cool. My horse was strong and fresh, for I had changed him at midday. The ground was rough with many stones, but we cared little for that. Beyond the next ridge, or the rise beyond that, or around the corner of the hill, was Ladysmith – the goal of all our hopes and ambitions during weeks of almost ceaseless fighting. We were going to be inside the town within an hour. The excitement of the moment was increased by the exhilaration of the gallop. Onward wildly, recklessly, up and down hill, over the boulders, through the scrub. We turned the shoulder of a hill, and there before us lay the tin houses and dark trees we had come so far to see and save.

The British guns on Caesar's Camp were firing steadily in spite of the twilight. What was happening? Never mind, we were nearly through the dangerous ground. Now we were all on the flat. Brigadier, staff, and troops let their horses go. We raced through the thorn bushes by Intombi Spruit.

Suddenly there was a challenge. 'Halt, who goes there?' 'The Lady-smith Relief Column', and thereat from out of trenches and rifle pits artfully concealed in the scrub a score of tattered men came running, cheering feebly, and some were crying. In the half light they looked ghastly pale and thin. A poor, white-faced officer waved his helmet to and fro, and laughed foolishly, and the tall, strong colonial horsemen, standing up in their stirrups, raised a loud resounding cheer, for then we knew we had reached the Ladysmith picket line.

Durban: 10th March 1900

Since the road by which Dundonald's squadrons had entered the town was never again closed by the enemy, the siege of Ladysmith may be said to have ended on the last day of February.

In the whole series of operations for the relief of Ladysmith the losses amounted to 300 officers and more than 5,000 men, out of a total engaged force of about 23,000, a proportion of rather more than twenty per cent. Nor had this loss been inflicted in a single day's victorious battle, but was spread over twenty-five days of general action in a period of ten weeks; and until the last week no decided success had cheered the troops.

On 3rd March the relieving army made its triumphal entry into Ladysmith, and passing through the town camped on the plain beyond. The scene was solemn and stirring. The streets were lined with the brave defenders, looking very smart and clean in their best clothes, but pale, thin, and wasp-waisted – their belts several holes tighter than was satisfactory.

Before the little Town Hall, the tower of which, sorely battered, yet unyielding, seemed to symbolise the spirit of the garrison, Sir George White and his staff sat on their skeleton horses. Opposite to them were drawn up the pipers of the Gordon Highlanders. The townsfolk, hollow-eyed but jubilant, crowded the pavement and the windows of the houses. Everyone who could find a flag had hung it out.

At eleven o'clock precisely the relieving army began to march into the town. First of all rode Sir Redvers Buller with his headquarters staff and an escort of the Royal Dragoons. The infantry and artillery followed by brigades, but in front of all, as a special recognition of their devoted valour, marched the Dublin Fusiliers, few, but proud.

Many of the soldiers, remembering their emerald island, had fastened sprigs of green to their helmets, and all marched with a swing that was wonderful to watch. Their Colonel and their four officers looked as happy as kings are thought to be. As the regiments passed Sir George White, the men recognised their former general, and, disdaining the rules of the service, waved their helmets and rifles, and cheered him with intense enthusiasm. Some even broke from the ranks. Seeing this the Gordon Highlanders began to cheer the Dublins, and after that the noise of cheering was continual, every regiment as it passed giving and receiving fresh ovations.

All through the morning and on into the afternoon the long stream of men and guns flowed through the streets of Ladysmith, and all marvelled to see what manner of men these were – dirty, war-worn, travel-stained, tanned, their uniforms in tatters, their boots falling to pieces, their helmets dinted and broken, but nevertheless magnificent soldiers, striding along, deep-chested and broad-shouldered, with the light of triumph in their eyes and the blood of fighting ancestors in their veins. It was a procession of lions. And presently, when the two battalions of Devons met – both full of honours – and old friends breaking from the ranks gripped each other's hands and shouted, everyone was carried away, and I waved my feathered hat, and cheered and cheered until I could cheer no longer for joy that I had lived to see the day.

On the evening after Buller's victorious army had entered the town I went to see Sir George White, and was so fortunate as to find him alone and disengaged. Sir George White told me how he had reached Natal less than a week before the declaration of war. He found certain arrangements in progress to meet a swiftly approaching emergency, and he had to choose between upsetting all these plans and entirely reconstructing the scheme of defence, or of accepting what was already done as the groundwork of his operations.

Sir Penn Symons, who had been commanding in the Colony, extravagantly underrated the Boer fighting power and laboured to impress his opinions on Sir George White, who, however, took a much more serious view of the situation, and was particularly disturbed at the advanced position of the troops. He wanted to withdraw them and Sir Archibald Hunter, his chief of staff, agreed with him.

They decided to ask Sir Walter Hely-Hutchinson what consequences would in his opinion follow a withdrawal. The Governor declared that 'loyalists' would be disgusted and discouraged; the results as regards the Dutch would be grave, and the effect on the natives, of whom there are some 750,000 in Natal and Zululand, might be disastrous.

On hearing this opinion expressed by a man of the Governor's ability and local knowledge, Sir Archibald Hunter said that it was a question 'of balancing drawbacks', and advised that the troops be retained at Glencoe. So the matter was clinched.

It is, therefore, worth while considering how far the Governor's judgment had been vindicated by events. The whole of the Klip River country rose, and many prominent Natal Dutch farmers joined the enemy. The loyalty of the natives alone exceeded the Governor's anticipations, and their belief in the British power and preference for British rule was found to stand more knocking about than those best able to judge expected. We have reaped a rich reward in this dark season for having consistently pursued a kindly and humane policy towards the Bantu races; and the Boers have paid a heavy penalty for their cruelty and harshness.

On the subject of holding Ladysmith Sir George White was quite clear. 'I never wanted to abandon Ladysmith; I considered it a place of primary importance to hold. It was on Ladysmith that both Republics concentrated their first efforts. Here, where the railways join, the armies of the Free State and the Transvaal were to unite, and the capture of the town was to seal their union.'

Exasperated at unexpected opposition – for they underrated us even more than we underrated them – they sacrificed around Ladysmith their chances of taking Pietermaritzburg and raiding all Natal; and it is moreover incontestable that in their resolve to take the town, on which they had set their hearts, they were provoked into close fighting and so suffered far heavier losses than could otherwise have been inflicted on so elusive an enemy in such broken country.

The General spoke with some bitterness of the attacks which had been made on him in the newspapers. He had always begged that the relieving operations should not be compromised by any hurry on his account, and he said, with earnestness, 'It is not fair to charge me with all the loss of life they have involved.' He concluded by saying, deliberately: 'It may be that I am an obstinate man to say so, but if I had the last five months to live over again I would not do otherwise than I have done.'

And then I came away and thought of the cheers of the relieving troops. Never before had I heard soldiers cheer like that. There was not much doubt about the verdict of the army on Sir George White's conduct of the defence, and it is one which the nation may gracefully accept.

THE STORY OF
IAN HAMILTON'S MARCH

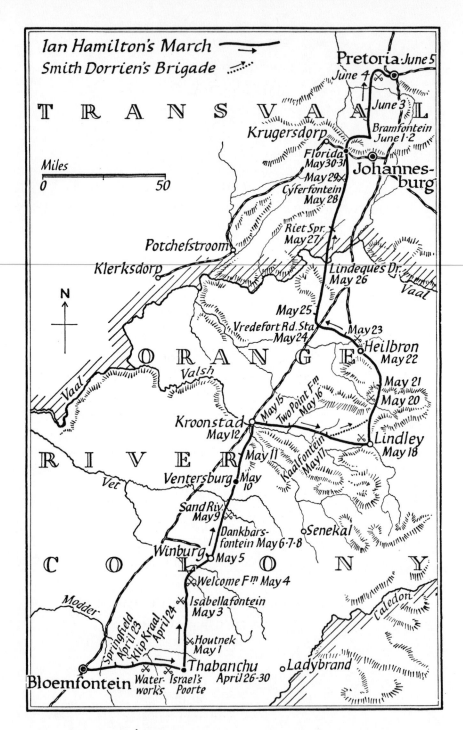

IAN HAMILTON'S ROUTE FROM BLOEMFONTEIN TO PRETORIA

In the train near Pieters, Natal: 31st March

Ladysmith, her garrison and her rescuers, were still recovering, the one from the effects of long confinement, the other from over-exertion. The war had rolled northward: the floods of invasion that had threatened to submerge the whole country had abated and re-ceded, so that the Army of Natal might spread itself out to feed and strengthen at its leisure and convenience on the reconquered territory.

Knox's (Ladysmith) Brigade went into camp at Arcadia, five miles west of the town. Howard's (Ladysmith) Brigade retired to the breezy plains south of Colenso. Clery's division – for the gallant Clery, re-covered from his sickness, had displaced the gallant and successful Lyttelton – moved north and encamped beyond Elands Laagte along the banks of Sunday's River. Hunter's division was disposed with one brigade at Elands Laagte and one at Tinta Inyoni. Warren established himself and his two brigades north of Ladysmith, along the railway line to the Orange Free State. Brocklehurst, with the remnants of what had once been almost a Cavalry Division, and now could scarcely mount three squadrons, occupied a neighbouring plain, sending his regiments one by one to be re-horsed; and around all this great army, resting after its labours and preparing for fresh efforts, the cavalry brigades of Dundonald and Burn-Murdoch drew an immense curtain of pickets and patrols which extended from Acton Homes in the east, through Bester's Station right round to Wessels Nek and further still, and which enabled the protected soldiers within to close their eyes by night and stretch their legs by day.

Meanwhile, the burghers had all retreated to the Drakensberg and the Biggarsberg and their scattered line stretched in a vast crescent even around our widely extended front from the Tintwa Pass, through Waschbank to Pomeroy.

After the relief of Ladysmith four courses offered themselves to Sir Redvers Buller. To stand strictly on the defensive in Natal and to send Lord Roberts every man and gun who could be spared; to break into the Free State by forcing Van Reenen's Pass or the Tintwa;

to attack the 12,000 Boers in the Biggarsberg, clear Natal, and invade the Transvaal through the Vryheid district; and, lastly, to unite and reorganise and co-operate with Lord Roberts's main advance either by striking west or north.

Which course would be adopted? I made inquiries. Staff officers, bland and inscrutable – it is wonderful how well men can keep secrets they have not been told – continued to smile and smile. It was necessary to go to more humble sources for truth, and after diligent search I learned from a railway porter, or somebody like that, that all attempts to repair the bridge across the Sunday's River had been postponed indefinitely. This, on further inquiry, proved to be true.

Now, what does this mean? It means, I take it, that no direct advance against the Biggarsberg is intended for some time; and as the idea of reducing the Natal Army to reinforce the Cape Colony forces has been definitely abandoned the western line of advance suggests itself.

It would be absurd to force Van Reenen's Pass with heavy loss of life, when by waiting until the main army has reached, let us say, Kroonstad, we could walk through without opposition; so that it looks very likely that the Natal troops will do nothing until Lord Roberts's advance is more developed, and that then they will enter the Free State and operate in conjunction with him. At any rate there will be a long delay.

Therefore, I said to myself, I will go to Bloemfontein, see all that may be seen there and on the way, and rejoin the Natal Army when it comes through the passes.

I left the camp of Dundonald's Brigade early in the morning of the 29th of March, and riding through Ladysmith, reached the railway station and caught the 10 a.m. down train.

The train started across the well-known ground, and how fast and easily it ran. Already we were bounding through the scrub in which a month before Dundonald's leading squadrons, galloping in with beating hearts, had met the hungry picket line.

Intombi Spruit hospital camp was reached in a quarter of an hour. Hospital camp no longer, thank goodness! Two days before I left the town the last of the 2,500 sick had been moved down to the great hospital and convalescent camps at Mooi River and Highlands.

We sped swiftly across the plain of Pieters, and I remembered how

I had toiled across it, some five months before, a miserable captive, casting longing eyes at the Ladysmith balloon, and vigilantly guarded by the Boer mounted escort. Then the train ran into the deep ravine between Barton's Hill and Railway Hill, the ravine the cavalry had 'fanned' on the day of the battle, and, increasing its pace as we descended towards the Tugela, carried us along the whole front of the Boer position. Signs of the fighting appeared on every side. Biscuit tins flashed brightly on the hillside like heliographs. In places the slopes were honeycombed with little stone walls and traverses, masking the sheltering refuges of the infantry battalions during the week they had lain in the sun-blaze exposed to the cross fire of gun and rifle. White wooden crosses gleamed here and there among the thorn bushes. The dark lines of the Boer trenches crowned the hills. The train swept by – and that was all.

I knew every slope, every hillock and accident of ground, as one knows men and women in the world. Here was good cover. There was a dangerous space. Here it was wise to stoop, and there to run. Behind that steep kopje a man might scorn the shrapnel. Those rocks gave sure protection from the flanking rifle fire. Only a month ago how much these things had meant.

The train steamed cautiously over the temporary wooden bridge at Colenso and ran into the open country beyond. On we hurried past the green slope where poor Long's artillery had been shot to bits, past Gun Hill, whence the great naval guns had fired so often, through Chieveley Camp, or rather through the site of Chieveley Camp, past the wreck of the armoured train – still lying where we had dragged it with such labour and peril, just clear of the line – through Frere and Estcourt, and so, after seven hours' journey, we came to Pietermaritzburg.

After waiting in Pietermaritzburg long enough only to dine, I proceeded by the night train to Durban, and was here so fortunate as to find a Union boat, the *Guelph*, leaving almost immediately for East London.

Bethany: 13th April

If you go to sleep when the train leaves East London, you should wake, all being well, to find yourself at Queenstown.

Nothing in the town impresses the traveller, but at the dining-room of the railway station there is a very little boy, about twelve years old, who, unaided, manages to serve, with extraordinary despatch and a grand air, a whole score of passengers during the brief interval allowed for refreshments.

Five months earlier I had passed along this line, hoping to get into Ladysmith before the door was shut, and had been struck by this busy child. Much had happened in the meantime, not so far from where he lived. But here he was still – the war had not interfered with him, Queenstown was beyond the limit.

At Sterkstroom a line of empty trenches, the Red Cross flag over a hospital, and an extension to the cemetery enclosure showed that we had crossed the line between peace and war. Passing through Molteno the train reached Stormberg.

At Stormberg I changed my mind or, rather – for it comes to the same thing and sounds better – I made it up.

I heard that no immediate advance from Bloemfontein was likely or even possible for a fortnight. Therefore, I said, I will go to Capetown, and shelter for a week at 'The Helot's Rest'.

So to Capetown I went accordingly – seven hundred miles in forty-eight hours of bad trains over sections of the line only newly reopened. Capetown at this present time is not an edifying place. It is simply a centre of intrigue, scandal, falsehood, and rumour.

The visitor stays at the Mount Nelson Hotel, if he can be so fortunate as to secure a room. At this establishment he finds all the luxuries of a first-class European hotel without the resulting comfort. There is a good dinner, but it is cold before it reaches him; there is a spacious dining-room, but it is overcrowded; there are clean European waiters, but they are few and far between.

The whole town was overrun with amateur strategists and gossiping women. There were more colonels to the acre than in any place outside the United States, and if the social aspect was unattractive, the political was scarcely more pleasing.

Party feeling ran high. Some of the British section, those tremendous patriots who demonstrate but do not fight, had just distinguished themselves by mobbing Mr Schreiner in the streets.

The Dutch section, some of them the men who, risking nothing themselves, had urged the Republics to their ruin, all of whom had smiled and rubbed their hands at the British reverses, sat silent in public, but kept a strict watch on incoming steamers for members of Parliament and others of more influence than guile, and whispered honeyed assurances of their devotion to the Empire, coupled with all sorts of suggestions about the settlement.

Let no one stay long in Capetown now who would carry away a true impression of the South Africans. There is too much shoddy worn there at present.

Only at Government House did I find the Man of No Illusions,[1] the anxious but unwearied Pro-consul, understanding the faults and the virtues of both sides, measuring the balance of rights and wrongs, and determined – more determined than ever – to use his knowledge and his power to strengthen the Imperial ties.

The spell of the great movements impending in the Free State began to catch hold of me before I had travelled far on the line towards Bloemfontein. The one passenger train in the day stopped at Bethany. I got out. To go on was to reach Bloemfontein at midnight. Better, then, to sleep here and proceed at dawn.

'Are there many troops here?' I asked. They replied, 'The whole of the Third Division.' 'Who commands?' 'Gatacre.' That decided me.

I knew the General slightly, having made his acquaintance up the Nile in pleasant circumstances, for no one was allowed to pass his mess hungry or thirsty. I was very anxious to see him and hear all about Stormberg and the rest of the heavy struggle along the eastern line of rail. I found him in a tin house close to the station. He received me kindly, and we had a long talk.

I thought him greatly altered from the dashing, energetic man I had known up the river, or had heard about on the frontier or in plague-stricken Bombay. Four months of anxiety and abuse had left

[1] Lord Milner.

their mark on him. The weary task of keeping things going with utterly insufficient resources, and in the face of an adroit and powerful enemy in a country where every advantage lay with the Boer, had bowed that iron frame and tired the strange energy which had made him so remarkable among soldiers. But when he thought of the future his face brightened. The dark days were over. He had his whole division at last. Moreover, there was prospect of immediate action. So I left him, for it was growing late. Early next morning he was dismissed from his command and ordered to England, broken, ruined, and disgraced.

I will not for one moment dispute the wisdom or the justice of his removal. In stormy weather one must trust to the man at the helm, and when he is such a man as Lord Roberts it is not a very hard thing to do. But because General Gatacre has been cruelly persecuted in England by people quite ignorant of the difficulties of war in this country, it is perhaps not out of place to write a few words of different tenor.

Gatacre was a man who made his way in the army, not through any influence or favour, but by sheer hard work and good service. Wherever he had served he had left a high record behind him. On the Indian frontier he gained the confidence of so fine a soldier as Sir Bindon Blood, and it was largely to his reputation won in the Chitral Expedition that his subsequent advancement was due. At Bombay in 1897 he was entrusted with the duty of fighting the plague, then first gripping its deadly fingers into the city.

Gatacre's part in the Soudan campaign has been described at length elsewhere. His courage has never been questioned, because the savage critics did not wish to damage their cause by obvious absurdities. If I were to discuss his tactics in the Boer war here I should soon get on to ground which I have forbidden myself. It is sufficient to observe that Gatacre retained the confidence and affection of his soldiers in the most adverse circumstances. When the weary privates struggled back to camp after the disastrous day at Stormberg they were quite clear on one point: 'No one could have got us out but him.' Two days before he was dismissed the Cameron Highlanders passed through Bethany, and the men recognised the impetuous leader of the Atbara charge; and, knowing he had fallen among evil days, cheered him in the chivalry of the common man. The poor General was much moved at this spontaneous greeting.

Exit General Gatacre, and I suppose there are, here and there, notes of triumph. But among them I will strike a note of warning. If the War Office breaks generals not so much for incapacity as for want of success with any frequency, it will not find men to fight for it in brigade and divisional commands. Every man who knows the chances of war feels himself insecure. The initiative which an unsympathetic discipline has already killed, or nearly killed, in younger officers, will wither and die in their superiors. You will have generals as before, but they will not willingly risk the fruits of long years of service in damnable countries and of perils of all kinds. They will look at the enemy's position. They will endeavour to divide responsibility. They will ask for orders or instructions. But they will not fight – if they can possibly help it, and then only on the limited liability principle, which means the shedding of much blood without any result.

Bloemfontein: 16th April

After a decent interval let the curtain rise on a new act. The scene and most of the characters are different, but it is the same play. The town – a town of brick and tin – stands at the apparent edge of a vast plain of withered grass, from whose inhospitable aspect it turns and nestles, as if for protection, round the scrub-covered hills to northward. From among the crowd of one-storied dwelling-houses, more imposing structures, the seats of Government and commerce, rise prominently to catch the eye and impress the mind with the pleasing prospect of wealthier civilisation. The dark hills – their uncertain outline marked at one point by the symmetrical silhouette of a fort – form the background of the picture: Bloemfontein, April 1900.

It is five o'clock in the afternoon. The market-square is crowded with officers and soldiers listening to the band of the Buffs. Every regiment in the service, every Colony in the Empire is represented;

all clad in uniform khaki, but distinguished by an extraordinary variety of badges.

The inhabitants – bearded burghers who have made their peace, townsfolk who never desired to make a quarrel – stand round and watch complacently. After all, there are worse things than to be defeated. Demand is keen, the army is wealthy, and prices are high. Trade has followed hard on the flag which waves from every building; and, whether it be for merchandise or farm produce, the market is buoyant.

The officers congregate about the pretentious building of the club, and here I find acquaintances gathered together from all the sentry beats of the Empire.

The conversation stops abruptly. Everyone looks round. Strolling across the middle of the square, quite alone, was a very small grey-haired gentleman, with extremely broad shoulders and a most un-bending back. He wore a staff cap with a broad red band and a heavy gold-laced peak, brown riding boots, a tightly fastened belt, and no medals, orders, or insignia of any kind. But no one doubted his identity for an instant, and I knew that I was looking at the Queen's greatest subject, the commander who had in the brief space of a month revo-lutionised the fortunes of the war, had turned something like despair into almost inordinate triumph.

Such was the scene on the afternoon of my arrival in Bloemfontein. What of the situation?

By the rapid invasion of their territories, by the staggering blows which they had been dealt at Kimberley, Paardeberg, Poplar Grove, and Driefontein, and by the bad news from Natal, the Boers in the Free State were demoralised. If we could have pressed them unceasingly the whole country would have been conquered to the Vaal River. Encouraged by Lord Roberts's Proclamation, and believing that all resistance in the Southern Republic was at an end, great numbers of Free Staters returned to their homes, took the oath of neutrality, and prepared to accept the inevitable.

But while the army waited, as it was absolutely forced to wait, to get supplies, to get horses – to get thousands of horses – to give the infantry new boots, and all arms a little breathing space, the Boers recovered from their panic, pulled themselves together, and, for the moment, boldly seized the offensive.

Great, though perhaps temporary, were the advantages which they gained. The belief that the war in the Free State was at an end, which had led so many of the burghers to return to their farms, was shared to some extent by the British commander, and loudly proclaimed by his colonial advisers. To protect the farmers who had made their peace the Imperial forces were widely extended. A line was drawn across the Free State from Fourteen Streams, through Boshof, Bloemfontein, and Thabanchu, south of which it was assumed that the country was pacified and conquered.

Meanwhile Olivier and the southern commando, recalled from their operations in the Cape Colony, were making a hurried and, as it seemed, a desperate march to rejoin the main Boer forces. They expected the attack of the same terrible army which had already devoured Cronje; nor was it until they reached Ladybrand and found only Pilcher with a few hundred men snapping at their heels that they realised that the bulk of the British troops were for the moment practically immobile at Bloemfontein. Then they turned.

Pilcher fled warily before them, and fell back on Broadwood's Brigade, near Thabanchu. With renewed courage and strong reinforcements from their friends north of the line of occupation they pressed on. Broadwood was compelled to fall back on the Ninth Division, which was camped west of the waterworks. He made a twenty-mile march at night and laagered in the small hours of the morning, thinking, as most people would think, that pursuit was for the time being shaken off. Morning broke, and with it a Boer cannonade.

I do not intend to be drawn into a detailed description of the action that followed. For many reasons it deserves separate and detailed consideration, chiefly because it shows the Boer at his very best: crafty in war and, above all things, deadly cool. In a word, what happened was this: the shells crashed into the laager. Everyone said, 'Take the blasted wagons out of the shell fire. We will cover their retreat'; which they did most beautifully. The said wagons hurried out of the shell fire only to fall into the frying-pan of an ambuscade. Guns, prisoners, and much material fell into the hands of the Boers. The Ninth Division retreated suddenly – too suddenly, say the army, with other remarks which it is not my business to transcribe – on Bloemfontein, and the force of the storm fell on Gatacre.

Gatacre had a post at Dewetsdorp: three companies of the Royal Irish Rifles, two of Mounted Infantry. So soon as he heard of the retirement of the Ninth Division he sent orders by many routes for his post to fall back too. They fell back accordingly; but at Reddersburg the net closed round them. Let us judge no man harshly or in ignorance. Fighting followed. With a loss of eight killed and thirty-one wounded, the retreating troops surrendered when relief was scarcely five miles away. Everything curled back on to Bloemfontein and the railway line, which it was *vital* to hold. Reinforcements were thrust to the front to meet the emergency: Rundle, with the Eighth Division, was diverted from Kimberley to Springfontein; Hunter, with the Tenth Division (our old friends the Irish and Fusilier Brigades), started from Natal, thus condemning Buller to the strict defensive, and the Boers swept southward.

Now, in accordance with the terms of Lord Roberts's Proclamation, many farmers of the Free State, fighting men of the Boer Army – that is to say, who had thought that all was up: deserters, in other words – had come into the British posts, made their submission, taken the oath, and returned to their farms. The Boers were very angry with these people. What protection could we give them? Some, it is said – it may be a lie – were shot by the enemy. Most of them, from fear or inclination, rejoined their commandos.

The whole of the right-hand bottom corner of the Free State was overrun. Other Boers approached the rebel districts of Cape Colony. The lately penitent rebels stirred, are stirring.

Before Dewetsdorp: 21st April

When the incursion of the Boers into the recently pacified districts became known, the Eighth Division (Rundle) was diverted from Kimberley, whither it was proceeding, and concentrated at Springfontein. The Third Division (Chermside, in supersession of Gatacre) massed at Bethany. Still more troops were needed to guard the line and clear the country.

Sir Redvers Buller was asked whether he could co-operate by forcing Van Reenen's Pass and bringing pressure on the enemy's line of retreat. His position in the centre of the triangle of Natal was, however, an inconvenient one. The strategic advantages possessed by the Boers in this scene of the war have before been noticed. But it may be worth while to explain them again.

The enemy possess the superiority of an enveloping frontier. If Sir Redvers Buller moves west through Van Reenen's Pass to make the diversion required in the Free State, down will come the Boers from the Biggarsberg on his communications and into South Natal. If he moves north to attack the Biggarsberg positions in order to clear Natal he will cut the Boers on his left flank and line.

According to the best information there are 3,000 Boers on the Drakensberg Passes, and 10,000 on the Biggarsberg. Buller, therefore, would have preferred to mask Van Reenen's with the Ladysmith Division (Fourth, Lyttelton), which was getting well and strong again, and move northwards with the Second, Fifth, and Tenth Divisions. He did not consider until northern Natal should be cleared that he could safely move westward. On the other hand, the need in the Free State was urgent, and it was therefore arranged that the Tenth Division (Hunter) should come by sea to East London – one brigade to replace the division diverted from Kimberley, one brigade to Bethulie, and that the rest of the Natal Field Army should remain strictly on the defensive until the situation was materially altered.

Practically, therefore, five brigades of troops were available for the operations in the right-hand bottom corner: Hart, with a brigade of Hunter's division at Bethulie, the Third and Eighth Divisions under Chermside and Rundle at Springfontein and Bethany. Besides these powerful bodies, which were quite independent of the communication troops or the Bloemfontein army, there were 1,400 yeomanry and mounted infantry under General Brabazon, and Brabant's Colonial Brigade, about 2,500 strong.

Such was the situation when I left Bloemfontein on the morning of the 17th. I came by rail to Edenburg, trekked from there in drenching rains, most unusual for this time of year, and, resting for the night at Reddersburg, caught up the marching column in its camp, about eleven miles from Dewetsdorp, on the night of the 19th.

The position of the various troops was then as follows: Rundle, with eight battalions, four batteries, and 1,500 horse at Oorlogs Poort, about twelve miles from Dewetsdorp; Campbell, with two battalions and a battery near Rosendal, marching to join him; the Grenadier Guards double marching through Reddersburg to catch up the main force; Hart, with four battalions in Rouxville; Brabant, with 1,000 horsemen eight miles north of Rouxville; Dalgety, with a garrison of 1,500 men, holding Wepener.

So far as could be learned the enemy had about 7,000 men with twelve guns south of the Bloemfontein–Thabanchu line under Commandants Olivier and De Wet, and with this force, which made up in enterprise and activity what it lacked in numbers or material, they were attempting to blockade and attack Wepener, to bar the road of Rundle's column to Dewetsdorp, and to check Brabant and Hart at Smithfield. Besides proposing this ambitious programme, the Boers sent their patrols riding about the country commandeering all pacified farmers under threats of death.

We had a very pleasant ride from Reddersburg, and it was evening when we rounded the shoulder of a grassy hill and saw the camp of the main British column before us. It lay about the foot of a prominent knoll rising from a broad plain, which was in striking contrast to the mountains of Natal, and seemed to promise ample opportunity to the regular soldier. I presented myself to Sir Leslie Rundle, who received me courteously, and briefly explained the outlines of the situation. We had arrived in the nick of time. The whole force would march at dawn. The scouts had exchanged shots during the day. The Kaffir spies reported that the enemy would fight on the morrow. What could be better? So with much satisfaction we went to bed.

There was a biting chill in the air when the first light of dawn began to grow in the sky. The South African winter was drawing near. But the sun soon rose, and we shivered no longer. The cavalry were early astir, and by half past five all were in motion. I started a little later, but it was not long before I overtook them.

We were moving along in a wide formation, which secured us against all possibilities of surprise, when suddenly I noticed that the scouts far in front were halted.

'Tit-tat, tit-tat': two shots from a high plateau to the right. Shots fired towards you, I must explain, make a double, and those fired away from you a single, report.

We had flushed one of the enemy's outposts. Riding nearer, I could see their figures – seven in all – exposed on the skyline. This showed they were only an outpost, and wished to make us believe they were more. When the Boer is in force he is usually invisible. Still, the position was a strong one, and it is always a possibility worth considering with the Boer that he may foresee your line of thought, and just go one step further, out of contrariness. General Brabazon therefore halted his centre squadrons and detached a turning force of three companies of yeomanry to the right.

We waited, watching the scouts exchange shots with the Boer picket, and watching – for it was a very pretty sight – the yeomanry spread out and gallop away to the flank like a pack of hounds in full cry, each independent, yet the whole simultaneous. In a quarter of an hour they were scrambling up the steep sides of the plateau almost in rear of the obstructive picket, which hurriedly departed while time remained. Then the centre swung forward, and the whole cavalry force advanced again, the greater part of it moving on to the plateau, where a running fight with the Dutch outposts now commenced at long range. After an hour of this sort of thing we were in possession of practically the whole of the plateau, which turned out to be of large extent.

Beyond it, commanding it, essential to it, yet not of it, was a steep rocky kopje. The swift advance and the necessity of pressing the enemy had left the infantry a long way behind. The General felt, however, that this point must be secured. McNeill made a dash for it with the scouts. The yeomanry galloped off to the right again, as if about to surround it, and the Boers allowed themselves to be bounced out of this strong and important position, and scampered away to a smooth green hill a mile in rear. Brabazon made haste to occupy the captured kopje in force, and did so just in time, for as soon as the turning force of yeomanry and a company of mounted infantry approached the green hill, the musketry suddenly grew from an occasional drip into a regular patter, and there was the loud boom of a field gun. We had found the main Boer position, and the cavalry came to a standstill.

We had now to wait for the infantry, and they lagged on the road. The enemy now directed a very sharp fire on the captured kopje. Several soldiers were carried wounded off the top of the hill. Others had to lie where they were struck because it was not possible to move them while the fire was so accurate.

The infantry still lagged on the road, but at about two o'clock Sir Leslie Rundle himself arrived. Rundle considered that the retention of the kopje was of first importance, and Sir Herbert Chermside, his second in command, fully agreed with him. But the infantry of the advanced guard were alone near enough. It was decided to push them on. At this moment a reassuring message arrived from Brabazon engaging that he could hold his own, and hoping the infantry would not be hurried so as to lose their breath.

Everyone was very cheerful after this, and when at last the leading battalion – the Worcester Regiment – marched to the kopje all were able to admire the fine cool way in which they crossed the dangerous ground behind it. When the infantry had relieved the mounted men the latter withdrew to safer positions, and as the evening was drawing on the action came to an end – by mutual consent and by the effective intervention of the British artillery.

Camp before Dewetsdorp: 22nd April

It seems that my fortunes in this land are to be a succession of adventures and escapes, any one of which would suffice for a personal experience of the campaign. I acquit myself of all desire to seek for these. Indeed, I have zealously tried to avoid all danger except what must attend a War Correspondent's precarious existence. But these hazards swoop on me out of a cloudless sky.

However, I will tell the tale of the doings of the army, and what happened to me shall fill its proper place.

The night of the 20th passed quietly, but the Boers were awake with the sunrise and saluted us with discharges of the pom-pom, which, as far as I could see, did no harm to anyone. In the night the Dutchmen had been busy, and the black lines of entrenchments marked the hillsides. When I inquired whether there would be a battle or not that day, staff officers pointed over the veldt to a column of dust which was coming slowly nearer.

General Campbell, with three battalions (including two of her Majesty's Guards) and a battery, was marching to join the main column. It was necessary, in view of the entrenchments and the approaching reinforcements, to wait until the force was complete. The event would be decided on the morrow, and meanwhile Brabazon and the mounted troops – cavalry, I shall call them – were to make a reconnaissance of the Boer left.

The brigade, which included the mounted infantry, and was about 1,000 strong, moved southward behind the outpost line and, making a rapid and wide circuit, soon came on the enemy's left flank. Here we waited while patrols were pushed out and while Brabazon was clearing his own right by a still wider turning movement. The patrols soon drew the fire of the Boer pickets, and the rifle shots began to ring out in the clear cool air of the morning.

Meanwhile the flanking movement was in progress, and as the ground to our right was gradually made good and secured by Colonel Sitwell, Brabazon pushed his centre forward until McNeill's scouts were cantering all over the slopes, and hunting such of the enemy as tarried to safer and more remote positions. At last we arrived at the edge of the swell of ground. It fell steeply towards a flat basin, from the middle of which rose a most prominent and peculiar kopje. In-visible behind this was Dewetsdorp. Round it stood Boers, some mounted, some on foot, to the number of about 200.

Our rapid advance, almost into the heart of their position, had disturbed and alarmed them. They were doubtful whether this was reconnaissance or actual attack. They determined to make certain by making an attempt to outflank the outflanking cavalry; and no sooner had our long-range rifle fire compelled them to take cover behind the hill than a new force, as it seemed, of two hundred rode into the open and, passing across our front at a distance of, perhaps, 2,000 yards, made for a white stone kopje on our right.

Angus McNeill ran up to the General: 'Sir, may we cut them off? I think we can just do it.' The scouts pricked up their ears. The General reflected. 'All right,' he said, 'you may try.'

'Mount, mount, mount, the scouts!' cried their impetuous officer, scrambling into his saddle. Then, to me, 'Come with us, we'll give you a show now – first-class.'

A few days before, in an unguarded moment, I had promised to follow the fortunes of the scouts for a day. I looked at the Boers: they were nearer to the white stone kopje than we, but, on the other hand, they had the hill to climb, and were probably worse mounted. It might be done, and if it were done – I thought of the affair of Acton Homes – how dearly they would have to pay in that open plain. So I got on my horse and we all started – forty or fifty scouts, McNeill and I, as fast as we could, by hard spurring, make the horses go.

It was from the very beginning a race, and recognised as such by both sides. As we converged I saw the five leading Boers, better mounted than their comrades, outpacing the others in a desperate resolve to secure the coign of vantage. I said, 'We cannot do it'; but no one would admit defeat or leave the matter undecided.

We arrived at a wire fence 100 yards – to be accurate, 120 yards – from the crest of the kopje, dismounted, and, cutting the wire, were about to seize the precious rocks when – as I had seen them in the railway cutting at Frere, grim, hairy, and terrible – the heads and shoulders of a dozen Boers appeared; and how many more must be close behind them?

There was a queer, almost inexplicable, pause, or perhaps there was no pause at all; but I seem to remember much happening. First the Boers – one fellow with a long, drooping, black beard, and a chocolate-coloured coat, another with a red scarf round his neck. Two scouts cutting the wire fence stupidly. One man taking aim across his horse, and McNeill's voice, quite steady: 'Too late; back to the other kopje. Gallop!'

Then the musketry crashed out, and the 'swish' and 'whirr' of the bullets filled the air. I put my foot in the stirrup. The horse, terrified at the firing, plunged wildly. I tried to spring into the saddle; it turned under the animal's belly. He broke away, and galloped madly off. Most of the scouts were already 200 yards off. I was alone, dismounted, within the closest range, and a mile at least from cover of any kind.

One consolation I had – my pistol. I could not be hunted down unarmed in the open as I had been before. But a disabling wound was the brightest prospect. I turned, and, for the second time in this war, ran for my life on foot from the Boer marksmen, and I thought to myself, 'Here at last I take it.' Suddenly, as I ran, I saw a scout. He came from the left, across my front; a tall man, with skull and cross-bones badge, and on a pale horse. Death in Revelation, but life to me.

I shouted to him as he passed: 'Give me a stirrup.' To my surprise he stopped at once. 'Yes,' he said shortly. I ran up to him, did not bungle in the business of mounting, and in a moment found myself behind him on the saddle.

Then we rode. I put my arms round him to catch a grip of the mane. My hand became soaked with blood. The horse was hard hit; but, gallant beast, he extended himself nobly. The pursuing bullets piped and whistled – for the range was growing longer – overhead.

'Don't be frightened,' said my rescuer; 'they won't hit you.' Then, as I did not reply, 'My poor horse, oh, my poor —— horse; shot with an explosive bullet. The devils! But their hour will come. Oh, my poor horse!'

I said, 'Never mind, you've saved my life.' 'Ah,' he rejoined, 'but it's the horse I'm thinking about.' That was the whole of our con-versation.

It was with a feeling of relief that I turned the corner of the further kopje and found I had thrown double sixes again.

Well satisfied with my brief experience with the scouts, I returned to General Brabazon. While we had been advancing deeply into the Boer flank, they had not been idle, and now suddenly, from the side of the solitary kopje behind which they had collected, three guns came into action against us. For ten minutes the shell fire was really hot. But fate was in a merciful mood that day, for we had but one man killed and five or six – including the General's orderly – wounded by them.

It was, however, evident that this could not endure. Brabazon had not cared to bring his own two guns into such an advanced position, because they were not horse guns, and might not be able to get away safely if the Boers should make a strong counter-attack.

Without guns it was useless to stay, and Brabazon decided to with-draw the reconnaissance, and did so most successfully.

Bloemfontein: 1st May

The object of the operations was to clear the right-hand bottom corner of the Orange Free State of the Boers, and, if the enterprise prospered and the fates were kind, to cut off and capture some part of their forces. In all five columns were in motion. Ian Hamilton, with 2,000 mounted infantry, was ordered to demonstrate against the waterworks position. French, supported by Pole-Carew, was instructed to move on Leeukop. Rundle, in conjunction with Hart and Brabant from the southward, was to force his way to Dewetsdorp and to relieve Wepener. What befell his column on 20th and 21st April has already been described. The attack on the Boer position in front of Dewetsdorp had not been made on the 20th because Sir Herbert Chermside pointed out that the infantry were fatigued with marching, and it was thought better to wait for Campbell's Brigade, which would arrive at sundown.

The 22nd was to be the day of battle. Meanwhile Sir Leslie Rundle had telegraphed to Lord Roberts describing the horseshoe position of the enemy, and its strength, explaining that with the small mounted force at his disposal any attack which he might make would develop into something very like a frontal attack, and would be costly. When this telegram reached Bloemfontein it was apparently mis-understood. 'Rundle is hung up,' they said. Hence the reply which arrived in the dead of night, and prevented the attack of the 22nd. 'Wait till you get into touch with Pole-Carew,' or words to that effect. So the powerful force – almost equal in strength to that with which Sir George White had resisted the first fury of the Boers when, with 25,000 men under the Commandant-General himself, they burst into Natal – was relegated to some days of waiting in front of a position held by scarcely 2,500 men.

The 23rd passed quietly for times of war, and the Boer riflemen and artillerists fired busily till dusk without doing much harm.

The morning of the 24th was unbroken by a single shot. Rundle, now in touch with Pole-Carew, swung his division to the left, pivoting on Chermside, to whom he entrusted the defence of the plateau.

Brabazon with his mounted brigade formed the extreme outer flank of this sweeping movement. His orders were to join French, who drove inward from the north, somewhere behind Dewetsdorp on the Modder River. So we started, and, with much caution and the pomp of war, turned the enemy's left, and in solemn silence bore down on the flank and rear of his position.

Meanwhile, Chermside on the plateau was struck by the entire cessation of fire from the Boer lines opposite to him. He sent scouts to reconnoitre. Single men crept up the hill, looked into the trenches, and found – nothing. The Boers had retreated swiftly in the night. They enjoyed good information of all our movements and designs: and delayed us with the appearance of strength until the last minute. On the night of the 22nd they sent off their wagons towards Thabanchu. On the 23rd they made their effort against Wepener, and attacked the garrison heavily, and on the night of the 24th, having failed at Wepener, they performed a masterly retreat, the assailants of Wepener marching northwards via Ladybrand, the covering force at Dewetsdorp moving on Thabanchu.

And so it was that when, as directed, Brabazon circled round the enemy's left flank and struck the Modder River – here only a rocky ditch with occasional pools of mud – and when French, moving from Leeukop round and behind their right flank, met him, they found the Dutch already departed, and Dewetsdorp again under the Union Jack.

The movements which followed the occupation of Dewetsdorp need not take long in the telling. French's occupation of the town instead of pursuing the enemy was not in accordance with the Commander-in-Chief's ideas, and the cavalry leader was forthwith ordered to follow the Boers at his best pace to Thabanchu. He started accordingly at daylight on the 25th, and Rundle with the Eighth Division followed at noon. Chermside remained at Dewetsdorp with part of the Third Division, and was entrusted with the re-establishment of order through the disturbed districts.

Brabazon marched on Wepener and collected the garrison. Their defence of seventeen days, under continual rifle and shell fire, in hastily dug trenches, which they were unable to leave even at night; exposed to several fierce attacks; in spite of heavy losses and with uncertain prospects of relief, will deserve careful attention when full accounts are published.

Bringing the defenders with him, and having communicated with Hart and Brabant, Brabazon returned to Dewetsdorp, and was ordered to move thence to Thabanchu. Pole-Carew and the Eleventh Division returned to Bloemfontein to take part in the main advance.

The Boers made good their retreat. They took with them twenty-five prisoners of the Worcester Regiment, who had blundered into their camp before Dewetsdorp, armed only with cooking pots, which they meant to carry to their regiment on 'Brab's kopje', and great quantities of sheep and oxen. They halted in Ladybrand, and to the north and east of Thabanchu, in a most pugnacious mood. Indeed, they had no reason to be discontented with the result of their southern incursion.

They had captured seven guns and nearly 1,000 prisoners. They had arrested and carried off a good many farmers who had laid down their arms and made their peace with the British Government. They had harried all who received the troops kindly, had collected large quantities of supplies, which they had sent north, and, lastly, had delayed the main advance by more than five weeks.

Winburg: 8th May

Of all the operations which had been intended against the enemy to the east of the railway, Hamilton's advance towards the waterworks position, being the most northerly, was to have been the least earnestly pressed. The orders were: 'If you find the waterworks weakly held, which is not likely, you may try to occupy them, and, in the event of success, may call up Smith-Dorrien's brigade to strengthen you.'

On this, General Ian Hamilton, who now commanded the imposing, but somewhat scattered, Mounted Infantry Division, started from Bloemfontein on the 22nd of April with about 2,000 Light Horse, Australians, and mounted infantry, and one battery of horse artillery.

On the 23rd he arrived before the waterworks, reconnoitred them, found them weakly held, or at any rate, thought he could take them, attacked, and before dark made himself master of the waterworks themselves, and of the drift over the river which led to the hills beyond, into which the enemy had retired. Smith-Dorrien's brigade was called up at once, arrived after dark, and the next morning the force crossed at the drift, and the whole position was occupied. The news of the capture of this strong and important place, which secures the Bloemfontein water supply, was received with great satisfaction.

Round Dewetsdorp it became evident that the Boers had evaded the intercepting columns and were making their way northwards by Thabanchu. Sir Ian Hamilton suggested that he should be permitted to advance himself and occupy Thabanchu. Permission, and with it a field battery, was given, and, on the 25th of April, the column moved out of the waterworks position towards Thabanchu.

The country to the east of Bloemfontein is at first smooth and open. To anyone unaccustomed to the South African veldt the great plains of brownish grass appear to offer no obstacle to the free movement of cavalry or artillery; nor is it until one tries to ride in a straight line across them that the treacherous and unimagined donga or the awkward wire fence interposes itself. But beyond the Modder River, on which the waterworks are situated, the surface of the ground becomes rocky and hilly, and the country uprears itself in a succession of ridges to the rugged and lofty peaks of Basutoland.

Thabanchu, a town of comparative commercial importance in the Orange Free State, and of undoubted strategic value, stands at the foot of the precipitous feature that bears its name. It is approached from the direction of Bloemfontein by a long, broad, flat-bottomed valley, whose walls on either side rise higher and higher by degrees as the road runs eastward. The eastern end of this wide passage is closed by a chain of rocky kopjes, whose situation is so curious and striking that they seem to be devised by nature to resist the advance of an invader. The kopjes, rising abruptly from the flat glacis-like ground, are a strong rampart, and the whole position, resting on apparently secure flanks, creates a most formidable barrier, which is called locally Israel's Poorte.

Along the valley, on the 25th of April, Hamilton proceeded to march with his entire force, Ridley and the mounted infantry being a considerable distance in front of the main body. At ten o'clock a heavy fire of musketry and artillery was opened at an extreme range from the hills on the left-hand side of the column. Ignoring this, Ridley continued his march, and Hamilton followed, until, at a little after eleven o'clock, both were brought to a standstill before the Israel's Poorte position, which was found to be occupied by the enemy, estimated at 800 strong, with several guns.

After a personal reconnaissance, and in spite of a most disquieting report that the Boers had just been reinforced by 'two thousand men in four lines', the General resolved to attack. His plan was simple but effective. The front was to be masked and contained by a sufficient force of infantry and all the guns. The rest of the troops were to stretch out to the left and swing to the right, the infantry along the left-hand wall of the valley, the mounted men actually the other side of the wall.

Accordingly, the Canadian Regiment and the Grahamstown Volunteers (Marshall's Horse) moved forward in extended order – twenty-five yards interval between men – to within about 800 yards

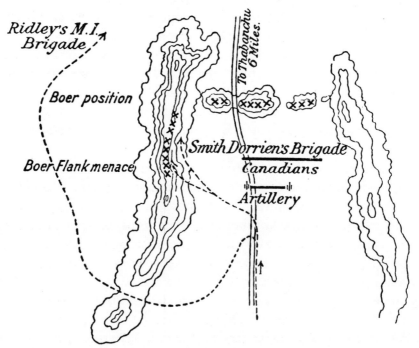

THE ACTION AT ISRAEL'S POORTE, 25TH APRIL

of the enemy's position, and here, just out of the range of serious harm, they lay down and opened a continuous musketry fire. Both batteries came into action forthwith and shelled the crest line with satisfactory energy. Smith-Dorrien, with the remaining three battalions of his brigade, moved to the left, and began working along the ridges. Ridley, breaking out of the valley into the more open ground beyond, began to move against the enemy's line of retreat.

Four hours passed, during which the Boers indulged the hope that the frontal attack would be pushed home, and at the end of which they found their right flank turned and their rear threatened. Immediately, with all the hurry of undisciplined troops who feel a hand on their communications, they evacuated the position, and, running to their horses, galloped away. The Canadians and Grahamstown Volunteers thereupon arose and occupied the line of kopjes, and thus the door was opened and the road to Thabanchu cleared.

General Hamilton, pushing on, entered Thabanchu the same night, and the British flag was again hoisted over the town. On the 26th French and his cavalry, covering the march of Rundle's (Eighth) Division, arrived, and, since he was a lieutenant-general, took the command out of Hamilton's hands for a time.

I had come northwards from Dewetsdorp with the cavalry brigades, and was an eye-witness of the operations round Thabanchu which occupied the 26th and 27th. Thabanchu Mountain is a lofty and precipitous feature of considerable extent, and, towards the south, of indefinite shape. To the north, however, it presents a wide bay, on whose grassy shores rising from the more arid plain the Boer laagers were reported to stand. The enemy held the crest of the crescent-shaped mountain with guns and riflemen, and in order that no one should pry behind it they extended on their right a few hundred trustworthy fellows, who, working in the most scattered formation, gave to their position an enormous front of doubtful strength.

On the afternoon of the 26th, with a view to further operations on the following day, a force of mounted infantry, supported by galloping Maxims and a horse battery, was sent to reconnoitre, and if possible to hold the hill, henceforward called 'Kitchener's Horse Hill'. The troops gained possession of the feature without fighting, though a few Boers were seen galloping along the ridges to the right and left, and an intermittent musketry fire began. A garrison to hold the hill was detailed, consisting of Kitchener's Horse, a company of the Lincoln Mounted Infantry, and two Maxim guns; but just as the sun sank this plan was changed by the officer commanding the force, and the whole were ordered to retire into Thabanchu. On the Indian frontier it is a cardinal rule to retire by daylight and sit still when overtaken by night in the best position at hand. In this war experience has shown that it is usually better to remain on the ground, even at a heavy cost, until it is quite dark, and then to retreat, if necessary. But the teaching of both wars is in complete agreement on one point: twilight is the worst time of all to retire.

The consequences of this ill-timed change of plan were swift. The Boers saw the retrograde movement, and pressed boldly forward, and Kitchener's Horse, finding themselves closely engaged, were unable to move. A sharp and savage little fight followed in the gloom. The Boers crept quite close to the soldiers, and one fierce greybeard was shot through the head eight paces from the British firing line, but not until after he had killed his man. The reports which reached the town, that Kitchener's Horse were 'cut off' on a kopje four miles from camp, induced General French to send the Gordon Highlanders to their relief. This battalion started at about ten o'clock, and were put on their road to the northward. But in the darkness and the broken ground they lost their way, marched five miles to the south, occupied another hill, and did not rejoin the command until the afternoon of the next day, an absence which, since no inquiries could discover them, caused much anxiety. Kitchener's Horse meanwhile, under Major Fowle, of the 21st Lancers, made a plucky defence, beat off the Boers, and managed at about eleven o'clock to effect their retreat undisturbed.

Very early the next morning the whole force marched out of the town, and French's operations were this day designed to compel the enemy to retreat from his positions in rear of Thabanchu Mountain, and if possible to surround some part of his force. The information at General French's disposal could not, however, have been very accurate, for in my telegram of the 26th I wrote that 'more than 2,000 Boers' were collected to the north of Thabanchu, and the Press Censor erased this and substituted the words 'small parties'.

The plan was clear and vigorous. Gordon's cavalry brigade was to move to the right, round the east of Thabanchu Mountain, and force their way into the plains behind it. Hamilton was to push back the weak Boer right, and open the way for Dickson's cavalry brigade to pass through and join hands with Gordon. Rundle, whose infantry were tired from their long march from Dewetsdorp, was to demonstrate against the Boers' centre and hold the town.

The action opened with the re-occupation of Kitchener's Horse Hill by Smith-Dorrien's infantry brigade, who advanced in determined style, and by a sweeping movement of Ridley's mounted infantry. Both these undertakings, which were directed by Hamilton, prospered. The Boer right, which was very thin, was brushed aside, and the road for the cavalry was opened. At, and not until, nine o'clock, French's leading squadrons began to appear on the plain, and by ten the whole of Dickson's brigade had passed through the gap and were safely extended in the undulating plains beyond.

Wishing to see, for the first time, cavalry and horse artillery working in suitable country, I rode down from my post of observation on Kitchener's Horse Hill and trotted and cantered until I caught up the squadrons. It was evident that the left enveloping arm was making good progress. Already we could almost look into the bay behind Thabanchu Mountain. If Gordon were only getting on as well we might join hands with him, and enclasp a goodly catch of prisoners. So the brigade continued to advance from ridge to ridge, and presently Boers began to gallop across the front to escape, as was thought, from the net we were drawing round them. The enemy did not fly very far, but gathered together in what soon became considerable numbers outside the net, near a peaked hill, which does not appear in my sketch, but which the reader may bear in mind as lying to the left rear of the turning cavalry.

At last Dickson's advance reached a point between Thabanchu Mountain and the peaked hill, so that no more Boers could escape by that road; and we saw the others, three or four hundred in number, riding about, up and down, or round and round in the bay, like newly-caught rats in a cage.

At this everyone became very excited. 'Only a few more men and we might make a bag.' Where could men be found? Somebody suggested asking Hamilton. The helio twinkled: 'Come and help us make a bag,' it said, in somewhat more formal language. And Hamilton came forthwith, leaving positions which were of much value; collecting every man he could lay his hands on; he hurried to seize and line the northern spurs of Thabanchu Mountain, prepared to risk much to strike a heavy blow.

The movement of infantry and guns to support him encouraged

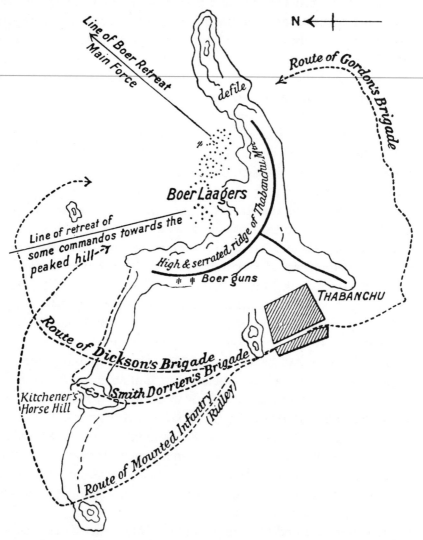

FRENCH'S OPERATIONS ROUND THABANCHU, 26TH AND 27TH APRIL

Dickson to press still further forward, and the whole brigade advanced nearly another mile. At length we overtopped a smooth ridge, and found ourselves looking right into the bay or horseshoe of mountains. Now at last we must see Gordon. 'There he is,' cried several voices, and looking in the direction shown I saw a majestic body of horse streaming out of the centre of the bay towards the north-west. But was it Gordon? At least 4,000 mounted men were riding across our front, hardly two miles away. Surely no brigade was so numerous. Yet such was the precision of the array that I could not believe them Boers.

Boers, however, they proved to be; for two large puffs of smoke leapt from the tail of the column, and two well-aimed shells burst near our horse battery. At the same time patrols from the left rear hurried in with the news that the Boers who had already escaped from our imagined 'trap' were advancing in force, with two more guns, to cut us from the rest of the army.

As for Gordon, there was no longer any doubt about his fortunes. Far away to the eastward the horseshoe wall of mountains dipped to a pass, and on the sides of this gateway little puffs of smoke, dirty brown against the darkening sky, showed that Gordon was still knocking with his artillery at the door, and had never been able to debouch in the plains behind it. Moreover, the dangerous hour of twilight was not long distant. Dickson determined to retreat while time remained, and did so without any unnecessary delay. Whereat the Boers came down on our rear and flank, opening furious fire at long range, and galloping eagerly forward, so that the brigade and its guns, so far from entrapping the enemy, were all but entrapped themselves.

Hamilton, who had taken some risks in order to promote the expected entrapping, had now to think of himself. First, the Boer advance must be stopped, and, secondly, the force which had, in the hopes of grasping the Boers, let go its hold on Kitchener's Horse Hill, must be withdrawn within the Thabanchu picket line. The General, however, was equal to both requirements. Judiciously arranging some force of infantry and guns, he peppered the advancing Boers heavily, so that at 800 yards they wheeled about and scurried to the shelter of adjacent kopjes. This advantage restored the situation. Hamilton remained on the ground till dark, and then, with the whole of Ridley's and Smith-Dorrien's commands, returned safely into Thabanchu.

The Boers were prepared to retreat from Thabanchu, but they proposed to do so in their own time, and it was quite evident that we had not succeeded in any way in hindering or preventing them. It was also clear that, far from being 'in small parties', their strength was nearly 6,000, so that on the whole we might congratulate ourselves on having moved in ignorance and taken no great hurt.

On the evening of this instructive, but unsatisfactory, day, Hamilton received orders from Lord Roberts to march north on Winburg in conformity with the general advance of the army. French remained for some days at Thabanchu, but attempted no further serious operations against the enemy.

Winburg: 8th May (continued)

Ian Hamilton's orders were to march north from Thabanchu on Winburg by the Jacobsrust road, and he was expected to reach his destination by the 7th of May. The column with which he started from Thabanchu was composed of Smith-Dorrien's 19th Infantry Brigade, Ridley's Mounted Infantry Brigade, and two batteries of artillery; but at Jacobsrust he would receive a strong reinforcement, consisting of Bruce-Hamilton's 21st Brigade of Infantry, Broadwood's Cavalry Brigade, two batteries of field and one of horse artillery, and two 5-in. guns. This accession would raise his force to a total of 7,500 infantry, 4,000 mounted men, and thirty-two guns. The first thing was to reach Jacobsrust, and effect the junction with Bruce-Hamilton's force.

The Thabanchu column started at daybreak on the 30th of April, and when it was within three or four miles of Houtnek Poort the enemy suddenly unmasked field guns and opened a long range fire with them from the east on the right flank of the marching troops. Colonel Bainbridge, with the 7th Corps of Mounted Infantry, wheeled up to contain this force of the enemy, and at the same time De Lisle – of polo fame – pushed forward with the 6th Corps and the New Zealanders, and seized a commanding position about 2,000 yards south of the actual nek. Colonel Legge, meanwhile advancing on the left front, noticed that Thoba Mountain was weakly held by the enemy, and thereupon ordered Kitchener's Horse to attack it, thus antici-pating the order which the General was himself about to send. These dispositions enabled a deliberate view of the situation to be taken.

The pass of Houtnek consists of two parallel grassy ridges separated by a smooth shallow valley a little more than a mile across, and devoid of cover. On the east the pass runs up into sharp rocky kopjes, strengthened by successive lines of stone walls trailing away towards the main laagers of the enemy. Both the centre and the left flank of the Boer position refused all opportunity of attack. The Dutch right

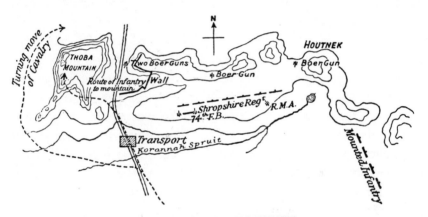

THE ACTION OF HOUTNEK

was scarcely more encouraging. On the west of the pass rose the great mountain of Thoba, an uneven battlefield, better suited to Boers than to British troops. Yet as it was on Hamilton's safer flank, dominated the rest of the enemy's position, could be turned by mounted troops making a very wide detour, and being, moreover, the only way, the General resolved to attack it.

At 9.30 the infantry began to come up, and at ten o'clock the ap-proaches to the Boer position were strongly occupied. As soon as Kitchener's Horse were seen to have made good their footing on Thoba Mountain, Hamilton ordered General Smith-Dorrien to support them with part of his brigade, two companies of the Shrop-shires, the Gordon Highlanders, and four companies of the Canadians being successively worked up on to the hill under heavy shell fire. This practically disposed of the whole force, which was soon engaged all along the line, the mounted infantry holding the enemy off the right and right rear, the Cornwalls guarding the baggage, one-half Smith-Dorrien's brigade containing the front, and the other half with Kitchener's Horse pushing the flank attack on Thoba Mountain.

As soon as the Boers understood the designs of the British on Thoba they made a strong effort to regain and hold that important feature. About two o'clock, some 150 of the German corps of the Boer force advanced from the northern point of Thoba in four lines across the table top to drive the British off the hill. So regular was their order that it was not until their levelled rifles were seen pointing south that they were recognised as foes, and artillery opened on them. In spite of an accurate shell fire they continued to advance boldly against the highest part of the hill, and, meanwhile, cloaked by a swell of the ground, Captain Towse, of the Gordon Highlanders, with twelve men of his own regiment and ten of Kitchener's Horse, was steadily moving towards them.

The two forces, strangely disproportioned, drew near to each other. Neither was visible to the other. The unexpected collision impended. From every point field glasses were turned on the spectacle, and even hardened soldiers held their breath. At last, with suddenness, both parties came face to face at fifty yards' distance. The Germans, who had already made six prisoners, called loudly on Captain Towse and his little band to surrender. A furious splutter of musketry broke out at once, and in less than a minute the long lines of the enemy recoiled in confusion, and the top of the hill was secured to the British.

Captain Towse, for his conspicuous gallantry, and for the extraordinary results which attended it, has been awarded the Victoria Cross; but, in the moment when his military career was assured by a brilliant feat of arms, it was terminated by a bullet which, striking him sideways, blinded him in both eyes.

As the day wore on without the British making good their hold on Thoba Mountain the enemy gathered in a more and more threatening attitude on the right of the column, and by four o'clock at least 1,500 men were collected, with guns and 'pom-poms', which threw shell into the rearguard and transport. Hamilton, however, was determined to fight the matter out. He therefore directed that all troops should post guards on their front, lie down wherever darkness found them, and prepare to renew the action at daybreak. He then telegraphed to General French for some assistance, the need of more mounted troops being painfully felt.

At dawn on May-day fighting recommenced, and soon after six o'clock parties of the Gordons and Canadians succeeded in gaining possession of the two peaks of Thoba Mountain. Besides this, half a company of the Shropshires, under Colour-Sergeant Sconse, managed to seize the nek between them, and though subjected to a severe cross fire, which caused in this small party ten casualties out of forty, maintained themselves stubbornly for four hours. The points which dominate the flat top of the mountain were thus gained.

Meanwhile reinforcements, consisting of the 8th Hussars, a composite Lancer regiment, the East Yorkshire, and a field battery, had arrived from Thabanchu, and the approach of Bruce-Hamilton's force from the direction of Kranz Kraal was also felt. General Ian Hamilton now ordered Colonel Clowes, commanding the cavalry, to move right round Thoba Mountain and threaten the Boer line of retreat as a preliminary and accompaniment of the main infantry assault, which had now become inevitable. Clowes's force was strengthened by the addition of a horse battery.

At about 8 a.m. General Smith-Dorrien had himself gone up to the top of Thoba Mountain to direct personally when the time should come. A little before one o'clock, the progress of the cavalry being satisfactory, he determined to settle the matter, so that if successful the force might get its baggage over the pass before dark. He therefore formed a line of infantry right across the plateau, two companies of the Shropshires in the centre, and one and a half companies of the Gordons on either flank. The advance was sounded.

The troops moved forward with alacrity. For a few moments the fire was heavy, but the Boers knew themselves bested, and on the soldiers raising the cheer that precedes the actual assault they rushed to their horses, and the whole of Thoba Mountain was won. The rest of the position now became untenable, and the enemy promptly evacuated it, galloping swiftly back in the direction of Jacobsrust.

The next day the junction between the columns was effected, and

Ian Hamilton's force formed, with reference to the main advance, the army of the right flank, and was composed as follows:

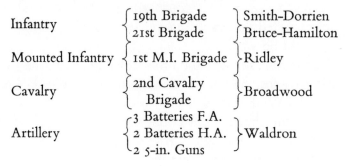

Infantry	19th Brigade	Smith-Dorrien
	21st Brigade	Bruce-Hamilton
Mounted Infantry	1st M.I. Brigade	Ridley
Cavalry	2nd Cavalry Brigade	Broadwood
Artillery	3 Batteries F.A. 2 Batteries H.A. 2 5-in. Guns	Waldron

This force was supported by the Highland Brigade and two 4·7 naval guns, under General Colvile, who was directed to follow the leading column at a distance of ten miles. Hamilton proposed to march forward on the 2nd of May, but an order from headquarters enjoined a halt; nor was it until the afternoon of the 3rd that the force reached Jacobsrust, as it is called by the inhabitants; Isabellafontein, as our maps record.

On the 4th of May the whole army moved forward again, Lord Roberts passing through Brandfort towards Smaldeel, Hamilton continuing his march on Winburg. Scarcely had the troops left camp when a patter of musketry warned the General that his cavalry had become engaged. Riding forward, he was the witness of a very dashing cavalry exploit. Across the line of advance was drawn up a strong force of the enemy, estimated at 4,000 men and thirteen guns. These, in a good position along a range of wooded bluffs, promised a sufficient task for the troops during the day. But now, suddenly, from the direction of Brandfort, a new army of Boers began to appear, riding swiftly down to join hands with their comrades athwart the road, and fall on the left flank of the column.

The thing was urgent, and perhaps vital. But between the fast converging Boer forces, at the angle where they would meet, ran a long ridge of indefinite extent. General Broadwood at once, without a moment's delay, galloped forward, and with two squadrons of the Guards' Cavalry and two of the 10th Hussars seized it. The Boers were already scrambling up its lower slopes. A sharp fight immediately opened. Kitchener's Horse, hurrying up in support, occupied a further point of the ridge, and the Dutch, after a determined but futile attempt to clear the hill, fell back. The junction of the two Boer columns was prevented.

It was not expected that so strong a position as the bluffs behind the Vet River would be yielded without a shot fired. This, nevertheless, proved to be the case, for when, on the morning of the 6th, Hamilton resumed his advance, he found that no force of the enemy stood between him and Winburg.

He therefore sent, shortly after noon, a staff officer, Captain Balfour to wit, under flag of truce, with a letter to the mayor of the town summoning him forthwith to surrender the town and all stores therein, and promising that if this were done he would use every effort to protect private property, and that whatever foodstuffs were required by the troops should be paid for. This message, which was duly heralded by the sound of a trumpet, concluded by saying that unless an acceptance was received within two hours the General would understand that his offer had been declined.

Thus accredited, Captain Balfour made his way into the town and was soon the centre of an anxious and excited crowd of burghers and others who filled the market-square. The mayor, the landdrost, and other prominent persons – indeed, all the inhabitants – were eager to avail themselves of the good terms, and a satisfactory settlement was almost arranged when, arriving swiftly from the north-east, Philip Botha and a commando of 500 men, mostly Germans and Hollanders, all very truculent since they were as yet unbeaten, entered the town.

A violent and passionate scene ensued. Botha declared he would never surrender Winburg without a fight. Dissatisfied with the attentions paid him by Captain Balfour, he turned furiously on him and rated him soundly. Several of the Free Staters had asked what would be done to them if they laid down their arms. Balfour had replied that they would be permitted to return to their farms, unless actually captured on the field. This Botha held to be a breach of the laws of war, and he thereupon charged the officer with attempting to suborn his burghers. What had he to say that he should not be made a prisoner? 'I ask favours of no Dutchman,' replied Balfour.

'Arrest that man!' shouted Botha, in a fury; 'I shall begin shooting soon.' At these shameful words a great commotion arose. The women screamed, the mayor and landdrost rushed forward in the hopes of averting bloodshed. The Boers raised their rifles in menace, and the unarmed British envoy flourished his white flag indignantly.

For several minutes it seemed that an actual scuffle, possibly a tragedy, would occur. But the influence of the townsfolk, who knew that their liberty and property lay in the hands of the Imperial General, and that the great siege guns were even then being dragged into effective range, prevailed, and Philip Botha, followed by his men, galloped furiously from the square towards the north.

That afternoon General Ian Hamilton entered Winburg at the head of his troops. Under a shady tree outside the town the mayor and landdrost tendered their submission and two large silver keys. The Union Jack was hoisted in the market-place amid the cheers of the British section of the inhabitants, and, as each battalion marching through the streets saw the famous emblem of pride and power, bright in the rays of the setting sun, these feeble or interested plaudits were drowned in the loud acclamations of the victorious invaders.

Kroonstad: 16th May 1900

Ian Hamilton, in spite of the long marches his troops had made, was impatient to push on from Winburg without delay, and, following the track to Ventersburg, to seize the drifts across the Sand River, twenty miles to the north. The great speed of his last movement had outpaced the Boers, and their convoys were struggling along abreast of, and even behind, the British column, trying vainly to slip across our front, and join the burgher forces accumulating for the defence of Kroonstad. By marching forthwith – great though the strain might be – the General hoped to secure the bloodless passage of the river, and perhaps cut up some of these same toiling convoys. Accordingly, having collected from the town about three days' stores, he set his brigades in motion on the afternoon of the 6th, and marched nine miles towards the Sand.

But Lord Roberts had decided to remain at Smaldeel until his temporary bridge over the Vet river was made and the trains running, and he did not choose to run the risk of the Boers concentrating all their forces upon any single division of his army, such as would be incurred if Hamilton pushed forward alone.

To us it seemed a great pity to wait; but to the Chief, in whose eyes the army of the right flank was but one column of that far-flung line which stretched from Rundle near Senekal, along the front of the main army to Methuen near Boshof, Hunter at Warrenton, and Mahon far away on the fringe of the Kalahari Desert, it must have been a very small matter. So I have no doubt that it was right to make us halt on the 7th and 8th.

On the former of these two days of rest Lord Roberts sent for General Hamilton to meet him at a point on the branch railway line midway between Winburg and Smaldeel, and they had a long private conference together. On the 9th, the whole army marched forward again towards the Sand River.

The march was not a long one, and by midday we reached the halting-place, a mile south of the river. The headquarters were fixed in a large farm which stood close to the wagon-track we followed.

This farmhouse was certainly the best purely Dutch homestead I have ever seen in the 500 miles I have ridden about the Free State. It was a large square building, with a deep veranda, and a pretty flower-garden in front, and half a dozen barns and stables around it. The construction of a dam across the neighbouring spruit had formed a wide and pleasant pool, in which many good fat ducks and geese were taking refuge from the wandering soldier. On all sides but the front of the farm, rose a thick belt of fir-trees. Within the house the ground floor was divided into three excellent bedrooms, with old-fashioned feather-beds and quaint wooden bedsteads, a prim but spacious parlour, a kitchen, pantry, and store-room. The parlour deserved the greatest attention. The furniture was dark and massive. The boards of the floor were deeply stained. In the middle was a good carpet upon which an ample oval table stood. The walls were hung with curious prints or coloured plates, and several texts in Dutch. One pair of plates I remember represented the ten stages of man's life and woman's life, and showed both in every period from the cradle to the grave, which latter was not reached until the comfortable age of one hundred.

The inmates of the farm consisted of the old man, a venerable gentleman of about sixty years, his dame, a few years younger, three grown-up daughters, a rather ill-favoured spinster sister, and seven or eight children or grandchildren of varying ages.

The General politely requested shelter for the night, and a bedroom and the parlour were placed at his disposal; not very enthusiastically, indeed, but that was only natural. The staff settled down in the veranda so as not to disturb the family. Ian Hamilton, keenly interested in everything, began at once to ask the old lady questions through an interpreter. When the General inquired about her youngest fighting son – a boy of fourteen – her sour face showed signs of emotion, and the conversation ended for the day. On the morrow, however, just before he crossed the river, he had to come back to the telegraph-tent pitched near the farm, and found time to see her again.

'Tell her,' he said to the interpreter, 'that we have won the battle today.'

They told her, and she bowed her head with some dignity.

'Tell her that the Dutch will now certainly be beaten in the war.'

No response.

'Perhaps her sons will be taken prisoners.'

No answer.

'Now tell her to write down on a piece of paper the name of the youngest, and give it to my aide-de-camp; and then when he is captured she must write to me or to the Hoofd-General, and we will send him back to her, and not keep him a prisoner.'

She thawed a little at this, and expressed a hope that he had been comfortable while beneath her roof, and then – for the guns were still firing – he had to hurry away. But the aide-de-camp remained behind for the paper.

The news that small parties of Boers were engaging our right flank guard did not prevent Hamilton riding over to meet the Chief, nor tempt us to quit the cool veranda of the farm; but when, suddenly, at about three o'clock, fifty shots rang out in quick succession, scarcely 500 yards away, everyone got up in a hurry, and, snatching pistols and belts, ran out to see what mischance had occurred. The scene that met our eyes was unusual. Down the side of the hill there poured a regular cascade of antelope – certainly not less than 700 or 800 in number – maddened with fear at finding themselves in the midst of the camp, and seeking frantically for a refuge. This spectacle, combined with the hope of venison, was too much for the soldiers, and forthwith a wild and very dangerous fire broke out, which was not stopped until fifteen or twenty antelopes were killed, and one Australian mounted infantryman wounded in the stomach.

Thus disturbed, I thought it might be worth while to walk up to the outpost line and see what was passing there. When I reached the two guns which were posted on the near ridge, the officers were in consultation. Away across the Sand River, near two little kopjes, was a goodly Boer commando. There were about 150 horsemen, with five ox-wagons and two guns. The horses were grazing, but not off-saddled. The men were lying or sitting on the ground. Evidently they thought themselves out of range. The subaltern commanding the guns was very anxious to fire – 'really think I could reach the brutes'; but he was afraid he would get into trouble if he fired his guns at any range greater than artillery custom approves. His range finders said '6,000'. Making allowances for the clear atmosphere, I should have thought it was more. At last he decided to have a shot. 'Sight for 5,600, and let's see how much we fall short.' The gun cocked its nose high in the air and flung its shell accordingly. To our astonishment the projectile passed far over the Boer commando, and burst nearly 500 yards beyond them: to our astonishment and to theirs. The burghers lost no time in changing their position. The men ran to their horses, and, mounting, galloped away in a dispersing cloud. Their guns whipped up and made for the further hills. The ox-wagons sought the shelter of a neighbouring donga. Meanwhile, the artillery subaltern, delighted at the success of his venture, pursued all these objects with his fire, and using both his guns threw at least a dozen shells among them. Material result: one horse killed. This sort of artillery fire is what we call waste of ammunition when we do it to others, and a confounded nuisance when they do it to us. Even as it was an opportunity was lost. We ought to have sneaked up six guns, a dozen if there were a dozen handy, all along the ridge, and let fly with the whole lot, at ranges varying from 5,000 to 6,000 yards with time shrapnel. Then there would have been a material as well as a moral effect. 'Pooh,' says the scientific artillerist, 'you would have used fifty shells, tired your men, and disturbed your horses, to hit a dozen scallawags and stampede 150. That is not the function of artillery.' Nevertheless, function or no function, it is war, and the way to win war. Harass, bait, and worry your enemy. Once he is more frightened of you than you are of him, all your enterprises will prosper.

In the evening the General returned from his conference with Lord Roberts, and told us the passage was to be forced on the morrow all along the line. The army of the right flank would cross by the nearest drift in our present front. The Seventh Division inclining to its right would come into line on our left. The Field Marshal, with the Guards and the rest of Pole-Carew's division, would strike north along the line of the railway. French, with two cavalry brigades and Hutton's mounted infantry brigade, was to swing around the enemy's

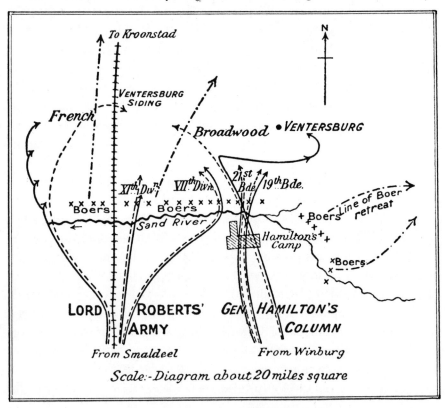

THE PASSAGE OF THE SAND RIVER

right and push hard for Ventersburg siding. Broadwood from our flank, with the Second Cavalry Brigade, and such of the Second Mounted Infantry Brigade as could be spared, was to be thrust through as soon as the Boer front was broken, and try to join hands with French, thus, perhaps, cutting off and encircling the Boer right. The diagram on page 514 will help to explain the scheme.

The operation of the next day was one of the largest and most extended movements of the war, although, probably from this cause, it was attended by very little loss of life. Upon the British side six infantry and six mounted brigades, with rather more than 100 guns, were brought into action along a front of over twenty-five miles. The Boers, however, still preserved their flanks. Upon the west they succeeded in holding up French, and on the east they curled round Hamilton's right and rear so that his action was of a piercing rather than a turning nature. But in thus amazingly extending their scanty forces, which, altogether, did not number more than 9,000 men, with twenty-five guns, the enemy became so weak all along their front that the attacking divisions broke through everywhere, as an iron bar might smash thin ice, with scarcely any shock.

On the evening of the 10th, the British forces, in their extended line, lay spread along the south bank of the river, just out of cannon-shot of the Boer positions on the further side. French, indeed, did not rest content with securing his ford twelve miles to the west of the railway, but pushed his two brigades across before dark. The wisdom of this movement is disputed. On the one hand, it is contended that by crossing he revealed the intention of the Commander-in-Chief, and drew more opposition against himself the next day. On the other, it is urged that he was right to get across unopposed while he could, and that his purpose was equally revealed, no matter which side of the river he stayed. During the night Ian Hamilton, at the other end of the line, seized the drift in his front with a battalion, which promptly entrenched itself. Tucker, who proposed to cross near the same point, despatched the Cheshire regiment for a similar purpose. The single battalion was sufficient; but the importance and wisdom of the movement was proved by the fact that the enemy during the night sent 400 men to occupy the river bank and hold the passage, and found themselves forestalled.

At daybreak the engagement was begun along the whole front. I am only concerned with Ian Hamilton's operations; but, in order that these may be understood, some mention must be made of the other forces. French advanced as soon as it was light, and almost immediately became engaged with a strong force of Boers, who barred his path. A sharp cavalry action followed, in which the Boers fought with much stubbornness. French persevered throughout the day, gaining ground gradually to the north. Although his casualties numbered more than a hundred, he was still some distance from Ventersburg siding at nightfall.

Ian Hamilton began his action at half past five, with his heavy guns, which shelled the opposite heights leisurely, while the infantry and cavalry were moving off. The Boer position before us ran along a line of grassy ridges, with occasional kopjes, which sloped up gradually and reached their summits about a mile from the river. But besides this position, which was the objective of the force, the Boers, who held all the country to the east, began a disquieting attack along our right and right rear, and although the mounted infantry, and principally Kitchener's Horse, under Major Fowle, held them at arm's length throughout the day, the firing in this quarter caused the General some concern.

At six o'clock the Twenty-first Brigade began to cross the river, and Bruce-Hamilton, stretching out to his left, soon developed a wide front. The Boers now opened fire with two or three field-guns and a 'pom-pom', which latter was quickly silenced by our heavy pieces. At the same time, the Nineteenth Brigade, who were containing the enemy's left, became engaged with their skirmishers in the scrub by the river. The four batteries of field artillery also came into action, and were pushed forward across the drift as soon as sufficient space was gained by the infantry. At a little after seven the head of General Tucker's division appeared on the plain to our left, and that determined officer thrust his men over the river in most vigorous style. Moreover, seeing Bruce-Hamilton committed to an assault, he swung two of his own batteries round to the eastward, and so rendered us material assistance.

Both Smith-Dorrien, who directed the two infantry brigades, and Ian Hamilton were fully alive to the grave dangers of crowding too

many troops on to a narrow front, and the infantry attack was very
sparingly fed with supports, until it became completely extended.
This condition was attained about eleven o'clock, when the Camerons
were sent across the river to clear the scrub and prolong the line to
the right. Bruce-Hamilton and the whole of the assaulting infantry

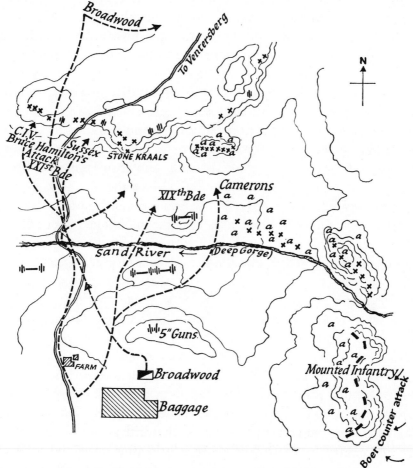

IAN HAMILTON'S ACTION AT THE SAND RIVER

rose up and advanced together upon the enemy's position, covered
by the heavy fire of twenty-six guns. By noon the whole of the
heights beyond the Sand were in the British possession.

Ian Hamilton had meanwhile ordered baggage and cavalry to cross.
Broadwood was over the enemy's position almost as soon as the

infantry. He proceeded to move in the direction of Ventersburg siding. The enemy, however, had covered themselves with a strong rearguard, and the cavalry were soon opposed by three guns and a force of riflemen of considerable numbers. Whether Broadwood would have thought it worth while here to order a charge, is uncertain; for at this moment a misunderstanding arose which induced him to change his plans altogether.

The Boer pressure on our right rear had been growing stronger and stronger all the morning, and at length Hamilton, wishing to check the enemy sharply, so as to draw his rearguard over the river after his baggage, told his chief of artillery to find him a battery. Now it happened that only one of the two horse batteries, 'P', had been able to go with the cavalry, the other, 'Q', being too tired to keep up. The chief of artillery therefore proposed to send for the tired battery. Unfortunately, by some mistake, either in giving or taking the order, the orderly was sent for 'P' instead of 'Q'. Broadwood, who knew that Hamilton would never deprive him of his guns except for some very urgent reason, sent them at once, abandoned his movement to the north-west, which indeed was now impracticable without artillery, and concluding that the rearguard was seriously involved, turned sharply to the east to assist them. Explanations arrived too late to make it worth while to revert to the original plan, and, perhaps, seeing that French was unable to make Ventersburg siding, it was just as well that Broadwood did not try alone.

Broadwood's latest movement, or the action of the artillery, or the knowledge that the British had successfully forced the passage of the river at all points, induced the Boers who were assailing the rearguard to desist, and the musketry in that quarter gradually died away. Meanwhile, by the exertions of Lieutenant-Colonel Maxse, the baggage had mostly been dragged across the river, and Ian Hamilton made haste to overtake his victorious infantry, who had already disappeared into the valley beyond the enemy's position. By the time that we reached the top of the high ground, Bruce-Hamilton's leading battalions were nearly a mile further on, and the tail of Broadwood's brigade was vanishing in a high cloud of dust to the eastward. The City Imperial Volunteers, who had lost a few men in the attack, were resting on the hill after their advance, and eating their biscuits. There were a few prisoners – Transvaalers for the most part – who had surrendered when the troops fixed bayonets. Four miles away to the north-east the trees and houses of Ventersburg rose from a grassy hollow.

The General decided to bivouac in the valley beyond the enemy's position, and to set his pickets upon the hills to the northward. He also sent an officer with a flag of truce into Ventersburg to demand the surrender of the town, and directed Broadwood to detach a regiment and some mounted infantry to occupy it, should the enemy comply.

Hoping to secure some supplies, particularly bottled beer, before everything should be requisitioned by the army, I rode forward after the flag of truce had gone in and waited where I could see what followed. When, about an hour later, a cavalry force began to advance from the direction of Broadwood upon the town, I knew that all was well, and trotted on to join them. My road led me within a few hundred yards of the town, but, luckily for me, I did not enter it alone, and hurried to join the troops. All of a sudden the ominous patter of rifle shots broke the stillness of the evening, and, turning to where the sound came, I saw a score of Boers standing on the sky-line about a mile away and firing at the advancing cavalry, or perhaps, for I was much nearer, at me. The next minute there galloped out of the town about a score of Dutchmen, who fled in the direction of their friends on the western sky-line. Had I ridden straight into the town I should have run into these people's jaws. I lost no time in joining the cavalry, and entered the streets with the squadron of Blues. It was a miserable little place, not to be compared with Winburg. There were a few good stores and a small hotel, where I found what I sought; but the whole town was very dirty and squalid.

Night put an end to all skirmishing, and under its cover the Boers retreated – the greater part to Kroonstad, which, be it remembered, they meant to hold to the death; but a considerable proportion to the east, where they collected with the commandos under Christian de Wet.

All our beasts were so exhausted that few of the regiments got their baggage that night, and hence it was impossible to make an early start next morning. But it was known that the Field-Marshal meant to reach Kroonstad on the next day, and the information at our disposal indicated that the Boers were entrenching a strong position along a line of wooded bluffs called the Boschrand, just south of the town.

We moved at eleven o'clock, heading direct for Kroonstad, and persevered for two hours after the sun had set, making in all nearly seventeen miles. The country to our left was flat and open, and as we converged upon the main army we could see, like red clouds with the sunset behind them, the long parallel lines of dust which marked the marches of the Seventh and Eleventh Divisions; and we knew besides, that, beyond both columns and west of the railroad, French was driving his weary squadrons forward upon another wide swoop. The army drew together in the expectation of a great action. But for all our marching we could never make up the extra distance we had to cover in coming diagonally from the flank, and as darkness fell we realised that the Seventh Division was drawing across our front, and that Pole-Carew with the guard was striding along ahead of us all. That night Lord Roberts slept at America siding, scarcely six miles from the Boschrand position.

Ian Hamilton marched on again at dawn, transport and convoys struggling along miles behind, and the fine-drawn yet eager infantry close upon the heels of the cavalry screen. At times we listened for the sound of guns, for if the enemy stood, the Field-Marshal must come into contact with them by eight o'clock. And when, after nine o'clock, no cannonade was heard, the rumour ran through the army that the Boers had fled without giving battle.

At eleven a message from Lord Roberts reached General Broadwood to say that it did not matter by which road Hamilton's column marched in, as the enemy was not holding his positions. Thereupon I determined, since there was to be no battle, to see the capture of Kroonstad, and being mounted on a fresh pony I had bought at Winburg, I soon left the cavalry behind, caught up the rear of Tucker's transport, pushed on four or five miles along the line of march of his division, struck the tail of the Eleventh Division, and finally overtook the head of the infantry columns about three miles from the town.

Lord Roberts entered Kroonstad at about midday with all his staff. The Eleventh Division, including the Guards' Brigade, marched past him in the market-square, and then, passing through the town, went into bivouac on the northern side. The rest of the army halted south of Kroonstad. Gordon's cavalry brigade a mile from the town; the Seventh Division and Ian Hamilton's force three miles away, in a wide valley among the scrub-covered, trench-rimmed hills the Boers had not dared defend. French, whose turning movement had again been obstinately opposed, reached the railway line north of the town too late to intercept any rolling stock. Indeed, Major Hunter Weston, a daring and enterprising engineer, arrived at the bridge he had hoped to blow up only to find that it had been blown up by the enemy.

Thus, by one long spring from Bloemfontein, Kroonstad, the new capital of the Free State, was captured.

Heilbron: 22nd May 1900

Having arrived at Kroonstad, Lord Roberts determined to halt until his supplies were replenished and the railway line from Bloemfontein in working order. Moreover, in the expectation of a general action outside the town, he had concentrated all his troops and had drawn the army of the right flank close in to the main force. Before he advanced again towards the enemy's position on the Rhenoster River, he wished to extend his front widely, as he had done in the previous operation. The scheme of advance by converging columns required a pause after each concentration before the movement could be repeated; so that while the Field-Marshal himself remained stationary his energetic Lieutenant was again on the move.

General Ian Hamilton, with the same troops as before and an addition of four 'pom-poms', started from his camp outside Kroonstad on the 15th, and after a short march encamped on the eastern side of the town preparatory to moving on Lindley, whither President Steyn had withdrawn. The question of supplies was a very troublesome one, and it was no light matter to thrust out fifty miles into a hostile country with only three and a half days' food and forage in hand. Meat in plenty could be found everywhere, but the stores of farinaceous goods which the farm-houses might contain were insufficient and precarious. Even the benefits of the abundant meat supply were to some extent discounted by the scarcity of wood, for it is not much satisfaction to a soldier to be provided with a leg of mutton if he has no means of cooking. The deficiencies were hardly made good by the arrival of a small convoy, the greater part of which consisted of disinfectants for standing camps, and the rest – so valuable in a grass country – of compressed hay.

Nevertheless, being determined, and trusting, not without reason, in his supply officer, Captain Atcherley, Hamilton started on the 16th, and the infantry bivouacked eighteen miles from Kroonstad on the Lindley road – it would perhaps be less misleading to write track. The cavalry brigade with one corps of mounted infantry under Broadwood were pushed ten miles further on, and seized a fine iron bridge, not marked on any map, which spans an important spruit at Kaalfontein. Here trustworthy information was received that a large force of Boers with guns was retreating before Rundle's column (Eighth Division) northwards upon Lindley, and deeming it important to occupy the town before they arrived, Hamilton ordered the cavalry to hurry on and take possession of the heights to the north of it. It was a double march when ordinary marches were long. The result, however, justified the effort. Broadwood 'surprised' – the word is taken from the Boer accounts – Lindley on the 17th. Scarcely fifty Boers were at hand to defend it. After a brief skirmish the town surrendered. The British loss was three men wounded. Broadwood then retired as directed by his chief to the commanding hill to the north to bivouac. This hill may for convenience be called 'Lindley Hill' in the subsequent narrative.

The infantry and baggage also made a long march on the 17th, but as the road was obstructed they were still fourteen miles from Lindley when night closed in. Even then the transport was toiling on the road, and a large part of it did not come in, and then in an exhausted condition, until after midnight. I wonder how many people in England realise what a spruit is, and how it affects military operations. Those who live in highly developed countries are accustomed to find the road running serenely forward across the valleys, and they scarcely notice the bridges and culverts over which it passes. All is different in

South Africa. The long column of transport trails across the plain. The veldt in front looks smooth and easy going. Presently, however, there is a block. What is the matter? Let us ride forward to where the single string of wagons merges in a vast crowd of transport, twenty rows abreast, mule carts, Cape carts, ox-wagons, ambulances, and artillery, all waiting impatiently, jostling each other, while drivers and conductors swear and squabble. Here is the spruit – a great chasm in the ground, fifty feet deep, a hundred yards from side to side. The banks are precipitous and impassable at all points except where the narrow single track winds steeply and unevenly down. The bottom is a quagmire, and though the engineers are doing their best to level and improve the roadway, it is still a combination of the Earl's Court water chute and the Slough of Despond. One by one, after a hot dispute for precedence, the wagons advance. The brakes must be screwed up to their tightest grip lest the ponderous vehicles rush forward down the slope and overwhelm their oxen. At the bottom like a feather bed lies the quagmire. Here one wagon in every three sticks. The mules give in after one effort – unworthy hybrids. The oxen strain with greater perseverance. But in the end it is the man who has to do the hauling. Forthwith come fatigue parties of weary men – it has been a long march already to soldiers fully equipped. Drag ropes are affixed, and so with sweat, blood, and stretching sinew, long whips cracking and whistling, white men heaving and natives yelping encouragement, another wagon comes safely through. And there are seven miles of transport!

On the morning of the 18th it was arranged that Smith-Dorrien should be left where he was (twelve miles west of Lindley) with his own brigade, one battery, and a corps of mounted infantry to help in the expected convoy, and should cut off the corner and rejoin the column at the end of its first march towards Heilbron. Ian Hamilton with the rest of the troops then moved on to Lindley. The march lay through the same class of country hitherto traversed – a pleasant grassy upland which, if not abundantly supplied with water by nature, promised a rich reward to man, should he take the trouble to construct even the simplest irrigation works. Spruits ran in all directions, and only required an ordinary dam, like the *bunds* the peasants build in India, to jewel each valley with a gleaming vivifying lake. But at present the countryside is so sparsely populated that the energies of its inhabitants could not produce much effect upon the landscape. The unamiable characteristic of the Boer, to shun the sight of his neighbour's barn, has scattered the farms so widely that little patches of tillage are only here and there to be seen, and the intervening miles lie neglected, often not more than twenty acres of a six thousand acre property being brought into cultivation, which seems rather a pity.

At length the track, which had been winding among the smooth undulations, rounded an unusually steep hillock of kopje character, and we saw before us at the distance of a mile the pretty little town of Lindley. The houses – white walls and blue-grey roofs of iron – were tucked away at the bottom of a regular cup, and partly hidden by the dark green Australian trees. We rode first of all to Broadwood's headquarters, following the ground wire which led thither. Arrived there we learned the news. Boer laagers and Boer patrols had been found scattered about the country to the south-east and north-east. There was occasional firing along the picket line. The town had upon most searching requisition yielded nearly two days' supply, and, most important of all, Piet De Wet, brother of the famous Christian, had sent in a message offering to surrender with such of his men as would follow his example, if he were permitted to return to his farm. Broadwood had at once given the required assurance, and Hamilton on his arrival had wired to Lord Roberts fully endorsing the views of his subordinate, and requesting that the agreement might be confirmed. The answer came back with the utmost despatch, and was to the effect that surrender must be unconditional. De Wet, it was remarked, was excluded from the favourable terms of the Proclamation to the burghers of the Orange Free State, by the fact that he had commanded part of the Republican forces. He could not therefore be permitted to return to his farm. I need not say with what astonishment this decision was received. The messenger carrying the favourable answer was luckily overtaken before he had passed through our picket line and the official letter was substituted. Piet De Wet, who awaited the reply at a farm-house some ten miles from Lindley, found himself presented with the alternative of continuing the war or going to St Helena, or perhaps Ceylon; and as events have shown he preferred the former course to our loss in life, honour, and money.

Lindley is a typical South African town, with a large central market-square and four or five broad unpaved streets radiating therefrom. There is a small clean-looking hotel, a substantial gaol, a church and a school-house. But the two largest buildings are the general stores. These places are the depôts whence the farmers for many miles around draw all their necessaries and comforts. Owned and kept by English-men or Scotchmen, the variety of their goods is remarkable. You may buy a piano, a kitchen range, a slouch hat, a bottle of hair wash, or a box of sardines over the same counter. The two stores are the rival Whiteley's of the countryside; and the diverse tastes to which they cater prove at once the number of their customers, and the wealth which even the indolent Boer may win easily from his fertile soil.

Personally I sought potatoes, and after patient inquiry I was directed to a man who had by general repute twelve sacks. He was an English-man, and delighted to see the British bayonets at last. 'You can't think,' he said, 'how we have looked forward to this day.'

I asked him whether the Dutch had ill-used him during the war.

'No, not really ill-used us; but when we refused to go out and fight they began commandeering our property, horses and carts at first and latterly food and clothing. Besides, it has been dreadful to have to listen to all their lies and, of course, we had to keep our tongues between our teeth.'

It was evident that he hated the Boers among whom his lot had been cast with great earnestness. This instinctive dislike which the British settler so often displays for his Dutch neighbour is a perplexing and not a very hopeful feature of the South African problem. Presently we reached his house (where the potatoes were stored). Above the doorway hung a Union Jack. I said –

'I advise you to take that down.'

'Why?' he asked, full of astonishment. 'The British are going to keep the country, aren't they?'

'This column is not going to stay here for ever.'

'But surely they will leave some soldiers behind to protect us, to hold the town.'

I told him I thought it unlikely. Ours was a fighting column. Other troops would come up presently for garrison duty. But there would probably be an interval of at least a week. Little did I foresee the rough fighting which would rage round Lindley for the next three months. He looked very much disconcerted; not altogether without reason.

'It's very hard on us,' he said after a pause. 'What will happen when the Boers come back? They're just over the hill now.'

'That's why I should take the flag down if I were you. If you don't fight, keep your politics till the war is over!' He looked very disappointed, and I think was asking himself how much his enthusiasm had compromised him.

The next morning before breakfast-time there was firing in the picket line south of Lindley. The patter of shots sounded across the valley, and upon the opposite slopes the British patrols could be seen galloping about like agitated ants. I was at the moment with General Hamilton. He watched the distant skirmish from his tent door for a little while in silence. Then he said:

'The scouts and the Kaffirs report laagers of the enemy over there, and over there, and over there' (he pointed to the different quarters). 'Now either I must attack them today or they will attack me tomorrow. If I attack them today, I weary my troops; and if I don't we shall have to fight an awkward rearguard action to get out of this place tomorrow.'

He did not say at the time which course he meant to follow, but I felt quite sure he would not take his troops back very far to the south or south-east to chastise impalpable laagers. We were running on schedule time and had to make our connections with the main army. So I was not surprised when the day passed without any movement on our part.

Very early on the 20th the brigades were astir, and as soon as the light was strong Broadwood's cavalry began to stream away over the northern ridges. The guns and the greater part of the infantry followed them without delay, so that by seven o'clock the great column of transport was winding round the corner of Lindley Hill on the road to Heilbron.

The full light of day had no sooner revealed the march of the troops than the watching Boers began to feel and press the picket line: and an intermittent musketry spread gradually along the whole three-quarter circle round Lindley. At eight o'clock our troops evacuated the town itself, at nine, the convoy being nearly round Lindley Hill, the pickets commenced to draw in. This was a signal for a decided increase in the firing. No sooner were the outposts clear of the town than the Boers in twos and threes galloped into it and began to fire from the houses. All kinds of worthy old gentlemen, moreover, who had received us civilly enough the day before, produced rifles from various hiding-places and shot at us from off their verandas. Indeed, so quickly did the town revert to the enemy's hands that Somers Somerset, the despatch-rider of *The Times*, was within an ace of being caught. He had arrived late the night before, and having found a comfortable bed at the hotel went to sleep without asking questions. The next thing he remembers is the landlord rushing into his room and crying in great excitement that the Boers were in the town. He scrambled into his clothes and, jumping on his horse galloped through the streets. History does not record whether he retained his presence of mind sufficiently to settle his hotel bill.

The General and his staff had watched the beginnings of the action from the now deserted camping ground, a dirty waste, littered with rubbish and dotted with the melancholy figures of derelict horses and mules. So soon as the retiring pickets drew north of the town, he mounted and made his way to the top of Lindley Hill. From this commanding table-top the whole scene of action, indeed the whole surrounding country, was visible. At our feet beyond the abandoned bivouac lay the houses of Lindley giving forth a regular rattle of musketry. On either side, east and west, rose two prominent kopjes held by companies of mounted infantry briskly engaged. The tail of the transport serpent was twisting away into safety round the base of our hill. Far away on the broad expanse of down parties of Dutch horsemen cantered swiftly forward; and along a road beyond the eastern kopje rose a steady trickle of mounted men. They moved in true Boer fashion – little independent groups of four and five, now and then a troop of ten or a dozen, here and there a solitary horseman riding back against the general flow. At no particular moment were more than thirty to be seen on the mile of dusty road. Yet to an experienced eye the movement seemed full of dangerous significance.

One became conscious of a growing accumulation of force somewhere among the hills to the eastward. The General, who had served on the Indian frontier, understood rearguard actions, and his face was grave. The Boers knew what they wanted. There was an air of decision about their movements which boded no good to rear or right flank guard. Gallopers were sent off, one to warn the right corps of mounted infantry, another to bid the main body of the force go dead slow, another to the threatened eastern kopje to learn the state of affairs there. The rearguard battery was brought up on to the table-top, and came into action. This was, I think, the key of the situation. This battery planted on Lindley Hill, and casting its shells now in one direction, now in another, compelled the assailants to keep their distance, and helped the pickets into safety and new positions further back.

But now, the rearguard having disengaged itself from Lindley town the General's place was with his main body, and we set off to trot and gallop the seven miles that intervened between the head and tail of our force. The firing in front had ceased before we came up.

We were just congratulating ourselves upon the success of these curious operations – curious because the drill books do not contemplate both sides fighting rearguard actions at the same time – when half a dozen riderless horses galloped in from somewhere miles away on the right flank. Evidently sharp fighting was proceeding there; the flow of Boers had meant mischief. The peaceful landscape told no tale. No sound of musketry nor sign of action could be distinguished. Indeed, in this scattered warfare one part of a force may easily be destroyed without the rest even knowing that a shot has been fired. 'Why scatter them?' asks the armchair strategist. 'Because if you don't scatter, and haven't got soldiers who are good enough to act when scattered, you will all get destroyed in a lump together.'

The General sent directions to the rearguard to communicate with the flank guard; kept another corps of mounted infantry handy to support either if necessary, and turned his attention to getting his brigades across the Rhenoster River. While this was proceeding the head of Smith-Dorrien's column, which had marched prosperously from their bivouac near Kaalfontein, came into view, and the Army of the Right Flank stood again united, a fact which suggests some consideration of its functions in the general scheme of Lord Roberts's advance.

After Kroonstad had been captured the republican forces on the railway retreated to the line of the Rhenoster. Half a mile to the north of this river there rises abruptly from the smooth plain a long line of rocky hills, and in this strong position the Boers had determined to make a stubborn stand. Any force advancing along the railway would indeed have found it a difficult and costly business to cross the river and dislodge an enemy so posted. Other low hills trending away to either flank would have made any turning movement an exceedingly extended and probably a useless operation, for the enemy being on the inside of the circle would have been able to confront the attack wherever it might fall. But the Rhenoster River rises considerably south of the point where it intersects the railway; and so soon as Ian Hamilton's force was across it, the Boers holding the kopjes position were in considerable danger of being cut off. The effect of our crossing the Rhenoster between Lindley and Heilbron should therefore be to clear the march of the main army. All fell out as Lord Roberts had expected; although the Boers had made great preparations to defend Rhenoster, had constructed strong entrenchments and made sidings to detrain their heavy guns, they evacuated the whole position without a shot being fired, compelled by the movement of a column forty miles away to their left flank.

All who understood the scope and cohesion of the operations were delighted at the prospect of getting across the Rhenoster River. The General was determined, rear and flank guard actions notwithstanding, to have his army and transport over that night: and two practicable crossings having been found, infantry, cavalry, guns and baggage began to push across. The last was now increased by the arrival of Smith-Dorrien, who brought with him a much needed convoy with sufficient supplies to carry us on to Heilbron and a march beyond.

Late in the evening came the news from the right flank guard. They had waited, fearing to expose the rearguard to a flank attack. The rearguard had made good its retreat. A gap had sprung up between the two bodies. The vigilant Boers had pounced in and stampeded the horses of one mounted infantry company. A sharp, fierce fight followed; the rearguard hearing the fusillade swung in to help. Ultimately the Boers were checked sufficiently to enable rear and flank guards to draw inwards together and draw off: but it was by general agreement of participants a very unpleasant affair. The local advantage rested with the Boers, who hit or captured the greater part of the squadron, including twenty wounded. Concerning these latter, Piet De Wet sent in a flag of truce during the night offering to hand them over if ambulances were sent, and several wounded Boers whom we had taken were given up. This was accordingly done. The army bivouacked on the north bank of the Rhenoster within two marches of the town of Heilbron, upon which it was now designed to move.

Heilbron: 22nd May (continued)

Heilbron lies in a deep valley. About it on every side rolls the grassy upland country of the Free State, one smooth grey-green surge beyond another, like the after-swell of a great gale at sea; and here in the trough of the waves, hidden almost entirely from view, is the town itself, white stone houses amid dark trees, all clustering at the foot of a tall church spire. It is a quiet, sleepy little place.

The President, his secretaries, and his councillors arrived one morning from Lindley, bringing the 'seat of Government' with them in a Cape cart. For nearly a week Heilbron remained the chief town. Then, as suddenly as it had come, the will-o'-the-wisp dignity departed, and Steyn, secretaries, councillors, and Cape cart, hurried away to the eastward, leaving behind them rumours of advancing hosts – and (to this I can testify) three bottles of excellent champagne. That was on Sunday night. The inhabitants watched and wondered all the next day.

On the Tuesday morning, shortly after the sun had risen, Christian De Wet appeared with sixty wagons, five guns, and 1,000 burghers, very weary, having trekked all night from the direction of Kroonstad, and glad to find a place of rest and refreshment. 'What of the English?' inquired the newcomers, and the Heilbron folk replied that the English were coming, and so was Christmas, and that the country to the southward was all clear for ten miles. Thereat the war-worn commando outspanned their oxen and settled themselves to coffee. Forty minutes later the leading patrols of Broadwood's brigade began to appear on the hills to the south of the town.

Looked at from any point of view, the British force was a formidable array: Household Cavalry, 12th Lancers and 10th Hussars, with P and Q Batteries Royal Horse Artillery (you must mind your P's and Q's with them), two 'pom-poms', and two galloping Maxims; and, hurrying up behind them, Light Horse, Mounted Infantry, Nineteenth and Twenty-first Brigades, thirty field-guns, more 'pom-poms', two great 5-in. ox-drawn siege pieces ('cow guns' as the army calls them), and Ian Hamilton.

The cavalry halted on the hills for a while, the General being desirous of obtaining the formal surrender of Heilbron, and so preventing street-fighting or bombardment. An officer was despatched with a flag of truce and a trumpeter; message most urgent, answer to be given within twenty minutes; but all these things take time. Flags of truce (prescribe the customs of war) must approach the enemy's picket line at a walk; a mile and a half at a walk – twenty minutes; add twenty for the answer, ten for the return journey, and nearly an hour is gone. So we wait impatiently watching the two solitary figures with a white speck above them draw nearer and nearer to the Boer lines; 'and,' says the brigadier, 'bring two guns up and have the ranges taken.'

There was just a chance that while all were thus intent on the town, the convoy and commando might have escaped unharmed, for it happened that the northern road runs for some distance eastward along the bottom of the valley, concealed from view. But the clouds of dust betrayed them.

'Hullo! what the deuce is that?' cried an officer.

'What?' said everyone else.

'Why, that! Look at the dust. There they go. It's a Boer convoy. Gone away.'

And with this holloa the chase began. Never have I seen anything in war so like a fox hunt. At first the scent was uncertain, and the pace was slow with many checks.

Before us rose a long smooth slope of grass, and along the crest the figures of horsemen could be plainly seen. The tail of the wagon

train was just disappearing. But who should say how many rifles
lined that ridge? Besides, there were several barbed-wire fences, which,
as anyone knows, will spoil the best country.

Slowly at first, and silently besides; but soon the hounds gave tongue.
Pop, pop, pop – the advanced squadron – Blues – had found something
to fire at, and something that fired back, too; pip-pop, pip-pop came
the double reports of the Boer rifles. Bang – the artillery opened on
the crest-line with shrapnel, and at the first few shells it was evident
that the enemy would not abide the attack. The horsemen vanished
over the sky-line.

We were over the first big fence, and now the scent improved.
Beyond the first ridge was another, and behind this, much nearer
now, dust clouds high and thick. The General galloped forward himself to the newly captured position and took a comprehensive view.
'Tell the brigade to come here at once – sharp.'

But now the whole hunt swung northward towards a line of
rather ugly looking heights. Broadwood looked at them sourly. 'Four
guns to watch those hills, in case they bring artillery against us
from them.' Scarcely were the words spoken, when there was a flash
and a brown blurr on the side of one of the hills, and with a rasping
snarl a shell passed overhead and burst among the advancing cavalry.
The four guns were on the target without a moment's delay.

The Boer artillerists managed to fire five shots, and then the place
grew too hot for them – indeed, after Natal, I may write, even for
them. They had to expose themselves a great deal to remove their
gun, and the limber and its six horses showed very plainly on the
hillside, so that we all hoped to smash a wheel or kill a horse, and
thus capture a real prize. But at the critical moment our 'pom-poms'
disgraced themselves. They knew the range, they saw the target. They
fired four shots; the aim was not bad. But four shots – four miserable
shots! Just pom-pom, pom-pom. That was all. Whereas, if the Boers
had had such a chance, they would have rattled through the whole
belt, and sent eighteen or twenty shells in a regular shower. So we
all saw with pain how a weapon, which is so terrible in the hands of
the enemy, may become feeble and ineffective when used on our
side by our own gunners.

After the menace of the Boer artillery was removed from our right flank, the advance became still more rapid. Batteries and squadrons were urged into a gallop. Broadwood himself hurried forward. We topped a final rise.

There, crawling up the opposite slope, clear cut on a white roadway, was a long line of wagons – ox-wagons and mule-wagons – and behind everything a small cart drawn by two horses. All were struggling with frantic energy to escape from their pursuers. But in vain.

The batteries spun round and unlimbered. Eager gunners ran forward with ammunition, and some with belts for the 'pom-poms'. There was a momentary pause while ranges were taken and sights aligned, and then —— ! Shell after shell crashed among the convoys. Some exploded on the ground; others, bursting in the air, whipped up the dust all round mules and men. The 'pom-poms', roused at last from their apathy by this delicious target and some pointed observations of the General, thudded out strings of little bombs. For a few minutes the wagons persevered manfully. Then one by one they came to a standstill. The drivers fled to the nearest shelter, and the animals strayed off the road or stood quiet in stolid ignorance of their danger.

Such was the affair of Heilbron, and it was none the less joyous and exciting because, so far as we could learn, no man on either side was killed, and only one trooper and five horses wounded. Then we turned homewards.

Heilbron had one memory for me, and it was one which was now to be revived. In the hotel – a regular country inn – I found various British subjects who had been assisting the Boer ambulances – possibly with rifles. It is not my purpose to discuss here the propriety of their conduct. They had been placed in situations which do not come to men in quiet times, and for the rest they were mean-spirited creatures.

While the republican cause seemed triumphant they had worked for the Dutch, had doubtless spoken of 'damned rooineks', and used other similar phrases; so soon as the Imperial arms predominated they had changed their note; had refused to go on commando in any capacity, proclaimed that Britons never should be slaves, and dared the crumbling organism of Federal government to do its worst.

We talked about the fighting in Natal which they had seen from the other side. The Acton Homes affair cropped up. You will remember that we of the irregular brigade plumed ourselves immensely on this ambuscading of the Boers – the one undoubted score we ever made against them on the Tugela.

'Yes,' purred my renegades, 'you caught the damned Dutchmen fairly then. We were delighted, but of course we dared not show it.' (Pause.) 'That was where De Mentz was killed.'

De Mentz! The name recalled a vivid scene – the old field-cornet lying forward, grey and grim, in a pool of blood and a litter of empty cartridge cases, with his wife's letter clasped firmly in his stiffening fingers. He had 'gone down fighting'; had had no doubts what course to steer. I knew when I saw his face that he had thought the whole thing out. Now they told me that there had been no man in all Heilbron more bitterly intent on the war, and that his letter in the 'Volksstem', calling on the Afrikanders to drive the English scum from the land, had produced a deep impression.

'Let them,' thus it ran, 'bring 50,000 men, or 80,000 men, or even' – it was a wild possibility – '100,000, yet we will overcome them.' But they brought more than 200,000, so all his calculations were disproved, and he himself was killed with the responsibility on his shoulders of leading his men into an ambush which, with ordinary precautions, might have been avoided. Such are war's revenges. His widow, a very poor woman, lived next door to the hotel, nursing her son who had been shot through the lungs during the same action. Let us hope he will recover, for he had a gallant sire.

Johannesburg: 1st June

On the 24th of May, Ian Hamilton's force, marching west from Heilbron, struck the railway and joined Lord Roberts's main column. The long marches, unbroken by a day's rest, the short rations to which the troops had been restricted, and the increasing exhaustion of horses and transport animals seemed to demand a halt. But a more imperious voice cried 'Forward!' and at daylight the travel-stained brigades set forth, boots worn to tatters, gun horses dying at the wheel, and convoys struggling after in vain pursuit – 'Forward to the Vaal'.

And now the Army of the Right Flank became the Army of the Left; for Hamilton was directed to move across the railway line and march on the drift of the river near Boschbank.

We crossed the Vaal on the 26th prosperously and peacefully. Broadwood, with his cavalry, had secured the passage during the previous night, and the infantry arriving found the opposite slopes in British hands. Moreover, the engineers, assisted by the strong arms of the Blues and Life Guards, had cut a fine broad road up and down the steep river banks.

Once across we looked again for the halt. Twenty-four hours' rest meant convoys with full rations and forage for the horses. But in the morning there came a swift messenger from the Field-Marshal: main army crossing at Vereeniging, demoralisation of the enemy increasing, only one span of the railway bridge blown up, perhaps Johannesburg within three days – at any rate, 'try', never mind the strain of nerve and muscle or the scarcity of food.

Forward again. That day Hamilton marched his men eighteen miles – ('ten miles', say the text-books on war, 'is a good march for a division with baggage', and our force, carrying its own supplies, had ten times the baggage of a European division!) – and succeeded besides in dragging his weary transport with him. By good fortune the cavalry discovered a little forage – small stacks of curious fluffy grass called manna, and certainly heaven-sent – on which the horses subsisted and did not actually starve. All day the soldiers pressed on, and the sun was low before the bivouac was reached.

At first, after we had crossed the Vaal, the surface of the country was smooth and grassy, like the Orange River Colony, but as the column advanced northwards the ground became broken – at once more dangerous and more picturesque. Dim blue hills rose up on the horizon, the rolling swells of pasture grew sharper and less even, patches of wood or scrub interrupted the level lines of the plain, and polished rocks of conglomerate or auriferous quartz showed through the grass, like the bones beneath the skin of the cavalry horses. We were approaching the Rand.

On the evening of the 27th, Hamilton's advance guard came in touch with French, who, with one mounted infantry and two cavalry brigades, was moving echeloned forward on our left in the same relation to us as were we to the main army.

The information about the enemy was that, encouraged by the defensive promise of the ground, he was holding a strong position either on the Klip Riviersberg, or along the line of the gold mines crowning the main Rand reef. On the 28th, in expectation of an action next day, Hamilton made but a short march. French, on the other hand, pushed on to reconnoitre, and, if possible, to pierce the lines that lay ahead.

I rode with General Broadwood, whose brigade covered the advance of Hamilton's column. The troops had now entered a region of hills which on every side threatened the march and limited the view.

At nine o'clock we reached a regular pass between two steep rocky ridges. From the summit of one of these ridges a wide landscape was revealed. Northwards across our path lay the black line of the Klip Riviersberg, stretching to the east as far as I could see, and presenting everywhere formidable positions to the advancing force. To the west these frowning features fell away in more grassy slopes, from among which, its approach obstructed by several rugged under-features, rose the long smooth ridge of the Witwatersrand reef. The numerous grass fires which attend the march of an army in dry weather – the results of our carelessness, or perhaps, of the enemy's design – veiled the whole prospect with smoke, and made the air glitter and deceive like the mirages in the Soudan. But one thing showed with sufficient distinctness to attract and astonish all eyes. The whole crest of the Rand ridge was fringed with factory chimneys. We had marched nearly 500 miles through a country which, though full of promise, seemed to European eyes desolate and wild, and now we turned a corner suddenly, and there before us sprang the evidences of wealth, manufacture, and bustling civilisation. I might have been looking from a distance at Oldham.

The impression was destroyed by the booming of shotted guns. French was at work. The haze and the distance prevented us from watching closely the operations of the cavalry. The dark patches of British horsemen and the white smoke of the Dutch artillery were the beginning and the end of our observations. But, even so, it was easy to see that French was not making much progress.

As the afternoon wore on the loud reverberations of heavy cannon told that the Boers had disclosed their real position, and we knew that something more substantial than cavalry would be required to drive them from it. In the evening French's brigades were seen to be retiring across the Klip River, and the night closed in amid the rapid drumming of the Vickers-Maxims covering his movement, bringing with it the certainty of an infantry action on the morrow.

At twelve o'clock a despatch from the cavalry division reached Hamilton. French's messenger said that the cavalry were having a hot fight and were confronted by several 40-pounder guns, but the stout-hearted commander himself merely acquainted Hamilton with his orders from headquarters, to march via Florida to Driefontein, and made no allusion to his fortunes nor asked for assistance. Indeed, as we found out later, his operations on the 28th had been practically confined to an artillery duel, in which, though the expenditure of ammunition was very great, the casualties were fortunately small.

But the Boers, seeing the cavalry retire at dusk, claimed that they had repulsed the first attack; their confidence in the strength of the Rand position was increased.

The orders from headquarters for the 29th were such as to involve certain fighting should the enemy stand. French, with the cavalry division, was to march around Johannesburg to Driefontein; Ian Hamilton was directed on Florida; the main army, under the Field-Marshal, would occupy Germiston and seize the junctions of the Natal, Cape Colony, and Potchefstroom lines. These movements, which the chief had indicated by flags on the map, were now to be executed – so far as possible – by soldiers on the actual field.

The operations of the main army are not my concern; but it is necessary to state the result, lest the reader fail to grasp the general idea, and, while studying the detail, forget their scale and meaning.

Advancing with great speed and suddenness through Elandsfontein, Lord Roberts surprised the Boers in Germiston, and after a brief skirmish drove them in disorder from the town, which he then occupied. So precipitate was the flight of the enemy, or so rapid the British advance, that nine locomotives and much other rolling stock were captured, and the line from Germiston southward to Vereeniging was found to be undamaged. The importance of these advantages on the success of the operations can scarcely be over-estimated. The problem of supply was at once modified.

French had camped for the night south of the Klip River, just out of cannon shot of the enemy's position, and at eight o'clock on the morning of the 29th he moved off westward, intending to try to penetrate, or, better still, circumvent, the barrier that lay before him.

Such ground as he had won on the previous day he held with mounted infantry, and thus masking the enemy's front he attempted to pierce if he could not turn his right. For these purposes the force at his disposal – three horse batteries, four 'pom-poms', and about 3,000 mounted men – was inadequate and unsuited. But he knew that Ian Hamilton, with siege guns, field guns, and two infantry brigades, was close behind him, and on this he reckoned.

Firing began about seven o'clock, when the Boers attacked the mounted infantry corps holding the positions captured on the 28th, and who were practically covering the flank movement of the rest of the cavalry division and the march of Hamilton's column. The mounted infantry, who were very weak, were gradually compelled to fall back, being at one time enfiladed by two Vickers-Maxims and heavily pressed in front.

But their resistance was sufficiently prolonged to secure the transference of force from right to left. By ten o'clock French had gone far enough west to please him, and passing round the edge of a deep swamp turned the heads of his regiments sharply to their right (north), and moved towards the Rand ridge and its under-features.

By the vigorous use of his horse artillery he cleared several of the advanced kopjes, and had made nearly two miles progress north of the drainage line of the Klip River, when he was abruptly checked. A squadron sent forward against a low fringe of rocks, clumping up at the end of a long grass glacis, encountered a sudden burst of musketry fire, and returned, pursued by shell, with the information that mounted men could work no further northwards.

Meanwhile Hamilton, who had determined to lay his line of march across the Doornkop ridges, and whose infantry, baggage, and guns were spread all along the flat plain south of the Klip, was drawing near. French halted his brigades and awaited him. The instructions from headquarters defined very carefully the relations which were to be observed between the two Generals. They were to co-operate, yet their commands were entirely separate. Should they attack the same hill at once, French, as a lieutenant-general and long senior to Hamilton, would automatically assume command.

French was joined by Hamilton at one o'clock, and French explained the difficulty of further direct advance. He must move still more to the west. On the other hand, Hamilton, whose force was eating its last day's rations, could make no longer detour, and must break through there and then – frontal attack, if necessary. So the cavalry division moved to the left to co-operate with the infantry attack by threatening the Boer right, and, in order that this pressure might be effective, Hamilton lent Broadwood's brigade and two corps of mounted infantry to French for the day. He himself prepared to attack what stood before him with his whole remaining force.

By two o'clock the cavalry in brown swarms had disappeared to the westward, both infantry brigades were massed under cover on the approaches of the Rand ridge, and the transport of the army lay accumulated in a vast pool near the passage of the Klip – here only a swamp, but further east a river. The artillery duel of the morning had died away. The firing on the right, where the mounted infantry still maintained themselves, was intermittent. The reconnaissance was over. The action was about to begin, and in the interval there was a short, quiet lull – the calm before the storm.

At three o'clock precisely the infantry advanced to the attack. Major-General Bruce-Hamilton directed the left attack with the Twenty-first Brigade, and Colonel Spens the right with the Nineteenth Brigade. The whole division was commanded by General Smith-Dorrien. The lateness of the hour gave scarcely any time for the artillery preparation, and the artillery came into action only a few minutes before the infantry were exposed to fire.

It must be noticed that the combination of the batteries and the support which they afforded to the attack were scarcely so effective as might have been expected from the number of guns available. But the General commanding a mixed force is bound to trust the various specialists under him, at least until experience has shown them to be deficient in energy or ability.

Each brigade occupied a front of more than a mile and three-quarters, and the files of the first line of skirmishers were extended no less than thirty paces. Bruce-Hamilton, with the left attack, started a little earlier than the right brigade, and, with the City Imperial Volunteers in the first line, soon had his whole command extended on the open grass.

A few minutes after three, French's guns were heard on the extreme left, and about the same time the firing on the right swelled up again,

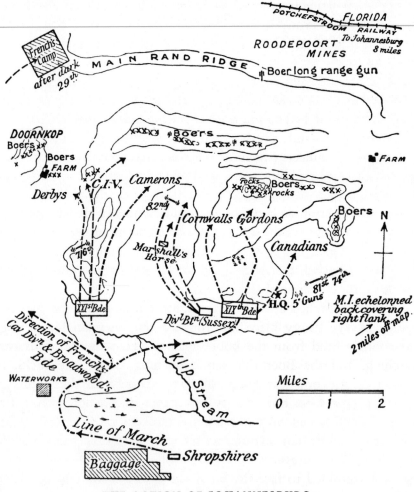

THE ACTION OF JOHANNESBURG

so that by the half-hour the action was general along the whole front of battle – an extent of a little over six miles.

The left attack, pressed with vigour, and directed with skill by General Bruce-Hamilton, led along a low spur, and was designed to be a kind of inside turning movement to assist the right in conformity with the cavalry action now in full swing. The City Imperial Volunteers moved forward with great dash and spirit, and in spite of worrying fire from their left rear, drove the Boers from position after position. While there is no doubt that French's pressure beyond them materially assisted their advance, the rapid progress of this Twenty-first Brigade entitled them and their leader to the highest credit. The Cameron Highlanders and the Sherwood Foresters supported the attack. But it was on the right that the fighting was most severe.

The leading battalion of the Nineteenth Brigade chanced – for there was no selection – to be the Gordon Highlanders; nor was it without a thrill that I watched this famous regiment move against the enemy. Their extension and advance were conducted with machine-like regularity. The officers explained what was required to the men. They were to advance rapidly until under rifle fire, and then to push on or not as they might be instructed.

Gradually the whole battalion drew out clear of the covering ridge, and long dotted lines of brown figures filled the plain. At this moment two batteries and the two 5-in. guns opened from the right of the line, and what with the artillery of French and Bruce-Hamilton there was soon a loud cannonade.

The Dutch replied at once with three or four guns, one of which seemed a very heavy piece of ordnance on the main Rand ridge, and another fired from the kopje against which the Gordons were marching. But the Boer riflemen, crouching among the rocks, reserved their fire for a near target. While the troops were thus approaching the enemy's position, the two brigades began unconsciously to draw apart. Colonel Spens' battalions had extended further to the right than either Ian Hamilton or Smith-Dorrien had intended. Bruce-Hamilton, pressing forward on the left, found himself more and more tempted to face the harassing attack on his left rear. Both these tendencies had to be corrected. The Gordons were deflected to their left by an officer, Captain Higginson, who galloped most pluckily into the firing line in spite of a hail of bullets. Bruce-Hamilton was ordered to bear in to his right and disregard the growing pressure behind his left shoulder. Nevertheless a wide gap remained. But by this mischance Ian Hamilton contrived to profit. Smith-Dorrien had already directed the only remaining battalion – the Sussex – to fill up the interval, and the General-in-Chief now thrust a battery forward through the gap, almost flush with the skirmish line of the infantry on its left and right.

The fire of these guns, combined with the increasing pressure from the turning movements both of Bruce-Hamilton and French, who was now working very far forward in the west, weakened the enemy's position on the kopje which the Gordons were attacking. Yet, when every allowance has been made for skilful direction and bold leading, the honours, equally with the cost of the victory, belong more to the Gordon Highlanders than to all the other troops put together.

The rocks against which they advanced proved in the event to be the very heart of the enemy's position. The grass in front of them was burnt and burning, and against this dark background the khaki figures showed distinctly. The Dutch held their fire until the attack was within 800 yards, and then, louder than the cannonade, the ominous rattle of concentrated rifle fire burst forth. The black slope was spotted as thickly with grey puffs of dust where the bullets struck as with advancing soldiers, and tiny figures falling by the way told of heavy loss. But the advance neither checked nor quickened.

With remorseless stride, undisturbed by peril or enthusiasm, the Gordons swept steadily onward, changed direction half left to avoid, as far as possible, an enfilade fire, changed again to the right to effect a lodgment on the end of the ridge most suitable to attack, and at last rose up together to charge. The black slope twinkled like jet with the unexpected glitter of bayonets. The rugged sky-line bristled with kilted figures, as, in perfect discipline and disdainful silence, those splendid soldiers closed on their foe.

The Boers shrank from the contact. Discharging their magazines furiously, and firing their guns twice at point-blank range, they fled in confusion to the main ridge, and the issue of the action was no longer undecided.

Still the fight continued. Along the whole infantry front a tremendous rifle fire blazed. Far away to the left French's artillery pursued the retreating Boers with shells. The advanced batteries of Hamilton's force fired incessantly. The action did not cease with the daylight. The long lines of burning grass cast a strange, baleful glare on the field, and by this light the stubborn adversaries maintained their debate for nearly an hour.

At length, however, the cannonade slackened and ceased, and the rifles soon imitated the merciful example of the guns. The chill and silence of the night succeeded the hot tumult of the day. Regiments assembled and re-formed their ranks, ambulances and baggage wagons crowded forward from the rear, the burning veldt was beaten out, and hundreds of cooking fires gleamed with more kindly meaning through the darkness.

The General rode forward, to find the Gordons massed among the rocks they had won. The gallant Burney, who commanded the firing line, was severely wounded. St John Meyrick was killed. Nine officers and eighty-eight soldiers had fallen in the attack; but those that remained were proud and happy in the knowledge that they had added to the many feats of arms which adorn the annals of the regiment. Ian Hamilton spoke a few brief words of thanks and praise to them – 'the regiment my father commanded and I was born in' – and told them that in a few hours all Scotland would ring with the tale of their deeds. And well Scotland may, for no men of any race could have shown more soldier-like behaviour.

Owing to the skilful conduct of the attack, the losses, except among the Gordons, were not severe – in all about 150 killed and wounded. The result of the fight – the action of Johannesburg, as we called it – was the general retreat of all the enemy west of the town under Delarey and Viljoen northwards towards Pretoria, and, in conjunction with the Field-Marshal's movements, the surrender of the whole of the Witwatersrand.

French, continuing his march at dawn to Driefontein, captured one gun and several prisoners. Ian Hamilton entered Florida, and found there and at Maraisburg sufficient stores to enable him to subsist until his convoys arrived.

Johannesburg: 2nd June

Morning broke and the army arose ready, if necessary, to renew the fight. But the enemy had fled. The main Rand ridge still stretched across our path. Its defenders had abandoned all their positions under the cover of darkness. Already French's squadrons were climbing the slopes to the eastward and pricking their horses forward to Elands-fontein (north). So Hamilton's force, having but six miles to march to Florida, did not hurry its departure, and we had leisure to examine the scene of yesterday's engagement. Riding by daylight over the ground of the Gordons' attack, we were still more impressed by the difficulties they had overcome. From where I had watched the action the Boers had seemed to be holding a long black kopje, some forty feet high, which rose abruptly from the grass plain. It now turned out that the aspect of steepness was produced by the foreshortening effects of the burnt grass area; that in reality the ground scarcely rose at all, and that what we had thought was the enemy's position was only a stony outcrop separated from the real line of defence by a bare space of about 200 yards.

I had not ridden a hundred yards further, when a melancholy spectacle broke upon the view. Near a clump of rocks eighteen Gordon Highlanders lay dead in a row. Their faces were covered with blankets, but their grey stockinged feet – for the boots had been removed – looked very pitiful. There they lay stiff and cold on the surface of the great Banket Reef. I knew how much more precious their lives had been to their countrymen than all the gold mines the lying foreigners say this war was fought to win. And yet, in view of the dead and the ground they lay on, neither I nor the officer who rode with me could control an emotion of illogical anger, and we scowled at the tall chimneys of the Rand.

The whole of Hamilton's force had marched by ten o'clock, but even before that hour the advanced guard had passed through Florida and picketed the hills beyond. Florida is the Kew Gardens of Jo-hannesburg. A well-built dam across a broad valley has formed a deep and beautiful lake. Carefully planted woods of Australian pines offer a welcome shade on every side. The black and white pointed chimneys of the mine buildings rise conspicuous above the dark foliage. There is a small but comfortable hotel, called 'The Retreat', to which on Sundays, in times of peace, the weary speculators whose minds were shattered by the fluctuations of the Exchange were wont to resort for rest or diversion. Everywhere along the reef the signs of industry and commerce were to be seen. Good macadamised roads crossed each other in all directions; flashy advertisements caught the eye. A network of telegraphs and telephones ran overhead. The ground was accurately marked out with little obelisks of stone into 'Deeps' and 'Concessions', and labelled with all the queer names which fill the market columns of the newspapers.

Since the soldiers had eaten their last day's rations, and the only food they had had that morning came from any odds and ends the regiments might have saved, it was imperative to find some supplies. The Field-Marshal had ordered that no troops should enter Johannesburg until he should specially direct; but, finding little to eat in Florida, Hamilton sent his supply officer and a squadron as far as Maraisburg; whence they presently returned with a quantity of tinned rabbit and sardines, and with the news that the Boers were said to be occupying a position near Langlaagte mine.

During the morning we caught a train and some prisoners. The train was returning from Potchefstroom, guarded by six armed burghers, and on rifles being pointed, it stopped obediently and surrendered. Among them was Commandant Botha – not Louis or Philip – but Botha of the Zoutspansberg commando, a brave and honest fellow, who had fought all through the war from Talana Hill until the last action; but who was quite content that Fate had decided he should fight no more. Hearing of him under guard, and near headquarters, I went to see him. He displayed no bitterness whatever, and seemed quite prepared to accept the decision of war. While we were chatting, one of the other Boer prisoners, who had been looking hard at us, said, suddenly, in very good English:

'The last time I saw you, you were in my position and I in yours.'

He then went on to tell me that he had been in the commando that destroyed the armoured train. 'I felt very sorry for you that day,' he said.

I remarked that it was much worse to be taken prisoner at the beginning of a war than near the end, as he was.

'Do you think this is the end?' asked the Commandant quickly.

'I should ask you that.'

'No, no – not yet the end. They will fight a little more. Perhaps they will defend Pretoria – perhaps you will have to go to Lydenburg; but it will not be very long now.'

And then, since both he and his companion had been through the Natal campaign, we fell to discussing the various actions. Ian Hamilton came up while we were talking. I had just told the Commandant that we considered the Boers had made a fatal strategic mistake in throwing their main strength into Natal, instead of merely holding the passes, masking Mafeking and Kimberley, and marching south into the colony with every man and gun they could scrape together. He admitted that perhaps that might be so; 'but,' said he, 'our great mistake in Natal was not assaulting Ladysmith – the Platrand position, you know – the day after our victory at Lombard's Kop. We blame Joubert for that. Many of us wanted to go on then. There were no fortifications; the soldiers were demoralised. If once we had taken the Platrand (Caesar's Camp) you could not have held the town. How many men had you on top of it?'

'Only a picket for the first week,' said the General.

'Ah! I knew we could have done it. What would have happened then?'

'We should have had to turn you out.'

The Commandant smiled a superior smile. The General continued: 'Yes – with the bayonet – at night; or else, as you say, the town could not have been held.'

'Presently,' said Botha, 'you pulled yourselves together, but for three days after Nicholson's Nek there was no fear of bayonets. If we had stormed you then – (then we had all our men and no Buller to think about) – you would not have been able to turn us out.'

Hamilton reflected. 'Perhaps not,' he said, after a pause. 'Why didn't Joubert try it?'

'Too old,' said Botha, with complete disdain; 'you must have young men for fighting.'

That was, so far as I remember, the end of the conversation; but, a fortnight later, I met Botha a free man in the streets of Pretoria. He told me he had been released on parole, so that evidently his frank manliness had not been lost upon the General.

After lunch I became very anxious to go into, and, if possible, through, Johannesburg. An important action had been fought, witnessed by only two or three correspondents; and since the enemy lay between the force and the telegraph wire no news could have been sent home. Hamilton, indeed, had sent off two of Rimington's Guides early in the morning with despatches; but they were to make a wide sweep to the south, and it was not likely, if they got through at all, that they would reach Lord Roberts until late. The shortest, perhaps the safest, road lay through Johannesburg itself. But was the venture worth the risk? While I was revolving the matter in my mind on the veranda of the temporary headquarters, there arrived two cyclists from the direction of the town. I got into conversation with one of them, a Frenchman, Monsieur Lautré by name. He had come from the Langlaagte mine, with which undertaking he was connected. There were no Boers there, according to him. There might or might not be Boers in the town. Could a stranger get through? Certainly, he thought, unless he were stopped and questioned. He undertook there and then to be my guide if I wished to go; and it being of considerable importance to get the telegrams through to London, I decided, after a good many misgivings, to accept his offer. The General, who wanted to send a more detailed account of his action, and to report his arrival at Florida, was glad to avail himself even of this precarious channel. So the matter was immediately settled. Lautré's friend, a most accommodating person, got off his bicycle without demur and placed it at my disposal. I doffed my khaki and put on a suit of plain clothes which I had in my valise, and exchanged my slouch hat for a soft cap. Lautré put the despatches in his pocket, and we started without more ado.

The tracks were bad, winding up and down hill, and frequently deep in sand; but the machine was a good one, and we made fair progress. Lautré, who knew every inch of the ground, avoided all highways, and led me by devious paths from one mine to another, around huge heaps of tailings, across little private tram lines, through thick copses of fir trees, or between vast sheds of machinery, now silent and idle. In three-quarters of an hour we reached Langlaagte, and here we found one of Rimington's scouts pushing cautiously forward towards the town. We had a brief parley with him, behind a house, for he was armed and in uniform. He was very doubtful of the situation ahead; only knew for certain that the troops had not yet entered Johannesburg. 'But,' said he, 'the Correspondent of *The Times* passed me more than two hours ago.'

'Riding?' I asked.

'Yes,' he said, 'a horse.'

'Ah,' said my Frenchman, 'that is no good. He will not get through on a horse. They will arrest him.' And then, being quite fired with the adventure: 'Besides, we will beat him, even if, unhappily, he escape the Boers.'

So we hurried on. The road now ran for the most part down hill, and the houses became more numerous. At length we turned into a regular street.

'If they stop us,' said my guide, 'speak French. Les Français sont en bonne odeur ici. You speak French, eh?'

I thought my accent might be good enough to deceive a Dutchman, so I said yes; and thereafter our conversation was conducted in French.

We avoided the main thoroughfares, bicycling steadily on through the poorer quarters. Johannesburg stretched about me on every side, silent, almost deserted. Groups of moody-looking people chatted at the street corners, and eyed us suspiciously. All the shops were shut. Most of the houses had their windows boarded up. The night was falling swiftly, and its shades intensified the gloom which seemed to hang over the town, on this the last day of its Republican existence.

Suddenly, as we crossed a side lane, I saw in the street parallel to that we followed three mounted men with slouch hats, bandoliers, and that peculiar irregular appearance which I have learned to associate with Boers. But to stop or turn back was now fatal. After all, with the enemy at their gates, they had probably concerns of their own to occupy them. We skimmed along unhindered into the central square, and my companion, whose coolness was admirable, pointed me out the post office and other public buildings, speaking all the time in French. The slope now rose against us so steeply that we dismounted to push our machines. While thus circumstanced I was alarmed to hear the noise of an approaching horse behind me. With an effort I controlled my impulse to look back.

'*Encore un Boer,*' said Lautré lightly. I was speechless. The man drew nearer, overtook and pulled his horse into a walk beside us. I could not help – perhaps it was the natural, and, if so, the wise, thing to do – having a look at him. He was a Boer sure enough, and I think he must have been a foreigner. He was armed *cap-à-pied*. The horse he rode carried a full campaigning kit on an English military saddle. Wallets, saddle-bags, drinking-cup, holsters – all were there. His rifle was slung across his back, he wore two full bandoliers over his shoulders and a third round his waist – evidently a dangerous customer. I looked at his face and our eyes met. Then he turned away carelessly. Presently he set spurs to his horse and cantered on. I breathed again freely. Lautré laughed.

'There are plenty of cyclists in Johannesburg,' he said. 'We do not look extraordinary. No one will stop us.'

We now began to approach the south-eastern outskirts of the town. If the original scheme of advance had been carried out, Lord Roberts's leading brigade should be close at hand. Lautré said, 'Shall we inquire?' But I thought it better to wait. As we progressed the streets became still more deserted, and at last we found ourselves quite alone. For more than half a mile I did not see a single person. Then we met a shabby-looking man, and now, no one else being in sight, the night dark, and the man old and feeble, we decided to ask him.

'The English,' he said with a grin, 'why, their sentinels are just at the top of the hill.'

'How far?'

'Five minutes – even less.'

Two hundred yards further on three British soldiers came in sight. They were quite unarmed, and walking casually forward into the town. I stopped them and asked what brigade they belonged to. They replied Maxwell's.

'Where is the picket line?'

'We haven't seen no pickets,' said one of them.

'What are you doing?'

'Looking for something to eat. We've had enough of 'arf rations.'

I said, 'You'll get taken prisoners or shot if you go on into the town.'

'Wot's that, guvnor?' said one of them, deeply interested in this extraordinary possibility.

I repeated, and added that the Boers were still riding about the streets.

'Well, then, I ain't for it,' he said with decision. 'Let's go back and try some of them 'ouses near the camp.'

So we all proceeded together.

I discovered no picket line at the edge of the town. Maxwell must have had one somewhere, but it certainly did not prevent anyone from passing freely; for we were never challenged, and, walking on, soon found ourselves in the middle of a large bivouac. I now became of some use to my companion, for if he knew the roads I knew the army. I soon found some officers of my acquaintance, and from them we learned that Lord Roberts's headquarters were not at Elandsfontein (south), but back at Germiston, nearly seven miles away. It was now pitch dark, and all signs of a road had vanished; but Lautré declared he knew his way, and, in any case, the messages – Press and official – had to go through.

We left the camp of Maxwell's brigade and struck across country in order to cut into the main southern road. A bicycle now became a great encumbrance, as the paths wound through dense fir woods, obstructed by frequent wire fences, ditches, holes, and high grass. Lautré, however, persisted that all was well, and, as it turned out, he was right. After about an hour of this slow progress we reached the railway, and, seeing more camp fires away to the left, turned along it. Half a mile in this direction brought us to another bivouac, which we likewise entered unchallenged. I asked a soldier whose brigade he belonged to, but he did not know, which was painfully stupid of him. A group of officers were gathered round an enormous fire a few yards away, and we went up to them to ask. Chance had led me to General Tucker's mess. I had known the commander of the Seventh Division in India, when he was stationed at Secunderabad, and he welcomed me with his usual breezy courtesy. He had been sent off with his leading brigade late in the afternoon to try to join hands with French, and so complete the circle round Johannesburg; but darkness had curtailed his march. Besides this, no communications having yet come through from the cavalry, he was uncertain where French was.

From him I got some whisky and water, and clear directions to the Field-Marshal's headquarters. They were, it appeared, two miles beyond Germiston, a mile and a half west of the road, in a solitary house on a small hill which stood beyond a large tank. And in case these indications might have been of little avail in the dark, he led us a few feet up the slope, and there we saw that, on the blackness of the night, flamed a regular oblong of glittering lights. It was the camp of the Eleventh Division. Somewhere near that were the Chief's headquarters. Thus instructed, we resumed our journey.

Another half-hour of walking brought us, as Lautré had promised, to a good firm road, and the bicycles quickly made amends for their previous uselessness. The air was cold, and we were glad to spin along at a fair ten miles an hour. At this rate twenty minutes brought us into Germiston. Not knowing where I should be likely to find dinner, or a bed, I dismounted opposite the hotel, and, seeing lights and signs of occupation, went inside. Here I found Mr Lionel James, the principal Correspondent of *The Times*. I asked him if his subordinate had arrived from Hamilton's force. He said 'No'; and when I told him he had started two hours in front of me, looked much concerned; whereat the Frenchman could not conceal a heartless grimace. I offered to give him some account of the action for his own use (for what is more detestable than a jealous journalist?), but he said that I had had the good luck to come through, and that he would not think of depriving me of my advantage.

We dined hastily and not too well, secured the reversion of half the billiard table, should all other couches fail, and set out again, this time tired and footsore. After two miles of dusty track the camp was reached. I found more officers who knew where Army Headquarters were, and at last, at about half past ten, we reached the solitary house. We sent the despatches in by an orderly, and after a few minutes Lord Kerry came out and said that the Chief wanted to see the messengers.

Now, for the first time in this war, I found myself face to face with our illustrious leader. The room was small and meanly furnished, and he and his staff, who had just finished dinner, sat round a large table which occupied the greater part of the floor.

The Field-Marshal rose from his place, shook hands, and bade us, in most ceremonious fashion, to be seated. He had read half of Hamilton's despatch.

'The first part of this,' he said, 'we know already. Two guides – Rimington's, I think – got in here about an hour ago. They had a dangerous ride, and were chased a long way, but escaped safely. I am glad to hear Hamilton is at Florida. How did you get through?'

I told him briefly. His eye twinkled. I have never seen a man before with such extraordinary eyes. The face remains perfectly motionless, but the eyes convey the strongest emotions. Sometimes they blaze with anger, and you see hot yellow fire behind them. Then it is best to speak up straight and clear, and make an end quickly. At others there is a steel grey glitter – quite cold and uncompromising – which has a most sobering effect on anyone who sees it. But now the eyes twinkled brightly with pleasure or amusement or approbation, or, at any rate, something friendly.

'Tell me about the action,' he said.

So I told him all I knew, much as it is set down in these pages, though not nearly at such length; but I don't think the tale lost in the telling. From time to time he asked questions about the artillery concentration, or the length of front of the infantry attack, and other technical matters, on which I was luckily well-informed. Then he asked what we proposed to do. Lautré said he would go back forthwith; but the Chief said, 'Much better stay here for the night; we will find you beds'; so of course we stayed. He asked me whether I meant to go back next morning. I said that as I had got my messages to the telegraph office I thought, upon the whole, that I would not run any more risks, but wait and see the British occupation of the town. He laughed at this, and said that I was quite right, and would be very ill-advised to be caught again. Then he said that he would send a letter to Hamilton in the morning, bade us all 'good night', and retired to his wagon. I, too, found a comfortable bed – the first for a month – and being thoroughly worn out soon fell asleep.

Pretoria: 8th June

The Commander-in-Chief had good reasons – how good we little knew – for wishing to push on at once to the enemy's capital, without waiting at Johannesburg. But the fatigue of the troops and the necessities of supply imposed a two days' halt. On the 3rd of June the advance was resumed. The army marched in three columns. The left, thrown forward in echelon, consisted of the Cavalry Division under French; the centre was formed by Ian Hamilton's force; and the right or main column nearest the railway comprised the Seventh and Eleventh Divisions (less one brigade left to hold Johannesburg), Gordon's cavalry brigade, and the Corps Troops all under the personal command of the Field-Marshal.

All the information which the Intelligence Department could collect seemed to promise a bloodless entry into the capital. So strong was the evidence that at dawn on the 4th of June Hamilton's column was diverted from its prescribed line of march on Elandsfontein[1] and drawn in towards the main army, with orders to bivouac on Pretoria Green, west of the town.

At ten o'clock it was reported that Colonel Henry, with the corps of mounted infantry in advance of the main column, was actually in the suburbs of Pretoria without opposition. The force continued to converge, and Ian Hamilton had almost joined Lord Roberts's force when the booming of guns warned us that our anticipations were too sanguine. The army had just crossed a difficult spruit, and Colonel Henry with the mounted infantry had obtained a lodgment on the heights beyond. But here they were sharply checked. The Boers, apparently in some force, were holding a wooded ridge and several high hills along the general line of the southern Pretoria forts.

Determined to hold what he had obtained, Lord Roberts thrust his artillery well forward, and ordered Ian Hamilton to support Colonel Henry immediately with all mounted troops. This was speedily done. The horsemen galloped forward, and, scrambling up the steep hillsides, reinforced the thin firing line along the ridge. The artillery

[1] Yet another Elandsfontein, situated to the west of Pretoria.

of the Seventh Division came into action in front of the British centre.
The Boers replied with a brisk rifle fire, which reached all three batteries, and drew from them a very vigorous cannonade.

Meanwhile the infantry deployment was proceeding. The 14th
Brigade extended for attack. Half an hour later Pole-Carew's batteries
prolonged the line of guns to the right, and about half past two the
corps and heavy artillery opened in further prolongation. By three
o'clock fifty guns were in action in front of the main army, and both
the Seventh and Eleventh Divisions had assumed preparatory formations. The balloon ascended and remained hanging in the air for an
hour – a storm signal.

During this time Hamilton was pushing swiftly forward, and
Smith-Dorrien's 19th Infantry Brigade occupied the line of heights,
and thus set free the mounted troops for a turning movement. The
21st Brigade supported. The heights were so steep in front of Hamilton
that his artillery could not come into action, and only one gun and
one 'pom-pom' could, by great exertion, be dragged and man-
handled into position. The fire of these pieces, however, caught the
Boers holding the wooded ridge in enfilade, and was by no means
ineffective.

So soon as Hamilton had collected the mounted troops he sent them
to reinforce Broadwood, whom he directed to move round the
enemy's right flank. The ground favoured the movement, and by half
past four the cavalry were seen debouching into the plain beyond
the Boer position, enveloping their flank and compromising their
retreat.

Towards four o'clock the cannonade all along the front had died
away, and only the heavy artillery on the right of Pole-Carew's
Division continued to fire, shelling the forts, whose profile showed
plainly on the sky-line, and even hurling their projectiles right over
the hills into Pretoria itself. So heavy had the artillery been that the
Boers did not endure, and alarmed as well by the flank movement
they retreated in haste through the town; so that before dusk their
whole position was occupied by the infantry without much loss.
Night, which falls at this season and in this part of the world as early
as half past five, then shut down on the scene, and the action – in
which practically the whole Army Corps had been engaged – ended.

The fact that the forts had not replied to the British batteries showed that their guns had been removed, and that the Boers had no serious intention of defending their capital. The Field-Marshal's orders for the morrow were, therefore, that the army should advance at daybreak on Pretoria, which it was believed would then be formally surrendered.

As soon as the light allowed the army moved forward. The Guards were directed on the railway station. Ian Hamilton's force swept round the western side. Wishing to enter among the first of the victorious troops the town I had crept away from as a fugitive six months before, I hurried forward, and, with the Duke of Marlborough, soon overtook General Pole-Carew, who, with his staff, was advancing towards the railway station. We passed through a narrow cleft in the southern wall of mountains, and Pretoria lay before us – a picturesque little town with red or blue roofs peeping out among masses of trees, and here and there an occasional spire or factory chimney. Behind us, on the hills we had taken, the brown forts were crowded with British soldiers. Scarcely two hundred yards away stood the railway station.

We were naturally very anxious to know what had befallen our comrades held prisoners all these long months. Rumour said they had been removed during the night to Waterfall Boven, 200 miles down the Delagoa Bay line. But nothing definite was known.

The Duke of Marlborough, however, found a mounted Dutchman who said he knew where all the officers were confined, and who undertook to guide us, and without waiting for the troops, who were advancing with all due precautions, we set off at a gallop.

The distance was scarcely three-quarters of a mile, and in a few minutes, turning a corner and crossing a little brook, we saw before us a long tin building surrounded by a dense wire entanglement. Seeing this, and knowing its meaning too well, I raised my hat and cheered. The cry was instantly answered from within. What followed resembled the end of an Adelphi melodrama.

The Duke of Marlborough called on the commandant to surrender forthwith. The prisoners rushed out of the house into the yard, some in uniform, some in flannels, hatless or coatless, but all violently excited. The sentries threw down their rifles. The gates were flung open, and while the rest of the guards – they numbered fifty-two in all – stood uncertain what to do, the long-penned-up officers surrounded them and seized their weapons. Someone – Grimshaw of the Dublin Fusiliers – produced a Union Jack (made during imprisonment out of a Vierkleur). The Transvaal emblem was torn down, and, amid wild cheers, the first British flag was hoisted over Pretoria. Time 8.47, 5th June.

The commandant then made formal surrender to the Duke of Marlborough of 129 officers and 39 soldiers whom he had in his custody as prisoners of war, and surrendered, besides himself, 4 corporals and 48 Dutchmen. These latter were at once confined within the wire cage, and guarded by their late prisoners; but, since they had treated the captives well, they have now been permitted to take the oath of neutrality and return to their homes.

At two o'clock Lord Roberts, the staff, and the foreign attachés entered the town, and proceeded to the central square, wherein the Town Hall, the Parliament House, and other public buildings are situated. The British flag was hoisted over the Parliament House amid some cheers. The victorious army then began to parade past it, Pole-Carew's division, with the Guards leading, coming from the south, and Ian Hamilton's force from the west. For three hours the broad river of steel and khaki flowed unceasingly, and the townsfolk gazed in awe and wonder at those majestic soldiers, whose discipline neither perils nor hardships had disturbed, whose relentless march no obstacles could prevent.

With such pomp and the rolling of drums the new order of things was ushered in. The former Government had ended without dignity. One thought to find the President – stolid old Dutchman – seated on his stoep reading his Bible and smoking a sullen pipe. But he chose a different course. On the Friday preceding the British occupation he left the capital and withdrew along the Delagoa Bay Railway, taking with him a million pounds in gold, and leaving behind him a crowd of officials clamouring for pay, and far from satisfied with the worthless cheques they had received, and Mrs Kruger, concerning whose health the British people need not further concern themselves.

Pretoria: 14th June

The feeble resistance which the Boers offered to our advance from Bloemfontein favoured the hope that with the fall of Pretoria they would sue for peace, and after the almost bloodless capture of the town there was a very general tendency to regard the war as practically over.

The successes gained in the Free State by the redoubtable Christian De Wet, and the cutting of the communications near Rhenoster, awoke everyone to the fact that further exertions were required. Though the Boers under Botha had made but a poor resistance in front of their capital, they were encouraged by the news from the Free State to adopt a more defiant attitude, and to make what we hope has been almost a final effort. As to that I will not be sanguine; but it is certain that, whereas on the 7th and 8th of June the Boer leaders in the Transvaal were contemplating surrender, on the 9th and 10th they were making all kinds of bold schemes to harass and even entrap the British Army.

On the 7th the news ran through the camp that Mrs Botha had come through the lines with some mission on her husband's behalf, and General Schoeman had himself made very decided overtures. On the 8th, therefore, an armistice was observed by both sides, and a conference on Zwaar Kop, where Lord Roberts was to meet the Republican generals, was arranged for the 9th; but when the 9th came circumstances had changed. The Field-Marshal had actually his foot in the stirrup ready to ride to the meeting-place, when a messenger arrived from Botha declining, unless Lord Roberts had some new proposal to make, to enter into any negotiations. The consequence of this was an immediate resumption of active operations.

The military situation was, briefly, that Lord Roberts's army was spread around and in Pretoria in various convenient camping grounds, with the greater part of its force displayed on the east and north-east sides of the town; and that the Boers, under Botha and De la Rey, to the number of about 7,000, with twenty-five guns, held a strong position some fifteen miles to the east astride the Delagoa Bay Railway.

It was evident that on any grounds, whether moral or material, it was not possible for the conquering army to allow the capital to be perpetually threatened by the enemy in organised force, and, indeed, to be in a state of semi-siege.

With the intention, therefore, of driving the enemy from the neighbourhood, and in the hope of capturing guns and prisoners, a large series of combined operations was begun. Practically all the available troops were to be employed. But the army which had marched from Bloemfontein had dwindled seriously from sickness, from casualties, and, above all, from the necessity of dropping brigades and battalions behind it to maintain the communications. It was necessary to leave the Fourteenth Brigade to hold Johannesburg, and now the Eighteenth Brigade became perforce the garrison of Pretoria, thus leaving only the Eleventh Division, the corps troops, and Ian Hamilton's force free for field operations.

The Eleventh Division numbered, perhaps, 6,000 bayonets with twenty guns. Ian Hamilton's force had lost Smith-Dorrien's brigade, which was disposed along the line between Kroonstad and Pretoria, and though strengthened by the addition of Gordon's cavalry brigade did not number more than 3,000 bayonets, 1,000 sabres, and 2,000 rifle-armed cavalry, with thirty guns. But the shrinkage had been greatest among the mounted troops. French's command of a cavalry division, which should have been some 6,000 mounted men, was scarcely, even with part of Hutton's brigade of mounted infantry, 2,000. The two cavalry brigades with Ian Hamilton mustered together only 1,100 men, and Ridley's mounted infantry, whose nominal strength was at least 4,000, was scarcely half that number in actuality. Brigades, therefore, were scarcely as strong as regiments, regiments only a little stronger than squadrons, and the pitiful – absurd if it had not been so serious – spectacle of troops of eight and ten men was everywhere to be seen. It must, therefore, be remembered that though the imposing names of divisions and brigades might seem to indicate a great and powerful force, the army at Lord Roberts's disposal was really a very small one.

The enemy's position ran along a high line of steep and often precipitous hills, which extend north and south athwart the Delagoa Bay line about fifteen miles east from Pretoria, and stretch away indefinitely on either side. The plan of the Field-Marshal was to turn both flanks with cavalry forces, and to endeavour to cut the line behind the Boers, so that, threatened by the attack of the infantry in front, and their retreat compromised, they would have to fall back, probably without being able to save some, at least, of their heavy guns.

French was directed to make a wide sweep round the enemy's right flank north of the railway. Pole-Carew, with the Eighteenth Brigade and the Guards, was to advance frontally along the railway; Ian Hamilton to move parallel to him about six miles further south; and Broadwood, who, with the rest of the mounted troops, formed part of Hamilton's force, was to endeavour to turn the enemy's left.

On the 11th, the whole army was in motion. French on the extreme left of the British front, which was extended from flank to flank about sixteen miles, soon came in contact with the Boers, and he became sharply engaged. It was not until nightfall that he was able to make any progress. Pole-Carew, with the Eleventh Division, moved eastward along the railway, and engaged the enemy with his long-range guns, to which the Boers replied with corresponding pieces, including a 6-in. gun mounted on a railway truck. Though an intermittent bombardment continued through the day, the operations in the centre were confined to a demonstration.

Meanwhile Broadwood and Ian Hamilton, advancing on the right, found that the Boers, besides occupying the whole line of the Diamond Hill plateau, had also extended their left flank, which was composed of the Heidelberg commando and other South Transvaal burghers, far beyond the reach of any turning movement, and for this reason the operations to the British right and right centre became of a piercing rather than of an enveloping nature. Hamilton endeavoured to hold off the enemy's unduly extended left by detaching a battalion, two field guns, and Gordon's cavalry brigade with its horse battery, in the direction of the Tigerspoort ridges. Ridley's brigade of mounted infantry curved inwards towards the railway, and while these two forces struck out, like the arms of a swimmer, Broadwood's brigade was intended to push through the gap thus made.

A dropping musketry and artillery fire began shortly after eight o'clock along the front of the force engaged in containing the Boers near Tigerspoort, and half an hour later Ridley's brigade was engaged

along the southern slopes of Diamond Hill. Meanwhile, Broadwood
was advancing steadily to the eastward, and crossing a difficult spruit
debouched into a wide, smooth, grass plain, surrounded by hills of
varying height, at the eastern end of which was a narrow gap. Through
this the line of march to the railway lay. He became immediately
engaged with the Boers round the whole three-quarters of the circle,
and a scattered action, presenting to a distant observer no picturesque
features, and yet abounding in striking incidents, began. The Boers
brought seven guns, so far as we could observe, against him, and since
the fire of these pieces was of a converging nature, the cavalry was
soon exposed to a heavy bombardment.

In spite of this, Broadwood continued to push on. The country
was well suited for cavalry action, and the gap, or 'poort', as it is
called in this country, plainly visible among the hills to the eastward,
encouraged him to try to break through. Accordingly, at about

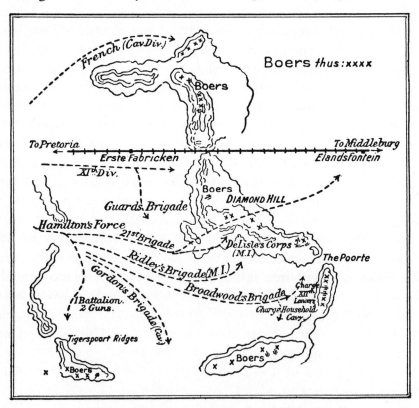

OPERATIONS AT DIAMOND HILL—I

eleven o'clock, he brought two horse-guns into a very forward position, with the design of clearing his road by their fire. The Boers, however, fought with a stubbornness and dash which had long been absent from their tactics. They were in this part of the field largely composed of Germans and other foreigners, of colonial rebels and of various types of irreconcilables.

No sooner had these two guns come into action than a very ugly attack was made on them. The ridge from which they were firing was one of those gentle swells of ground which, curving everywhere, nowhere allows a very extended view; and the Boers, about 200 strong, dashed forward with the greatest boldness in the hope of bringing a close musketry fire to bear on the gunners and of capturing their pieces. So sudden was the attack that their heads were seen appearing over the grass scarcely 300 yards away. In these circumstances the guns fired case shot, but though they prevented the Boers from coming nearer, it was evident that the position was still critical. Broadwood was compelled, therefore, to ask the 12th Lancers to charge.

Its effect was instantaneous. Though the regiment scarcely numbered 150 men, the Boers fled before them – those who were threatening the guns towards the south, and those immediately in the line of the charge eastward and northward, towards Diamond Hill. Had the horses been fresh and strong a very severe punishment would have been administered to the enemy; but with weary and jaded animals they were unable to overtake the mass of fugitives who continued to fly before them. But now in pursuit the regiment gradually came nearer to the enemy's main position, and drew a heavy fire on their left flank.

Seeing this, and having attained the object with which he had charged – the immediate relief of the guns – Lord Airlie gave the order 'files about', and withdrew his regiment before it became too seriously involved. As he issued this command he was struck by a heavy bullet through the body, and died almost immediately. The scanty squadrons returned in excellent order to the positions they had won, having lost in the charge, and mostly in the retirement, 2 officers, 17 men, including a private of the 10th Hussars, who managed to join in, and about 30 horses.

Meanwhile a large force of Boers who were already engaging the

17th Lancers and the rest of Gordon's brigade, but who were apparently doubtful of attacking, seeing the advance checked, now swooped down and occupied a kraal and some grassy ridges whence they could bring a heavy enfilading fire to bear. Broadwood, who throughout these emergencies preserved his usual impassive composure, ordered the Household Cavalry to 'Clear them out'.

The troopers began immediately to dismount with their carbines, and the General had to send a second message to them, saying that it was no good firing now, and that they must charge with the sword. Whereupon the Life Guardsmen scrambled back into their saddles, thrust their hated carbines into the buckets, and drawing their long swords, galloped straight at the enemy. The Boers, who in this part of the field considerably outnumbered the cavalry, might very easily have inflicted severe loss on them. But so formidable was the aspect of these tall horsemen, cheering and flogging their gaunt horses with the flat of their swords, that they did not abide, and running to their mounts fled in cowardly haste, so that, though eighteen horses were shot, the Household Cavalry sustained no loss in men.

These two charges, and the earnest fashion in which they were delivered, completely restored the situation; but though Broadwood maintained all the ground he had won, he did not feel himself strong enough, in face of the severe opposition evidently to be encountered, to force his way through the poort.

At about noon the Field-Marshal, who was with the Eleventh Division, observing an apparent movement of the enemy in his front, concluded that they were about to retreat, and not wishing to sacrifice precious lives if the strategic object were attained without, sent Ian Hamilton a message not, unless the resistance of the enemy was severe, to weary his men and horses by going too far. Hamilton, however, had seen how closely Broadwood was engaged, and fearing that if he stood idle the enemy would concentrate their whole strength on his cavalry commander, he felt bound to make an attack on the enemy on the lower slopes of Diamond Hill, and so hold out a hand to Broadwood.

He therefore directed Bruce-Hamilton to advance with the Twenty-first Brigade. This officer immediately set his battalions in motion. The enemy occupied a long scrub-covered rocky ridge below the main line of hills, and were in considerable force. Both batteries of artillery and the two 5-in. guns came into action about two o'clock. The Sussex Regiment, moving forward, established themselves on the northern end of the ridge, which was well prepared by shelling, and while the City Imperial Volunteers and some parts of the mounted infantry, including the Corps of Gillies, held them in front, gradually pressed them out of it by rolling up their right.

There is no doubt that our infantry have profited by the lessons of this war. The widely extended lines of skirmishers moving forward

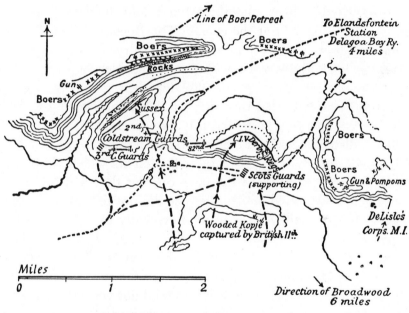

OPERATIONS AT DIAMOND HILL — 2

almost invisible against the brown grass of the plain, and taking advantage of every scrap of cover, presented no target to the Boer fire. And once they had gained the right of the ridge it was very difficult for the enemy to remain.

Accordingly at 3.30 the Boers in twenties and thirties began to abandon their position. Before they could reach the main hill, however, they had to cross a patch of open ground, and in so doing they were exposed to a heavy rifle fire at 1,200 yards from the troops who were holding the front.

The City Imperial Volunteers then occupied the whole of the wooded ridge. One poor little boy, scarcely fourteen years old, was found shot through the head, but still living, and his father, a very respectable-looking man, who, in spite of his orders from the field-cornet, had refused to leave his son, was captured; but with these exceptions the Boers had removed their wounded and made good their retreat to the main position. It being now nearly dark the action was broken off, and having strongly picketed the ground they had won, the infantry returned to their wagons for the night.

It was now imperative to carry the matter through, and in view of the unexpected obstinacy of the enemy, the Field-Marshal directed Pole-Carew to support Hamilton with the Brigade of Guards in his attack the next day.

Early the next morning Hamilton's infantry moved forward and re-occupied the whole of the ground picketed the previous night. On the right De Lisle's corps of mounted infantry prepared to attack; the cavalry maintained their wedge-like position, and exchanged shots all along their front with the Boers; but no serious operations were begun during the morning, it being thought better to await the arrival, or, at least, the approach, of the brigade which had been promised.

During this interval the Boers shelled our batteries heavily with their long range 30-pounder guns, and General Ian Hamilton, who was sitting on the ground with his Staff near the 82nd Field Battery, was struck by a shrapnel bullet on the left shoulder. Fortunately, the missile did not penetrate, but only caused a severe bruise with numbness and pain, which did not, however, make it necessary for him to leave the field.

At one o'clock the leading battalion of the Guards was observed to be about four miles off, and Bruce-Hamilton's brigade was therefore directed to attack. The Derbyshire Regiment, which had been briskly engaged during the morning, advanced up a flat tongue of land on the right. The City Imperial Volunteers moved forward in the centre, and the Sussex on the British left. Though this advance was exposed to a disagreeable enfilade fire from the Boer 'pom-pom', the dispersed formations minimised the losses, and lodgments were effected all along the rim of the plateau. But once the troops had arrived here the fight assumed a very different complexion.

The top of the Diamond Hill plateau was swept by fire from a long rocky kopje about 1,800 yards distant from the edge, and was, moreover, partially enfiladed from the enemy's position on the right. The musketry immediately became loud and the fighting severe. The City Imperial Volunteers in the centre began to suffer loss, and had not the surface of the ground been strewn with stones, which afforded good cover, many would have been killed and wounded. Though it was not humanly possible to know from below what the ground on top of the hill was like – we were now being drawn into a regular rat-trap. It was quite evident that to press the attack to an assault at this point would involve very heavy loss of life, and, as the reader will see by looking at the rough plan I have made, the troops would become more and more exposed to enfilade and cross-fire in proportion as they advanced.

After what I had seen in Natal the idea of bringing guns up on to the plateau to support the infantry attack when at so close a range from the enemy's position seemed a very unpleasant one. But General Bruce-Hamilton did not hesitate, and at half past three the 82nd Field Battery, having been dragged to the summit, came into action against the Boers on the rocky ridge at a distance of only 1,700 yards.

This thrusting forward of the guns undoubtedly settled the action. The result of their fire was immediately apparent. The bullets, which had hitherto been whistling through the air at the rate of perhaps fifteen or twenty to the minute, and which had compelled us all to lie close behind protecting stones, now greatly diminished, and it was possible to walk about with comparative immunity. But the battery which had reduced the fire, by keeping the enemy's heads down, drew most of what was left on themselves. Ten horses were shot in the moment of unlimbering, and during the two hours they remained in action, in spite of the protection afforded by the guns and wagons, a quarter of the gunners were hit. Nevertheless, the remainder continued to serve their pieces with machine-like precision, and displayed a composure and devotion which won them the unstinted admiration of all who saw the action.

About four o'clock General Ian Hamilton came himself to the top of the plateau, and orders were then given for the Coldstream Guards to prolong the line to the left, and for the Scots Guards to come into action in support of the right. Two more batteries were also brought forward, and the British musketry and artillery being now in great volume, the Boer fire was brought under control. Ian Hamilton did not choose to make the great sacrifices which would accompany an assault, however, nor did his brigadier suggest that one should be delivered, and the combatants therefore remained facing each other at the distance of about a mile, both sides firing heavily with musketry and artillery, until the sun sank and darkness set in.

Worsted in the fire fight, with three parts of their position already captured, and with the lodgment effected by Colonel De Lisle's corps on the left threatening their line of retreat, the Boers retreated during the night in good order from the whole length of the position which they occupied, and marched eastward along the railway in four long columns. When morning broke the silence proclaimed the British the victors.

By the unbroken success of his strategy Lord Roberts had laid the Boer Republics low. We had taken possession of the Rand, the bowels whence the hostile Government drew nourishment in gold and munitions of war. We had seized the heart at Bloemfontein, the brain at Pretoria. The greater part of the railways, the veins and nerves, that is to say, was in our hands. Yet, though mortally injured, the trunk still quivered convulsively, particularly the left leg, which, being heavily booted, had already struck us several painful and un-expected blows.

To make an end two operations were necessary: first, to secure the dangerous limb, and, secondly, to place a strangling grip on the windpipe somewhere near Komati Poort. The second will, perhaps, be the business of Sir Redvers Buller and the glorious Army of Natal. The first set Hamilton's brigades in motion as part of an intricate and comprehensive scheme, which arranged for the permanent garrisoning of Frankfort, Heilbron, Lindley, and Senekal, and directed a simultaneous movement against Christian De Wet by four strong flying columns.

I had determined to return to England; but it was with mixed feelings that I watched the departure of the gallant column in whose good company I had marched so many miles and seen such successful fights. Their road led them past Lord Roberts's headquarters, and the old Field-Marshal came out himself to see them off. First the two cavalry brigades marched past. They were brigades no longer; the Household Cavalry Regiment was scarcely fifty strong: in all there were not 1,000 sabres. Then Ridley's 1,400 mounted infantry, the remnants of what on paper was a brigade of nearly 5,000; thirty guns dragged by skinny horses; the two trusty 5-inch 'cow-guns' behind their teams of toiling oxen; Bruce-Hamilton's infantry brigade, with the City Imperial Volunteers, striding along – weary of war, but cheered by the hopes of peace, and quite determined to see the matter out; lastly, miles of transport: all streamed by, grew faint in the choking red dust, and vanished through the gap in the southern line of hills. May they all come safely home.